Robert R. Clewis (Ed.)
Reading Kant's Lectures

Robert R. Clewis (Ed.)

Reading Kant's Lectures

—

DE GRUYTER

Cover image
This relief bust (4.6 cm) was executed from life in 1782 by Paul Heinrich Collin (1748–89), a highly skilled local artist who, along with his brother, owned a ceramics factory in Königsberg. Collin knew Kant relatively well, as both he and Kant were regular Sunday dinner guests in the Motherby home. Ludwig Ernst Borowski, a close associate of Kant's and one of his early biographers, thought that the Collin relief best captured Kant's image (Borowski 1804: 177). Copies of this bust were available for sale in various sizes and materials (plaster, stoneware, wax), and the image also appeared on vases by the Collin brothers and in the production of several medallions (by Abramson in 1784 and 1804). The image here reproduced first served as the frontispiece to volume 7 of *Kant-Studien* (1902), and was of a bust then privately owned (in Berlin). An image of a different casting can be found in Clasen (1924: 30).

ISBN 978-3-11-099542-8
e-ISBN (PDF) 978-3-11-034533-9
e-ISBN (EPUB) 978-3-11-038449-9

Library of Congress Cataloging-in-Publication Data
A CIP catalog record for this book has been applied for at the Library of Congress.

Bibliographic information published by the Deutsche Nationalbibliothek
The Deutsche Nationalbibliothek lists this publication in the Deutsche Nationalbibliografie; detailed bibliographic data are available on the Internet at http://dnb.dnb.de.

© 2022 Walter de Gruyter GmbH, Berlin/Boston
This volume is text- and page-identical with the hardback published in 2015.
Typesetting: epline, Kirchheim unter Teck
Printing: CPI books GmbH, Leck

♾ Printed on acid-free paper
Printed in Germany

www.degruyter.com

The portrait of Kant is reproduced with the kind permission of Bayerische Staatsbibliothek München, Germany: Portr.R. Kant, Immanuel (3).

Contents

Preface and Acknowledgments —— XI

List of Abbreviations —— XIII

Robert R. Clewis
Editor's Introduction —— 1

I Metaphysics

Steve Naragon
Chapter 1: Reading Kant in Herder's Lecture Notes —— 37

Courtney D. Fugate
Chapter 2: The Unity of Metaphysics in Kant's Lectures —— 64

Dennis Schulting
Chapter 3: Transcendental Apperception and Consciousness in Kant's Lectures on Metaphysics —— 89

Corey W. Dyck
Chapter 4: Beyond the Paralogisms:
The Proofs of Immortality in the Lectures on Metaphysics —— 115

II Logic

Huaping Lu-Adler
Chapter 5: Constructing a Demonstration of Logical Rules, or How to Use Kant's Logic Corpus —— 137

Riccardo Pozzo
Chapter 6: Kant's Latin in Class —— 160

III Moral Philosophy

Oliver Sensen
Chapter 7: The Supreme Principle of Morality —— 179

Faustino Fabbianelli
Chapter 8: Kant's Concept of Moral *Imputatio* —— 200

IV Anthropology

Paul Guyer
Chapter 9: Play and Society in the Lectures on Anthropology —— 223

Alix Cohen
Chapter 10: From Faking It to Making It: The Feeling of Love of Honor as an Aid to Morality —— 243

V Pedagogy

Werner Stark
Chapter 11: Immanuel Kant's *On Pedagogy*: A Lecture Like Any Other? —— 259

Susan Meld Shell
Chapter 12: Reading Kant's *Lectures on Pedagogy* —— 277

VI Philosophical Encyclopedia

John Zammito
Chapter 13: Philosophy for Everyman: Kant's Encyclopedia Course —— 301

VII Natural Law/Right

Frederick Rauscher
Chapter 14: Did Kant Justify the French Revolution Ex Post Facto? —— 325

Günter Zöller
Chapter 15: "Without hope and fear": Kant's *Naturrecht Feyerabend*
on Bindingness and Obligation —— 346

VIII Natural Theology

Stephen R. Palmquist
Chapter 16: Kant's Lectures on Philosophical Theology –
Training-Ground for the Moral Pedagogy of *Religion*? —— 365

Norbert Fischer
Chapter 17: Kant as Pastor —— 392

IX Mathematics

Antonio Moretto
Chapter 18: Herder's Notes on Kant's Mathematics Course —— 418

X Physics

Christian Onof
Chapter 19: Kant's Lectures on Physics and the Development
of the Critical Philosophy —— 461

Henny Blomme
Chapter 20: Kant's Conception of Chemistry in the Danziger Physik —— 484

XI Physical Geography

Robert B. Louden
Chapter 21: The Last Frontier: Exploring Kant's Geography —— 505

Robert R. Clewis
Chapter 22: Kant's Natural Teleology?
The Case of Physical Geography —— 526

References —— 553

List of Illustrations —— 584

Contributors —— 585

Name Index —— 589

Subject Index —— 595

Preface and Acknowledgments

This project was made possible in part by a fellowship from the Alexander von Humboldt Foundation, which I used during a research stay at Ludwig-Maximilians-Universität München between 2012 and 2014, and a Kristeller-Popkin Travel Fellowship from the *Journal of the History of Philosophy*. I would like to thank my colleagues at Lehrstuhl für Philosophie II, and especially my Humboldt host, Günter Zöller, for making my research stay at LMU Munich so pleasant and productive. I would like to express sincere gratitude to Kristina Maschek for her help with logistical and related matters.

I became particularly interested in Kant's lectures after having translated the "Mrongovius" anthropology lecture from 1784/85, in Kant's *Lectures on Anthropology* (Cambridge University Press, 2012), edited by Robert Louden and Allen Wood and part of The Cambridge Edition of the Works of Immanuel Kant. Translating that transcription increased my already growing interest in Kant's lectures on anthropology, which led to a larger project on aesthetics and teleology in Kant's lectures. With this broader project on the lectures in mind, in May 2013 I helped organize a conference called "Kant as Lecturer-Philosopher: Connections between his Lectures and Philosophy" at LMU Munich, which in turn eventually led to the vision for this book. I therefore owe a great debt to Robert Louden and Allen Wood (and to the series co-editor, Paul Guyer) for their invitation to translate.

In Munich I encountered many wonderful scholars, academics, and philosophers; in particular I am grateful to have met Peter Adamson, Stephan Hartmann, Hannes Leitgeb, Gregor Schneider, Dennis Schulting, and Dietmar Zaefferer. I also sincerely thank Heinrich Meier for inviting me to attend the lectures at the Carl Friedrich von Siemens Foundation in Munich. Robert Pippin, a Visiting Scholar at that foundation at the time, played a (surely unintentional) role in this book's conception: an email from him, containing a kind and generous comment on the LMU conference sharing the theme of this book, encouraged me to produce this volume. For their papers and discussions, without which this work would not have come into being, I am grateful to the nine speakers at that 3–4 May 2013 conference: Reinhard Brandt, Vittoria Cassata, Faustino Fabbianelli, Norbert Fischer, Steve Naragon, Dennis Schulting, Werner Stark, Karsten Thiel, and Günter Zöller. I am, moreover, extremely indebted to the 21 authors of this volume's chapters; many authors went far beyond writing chapters, offering valuable advice on the book, sharing information about Kant's lectures or the student notes, commenting on each other's translations, chapters, and so on.

I am extremely grateful to Steve Naragon for sharing his wide knowledge at all phases of this project, from conception to the final stages of book production, and to Werner Stark for quickly answering countless questions and granting access to the manuscripts in the Marburger Kant-Archiv. For translating three of the volume's chapters, or for reading over translations, I thank Christian Göbel, Frederick Van Fleteren, Giorgio Galbussera, and Franz-Alois Fischer, in addition to the chapter authors themselves. For allowing me to present material from my chapter, I am indebted to the scholars in Günter Zöller's research seminar at LMU Munich in 2013, participants at the First Annual Kant Conference at KU Leuven, and students in David Kim's graduate seminar at the University of Pennsylvania, where I was a Visiting Scholar in 2015.

For allowing me access to manuscripts, I gratefully acknowledge the assistance of the Archiv der Berlin-Brandenburgischen Akademie der Wissenschaften, Colombia University, Marburger Kant-Archiv, Staatsbibliothek zu Berlin – Preußischer Kulturbesitz, and the University of Pennsylvania. For granting permission to include page reproductions or images, I thank the libraries of the University of Pennsylvania, University of Tartu, Staatsbibliothek zu Berlin – Preußischer Kulturbesitz, PAN Biblioteka Gdańska, and Bayerische Staatsbibliothek.

For advice and support at all stages of book production, I owe debts of gratitude to the editors at Walter de Gruyter, especially Gertrud Grünkorn and Christoph Schirmer, and to copy-editor Konrad Vorderobermeier.

I am grateful to my colleagues at Gwynedd Mercy University for the support they have shown me. I owe a large debt of gratitude to Wayne Huss, Lisa McGarry, and Frank Scully, Jr. for encouraging and facilitating this research; I sincerely thank my philosophy colleague Patrick Messina for taking over some of my administrative duties when I was in Germany. Moreover, I am indebted to Amanda Pirrone for her careful assistance in preparing this book. Needless to say, I am solely responsible for whatever errors or deficiencies are still to be found in it.

My deepest gratitude of all goes to my wife Elisa Schwab, who, along with my family, put up with me during countless hours spent working on this volume: this book is dedicated to her.

List of Abbreviations

Citations of Kant's writings are typically from the works by Immanuel Kant in the Academy Edition (*Akademie-Ausgabe*) of his collected works, *Kant's gesammelte Schriften* (1900–), edited by the Royal Prussian, subsequently German, then Berlin-Brandenburg Academy of Sciences, in 29 volumes.

The following abbreviations of Kant's works stem from the ones adopted by *Kant-Studien* (Walter de Gruyter). Nearly all abbreviations refer to writings in volumes of the *Akademie-Ausgabe* (AA); the relevant AA volume is listed below after each text. The few exceptions to this are indicated below (see the References list for full bibliographic information.)

Citations use arabic numerals to indicate first the AA volume, then page, then (if applicable) line numbers. For instance, "Danziger Physik 29.1,1: 118.10–11" refers to the Danziger Physik lecture transcription in volume 29.1,1 of the *Akademie-Ausgabe*, page 118, lines 10 to 11. Following convention, references to the first *Critique*, or *Kritik der reinen Vernunft*, use the standard A/B page numbers, where "A" refers to the first edition (published in 1781) and "B" to the second edition (1787). Kant's *Reflexionen* are cited by means of the abbreviation "Refl" followed by the customary *Akademie* number. Translations of these writings are generally taken (when possible) from The Cambridge Edition of the Works of Immanuel Kant (Cambridge University Press, 1992–). Unless otherwise stated, translations into English of other texts than Kant's are from the authors (or translators) themselves.

Abbreviations of Kant's works

AA	Akademie-Ausgabe
Anth	Anthropologie in pragmatischer Hinsicht (AA 07)
BBM	Bestimmung des Begriffs einer Menschenrace (AA 08)
BGSE	Bemerkungen in den Beobachutngen über das Gefühl des Schönen und Erhabenen (AA 20)
BDG	Der einzig mögliche Beweisgrund zu einer Demonstration des Daseins Gottes (AA 02)
Br	Briefe (AA 10–13)
DfS	Die falsche Spitzfindigkeit der vier syllogistischen Figuren erwiesen (AA 02)
EaD	Das Ende aller Dinge (AA 08)
EACG	Entwurf und Ankündigung eines Collegii der physischen Geographie (AA 02)
EEKU	Erste Einleitung in die Kritik der Urteilskraft (AA 20)
GMS	Grundlegung zur Metaphysik der Sitten (AA 04)
GSE	Beobachtungen über das Gefühl des Schönen und Erhabenen (AA 02)
GUGR	Von dem ersten Grunde des Unterschiedes der Gegenden im Raume (AA 02)
HN	Handschriftlicher Nachlass (AA 14–23)
IaG	Idee zu einer allgemeinen Geschichte in weltbürgerlicher Absicht (AA 08)
KpV	Kritik der praktischen Vernunft (AA 05)
KrV	Kritik der reinen Vernunft
KU	Kritik der Urteilskraft (AA 05)
Log	Logik (AA 09)
LV	Logik-Vorlesung: Unveröffentlichte Nachschriften (Kant 1998c)

MAM	Mutmaßlicher Anfang der Menschheitsgeschichte (AA 08)
MAN	Metaphysische Anfangsgründe der Naturwissenschaft (AA 04)
MonPh	Metaphysicae cum geometria iunctae usus in philosophia naturali, cuius specimen I. continet monadologiam physicam (AA 01)
MpVT	Über das Mißlingen aller philosophischen Versuche in der Theodicee (AA 08)
MS	Die Metaphysik der Sitten (AA 06)
MS/RL	Die Metaphysik der Sitten / Metaphysische Anfangsgründe der Rechtslehre (AA 06)
MSI	De mundi sensibilis atque intelligibilis forma et principiis (AA 02)
NEV	Nachricht von der Einrichtung seiner Vorlesungen in dem Winterhalbenjahre von 1765–1766 (AA 02)
NG	Versuch, den Begriff der negativen Größen in die Weltweisheit einzuführen (AA 02)
NLBR	Neuer Lehrbegriff der Bewegung und Ruhe und der damit verknüpften Folgerungen in den ersten Gründen der Naturwissenschaft (AA 02)
NTH	Allgemeine Naturgeschichte und Theorie des Himmels (AA 01)
OP	Opus Postumum (AA 21 and 22)
Päd	Pädagogik (AA 09)
PG	Physische Geographie (AA 09)
PhilEnz	Philosophische Enzyklopädie (AA 29)
PND	Principiorum primorum cognitionis metaphysicae nova dilucidatio (AA 01)
PR	Philosophische Religionslehre nach Pölitz (2nd edn., 1830; reprinted in Kant 1982)
Prol	Prolegomena zu einer jeden künftigen Metaphysik (AA 04)
Refl	Reflexion (AA 14–19)
RezMoscati	Recension von Moscatis Schrift: Von dem körperlichen wesentlichen Unterschiede zwischen der Structur der Thiere und Menschen (AA 02)
RGV	Die Religion innerhalb der Grenzen der bloßen Vernunft (AA 06)
RL	Metaphysische Anfangsgründe der Rechtslehre (AA 06)
SF	Der Streit der Fakultäten (AA 07)
TG	Träume eines Geistersehers, erläutert durch Träume der Metaphysik (AA 02)
TP	Über den Gemeinspruch: Das mag in der Theorie richtig sein, taugt aber nicht für die Praxis (AA 08)
UD	Untersuchung über die Deutlichkeit der Grundsätze der natürlichen Theologie und der Moral (AA 02)
ÜE	Über eine Entdeckung, nach der alle neue Kritik der reinen Vernunft durch eine ältere entbehrlich gemacht werden soll (AA 08)
ÜGTP	Über den Gebrauch teleologischer Principien in der Philosophie (AA 08)
V-Anth/Busolt	Vorlesungen Wintersemester 1788/1789 Busolt (AA 25)
V-Anth/Collins	Vorlesungen Wintersemester 1772/1773 Collins (AA 25)
V-Anth/Fried	Vorlesungen Wintersemester 1775/1776 Friedländer (AA 25)
V-Anth/Mensch	Vorlesungen Wintersemester 1781/1782 Menschenkunde, Petersburg (AA 25)
V-Anth/Mron	Vorlesungen Wintersemester 1784/1785 Mrongovius (AA 25)
V-Anth/Parow	Vorlesungen Wintersemester 1772/1773 Parow (AA 25)
V-Anth/Pillau	Vorlesungen Wintersemester 1777/1778 Pillau (AA 25)
V-Lo/Bauch	Logik Bauch (LV 1)

V-Lo/Blomberg	Logik Blomberg (AA 24)
V-Lo/Busolt	Logik Busolt (AA 24)
V-Lo/Dohna	Logik Dohna-Wundlacken (AA 24)
V-Lo/Hechsel	Logik Hechsel (LV 2)
V-Lo/Philippi	Logik Philippi (AA 24)
V-Lo/Pölitz	Logik Pölitz (AA 24)
V-Lo/Warschauer	Warschauer Logik (LV 2)
V-Lo/Wiener	Wiener Logik (AA 24)
V-Mo/Collins	Moralphilosophie Collins (AA 27)
V-Mo/Mron	Moral Mrongovius (AA 27)
V-Met/Arnoldt	Metaphysik Arnoldt (K 3) (AA 29)
V-Met/Dohna	Metaphysik Dohna (AA 28)
V-Met/Herder	Metaphysik Herder (AA 28)
V-Met-K2/Heinze	Metaphysik K2 (Heinze, Schlapp) (AA 28)
V-Met-K3/Arnoldt	Metaphysik K3 (Arnoldt, Schlapp) (AA 28)
V-Met-L1/Pölitz	Metaphysik L1 (Pölitz) (AA 28)
V-Met-L2/Pölitz	Metaphysik L2 (Pölitz, Original) (AA 28)
V-Met/Mron	Metaphysik Mrongovius (AA 29)
V-Met/Schön	Metaphysik von Schön, Ontologie (AA 28)
V-Met/Volckmann	Metaphysik Volckmann (AA 28)
V-MS/Vigil	Die Metaphysik der Sitten Vigilantius (AA 27)
V-NR/Feyerabend	Naturrecht Feyerabend (AA 27)
V-PG	Vorlesungen über Physische Geographie (AA 26)
V-Phil-Th/Pölitz	Philosophische Religionslehre nach Pölitz (AA 28)
V-PP/Herder	Praktische Philosophie Herder (AA 27)
V-PP/Powalski	Praktische Philosophie Powalski (AA 27)
V-Th/Volckmann	Natürliche Theologie Volckmann nach Baumbach (AA 28)
VBO	Versuch einiger Betrachtungen über den Optimismus (AA 02)
VKK	Versuch über die Krankheiten des Kopfes (AA 02)
VT	Von einem neuerdings erhobenen vornehmen Ton in der Philosophie (AA 08)
VvRM	Von den verschiedenen Racen der Menschen (AA 02)
WA	Beantwortung der Frage: Was ist Aufklärung? (AA 08)
WDO	Was heißt sich im Denken orientiren? (AA 08)
ZeF	Zum ewigen Frieden (AA 08)

Abbreviations of works by other authors

G   Leibniz, Gottfried: *Die philosophischen Schriften*, ed. Carl Immanuel Gerhardt. Berlin: Weidmann 1875–90.
PE   Wolff, Christian: *Psychologia empirica*. Frankfurt and Leipzig: Rengersche Verlagsbuchhandlung 1738.
PRa   Wolff, Christian: *Psychologia rationalis*. Verona: Ramanzini 1737.
VG   Wolff, Christian: *Vernünfftige Gedancken von Gott, der Welt und der Seele des Menschen, auch allen Dingen überhaupt*. Frankfurt and Leipzig: [unknown] 1733.

Editor's Introduction

Robert R. Clewis

Today it is unexceptional for professional philosophers to teach at a university, but this was of course not always the case.[1] The practice of teaching philosophy at the 'western' institution of higher education, broadly-understood, has a long history that dates at least as far back as Plato's Academy and Aristotle's Lyceum. Elisabeth of Bohemia, Spinoza, and Leibniz were not university professors or lecturers; Hegel, Russell, Arendt, and Rawls at some point (even if in different ways) were. With the aim of understanding Kant's philosophy more profoundly, the twenty-two chapters of *Reading Kant's Lectures* together examine Immanuel Kant as a university professor of eleven distinct disciplines.

As early as the nineteenth century and early twentieth century, studies of Kant (e. g., Erdmann 1880; Paulsen 1899; du Prel 1889; Heinze 1894; Adickes 1911, 1913, 1924–25; Arnoldt 1908–09) took into account his university teaching and lectures, and in the early and middle decades of the twentieth century (Vorländer 1924; Beck 1979) a consideration of Kant's academic activity was certainly not absent.[2] There was indeed interest in this side of Kant even during his lifetime, as the (sometimes lucrative)[3] publication of his anthropology (1798), logic (1800), physical geography (1802), and pedagogy (1803) lectures attest, whatever problems those editions might have.[4] Yet in some ways, these early publications do not so much reflect scholarly interest in the lectures as an interest in publishing the material. Even the publications a few decades later by Pölitz and "Starke" (i. e., Bergk) arguably had less to do with scholarly interest and more to do with selling books. More serious scholarship seems to have begun near the end of that century, with Erdmann, du Prel, Arnoldt, and Heinze.

---

1 This book was generously supported in part by a Fellowship from the Alexander von Humboldt Foundation; for a period between 2012 and 2014, I had a research stay at Ludwig-Maximilians-Universität München. I would especially like to thank my host at LMU Munich, Günter Zöller.
2 See also the standard biographies such as Cassirer 1918 and Kuehn 2001a; Zammito 2002; and Kuehn 2001b. For Kant as a lecturer, see Jachmann 1993: 116–20; Stark 1995; Ameriks and Naragon in Kant 1997b; and section 4 of this Introduction.
3 Vollmer and Rink, for instance, competed to be the first to publish Kant's lectures on physical geography, with Kant intervening to back Rink officially.
4 For a consideration of questions concerning the pedagogy (1803) and physical geography (1802) editions, see this volume's chapters by Stark and by Louden, respectively.

The primary source materials available – in archives, in digital form,[5] in publications of the transcriptions in German (e. g., Kant 2009b), in a growing body of English translations (Kant 2012a; Kant 2012c, and Kant 2016)[6] and of the 'textbooks' Kant used in his courses (e. g., Baumgarten 2013) – has increased considerably in recent decades.[7] Accompanying this, there is currently a sizeable and intensifying interest in examining Kant's lectures to characterize or contextualize his claims in anthropology, ethics, metaphysics, logic, theology, political philosophy, and science.[8] Yet unlike this book, most of these studies do not attempt to cover *every* major area of Kant's academic teaching in connection with his philosophy or intellectual activity.[9] One of this volume's primary aims is to provide such comprehensive coverage, viz., to understand Kant's philosophy through his university lectures not only in more strictly 'philosophical' areas but also in other fields, thereby contributing to a more complete picture of Kant's thought – including pedagogical, scientific, political, and religious perspectives. The main objective is thus not to provide an institutional history of Albertina University of Königsberg where Kant taught, nor to locate Kant in the long, complex trajectory of philosophers as educators, nor to offer a biographical sketch of Kant as teacher. Although the reader may very well become more familiar with the history of the university, of science, of ideas, or with Kant's life along the way, a chief aim is to learn about Kant's philosophical or intellectual activity and its development. The focus, then, is unabashedly on Kant.

In the following, I describe the volume's goals (section 1) and the 'use and abuse' of the notes or transcriptions (section 2).[10] I explain more precisely what

---

5 E. g., the student transcriptions of Kant's physical geography lectures have been available at the Kant-Arbeitsstelle of the Berlin-Brandenburgische Akademie der Wissenschaften since 2007 (see BBAW 2007). Access requires username and password, granted upon making an inquiry to the Arbeitsstelle.
6 E. g., the series The Cambridge Edition of the Works of Immanuel Kant in Translation (1992–). Kant 2012c contains the 1802 physical geography edited by F. T. Rink.
7 For details on, e. g., Kant's teaching, colleagues, and courses, see the extremely useful websites at Stark 2015 and Naragon 2015a. See also (*passim*) Stark 1993; and Louden 2000: 4 f.
8 E. g., consider Cambridge University Press's valuable Critical Guide series on Kant's lectures, such as Denis and Sensen 2015 (on the lectures on ethics) and Cohen 2014 (anthropology). See also *Kant's Lectures* (Dörflinger et al. 2015).
9 The topic of this volume is Kant's philosophy and intellectual commitments, arguments, views, etc., understood in a broad way, one that might not map directly onto the contemporary sense of the discipline known as 'philosophy'. For the sake of readability, I will not write 'intellectual, philosophical, etc.' every time this broad sense of his intellectual activity is meant.
10 I make no claim to originality concerning the historical points covered in this Introduction. For details, see the sources cited herein.

the lecture notes are (section 3). I sketch Kant as a lecturer (section 4) and conclude with a remark about the proposed way of approaching Kant (section 5). Finally, I summarize each of the chapters, to which the reader might turn for a concrete sense of the contents (section 6).

1 Aims of the volume

Immanuel Kant (1724–1804) lectured for 41 years or 82 semesters: he first began lecturing in the winter[11] semester 1755/56 and continued until the summer semester 1796.[12] A central aim of *Reading Kant's Lectures* is to examine every major area of Kant's lectures in light of his pre-Critical and Critical philosophical writings or published works.

This is not the place to take a stand on a crucial topic for the history and historiography of philosophy, namely, the merits and shortcomings of a 'presentist' approach that appropriates historical problems from the history of philosophy in order to 'solve' or at least clarify today's philosophical problems, and of a 'contextualist' approach that sets up its philosophical discussion with careful attention to the intellectual, social, and cultural contexts of the thinker in question, taking seriously the materiality of philosophical writing – its texts, audiences, and institutions. Conceiving of the topic in this limited way may very well create a false dichotomy, and in any case this issue merits analysis in its own right, and indeed has recently been addressed in book-length studies (e. g., Lærke, Smith, and Schliesser 2013). Here I simply suggest that studying Kant's intellectual activity in its lecturing context can allow us to discover and assess overlooked alternatives to our interpretations and reception of his thought. It may expose some fundamental assumptions of our readings – and even some misreadings. By definition, some claims about Kant – for instance, claims about his intellectual development – need to be studied diachronically and in their full and proper context. The lecture notes, when duly supplemented by his published writings, *Reflexionen*, and letters, and when they are exactly or at least approximately dated (ideally allowing for comparison with other transcriptions from the same

---

[11] The German academic calendar in Kant's day was (as it is now) divided into summer and winter semesters. The summer semester began about two weeks after Easter, and the winter semesters began about two weeks after St. Michael's (29 September) and continued into the following spring.
[12] Kant stopped about half way through this semester. 23 July appears to have been his last day; he normally would have been teaching until the second week of September.

period), offer an indispensable record for analysis here. Moreover, it is not simply that, as many commentators have noted, Kant lectured on a wide range of topics for a period spanning four decades and uninterrupted, amazingly, by sabbatical leave. It is also that the suggestion that the aim of the Critical philosophy *as such* is pedagogical, or, in the words of Felicitas Munzel, that "the Critical philosopher is the educator" (1999: 254; cf. Munzel 2012), deserves serious consideration.

The volume as a whole gives an overview of Kant's lectures, at times orienting the reader to past or recent scholarship on the lectures and important interpretive positions, at other times pushing the secondary literature forward or in a new direction, or presenting the author's reconstruction or interpretation of the argument or theme. As Steve Naragon[13] points out in the opening chapter, although we should be aware of concerns with the reliability of certain lecture notes, if these student transcriptions are read in light of Kant's published writings, the transcriptions can offer a new perspective into Kant's philosophical development, clarify points in the published texts, consider topics not discussed there, depict the philosophical and intellectual background in more detail, and are sometimes more accessible to readers than the published works (cf. Naragon 2015j).

This volume can provide a deeper understanding of the breadth of Kant's teaching and his courses' contents, show how some of his philosophical views are presented in his lectures, and reveal what his lectures tell us about some of the positions defended in the published writings. Moreover, readers may also indirectly learn about the authors from whom Kant is drawing and whose textbooks he used, a list that would include works by Achenwall, Basedow, Baumgarten, Bock, Eberhard, Erxleben, Feder, Karsten, Meier, Meiners, and Wolff.[14] During Kant's day, the use of assigned textbooks for lectures was mandatory (though the geography course, where he was permitted to use his own notes, was an exception to this). This requirement placed constraints on what Kant could and could not say, leading to lectures made up of interspersed analytical or critical commentary on a textbook. Hence lectures were often a mixture of his own views and those of the textbook author, as Kant's occasional references to "the author" indicate.

How one counts up Kant's academic teaching will inevitably contain a degree of arbitrariness. This volume divides his lecturing into eleven distinct areas: metaphysics, logic, moral philosophy, anthropology, 'philosophical encyclopedia', pedagogy, natural law or natural right (*Naturrecht*), natural theology, math-

---

[13] This Introduction is thoroughly indebted to Steve Naragon; much of the textual and historical information in it relies heavily on his work. I also thank him for his input at all stages of writing and publishing this book.

[14] For a list of the textbooks Kant used, see Naragon 2015f.

ematics, physics, physical geography. Structurally, the book unfolds in this order, beginning with three core areas of philosophy.[15] There is at least one chapter for each area, and sometimes more: the course on metaphysics, for instance, receives four chapters, followed by logic. Kant after all was professor *ordinarius* of Logic and Metaphysics; he lectured on logic 56 times and metaphysics 53 times, making these the two disciplines he taught most frequently.

At the same time, in paying attention to under-examined areas such as his lectures on mathematics, physics, philosophical encyclopedia, and physical geography, I hope the volume adds to the growing scholarship on Kant as lecturer. While Kant's *philosophy* of math in the *Critique of Pure Reason*, or philosophy of science in the *Metaphysical Foundations of Natural Science*, has justifiably been much covered in older and more recent studies, his lectures in these areas arguably merit deeper examination. Perhaps we can learn something about Kant's philosophical views by looking at his teaching and in particular at a course's aims, format, content, and textbooks. Some themes that shape the volume are, therefore: a wider appreciation of the perhaps *fluid* nature of the boundaries between Kant's teaching and philosophical writing, and between the disciplines he taught – he discussed, e.g., chemistry in the physics course and philosophical encyclopedia course; an increased historiographical awareness of Kant's intellectual and institutional contexts, especially insofar as it shaped his own philosophical development; an examination of lesser known lecture notes (e.g., on mathematics, philosophical encyclopedia) that may be of scholarly value yet have been relatively under-examined; and a reassessment of the more well-known notes.

All areas of Kant's university teaching are covered here by an international team of experts. Given the breadth of coverage, the number of essays in each area of Kant's teaching had to be limited. Although this book cannot have the depth of a volume devoted to a single discipline, such as the notable volumes by Denis and Sensen (2015) and Cohen (2014), I hope that what may have been lost in depth of focus is amply regained in coverage and breadth.

---

[15] Kant never lectured directly on 'aesthetics' in the third *Critique*'s sense concerning an analysis of the judgments of beauty and the sublime, although some of its content appeared in his lectures, especially those on logic and anthropology. Still, Stuckenberg claims that it is probable that Kant "lectured on 'The Emotion of the Beautiful and the Sublime', on which subject a small volume by him appeared in 1764" (Stuckenberg 1882: 72), but it is hard to find concrete evidence of his teaching such a course. In any case, if its content were similar to Kant's *Observations* (1764), such a course would have significantly overlapped with Kant's later anthropology course (first taught in 1772/73).

There are other necessary limitations. For instance, the volume does not address Kant's period as a tutor for families before he returned to the Albertina in 1755. And although every area of Kant's lecturing is covered, the volume, with the exception of Riccardo Pozzo's chapter, does not emphasize Kant's practice sessions (i.e., *repetitoria, examinatoria, disputatoria*),[16] since their content mostly overlaps with the lectures and since the *repetitoria* offer less material to examine. Moreover, the chapters only tangentially refer to Kant's marginal notes (*Reflexionen*) and letters and, when they do, they do so mainly to support their arguments concerning Kant's lectures and student transcriptions. This is in no way to diminish the importance of Kant's *Reflexionen* and correspondence, since after all, unlike the student notes, they were written by Kant's own hand, but only to say that it would have constituted another project – one, I might add, that would have been less timely than the present one, since the *Akademie-Ausgabe* has recently published Kant's lectures (most recently in 1997c, 2009b) and will continue to do so in the near future. Having been put on hold since 1983, with Kant 1997c the completion of the fourth *Abteilung* (Division) of the *Akademie-Ausgabe* has been taken up again.

In order to announce what he would be teaching and to gain student interest, Kant published approximately seven[17] announcements of his lectures, and insofar as these announcements are relevant to Kant's lectures, some of this volume's chapters mention them. They are, with the relevant passages in parentheses (following Naragon 2015d):

1. *Neue Anmerkungen zur Erläuterung der Theorie der Winde*: program for summer semester 1756 (TW 1: 502 f.)
2. *Entwurf und Ankündigung eines Collegii der physischen Geographie*: program for summer semester 1757 (EACG 2: 4; 9 f.)
3. *Neuer Lehrbegriff der Bewegung und Ruhe*: program for summer semester 1758 (NLBR 2: 25)

---

16 We have only sporadic evidence of these prior to 1770, but Kant is shown to have offered one nearly every semester after that, and we have reason to believe that he always offered these practicals (Naragon 2015a; see Borowski, quoted in Reicke 1860: 32; reprinted in Malter 1990: 43).
17 The total number depends on whether one excludes or includes *Neue Anmerkungen* (omitted by Kant 2007: 497 n. 2); *Die falsche Spitzfindigkeit* (counted by neither Kowalewski at Kant 2000a: 139 f. nor Kant 2007: 497 n. 2, yet suggested by Pozzo); and/or *Versuch den Begriff der negativen Größen* (counted by neither Naragon nor Kant 2007 nor Kowalewski, but suggested by Pozzo). Cf. Kowalewski's classification at Kant 2000a: 139 f.; and Kant 2007: 497 n. 2 (which lists five total, omitting *Neue Anmerkungen* and *Die falsche Spitzfindigkeit* from the seven listed here). Pozzo's chapter in this volume suggests counting *Die falsche Spitzfindigkeit* and *Negativen Größen*.

4. *Versuch einiger Betrachtungen über den Optimismus*: program for winter semester 1759/60 (VBO 2: 35)
5. *Die falsche Spitzfindigkeit der vier syllogistischen Figuren erwiesen*: program for winter semester 1762/63 (DfS 2: 57)
6. *Nachricht von der Einrichtung seiner Vorlesungen in dem Winterhalbenjahre von 1765–1766*: program for winter semester 1765/66 (NEV 2: 305–13)
7. *Von den verschiedenen Racen der Menschen*: announcement of the physical geography course for summer semester 1775 (VvRM 2: 443)

It should be noted, however, that the material contained in these announcements is not always useful for understanding his philosophy in light of his lectures, and that the passages concerning his lectures can be quite brief.

What areas did Kant teach, and how many times?[18] Table 1 summarizes the disciplines he taught and the frequency of his teaching.

These numbers leave aside Kant's practicals or *repetitoria*.[19] Moreover, the table is generous with the data, as it includes all courses that likely took place. In his university career, Kant apparently offered five additional, unnamed *privatissima*, or courses of lectures offered privately to a closed group of 'non-traditional students': 1767, 1769, 1769/70 (twice), and 1770/71. (These 'students' might have been a few army officers, the instruction occurring in a private parlor.) If the five unnamed *privatissima* are included, the total number of courses taught comes to 284, for an average (over 82 semesters) of 3.5 courses per semester (Naragon 2015b).[20]

---

[18] I cannot here go into detail regarding the periods, dates, or schedule of Kant's university teaching. For the university course catalog, see Oberhausen and Pozzo 1999. For when and how often Kant taught, see Naragon 2015b. For Kant's teaching career, see the biographical works in footnote 2. For details concerning Kant's students (number, level of preparation, background, etc.), see Naragon 2015a. On Kant and his city, Königsberg, see Stavenhagen 1949.

[19] For details and sources on practicals, see Naragon 2015l. This Introduction does not focus on the differences between the public, private, or very private (*privatissima*) lectures.

[20] For more on what courses Kant taught, when, and the textbooks Kant used, see Oberhausen and Pozzo 1999; Stark 1993; and Naragon 2015a.

Table 1: Discipline and Frequency of Courses Kant Taught[21]

Course	Number of Times Taught
Logic	56
Metaphysics	53
Geography	49
Moral Philosophy	28
Anthropology	24
Physics	21
Mathematics	15
Natural Law/Right	12
Philosophical Encyclopedia	10
Natural Theology	4
Pedagogy	4
Mechanics[i]	2
Mineralogy[ii]	1
Total	279

2 On the use and abuse of the lecture notes

The student lecture notes or transcriptions that derive from Kant's lectures and teaching should *not* be read as pure reports of Kant's beliefs or statements, for they can involve a tricky mix of source text (the assigned textbook), the student or transcriber or copyist, and Kant himself. At least *prima facie*, therefore, the

---

21 This table is based on Naragon 2015b, which in turn stems from Arnoldt and his editor Schöndörffer (Arnoldt 1908–09).

i Kant is listed as having lectured on *mechanics* for 1759/60 and 1761. In organizing this book I have not given mechanics its own section but considered it to be a part of mathematics, as it was included in that course's textbook, Christian Wolff's *Auszug aus den Anfangs-gründen aller Mathematischen Wissenschaften, zu Bequemerem Gebrauche Der Anfänger, auf Begehren verfertiget* (see Martin 1967). During the Russian occupation of his city, Kant may have also offered a private course (*privatissimum*) to Russian officers on *fortification*, a topic covered by Wolff's *Auszug*, from which Kant likely would have used the relevant section (cf. Stark 1993: 322; Vorländer 1924, vol. 1: 89; Malter 1990: 41; Naragon 2015a).

ii Kant apparently offered a course on *mineralogy* during winter semester 1770/71. The subject matter would have overlapped with physical geography, and this course appears to have served as a substitute since Kant did not offer physical geography that semester. I have not devoted a section to mineralogy mostly because the topic was covered in the geography course, which receives a section in the present volume.

lecture notes should be viewed as supplemental rather than primary. However, even if a set of notes should not be seen as a verbatim record, it is reasonable to view the lecture transcription as giving a good idea of the content of the course in question. I would submit that the transcriptions of the lectures, when read with proper attentiveness and when compared to Kant's published writings as well as to the appropriate *Reflexionen*, letters, and (independent) transcriptions from the period, can be of philosophical, in addition to historical, interest. If we aim to understand Kant's philosophical concepts, doctrines, and arguments, it would be a mistake to ignore or repudiate the student transcripts solely on the grounds that Kant did not pen them.

Nevertheless, it should always be kept in mind that there are potential issues posed by the notes, and these should be considered on a case-by-case basis. Possible problems include textual corruptions, illegible words (due, say, to smudge marks and ink blots), missing or torn pages, spelling errors, outdated orthography, and errors introduced by either the auditor or copyist (who may not have heard the lecture). There are also dating issues; it is not always possible to determine exactly on which semester a lecture transcription was based. The date of composition of the notes may very well differ from the date of the course, the 'source lecture' of the notes: often the notes were copied or re-copied years after the lecture had taken place (see section 3). Any date that is written on a title page should be taken with a grain of salt, as the date could be referring to any number of things, and only occasionally is it in fact the date of the source lecture. About a century ago, Erich Adickes put the point well:

> The copying and compiling of notebooks from Kant's lectures (with various changes entering with their production) was a flourishing branch of industry in Königsberg, such that with no set of notes can we, without further study, assume uniformity (descent from a single set of lectures) or the reliability of any dates (found on the title page or elsewhere); nor can one assume, over a section of text of any length, that one is reading Kant's own words. (Adickes 1913: 8; trans. Naragon 2015g)

Moreover, there may also be issues associated with the printing process and editorial decisions made by the editors of the *Akademie-Ausgabe* when preparing the student transcripts. For instance, the editing carried out in the 1960s and 1970s by the late Academy editor Gerhard Lehmann (volumes 24, 27, 28, 29) was 'consistently negligent' or even misleading[22] – in contrast to the meticulous work demonstrated in volumes 25 (anthropology) and 26 (physical geography). (Werner

---

[22] Apart from often unhelpful and misleading introductory essays, his philological notes were haphazard and often wrong, he occasionally (and unknowingly) would re-arrange pages, he

Stark and Reinhard Brandt co-edited volume 25, and Stark is editing volume 26 in collaboration with Brandt.)

Adding yet another layer to this complicated situation, there are problems associated with publications of Kant's lecture notes *during* Kant's lifetime, by Kant's contemporaries Jäsche (logic) and Rink (pedagogy, physical geography). Indeed, such publications arguably stand in a category of their own, since they were published during Kant's lifetime (hence count as 'publications') but are really compendia of student notes or drafts rather than genuine Kantian works.[23] Kant had very little to do with these editions on logic, pedagogy, and geography, agreeing to them, but apparently little more than that. In comparison with the student notes, these published texts are in some ways *more* puzzling and difficult for scholars to work with than the student transcriptions (manuscripts). For rather than existing as available manuscripts, the textual bases or source notes of the Jäsche logic and Rink pedagogy and physical geography are either uncertain, lost, or unclearly stated by the editor.[24] This does not imply that we should completely ignore these editions[25] – indeed Lu-Adler, Stark, Shell, and Louden here make a positive use of them – but that we should bear in mind their potential problems.

Scholars and editors have disputed the value of the transcriptions since nearly the beginning of Kant studies. To help us further understand the limits and proper uses of the transcriptions, and to help us see why and how we should read the lecture notes, I present their controversial reception by Rosenkranz/Schubert, Sonderling, Dilthey, and Wundt (cf. Kant's own view of student notetaking in a 1778 letter to Herz, Br 10: 242). Rosenkranz and Schubert, in the Preface to their 1838 edition of Kant's collected writings, were skeptical about the transcriptions

---

routinely failed to properly mark marginalia and other significant features of the manuscripts, and would typically commit several transcriptional errors on every page.

23 On the issues associated with Jäsche's and Rink's editions, see this volume's chapters by Lu-Adler (logic), Shell (pedagogy), Stark (pedagogy), and Louden (geography).

24 In the case of the Rink geography, we know, even if Rink never stated this clearly, that it is an amalgam, based on texts that closely resemble the "Holstein" (1757–59) and the "Kaehler" (1775). Rink did not have those manuscripts, but worked from the (now lost) *Diktattext* (which resembles "Holstein") and a set of notes (also lost) that shares an ancestral manuscript with "Kaehler."

25 The *Anthropology from a Pragmatic Point of View* (1798) stands in much better shape than these editions by Rink and Jäsche, which are much more like the student transcriptions, and sometimes of *less* value, given the tampering by the editors. Kant actually published the 1798 work and we have his working manuscript (the "Rostock") for comparison. Nevertheless, it seems advisable, given the breadth of coverage of the lectures in *Vorlesungen über Anthropologie* (Kant 1997c), to consult the latter as well since they, *inter alia*, allow us to document changes in the course's structure and content. Several of these clearly dated (and well annotated) lecture notes were recently translated into English (Kant 2012a).

published after Kant's death and therefore chose not to include them in their edition. However, they had in mind the *published* lecture notebooks, specifically, the ones on physical geography edited by Vollmer, on religion edited by Pölitz (1817; 1831 [*sic*]), on metaphysics edited by Pölitz in 1821, and on anthropology edited by Friedrich Christian Starke in 1831. In other words, the alleged problem was not necessarily with the handwritten lecture transcriptions per se, but with these early editions of them. And even they admitted: "We do not deny the value of these writings; the lectures on metaphysics in particular appear to offer us a very accurate picture of Kant's lecturing" (Rosenkranz and Schubert 1838–42, vol. 1: x). Nevertheless, they claimed that, with the exception of possible misunderstandings and addenda on the part of a transcriber, "these writings [the early editions of the lectures] still essentially contain nothing that is not already to be found in the other writings"; note that this may very well be taken as a good *reason* to examine (reliable) editions of the lecture transcriptions, since we might profit from and more clearly understand another formulation or restatement of Kant's position (as the first paragraph of Henny Blomme's chapter in this volume suggests). In any case, their claim is surely off the mark if generalized to apply to all lecture transcriptions, for the latter contain key substantive claims that do not appear in Kant's published works. Moreover, as Erich Adickes noted, the lectures can be useful in characterizing the development of Kant's thought (1896: 579 f.), especially in areas (e. g., aesthetic theory) in which the published writings offer less material (or appear quite late) and can be fruitfully supplemented by the lectures (e. g., on anthropology or logic).

In fact, Jakob Sonderling goes toward the other extreme. Sonderling insists that, even in the Critical period, Kant held a variety of positions in the lectures that were superseded by the Critical writings, and, perhaps more controversially, that to a certain extent Kant led a *double life* in his teaching activity and in his writing (Sonderling 1903: 6 f.)

Although there are undoubtedly discrepancies between Kant's lectures and published writings, Sonderling's assessment seems only slightly more accurate than the (generalized) view of Rosenkranz and Schubert. For, as Pozzo notes in his chapter (following Hinske 1998: 30), the assertion of a "double life" and consequent rigid separation between Kant's teaching and writing seems to be too strong. The best hermeneutic position seems to be somewhere between the "double life" and "direct correspondence" views. In any case, it is hard to make broad statements of any value without considering a transcription's context, characteristics, content, and genesis. In other words, a historically sensitive analysis would carefully examine each text in its own particular context – what Kant was claiming, in what year, and in what course; whether there are variant readings or similar transcriptions; the origin and history of the transcription in question, the identity and alleged reliability of the transcriber (if not anonymous); and whether Kant makes similar claims in other places, i. e., in letters, published writings, or *Reflexionen*.

Unlike all preceding collected editions of Kant's works, the *Akademie-Ausgabe* included the lectures. In the preface to the edition's first volume, Wilhelm Dilthey, who served as its first editor and was himself a philosopher of notable interest, claims that the lectures are important for three reasons:

> They serve the edition by adding the material in the lectures to the context of his system that is otherwise provided by Kant's published writings .... At the same time this [D]ivision [of the lectures] offers an essential enrichment of the material for the developmental history of Kant ... Finally, one can attain through this long series of lectures an intuitive picture of Kant's teaching activity, his lectures, and the pedagogical side of his influence on the circle of his auditors. (AA 1: xiv; trans. Naragon 2015h)

Dilthey maintains that, from the time Herder was Kant's student to the last years of Kant's academic career, "the lecture notebooks accompany the development of the Critical philosophy" (AA 1: xiv). In fairness to opponents of his position, however, Dilthey also summarizes the potential problems with using the lecture notes:

> The most important among these is the uncertainty of this kind of transmission; never can such a notebook be seen as an authentic document of Kant's spoken word. It can also never be inferred, according to the pedagogical aims of lectures over which he himself quite emphatically declared, that he completely expressed his attained standpoint in the flow of the development of thinkers covered in his lectures .... And this is all the more necessary given the uncertainty of the time from which the material of the then published lectures arose, and over the accuracy of its reproduction. (AA 1: xiv; trans. Naragon 2015h)

Finally, Max Wundt criticized Paulsen's use (1899) of the Pölitz metaphysics lectures, raising questions regarding their lectures in general:

> And further, with these lectures we are everywhere dependent upon the insight, diligence, and care of the notetaker, unknown quantities of which we do not know how to take into account.... The lectures on metaphysics in particular seem rather carelessly written down. We never know how far we should trust the notetaker. Does he offer us everything? Does he omit the more difficult discussions? Sometimes one almost gets the impression that certain dogmatic doctrines are being offered to us for which, however, the connected critique of Kant's was omitted as too difficult. In general, it is easier to follow the description of some definite content than it is its justification. Because of this the lectures attain without doubt a more dogmatic stamp than was the intention of the lecturer. But, in addition to that, and despite all our troubles, we cannot determine the time these notes were written – or better, times, for there are certainly several notes produced at different times and then worked together. (Wundt 1924: 5 f., 9 f.; trans. Naragon 2015h)

Most of these points are by now familiar to the reader. On the dating problem, Wundt appears to be too skeptical, as many transcriptions can be dated quite accurately, though this naturally depends on the transcription in question. More interestingly, Wundt casts doubt on whether we can trust the transcriber, who may have omitted some important claims or arguments, especially the more difficult material. Again, this problem can often be solved by looking at various readings and the contents of contemporary lecture notes. But Wundt is right that the fact that Kant used a textbook (e. g., Baumgarten's *Metaphysica*) is bound to give the lecture notes a more dogmatic flavor. Still, Kant apparently strived to make his lectures as interesting as possible, and was aware of the pedagogical shortcomings of adopting a dry and 'scholastic' tone and method (see section 4). A given set of lecture notes is indeed likely to be, in varying degrees, some mixture of Kant, the textbook author, and the original auditor's interpretations of Kant (and, when applicable, later transcribers, copyists, or even editors). The key, in a given case, is to figure out what components make up the mix. While it is at times difficult, we need not assume it is impossible.

Wundt makes a different, nonetheless skeptical point about the Dohna notes published by Kowalewski, namely, that it is quite "self-explanatory" or obvious that the notebooks of a fifteen-year old student could not reveal to us any surprising new insights into Kant's theory.[26] In addition to noting the slightly *ad hominem* nature of this remark, I point out that scholars cannot know whether there are any new and surprising insights in the lecture transcriptions *until one examines the transcriptions* – a quite obvious point, yet one too easily forgotten. If this is correct, we should not dismiss or ignore the student notes outright. And even if the results or findings are not *surprising*, they could still be intellectually interesting, have scholarly value beyond their considerable historical interest, and help us understand Kant's intellectual development. For these reasons, I would submit that the lecture notes, despite the noted problems, merit our attention.

Moreover, true to the original vision of the first editors and Dilthey, the *Akademie-Ausgabe* published Kant's lectures on anthropology (1997c) and is completing its edition of the lectures on physical geography (2009b; forthcoming). As noted, the contemporary community of Kant scholars appears to be taking more and more interest in the lectures, even if, in some form, much of the material has been around for centuries. Many of Kant's lectures on logic, metaphysics, anthropology, and pedagogy have been translated into French, Italian, Spanish,

---

[26] Wundt assumes that these notes were written by Dohna rather than by his *Hofmeister*, who would have been older. In any case, these notes are not all written in the same hand.

English, and other languages. While interest in the lectures is hardly novel, lately there has been a considerable increase in such translations as well as articles and monographs. Moreover, some topics might benefit from more clarity or study, e. g., Kant's accounts of race in the anthropology and geography notes, which are justly controversial (e. g., see Mikkelsen 2013; Elden and Mendieta 2011; Kleingeld 2007). This debate, which likely will not subside anytime soon, has arguably been carried out either with insufficient attention to the genesis and context of the transcriptions, or, more philosophically, to the (e. g.) teleology and philosophy of nature presented in them, leaving further areas to explore. Finally, some of the lectures examined in this book (physics, mathematics, and philosophical encyclopedia) have never been fully translated into English or have been relatively neglected – for instance, the physics lectures stood out in that they were missing an abbreviation in the *Kant-Studien* list that was the basis for the abbreviations used in this volume – so there is an opportunity to learn from relatively overlooked areas of Kant's intellectual activity.

3 What, after all, is a lecture note?

Nachschrift is best used as a generic term containing three distinct kinds: the original notes, a fair copy of these notes, and copies made from a second set of notes. There is, of course, considerable latitude in how these terms are used, which can create considerable confusion. Here I have followed the senses described by Naragon (2015i), and a detailed treatment of these terms can also be found in Stark (1993).

A set of original notes (*Mitschrift*; also called the *Urschrift*, or original written text) is a manuscript actually prepared in the lecture hall. Such original notes are typically marked by many abbreviations and truncated sentences, hurried handwriting that is usually if not always in pencil, and often found on odd scraps of paper. Very few of the extant Kant *Nachschriften* – perhaps only those from Herder – were written in the classroom.

A fair copy or clean copy (*Reinschrift*) is a manuscript prepared at home from a set of original notes, typically in a neater hand, with fewer abbreviations and truncated sentences, always in ink, and with fewer spelling and grammatical errors. Margins are sometimes carefully prepared by creasing the pages, and headings are often included with decorative or ornamental script. The purpose is to create a manuscript that is easier to read, better organized, and with fewer errors. These fair copies might then be carried into the classroom, and occasionally amended by their author. The *Nachschriften* prepared by Dohna-Wundlacken, Mrongovius, and Vigilantius are good examples of fair copies, and the Vigilantius notes, in particular, suggest the addition of contemporary marginalia, possibly stemming from the *repetitoria* sessions that Kant held.

A copy (*Abschrift*) is a manuscript that was copied from another written text, either for one's own use, or for sale to another student. Such copies may remove obvious errors from the text, but the intention here, ultimately, is to duplicate a text – and quite often the copyist was too ignorant to make any corrections; in general, a copyist is more likely to introduce errors. Typical indicators that a manuscript is a copy are: spaces left blank where the original text was illegible, words or entire lines written twice (or else omitted altogether), various non-phonetic misspellings of proper names or philosophical terms suggesting that the writer was not present at the lecture, and may have little sense or knowledge of the context of the material. The existence of nearly verbatim *Nachschriften* would indicate that one of them was copied from the other, or that both are copies of some common ancestor. Similarly, as copies are made of copies, the copy errors accumulate; here one must make use of various philological techniques to determine relationships among the notes, and in this fashion determine which is closest to the original set of notes.

We should keep in mind the difference between the mere copying of a manuscript (with all the normal errors creeping in) and some new composition, where a new manuscript is created from two or more source manuscripts. We can safely assume that most clean copies (*Reinschriften*) would have been prepared shortly after the source lecture – and then might be copied and re-copied thereafter. Every so often, there is a *Nachschrift* that is composed from several manuscripts, and thus potentially long after the relevant source lectures. More typically, a student walks into the lectures with a copy from a previous set of notes (and thus, from an earlier source lecture), and then adds his own marginalia. In such a case, the main text and the marginalia would have different source lectures.

As one can imagine, taking, copying, and selling lecture notes was commonplace in eighteenth-century German universities. There was a considerable business in the production and sales of notes from Kant's lectures in particular. Kant himself was involved in procuring lecture notes for acquaintances, as his 1778 correspondence with Marcus Herz and Minister von Zedlitz reveals. Notes were copied either by a student from some other set of notes or else were 'professionally' copied and sold.[27] There was a demand for these notes by people who could not attend Kant's lectures, and it is easy to imagine students bringing purchased copies of notes into Kant's classroom.

---

27 On the acquisition and copying of notes by students, see Adickes (1911: 33–44) and Lindemann-Stark (1990: 75–7).

Table 2 reveals the total manuscripts (including those that were once extant) and manuscripts that are currently available, i. e., not lost or destroyed (Naragon 2015j). The important ways of "being available" include the following: (1) we have the original manuscript, (2) we possess some more recent copy written out by a Kant scholar (such as Reicke, Adickes, Menzer), e. g., when the original later went missing during the second World War, or (3) we have a published version of the text (where the original has gone missing). It may also be useful to know if any of these are available digitally, but it is of less importance than these original material documents.

Table 2: Availability of Manuscripts[28]

Discipline	Total Manuscripts	Total available
Anthropology	47	36
Physical Geography	36	32
Logic	26	19
Moral Philosophy	23	14
Metaphysics	17	13
Natural Theology	5	5
Physics	3	3
Philosophical Encyclopedia	3	1
Natural Law/Right	2	1
Pedagogy	1	1
Mathematics	1	1
Total	164	126

It is noteworthy that the disciplines that have the most total manuscripts are anthropology (47) and physical geography (36), and that these disciplines are likewise first and second in terms available today (anthropology: 36; geography: 32). The two fields can be seen as 'twin' (non-identical of course) disciplines – not only in that Kant taught geography in the summer semester and (starting in 1772/73) anthropology in the winter semester, but also since he conceived of both

---

28 Some of these numbers (based on Naragon 2015j) are deceptively high, as they include fragments and selections as well as complete manuscripts. Moreover, there is no guarantee that all of these manuscripts are numerically distinct, and many of the texts share common ancestors. The numbers are also subject to change with new discoveries. For commentary as well as complete lists of published and unpublished notes, see Naragon 2015a.

as 'worldly' and pragmatic rather than 'scholastic' disciplines, which likely contributed to their popularity and increased the demand for a copy.[29]

The present volume contains – among other figures – photographical reproductions of pages from the Herder mathematics, Herder metaphysics, "Naturrecht Feyerabend," and "Danziger Physik" transcriptions, along with translations of the notes penned on those pages. It also includes reproductions from Kant's own copy of Meier's *Auszug* and Baumgarten's *Metaphysica* as well as of a page from the printed edition of Kant's *Religion*. These reproductions and translations are included mainly as 'embellishments' offering a sense of how the transcriptions or books looked, but they may also facilitate a better understanding of the transcriptions or, in the case of Baumgarten and Meier, of how Kant used these books. In any case, they should not be taken as objects of commentary by the corresponding chapters.

4 A thrill or a yawn? Kant as lecturer

I now turn briefly to Kant in the classroom – an aspect that, even if largely biographical, fleshes out the context of his lectures. Kant was a private lecturer (*Privatdozent*) for fifteen years (1755–70) before becoming professor *ordinarius* of Logic and Metaphysics in 1770. Kant had a reputation, at least during his prime, for being a fascinating and inspiring teacher and lecturer.[30] There are many anecdotes of the contemporary accounts of Kant as a professor, but I limit myself to just a few – representing the beginning, middle, and end of Kant's teaching career.

Johann Gottfried Herder attended Kant's courses between 1762 and 1764. In a widely quoted passage from *Letters on the Advancement of Humanity* (Letter 79), Herder wrote, decades after he had left the university:

> I have had the good fortune to know a philosopher who was my teacher. He in his most vigorous manhood had the cheerful liveliness of a youth that will, I believe, accompany him into his old age. His brow, built for thinking, was the seat of indestructible serenity and joy, talk rich in ideas issued from his lips, joking, humor and wit were at his disposal, and his teaching lectures were the most amusing entertainment. He examined with as much spirit Leibniz, Wolff, Baumgarten, and Hume, as he followed the development of physics, the laws of nature as expounded by Kepler and Newton, and as he responded to the writings of Rousseau which were then appearing, his *Emile* and his *Heloise*, and every new discovery

---

29 On this point, see my chapter in this volume, especially its conclusion.
30 See Malter (1990) for a collection of texts on Kant's life. See also Naragon 2015e.

he assessed, and he always returned to the genuine knowledge of nature and to the moral value of man. The history of man, of peoples, and of nature, mathematics, and experience were the founts from which he enlivened his lectures and his conversation; nothing worth knowing left him indifferent, no cabal, no sect, no personal gain, no vain ambition had the least attraction for him as contrasted with the expansion and elucidation of truth. He encouraged and forced one agreeably to think for oneself. Domineering was foreign to his nature. This man whom I name with the greatest gratitude and respect is Immanuel Kant. (Herder 1877–1913, vol. 17: 404; Herder 1991: 424 f.; reprinted in Malter 1990: 57; trans. modified from Friedrich 1949: xxii)

Herder, about three years before his death and – strikingly – after a bitter break with Kant, reflects on himself in the third person, in the preface to *Kalligone* (1800):

> For more than thirty years I have known a youth [viz., Herder] who heard all of the lectures, some more than once, of the *founder of the Critical philosophy* himself – and indeed in his early, flourishing years. The youth marveled over the teacher's dialectical wit, his political as well as scientific acumen, his eloquence, [and] his intelligent memory. (Herder 1998: 651 f.; reprinted in Malter 1990: 59 f.; trans. Naragon 2015e, modified)

Kant's *self*-assessment is also worth quoting. In a late 1773 letter to Marcus Herz, who had just written a review of Ernst Platner's *Anthropology*, Kant comments on his course on anthropology, which he was then teaching for the second time, having first taught it in winter semester 1772/73.

> I have read your review of Platner's *Anthropologie*. I would not have guessed the reviewer myself but now I am delighted to see the evident progress of his skill. This winter I am giving, for the second time, a lecture course on *Anthropologie*, a subject that I now intend to make into a proper academic discipline. But my plan is quite unique. I intend to use it to disclose the sources of all the [practical] sciences, the science of morality, of skill, of human intercourse, of the way to educate and govern human beings, and thus of everything that pertains to the practical. I shall seek to discuss phenomena and their laws rather than the foundations of the possibility of human thinking in general. Hence the subtle and, to my view, eternally futile inquiries as to the manner in which bodily organs are connected with thought I omit entirely. I include so many observations of ordinary life that my auditors have constant occasion to compare their ordinary experience with my remarks and thus, from beginning to end, find the lectures entertaining and never dry. In my spare time, I am trying to prepare a preliminary study for the students out of this very pleasant empirical study, an analysis of the nature of skill (prudence) and even wisdom that, along with physical geography and distinct from all other learning, can be called knowledge of the world. (Letter 79; Br 10: 145 f. [Kant 1999: 141]; reprinted in Malter 1990: 126 f.)

Yet some *Reflexionen*, dated by Erich Adickes to around 1776, reveal that Kant was sometimes unhappy with his delivery and method when it came to logic and metaphysics, leading him to re-assert a distinction between useful, 'worldly' knowledge (which included anthropology and geography) and dry, 'scholastic' philosophy (e. g., logic and metaphysics). According to Refl 4989, Kant thought that his method of delivery had a disadvantageous form and appeared to be scholastic and dry (AA 18: 53). But it was apparently not just a matter of delivery. According to contemporaneous reflections on logic (Refl 2050–2052), Kant distinguished between "popular" methods that are necessary for "application" and for life, and those "suited for the school" (AA 16: 213 f.) – a theme also taken up by John Zammito's contribution to this volume.

Johann Georg Hamann, in a letter to Herder dated 26 October 1783, wrote that Kant was then (i. e., in winter semester 1783/84) lecturing on philosophical theology "to an amazing throng of auditors" (Malter 1990: 240). But in a 21 September 1791 letter to Karl Leonard Reinhold, one of Kant's earliest defenders, Kant admits that lecturing is becoming more difficult for him due to a deterioration in health and physical strength that began about two years earlier, that is, around 1789, even if he could still write and think without interruption in the mornings for two or three hours, before being forced to take breaks and work in intervals (Letter 487; Br 11: 288). Indeed, on Monday, 4 July 1791, Johann Gottlieb Fichte audited Kant's lecture and was thoroughly unimpressed. He entered into his diary that Kant, 67 years old at the time, "seemed sleepy to him" during their meeting (Malter 1990: 372). In a contemporaneous letter, Fichte confessed that he did not know whether Kant (the main reason Fichte had travelled to Königsberg) would help him much, since he considered his lectures to be less useful than his writings, and noted that Kant struck him as worn out and frail (Malter 1990: 375).

Finally, for a report on the usefulness of even late lectures in understanding Kant's publications, consider the words of an auditor of a summer semester 1795 logic course. In that semester Kant lectured on logic (50 auditors), physical geography (33 auditors), and offered a practicum for fifteen logic students. In a letter dated 30 April 1795, Wenzel Johann Gottfried von Purgstall (1773–1812), an Austrian nobleman, wrote to Wilhelm Joseph Kalmann, one of Reinhold's friends, noting that the logic course helped him better understand all three *Critiques*.

> One never leaves his auditorium without bringing home some elucidating hint into his writings, and it is as though one arrived at the easiest and shortest way to understanding many difficult sentences in the *Critiques of Pure and Practical Reason* …. Once one has come so far as to understand his *voice*, then it is not so difficult to understand his *thoughts*. He spoke last about *space* and *time*, and it was as though I had never understood anyone as I understand him; and now he is in that part of his *Logic* where he needs to discuss *cognition*. This gives him the opportunity to discuss their perfection, and to discuss logical, aesthetic, and other sorts of cognitions. He then discussed the main concepts, I believe, of the beautiful out of the *Critique of the Power Judgment*, and this so easily and understandable and entertainingly as can hardly be imagined. From this alone one can well imagine

how interesting it would be to hear his entire course, for then one would be easily made acquainted with *all* of his ideas. (Hügelmann 1879: 608–10; reprinted in Malter 1990: 418–21; trans. Naragon 2015e)

It is noteworthy that although Kant never offered a course in 'aesthetics',[31] he apparently discussed its themes and topics (beauty, judgment, etc.) while lecturing on logic.

5 Concluding unscientific remark

No doubt this volume has omitted a noteworthy topic or missed some intriguing angle, but thankfully the reader can consult the growing body of scholarship in this area of Kant studies. I hope this volume opens up some new questions and offers some compelling answers about Kant's philosophy in light of his university teaching. We might then, possibly, better understand Kant's philosophical positions and even some of his scientific doctrines, and, at least *indirectly*, more clearly articulate our own philosophical arguments, and defend or countervail contemporary philosophical positions with more historical self-awareness. How tightly one reads this 'indirectly' depends on one's view of the relation between philosophy and the history of philosophy as I hinted in the first section – a complex topic to be sure. Nevertheless, the reader can probably perceive, in the recent and apparently growing outpouring of editions, translations, guides, and studies of Kant, including this volume itself, a strong attraction among contemporary scholars to the view that many philosophical questions are formulated in concepts, themes, and questions inherited from the past and, in the case of contemporary 'western' philosophy, inherited from Kant in particular, and that both the philosophical traditions and Kant should therefore continue to be studied and re-interrogated, interpreted and re-interpreted.

But rather than refining and pursuing this point, I shall close with a final, fanciful thought. One of the values of studying the history of philosophy is arguably to expose and understand the philosophical presuppositions of our own day and, in Bernard Williams's phrase, "to make the familiar strange again" (2006: 260), including how those assumptions are formed and shaped by a philosopher's way of writing, communicating, or teaching philosophy. In this vein, it might be worthwhile to see how academic philosophy – including teaching and writing philosophy and the 'publish or perish' climate that can invade the

---

31 See footnote 15 above.

latter – has evolved through the ages, to reveal what sociological, economic, political, or cultural pressures have been placed on the practice of philosophy. Perhaps this book's 'method' or line of questioning could be fruitfully applied to other thinkers. What would a similar volume on Aristotle or Simplicius, Plotinus or Proclus, Averroes or Aquinas, Baumgarten or Hutcheson, Fichte or Hegel, or Arendt or Rawls, look like? How did their philosophical and academic lives differ from Kant's – and from our own? More importantly – to philosophers at any rate – what philosophical conclusions can we draw from this? To pose such questions is in no way to reduce philosophy and philosophical reason to such pressures and circumstances (how, after all, could posing a question do *that*?), but it is, at the very least, to acknowledge them.

6 Overview of the chapters

The following chapters naturally vary in scope and method, contextualizing and philosophizing in different ways and from diverse perspectives (some having a narrower, some a broader focus), but a principal goal, as noted, is to gain a more informed interpretation of Kant's lectures by considering the connection between the student notes and his published works or philosophical writings – at least so far as this is feasible or helpful given the discipline in question. The first section examines metaphysics.

Steve Naragon uses Herder's notes from Kant's metaphysics lectures as an illustration of the general problem of distinguishing three possible voices in the text: Kant, Baumgarten, and Herder. Naragon first makes general observations on the scholarly use of the student notes from Kant's classroom and a few specific observations on the importance of the Herder notes. He then reviews the discussion of *real* and *logical* grounds found in the notes, to illustrate how much of Kant's voice can actually be found in the Herder notes. Naragon concludes that there is a considerable overlap of material between the lecture notes and Kant's published works, as well as a steady engagement by Kant with other philosophers of his day.

Courtney Fugate, co-translator (with John Hymers) of Baumgarten's *Metaphysica* (Baumgarten 2013), which Kant also used in his course on anthropology and theology, examines the challenge that the notion of metaphysics as a science would have posed for Kant as a lecturer. How did Kant's understanding of the nature and unity of metaphysics change over the years? How does this relate to the traditional conception of metaphysics found in Baumgarten's textbook? And how did Kant understand the relationship between metaphysics and his emerging Critical philosophy? Fugate examines how Kant's response to this challenge evolved during his teaching career. He compares the extant transcriptions between 1764 and the 1780s, paying attention to the relationship between the way Kant frames the lectures for his students, and how Kant selects from, rejects, and modifies various parts of Baumgarten's textbook while partially adopting some of them as his own.

Dennis Schulting focuses on transcendental apperception and the notion of 'consciousness' in the metaphysics lectures contemporaneous with Kant's Critical phase. He looks at the Leibnizian and Wolffian background of Kant's theory of apperception, and the usage and occurrence of the term 'consciousness' in the lecture notes and in Kant's pre-Critical published work. He addresses aspects of the theory of obscure representations in order to clarify Kant's distinction between apperception and mere consciousness. He then examines how Kant's conception of 'consciousness' develops from the pre-Critical Herder and Pölitz metaphysics lectures to the lectures of the Critical period, viz., the Metaphysik von Schön and Mrongovius, where the notion of 'apperception' first crops up and which show that Kant departs from the Leibnizian-Wolffian conflation of apperception and consciousness, although there appears to be some carry-over from the pre-Critical lectures. After considering an ambiguity about the relation between inner sense and transcendental apperception in the Mrongovius notes, Schulting concludes that Kant espouses a gradual conception of consciousness in line with Leibniz's gradual conception of perceptions.

Corey Dyck considers how Kant's treatment of rational psychology in the lectures serves as a complement to the discussion in the first *Critique*. Dyck holds that the discussions preserved in the student notes expand on key aspects of Kant's criticism of the rational psychologist, and that they prove particularly useful in illuminating Kant's developing criticisms of the arguments for the soul's immortality, an issue on which Kant has comparatively little to say in the first *Critique*. Moreover, Dyck contends that the discussions in the notes also aid in understanding the basis for, and implications of, Kant's surprising endorsement of a doctrinal belief in immortality grounded on a teleological argument, that is, on a consideration of the human being as a natural rather than a moral being.

Huaping Lu-Adler discusses some problems with Kant's logic corpus while recognizing its richness and potential scholarly value. She examines the Jäsche *Logik*, Wiener Logik, Logik Dohna-Wundlacken, and other lecture notes, and several logic Reflections, holding that in these texts Kant presents logic as reason's a priori cognition of the purely formal conditions of thinking (hence as a kind of intellectual self-cognition). She explicates Kant's conception of logic, aiming to shed light on three main issues: what Kant thinks should be included in logic proper, given that he used Georg Friedrich Meier's *Auszug aus der Vernunftlehre* as the basis for his logic lectures but also went beyond it in significant ways; how we should understand Kant's attitude toward Aristotle's logic and in what sense he views the latter as complete *by nature* while departing from its teachings at various significant points; and how we should interpret Kant's view about the nature, subject matter, ground, and scope of logic. She proposes and explains a methodical way to approach Kant's writings on logic. She then applies her innovative proposal by showing how one can use various materials from the corpus to construct a Kantian demonstration of the formal rules of thinking lying at the base of Kant's Metaphysical Deduction. Potentially opening up new lines of research, she suggests that the same proposal can be fruitfully iterated with respect to other topics. After presenting and applying her method, Lu-Adler considers other modern notions of logic (e. g., Locke's and Wolff's), with which Kant contrasts his own, but whose ideas he sometimes weaves into his own concept of logic.

Riccardo Pozzo examines Kant's usage of Latin in his classroom, exploring the evolution of the logic "text" from an interleaved handbook (*durchschossenes Handbuch*) to a student lecture transcription (*Vorlesungsnachschrift*), and relates Kant's pedagogical activities and aims to the first *Critique*. Pozzo starts with some definitions pertaining to literary genres, passes through institutional requirements concerning scheduling and textbooks, and ends with Kant's use of Latin in class, documented by the substantial number of Latin lines written by Kant in his interleaved copy of Meier's *Auszug*, which derives from Kant's practice of dictating in Latin during his *repetitoria*. Pozzo explains Kant's reasons for sticking to Latin and looks at how these passages ended up in the *Nachschriften*. Finally, he considers Kant's *Critique of Pure Reason* as having been originally conceived as a textbook for lectures on aesthetics (i. e., on space and time), logic, and metaphysics.

Oliver Sensen traces the development of Kant's supreme principle of morality throughout the student lecture notes and spells out Kant's argument for the supreme principle. While Kant formulates the content of obligation as early as the 1760s, and while his critique of alternative theories changes little over time, he comes close to proposing the *source* of the supreme principle in the Collins lectures (mid-1770s), but does not yet have the concept of autonomy and respect for the moral law as moral motivation. It is only with the *Groundwork* and the contemporaneous Mrongovius II lecture notes that Kant's positive solution is fully worked out, Sensen argues. If so, the moral philosophy lectures elucidate Kant's argument for the supreme principle of morality. While presenting his claims, Sensen sketches the background of the four groups of Kant's lectures on ethics, and he offers a possible explanation of what caused Kant to change his views on moral motivation.

Faustino Fabbianelli reconstructs the different lines of Kant's theory of moral imputation (*imputatio*). He claims that Kant offers different models of imputation by virtue of which one and the same action can be judged differently; he names these the *absolute* model of imputation and the *relative* model, according to which there are degrees of freedom. Fabbianelli argues that the variations in Kant's theory reflect Kant's different views of the role of reason and empirical experience, and that the fluctuations are not simply a function of the level and status of philosophical reflection, but are also consequences of Kant's discussion with key philosophical figures such as J. A. H. Ulrich, C. C. E. Schmid, and K. L. Reinhold. Fabbianelli compares Kant's lectures with his published works on imputation, and he evaluates the two kinds of texts in light of the critical or sympathetic writings of Kant's contemporaries.

Paul Guyer turns to Kant's lectures on anthropology to help us understand Kant's claims about play and society published in the *Critique of the Power of Judgment*. He focuses on three transcriptions: Collins, from the first time Kant gave the course (1772/73), Friedländer (1775/76), and Mrongovius (1784/85). Guyer considers these lecture transcriptions to be important sources for the development of Kant's aesthetic theory, both with regard to play in response to, and in creating, beauty, and with respect to the interest we take in taste. Guyer concludes that Kant's discussions of aesthetics in the lectures shed light on the central concepts of his mature aesthetic theory, those of the free play of our cognitive powers as the underlying source of our pleasure in *beauty* on the one hand, and of the judgment of *taste* on the other as an assessment of the universal shareability of such pleasure and as the basis of a further social interest in beauty.

Alix Cohen observes that by encouraging the development of the feeling of the love of honor, not only do Kant's lectures on anthropology go against traditional portrayals of his ethics as anti-emotions, they approve of a feeling that is literally self-centered since it consists in desiring that one's self be valued. To make sense of this claim, Cohen argues that the feeling of the love of honor has a dual nature, as a means to preserve the species and as an aid to morality. She begins by exploring the *social* role of honor, leading her to argue that while its aim is to preserve the mere appearance of respect, it thereby fosters genuine respect. She then turns to its *moral* role, arguing that it is an 'aid' to morality in the strongest possible sense of the term, since it both prompts the conception of self-esteem and motivates agents to become worthy of honor. On this basis, she suggests that a shift transforms the natural function of the feeling of love of honor from an inclination to fake virtue to an inclination that aids it. She concludes that the perspective of Kant's lectures on anthropology differs in important and meaningful ways from his Critical position, for the lectures are not concerned with rationality in general, but rather with the embodied human agent.

Werner Stark examines the origin, structure, and aim of the course on education, which Kant taught four times (1776/77, 1780, 1783/84, 1786/87). Friedrich Theodor Rink, Kant's younger colleague and former student, edited and published *Immanuel Kant: On Pedagogy* (1803). On the latter's existence and purpose, Stark warns that it is *not* a student transcription (*Nachschrift*) of a lecture allegedly given by Kant in the 1780s; that there is *no* compelling evidence for Rink's claim that the text is made up of Kant's personal notes written down for his lecture; yet that Weisskopf's (1970) view that the text basically consists of Rink's compilation of heterogeneous parts is also *not* sufficiently justified. On the positive side, Stark argues that we can discern a different aim and origin if we keep in mind the Prussian school reforms and the pedagogical discussions at the Albertina's Faculty of Philosophy in the 1780s and 90s. *On Pedagogy* can also be seen as a counter-proposal to the Latin school Kant attended. We may assume, Stark concludes, that *On Pedagogy* belongs to the broad context preceding *The Conflict of the Faculties*, and that in it Kant adopts positions that are put *ad acta* no later than 1798.

Susan Meld Shell acknowledges that the text that has come down to us as Rink's *Lectures on Pedagogy* (or *Immanuel Kant: On Pedagogy*) has had a long and checkered career. Despite its known defects, Shell argues, *Lectures on Pedagogy* (1803) is of greater philosophic interest than has been generally recognized. Read with care, and against the backdrop of Kant's shifting political setting, the *Lectures on Pedagogy* evinces an intimate connection with major themes of Kant's published writings during the late 1780s and 90s, especially *Religion within the Boundaries of Mere Reason* (1792), and *Anthropology from a Pragmatic Point of View* (1798). The long-brewing contest over popular education in Prussia had reached a state of crisis during Kant's final decade of professional activity, with serious, and potentially grave, implications for his own life work. The course, Shell maintains, specifically addresses that crisis while also reflecting Kant's ongoing concern to reconcile freedom and lawful necessity, a concern that reaches back to his earliest reading of Rousseau's *Emile* in the mid-1760s.

John Zammito holds that the lecture notes on philosophical encyclopedia – even in their fragmentary 1775 form – offer us insight into the transition from the Kant of the 1760s, the Kant of Popular philosophy, to the Kant of the Critical philosophy. He contends that the philosophical encyclopedia course was an expression of Kant's transient interest in Popular philosophy and a casualty of his Critical turn. Zammito sees the course as a clear instance of Kant's pedagogical privileging of "philosophy for the world" over "philosophy for the schools," but notes that it is also problematic in its affirmation of a historical approach to philosophy, largely inconsistent with Kant's wider conception of philosophy as something that must be practiced personally rather than studied empirically. Zammito adds that Kant's attitude towards aesthetic-literary elegance and analytical rigor is a crucial yet puzzling issue raised by this course material. Finally, Zammito argues that Kant's disenchantment with Johann Feder (whose textbook he used in the course) and Feder's colleagues and their program of psychological displacement of philosophy, culminating in the bitter quarrel over the Göttingen review of the first edition of the *Critique of Pure Reason* (1781), helps explain Kant's abandonment of the course.

Frederick Rauscher turns to Kant's lecture on natural right (or natural law),[32] "Naturrecht Feyerabend" (1784), the only preserved transcription of Kant's course on natural right or law (*Naturrecht*) and which Rauscher translated for The Cambridge Edition of the Works of Immanuel Kant. Rauscher reviews the transcript's dating, content, background, and relation to Kant's published writings. The philosophical discussion in his chapter focuses on Kant's views of sovereignty, representation, and monarchy. Rauscher argues that at the time of the summer 1784 course Kant was *not* in fact committed to a view that would justify his later claim, concerning the French Revolution, that when the King of France called the Estates General into session, the monarch transferred sovereignty back to the people.

Günter Zöller's chapter on "Naturrecht Feyerabend" presents Kant's doctrine of the grounds of 'bindingness' (*Verbindlichkeit*) in law and ethics. Zöller places the transcription's account of *Verbindlichkeit* against the background of the civil-law tradition of *obligatio*. He puts it in the context of Kant's general enterprise of developing the foundational concepts of moral philosophy and ethics on the basis of technical terms drawn from law and politics. Zöller addresses the parallel between Plato's and Kant's attempts to establish *ethical* principles on a presumed analogy with the form and function of rules in politics and law. He presents Roman law's doctrine of (private) *obligatio* as the generic binding force of law. Zöller examines the transcription's dissociation of ethical obligation from hope and fear as mechanisms of psychosocial constraint. Finally, the lecture's position on the *inter*subjectivity and *intra*subjectivity of law and ethics, respectively, is shown to differ from the account in Kant's contemporaneous *Groundwork of the Metaphysics of Morals* (1785).

---

[32] *Recht* is notoriously difficult to translate. While Frederick Rauscher (like Mary Gregor, in The Cambridge Edition's *Practical Philosophy*) prefers to translate *Naturrecht* as "natural right" to stress its connection to Kant's other uses of *Recht*, Günter Zöller prefers "natural law," pointing out that *Naturrecht* has a disciplinary function and that Kant is writing in the natural law tradition. (For details, see their chapters.) Needless to say, this difficult terminological-philosophical issue cannot be settled here, but the reader should keep in mind that the best translation of the term remains controversial.

Stephen Palmquist asks how serious Kant was about his suggestion, found in the first edition Preface to *Religion*, that he hoped his book would be suitable for use as compulsory reading for a philosophy class that theology students of the future would be required to take in their final year of study. Palmquist's chapter begins by sketching the pedagogical themes that develop progressively throughout *Religion* and become more prominent as the text proceeds. He then turns to Kant's own lectures, especially the Pölitz lecture on the philosophical doctrine of religion, to answer two key questions. First, do the student notes for lectures delivered prior to 1792 provide evidence that Kant followed his own, subsequently articulated, theory of moral-religious pedagogy when he taught university courses relating to religion and theology? And second, do the lectures notes provide any evidence that Kant's views on moral pedagogy *within a religious community* predated his writing of *Religion*?

Norbert Fischer focuses on the Pölitz edition of Kant's lectures on the philosophical doctrine of religion. Fischer's thesis is that some elements of the Critical philosophy can be seen as a kind of "pastoral service" for the educated. He argues that while this feature is already evident in Kant's published works, it is even more obvious in Kant's lectures and especially in his remarks about the "purpose of creation." The Pölitz transcription, Fischer holds, not only allows us to make sense of passages in Kant's publications, but also makes connections between the Critical philosophy and life. Fischer discusses key elements of Kant's philosophy of religion in his published works, focuses on Kant's analysis of religion in Pölitz, and finally comments on the account of some central Christian themes found in the lecture.

Antonio Moretto turns to the mathematics lecture notes written by Kant's famous student, Johann Gottfried Herder.[33] In his first years as *Privatdozent* Kant offered a course on mathematics nearly every semester, but for some (apparently unknown) reason suddenly stopped teaching it after winter semester 1763/64. Jus-

---

[33] Our only lecture notes from Kant's mathematics lectures come from Herder; it is *possible*, however, that these notes stem from another professor's lectures, not Kant's (Naragon 2015k). The full professor of mathematics during Herder's student years, Christoph Langhansen, was offering public lectures on arithmetic, geometry, trigonometry, and astronomy in a two-semester sequence at this time, and Herder's poverty would speak in favor of his attending these public lectures. However, we lack positive evidence that Herder attended Langhansen's mathematics lectures, and Kant was presumably allowing Herder to attend his classes for free. Karl Christiani, full professor of practical philosophy and Langhansen's son-in-law, was also offering occasional private courses on mathematics at the time. Moreover, Herder is reported to have diligently attended the lecture of F. J. Buck, who taught mathematics during this time using Wolff's *Anfangsgründen* (Böttiger 1838: 128).

tified or not, this set of notes has received relatively scant scholarly attention. In examining "Mathematik Herder," Moretto explores how, for his 1762/63 lectures on mathematics, Kant used Wolff's *Auszug aus den Anfangsgründen aller mathematischen Wissenschaften* to outline the structure of mathematics. Moretto considers the distinction between *pure* and *applied* mathematics in relation to the status of mathematics in Kant's day, revealing in particular the influence of Abraham Gotthelf Kästner. Moretto also examines ties between the conception of math adopted in this pre-Critical text and the later and more familiar account typically associated with Kant: the concept of magnitude connected with the categories of unity and plurality; *mathesis universalis* as universal science of magnitudes; the regard for the applied part of mathematics (*mathesis applicata*); the consideration of algorithms that show how natural numbers are reducible to additions of units; and a regard for sensible images in arithmetic.

Christian Onof examines the student notes on Kant's lectures on physics, which Kant began teaching in winter semester 1755/56. Kant's earliest publications were largely in physics or physical geography, and he taught physics for decades. Onof discusses the Friedländer or "Berliner Physik" transcription (from around 1775 or 1776) and the Mrongovius or "Danziger Physik" transcription (1785). He analyzes a number of themes central to Kant's interest in natural philosophy, including the infinite divisibility of matter, impenetrability, and repulsive and attractive forces. To shed light on Kant's writings on natural science, above all the *Metaphysical Foundations of Natural Science* (1786) composed around this time (see the letter to Schütz, 13 September 1785; Br 10: 406.26–27), Onof focuses mainly on the Danziger Physik, discussing passages that reveal the development of a Critical approach.

Henny Blomme also discusses Kant's lectures on physics, concentrating on Kant's relationship to late eighteenth-century and nineteenth-century developments in chemistry as reflected in the Danziger Physik. He holds that these developments were the main reason why, after having used Erxleben's *Anfangsgründe der Naturlehre* (1772) for several years, Kant switched to Karsten's *Anleitung zur gemeinnützlichen Kenntniß der Natur* (1783). Unlike Karsten, Kant stressed the importance of a clear division between physics and chemistry. Blomme argues that because the current conception of what it means to be a science radically differs from Kant's, it is difficult for us to understand his evaluation of the scientific status of chemistry. Accordingly, few contemporary scholars have been able to explain why, in *Metaphysical Foundations*, Kant claimed that chemistry would likely never be more than 'a systematic art'. Accordingly, Blomme gives a brief history of the theories of elements and principles; situates the Danziger Physik with regard to contemporaneous chemistry; explains what turns a 'doctrine of nature' into a proper science; characterizes Kant's conception of a special metaphysics of corporeal nature; asks why Kant needs a fundamental determination of matter; offers a reconstruction of Kant's conception of 'empirical affection' and its role in *Metaphysical Foundations*, taking into account Kant's theory of change and motion; and, finally, considers whether Kant would have considered organic chemistry to be a proper science.

In the penultimate chapter, Robert Louden tells us why we should devote scholarly attention to Kant's lectures on geography, including even the Rink edition. A complete English translation of Rink's edition of Kant's *Physical Geography* was published in 2012 (Kant 2012c; cf. Bolin 1968), and several significant transcriptions of Kant's classroom lectures on physical geography are still forthcoming in volume 26 of the *Akademie-Ausgabe* of his collected writings. So, why has Kant's work on geography suffered from so much neglect? Contrary to received scholarly wisdom, Louden argues that the main cause of the neglect is *not* Rink's editorial sloppiness. Rather, Kant's physical geography has simply not been considered to be as important as his contributions to metaphysics, logic, ethics, theology, or anthropology. Louden argues that Kant's *Physical Geography* deserves our scholarly respect, and he presents four reasons for taking it seriously.

Finally, in my own chapter I explore to what extent Kant's developing Critical philosophy influenced his lectures on physical geography – given between summer semester 1756 (Kant's second semester of university teaching) and 1796 (his last) – as well as the corresponding lecture announcements and essays on race and teleology. The chapter examines Kant's conceptions of organisms and animals, nature's agency, and apparent design in these writings and physical geography *Nachschriften* (not Rink's edition) from the 1750s to 1790s: manuscripts Holstein, Kaehler, Dönhoff, and Dohna. I maintain that methodological distinctions between empirical science and pure, transcendental philosophy, and between 'popular', worldly philosophy and 'scholastic' philosophy, are crucial for understanding his use of teleological principles in the geography course. I show that Kant applies teleological principles to nature in a rather 'direct' fashion in these lectures, although this should not be taken to mean that he considers the teleological judging of organisms to be incompatible with judging them mechanistically.[34]

---

[34] For comments on the main sections of this Introduction, I am especially grateful to Henny Blomme, Steve Naragon, Stephen Palmquist, Dennis Schulting, Oliver Thorndike, and Günter Zöller.

I | **Metaphysics**

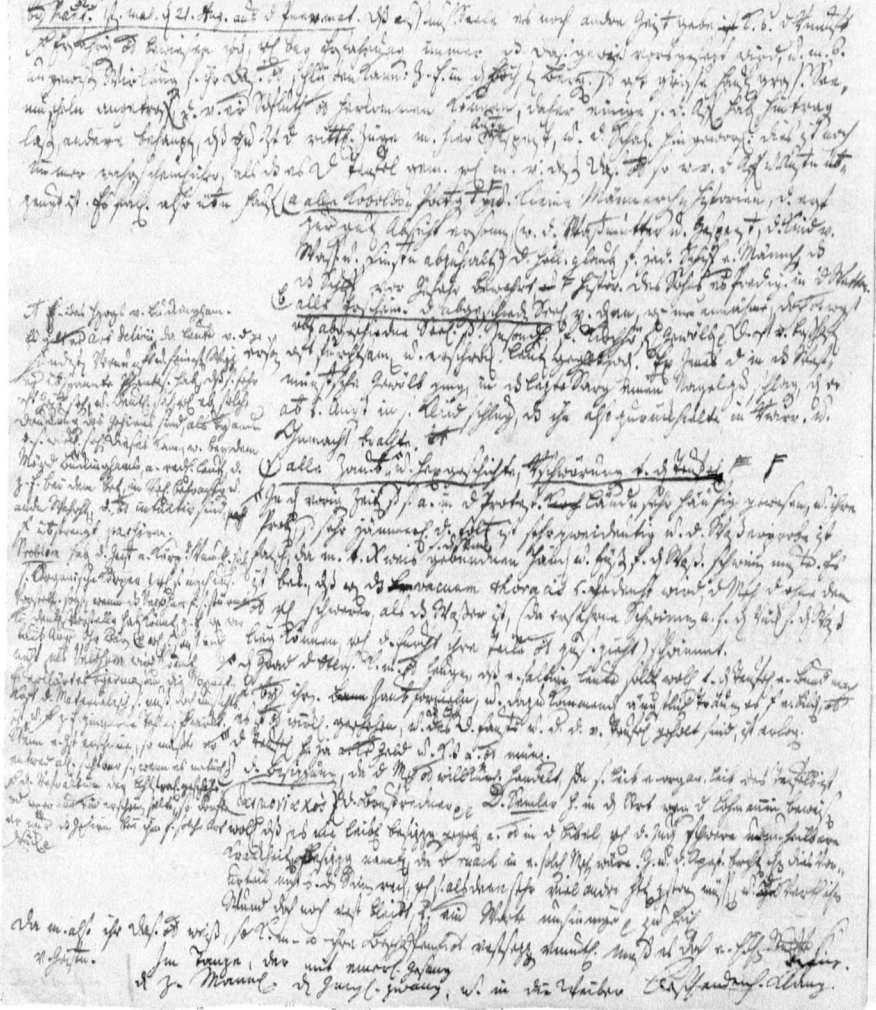

Fig. 1: Reproduction of a page from Herder's first day of notes from Kant's metaphysics lectures (cf. AA 28: 148–50). Page 32 of a 140-page notebook begins: "bey Kant. 1sten mal. den 21. Aug. aus der Pneumatologie." Reproduced with the kind permission of Stiftung Preußischer Kulturbesitz, Berlin, Germany. Call number: NL-Herder XXVI.5. Steve Naragon's translation of the text follows; the German text is also given.

Transcription of the Text in Fig. 1
bey Kant. 1sten mal. den 21. Aug. aus der Pnevmatologie

Daß ausser unserer Seele es noch andre Geister gebe, kann aus der Vernunft durch Erfahrung nicht bewiesen werden, weil bey Erfahrungen immer das Dasein gewiß vorausgesezt wird, und man aus ungewißen Wirkungen auf ihr Dasein nicht schlüßen kann: Z. E. in den höchsten Bergen sind oft grosse haufen grosser Seemuscheln angetroffen, die von einer Sindfluth nicht herkommen können, daher einige sie die Affen haben hintragen laßen, andere behaupten, daß zu Zeit der ritterlichen Züge man hier Austern gespeist, und die Schalen hingeworfen. Dies ist noch immer wahrscheinlicher, als daß es Der Teufel gemacht weil man von deßen Dasein nicht so wie von der Affen und Austern überzeugt ist. Es fallen also übern haufen:

α) alle Kobolds Poltergeister (historie des Sohns eines Prediger in der Wetterau) und kleine Männerchen Historien, die erst zur guten Absicht ersonnen, (wie die Waßermütter und Gespenster, die Kinder vom Waßer und Finstern abzuhalten). Die Holländer glauben auf jedem Schiff ein Männchen, das das Schiff vor Gefahr bewahrt,

β) alle Erscheinungen der abgeschiedenen Seelen, von den, wenn mans annähme, doch nicht weiß obs abgeschiedne Seelen sind. Insonderheit auf Kirchhöfen, Gewölben etc. Die oft von boßhaften ersonnen oft [von] furchtsamen und erschrocknen Leuten geglaubt werden. Exempel Jenes der in das Westmünstersche Gewölb ging, in das lezte Sarg einen Nagel zu schlagen, den er aber aus Angst in sein Kleid schlug, das ihn also zurückhielte, in Verwirrung und Ohnmacht brachte.

{Anmerkung E. des Herzogs von Buckingham. Es gibt eine Art delirii, da leute von der gesundesten Vernunft und feinste Wizz eine überspannte Phantasie haben, daß sie sehr oft Geister sehen, und deutlich sehen, weil eben solche Drückungen des Gehirns sind, als bey andern die sie wirklich sehen. Dieses kann, wie bey dem Mörder Buckinghams, auch redlichen Leuten, die z. E. bei dem beten, in Religionsbetrachtungen und andern Wahrheiten, die nicht intuitiv sind, sich überanstrengt, passiren.}

γ) alle Zauber- und Hexengeschichte, Verschwörung mit dem Teufel. Den Grad der Gottlosigkeit kann man nicht leugnen, daß einfaltige leute sollten wollen mit dem Teufel ein Bund machen auch bey ihren Zauberformeln, und dazu kommenden ängstlichen Träumen es sich einbilden, aber es ist nicht wirklich geschehen, und das leben des D. Fausts und die die vom Teufel geholt sind, ist erlogen. Der Teufel hat ja auch kein Geld und kanns auch nicht münzen.

In den vorigen Zeiten sind sie auch in der Protestantischen Ländern sehr häufig gewesen, und ihre Proben, sind sehr jämmerlich. Die folter ist sehr zweideutig und die Waßerprobe ist falsch; da man mit kreuzweis auf den Rucken gebundnen Händen und Füßen auf den Waßer schwimen muste. Es ist bekannt, daß wenn das vacuum thoracis ausgedehnt wird; der Mensch der ohne dem nicht viel schwerer, als das Waßer ist, (da erfahrne Schwimmer auch auf den Rücken auf den Waßer liegen können, weil die furcht, ihre Teile nicht zusammenzieht) schwimmt.

δ) die Besizzungen, da der Mensch nicht willkürlich handelt, sondern sein leib ein organischer leib des Teufels ist (δαιμονιακοσ) die Brustredner etc. etc. D. Semler hat in den Streit wegen der Lohmannin beweisen wollen, daß es nie leibliche besizzungen gegeben, auch nicht in der Bibel, weil die Juden schwere und unheilbare Krankheiten, Besizzungen nannten, da der ruach in ein solchen Menschen wäre. Jesus und die Apostel brauchten ihnen dies Vorurteil nicht aus dem Sinn reden, weil sie alsdenn sehr viel andre hätten zerstören müssen, und der Werth ihrer Wunder doch noch vest bleibt, mit einem Worte unsinnige etc. zu heilen.

{Problem: haben die Geister auch Körper? Vermutlich haben sie Organische Körper 1) weil sie nach unserer Vorstell.ung sonst, wenn das Universum auf sie stürmte keine deutlichen Vorstellungen haben könnten, z.E. wenn wir lauter Auge Ohr wären 2) weil sie sonst wohl nicht ins Universum wirken könnten. Es erklärt es einigermaßen die Magnetkraft die Materialisch sein muß, doch unsichtbar ist und durch z.E. zinzerne Teller durchwirkt. Wenn ein Geist erschiene, so müßte er entweder allen sichtbar sein, wenn es natürlich durch die Refraktion der lichtstralen geschähe, oder wenn er nur einem erscheinen sollte, so dörfte er nur das Gehirn bei ihm auf solche Art drücken etc.}

Da man also ihr Dasein nicht weiß, so kann man auch ihre Beschaffenheit nicht vestsezzen, vermutlich muß es doch ein höhere Stuffe sein von Geistern.

English Translation
with Kant the first time, August 21st, from the pneumatology.

That there might be yet other spirits besides our own souls cannot be proven by reason through experience, because with experiences existence is always presupposed with certainty, and one cannot infer their existence from uncertain effects. E. g., in the highest mountains one often finds large piles of sea mussels that could not have come from the biblical flood, therefore some maintain that apes carried them there, others that, during the time of the Crusades, they dined here on oysters and threw away the shells. This is always more likely than that the devil made them, since one is not as convinced of his existence as of apes and oysters. The following are, therefore, to be rejected:

(α) all kobolds, poltergeists (story of the son of a preacher in the Wetterau) and stories of little men, first thought up with good intentions (like the water-mother and ghosts that keep children away from water and the dark). The Dutch believe that a little man aboard each ship protects that ship from danger.

(β) <u>all appearances of departed souls</u>, of which, if one accepts it, one still does not know whether they are departed souls. Especially in churchyards, burial vaults, etc. Often thought up by malicious people and believed by the fearful and horrified. <u>Example</u>: the person who entered the Westminster vault to hammer a nail into the last sarcophagus, but in his fear nailed through his own clothing, holding him fast, so that he became confused and fainted.

{Note. Example of the Duke of Buckingham. There is a kind of *delirii* [delirium], where people with the healthiest reason and finest wit have an overstretched fantasy and thus often see spirits, and see them distinctly, because the very same impressions are made in the brain as when they really see things. As with the murder of Buckingham, this can also happen to honest people who overstrain themselves, e. g., in prayer, in religious observations and other truths that are not intuitive.}

(γ) <u>all tales of wizards and witches and oaths with the devil</u> One cannot deny a degree of godlessness, that simple people should want to make a pact with the devil, also with their magic formulas and the anxious dreams that imagine it; but it did not really happen, and the life of Dr. Faust and of those fetched by the devil are all fabricated. The devil also has no money, nor can he mint it.

In previous times they were quite frequent, in the Protestant lands as well, and the trials were horrible. Torture is very ambiguous and the trial by water is false – that one must float on one's back in the water with hands and feet bound cross-wise. It is known that when the *vacuum thoracis* [chest cavity] is extended that the human – who is not much heavier than water anyway – will float (here experienced swimmers can also lie on their backs in the water, because they do not curl themselves up out of fear).

(δ) <u>possessions</u>, where a human being does not act voluntarily, but rather his body is the organic body of the devil (δαιμονιακοσ [Greek: demon]), who speaks from the chest, etc. etc. Dr. Semler wanted to prove in his argument regarding Miss Lohmannin that there never were bodily possessions, also not in the Bible, because the Jews called any serious and untreatable illness a 'possession', that there was a *ruach* [Hebrew: spirit] in such people. Jesus and the Apostles did not try to stop this prejudice, because then they would also have had to stamp out much more, and the value of their miracles still remains firm, to be able to heal the insane, etc., with a word.

{<u>Problem</u>: do the spirits also have bodies? Presumably they have organic bodies (1) because otherwise, according to our representations, they would not be able to have any distinct representations when the *universum* [universe] impressed upon them, e. g., if we were mere eyes [or] ears. (2) because otherwise they would not be able to act in the *universum* [universe]. Some of this could be explained with magnetic power, which must be material and yet is invisible and is able to act, e.g., through a tin plate. If a spirit were to appear, then it would have to be either visible to everyone, if it happened naturally through the refraction of light-rays, or if it appeared to only one, then only his brain would need to be affected, etc.}

Therefore, because one does not know of their existence, one also cannot determine anything about their constitution, although presumably it must be a higher order of spirits.

Chapter 1
Reading Kant in Herder's Lecture Notes

Steve Naragon

It would be pleasant to imagine when reading the various student notes from Kant's lectures – those written down by Herder, for instance, in the 1760s – that we were reading notes that Kant himself might just as well have written himself and then read aloud to the class – that the students were acting merely as stenographers of greater or lesser skill. Such pleasant thoughts are quickly dissipated by obvious worries, however. To take as an example Herder's notes from Kant's metaphysics lectures, the notes I wish to discuss here: Are we reading Kant's unadulterated words (if perhaps not all of them) as spoken in the classroom? Or are we reading Herder's thoughts about Kant or about the Baumgarten text from which Kant was lecturing? And even if these words (or at least most of them) *are* Kant's, how many are just a re-hashing of Baumgarten, as opposed to Kant's own views on the topic at hand?

These are reasonable worries, and completely disentangling the principal voices – Kant, Herder, and Baumgarten – is likely a lost cause; but by comparing Herder's notes against Kant's publications of that period, and Kant's own notes jotted down in his copy of Baumgarten, as well as the Baumgarten text itself, we most definitely find unambiguous strands of Kant's voice in the notes.

In what follows, I will offer a few general observations on the scholarly use of the student notes from Kant's classroom, and a few more specific observations on the importance of the Herder notes in particular, before reviewing the discussion of real and logical grounds, using this as one example of how much of Kant we can find in the Herder notes. What we discover is a considerable overlap of material between the lecture notes and Kant's published works, as well as a steady engagement with other philosophers of his day.

Kant's discussion of ground or reason (German: *Grund*; Latin: *ratio*) first appears in his *New Elucidation* (1755), the first of three public Latin defenses that Kant presented during his teaching career in Königsberg, and it is here that he claims to prefer the term 'determining ground' over Wolff's 'sufficient ground' (or 'sufficient reason'). Kant began to use the terms 'real ground' and 'logical ground' in *Negative Magnitudes* (1763) and *Only Possible Argument* (1763), and continued to make use of them in various ways throughout his career. The connection between a real ground and its consequence is what we usually call a 'causal relationship', and the connection between a logical ground and its consequence we call a 'logical inference'. This distinction between real and logical grounds eventually made its way into the Critical philosophy, among other things marking the distinction between the synthetic and the analytic. Baumgarten's text does not distinguish the logical from the real, and Kant's insertions of this into his lectures is a constant thread running through the Herder notes.

Kant was not the first to discuss this concept of a real ground in his generation of philosophers – Crusius, for instance, devotes several pages to it in his *Entwurf der nothwendigen Vernunft-Wahrheiten* (1745) – but Kant believed that his use of the concept, and how it was to be distinguished from a logical ground, was something new under the sun – and we find all this echoed and amplified in Herder's notes from Kant's classroom.

1 On using the student notes

We have mention of over 160 sets of notes from Kant's classroom, of which 126 survive in some form or other, either as fragments or in their entirety. They stem from eleven different course-subjects, although most of the notes are from Kant's lectures on anthropology, physical geography, logic, metaphysics, and moral philosophy, and they extend from 1762 (seven years after Kant began lecturing) all the way up until his last semester in the summer of 1796. A great many of the notes are copies and compilations of other notes, and thus are somewhat removed from the classroom, and with roughly half of the notes we have no idea of the original author's identity. Similarly, with many of these notes the semester of the source-lecture is a point of conjecture and considerable debate. Often the notes stem from different lectures, as compilations; sometimes a completed set of notes has marginalia added from the lectures of a later semester.

How closely are these notes related to Kant? As Adickes wrote about one hundred years ago:

> The copying and compiling of notebooks from Kant's lectures (with various changes entering with their production) was a flourishing branch of industry in Königsberg, such that with no set of notes can we, without further study, assume uniformity (descent from a single set of lectures) or the reliability of any dates (found on the title page or elsewhere); nor can one assume, over a section of text of any length, that one is reading Kant's own words. (Adickes 1913: 8)

This is not encouraging news; nor are the various accounts of these notes from Kant and others. For instance, in an October 1778 letter to his former student Marcus Herz, who had asked Kant to send him sets of notes from his logic and metaphysics lectures, Kant replied:

> Those of my students who are most capable of grasping everything are just the ones who bother least to take explicit and verbatim notes; rather, they write down only the main points, which they can think over afterwards. Those who are most thorough in note-taking are seldom capable of distinguishing the important from the unimportant. They pile a mass of misunderstood stuff under what they may possibly have grasped correctly. (Br 10: 242 [Kant 1999: 170])

Kant's former student and later biographer, Reinhold Bernhard Jachmann, provided a brief summary of the different courses offered by Kant, and had this to say about the metaphysics lectures:[1]

> The metaphysics course was also illuminating and pleasant, considering the difficulty of the subject for the beginning thinker. Kant was especially artful in arranging and defining metaphysical concepts, whereby he would attempt to think through the subject in front of his students, just as though he were beginning himself – gradually adding new limiting concepts, little by little improving the explanations already considered, and finally reaching the finished concept which he had thoroughly exhausted and illuminated from all sides – thus acquainting the closely attentive student not just with the subject, but also with methodical thinking. Whoever did not understand this way of his would take his first explanation as the correct and fully exhaustive one, and so would not follow him very closely after that, thus collecting mere half-truths – just as several sets of student notes have convinced me. (Jachman 1804: 29 f.)

Given these various problems with the notes, one could not be blamed for questioning their value altogether; but my intention is to inspire caution, rather than outright dismissal. A judicious use of the notes offers all sorts of advantages, of which five come readily to mind:
- They clarify or develop points made in Kant's published writings.
- They consider topics not discussed in any of the published writings.
- They provide a much broader philosophical context against which these writings are to be understood.
- They offer a new perspective into Kant's intellectual development.[2]

---

[1] Jachmann matriculated at the university on 11 April 1783, and was possibly Kant's amanuensis from 1788–94, so his acquaintance with Kant's lectures would have stemmed from the 1780s and 90s.

[2] As Dilthey wrote in the preface to vol. 1 of the *Akademie-Ausgabe* of Kant's writings: "This [D]ivision [of student lecture notes] offers an essential enrichment of the materials for the history of Kant's development. From the time when Herder was his most ardent student, until the last years of his academic career, the lecture notebooks accompany the development of the Critical philosophy" (AA 1: xiv).

– And finally, they are in some sense more accessible to the non-specialist, as would have been fitting for a classroom presentation.

In what follows, however, my goal is simply to understand better the relationship between Herder's notes, Kant's publications, and Baumgarten's metaphysics text.

2 Why are the Herder notes special?

Among the more than one-hundred sets of notes that we have from Kant's classrooms, Herder's notes enjoy a special standing, and this for at least six reasons: (1) they are early, (2) they are the only notes that are early, (3) they are direct from the classroom, (4) they are our only notes with multiple drafts, (5) they are extensive, and (6) they are Herder's. I will say a few words about each of these points.

(1) They are early

Johann Gottfried Herder (1744–1803) arrived in Königsberg (now: Kaliningrad, Russia) in the summer of 1762,[3] having traveled from his birthplace of Mohrungen (now: Morag, Poland), a town of a little over 1,000 inhabitants and lying 100 kilometers south and a little west of Königsberg. The university at Königsberg was in the second half of the summer semester when Herder matriculated on 10 August 1762, and with that semester Kant was finishing up his 7th year of teaching at the university. Herder claims to have attended all of the courses that Kant offered,[4] remaining for four full semesters and then leaving on 22 November 1764, in the middle of the winter semester (1764/65) probably not long before the month-long Christmas recess, to assume a teaching position at the cathedral school in Riga. So he could have sat in Kant's classroom during as many as six different semesters.[5]

---

[3] There is some uncertainty about when Herder actually arrived in Königsberg, but not when he first attended Kant's lectures.

[4] In the "Preface" to his *Kalligone* (1800; reprinted in Herder 1998: 651 f.). Kant was Herder's most significant, but not his only, instructor. Herder also heard dogmatics with T.C. Lilienthal, church history with D.H. Arnoldt, philology with G.D. Kypke, physics with J.G. Teske, mathematics and physics with F.J. Buck, and possibly New Testament with Christoph Langhansen and F.S. Bock; see Herder (1846: 127, 137), Kühnemann (1912: 19), and Dobbek (1961: 92–5). In a letter from early 1768, Herder offered a brief account of his university course-work: "philosophy according to its parts with Magister Kant, philology with Professor Kypke, theology in its various fields with Doctor Lilienthal and Arnold [sic]" (Herder 1977–96, vol. 1: 95).

[5] Following Melanchthon's innovations, the academic calendar of the Protestant universities

Table 1: Kant's teaching schedule during Herder's student years

	Metaphysics	Physical Geography	Moral Philosophy	Mathematics	Logic	Physics
1762	X			(?)	X	
1762/63	X			X	X	
1763				X	X	X
1763/64	X	X	X	(private)	X	
1764	Wed./Sat. 10–12	10–11			9–10	
1764/65	11–12		10–11		9–10	8–9

With the noted exception, meeting times occurred on Monday, Tuesday, Thursday, and Friday.

Herder first attended Kant's classroom on 21 August 1762[6] – Kant was lecturing on metaphysics. It is likely that the university had been in summer recess when Herder matriculated, and that classes had just resumed in late August. The metaphysics notes that Herder wrote down stem from at least two different semesters, and possibly more. Kant is presumed to have lectured on metaphysics five times during Herder's stay: 1762, 1762/63, 1763/64, 1764, and 1764/65. We know that a few of these notes come from the end of the 1762 semester, while the vast majority of the notes come from one or two later semesters, with most of the evidence pointing to 1763/64 and 1764.

Kant was composing some interesting material in the early 1760s,[7] and much of this is reflected in Herder's notes. During Herder's first month in Königsberg, Kant would have completed *The False Subtlety of the Four Syllogistic Figures* (1762), since it appears to have served as a lecture announcement for winter

---

was arranged by semester, with Michaelmas (29 September) and Easter serving as the end-points for the summer and winter semesters. At Königsberg there was normally a recess of about two weeks at Michaelmas and three weeks at Easter, as well as one-month recesses near the middle of each semester (Dog Days in summer, Christmas in winter).
In the table given here, 'X' means that there is good evidence that the course took place. The times are given, when known. In 1764, Kant taught Metaphysics on Wednesdays and Saturdays from 10–12; the other courses were taught on the "normal days" (Monday, Tuesday, Thursday, Friday) for one hour each.
6 As we learn from his journal entry on page 32 of his *Brown Notebook* (NL-Herder XXVI.5), reprinted at AA 28: 148 (and reproduced and translated in this volume; see Fig. 1), Herder memorializes this event a second time at the top of page 123, in an otherwise isolated entry: "den 21. August bei Kant das Collegium angefangen."
7 Profitably explored in Laywine 1993, Schönfeld 2000, and Watkins 2005.

semester 1762/63, Herder's first full semester at the university. *The Only Possible Argument in Support of a Demonstration of the Existence of God* (1763) would have been completed shortly after that, probably in October of 1762, since it was published shortly after mid-December.[8] *The Inquiry concerning the Distinctness of the Principles of Natural Theology and Morality* (1764) – Kant's so-called "Prize Essay" awarded second place by the Prussian Academy of Sciences – was completed shortly before 31 December 1762, the deadline for submission;[9] and the *Attempt to Introduce the Concept of Negative Magnitudes into Philosophy* (1763) was completed by 3 June 1763, the date it was handed to the philosophy dean (Christiani) for censoring. Perhaps of greatest interest for Herder was Kant's *Observations on the Feeling of the Beautiful and Sublime* (1764), an essay Herder appreciated during his first years away from Königsberg.[10] Kant's *Dreams of a Spirit-Seer* (1766) was also begun during Herder's student days, and Herder's review of the book appeared in the 3 March 1766 issue of Kanter's *Königsbergsche Gelehrte und Politische Zeitungen*.[11]

(2) They are the only notes that are early

These are the only notes that we have from Kant's early years as a *Privatdozent*. Kant most likely began lecturing with the winter semester of 1755/56, and taught as a *Privatdozent* for fifteen years before accepting the Logic and Metaphysics professorship in May 1770, the summer of 1770 marking his first semester as a professor. Kant taught four to six classes each semester during the 50s and 60s – as best we can tell from the records – and this dropped down to four to five during the early 70s, and eventually to only three per semester after that (with some exceptions). Beginning with 1770, Kant alternated between a course on logic in

---

8 This is based on Walford's arguments (Kant 1992: lix). Gaier (in Herder 1985: 845) views Herder's "Essay on Being" as a criticism of Kant's essay, and Martin (1936: 295) dates the essay to possibly the second half of 1763, but more likely 1764. See Gaier's transcription of Herder's essay in Herder (1985: 9–21), and his commentary and notes (Herder 1985: 844–69).
9 Beiser (1987: 151) traces influences from this essay to Herder's *Ideen zur Philosophie der Geschichte der Menschheit* (1784–91).
10 This essay was completed by 8 October 1763 (the Saturday before the winter semester classes began), the date he submitted it to the philosophy dean (F. S. Bock) for censoring. See Herder's letter of 21 May 1765, to Hamann (Herder 1977–96, vol. 1: 45): "I am noticeably profiting from this writing of my teacher, whom I value more and more ..."; and his November 1768 letter to Kant: "May your account of the *Good* contribute to the culture of our century as much as your account of the *Sublime and the Beautiful* has done" (AA 10: 77).
11 Reprinted at Herder 1877–1913, vol. 1: 125–30.

the summer and on metaphysics in the winter, with various other courses sprinkled in, but always including a course on physical geography in the summers and on anthropology in the winters. Prior to that, in the 50s and 60s, Kant taught a course on logic, metaphysics, physical geography, and mathematics nearly every semester (although he abruptly quit teaching mathematics in 1763). By my count, 46 % of Kant's courses occurred *before* he was made a full professor in 1770.[12]

Despite all that teaching during his years as a *Privatdozent*, the only notes that remain are those from Herder's hand, thus from summer 1762 to fall 1764. The next notes that we have come from Kant's 1770 physical geography lectures and his logic lectures from the early 1770s.

(3) They are direct from the classroom

Herder's notes are the only notes that we have written in pencil, and very likely the only notes written in the classroom. Various other notes were written out by auditors whom we know attended Kant's lectures – those by Mrongovius, Dohna, Volckmann, von Schön, and Vigilantius, for instance – but these are all, at best, fair copies re-written at home from notes taken down in the lecture.

Most of Herder's notes written in pencil are in the smaller 8° format, while the 4° notes are primarily in ink, neatly written and with a wide margin on the side for additions. It seems likely that all the notes in pencil were written in the classroom, and perhaps also the 8° sheets written in ink, as these also lack margins and have a rushed appearance.

Certain features of the content of the notes suggest a closeness with the classroom as well. For instance, there is a long passage in the Ontology section at V-Met/Herder 28: 21 that concerns §159 of Baumgarten that is nearly verbatim with a note that Kant had written in his own copy of Baumgarten, next to §159. Here we have what appears to be a clear example of Kant reading a passage of a prepared note to students (and thus at least one instance of "Kant reading Kant in Herder's notes").

We even have several accounts of Herder sitting in Kant's classroom, two recorded by classmates of his – Karl Gottlieb Bock and Jakob Friedrich Wilpert. Bock (1746–1829) matriculated at Königsberg a month after Herder (on 27 September 1762), and forty-three years later in 1805 offered these memories of their student days together:

---

[12] That is, 128 courses from a career total of 279 (these are soft numbers, given the gaps in the records).

> Kant offered to let him hear, free of charge, all his lectures on logic, metaphysics, moral philosophy, mathematics, and physical geography. It was here, in the years 1763 and 1764, that he made his acquaintance. We heard Kant's lectures together and he still wrote to me about this in a letter of 11 August 1788, on his way to Italy from Nürnberg: "I can still see you before me, real as life, sitting at the table at which I also sat. Where has the time gone?"
>
> With strained attentiveness he took in every idea, every word of the great philosopher, and at home ordered his thoughts and expression. He often shared these notes with me and we would discuss them in an isolated summerhouse in a seldom-visited public garden by the Alt-Roßgarten church. (Herder 1846: 133 f.; Herder's letter to Bock is printed in Herder 1977–96, vol. 6: 20–22)

Bock goes on to recall an especially lively lecture where Kant quoted from his favorite poets (Pope and Haller) to illuminate certain points on the nature of time and eternity. Herder was so moved by this that he returned to his room, set Kant's lecture down in verse, and handed it to Kant the following morning before the lecture began. Kant was so impressed by Herder's poem that he read it aloud "with fiery praise" to the class. The poem is lost, but if Bock is correct that it "sprang out of Kant's lecture on time and space like Minerva from Jupiter's head,"[13] then Herder presumably found poetic inspiration sitting in Kant's metaphysics lectures – a rather stark contrast with the observation made by Herder's widow that he "most preferred hearing Kant talk about astronomy, physical geography, and in general about the great laws of nature," but that "he had much less taste for the metaphysics lectures …. After many of these metaphysical lectures he would hurry outside with some poet or Rousseau, or some such author, so as to free himself of the impressions that agreed so little with his mind" (Maria Herder 1830, pt. 1: 68 f.).

Jakob Friedrich Wilpert (1741–1812), later a two-time mayor of Riga, recalled attending with Herder

> … Kant's lectures on metaphysics, moral philosophy, and physical geography. We sat at a table[14]; at that time he was shy and quiet, his gait was stooped and quick, his eyes often sick-looking; from his appearances, one could see that he was poor; but his spirit was rich,

---

[13] The phrase is from Bock's letter to Herder (now lost), dated 9 April 1788; the relevant passage is quoted in Herder (1846: 113 f.). See Emil Herder's gloss on Bock's story (1846: 135 f.), and also J. G. Herder's letter to Scheffner of 31 October 1767 (Herder 1977–96, vol. 1: 94) indicating that he no longer has the poem, and that he now regards it as "a belch from a stomach overloaded with Rousseau's writings." Dobbek (1961: 220 n. 166) believes Bock misremembered the poem's topic, and that it was actually the first part of Herder's "Der Mensch."

[14] The tables in the lecture halls were generally reserved for those students wishing to take notes.

even then – and when he discussed the lectures of his teachers, it was so thorough and firm, that he commanded respect and affection from his colleagues. We all heard dogmatics together from Dr. Lilienthal; otherwise I didn't have any closer relations with him. (Herder 1846: 137)

In Karl August Böttiger's (1760–1835) journal entry of 2 December 1798, we find a reminiscence that Herder shared with him from his student days:

> Kant shone from the lectern, a god to all. The Livland and Curland students heard him alone, as they pursued only gallant studies. But he spoke a lot of confusing things as well. Herder could make use of his lectures only by noting the main points in the classroom, and then setting out and re-working what he had heard in his own way once back home. (Böttiger 1838: 128)

Finally, near the end of his life, in the latter years of a bitter falling out with Kant, Herder offers one more glimpse of his student days with Kant:

> For more than thirty years I've known a youth [viz., Herder himself] who heard all of the lectures, some more than once, of the *founder of the Critical philosophy* himself – and indeed in his early, flourishing years. The youth marveled over the teacher's dialectical wit, his political as well as scientific acumen, his eloquence, his intelligent memory; he was never at a loss for words; his lectures were meaningful conversations with himself. But the youth soon noticed that, when he set aside the gracefulness of the presentation, he would become wrapped in one of its dialectical webs of words, within which he himself was no longer able to think. He therefore set himself the strict task, after each hour of careful listening, of changing it all into his own words, making no use of pet words or phrases of his teacher, and even diligently to avoid this. (Herder 1998: 651 f.)[15]

(4) They are our only notes with multiple drafts

As mentioned above, some of the notes are in pencil, some in ink. Most of the 4° notes are in ink, and these are written neatly (although with frequent abbreviations) and with wide margins, but roughly half of the smaller 8° notes are also written in ink, and these are highly abbreviated and without margins, just like the notes written in pencil. It is nearly certain that the notes in pencil were written down in the classroom, and very likely that all of the notes in the 8° format. There are eight instances of overlapping text in Herder's metaphysics notes. Some of this overlap is likely due to Herder attending the lectures over two or more different

---

[15] This passage comes from the preface to Herder's *Kalligone* (1800) and in a footnote to the first sentence of this passage, Herder adds a list of Kant's publications from the years he studied with him.

semesters, but at least one overlap is due to one of the manuscripts (written in pencil, printed at V-Met/Herder 28: 843–49) serving as an earlier draft for the other manuscript (written in ink, printed at V-Met/Herder 28: 22–30).

(5) They are extensive

Once Herder's metaphysics notes are sorted out and properly ordered, we find ourselves with a nearly complete set that compares quite favorably with later sets of notes in our possession. For instance, Herder's is the third longest set of metaphysics notes from Kant's classroom (the Metaphysik L_1 is roughly 15 % longer, and the Metaphysik Mrongovius about 27 % longer). The Herder notes are weighted more towards ontology and empirical psychology, while Metaphysik L_1 is weighted more towards rational psychology and natural theology, and Metaphysik Mrongovius has a much larger introductory section, and relatively larger sections on ontology and empirical psychology.

(6) They are Herder's

Herder is not the only student from Kant's classroom who would later go on to distinguish himself (one thinks of L. E. Borowski, Theodor von Hippel, Marcus Herz, and Theodor von Schön, among others), but Herder is still one of a small number, and of these he was certainly the most significant in the world of letters.

3 Five brief cautions on using the Herder notes

There are four basic problems with the notes as they currently appear in volume 28 of the *Akademie-Ausgabe*, as well as a fifth general worry about Herder. The four problems are a result of Lehmann's editorial efforts: he duplicated the material between the two parts of volume 28, he included material that is likely not from Kant's lectures, he was careless in his transcription, and the editorial apparatus is wanting. The fifth general worry is that Herder was a budding genius, and that he might therefore have included his own reflections in his notes.

(1) Duplication of material

Volume 28 of the *Akademie-Ausgabe* was published in two partial volumes: one in 1968 and one in 1970. While preparing the 1968 volume, Lehmann lacked the manuscripts included in NL-Herder XXV. 46a (now housed in Berlin at the Staatsbibliothek Preußischer Kulturbesitz), but much of this missing material had been copied out by Paul Menzer in the first decade of the last century, and so Lehmann included Menzer's copy in the 1968 volume. This was unfortunate, however, for two reasons. First, Menzer's copy was extremely rough and certainly not intended for publication (those passages that Menzer incorporated into his own published writings are much more accurately transcribed). Second, included in Menzer's copy are occasional stray notes intended for his own use, which Lehmann inadvertently included as part of Herder's notes (e. g., V-Met/Herder 28: 85, 101).

Once the missing set of Herder manuscripts was located, Lehmann prepared a new transcription and included it in the 1970 volume. While Lehmann's new transcription is nearly always superior to Menzer's rough transcription, it is not uncommon to find scholars citing the Menzer copy published in the 1968 volume, apparently unaware of the better transcription.

(2) Inclusion of material not clearly stemming from Kant's lectures
Other than the extranea inserted with Menzer's copy of Herder's notes, one also finds Lehmann including material that is most likely not from Kant's classroom: a variety of pages from a student note book that are either almost certainly from some other lecturer, or were early drafts of an essay of Herder's, but in any event most likely do not stem from Kant's metaphysics lectures (cf. V-Met/Herder 28: 935–46, as well as V-Met/Herder 28: 53–5, which appears to be a study by Herder of Kant's *New Elucidation* of 1755).

(3) Poor transcription
The Herder manuscripts are often difficult to read. A majority of the words are abbreviated, most are hastily written, and some of the penciled text has been rubbed away. Unlike many of the other student notes from Kant's classroom, these were not prepared by a professional copyist, and consequently a good transcription requires extraordinary care. This in part explains why there are, on average, two to three transcriptional errors on every page of Lehmann's published text in the *Akademie-Ausgabe*. Some of the errors are trivial, but many are not, and result in a deformation of the meaning. A different sort of error occurs at the manuscript page break indicated on V-Met/Herder 28: 930, where Lehmann splices together two broken sentences across the break. A closer inspection of the text makes it clear that one or more pages of missing text stand between these two sentence fragments.

(4) Poor editorial apparatus

Finally, the introductory material explaining the metaphysics notes borders on the opaque, his "Textänderungen und Lesearten" are riddled with errors large and small, and the marginal pagination that is supposed to reflect the pagination of the various manuscripts is often arbitrarily sequenced.

If we remove the duplicated material and other foreign matter, a proper ordering of the notes would look something like this (using the *Akademie-Ausgabe* pagination): (A) 5–53, (B) 850–75, 875–86, 137–38, 922–23, and (C) 886–922 form three core sections of the notes, to which additional material, perhaps stemming from other semesters, can be added. With (A) belongs the material from 155–58 and 843–49, with (B) the material from 924–28, 143–44, 145–48, and 928–31, with (C) the material from 144–45, and 148–51. From this list of page numbers one can appreciate the difficulties that any scholar faces when attempting to make an appropriate use of these notes as they presently stand in the *Akademie-Ausgabe*.

(5) Herder's own authorial insertions

As for assessing the content of these notes and how closely they correspond with what Kant actually said in his lectures, it will do well to recall those three comments made near the end of Herder's life, quoted above, that suggested that Herder would write down only the main points in class, and then at home re-write the notes in his own words.

4 Baumgarten's *Metaphysica*

Professors were required to lecture from textbooks, and Kant chose to base his metaphysics lectures on Alexander Baumgarten's successful and widely used Latin textbook *Metaphysica* (4th edition: 1757; 1st edition: 1739).[16] Kant used the 4th edition during most of his career (this is the edition reprinted at AA 15: 5–54 and AA 17: 5–226). Several other popular metaphysics textbooks were available to Kant – he made use of a text by Baumeister for a few semesters during his early years of teaching, and Crusius wrote a textbook often used by other professors at Königsberg – but Kant strongly preferred Baumgarten and by 1759 was

---

[16] Fortunately for the non-Latin reader, this text has recently been made available in both a Latin-German edition (Baumgarten 2011) and in an English edition (Baumgarten 2013).

using that exclusively and for the remainder of his forty-year teaching career. Kant called it the "most useful and foundational of all textbooks of its kind" (TW 1: 503).

Baumgarten was a professor at Halle (from 1737–40) and then at Frankfurt/Oder (from 1740–62), and was intellectually aligned with Christian Wolff's rationalism, although he emphasized certain aspects of Leibniz's metaphysics that were downplayed or rejected by Wolff – for instance, in his offering a proof of the doctrine of pre-established harmony. Kant clearly held Baumgarten in high regard. In the *New Elucidation* (1755) Kant characterized "the penetrating Baumgarten" (PND 1: 397) as the "chief of the metaphysicians" (PND 1: 408); in his lecture announcement for winter semester 1765/66, Kant praised Baumgarten's metaphysics text for "the richness of its contents and the precision of its method" (NEV 2: 308); in the Logik Pölitz (dated c. 1780), Kant said of Baumgarten that "Wolff's logic was distilled by Baumgarten, a man who has contributed much here" (V-Lo/Pölitz 24: 509); and in the *Menschenkunde* anthropology notes (dated 1781–82), Baumgarten is characterized as "a man quite rich in material and succinct in its execution" (V-Anth/Mensch 25: 859).

Baumgarten divided his *Metaphysica* into 1,000 sections: §§ 1–3 presents a brief introduction to metaphysics, followed by the ontology (§§ 4–350), cosmology (§§ 351–500), psychology (§§ 501–799), and natural theology (§§ 800–1000). The psychology was further divided into two main sections: empirical psychology (§§ 504–739) and rational psychology (§§ 740–799). Kant later used this section on empirical psychology as a basis for his anthropology lectures (which he began offering with the 1772/73 winter semester).

5 Real grounds in Herder's notes

Baumgarten's textbook on metaphysics often stands front and center in Herder's notes and is rarely far from view. It determines for the most part the topics presented and their order of presentation. But there is also much material in the notes not found in Baumgarten, and these additions are typically made with no indication that Kant is disagreeing with Baumgarten or in some way amending him.

Kant also wrestles with other philosophers in these notes. Apart from Baumgarten – who is normally referred to as "the author" – Kant discusses Leibniz, Wolff, and Crusius in about a dozen different places. Newton and Descartes each receive seven mentions, Locke four, Malebranche three, Rousseau two, and rather interestingly, Hume makes only one appearance, and that in a discussion of moral sentiment.¹⁷ This neglect of Hume is somewhat strange, if his account of causality really was troubling Kant's mind during this period as much as is generally claimed.¹⁸

And this brings me to my last topic, as well as providing an opportunity to acknowledge a debt. It was while reading Eric Watkins's *Kant and the Metaphysics of Causality* (2005) that I was led to consider more closely the theme of real grounds in the Herder notes. A central thread in the first half of Watkins' book is the emergence and evolution of Kant's understanding of the concept of a real ground:

> After Hume's *Enquiry Concerning Human Understanding* was translated into German in 1755,¹⁹ Kant reacted by introducing a new metaphysical distinction between real and logical grounds, reinterpreting the ontological principles he had developed earlier in terms of real grounds and making the notion of a real ground fundamental to several principles that became central parts of his overall position in the early 1760s. (Watkins 2005: 10; Watkins elaborates and defends this claim on 166–70)

A bit later, Watkins writes:

> Hume helped Kant to see that, as a proponent of physical influx, he could not understand grounds as purely logical (as Wolff and Baumgarten had). As a result, he introduced the notion of a "real ground" and attempted to work out its consequences in *The Only Possible Argument in Support of a Demonstration of the Existence of God* (1763), the *Negative Magnitudes* (1763), and various *Reflexionen* of the period. (Watkins 2005: 103)

---

17 Herder recalled some of these figures in his homage to Kant (in his 79th "Letters on the Advancement of Humanity"): "In the same spirit with which he investigated *Leibniz, Wolf, Baumgarten, Crusius,* and *Hume,* and traced the laws of *Kepler, Newton,* and the *physicists* generally, he also examined the writings then appearing by Rousseau, namely, his *Emile* and his *Heloise*" (Herder 1877–1913, vol. 17: 404).

18 Hume's influence on the early Kant has been discussed extensively by Henrich (1967), Kreimendahl (1990), and more recently by Watkins (2005); see also Falkenstein's (1995) helpful discussion of Kreimendahl.

19 Hume discusses causality in both his *Treatise of Human Nature* (1739–40) and the more succinct *Enquiry Concerning Human Understanding* (1748; originally published as: *Philosophical Essays Concerning Human Understanding*). A German edition of the *Enquiry* appeared in 1755 (anonymously translated, and edited by Johann Georg Sulzer), and selections from the *Treatise* appeared in German in 1771 and 1772; a translation of the entire *Treatise* was not published until 1790–92. Kant appears not to have read texts in English, and it is unclear when Kant might have obtained a copy of the 1755 translation given the complications of the Russian occupation of Königsberg from 1758–62. Nonetheless, he had English-reading friends interested in Hume (J. G. Hamann since 1759; Joseph Green since 1765) and through whom he had ready access to Hume's ideas.

And finally:

> Kant had already explicitly accepted grounds as an integral part of his account as early as 1755 in the *Nova dilucidatio*. However, in that work Kant does not describe grounds as real. Starting around 1762 – presumably after having read Hume's *Inquiry* in translation – and continuing up throughout the rest of his pre-Critical period, Kant draws a distinction between logical and real grounds and makes real grounds into a fundamental feature of his metaphysics as he comes to see how important they are in providing an adequate account of a series of metaphysical issues .... Real grounds are pivotal to Kant's immediate response to Hume. (Watkins 2005: 162)[20]

Baumgarten lacked any concept of a real ground. His commitment to Leibniz's pre-established harmony meant that the ground of any change in a thing was always within that thing itself. All apparent connections between substances were logical in the sense that all predicates of a substance were inner determinations of that substance; the predicates were contained in the concept of the subject itself, allowing for all truths to be *analytically* true.[21]

Real grounds, and the wider distinction between the real and the logical that is built on this concept, are discussed primarily in the ontology section of the notes, but throughout the later sections as well, and it is arguably the most important concept being developed in Kant's early metaphysics. When reading the Herder notes, it is striking how often this topic appears, usually as an unspoken addition or amendment to a claim or definition in Baumgarten. I discuss this further below.

6 The grounds of others and Kant's response

Wolff and Baumgarten

Christian Wolff and Alexander Baumgarten both understand a ground as closely involved with the giving of an account or explanation. Wolff offers a definition in § 29 of his *Vernünfftige Gedancken* (1720):

---

[20] Longuenesse (1998: 351) also notes this new distinction between logical and real grounds and points to its occurrence in the Herder notes.
[21] This connection between logical vs. real grounds and the analytic vs. synthetic judgments is made in Reflections 3504, 5706, and 5707. The first, dated by Adickes to the late 1770s, reads: "A ground is either analytic (logical) or synthetic (real ground)" (AA 17: 28).

> *What a ground is and what is called grounded.* If a thing A contains in itself something from which one can understand why B is – B can be either something in A or outside A – one calls that which is to be found in A the **ground** of B. A itself is called the cause, and one says of B that it is grounded in A. The ground is that by which one can understand why something is, and the cause is a thing that contains the ground of another in itself.[22]

Wolff illustrates his definition with an example of a garden: Suppose the plants are flourishing and that this is due to the warmth of the air. In this case, the warmth of the air is what Wolff calls the *ground* of the flourishing, and the air itself (which is warm) is the *cause*. The ground of X (or of X being in a certain state) is that by which one understands X (either why it exists or why it is in a certain state).

Baumgarten appears to follow Wolff closely in his own definition in *Metaphysica* (1757), § 14:

> A GROUND (condition, hypothesis) is that from which it can be cognized why something is. Whatever has a ground, or of which something is the ground, is called the CONSEQUENCE, and is DEPENDENT on it. The predicate by which something is the ground or consequence or both, is the CONNECTION.

Neither of these definitions distinguishes between the *real* ground (the cause of a thing's existence or change in its state), the *logical* ground (the cause of the thing's possibility), or the *ideal* ground (the cause of our cognition of the thing).

Crusius

Crusius expanded this discussion of grounds by distinguishing real and ideal grounds in his *Entwurf der nothwendigen Vernunft-Wahrheiten* (1st edition: 1745).[23] The *real ground* of X (*principium essendi vel fiendi*) is the cause of the existence or becoming of X, while the *ideal ground* of X (*principium cognoscendi*) is the cause of our cognition "with conviction" of X (*Entwurf*, § 34):

> § 34. Anything that produces something else either in whole or in part, and insofar as it is viewed as such, is called a **ground** or **cause in the broad sense** (*principium, ratio*). For that reason efficacious causes are one kind of ground, whose necessity is clarified by the preceding (§ 15, § 29). But they are not the only kind. Therefore we must also consider here the other

---

22 This book is not listed in Kant's library (in Warda 1922), although he did have a copy of Wolff's Latin metaphysics, the *Philosophia prima sive Ontologia* (1730).
23 Kant owned the 1753 second edition of this work (Warda 1922: 47).

kinds of grounds. Namely, what one calls grounded and whose production is attributed to another is either only the cognition in the understanding or else the thing itself outside of our thoughts. Therefore a ground is either a ground of cognition, which can also be called an ideal ground (*principium cognoscendi*), or a real ground (*principium essendi vel fiendi*). A ground of cognition is what produces the cognition of something with conviction and so is viewed as such. A real ground is what produces or makes possible, either in whole or in part, the thing itself, outside of our thoughts. (Crusius 1745: 52 f.)

For Crusius, the ideal ground of X is just the cognitive ground, that is, whatever causes one's belief in X. But in the context of a Leibnizian pre-established harmony, the meaning of 'ideal ground' shifts: Here an ideal ground (or change or influence or connection) is where a change in one substance is caused by itself, but where this change tracks related changes in another substance (*as though* the first substance were influencing the second substance). This understanding of real and ideal runs parallel to Baumgarten's definition of real and ideal influence at *Metaphysica*, § 212:

If the passivity of the substance influenced by another is at the same time the action of the one acted upon, the PASSIVITY and INFLUENCE are said to be IDEAL. If, however, the passivity is not the action of the one being acted upon, the PASSIVITY and INFLUENCE are said to be REAL. (Baumgarten 1757: 64; and see Kant's comment on this in his Refl. 3581, 17: 71)

In the *Entwurf*, § 36, Crusius distinguished two kinds of real ground: *efficacious* causes and inefficacious or *existential* causes:

Further division of real grounds into efficacious causes and inefficacious real grounds or existential grounds. When a real ground produces or makes possible something outside of thought, it does so either by means of an efficacious force and, in that case, is called an **efficacious cause**. Or the laws of truth in general do not allow anything else other than that after certain things or certain of its properties have been posited, something else is now possible or impossible, or must be possible in this way and not otherwise. This kind of ground I will call the **inefficacious real ground** or also the **existential ground** (*principium existentialiter determinans*). Accordingly, an **existential ground** is one that makes something else possible or necessary through its mere existence due to the laws of truth. E. g., the three sides of a triangle and their relations to each other constitute a real ground of the size of its angle, but only an inefficacious or existential ground. By contrast, fire is an efficacious cause of warmth. (Crusius 1745: 54 f.)

An *efficacious* cause requires some action on the part of the cause while an *existential* cause exerts its influence simply by virtue of existing. For example, the sides of a triangle, as they are in the triangle, constitute an existential real ground of the angles of that triangle. Fire, on the other hand, is an efficacious real ground of the warmth that results.

Kant's response to Wolff, Baumgarten, and Crusius

Kant engages with both of these accounts in his published writings as well as in the classroom. The first discussion occurs in the *New Elucidation* (1755), where section two[24] begins with an account of ground: "That which determines a subject in respect of any of its predicates, is called the *ground*" (PND 1: 391), after which Kant distinguishes between *antecedent grounds* (or "ground of being/becoming"; the reason *why*) and *consequent grounds* (or "ground of knowing"; the reason *that*).[25] The antecedent ground gives an account for why something is (Kant's example: the elasticity in Descartes' "elastic globules" for explaining the finite speed of light), while the consequent ground is what makes our knowledge of the thing actual (e. g., the eclipses of the satellites of Jupiter give us evidence of the finite speed of light).

Kant follows this brief discussion with a criticism of the definition of 'ground' given by Wolff (and so *a fortiori* Baumgarten), which Kant finds to be circular. It is unhelpful, Kant writes, to define "the ground of X" as that which explains why X exists or why X has a certain predicate – for the word 'why' just means "for which ground" – turning Wolff's definition into the less-than-illuminating: "a ground is that by reference to which it is possible to understand *for which ground* something should be rather than not be" (PND 1: 393).[26]

This same criticism is repeated in Kant's classroom some eight years later, in a passage discussing Baumgarten, § 14:

> The author's description *of ground* is insufficient because of the word 'why' [*cur*], which just means 'from which ground.' Thus it is a hidden circle. (V-Met/Herder 28: 11)

Kant also favorably mentions Crusius in this passage of the *New Elucidation*, whom Kant invokes as support to drop all talk of "sufficient ground" (= "suffi-

---

[24] Section Two bears the title: "Concerning the principle of the determining ground, commonly called the principle of the sufficient ground."
[25] See also the recapitulation of this distinction in the Herder notes (V-Met/Herder AA 28: 54 f.).
[26] Kant also criticized Wolff's claim that it is possible for something (e. g., God) to be the ground of its own existence. Proposition Six of the *New Elucidation* (AA 1: 394) reads: "To say that something has the ground of its existence within itself is absurd." Kant does not name Wolff here, but it is presumably directed at his *Philosophia Prima* (§ 309) and *Theologia naturalis* (§ 28), and the Herder notes *do* mention Wolff: "*Wolff* is mistaken when he says: a thing has its ground in itself or in another" (V-Met/Herder AA 28: 13). Self-grounding is also implied in Baumgarten's *Metaphysica*, § 20, which argues that everything (and therefore God as well) has a ground, and we find in Kant's 3rd edition copy a note rejecting this notion of self-grounding.

cient reason") in favor of "determining ground" – and this is again repeated in the Herder notes (in a comment on Baumgarten, § 21):

> Therefore it would be better and more determinate to call it the determining ground (with Crusius), rather than, with *Wolf*, the sufficient ground. (V-Met/Herder 28: 54)

7 An insight of *Negative Magnitudes*[27]

Real grounds can conflict with each other

In a passage from the "Natural Theology" section of Herder's metaphysics notes, when Kant discusses the perfection of God, we come across the following complaint:

> The author [i.e., Baumgarten], Wolff, and almost no philosophers have paid attention here to the logical and real ground and conflict; and [they] viewed everything as logical. – Much is self-contradictory and impossible. Much conflicts with itself and is not impossible and not contradictory. Now one reality can conflict with another without contradicting it. (V-Met/Herder 28: 912)

Kant makes a similar point earlier in the notes during a discussion of Baumgarten's definition of ground (§ 14), where Kant notes that "there is no [logical] contradiction with pure positing or negating" (V-Met/Herder 28: 11).

Kant could have had his younger self in mind as well in his complaint above, for back in 1755 Kant also neglected to distinguish between *logical* and *real* grounds, a distinction that makes its first appearance in his *Negative Magnitudes* essay of 1763 – and this brings us up to the years when Herder was studying at the university.

What I find especially striking in the Herder notes is how constantly Kant remarks on this distinction between the logical and the real, especially throughout the ontology section, but later as well. Often without any indication that Baumgarten is being amended, Kant will insert various instances of this contrast between the logical and the real that was the centerpiece of the *Negative*

---

[27] Zinkin (2012) discusses yet another insight in the *Negative Magnitudes* (1763) essay, namely, that Kant's examples of negative magnitude with respect to our cognitive activity (e. g., of apparent mental repose, as discussed at AA 2: 199, or of desire at AA 2: 201) reveals an effort of the mind that – *pace* Hume – counts as an awareness or impression of a real force.

Magnitudes. While Baumgarten is the occasion for the notes and Herder is the note taker, the insertions making their way into the notes are all clearly Kant's.

Kant began his *Negative Magnitudes* (1763) with an extensive discussion of logical and real *opposition*, claiming that "attention has been exclusively and uniquely concentrated until now" upon logical opposition alone (NG 2: 171). A logical opposition is "where two contradictory predicates are ascribed to the same thing, resulting in "nothing at all" (a *nihil negativum*) – for instance, a two-dimensional figure that is both a square and a circle. In contrast, real opposition is "where two predicates of a thing are opposed to each other, but not through the law of contradiction" – for instance, two different motive forces pushing against an object, and resulting in what Kant calls a *nihil privativum* – the object does not disappear, but something is missing because of this opposition that otherwise would be present. Walking east on a train that is traveling west results in a *nihil privativum*; both motions are real, but they oppose each other. Kant is introducing here what he understands to be a new distinction and he takes great pains in that essay to explain it.

Real grounds are not based on the principle of identity

In the "General Remark" that concludes the *Negative Magnitudes*, Kant introduces a further distinction between logical and real grounds:[28]

> I call the first kind of ground a logical ground because its relation to the consequence is logical, namely, it can be distinctly seen to follow according to the rule of identity. The second kind of ground I call a real ground because, although this relation belongs to my true concepts, this kind of relation cannot at all be judged. (NG 2: 202)

In other words, the connection between a logical ground and its consequence can easily be found by analyzing the subject (or ground), which reveals the presence of the predicate (or consequence). But no such analysis is available for real grounds and their consequences; these relationships are simple, brute facts about the world.

Kant offers an argument for this distinction between logical and real grounds in a comment on a student essay.[29] The student had written that, for all he knew,

---

[28] In *The Only Possible Argument* (1763) we find logical and real ground being used, but not introduced or defined as such.

[29] Kant wrote four comments in all on this essay (Refl 3718–21), which Adickes dated to possibly the early 1760s, but which more probably stems from the 1780s, when Michael Friedländer was

the distinction between logical and real grounds was just a product of our "short-sightedness," and that if we had a better grasp of the real essence of things, then we would be able to analyze out every predicate, so that in the end all consequences would be logical, and not real. To this Kant replied:

> If the real consequence is contained in the real ground, and were posited through that according to the rule of identity, then it would be contemporaneous with it. All alterations are possible, therefore, only through the real relations of the grounds to their consequences, and the logical grounds are therefore distinguished from real grounds not by the limits of my cognition, but rather in themselves. (Refl 3719, 17: 266)

Kant illustrates the opacity of the relationship between real grounds and their consequences with three brief examples in the *Negative Magnitudes* essay (NG 2: 202):

> [1] The will of God contains the real ground of the existence of the world. The will of God is something. The world that exists is *something completely different*. Nonetheless, the one is posited by the other.

> [2] The state of mind in which I hear the name *Stagirite* is something, and it is in virtue of that something that something else, namely my thought of a philosopher, is posited.

> [3] A body A is in motion; another body B, lying in the direct path of A, is at rest. The motion of A is something; the motion of B is something else; and yet the one is posited by the other.

Kant delivers up essentially these same three examples in Herder's notes in order to make the same point – namely, that they portray relations not reducible to the principle of identity:

> [1 + 2] The connection between the logical ground and consequence can be grasped, but not that between the real ground, that when something is posited, something else is posited at the same time. Example: God wills! – The world comes about! – Julius Caesar! The name brings to mind the thought of the ruler of Rome. (V-Met/Herder 28: 12)

> [2 + 3] All our experience of how bodies affect each other is simply: one moving body moves another. No one doubts this, but the cause of the preceding strong motive power is in the laws of nature, which are inexplicable. With *each* interaction the cause is therefore inexplicable and especially when I apply this to the soul. (V-Met/Herder 28: 886)

> [1 + 3] Every determination of a thing that requires a real ground, however, is posited through something else, and the connection of a real ground with a real consequence is

---

at the university (the essay is bound with other Friedländer materials, and likely stems from Michael; I thank Werner Stark for pointing this out).

therefore not to be understood through the rule of identity, and also cannot be expressed with a judgment; it is rather a simple concept. E. g., the will of God is the real ground of the existence of the world, it is not a logical judgment using the rule of identity. For the world is not one and the same with God, but rather is a simple concept. This concept is called *power*, e. g., bodies pushing each other. (V-Met/Herder 28: 24)[30]

Real grounds are knowable either empirically or not at all

In the passage immediately following the quote above, Kant notes that the connections between real grounds and their consequences sometimes have the appearance of being logical (or analytic), but they are in fact cognizable only on the basis of experience:

> Our power of imagination produces again distinct concepts that one already had. This appears at first to be a logical proposition, but it is not; rather the predicate itself is here the relation of the real ground, etc. Only through experiences, not logically, can we comprehend the connection of the real ground. (V-Met/Herder 28: 24)

Kant will make the same point a few years later in his *Dreams of a Spirit-Seer* (1766):

> It is impossible ever to comprehend through reason how something could be a cause or have a force; rather, these relations must be taken from experience. For the rule of our reason extends only to comparison in accordance with *identity* and *contradiction*.... That my will moves my arm is no more intelligible to me than were someone to claim that my will could halt the moon in its orbit. The only difference between the two cases is this: I experience the former, whereas my senses have never encountered the latter. (TG 2: 370; see also Refl 3756, 17: 284 f., dated 1764–66)

Kant's grounds are not Crusius's grounds

After making the distinction between logical and real grounds in the *Negative Magnitudes*, Kant then describes Crusius' distinction between real and *ideal* grounds, noting that this is something entirely different:

> [T]he division made by *Crusius* between the ideal and the real ground is entirely different from my own. For his ideal ground is identical with the ground of cognition; and here it

---

[30] And in the discussion on Natural Theology, we find in a discussion of real and logical grounds that with the former, "we cannot comprehend the connection," which is why "physics is more difficult than arithmetic, and theology the most difficult" (V-Met/Herder AA 28: 911).

is easy to see that if I already regard something as a ground, I can infer from it the consequence. Therefore, according to his principles, the west wind is a real ground of rain clouds, and at the same time is also an ideal ground, since I am able to recognize and expect the latter by way of the former. But according to our concepts, the real ground is never a logical ground, and the rain is not posited by the wind in virtue of the rule of identity. The distinction between logical opposition and real opposition that we mentioned above is parallel to the distinction between the logical ground and the real ground under discussion here. (NG 2: 203)

This point is also echoed in the Herder notes in several places:

Crusius separates grounds into ideal and real. This division is entirely different, e.g., the world is the ideal ground of God. For the ideal ground is merely the ground of cognition. They are therefore subordinated in such a way that a real ground could at the same time be an ideal ground; but no real ground can be a logical ground and vice versa. For they are exactly opposed.

In all demonstrations and in mathematics the proofs are logical grounds. Crusius's bringing forth [das Hervorbringen] is just a real ground, e.g., God is a real ground of the world; the latter is not logically posited *per regulam identitatis* [through the rule of identity] because the world is not in God. (V-Met/Herder 28: 12)

With Crusius, the *ideal ground*, from which I can infer something, is therefore different than the *logical – quod continent rationem logicam per regulam identitates* [which contains the logical ground through the rule of identity]: every logical ground is ideal, not every ideal ground is logical. The real consequences give the cognitive ground to the real ground. *Adaequater* [adequate] *cognitive ground*, e.g., mathematics has this. E.g., self-interest is not a *principium adaequatum* [adequate principle] of vice. (V-Met/Herder 28: 37)

In the text just preceding this, Kant criticizes Crusius's definition of a ground as "anything that brings about something else" and then introduces his own division of grounds into logical and real:

Crusius describes a ground as that through which something is brought about. The word *to bring about* [*hervorbringen*] is much too composite [*zusammengesetzt*]: for not all effects are consequences, and not all powers are grounds.

Every *ground* is either logical, through which the consequence that is one and the same with it is posited as a predicate *per regulam identitatis* [through the rule of identity], or *real*, through which the consequence that is not one and the same with it is not posited *per regulam identitatis*. (V-Met/Herder 28: 11)

To support my claim about the ubiquity of this distinction between the logical and the real in Herder's notes, let me list a dozen more examples (where '§' refers to the Baumgarten paragraph under discussion):

§ 14: As part of his long commentary on Baumgarten's definition of 'ground', and in which Kant had already drawn the distinction between logical and real grounds (V-Met/Herder 28: 11), Kant also notes that repugnance can be either logical or real (V-Met/Herder 28: 12), thus echoing the opening pages of *Negative Magnitudes* (NG 2: 172).

§ 23: Baumgarten's argument that "everything has a consequence" brings Kant to add that "every consequence is either logical or real" (V-Met/Herder 28: 14).

§ 36: Baumgarten's discussion of affirmative and negative determination as realities and negations leads Kant to counter that some negations are in fact real, e. g., the real repugnance as discussed in *Negative Magnitudes* (V-Met/Herder 28: 14).

§ 81: Baumgarten defines 'opposites' as when something is posited and something else is thereby denied, which Kant then glosses with a distinction between logical and real opposition, which Kant further describes as positing the negative nothing and the privative nothing (V-Met/Herder 28: 16).

§ 101: Baumgarten offers a brief definition of 'necessary thing' (viz., that thing "whose opposite is impossible") and 'contingent thing' (viz., anything that is "not necessary"), and Kant responds approvingly, adding that every positing is either logical or real (V-Met/Herder 28: 18). Related here is Kant's Refl 3725, dated to the early 1760s and written next to Baumgarten, § 109:

> Absolute necessity is either logical: on account of the principle of contradiction, or real: not on account of the principle of contradiction. The former is the necessity of judgments. Or the necessity of the relation of the predicate and the subject. The latter is the necessity of the beings. 1. God is omnipotent. 2. God exists. The latter cannot be known (in itself) through the contradiction of opposites. The opposite of existing is not-being. But not-being, alone, does not contradict itself. Existence is not a predicate, therefore its opposite is not a predicate opposed to anything (Refl 3725, 17: 270).

§ 135: Baumgarten notes that "realities and negations are opposed to one another," and Kant continues with a distinction between logical and real cancellation (V-Met/Herder 28: 19 f.).

§ 192: Baumgarten defines 'inherence' as the existence of an accident, and 'subsistence' as the existence of a substance, to which Kant adds that the real ground of the accident is in the substance (V-Met/Herder 28: 25, and the first draft version at V-Met/Herder 28: 845).

§ 197: Baumgarten claims that the ground of an accident inhering in a substance is a "power in the wider sense" or a "sufficient ground," to which Kant adds that they require a "real ground," which he then distinguishes from logical grounds that simply follow from the rule of identity (V-Met/Herder 28: 24, and the first draft version at V-Met/Herder 28: 844).

§ 210: With respect to a long paragraph devoted to the definition of 'action' and 'passion', and in which Baumgarten repeats that the sufficient ground in a substance to bring about some alteration is called 'a power', Kant begins his comments with the observation that power is "the relation of a *real* ground to an accident" (V-Met/Herder 28: 26).

§§ 265–30: In a comment on Chapter 3 of Baumgarten, which concerns "the relations of things," Kant notes that "a distinction has been omitted here: the relation of a thing is either logical or real" (V-Met/Herder 28: 32).

§ 430: Baumgarten defines the "nature of a thing" as the sum of its internal determinations that underlie its accidents, and Kant is quick to call these the real grounds (V-Met/Herder 28: 49).

§ 806: In what appears to be a comment on this paragraph, where Baumgarten notes that "a most perfect thing is a most real thing," Kant notes that not all realities can be in the most real thing, bringing up his distinction between logical and real repugnance, as first discussed in *Negative Magnitudes* (V-Met/Herder 28: 150).

8 One more oddity and a conclusion

Given the important shift between *New Elucidation* (1755) and the essays of the early 1760s, it is surprising to find two pages of notes on the former among Herder's papers (printed at V-Met/Herder 28: 53–55). They were cataloged and published by Lehmann as notes from Kant's classroom, and while it is possible that they do in fact stem from his lectures, this seems unlikely, since they consist primarily of a sketchy outline of the first six propositions of *New Elucidation*, and they do not read at all like lecture notes. But it is odd in any event – either for Kant to be discussing this early essay so extensively in his lectures, or for Herder to bother with it.

So are there any take-away lessons from the above? First and most importantly, the constant interplay between commentary, criticism, and silent emendation of the Baumgarten text makes clear the indispensability of familiarizing ourselves with Baumgarten before making use of these student notes. Second, the frequency with which claims and arguments made in Kant's published writings also appear in the student notes suggests that these notes might help us to clarify those arguments. And finally, because of the one instance of multiple drafts in the Herder notes, we have some basis for discerning Herder's own insertions – and what we discover is that he did not substantially alter the notes, not even in their vocabulary. In general, however, disentangling student insertions from Kant's views will always be problematic, since any deviation in the notes that strays too far from the published views will, rightly or wrongly, be attributed to the student, rather than to Kant – and similarly with anything that is unintelligible.

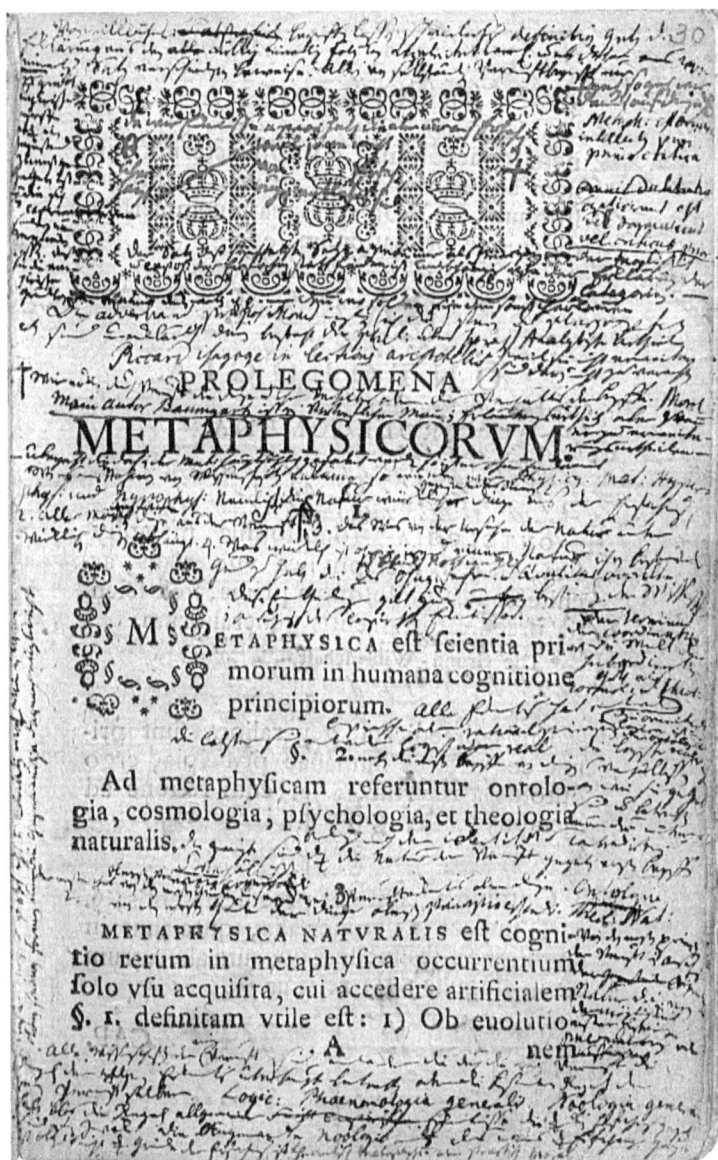

Fig. 2: Reproduction of page 1 ("Prolegomena") of Kant's copy of A. G. Baumgarten's *Metaphysica* (Halle, 1757, 4th edn.), with Kant's handwritten notes: Reflections 4159–66 (AA 17: 438–41), 4359–64 (AA 17: 519–20), 5124–25 (AA 18: 99), 5128 (AA 18: 100). Reproduced with the kind permission of the University of Tartu Library, Estonia. Call number: manuscript 93. Kant's personal copy of Baumgarten's *Metaphysica* is available at the University of Tartu Library website: http://hdl.handle.net/10062/32369. Accessed 22 April 2015.

Chapter 2
The Unity of Metaphysics in Kant's Lectures

Courtney D. Fugate

Some scholars have pointed to Kant's employment of Baumgarten's *Metaphysica* in his lectures on metaphysics, anthropology, and natural theology, over a span of nearly four decades, as evidence for his close and enduring ties with the metaphysical tradition.[1] This seems to be confirmed by Kant's explicit statements about metaphysics in his published writings. At the end of the Architectonic of Pure Reason, for instance, one can read that "metaphysics is also the culmination of all *culture* of human reason, which is indispensable," because it not only determines the ultimate end of the human being, but "must ground even the *possibility* of some sciences and the *use* of them all" (A850 f./B878 f.).

Notwithstanding this and similar evidence, many have remained skeptical whether such positive statements genuinely reflect Kant's considered view of the matter. There are many good reasons to take such suspicions seriously. First, and most obviously, Kant's statements about metaphysics are not always as unequivocally positive as the quote above suggests, particularly when he has in mind the form it had taken in his predecessors, among whom he regarded Baumgarten in particular to be the "Coryphaeus" (PND 1: 409). Secondly, it is hard to ignore the estimation of Moses Mendelssohn, one of the brightest proponents of the metaphysical tradition, when he famously refers – precisely in connection with metaphysics – to the "works ... of the all-crushing Kant" (Mendelssohn 1989: 469). Thirdly, and perhaps most fundamentally, it is not particularly clear what Kant actually takes metaphysics to be. In the Critical writings, he often describes metaphysics as "cognition *a priori,* or from pure understanding and pure reason" (Prol 4: 265) or as "an entirely isolated speculative knowledge of reason, indeed through mere concepts, which raises itself completely above any instruction by experience" (KrV Bxiv). In such cases, the reader might well suspect that Kant is thinking only of traditional metaphysics and is, through such a definition, craftily setting it up for a certain fall. For if the *Critique* shows that knowledge is only possible through the assistance of experience, then this would seem to show that

---

[1] See in particular Ameriks 1992, which reaches a similar conclusion as does this chapter. Ameriks, however, does not focus on Kant's conception of metaphysics, but rather on specific issues in ontology and rational psychology.

any supposed knowledge "through mere concepts," i.e., metaphysics, is actually impossible. Since Kant also claims at various points "that it is not at all metaphysics that I am doing in the *Critique*, but a whole new and as yet unattempted science" (Br 10: 340), the suspicion naturally arises that the "metaphysics" about which Kant speaks so positively in other contexts has little, if anything, to do with the kind found in Baumgarten's textbook.

Obviously, such suspicions can hardly be quelled by mining Kant's published writings, since it is precisely the consistency and genuineness of these that are at issue.[2] Fortunately, the copious notes taken by students attending Kant's lectures on metaphysics offer us another window into his views on the topic, one in which the desire to present a view more palatable for traditionalists would not be expected to arise. I thus propose in this chapter to examine these notes to see what Kant's position on metaphysics was at certain key points in his intellectual development, with the aim of answering three main questions: How did Kant's understanding of the nature and unity of metaphysics change over time? How does this relate to the traditional conception of metaphysics as this is expressed in Baumgarten's textbook? How did Kant understand the relationship between metaphysics and his emerging Critical philosophy? Taking a broader view of these questions, I examine and compare all of the extant lecture notes dating from the 1760s to the late 1780s. Due partly to limitations of space and partly to the poor quality of the notes themselves, I have chosen not to examine any sets of lectures dated later than this. Although these texts do indeed suggest Kant continued to revise his approach to metaphysics throughout the 1790s, it does not seem advisable to hazard a guess at the nature of this development based on the surviving evidence.

1 The Herder lecture notes

Let us begin our investigation with the set of notes penned by Kant's famous student, Johann Gottfried Herder, in first half of the 1760s.[3] These notes require considerable care when used, both because they were reworked by Herder at

---

[2] Naturally, after a thorough analysis of the content of the lecture transcripts has been completed, it would be useful to compare the results with Kant's published writings. Although I do not propose to do this in the present chapter, it should be noted that Kant's discussion of metaphysics in the lectures delivered after 1770 are evidently related closely in subject matter to the Architectonic of Pure Reason (A832–51/B860–79).
[3] On the origin and dating of the notes see "Translator's Introduction" in Kant 1997b. Exact dating of the notes will not be crucial for my argument.

home and because of certain irregularities that have come to light in their handling by the editors of the *Akademie-Ausgabe*.⁴ We will confine ourselves mainly to the introduction, which seems to have been handled adequately and, most importantly, concerns issues that can be checked against Kant's published writings from the same period.⁵

According to these notes, Kant opened his metaphysics course at this time with a general "prolegomena" which was to replace the "*prolegomena metaphysicorum*" of Baumgarten's original textbook. Kant's own prolegomena appears to fall rather neatly into four parts. He first treats the content of metaphysics (V-Met/Herder 28.1: 5.1–16), then the method for establishing its results (5.17–6.18), followed by a discussion of the method for presenting these results (6.18–38), and ends by considering the goal and character of the metaphysician (7.1–23).

In the first part, Kant follows Baumgarten in attempting to define the content or object (*Gegenstand*) of metaphysics. In Baumgarten's textbook, we read simply that: "METAPHYSICS is the science of the first principles in human knowledge" (Baumgarten 2013: §1). Baumgarten probably omitted any further elucidation of this definition in expectation that it would be understood easily by most academics using the textbook, and that these would be able to inform students of the necessary background in the lecture hall. Kant certainly would have known that by science was meant – to use Wolff's description – "an acquired proficiency for demonstrating what is being affirmed, or negated"⁶ (Wolff 1735: §594). He also would have known that this has two immediate implications. First, it implies that, as specifically and fully *demonstrated* knowledge or cognition, science must be certain, and so must be derived with certainty from principles that are already known to be certain. As Baumgarten's *Acroasis Logica* reads, "*science* is certain cognition based upon certain cognitions" (Baumgarten 1761: §2). The second implication Kant would have noted is that, since science is an acquired proficiency or *habitus*, a science of metaphysics must be the result of the conscious cultivation of a natural disposition already present innately in the human mind. This fact is underscored in §3 of Baumgarten's own prolegomena, where he distinguishes metaphysics as a science from what he calls "natural metaphysics" (*metaphysica naturalis*). Both share the same conceptual content. Yet natural metaphysics acquires knowledge of such simply by the common employment of concepts like substance, accident, and unity as this is required for everyday

---

4 See Naragon 2000 and Kant 1997b: xxix f.
5 For more on Kant's philosophical position at this time see Clewis 2014 and Henrich 1967.
6 "Si quis propositionem demonstrare noverit, is eam *scire* dicitur. Atque adeo *scientia* est habitus demonstrandi, quod affirmamus, vel negamus."

life and goes no further, whereas scientific metaphysics, as an artificial or skilled practice (*metaphysica artificialis*) aiming at metaphysical knowledge for its own sake, is devoted essentially to achieving the greatest possible clarification of metaphysical concepts and the most exact skill in demonstrating metaphysical principles.[7]

So Kant would have encountered metaphysics here not only in its traditional objective significance, but also in its subjective significance, i.e., as concerned not only with a delimited content, but also specifically with the extent to which this same content can be known demonstratively by human beings, whose intellects are necessarily finite. Thus, although there is no clearly subjectivist turn in Baumgarten's definition of metaphysics as the "science of the first principles in human knowledge," the subjective significance of these principles as being "firsts" specifically for *human* knowledge, was certainly at issue. One can see this immediately from Baumgarten's own suggestion in the Preface to the third edition of the *Metaphysica* that the very idea of first principles only makes sense to a finite mind such as our own. For an infinite mind knowing all things most scientifically, such as God's, all principles would imply each other such that there would be no first and no last (Baumgarten 2013: 80). Importantly, this is true not because first and last would be intuited simultaneously by such a being, but rather for the much deeper reason that the ground-consequence relation is itself perfectly symmetrical so that the very notion of an absolutely first or last thing only makes sense for a finite mind (Fugate 2014a).

In light of this, it is important to recognize that in the lecture notes Kant himself approaches metaphysics quite specifically from the standpoint of human knowledge. His method is to determine the real definition of metaphysics by applying Baumgarten's nominal definition of it as "the science of first principles in human knowledge" to the structure of human knowledge as it actually exists. In this way, Kant bases his definition on the analysis of specific observations regarding the *given* structure of human knowledge. All knowledge that we actually possess, he first notes, has a manifestly *composite* structure (V-Met/Herder 28.1: 5ff.). That is to say, any common cognition can always be broken down into at least two major components, namely into concepts and judgments. Furthermore, he observes that all common concepts can be further analyzed into simpler component concepts without which they would not be possible, until, presumably, one reaches some set of irresolvable, and thus absolutely first concepts. Here Kant departs from mere observation by introducing an a priori rational principle, namely that nothing composite can be infinitely divisible. From this he then

---

[7] See also Baumgarten 2013: 29f.

infers not only that there are, but indeed that there must be such first concepts in human knowledge. For if there are composite concepts, and no composite can be infinitely divisible, then there must be simple concepts as well. Due to the latter's being both the first and the most simple components of all other concepts, Kant refers to these variously as *principia sensu incomplexo* and as "irresolvable fundamental concepts" (*unzergliederliche Grundbegriffe*). Will there be one or several of these most basic concepts? Again, Kant looks to our actual knowledge for the answer: there must be several, he says, because fewer could not account for the complexity of the knowledge we actually possess (V-Met/Herder 28.1: 9). The case of judgments is exactly parallel: Since in human knowledge there are judgments requiring demonstration from still other judgments, then, assuming the principle that an infinite regress is impossible, there must be some first or "fundamental judgments" (*Grundurtheile*). And as judgments are essentially relations of concepts, these most basic judgments will be, he says, *principia sensu complexo*. Furthermore, since these judgments must be indemonstrable (*unbeweisliche*), if knowledge is really to be possible, their truth must be able to be made evident beyond all doubt in some other way than through demonstration.

With the help of a later section from the same set of lecture notes and part of another set also taken by Herder, we can confirm and slightly expand the general picture Kant paints here in the prolegomena. In these we again find Kant dividing knowledge into two primary components, concepts and judgments (V-Met/Herder 28.1: 155 ff.). Concepts are further divided into the non-fundamental or complex and the fundamental or *principia sensu incomplexo*. The latter, we read, are either derivative or primitive. What can this mean? How can fundamental concepts also be derivative? This must look like a transcriptional error until we notice that elsewhere in the notes Kant uses the designation "fundamental" (*fundamentale*) to refer specifically to what is basic in the order of human reasoning, not in the order of objects themselves. Thus what is fundamental for human knowledge is in many cases an empirical given.[8] Concepts that can only first be derived from experience and are subsequently employed as the initial principles of a science are in this sense fundamental concepts. Still, we treat these same principles as derived when we attempt to discover a scientific explanation of their truth. So fundamental principles in Kant's general sense can be regarded as derivative even within the same science. *Primitive* fundamental concepts, by contrast, are those that always play the role of "firsts" in their respective science, although these too Kant divides into the "relatively" and the "absolutely" primitive. This new division rests not on the role a principle plays within its respective science, but on

---

[8] See Clewis 2014: 198–203.

the placement of the science itself within the wider scope of human knowledge. Practical sciences, for instance, have their unique primitive fundamental principles and yet these principles are not for that reason fundamental with respect to human knowledge as a whole. The *absolutely* primitive fundamental concepts, however, will be those irresolvable and simple concepts that always serve as firsts in respect to *all* human knowledge. Among such concepts, Kant lists "existence," "something," "next to," "after" and "through another" (V-Met/Herder 28.1: 158). One part of metaphysics, according to Kant, will therefore consist in the scientific treatment of these absolutely primitive fundamental concepts.

In accordance with what we saw before, Kant also articulates in these texts a fuller account of his parallel division with regard to judgments, the only notable difference being that the absolutely primitive fundamental judgments are not, properly speaking, irresolvable into further parts (since every judgment is composed of concepts), but rather are indemonstrable through any more basic judgments. Unlike concepts, however, these judgments are subject to a further important division, namely into what are called formal and material principles. The formal absolutely primitive fundamental judgments, according to the notes, are those of identity and contradiction, which prescribe as a rule the manner or way that "all predicates are to be compared with the subject" of a given proposition (V-Met/Herder 28.1: 8). Their material counterparts, by contrast, prescribe as a rule "which predicates are to be compared with the subject." In other words, the material principles provide the content of our knowledge, which Kant further explains by saying that they provide the middle terms for our demonstrations of all other true judgments. If the formal principles provide the absolutely primitive rules of the form of true knowledge, the material ones provide the entire basis for our knowledge of whatever truth goes beyond the mere restatement of identity or contradiction. Among such material judgments, Kant lists for his students Crusius's principle that "everything that is, is somewhere and at some time" (V-Met/Herder 28.1: 9).[9] It is supposed to be true and indemonstrable, and yet it is also supposed to express a relation of identity between the *non-identical* concepts of existence and those of spatial and temporal location. According to the notes, another judgment of this kind is: "A complete space has three dimensions" (V-Met/Herder 28.1: 9).

This distinction can be clarified further by attending to the way Kant expresses the precise relation between such material principles and their formal counterparts in the notes. The material principles, he explains, being indemonstrable, clearly cannot be demonstrated through the primitive formal principles.

---

9 Of course, Kant thinks that this principle is actually false.

Yet since the formal principles are those of the form of absolutely all judgments whatsoever, the material ones must nevertheless stand under them as regards form (V-Met/Herder 28.1: 9 f.). Kant distinguishes these material principles from mere hidden identities or contradictions (whose truth can also be proven through the formal principles) by saying that they stand "immediately" under the formal principles. What Kant has in mind here is this: A hidden identity or contradiction not only stands under one of the formal principles, but can be reduced to it by means of a stepwise resolution of the concepts involved. In every such case, one will eventually end up with something roughly of the form "A is A" or "A is not A," and will thus be able to determine the truth or falsity of the original judgment. A primitive material principle, by contrast, will have to be indemonstrable and yet possess the form of either identity or contradiction "immediately," i. e., without such being provable by any further stepwise resolution to the formal principles. A second part of metaphysics will therefore accompany the earlier analysis of concepts and consist in the scientific treatment of precisely these primitive formal and material judgments.

As simple as this outline is, Kant thinks it can provide a sufficient basis for diagnosing the errors of his major predecessors and for developing a preliminary sketch of the proper method of metaphysics. The true method of metaphysics, which is the topic of the second part of the prolegomena, consists simply in learning to reliably recognize which principles are genuinely fundamental and which are not, and so must be further analyzed into their component concepts or judgments. There are thus precisely two ways to err systematically in metaphysics, which derive from the very structure of human knowledge as such (V-Met/Herder 28.1: 5). First, one can err by failing to recognize the most basic concepts and principles as being such. Since this will often lead us to attempt demonstrations of what is in principle indemonstrable, it also tends to corrupt the practice of demonstration. The second way to err is to accept as absolutely primitive principles those that are not such. This can prevent us from discovering any hidden contradictions or falsities, or lead us to incorrectly extend or restrict the scope of a concept. To avoid both kinds of error, the metaphysician must not begin with definitions or complete concepts of its objects, but rather with those features of objects that are most familiar and evident and proceed by analysis of these towards ever more complete concepts. According to Kant, two things are essential to such analysis, namely, that one accept the results with "exceptional decisiveness" even if they seem to contradict common sense and that one take pains to estimate with the "greatest honesty" the degree of one's certainty regarding a certain principle, as well as to acknowledge what remains to be shown (V-Met/Herder 28.1: 6).

As the body of the lecture notes shows in detail, Kant ascribed the key mistakes made by Wolff and Baumgarten to this first mode of error, and those of Crusius to the second (V-Met/Herder 28.1: 156 f.), thereby situating his own method as a sort of middle position (cf. Fugate 2014b). According to his account, Wolff and Baumgarten imitate mathematics and adduce arbitrary definitions, accepting none as materially irresolvable, and admit only a single principle of all knowledge, the principle of contradiction. Crusius, by contrast, correctly recognizes that it is impossible to account for the real content of our knowledge without admitting certain absolutely primitive material principles, indeed both irresolvable concepts and indemonstrable judgments. Yet he fails precisely by presenting as indemonstrable and certain many principles that he has not indeed fully analyzed himself. This can be due to a failure of attention or to an intentional misrepresentation of one's degree of certainty. If only we can avoid both these types of errors, then, on Kant's account, we should expect to be able to reach by analysis at least some most basic principles that are certain beyond any reasonable doubt. This knowledge will then constitute the entire content of metaphysics and will subsequently form the basis of all further scientific knowledge.

The third part of the prolegomena, concerning the popular presentation of metaphysical knowledge, need not detain us, since Kant himself treats it almost perfunctorily. In essence, Kant simply states that although metaphysics aims most centrally at the solidity of its knowledge, it can and should aim also at presenting its knowledge with beauty (V-Met/Herder 28.1: 6). This leads him naturally into the fourth part, where he discusses in some detail the goal and character of the metaphysician. This again follows largely from his description of method in the second part. The metaphysician, according to Kant, should not aim so much at producing philosophers and opinions, but rather at healthy understanding, i.e., the kind of *habitus* that is required in order to carry out metaphysical analysis properly and to present one's results honestly and publicly. This means that an essential function of the metaphysician is the avoidance of prejudices that would distract him from attending only to the content of the ideas or experiences being analyzed. These include prejudices in favor of the views of respected philosophers simply because they are respected or in favor of one's own opinions simply because they are one's own, as well as prejudices against the views of others simply because they are foreign or strike one as absurd. The genuine metaphysician will carefully consider contrary views, putting himself in the place of this other person and ascribing to them greater understanding than himself. When the metaphysician finds an error, they will not disregard it, but rather seek to understand its causes, because "every error is an actual phenomenon and appearance in the human soul" (V-Met/Herder 28.1: 7) and so has a real ground. The aim of the metaphysician, according to Kant, is thus to investigate and understand, and thereby more precisely correct for, the real cause of the prejudices within the mind that distract us from impartial analysis and lead to the dishonest presentation of our results. Metaphysics, as the lectures describe it, is nothing other than the scientific basis of all genuine science and can be acquired naturally by any sufficiently thorough, unprejudiced, and enlightened mind.

2 Assessment

In these notes, we see Kant presenting his students with a reasonably sophisticated and unified account of the content and method of metaphysics. Kant's insistence that we base our definition of metaphysics on an analysis of human knowledge, that in effect we reach a clear understanding of what it is before determining what it ought to be, points in the direction of what might be termed a subjective turn in his thought. On such an account, metaphysics is not only to provide human knowledge with a foundation, but metaphysics itself is to be defined by and limited to the role of providing such a foundation specifically for finite or human knowledge. It should be noted that Kant's procedure here is profoundly consistent: according to it we reach an understanding of metaphysics itself by the same method, and within the same limits, as we do all other particular metaphysical principles.

Nevertheless, by this method Kant reaches a conclusion that remains basically the same as Baumgarten's own definition of metaphysics as "the science of the first principles in human knowledge" (Baumgarten 2013: 99). Kant shows no skepticism regarding the possibility of erecting such a science, and remains committed to the existence of absolutely primitive fundamental principles. As we have seen, this commitment is based on the unexplained assumptions that composites cannot be infinitely divisible and that an infinite chain of true judgments relating serially as grounds to consequences is also intrinsically impossible. Where he departs from his Wolffian predecessors is when it comes to the question as to the number and nature of first principles. And here he sides with Crusius in holding that there must be several irresolvable primitive concepts and many indemonstrable primitive judgments, which provide the basis for all truths having any real content. Since the only way to secure the certainty of such principles is through an exact and unprejudiced analysis of what is most clear and evident in human knowledge itself, the primary goal of metaphysics becomes one of acquiring the skill for such an exact analysis of ideas and experiences. Where he departs from Crusius is in the exact details of this analysis with regard to some core metaphysical concepts. In all respects, then, Kant presents to his students the view of metaphysics one also finds expressed in *Inquiry concerning the Distinctness of the Principles of Natural Theology and Morality* and employed in *Attempt to Introduce the Concept of Negative Magnitudes into Philosophy* and other works of the early 1760s. On this basis, one can understand Kant's statement around the same time that he "can easily, through the slightest turn, induce the author, whose textbook has been chosen chiefly for the richness of its content and the precision of its instruction, i.e., A. G. Baumgarten, to follow the same path" (NEV 2: 308).

3 The lecture notes L_1

The Heinze extracts from Metaphysics L_1, which have been dated to the later part of the 1770s, also begin with a revision of Baumgarten's prolegomena. As in the Herder transcripts, Kant again sets the stage through an analysis of the uniquely composite structure of human knowledge. A piece of knowledge, he explains, can be combined (*verbunden*) with other pieces of knowledge in two basic ways or according to two different species (*Gattungen*) of combination, namely through *coordination*, as when they form co-parts of a common whole, or through *subordination*, as when they relate to one another as ground and consequence. From this there arises two kinds of limits (*Schranken*) to which human knowledge is necessarily subjected. The realm of coordinated knowledge, which is the province of history in a general sense, must be finite in scope due to the natural limit of human experience and memory. But the limits of its scope, Kant says, are nevertheless "entirely undetermined" (V-Met/L1 28.1: 171). It seems probable that by this last remark Kant simply means that, although the quantity of our historical knowledge will always be limited, what this specific limit might be is not determined by any feature essential to human knowledge. By contrast, the series of subordinated knowledge must not only be finite, he explains, but must also have a fixed highest and lowest term, which provide the boundary points respectively of an ascending progression towards the first or highest ground and a descending progression towards the last or lowest consequence. Interestingly, Kant observes that since we can proceed either way in such a series, it is possible in principle to designate either end as a priori and the other as a posteriori. Yet we do in fact identify experience preeminently with the a posteriori, and the reason for this is that we just happen to always cognize the lowest consequences through experience. Kant seems to recognize here that what is taken to be before and after in our knowledge derives not from its intrinsic structure, but rather from the fact that the human being is only ever able to know the last or lowest consequences through immediate experience, i.e., through direct acquaintance and not by coming to them through first principles. Therefore, what is first or prior subjectively considered, namely experience, is always what comes after or is posterior in the order of grounds and consequences, and this is no doubt a feature directly linked to the general finitude of human knowledge.

Yet, just as soon as Kant recognizes the dependency of the usual designation of the a priori and the a posteriori on a special feature of human knowledge, he proceeds to construct his definition of metaphysics on this very distinction. Since every human science is limited, Kant argues, and since this requires a limit both a priori and a posteriori, Baumgarten's definition is incomplete in at least two ways. First, it is ambiguous with regard to the a priori limit of the science. Many things can actually be considered "firsts" in human knowledge. Experience can provide us with what are first principles relative only to us. Likewise, every human science has its relatively first principles. To fix the definition, therefore, we must find a way to precisely distinguish the sense of "first" distinctive to metaphysical knowledge. Kant notes that the usual way to do this, namely, by referring metaphysics to the first principles of *all* human knowledge, is clearly inadequate. For in this case, there will only be one metaphysical concept, namely, of a thing in general, and one metaphysical judgment, the principle of contradiction (V-Met/L1 28.1: 172). Second, the definition fails entirely to designate the a posteriori limit of the science. If metaphysics is allowed to be some set of first principles beyond the absolutely first, then since anything can be considered first with respect to what follows it, the a posteriori limit will be a matter of choice. Kant rejects this proposal, for unstated reasons, asserting that metaphysics must be among those sciences whose limits are determined "by nature and by reason" (V-Met/L1 28.1: 172).

To precisely distinguish what he calls the "territory" of metaphysics from that of the other sciences, Kant introduces two key distinctions. The first distinction is between sciences that employ a rational principle of cognition and those that employ an empirical one. A rational science in this first sense acquires knowledge through the activity of the understanding, whereas an empirical science acquires knowledge through our being passively affected by external objects. The second distinction sounds very similar, but divides sciences not by their sources, but by means of the qualities of their objects, namely whether these are rational or merely empirical. A rational science in this second, objective sense, is one that concerns *pure* concepts and objects, i. e., those objects given through the pure self-activity of understanding and reason, whereas an empirical science in this sense is one that concerns *empirical* concepts and objects, i. e., those given to us through the passivity of our senses. According to the lecture notes, the science of metaphysics must be understood as being rational in both of these respects, thus as scientifically investigating pure or non-empirical objects based entirely on the pure activity of the understanding and reason. Yet this description fails to distinguish metaphysics from mathematics, which is also rational or pure in both method and object. As we will see below, in later sets of notes Kant distinguishes metaphysics as cognition through pure concepts from mathematics as cognition through the construction of concepts in pure intuition. If the notes accurately reflect his position at this time, then Kant has not yet reached this key formulation, but rather continues to rely on the Wolffian distinction, also found in Baumgarten, between philosophy as "the science of qualities in things" and mathematics as the science of the quantities in things (Baumgarten 1761: § 1; see also Baumgarten 2013: 21).

Here we meet for the first time what is perhaps the most radically original and enduring feature of Kant's understanding of metaphysics in the Critical period. As we have just seen, Kant does not simply reject Baumgarten's definition of metaphysics. He presses it into this new form by the application of even stricter criteria for the definition of a science. Kant simply assumes, likely for reasons similar to what we found in the Herder notes, that a science of metaphysics must be possible. For metaphysics *just means* the scientific basis for all rational science, and without rational science no certain, unified, or demonstrated knowledge would be possible at all. Since on Kant's present account all scientific or rational knowledge first becomes such through the *application* of the principles of the pure understanding and pure reason, metaphysics in one key sense is nothing other than the science of these principles considered on their own, i.e., it is the doctrine of rational science as such. The conception of metaphysics Kant presents here to his students thus not only retains essentially a reference to its traditional role as the "science of the first principles in human knowledge," but even seeks to strengthen this role by arguing that it must constitute an absolutely original and isolated science. However, by the same token, Kant also radically revises the traditional definition of metaphysics through this demand that it pick out a specific territory, or qualitatively distinct domain, defined by the very nature of human reason. Now if metaphysics must be possible and if it must pick out a territory heterogeneous from all the rest, then – so Kant argues – the only way to define it is by reference to the distinction between cognition that is based, at least in part, on empirical principles and that which is based entirely upon those that are pure (V-Met/L1 28.1: 172–73). Thus at the very basis of Kant's new definition of metaphysics is the clearly subjective distinction between representations that originate in the pure activity of our intellectual powers and those that originate from the impure passivity of our physical senses.[10] So the notes depict Kant

---

[10] On why this distinction should not be understood to be identical to the traditional distinction between innate and acquired representations, see Zöller 1998.

neither as seriously questioning whether metaphysics is really possible, nor as entirely rejecting the traditional definition of this science. Rather, they depict him as seeking to transform this definition under the constraint that metaphysics be a strictly delimited and therefore entirely pure science.

Returning to the text: Kant proceeds to elaborate on the foundational role that such a science as metaphysics must play with respect to scientific knowledge in general. Since metaphysics is the whole of science that is pure in both method and content, at least part of its function is analogous to that of logic. As Kant explains, "since logic treats the use of the understanding and reason, metaphysics is a logic of the use of the pure understanding and pure reason" (V-Met/L1 28.1: 173). Kant's thought here seems to be that just as logic studies and clarifies the laws that govern the use of understanding and reason in general, then, to the extent that there is a possible pure use of these faculties, the study of such pure laws will naturally fall to metaphysics as the science encompassing all study of pure objects (cf. A52–57/B77–82). Metaphysics will therefore include as part of its very content the rational science of the laws governing a possible pure use of understanding and reason. Now, all rational sciences, even those having an empirical object, are rational precisely insofar as they are based upon principles arising from the pure activity of understanding and reason. Leaving aside mathematics, they all therefore differ from metaphysics in that they apply such principles to empirically given objects, thereby applying the pure principles of knowledge (*principii cognoscendi*) studied by metaphysics to the empirical concepts gathered from experience. Hence, since metaphysics on its own treats the pure use of the understanding and reason and the pure concepts that derive from these, it will relate to all other rational sciences as pure science relates to applied sciences (V-Met/L1: 173). Later in the notes, for example, Kant explains:

> The concept of the soul is by itself a concept of experience. However, in rational psychology we take no more from experience than the mere concept of the soul, that we have a soul. The rest must be known from pure reason. That knowledge in which we depart from the guidance of experience is the metaphysical knowledge of the soul. (V-Met/L1 28.1: 263)

So "the object of metaphysics can indeed also be empirical objects, although it [i.e., metaphysics] must be derived from the universal grounds of pure reason" (V-Met/L1 28.1: 177). In the prolegomena to L_1, Kant also mentions under such applied metaphysics what he calls "the pure doctrine of body [*somatologia pura*], which can be regarded as a ground for explaining what we experience with our senses," i.e., for physics (V-Met/L1 28.1: 175), as well as natural theology (*theologia naturalis*), which we learn later "must presuppose an original being on account of the empirical use of reason" (V-Met/L1 28.1: 305).

Metaphysics, as Kant explains, will therefore have at least two divisions. It will first contain a science of a possible pure use of understanding and reason, i.e., a pure or "transcendental metaphysics" (V-Met/L1 28.1: 177), and secondly, under the title of applied metaphysics, it will include any particular sciences that apply pure understanding and reason to objects given in experience, though without relying on any further principles borrowed therefrom. According to the notes, there is also a third pure science namely, morals (*Moral*). Since Kant says nothing further of this in the notes, it is impossible to determine how he thought it relates to metaphysics, whether as a part or as something else besides. All that is clear is that Kant regards morals as sharing the distinctive feature of both mathematics and metaphysics, namely, absolute purity and independence from empirical principles.

Now pure metaphysics, as we have just seen, has the task of reflecting rationally on its own pure nature, because in this case both the method and object are rational or pure. The first question that arises here is "whether metaphysics is really a dogmatic science or only a guide and organon" (V-Met/L1 28.1: 173). In other words, is metaphysics only able to provide a foundation for other rational sciences, which to some extent must borrow their objects from empirical experience, or is it also able to produce its own rational knowledge of pure objects originally and from its own resources alone? Kant's well-known answer to this question is much less interesting than is the generality with which the question itself is framed in the lecture notes. As Kant explains, no knowledge is possible in the absence of experience. Yet metaphysics is by definition knowledge from principles of the pure understanding and pure reason, and this description applies whether we are speaking of it only in its role as the foundation of other rational sciences or in its possible role as a source of knowledge regarding some particular pure objects. So the question that naturally arises from this reflection – How is metaphysics possible? – really includes two related questions: How are pure principles of the possibility of rational knowledge regarding empirical objects possible? How is it possible for these same principles to provide knowledge of pure objects?

The original unity of these two questions can be seen from the way in which Kant attempts in the lecture notes to demonstrate that his revised definition of an absolutely pure science perfectly agrees with the ancient title, "metaphysics," which indicates that it a science of that which lies beyond physics, indeed beyond all experience. To understand this, we must observe that earlier in the notes Kant had described the absolutely first principles of knowledge as the "highest" principles, and those borrowed immediately from experience as the "lowest." He also explained in some detail at that point that the traditional picture of metaphysical knowledge and its relation to the other sciences has always been that of a ladder, and that the move from the a posteriori to the a priori is generally represented as an assent to first or highest principles. It is with this image in mind that Kant now explains that the science of pure knowledge, as the science of what lies essentially and absolutely above all empirical knowledge, agrees most precisely with the description of a science beyond physics. As the notes explain,

> It [metaphysics] is a science that in the same way lies outside of the field of physics, beyond it. And because pure rational concepts, which transcend [*übergehen*] experience, follow after the mixed appearances of physics, this science is correctly called metaphysics. (V-Met/L1 28.1: 174)

A reader coming to these notes directly from the *Critique of Pure Reason* might suppose that Kant is here speaking only of the dialectical ideas of pure reason. This would be natural enough, because in the absence of the image of the ladder Kant here provides, one would not think of identifying genuine synthetic knowledge a priori with what is above or beyond experience. But as the notes make abundantly clear, it is precisely in this image of assent to what lies beyond experience that the question of synthetic knowledge a priori and the question of the possibility of knowledge of pure objects stand unified. Both originate with the single question of the nature and possibility of metaphysical knowledge as pure knowledge. Although we will need to confirm this below in our examination of later sets of notes, this already provides considerable insight regarding the unity of Kant's definition of metaphysics in the Critical period. Metaphysics as a science that is pure both in form and object is one that lies essentially above or beyond experience. It will study as its first object the principles of the pure use of understanding and reason, i. e., the pure concepts and judgments that reason is able to make for itself without any dependence on experience. In their downward application to possible objects of experience, these pure concepts and judgments will provide the fundamental form of all the rational sciences. But pure metaphysics also generates for itself concepts of possible pure objects, which if known, must be known through those same pure principles that form the basis of applied metaphysics. If there are any rational sciences, then metaphysics must exist at least in this first function, as a "guide and organon" for experience, but it must be further determined whether it can also produce knowledge of pure objects on its own. Under the study of such objects, Kant lists transcendental cosmology and transcendental theology, which provide the basis in turn for the applied metaphysical sciences of rational somatology, rational psychology, and natural theology, which were mentioned above.

4 Assessment

This set of notes is particularly interesting because it gives us a first glimpse into how Kant sees metaphysics after the Critical turn, but also before the publication of the *Critique of Pure Reason*. As he does in the Herder transcripts, Kant presents his students with an essentially positive and well-unified conception of metaphysics as a science. In particular, we have seen that he combines the image of scientific knowledge as a ladder ascending towards first principles with a distinction between pure and empirical principles to explain the original unity of the question of the possibility of rational sciences regarding both empirical and pure objects. The question of synthetic judgments a priori, which form the basis of all rational science of objects of experience, as well as the question of a possible rational knowledge of pure objects, i. e., what Kant will later call the ideas of pure reason, both arise in the same assent to the pure basis of all human knowledge. In the first, the same principles are considered in their possible application to experience as are considered in a possible application to pure objects in the second. In accordance with this, Kant is able to speak of metaphysics in at least two related senses in these notes: first, as pure or transcendental metaphysics, which is pure in both method and object, and which therefore considers the pure faculty of knowledge itself, its sources, laws, and limits, as well as any pure objects it might be able to cognize on its own; secondly, as applied metaphysics, which encompasses all other genuine sciences.

In addition to clarifying Kant's understanding of the unity of metaphysics, these notes also provide insight into the natural evolution from the more traditional distinction between the a prior and the a posteriori, and the special sense this distinction takes in Kant's Critical writings. As we saw above, Kant recognizes the traditional distinction as a relative one. What is before and after in our knowledge depends largely upon our choice, and is a matter of comparison. Indeed, almost any principles can be considered a priori with respect to others that are shown to follow from them. As we also saw above, Kant found such a relative or comparative sense to be inadequate to serve in defining a science such as metaphysics, which must have an absolute territory defined by the nature of reason itself. On this basis, Kant seeks to delimit a special absolute sense of the a priori to describe the whole class of principles that have their source in the pure activity of the understanding and reason, and as such entirely exclude any dependency on experience. These are preeminently prior both for this reason, and because they correspond to the highest rung from which all other knowledge is represented as depending. By the same token, the a posteriori is no longer defined as what comes later, but as that whole class of principles that come later because they have their sources in empirical experience, which itself is represented always as the last consequence or lowest rung on the ladder of knowledge.

In addition, these notes also shed considerable light on the original source and meaning of the term "transcendental" in Kant's early Critical philosophy.[11] Metaphysics is, as Kant remarks, the same as the "trans physical" or what essentially goes beyond or transcends experience. According to Kant's revised definition of metaphysics as pure science or as science that is a priori in an absolute sense, a transcendental science is one that is rational in both method and object, and so lies beyond experience in this twofold sense. As we saw above, Kant mentions exactly three such sciences, namely, transcendental metaphysics, which has the pure understanding and pure reason as its object, transcendental cosmology, which has the "pure rational concept" of a whole that is not part of a still greater whole as its object, and transcendental theology, which has the pure rational concept of an original being as its object. All of these are transcendental precisely "because also the object, and not only the principles are an object of pure reason and not of experience" (V-Met/L1 28.1: 195).

5 The Mrongovius, Volkmann, and von Schön lecture notes[12]

These three sets of notes provide us with a clear picture of Kant's views on metaphysics in the mid-1780s. They agree on all essential points and share several distinctive features. All three begin by expanding on and refining the definition of metaphysics that we found in L_1, while adding to the prolegomena two further subsections, namely, on the history and the use of metaphysics, so that it now comprises three parts.[13] As he does in L_1, Kant here distinguishes between historical and scientific cognition, depicting the latter again as a kind of ladder that can be seen from two points of view. We can start either from below by basing our knowledge on experience, and ascending from this as a principle of cognition towards the true grounds; or we can begin from above, from principles of

---

[11] For a brief account of the background on this term, see Aertsen 2000, Hinske 1970a and 1970b, and the dated but classic studies, Knittermeyer 1920 and 1953/54.
[12] All translations here are my own. However, in respect to Mrongovius I have relied heavily on the edition and notes in Kant 1997b as well as the discussion of this text in Naragon 2000.
[13] The lack of such features in previous notes is very probably due to their having been lost, not an innovation on Kant's part in the Critical Period. A short historical sketch is included at the end of L_1 and the outline for Herder's second set of lecture notes contains divisions on the history and use of metaphysics, although the subdivisions show the content to have been quite different from what we find in the 1780s. See V-Met/Herder 28.1: 156 f.

being, and descend towards experience, which is the "lowest step in the series" (V-Met/Volckmann 28.1: 356). The former cognition is a posteriori, the latter a priori. Since descent through the whole series is impossible for human beings, the very possibility of scientific cognition presupposes that we must be able to isolate and secure its first members. From this arises the traditional definition of metaphysics:

> Such a project is modest; for since we have principles, and some of these must be terminal points [*termini*] a priori; we can ask about these. Such a science has long been thought of, and called metaphysics, and under this is understood: a science of the first principles of all other human knowledge. But this definition is not sufficiently determinate. (V-Met/Volckmann 28.1: 357)

This point reveals the first advancement over L_1. In all three sets of lecture notes, Kant is recorded as asserting that in order to have a science of any kind, one must have more than merely the interconnection in a series of grounds and consequences; one must also have an idea of the whole. Thus we read: "Every science must make up a system, a whole according to a previously discovered idea" (V-Met/Schön: 28.1: 463); "the system [of metaphysics] must be based on an idea, through which the parts, the connection of the parts, and the completeness of the parts is determined" (V-Met/Mron 29.1,2: 751); "to hang together as members and compose a whole, where no part can be taken away without damaging the idea of the whole and this systematic whole is called science" (V-Met/Volckmann 28.1: 357). In this idea, we find unified both the specific manner of connection among the members of the series and the limits to which this series is necessarily subject. The members not only stand to one another as ground and consequence, but as members composing a whole, where the place of any part is determined by its reciprocal relation to the others. Likewise, the limits to which the whole series is subject are fixed by the completeness exhibited in the coherence of all members into a whole in which there are no detectable or even possible gaps.

Now, just as in L_1, Kant here proceeds to examine the problems with the traditional definition, coming eventually to the conclusion that the only entirely determinate concept of metaphysics possible is that of the science of a priori principles in the absolute sense, or what is the same, "the science of the principles of pure cognition or only pure philosophy" (V-Met/Mron 29.1,2: 750).

> The whole of our pure knowledge a priori or our pure rational knowledge is metaphysics or it is a system of pure rational knowledge through mere concepts. Such a science is entirely separated by itself, entirely isolated; pure reason places itself entirely apart. (V-Met/Schön 28.1: 464)

This definition of metaphysics in terms of knowledge from pure concepts alone points to the second innovation over L_1, found in these lecture notes. Whereas in L_1 Kant distinguished mathematics from metaphysics, both of which are pure, by reference to their subject matter, namely quantitative and qualitative features of objects respectively, he now makes use of the distinction between pure concepts and pure intuitions. Metaphysics "is a system of pure rational knowledge through mere concepts," "but the use of reason is again twofold, either through mere concepts or through the construction of concepts; the former is philosophical, the latter mathematical and both employ pure concepts a priori" (V-Met/Schön 28.1: 464). With this, Kant has reached a fully determinate concept or idea by which to determine the specific content and limits of metaphysics; it is pure, not empirical, knowledge, from pure concepts alone, thus without any dependence even on pure intuitions.

Again, it is crucial to notice that when Kant speaks in these lectures of pure a priori knowledge, he clearly means to include all possible synthetic a priori concepts and judgments. It is thus clear that Kant does not mean to exempt from this description the concepts and principles justified by the *Critique of Pure Reason*. But how is this? Is it not the case that the employment of the categories requires a relation to, and thus is in some sense dependent upon, both the forms of pure intuition and the givenness of empirical objects to which they can correspond? To see why this is not the case, it must be clear that the question here is not one of justification, but of the original source of the cognitions. The specific unity prescribed by the categories is an absolutely pure and original source of unity in our cognitions that can be derived neither from intuition nor from experience. It is thus merely the *theoretical use* of the categories that should be understood as depending on pure intuition and possible experience, and not the categories themselves as absolute principles of thought of an object in general. Considered by themselves, these are original or unconditioned, pure and merely conceptual conditions of all thought in general. The question of the possibility of experience and the question of the possibility of knowledge of noumenal objects are therefore two branches of one question: *How is metaphysics as pure knowledge from mere concepts possible?* Indeed, even more fundamentally, the lectures make it clear that Kant regarded the critique of pure reason itself to be the purest part of metaphysics according to this definition. The reason for this is that it constitutes the only theoretical science possible that is purely rational with regard to both method and object, and so corresponds most essentially with Kant's radicalized definition of metaphysics. "The first part of metaphysics," we read in the Volckmann notes,

> is therefore the entire determination of our pure reason, the determination of its nature, and the boundaries of its faculties. This part can be called transcendental philosophy or the

critique of pure reason, where pure reason is its own object. This first part of metaphysics can also be called pure metaphysics, since one usually divides science in general into the pure and the applied part. (V-Met/Volckmann 28.1: 360)

And a few pages later:

If I consider the critique of our reason itself, insofar as it judges independently from all experience: then this is the genuine pure philosophy; for it justifies reason and shows how far it can reach independently from experience; and from this it follows at the same time that in every science in which reason rules, there must be a metaphysics. (V-Met/Volckmann 28.1: 362 f.)

Both of these passages are backed up in the von Schön and Mrongovius lectures. They identify the critique of pure reason with pure metaphysics, or with metaphysics according to the precise meaning of knowledge from mere concepts; for in it pure reason examines and criticizes only itself. Such a science is therefore pure or rational with respect to both method and object.

As the first quote in the paragraph above indicates, the relation between the critique of pure reason and the other rational sciences is being compared by Kant to the broader and better understood relation of the pure to the applied sciences. This is the third innovation in these notes over what we found in L_1. As we saw above, in L_1 the distinction Kant drew between pure and applied metaphysics corresponded to a distinction between the critique of pure reason as well as the system of all a priori concepts and judgments, on the one hand, and the application of this system to objects given empirically, on the other. Now, by contrast, Kant consistently identifies pure metaphysics with the critical examination of pure understanding and pure reason alone and applied metaphysics with the pure system of philosophy, which comprises the transcendental categories and principles, i. e., ontology, as well as the special metaphysics of nature and freedom (V-Met/Volckmann 28.1: 360, 364). This is a peculiar use of the pure-applied distinction, but seems to correspond to the difference between knowledge that is only directed towards the pure faculty of reason itself and that which is directed to the concepts and principles of this faculty in its possible relation to objects. So in pure metaphysics, or critique, we ask about the "origin, use, and boundaries" of a concept, whereas in ontology, one branch of applied metaphysics, we talk of objects in general, for example whether they must be substances or accidents (V-Met/Volckmann 28.1: 361).

A fourth innovation over what we saw in L_1 lies in Kant's greater clarity on the precise reason why all science must have its foundation in a metaphysics, including even experience itself. The reason for this is that the necessity of a concept or principle – cognition of which is what it means to know it rationally – can only have its source in pure reason. Pure reason is precisely reason insofar as it is a faculty of forming judgments entirely through itself and so independently from experience. Since no judgment drawn from experience as such can be necessary, if rational knowledge is possible, then so too must be knowledge from pure reason. Furthermore, if rational science is nothing other than necessarily and thus systematically connected cognitions, then a science will only be such to the extent that it draws its cognitions from metaphysics. In the Volckmann lectures we therefore read that "metaphysics is thus the philosophy of all sciences, since it prescribes the use of reason for every other science, and what is to be taken note of when we consider any science" (V-Met/Volckmann 28.1: 363). There must thus be a metaphysics in every rational cognition or in every genuine science, and so there will be a metaphysics of morals, of corporeal nature, of politics and even of mathematics (V-Met/Volckmann 28.1: 362 f.). As for experience:

> To see the necessity of something means to know it a priori from concepts: for we do not see the necessity of all when we see simply that it always happens, e. g., if we see that powder ignites on contact with fire. In order to see necessity, I must penetrate to the cause of this, which no experience teaches. Therefore cognition with consciousness of necessity is from concepts a priori. Experience provides only historical knowledge. Thus to this extent metaphysics is no mere figment of the mind. It rather has an object and provides knowledge from mere concepts a priori independently of all experience and this science has reality for its object. (V-Met/Schön 28.1: 469)

This completes our examination of the first part of the prolegomena found in the three sets of lecture notes under consideration, which cover the same material, though in more detail, that we found in L_1. As noted above, Kant seems at this time to have added two additional subsections to the prolegomena in the 1780s. In the first new section, Kant provides the student with a sketch of the history of metaphysics. For our present purposes, this subsection is not particularly remarkable except that it is clearly arranged by Kant to illustrate three things: that metaphysics itself is inevitable for human beings; that his newly formulated definition of metaphysics was that towards which all previous metaphysicians had been groping; and, finally, that these failed precisely because they misunderstood the nature of our cognitions through pure concepts, which could not be avoided in the absence of a critique of pure reason. Historically, metaphysics originates from an interest in the things that lie beyond nature, because it is upon these that all other things depend, including the future and fate of the human being itself. As the notes explain: "Reason would prefer to give up all other sciences before this one [i. e., metaphysics]. These questions concern its highest interest, and that reason should no longer concern us with them, would mean for it to cease being reason" (V-Met/Mron 29.1,2: 765). As products of pure understanding and reason, Kant explains, the concepts of such things arose easily and naturally among peoples. And as philosophy developed, metaphysicians came to recognize the distinction between the sensible and the intelligible and to speculate on the difference in the origin of our knowledge of these two kinds of things. All subsequent philosophers, on Kant's account, have either followed Plato, who assumed an intuition of intellectual things, or Aristotle, who denied such an intuition and derived all knowledge from the senses, but still recognized as intellectual at least the form of our concepts generated by reflection (V-Met/Mron 29.1,2: 760 f.). The former tradition naturally inclined toward mysticism in order to support its claims to knowledge, while the latter tended to fall into crude and inconsistent empiricism, since it could just as little account for the validity of its concepts.

As the notes tell us, "no one has even thought of a critique of pure reason until now" (V-Met/Mron 29.1,2: 764; cf. V-Met/Volckmann 28.1: 377). They have examined concepts and principles establishing the *quid facti*, but have not thought to ask about the *quid iuris*. Metaphysics would never have been needed, and neither would a critique of pure reason, if we were only concerned with its mathematical and empirical uses. However, because the interest of reason lies "concentrated" in reason's pure objects, and because here reason necessarily falls into dialectic with itself in the absence of a critique, the examination of the whole of reason's pure faculty becomes necessary (V-Met/Mron 29.1,2: 767). This critique of pure reason, which is just pure metaphysics, will thus have two parts: it will examine the possible immanent use of pure understanding in a transcendental analytic, and the possible transcendent use of it in a transcendental dialectic. Confirming what we found in L_1, it is clear that here too Kant regards metaphysics, or cognition from pure concepts alone, to encompass the principles of both an immanent and a transcendent use of pure reason:

> Metaphysics means the same as trans physical. Nature is the object of all possible experience. Now, here I can again have principles that are not borrowed from experience and these belong to metaphysics, e. g., that all alterations have their cause. So beyond physics there is again knowledge and so metaphysics as it were lies on an entirely different side of human knowledge. (V-Met/Schön 28.1: 469)

The examination of reason's ability to gain knowledge through principles that transcend experience will be as much an examination of the possible application of these to experience as it will be an examination of its possible application to pure objects.

This history leads directly to Kant's discussion of the uses of metaphysics in the third subsection of the prolegomena. Again, the details are not as relevant to our concerns in this chapter as is the general shape of the argument. Metaphysics, the notes explain, originally arose precisely from our interest in two pure objects, namely in God and another world (V-Met/Volckmann 28.1: 382). But critique shows that here metaphysics can in fact accomplish nothing, and indeed that such a science would not have arisen merely for the sake of its immanent use, because here reason always has experience with which to confirm its conclusions. As the notes further explain, the reason for such interest lies in the connection of these objects with morality. Like metaphysics itself, morality is based in the pure concepts of reason alone. But rather than providing principles of knowledge, it commands us through an absolutely necessary law to obey without consideration of our own happiness. "Morals is therefore a separated science, a practical and pure rational science that presupposes no principles of God or of another world" (V-Met/Volckmann 28.1: 383). It is "the knowledge of that which I unfailingly must do according to the principles of reason that concern my entire end. It is already given to us and requires no metaphysical principles and needs to presuppose neither God nor another world" (V-Met/Mron 29.1,2: 776). But as the notes explain, the human being cannot forgo all concern with happiness and the only way to make such a need consistent with the moral command is after all to assume the existence of God and of another life. So "the moral motives are, however, further strengthened through this, when I see that there is a God and another world" (V-Met/Mron 29.1,2: 776).

If these notes are accurate, then the interest that generates metaphysics derives in fact from something that is not intrinsically metaphysical, and this is the case even should we go beyond anything said explicitly in the notes and ascribe morality itself to metaphysics. The interest in God and another world is not a part of either speculative or moral metaphysics, because it is not a cognition, whether theoretical or practical, from pure concepts alone. It takes into account an empirical, indeed anthropological, principle, namely our inability to square our interest in happiness with the pure moral principle in the absence of such beliefs. "Metaphysics is therefore not the foundation of religion ... but rather the bulwark against the attacks of speculative reason" (V-Met/Mron 29.1,2: 776).

From this follows the final determination of the conception of metaphysics, which unifies its various functions in pursuit of one supreme function or end. By definition, metaphysics is cognition from pure concepts alone, and as such includes as its pure part the critique of the pure faculty of reason itself. This, again, has two parts, namely the examination of its possible immanent use and of its possible transcendent use. The examination of the latter leads to a merely negative conclusion, namely that metaphysics of pure or transcendent objects is impossible, that here there can be no knowledge, but only belief. But when viewed from the standpoint of the positive function this plays with respect to the highest practical end that reason sets for us, metaphysics becomes the science of the boundaries of human reason, the culture of all science, and the protector of pure reason's highest vocation:

> Metaphysics is the spirit of philosophy. It relates to philosophy as the *spiritus vini* to wine. It elucidates our elementary concepts and thereby makes us proficient to gain insight into all the sciences. In short, it is the greatest cultivation of human understanding. (V-Met/Mron 29.1,2: 940)

6 Conclusion

This examination of Kant's lectures has suggested several fundamental conclusions about his relationship with traditional metaphysics. First, we have seen that both before and after the Critical turn, Kant remains committed to the reality of metaphysical knowledge and is in possession of a highly articulated theory of its nature and unity. Indeed, Kant is so far from dispensing with metaphysics at this time, that according to his refined definition, it remains not only the unquestioned foundation of all real science, but under the title of "pure metaphysics," even comes to be identified with the critique of pure reason itself. Secondly, we have seen that even when Kant eventually comes to reject Baumgarten's definition of this science in the Critical period, he does so not because he rejects metaphysics, but only because he finds the definition too indeterminate. Kant thus arrives at his own definition through a natural refinement of the traditional definition through attention to the actual structure of human knowledge and the strict requirement that metaphysics describe a qualitatively distinct territory. Finally, we have seen that throughout Kant's discussion of metaphysics, the precise relation of metaphysics to moral philosophy has remained unclear. In some respects, he unquestionably ascribed the foundation of moral philosophy to metaphysics, understood as pure philosophy. On the other hand, in some passages he seems to exclude it from metaphysics, assigning to metaphysics itself the important but clearly subordinate role of cultivator and protector of reason's practical vocation. Accordingly, it seems that the ultimate unity of metaphysics remains to some extent an unresolved problem in Kant's lectures of the 1780s.

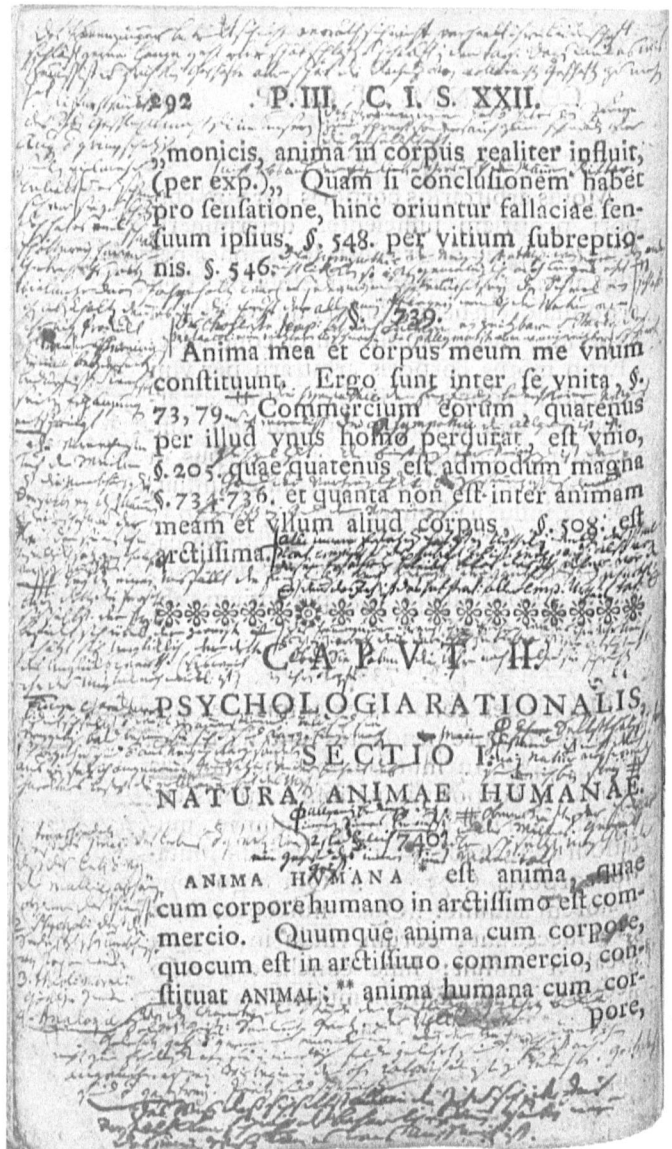

Fig. 3: Reproduction of page 292 ("Psychologia Rationalis") of Kant's copy of A. G. Baumgarten's *Metaphysica* (Halle, 1757, 4th edn.), with Kant's handwritten notes: Reflections 4230 (AA 17: 468–69), 4342 (AA 17: 512), 5453 (AA 18: 186), 5998 (AA 18: 420). Reproduced with the kind permission of the University of Tartu Library, Estonia. Call number: manuscript 93. Kant's personal copy of Baumgarten's *Metaphysica* is available at the University of Tartu Library website: http://hdl.handle.net/10062/32369. Accessed 22 April 2015.

Chapter 3
Transcendental Apperception and Consciousness in Kant's Lectures on Metaphysics

Dennis Schulting

I shall focus chiefly on the metaphysics lectures contemporaneous with Kant's Critical phase, namely the Mrongovius, Vigilantius, and von Schön lecture notes.[1] One sees in those lectures, more clearly than in the Herder and 1770s Pölitz lectures, that Kant takes Baumgarten just as a jumping-off point for presenting his own views. Often, and especially in the introductory parts, one has the impression that whole passages of the *Critique of Pure Reason* are paraphrased in the lectures alongside clarifications which provide us with helpful additional insight into central ideas of the Critical philosophy. Of course, topics that are less developed in the *Critique* itself, such as the specific ontological categories and their definition, are also broached in the later parts of the lectures. However, there appear to remain some carry-overs from the pre-Critical lectures (especially the 1770 Pölitz metaphysics). I shall look at one particular, though crucial, element – namely the relation between (transcendental) apperception and the notion of 'consciousness' – and explore to what extent, and in which contexts, apperception and consciousness are featured in the lectures and what changes (or not) between the pre-Critical and Critical phases of Kant's lecturing activity.

In Section 1, the theme of apperception and consciousness and their relation is introduced. I also address some terminological issues. In Section 2, I look briefly at the Leibnizian and Wolffian background of Kant's theory of apperception, and the usage and occurrence of the term 'consciousness' both in the lecture notes and in Kant's pre-Critical published work. I also discuss, again very briefly, aspects of the theory of obscure representations, in order to clarify Kant's

---

[1] A version of this chapter was first presented as a paper at the workshop *Kant as Lecturer/Philosopher: Connections between his Lectures and Philosophy*, at the Ludwig-Maximilians-Universität in Munich on 3–4 May 2013. I thank Steve Naragon, Reinhard Brandt, and Günter Zöller for their comments during the workshop and in particular Robert R. Clewis for the invitation to present the paper and for his helpful suggestions for improvements on a later draft. I am also especially grateful to Steve Naragon for very useful comments on a previous version of this article.

differentiation of apperception from consciousness tout court. In Section 3, I examine how Kant's conception of consciousness develops from the pre-Critical Herder and Pölitz metaphysics lectures to the lectures of the Critical period, specifically the Metaphysik von Schön and Mrongovius, where the notion of 'apperception' first crops up, and which show that Kant departs from the Leibnizian-Wolffian conflation of apperception and consciousness. Specifically, the newly forged link between apperception and transcendental logic is addressed. In the conclusion (Section 4), I briefly consider a lingering ambiguity about the relation between inner sense and transcendental apperception in the Mrongovius notes and, this notwithstanding, conclude that, in line with Leibniz's gradual theory of perceptions, Kant espouses a gradual theory of consciousness.

1 Introduction: Apperception and consciousness

One of the cornerstones of the transcendental philosophy is without doubt the notion of 'transcendental apperception'. In the A-Deduction in the *Critique of Pure Reason* (KrV), Kant calls it the "Radikalvermögen" of all our cognition (KrV A114),[2] a term not easily translatable into English (the German term refers to the Latin *radix*, meaning 'root', so 'root capacity' would be a potential translation for it).[3] It is associated closely with self-consciousness, more in particular with the well-known phrase with which the transcendental deduction of the categories proper, in its B-version, is introduced in § 16, namely "The *I think* must *be able* to accompany all my representations" (KrV B131). This "I think" is, as Kant says at KrV A354, "the formal proposition of apperception," and concerns the transcendental unity of self-consciousness, and so the "consciousness of oneself [*Bewußtsein seiner Selbst*]" (KrV B68; cf. Anth, § 4 note, 7: 134n).

Crucially, as Kant proceeds to argue in the Transcendental Deduction, transcendental apperception, as an act of the understanding, provides "the legislation for nature" (KrV A126), and is the subjective ground on which nature's lawfulness depends (cf. A127). Transcendental apperception is not only the necessary condition, or the subjective condition, under which we can *experience* nature and its objects, but, as Kant argues, also the sufficient condition for nature and its

---

2 References to KrV are by means of the standard A/B page numbers. All other references to Kant's works are to the *Akademie-Ausgabe* by means of the standard abbreviations followed by volume, page (and, occasionally, line) numbers, as noted in this volume's note on abbreviations.
3 In the Dutch translation of the *Critique* (Kant 2004c: 203) *Radikalvermögen* is aptly rendered *oervermogen*, which translates back into German as *Urvermögen*.

objects, insofar as nature qua nature or the objectivity of objects is concerned.[4] In other words, transcendental apperception is also an objective condition of experience. Kant's position might seem extreme, and smacking of phenomenalistic idealism, when he argues, in the conclusion of the A-Deduction, that the objects of which we have knowledge "are one and all in me, that is, are determinations of my identical self," which is "only another way of saying that there must be a complete unity of them in one and the same apperception" (KrV A129 [Kant 2003: 149]). However, what I believe Kant is claiming here is that, very generally put, knowledge of objects is intimately and necessarily bound up with a form of self-consciousness, an idea that I contend he picks up, at least partly, from the Wolffian tradition but on which at the same time he puts his own Critical slant. I return to this perhaps surprisingly Wolffian aspect in Section 2.

In this chapter, I have no space to discuss the details of Kant's theory of apperception and its pivotal role in the foundation of empirical knowledge (a topic I dealt with extensively in Schulting 2012). Here, I wish to focus on the extent to which Kant addresses transcendental apperception in the lectures on metaphysics that he gave in the 1780s and early 1790s, which have been published in volumes 28 and 29 of the *Akademie-Ausgabe*. (I shall also refer to relevant passages in the contemporary anthropology lectures.) Noticeable, first, is that Kant hardly ever uses the term 'apperception' (it occurs roughly 36 times in all of the metaphysics notes) and that where he uses it he never calls it '*transcendental* apperception', but always merely 'apperception'. More often, though, he refers to it just by the label that his rationalist predecessors in the German school used: 'consciousness', which presents a potential problem of confusing transcendental apperception with consciousness as such. This is mostly a matter of terminology, but, at least at first sight, it might be that Kant's view on consciousness in the lecture notes is still very much informed by the Wolffian conflationist view of consciousness, and that this is even carried over into the *Critique*, at least in the A-version, to the extent that Kant does not always carefully distinguish between the terms 'apperception' and 'consciousness'. This is an important issue, as from the very first reception of the first *Critique*, many commentators from Reinhold up until recent times[5] have taken Kant's principle of apperception to be a principle of consciousness, which confuses a chiefly epistemological principle with a

---

4 Of course, transcendental apperception is not the sufficient condition for the *existence* of objects as things in themselves (although transcendental apperception is the ground of the *determination* of the existence of things). On this topic, see further Schulting 2012: 50–9, 65 f.
5 For references to recent literature, see Schulting 2012: 155–65. For a critique of Reinhold (and others) on this score, see Ameriks 2000a and Schulting forthcoming b.

psychological condition. In the *Critique*, Kant makes it clear that transcendental conditions must be seen strictly separately from conditions that have to do with psychology (cf. e.g., KrV B152). But I believe that there are clear indications, also in the lecture notes, that Kant's use of the term 'consciousness' must be read as meaning 'apperception', in the Critical sense of transcendental apperception, or as meaning 'unity of consciousness', not just consciousness in any (mere) psychological sense (in terms of 'awareness' or 'sentience' or 'feeling of self').

Secondly – and this is related to the first issue – I believe that Kant does not think, as might be concluded from some of his statements, that in sensibility or inner sense, independently of transcendental apperception, there is no consciousness at all, more precisely, that mere sensible representations are unconscious or not conscious representations. Notice that, as far as I know, in most of its occurrences Kant does not use the term 'unconscious' and cognates intransitively but more in the sense of 'not being conscious of', and in fact hardly uses it at all (at one point in the anthropology lectures, he associates absolute unconsciousness with death).[6] In the *Critique*, Kant quite explicitly – and implicitly in some passages in the lectures of the Critical period (but see below Section 4) – keeps inner sense and *transcendental* apperception apart, where the former must be seen as equivalent to *empirical* apperception, which is "forever variable" and consists merely of a "stream of inner appearances" (KrV A107). The Critical Kant clearly distances himself from what was "customary in the systems of psychology" (KrV B153), referring to the broadly Wolffian tradition, which viewed inner sense as identical to apperception tout court. Inner sense is thus merely psychological, whereas transcendental apperception refers to a logical, formal consciousness.[7]

But the pre-Critical Kant just takes over whole the standard notion of 'inner sense' as referring to the consciousness of self generally or what later on is called 'self-consciousness' (or what in his Latin writings Wolff calls *apperceptio*), which

---

[6] The Friedländer anthropology (1775/76) reads: "The cessation of all sensation is unconsciousness. If one cannot get out of this state of sensation, then this is death. Sleep is the cessation of all sensation in a healthy state. It is an insensibility to and unconsciousness of outer objects" (V-Anth/Fried 25: 511 [Kant 2012a: 80]). Cf. Anth 7: 166 (§ 27), where Kant speaks of unconsciousness as "a foretaste of death" (Kant 2007: 277).

[7] Cf. Anth 7: 142: "The cause of these errors is that the terms *inner sense* and *apperception* are normally taken by psychologists to be synonymous, despite the fact that the first alone should indicate a psychological (applied) consciousness, and the second merely a logical (pure) consciousness" (Kant 2007: 255). Kant speaks simply of apperception here, but he means of course *transcendental* apperception, not empirical apperception, which is equivalent to inner sense (cf. KrV A107).

as said the Critical Kant first specifically differentiates as *transcendental* consciousness or apperception, on the one hand, and inner sense and empirical apperception on the other. And given that in the rationalist systems of psychology inner sense was identified with "consciousness strictly speaking," i.e., "the state of my soul" (Baumgarten 1983b: 16 f.), it does not seem unreasonable to expect Kant, in the Critical phase, to continue to associate his successor notion of transcendental apperception with "consciousness strictly speaking," thus giving rise to an ambiguity over the use and meaning of 'apperception' in contrast to 'consciousness' in the more technical, psychological sense. But we must note that, already early on, and in a way that compares with his later distinction between inner sense and apperception (more precisely, transcendental apperception), Kant also distinguishes between psychological and logical, formal consciousness.[8] And often it is also only this latter sense of consciousness that he is referring to when he uses the term 'consciousness'.

In the next section I explore the Leibnizian and Wolffian background of Kant's developing views, and examine also some passages in which Kant hints at self-consciousness in published work from the pre-Critical period. To get a clearer idea of Kant's views in this regard, I also briefly look at the Leibnizian-Wolffian theory of obscure representations, which Kant adopts.

2 Self-consciousness in the pre-Critical Kant and the Leibnizian and Wolffian background

As Reinhard Brandt (1994: 2) has pointed out, prior to and including the *Inaugural Dissertation* of 1770, apart from metaphysical questions regarding soul-body interaction, Kant appears uninterested in the topic of consciousness or self-consciousness as such or as a grounding faculty for knowledge in his published works

---

8 See, e.g., the Pölitz notes from the 1770s, V-Met-L1/Pölitz 28: 227. However, notice that here Kant might still be considered to be quite close to a Wolffian view of the self in that *conscientia psychologica*, which is a "*subjective* consciousness," "a forcible state," and not "discursive, but intuitive" (28: 227), is to be taken as consciousness of the self as such, i.e., of "the soul," "where we can intuit the substance immediately" (28: 226), whereas *conscientia logica* is only directed at objects, i.e., is an "*objective* consciousness," where "I am conscious of other cognitions [*bin ich mir anderer Erkenntnisse bewußt*]" (28: 227; all translations mine). It is this latter logical consciousness, which comes to be associated with transcendental apperception in the Critical period (see Section 3 below). The later Kant of course considers psychological consciousness to concern merely how I appear to myself in inner sense, not how I am as a substantial thing in itself (cf. B152 f., 157 ff.).

in the pre-Critical period, which is evidenced by the infrequent occurrence of the very term 'consciousness'.[9] Heiner Klemme (1996: 55 ff., esp. 59) has shown that Kant's subjective turn takes place in the early 1770s, which first becomes manifest in particular in the anthropology lectures of 1772/73 (Collins and Parow).[10] However, Kant does speak of 'inner sense' and hints at the cognitive function it has already in earlier works, such as in the conclusion to his work *The False Subtlety* of 1762, where he reflects on the "mysterious power ... which makes judging possible" as that which makes the difference between animals and human beings. He identifies this power as "the faculty of inner sense," which is "the faculty of making one's own representations the objects of one's thought" and is "a fundamental faculty [*Grundvermögen*]" that "can only belong to rational beings," and on which "the entire higher faculty of cognition is based" (DfS 2: 60 [Kant 1992: 104]). Likewise, in the 1763 essay *Negative Magnitudes*, Kant refers appreciatively to Leibniz's view of the soul's faculty of representation, or activity of the mind, as the foundation for conceptuality:

> There is something imposing and, it seems to me, profoundly true in this thought of Leibniz: the soul embraces the whole universe with its faculty of representation, though only an infinitesimally tiny part of these representations is clear. It is, indeed, the case that *concepts of every kind must have as the foundation on which alone they are based the inner activity of our minds* .... *The power of thought possessed by the soul must contain the real grounds of all concepts*, in so far as they are supposed to arise in a natural fashion within the soul. (NG 2: 199 [Kant 1992: 237]; emphasis added)

---

9 In the pre-Critical published works, the term *Bewußtsein* or the cognate *bewußt* occurs, in various contexts, in NTH 1: 366; GSE 2: 217, 237, 249; NG 2: 168, 182, 199; UD 2: 284, 286, 290, 299; and, befitting its thematics, most frequently in TG 2: 320, 332, 333, 337, 338, 339, 340. The Latin *conscientia* appears in PND 1: 401, 403, 406. The term *Selbstbewußtsein* as such does not occur in the pre-Critical corpus, although Kant does speak of "personal consciousness" (TG 2: 338). By comparison, in the early anthropology lectures Kant speaks of "consciousness of self-activity" (V-Anth/Collins 25: 10 [Kant 2012a: 17]) or of the "representation of I" as "the personality to be conscious of oneself" (V-Anth/Fried 25: 473 [Kant 2012a: 50]; cf. V-Anth/Pillau 25: 736).

10 Cf. V-Anth/Collins 25: 10: "The I is the foundation of the capacity for understanding and reason, and the entire power of cognition, for all these rest on my observing and inspecting myself and what goes on in me" (Kant 2012a: 17). See further the references in the note above. Klemme (1996: 59–62) makes the interesting claim that Kant was under the influence of Herz's critique of his earlier position in the *Inaugural Dissertation*. Klemme points out that Herz argued that there must be a "'first subject' ... which is numerically simple" in order to be able to conceive of "the unity that is the result of the comparison of representations." According to Klemme, Herz positions this "first subject" as "epistemic center."

And in the *Inquiry* of 1764, when comparing the method for metaphysics with Newton's method for natural science, he sees an important foundational, or at least facilitating, role for "inner experience" or "self-evident inner consciousness." Kant writes:

> The true method of metaphysics is basically the same as that introduced by Newton into natural science and which has been of such benefit to it. Newton's method maintains that one ought, on the basis of certain experience and, if need be, with the help of geometry, to seek out the rules in accordance with which certain phenomena of nature occur. Even if one does not discover the fundamental principle of these occurrences in the bodies themselves, it is nonetheless certain that they operate in accordance with this law. Complex natural events are explained once it has been clearly shown how they are governed by these well-established rules. Likewise in metaphysics: *by means of certain inner experience, that is to say, by means of an immediate and self-evident inner consciousness,* seek out those characteristic marks which are certainly to be found in the concept of any general property. (UD 2: 286 [Kant 1992: 259]; emphasis added)[11]

The above-quoted reference to Leibniz's view of the soul as the faculty of conscious representation or activity of the mind warrants a look at the backdrop against which Kant eventually, in the 1770s up to the *Critique*, develops his own theory of transcendental (self-)consciousness, or transcendental apperception. It is unlikely that on this point Kant was directly influenced by either Leibniz or Wolff apart from inheriting the existing terminology. Most probably the theory of transcendental apperception is original to Kant himself. Thiel (2011: 372–6) suggests that Mérian's account of 'original apperception' might have had some influence on Kant's conception of transcendental apperception. Kant must have known about Mérian's conception of apperception through Tetens' account of Mérian in his *Philosophische Versuche über die menschliche Natur und ihre Entwicklung* (1777), which Kant read. But notice that Kant's first use of the term 'apperception', whilst pointing out its epistemic grounding function that is later associated with its transcendental role, in the *Duisburg Nachlass* (Refl 4674, 17: 646 f. [1773–75]), predates his reading of Tetens. One of the very first occurrences of the term 'apperception' in the Kantian corpus is in Refl 4562 (17: 594), dated by Adickes between 1772 and 1776.

What is clear though is that Kant appropriates Leibniz's notion of 'apperception', which is first mentioned in the *New Essays* (G 5: 121, II.ix.4), by its cognate *s'appercevoir*, and later in the *Principles of Nature and Grace* (G 6: 600, §4) and

---

11 See also PND 1: 403.

Monadology (G 6: 608 f., § 14).[12] Apart from one occasion (§ 93), where he employs the term *apperceptibilitas*,[13] Baumgarten does not use the term 'apperception' or its cognate 'apperceive' in the *Metaphysica*, although he does mention the Latin equivalent in his *Acroasis logica*,[14] a copy of which Kant had in his possession (Warda 1922: 45). Baumgarten barely even discusses consciousness. Wolff employs the Latinized *apperceptio* in his *Psychologia empirica*.[15]

Leibniz[16] distinguishes between perception, which is "the inner state of the monad," and apperception, the latter defined as consciousness (*conscience*), or "the reflexive knowledge of that inner state" (*Principles*, G 6: 600, § 4; cf. *Monadology*, G 6: 608 f., § 14). Leibniz criticizes Locke's view of the ineliminably reflexive nature of perception, which is the view that it is "impossible for any one to perceive without perceiving, that he does perceive" (Locke, *Essay*, Book II, Ch. XXVII, § 9 [Locke 1975: 335]). As Leibniz points out, the view that any perception is a conscious perception is vulnerable to an infinite regress. In his response to the Lockean position, he writes:

> [I]t is not possible that we should always reflect explicitly on all our thoughts; otherwise the mind would reflect on each reflection *ad infinitum*, without ever being able to move on to a new thought. For example, in apperceiving some present feeling, I should have always to think that I think about that feeling, and further to think that I think of thinking about it, and so on *ad infinitum*. (*New Essays*, G 5: 108, II.i.§ 19; trans. amended)

However, Leibniz's valid objection that an infinite regress threatens if all of our thoughts were always reflected upon does not necessarily exclude the possibility that the first-order perception has some degree of (non-reflexive) conscious-

---

12 All references to Leibniz's works are to the edition by I. C. Gerhardt (Leibniz 1875–90), cited in the standard way by means of the abbreviation G followed by volume and page numbers, with sometimes an indication of book, chapter, and section numbers. The translation used for the *New Essays on Human Understanding* is Remnant and Bennett (Leibniz 1996). All other translations are mine.
13 I thank Steve Naragon for bringing this to my attention.
14 "Quae ens aliquod distinguit, illa APPERCIPIT, seu eorum sibi est conscium. Perceptio appercepta est COGITATIO …" (Baumgarten 1773, 'Prolegomena', § 3: 1 f.).
15 "Menti tribuitur *Apperceptio*, quatenus perceptionis suae sibi conscia est. / Apperceptionis nomine utitur *Leibnitius*: coincidit autem cum conscientia, quem terminum in praesenti negotio *Cartesius* adhibet" (Wolff, *Psychologia empirica* [PE], § 25: 17). See also PE, § 26, where Wolff provides the following example for apperception: "Dum jam scribo, conscius mihi sum me scribere. Quatenus mihi conscius sum actus scribendi, eundem appercipio …." According to Warda (1922), Kant had apparently no copy of the *Psychologia empirica* in his possession.
16 For my subsequent all-too-brief account of Leibniz and Wolff on consciousness, I rely on the in-depth studies of Wunderlich 2005: 18–46 and Thiel 2011: 279–314.

ness, i.e., a consciousness that is not an apperception (understood as reflexive consciousness). In fact, one could argue that the first-order perception must be conscious, in the non-reflexive sense, in order for a second-order, reflexive consciousness of that state at all to be possible.

For Leibniz, by contrast, apparently the perceptions that are not apperceived are themselves ex hypothesi unconscious. He calls these perceptions minute perceptions (*petites perceptions*) in the *New Essays*. In one notable passage, Leibniz writes about these perceptions in relation to apperception: "At every moment there is an infinity of perceptions in us, but without apperception and without reflection, that is, changes in the soul itself, which we do not apperceive [*dont nous ne nous appercevons pas*]" (*New Essays*, G 5: 46, preface; trans. mine). The standard reading takes Leibniz here to deny these minute perceptions the feature of 'being conscious'. Notice though that Leibniz here appears to equate "apperception" with "reflection," which suggests that a higher-order consciousness is at issue, not eo ipso excluding the possibility that the infinite amount of perceptions in us, which we do not apperceive, are nonetheless conscious perceptions at least *to some degree*. Jorgensen (2009: 242) argues indeed that "consciousness arises with sensation," not first with a higher-order reflection, pointing to a passage in the *Monadology* (G 6: 610; §23), where Leibniz writes that "on being awakened from a stupor, we *apperceive* our perceptions." Here, apperception clearly indicates first-order consciousness, not consciousness of the reflexive sort.[17]

However, as Thiel (2011: 300) justly observes, the official reading of Leibniz's position on the unconsciousness of minute perceptions raises the question of "how the conscious can arise from the unconscious." This is all the more problematic since, in conformity with the Law of Continuity (cf. Jorgensen 2009),[18] Leibniz believes that "noticeable [conscious] perceptions arise *by degrees* from ones that are too minute to be noticed" (*New Essays*, Preface, G 5: 49; emphasis added). Hence, Thiel rightly asks: "How can consciousness develop 'by degrees' from something that is totally unconscious ...?" (2011: 300). I shall come back to this central problem further below. I believe that the Critical Kant is able to avoid this problem precisely by disentangling the notion of inner sense, or consciousness strictly speaking (which Kant interprets as consciousness in a more

---

[17] See also a passage where Leibniz writes about a wild boar that is able to "apperceive," even though it does not have understanding or indeed a capacity for reflection (*New Essays*, G 5: 159, II.21, §5).
[18] Leibniz writes of this law: "The *Law of continuity* states that nature leaves no gaps in the orderings which she follows, but not every form or species belongs to each ordering" (*New Essays*, G 5: 286).

determinate psychological sense), from apperception as a formal consciousness or *conscientia logica*, namely, as *transcendental* apperception.

For Wolff, consciousness implies the capacity to distinguish. In the *German Metaphysics*, first published in 1720, his view is that we are conscious of things in so far as we distinguish them.[19] A representation is clear (*klar*) if we are able to distinguish various things from each other, and if in addition the parts of a thing are clear, then the representation is distinct (*deutlich*). Where a representation is not clear, it is obscure (*dunkel*), meaning that it is not conscious, which is similar to Leibniz's position on minute perceptions, which are not apperceived. Thus, since clarity consists in the distinction in the manifold of things and distinctness results from the clarity of their parts, clarity and distinctness of representation "ground" consciousness (VG, § 732: 457).[20] This relates to the view that isolated representations cannot be conscious ones. Given that consciousness is the capacity to distinguish, representations can only be conscious in their relation or coherence. That is, isolated and simple representations could not be differentiated from each other, since given their isolation a network of connectivity that is required for differentiation is missing; hence I could not be conscious *of* representations as isolated representations, and so isolated representations cannot be conscious. This is an important element of Wolff's view of consciousness.

But given that Wolff thinks that "*complete* obscurity ... cancels out consciousness [*hebet die völlige Dunckelheit das Bewustseyn auf*]" (VG, § 731: 457; emphasis added) and given the Leibnizian view that there are degrees to which a thought is more or less obscure,[21] it would appear to follow that while, as Wolff believes,

---

[19] See Wolff, *Vernünfftige Gedancken von Gott, der Welt und der Seele des Menschen, auch allen Dingen überhaupt* [VG], §§ 729–30: 454–6.

[20] In his copy of Meier's *Auszug aus der Vernunftlehre*, Kant refers to this Wolffian conception of consciousness already early on in Refl 1679 (1752–56): "To be conscious of a ~~thing~~ representation [*Sich einer ~~sache~~ Vorstellung bewust seyn*] is: to know that one has this representation, that is, to differentiate this representation from the others" (Refl 1679, 16: 80; trans. mine). See also the later account in the Logik Blomberg, § 13, V-Lo/Blomberg 24: 40. Interestingly, Meier distinguishes between "simple consciousness [*einfaches Bewußtseyn*]" and "multiple consciousness [*vielfaches Bewußtseyn*]," whereby the former relates to the consciousness of a representation or thing, whose parts (or manifold) cannot be distinguished, whereas the latter concerns a consciousness that includes consciousness of the inner parts of a thing or the manifold contained in the representation (*Vernunftlehre*, § 28 [Meier 1752a: 28 f.]).

[21] Obscurity is not an absolute value. This is confirmed by Kant in a passage in the Logik Blomberg (1770s), § 125 (V-Lo/Blomberg 24: 119), which says that something can never be "obscure in itself" but only "relatively," so that what is obscure "can become clear under certain circumstances, but not under others" (Kant 2004b: 93). However, this appears to concern logical obscurity only; elsewhere, Kant says that *psychological* obscurity *is* absolute. I come back to this

consciousness seems to consist in the *relation between* representations, that is, in the way that they are differentiated, these representations themselves must have a degree of some intensity that is *relative to* some degree that another, differentiated representation has. That is to say, the consciousness as relation consists in one degree being relative to another degree, so that the relation as consciousness would seem to lie in the degree to which one representation is conscious relative to another conscious representation on a scale of decreasing or increasing magnitudes. If the relation constitutes consciousness, then the *relata* must to some degree also amount to consciousness, on a scale of intensive magnitudes ranging from a total lack of consciousness (=0) being equivalent to complete obscurity, as Wolff himself suggests, to clear consciousness (=1). I shall return to this problem when I discuss Kant's view of consciousness.

Another important element of Wolff's view of consciousness is that it concerns a two-way relation: consciousness is not just consciousness of things but equally, and simultaneously, a *self*-consciousness. Any representation that is a perception of an object also always has a reflexive part, which is the element of apperception, and points to the subject of representation. Apperception is the consciousness of the self's own activity *in the consciousness of things*. This is again based on the definition of consciousness as the capacity to distinguish, for "in distinguishing objects from one another we become conscious of ourselves as distinct from the objects of which we are conscious" (Thiel 2011: 307 f.).[22] The subject is differentiated from objects precisely in her being conscious of those objects.[23] Thiel talks about self-consciousness as being "doubly derivative," that is, "it depends on the consciousness of objects, and on the consciousness of our mental act of distinguishing that is involved in the consciousness of objects" (Thiel 2011: 308). But it also means that, reciprocally, we could not be conscious of objects if we were not self-conscious. Notice that consciousness is broader in scope than apperception: consciousness can be of external objects or of one's

---

point further below and in Section 4. Wolff too admits the real possibility of perceptions that are totally obscure (Wolff, *Psychologia rationalis* [PRa], §§ 200–1: 93 f.). See also Claudio La Rocca (2007: 65–87) on obscurity in Kant and his rationalist predecessors.

22 See Wolff, PE, §§ 24–6: 17, and VG, § 729: 454 f.

23 "*Anima sibi sui conscia est, quatenus sibi conscia est suarum mutationum veluti actionum: nec aliter sibi conscia .... Dum enim attentionem nostram in hoc convertimus, quod rerum perceptarum nobis conscii sumus; nostri etiam nobis conscii sumus. Sed tum apperceptionem, actionem quandam animae, percipimus ...,* **& nos per eam tanquam subjectum percipiens ab objectis, quae percipiuntur, distinguimus, agnoscentes utique percipiens subjectum esse quid diversum a re percepta. Anima igitur sibi sui conscia est, quatenus sibi conscia est suarum mutationum**" (Wolff, PRa, § 12: 7; bold face mine).

own thoughts, whereas apperception is always an inner-directed consciousness that feeds off the consciousness of things (Wolff, VG, §730: 455 f.).

The Wolffian view of self-consciousness as derivative of the consciousness of representations of objects seems to be reflected in what Kant is reported as having said in the early Metaphysik L_1, namely, that the consciousness of self is "a knowing of that which belongs to me [*ein Wissen dessen, was mir zukommt*]," namely, that it is "a *representation of* my representations" (V-Met-L1/Pölitz 28: 227; trans. mine and emphasis added). The reflexivity inherent to representation, that is, the second-order representation of one's first-order representation of objects, is even more clearly expressed in a later lecture note (the Metaphysik Vigilantius), where the reflexivity ("the representation of my representation to myself") is also directly linked to apperception, a notion still absent from the early lectures:

> [W]hat representation is in itself, is inexplicable. A definition of that cannot be given because a representation can be explained only and in no other way than when one again represents a representation to oneself…. This action of the mind can be described as something in me that refers to something other. Now this relation of this something other in me is representation taken subjectively. **The representation is aimed in part *at the object*, to which I am referring, in part *at that action of the mind* through which I compare something in me with the object.** {Then one is occupied with the object in itself and its constitution, which must be wholly distinguished from the manner of representation of the subject, which involves the second, the action of the mind.}[24] This latter is called consciousness or the representation of myself insofar as I exhibit **the representation of my representation to myself**…. Consciousness is also called apperception, which accompanies the represented object. (V-Met/Vigil 29: 970 [Kant 2001: 441]; bold face mine)

Dyck (2011: 48) contends that Wolff's derivative conception of self-consciousness is "certainly a long way from Kant's well-known claim of an *original* apperception." But unlike Dyck I believe that, notwithstanding some crucial differences, Kant and Wolff are much closer in this particular respect, and not just the pre-Critical Kant of the Pölitz lectures quoted earlier (V-Met-L1/Pölitz 28: 227), but the Critical Kant too. In the Critical view, transcendental self-consciousness or apperception is after all an *objective* unity of consciousness defining an object in general (B137). *Mutatis mutandis*, this is similar to Wolff's view of self-consciousness being derivative of objective consciousness, in that for Kant there is only an original or transcendental self-consciousness insofar as there is an a priori synthesis of representations that defines an object (in general), simply because the

---

[24] The text part between curly brackets concerns marginal notes in the manuscript inserted in the main text in the Ameriks/Naragon translation in the Cambridge edition (Kant 2001) as well as the *Akademie* text.

transcendental unity of self-consciousness *constitutes* the objective unity of representations *by means of* a priori synthesis of one's own representations (B139). So, one could say that the self of transcendental self-consciousness is derivative of the synthesis that constitutes the objective unity among one's representations. The 'originality' of transcendental apperception must thus not be interpreted as if it were somehow *prior to* the objective unity of representations, nor is there, as Dyck claims, a "priority of the identity of the subject disclosed in transcendental self-consciousness to the mind's synthesis of its representations" (Dyck 2011: 49). In my view, this is too redolent of a Henrichian reading of the status of the identity of transcendental self-consciousness, which is putatively independent of, and prior to, an a priori synthesis of one's representations and a fortiori the *objective* unity of consciousness. Rather, it is the analytic unity of the identical self that is grounded on the "antecedently conceived" (B133n) synthetic unity that results from a priori synthesis. No identity of self obtains independently of, or prior to, the a priori synthesis that first constitutes an original-synthetic unity of self-consciousness, and hence grounds an objective unity of consciousness. In fact, the analytic and synthetic unities are mutually implicative aspects of the function of unity that underlies the identity of the self as the agent of any judgment, which is defined by the objective unity of apperception (see further Schulting 2012: 57–9, 89, *et passim*).

To some extent, Kant is also indebted to Wolff's theory of clear and distinct representation, though with some significant changes (i.e., unlike Wolff, for Kant the opposite of distinct is not confused, but indistinct; he equally opposes the view that the contrast between confusion/indistinctness and distinctness matches the distinction between sensibility and the understanding[25]). Relatedly, the pre-Critical Kant adheres to the Leibnizian-Wolffian theory of obscure representations and the traditional view that consciousness is a characteristic of the understanding and reason and not of sensibility.[26] Hence, "[o]bscure representations are those of which one is not conscious," "although I can infer that such representations, of which I am not conscious, are in me" (V-Anth/Fried [1775/76] 25: 479 [Kant 2012a: 55]). In various passages in the logic (V-Lo/Blomberg 24: 41, 119; V-Lo/Philippi 24: 410; cf. V-Lo/Pölitz 24: 511) as well as the anthropology

---

25 Cf. V-Anth/Fried 25: 482; see also Anth 7: 140n (§ 7).
26 Even in the Critical period, e. g., in Metaphysik Volckmann (1784/85), Kant holds that consciousness is unique to the intellect, and is not contained in "sensus, imaginatio" (V-Met/Volckmann 28: 449). However, in the Metaphysik Dohna (1792/93) Kant says that "[s]ense is the faculty of empirical intuitions for becoming **immediately conscious** of existence in space or in time" (V-Met/Dohna 28: 672 [Kant 2001: 374]; bold face mine).

lecture notes (V-Anth/Fried 25: 479; V-Anth/Mron [1784/85] 25: 1221; cf. V-Met/Mron 29: 879) Kant recounts the well-known example of the Milky Way, which I see clearly "as a white strip," but of whose individual stars I have no immediate awareness but only obscure representations, and also the example of the improvising musician who "must direct his reflection upon every finger he places, on playing, on what he wants to play, and on the new [music] he wants to produce," but is thereby not *directly* conscious of every single note he plays (V-Anth/Fried 25: 479 [Kant 2012a: 55]).[27] On this account, of representations that are obscure, such as individual stars or notes, I can only become conscious by inference, but as such they are unconscious. Consciousness and obscurity are mutually exclusive, since clarity, the opposite of obscurity, is the definition of consciousness. In the early Pölitz metaphysics notes we see this confirmed:

> As concerns objective consciousness, those representations which we have of objects of which one is conscious are called *clear* [*klare*] representations; those of whose features [*Merkmale*] one is also conscious, *distinct* [*deutliche*]; those of which one is not at all conscious, *obscure* [*dunkle*]. (V-Met-L1/Pölitz 28: 227 [Kant 2001: 46 f.])[28]

However, later, in the *Critique*, at least in its B-edition, Kant is critical of the traditional view that consciousness equates with clarity and that therefore we cannot at all be conscious of obscure representations, although in the Mrongovius anthropology (V-Anth/Mron 25: 1221), from 1784/85, and in e.g. the later Pölitz lectures (V-Met-L2/Pölitz 28: 584) Kant still states the view, in conformity with the traditional viewpoint, that I am *not* conscious of my obscure representations. It should be observed though that these statements were recorded before the publication of the B-edition of the *Critique* of 1787, where in the revised Paralogisms chapter Kant first presents his critique of the view that clarity equates with consciousness, and that by implication obscure representations must be unconscious ones (KrV B414 f.n; see further below). Here in the Anthropology notes, however, Kant also says that I am not *immediately* conscious of these obscure representations, that is, conscious of each individual star, not thereby excluding the possibility that some degree of consciousness must be involved even in the obscure representation of individual stars.[29]

---

[27] Cf. V-Lo/Blomberg 24: 119, § 124, on the notion of 'mediate consciousness'.
[28] See also the contemporary Logik Blomberg, V-Lo/Blomberg 24: 41 f., 118–20, and the later Logik Dohna-Wundlacken, V-Lo/Dohna 24: 702, 725.
[29] Cf. UD 2: 289 f. Since this concerns a pre-Critical work, it is unsurprising that Kant here confirms the standard Leibnizian-Wolffian view that "[o]bscure representations are representations of which we are not conscious." However, he talks about "obscure concepts" such as those we

In the *Critique* itself, Kant more clearly states his view that consciousness has a greater extension than the scope of clarity strictly speaking (cf. Wunderlich 2005: 141), or put more precisely, that clarity, and thus consciousness, comes in degrees, *relative to* obscurity. That is to say, also obscure representations that are accompanied by a weak consciousness which suffices to make certain distinctions between representations, but which falls short of second-order reflexive consciousness, or, apperception, must be possible. This is the position that Kant takes in the B-edition of the *Critique*, in a well-known note in the Paralogisms in which he criticizes the Wolffians. In contrast to the Wolffian conception – and this also relates to my point earlier about the essentially relational nature of consciousness – in the *Critique* Kant argues, in line with Leibniz's Law of Continuity, that between clear consciousness and total unconsciousness (what in the *Prolegomena* he labels "psychological darkness" [Prol 4: 307]) infinitely many degrees of consciousness exist:

> Clarity is not, as the logicians say, the consciousness of a representation; for a certain degree of consciousness, which, however, is not sufficient for memory, must be met with [*anzutreffen sein*] even in some obscure representations, because without any consciousness we would make no distinction [*Unterschied*] in the combination of obscure representations; yet we are capable of doing this with the marks of some concepts (such as those of right and equity, or those of a musician who, when improvising, hits many notes at the same time). Rather a representation is clear if the consciousness in it is sufficient for *a consciousness of the difference* [*des Unterschiedes*] between it and others. To be sure, if this consciousness suffices for a distinction [*Unterscheidung*], but not for a consciousness of the difference [*des*

---

have in deep sleep and, interestingly, observes that the term 'consciousness' is ambiguous, for either "one is not conscious that one has a representation, or one is not conscious that one has had a representation" (Kant 1992: 263). As Kant points out, the former means merely that one's representation is obscure, whereas the latter that one does not remember it. Now from the fact that one does not remember that one had a representation it does not follow that one was not conscious, to some degree, of the representation *while* asleep, e. g., while sleepwalking. Cf. TG 2: 338n, where Kant recounts the same example and surmises that "these representations may be clearer and more extensive than even the clearest of the representations we have when we are awake" (Kant 1992: 325). See the comparable account in the Metaphysik Herder of 1762–64, where it says: "The states of the soul while sleeping are not exhausted by dreams [*Die Zustände der Seele im Schlafe erschöpfen nicht die Träume*]. *We can have clear representations, which we do not know and therefore we think were not there*[.] – There is a kind of sleep, where sleeping persons perform certain arbitrary acts in accordance with their fantasies. The fact that they are sleeping shows their lack of sensation (e. g., one who had mere feeling but no consciousness at all) and *from the fact that we do not remember [anything] when we awake from a deep sleep, it does not follow that we were then not conscious of this*" (V-Met/Herder 28: 86; trans. mine and emphasis added). See also Schulting 2012: 183–6.

Unterschiedes], then the representation must still be called obscure. So there are infinitely many degrees of consciousness down to its vanishing. (KrV B414 f.n)

Because "a certain degree of consciousness ... must be met with even in some obscure representations," Kant here no longer identifies clarity with consciousness tout court, but rather with a consciousness of the second-order, namely a consciousness *of* the differentiation of representations.[30] The differentiation itself of representations is still accompanied by a degree of consciousness, which may range in intensity anywhere on a scale between 0 to 1, but one which falls short of the clear consciousness (=1) that accompanies a *recognition* of the differentiation. This gradual view of consciousness is confirmed in the contemporary and later metaphysics lecture notes, i. e., the von Schön, the Mrongovius, and the Vigilantius:

> Each sensation is considered as if it originated from zero just as much as it can also decrease again to zero; the sensation will never become completely nothing, even though for us it is dwindlingly small [*verschwindend*]: our sensations become gradually weaker until the lack of consciousness. Consciousness always requires a degree of differentiation [*Grad des Unterscheidens*]; now even if *this* consciousness [of the differentiation] vanishes, the sensation therefore still has a degree. (V-Met/Schön 28: 509; trans. mine and emphasis added)

> All reality has degree. There are degrees from sensation to thought, i. e., up to apperception, where I think myself with respect to the understanding. Something can have so little degree that I can scarcely notice it, but nonetheless I am still always conscious of it. There is, properly speaking, no largest and smallest in experience. (V-Met/Mron 29: 834 [Kant 2001: 192])

> It follows now from this, that the real, since it has its ground in sensation, therefore in the object of the senses, could not have its abode in the merely intellectual, therefore the degree of the real can thus be thought neither as greatest <*maximum*> nor as smallest <*minimum*>. On the other hand, it is certain that the modification of the degree of the intensive magnitude of the real quality must be infinite, *even if it can also be unnoticeable*. Therefore between the determinate degree A until 0=zero there must be found an infinite multitude

---

30 Confusingly, in MAN 4: 542, of course published just prior to the B-edition of the *Critique*, Kant still maintains that consciousness as such consists in the clarity of representations. It should also be noted that in the A-Deduction of 1781 Kant appears to still identify empirical consciousness with clarity (cf. A117n), suggesting that obscure representations are therefore unconscious. But what Kant presumably means here is not dissimilar to what he says in the note to B414, namely that clarity in the sense of consciousness is not restricted to apperceptive consciousness but "also extends," to put it in the terms of the account in the *Anthropology*, to the obscure representations, of which one is indirectly conscious, and which thus makes them "*distinct representations*" and so relatively clear, i. e., conscious to some degree (Anth, § 5, 7: 135 [Kant 2007: 246]). Cf. V-Lo/Dohna 24: 725: "Clarity is consciousness <not> only of representations in the whole but also of their partial representations" (Kant 2004b: 461).

of qualities of the real, *even if in an unnoticeable degree, e.g., knowledge, representations, yes even the consciousness of human beings have many degrees, without one being able to determine the smallest.* (V-Met/Vigil 29: 1000 [Kant 2001: 468]; emphasis added)

The crucial note to B414 in the B-edition Paralogisms is important for an assessment of Kant's relation to the traditional view of consciousness and the theory of obscure representations, and the development of his Critical notion of transcendental apperception, which we see reflected in the changes between his conception of inner sense and consciousness from the lectures on metaphysics in the 1770s (the Herder and early Pölitz notes) and the later lectures. I discuss this in the next section, while I return to the issue of obscurity towards the end of the chapter.

3 From the Herder metaphysics notes to the lectures from the Critical period: A developing conception of consciousness

In the early, pre-Critical lectures, the Metaphysik Herder and Metaphysik L_1, Kant still holds a view of consciousness that is largely Wolffian. Consciousness of inner sense is a consciousness of self or self-consciousness, and comes down to a concept of the 'I' as intelligence, which is the soul of which in addition we have provable knowledge as a substance separate from the body (V-Met-L1/Pölitz 28: 224 f.).[31] Kant simply distinguishes between *conscientia psychologica*, "where one is conscious merely of one's subject [*sich nur seines Subjects bewußt ist*]" (V-Met-L1/Pölitz 28: 227; trans. mine), and which is intuitive, and a discursive *conscientia logica*, which is directed at objects and which as objective consciousness is therefore constitutive of knowledge strictly speaking (this view also seems to be found in the later Mrongovius anthropology notes[32]). In line with Baumgarten's definition, in his *Metaphysica*, of inner sense as "consciousness strictly speaking" (Baumgarten 1983b: 16 f.), Kant takes over the standard idea among his rationalist predecessors that consciousness is to be identified with inner sense (V-Met/Herder 28: 901), which animals lack despite possessing a soul (V-Met-L1/Pölitz 28: 274);[33] animals only have "praevisio without consciousness" (V-Met/Herder 28:

---

[31] See again footnote 8 above.
[32] "We can divide our consciousness into subjective and objective consciousness. Our consciousness is subjective when we direct our thoughts to our existence and to our understanding itself; it is objective when we turn them to other objects" (V-Anth/Mron 25: 1219 [Kant 2012a: 351]).
[33] "With animal souls everything depends on consciousness, *which however they do not show*: but rather actions in accordance with a determinate plan, which they cannot change by means

862), and given that Kant associates consciousness with judging (V-Met/Herder AA 28: 853), animals apparently are not capable of judging either (cf. DfS 2: 60).[34]

After the publication of the *Critique*, the picture in the metaphysics lectures that we know from the Critical period changes accordingly. As already indicated in my introduction, Kant's view of inner sense changes, as well as his idea of the role of consciousness, which is more explicitly connected to the capacity to judge. Notice, however, that whereas Kant's view regarding inner sense changes, even in the *Critique* and especially in the A-version he continues to employ the general term *Bewustseyn* for the judgmental capacity of the understanding, which is unique to human beings.[35] Yet in almost all cases where Kant uses the term *Bewustseyn*, he means a higher form of consciousness, that is, transcendental apperception. Consciousness is now connected to the logical topic of the rules for unifying various representations in a judgment. For instance, in the Metaphysik Volckmann from 1784/85 we read that judgment is "the consciousness of the manifold representations of a unity in one consciousness [*das Bewustseyn der mannigfaltigen Vorstellungen einer Einheit in einem Bewußtseyn*]" (V-Met/Volck 28: 395; trans. mine). In other words, consciousness is more clearly connected to epistemology: cognition or knowledge is, according to the Metaphysik von Schön (mid-to-late 1780s), "the representation with consciousness, in relation to some object [*in Beziehung auf irgend ein Objekt*]," which must be contrasted with "subjective representations or sensations," by means of which we do not cognize any-

---

of a reflection upon their current state" (V-Met/Herder 28: 901; trans. mine and emphasis added); "Livestock ... does not have the inner sense to represent to itself its *statum repraesentationis*" (V-Met/Herder 28: 868; trans. mine); see also V-Met/Herder 28: 864, 911; "[H]owever much animal souls increase in their sensible faculties, consciousness of their self, inner sense, still cannot be attained thereby" (V-Met-L1/Pölitz 28: 276 [Kant 2001: 87]); "[W]e ascribe to [animals] a faculty of sensation, [reproductive] imagination, etc., but all only sensible as a lower faculty, and not connected with consciousness. We can explain all phenomena of animals from this outer sensibility and from mechanical grounds of their bodies, without assuming consciousness or inner sense" (V-Met-L1/Pölitz 28: 277 [Kant 2001: 88]); "Animals have senses and reproductive imagination …. The faculty of consciousness cannot be attributed to animals" (V-Met-L2/Pölitz 28: 594 [Kant 2001: 354]). On Kant on animal consciousness, see further McLear 2011.

34 In a *Reflexion* from around 1771 (Refl 4440, 17: 548), Kant appears to acknowledge that although they do not have the capacity to judge (*iudicandi*) strictly speaking, animals are capable of making distinctions (*diiudicandi*), meaning that they are capable of making a *iudicium sensitivum*, but not a *iudicium intellectuale*. I thank Steve Naragon for bringing this *Reflexion* to my attention.

35 Also in the later Metaphysik Mrongovius (V-Met/Mron 29: 888, 906), Kant still denies animals consciousness. See also V-Lo/Dohna 24: 689 f., 702.

thing (V-Met/Schön 28: 471; trans. mine). The connection between knowledge, the unity of consciousness, and objectivity is emphasized thus:

> Everything which we call knowledge [*Erkenntnis*] corresponds with the fact that it is a unity and a connection [*Verbindung*] of the manifold of representations. That is, many representations must be connected [*verbunden*] in one consciousness. The universality must concern the unity of consciousness in the synthesis, and this now is the thought of an object [*Objekte*], for I am only able to think by means of the fact that I bring unity of consciousness into the manifold of my representations .... (V-Met/Schön 28: 471; trans. mine)

Consciousness, more specifically the unity of consciousness, now defines the form of thought (V-Met/Schön 28: 472.3–5). Indeed, unity of consciousness, more precisely the consciousness of *objective* unity, now defines judgment, in conformity with the crucial passage at B137 in the B-Deduction (which confirms that the Metaphysik von Schön must be dated after 1786)[36]:

> Now judgment is the consciousness of the objective unity of various representations. Consequently, they [i.e., all acts of the understanding] contain the ways in which representations can be universally connected in one consciousness (V-Met/Schön 28: 472; trans. mine);

and, accordingly, the unity of consciousness corresponds with the categories:

> [A]ll pure concepts of the understanding [are] nothing ... but concepts of the unification of the manifold in one consciousness (V-Met/Schön 28: 482; trans. mine).

Consciousness, more in particular the consciousness of myself, as "a mere act <*actus*> of thinking" (V-Met/Vigil 29: 978 [Kant 2001: 448]), is now seen to be constitutive of the synthesis among the manifold representations in intuition and hence of the a priori concepts of knowledge, the view that Kant expounds in the *Critique* and is broadly reflected in the metaphysics lectures of the 1780s and 90s, such as in this passage in the late Metaphysik Vigilantius (1794/95):

> Concepts can also be thought *a priori* if they contain nothing but the concept of synthesis, i.e., of the composition of the manifold in representation in order to constitute a cognition, and this synthesis has unity, i.e., the consciousness of myself of the connection of the manifold in my representations .... The understanding alone has connected the manifold in the

---

36 On the other hand, in Metaphysik von Schön Kant still appears to hold on to the problematic view of judgments of perception, which he had proposed in the *Prolegomena* from 1783 but had abandoned after 1786 (see Pollok 2008; 2013). Nevertheless, it is clear that Graf von Schön matriculated only in October 1788, so that the notes must be of a date later than 1788 (although they might of course have been copied from earlier lectures).

representation, and the concept arose through the consciousness of the connection. On this rests the pure concept of the understanding: or *a priori* concept. The subject or the understanding maintains the consciousness itself of the connection of the manifold through the pure intuition of space and time. One thus calls the pure concepts of the understanding those which contain *synthetic unity* or the consciousness of the connection of the manifold in representation, or concepts of the unity of the manifold in synthetic representation. One predicates the pure concept of understanding as category – therefore this is the consciousness of the synthetic unity of the given manifold in representation. (V-Met/Vigil 29: 978 f. [Kant 2001: 448])

In the same Vigilantius notes, consciousness is identified as a "logical function," namely as a consciousness "of the unity of the manifold according to concepts" (V-Met/Vigil 29: 984 [Kant 2001: 453]).

Although the term 'apperception' itself only first appears in the lecture notes from the Critical period, Kant already used, and reflected on the epistemic role of, the term in the 1770s, most explicitly in the *Duisburg Nachlass*;[37] but these reflections did not carry over to the contemporary lectures: in Metaphysik L_1 (the 1770s Pölitz) no mention is made of apperception. But in the Mrongovius lecture notes, the first extant metaphysics lecture notes from right after the publication of the first edition of the *Critique*, explicit mention is made of the *Critique*,[38] which makes it likely that Kant used or at least referred to the *Critique* in his metaphysics lectures. By far the most occurrences of the term 'apperception' or the Latin *apperceptio* are, accordingly, in the Mrongovius lectures (by my count, 18 times out of roughly 36 times in all of the metaphysics lectures).[39] In contrast to the traditional view of inner sense as self-consciousness tout court, pure apperception is now differentiated from inner sense: in a *Reflexion* on anthropology (from around 1783–84) Kant notes that apperception is in fact not a "sense [*Sinn*]," "but

---

[37] See, e.g., Refl 4675 (May 1775), 17: 651.13–16: "The condition of all apperception is the unity of the thinking subject. From this flows the connection of the manifold in accordance with a rule and in a whole, since the unity of the function must suffice for subordination as well as coordination" (Kant 2005: 163). Or Refl 4677, 17: 658: "Everything that is *thought* as an object of perception stands under a rule of apperception, self-perception" (Kant 2005: 167).

[38] "The first and major representation is that of the I or the consciousness of my self, apperception (as Prof. Kant calls it in his *Critique*)" (V-Met/Mron 29: 878 [Kant 2001: 248]).

[39] The term 'apperception', appearing in the original text either as *apperceptio*, *apperceptio empirica*, *apperceptio pura*, *reine Apperception*, *empirische a/Apperception*, *intellectuelle Apperception*, or just *a/Apperception*, occurs 36 times in the entire corpus of metaphysics lecture notes published in the *Akademie-Ausgabe*. The term appears in the following places:
V-Met-L2/Pölitz 28: 584 (3x); 590 (1x); V-Met/Dohna 28: 654 (2x); 670 (2x); 673 (2x); Dohna Beilage, 28: 704 (1x); V-Met-K2/Heinze 28: 712 f. (5x); 735 (1x); V-Met/Mron 29: 834 (1x); 878 (3x); 879 (1x); 882 (2x); 884 (2x); 888 f. (8x); 906 (1x); V-Met/Vigil 29: 970 (1x).

[that] by means of [which] we are conscious of representations of both outer and inner sense." He writes further: "It [i.e., apperception] is merely the relation of all representations to their common subject, not to the object. The form of inner sense is time. The form of apperception is the formal unity in consciousness in general, which is [a] logical [unity]" (Refl 224, 15: 85; trans. mine). In conformity with Kant's position in the *Critique of Pure Reason*, inner sense is now identified as empirical apperception, as consciousness in the materially psychological sense, which sharply contrasts with a formal consciousness, i.e., transcendental apperception. In the Metaphysik Dohna (V-Met/Dohna 28: 670 f.), from the early 1790s and roughly contemporaneous with the published *Anthropology*,⁴⁰ Kant points out that the distinction between empirical and intellectual or pure apperception reflects the idea that it is the latter which is "self-determining" and the former which concerns myself as a "being whose existence is determined in time," i.e., in inner sense (Kant 2001: 372; cf. KrV B151 f.); or, in the words of Metaphysik K2 (also early 1790s), empirical apperception is "when I am conscious of myself by means of inner sense … (whereby I am *given* to myself [*hier muss ich mir selbst gegeben sein*])" (V-Met-K2/Heinze 28: 712 f.; trans. mine and emphasis added), which suggests the contrast between the spontaneity of transcendental apperception, which does the "self-determining," and the receptivity of empirical apperception that is highlighted in the *Critique*.

An important passage in the Mrongovius notes in the section on empirical psychology (rendered *Erfahrungspsychologie* in Meier's 1766 German translation of Baumgarten's *Metaphysica*), where Kant speaks explicitly of apperception, gives an excellent précis of the central line of reasoning of the Transcendental Deduction, that is, the argument that the unity of consciousness, or transcendental apperception, constitutes the general rule for concept formation and hence for the possibility of the representation of objects:

> A concept is the consciousness that the [same] is contained in one representation as in another, or that in multiple representations one and the same features are contained. This

---

40 Cf. Anth 7: 161 (§ 24): "Inner sense is not pure apperception, a consciousness of what the human being *does*, since this belongs to the faculty of thinking. Rather, it is a consciousness of what he *undergoes*, in so far as he is affected by the play of his own thoughts" (Kant 2007: 272); Anth 7: 153 (§ 15): "A representation through sense of which one is conscious as such is called *sensation*, especially when the sensation at the same time arouses the subject's attention to his own state" (Kant 2007: 265). At Anth 7: 141 (Kant 2007: 254), Kant contrasts a "*discursive*" or "logical consciousness," which is "pure apperception of one's mental activity," and "gives the rule," with "*intuitive* consciousness." See also Anth §§ 5, 6, 7. In the note to § 4 (Anth 7: 134n), empirical apperception is identified with inner sense.

thus presupposes consciousness or apperception .... Understanding is the faculty for bringing various representations under a rule. It rests on apperception. (It is the faculty for determining the particular by the general. With the higher cognitive power the cognitive faculty is considered not in relation to intuition, but rather to the unity of consciousness. This is the representation of one's representations and therefore is also called apperception. Without the consciousness of the sameness of a representation in many representations, no general rule would be possible. For a rule is a necessary unity of consciousness of a manifold of representations, relation of the manifold of representations to one consciousness.) But how are concepts possible through apperception? In that I represent to myself the identity of my apperception in many representations. The concept is a common perception <*perceptio communis*>, e. g., the concept of body. This applies to metal, gold, stone, etc. In this I represent to myself a one in a manifold. The logical function of this consists in generality. This is the analytic unity of apperception, and many in one is its synthetic unity. The analytic unity of apperception represents nothing new to us, but rather is merely conscious of the manifold in one representation. The synthetic [unity] deals with many, insofar as it is contained in one. As long as the understanding judges according to this it is a pure understanding. The understanding makes rules. From the multiple representations it draws out the general, that which is met in all. It is consequently also called the faculty of rules. Experience presupposes understanding because it is a connection of perceptions according to rules. It has *a posteriori* and *a priori* rules. (V-Met/Mron 29: 888 f. [Kant 2001: 256 f.])

Here, all the fundamental aspects of Kant's mature theory of knowledge, specifically the pivotal role played by transcendental apperception, come to the fore. Consciousness or apperception is explicitly linked to the theory of concepts, namely to the idea that by means of a general rule many particular representations are united under a general or common one, and a fortiori to the capacity to judge about objects, thus to the possibility of experience (see Schulting 2012: 99). The grounding role of consciousness is acknowledged in the sense that the activity of judging consists precisely in the consciousness of the unity among the manifold of one's own representations.[41] Herein, I believe, the connection with the quintessentially Wolffian reflexive conception of apperception as the "representation of one's representations" becomes apparent, which *mutatis mutandis* shows the reciprocal, or, mutually implicative relation between the subject of consciousness and the objects that it represents.

---

41 I expand on this topic in Schulting forthcoming a.

4 Conclusion: Transcendental apperception, consciousness, and obscure representations

However, a lingering ambiguity remains about the relation between inner sense and transcendental apperception in the Mrongovius notes, which might however have to do with an ambiguity affecting Kant's overall position on apperception, also in the *Critique* (see, e.g., KrV B140). For example, when in the Mrongovius lecture Kant says that "[a]pperception is the ground of inner sense" (V-Met/Mron 29: 882 [Kant 2001: 251]), he apparently means transcendental apperception, given that he equates inner sense with empirical apperception. But what does it mean that transcendental apperception is the ground of inner sense? Does it mean that it would not be possible to have an inner sense (in the Critical meaning) that is not grounded on transcendental apperception (in the case of animals, say)? That seems odd given that inner sense is *always* variable (KrV A107), and transcendental apperception is supposed to provide a measure of permanence to inner sense. If transcendental apperception provides a measure of permanence to inner sense, and inner sense is unconditionally grounded on transcendental apperception, then inner sense cannot be variable.[42] In addition to this ambiguity, it is also still claimed in the Mrongovius that "[c]onsciousness is the principle of the possibility of the understanding, *but not of sensibility*" and that the "self underlies consciousness and is what is peculiar to spirit" (V-Met/Mron 29: 878 [Kant 2001: 247]; emphasis added). This is reminiscent of the pre-Critical view of consciousness, which says that consciousness is exclusive to the understanding, and the idea that inner sense is identified as self-consciousness tout court, were it not for the occurrence of the term 'apperception' a bit later in the text (Kant 2001: 248), a term that, in the lecture notes that we know, was not used by Kant in his lectures prior to the publication of the *Critique*, and, as is clear from a later passage in the Mrongovius (V-Met/Mron 29: 888), refers strictly to unity of consciousness, not consciousness tout court.[43]

Whatever the case may be regarding these ambiguities, and to return to the topic of obscure representations that are supposedly unconscious, a notable

---

42 Naturally, Kant's Critical argument is to be taken modally: if and only if inner sense is determined in time, it is grounded on transcendental apperception. There is thus a real possibility that inner sense is not coextensive with transcendental apperception for some occurrent mental state.

43 It also conflicts with another passage in the Mrongovius, where it is pointed out that consciousness is *not* restricted to the understanding (and reason), e.g., when Kant talks about the feeling of pleasure: "Pleasure is thus the consciousness of the agreement of an object with the productive power of imagination of our soul" (V-Met/Mron 29: 891 [Kant 2001: 259]).

passage from the Vigilantius notes reveals Kant's Critical view regarding the continuous and gradual nature of consciousness:

> Just as the clarity of a representation can gradually become obscure so that finally the soul slumbers in it and thus its consciousness is lost little by little, so can all degrees of the powers of the human soul give way little by little, and when they have been diminished through all degrees, finally pass over into a nothing. Here is no leap <*saltus*>, but rather it observes the laws of continuity by descending through ever smaller degrees, between which there is always again a time. (V-Met/Vigil 29: 1037 f. [Kant 2001: 503])

Like passages from the Mrongovius, von Schön and elsewhere in the Vigilantius (as quoted in Section 2 above), this excerpt demonstrates that Kant has abandoned the official Leibnizian-Wolffian line[44] that obscure representations of which one is not (or not immediately) conscious are therefore unconscious. For in conformity with the Law of Continuity clarity and obscurity are not absolute values,[45] but have a lesser or greater comparative degree of intensive magnitude on a scale of 0 to 1, given that each individual representation, being a sensation ("each sensation is only a singular representation" [V-Met/Schön 28: 507; trans. mine]), is eo ipso conscious qua it necessarily having a certain intensive magnitude. This position is echoed in the Jäsche *Logic*, where Kant maintains that the intensive magnitude (concerning the "matter") of the different representations in the manifold of which I am aware can decrease, implying a *weaker* consciousness, not an instantaneous total lack of consciousness:

> And even with compound representations, too, in which a manifold of marks can be distinguished, indistinctness often derives not from confusion but from *weakness of consciousness*. Thus something can be distinct as to *form*, i.e., I can be conscious of the manifold in the representation, but the distinctness can diminish as to *matter* if the degree of consciousness becomes smaller, although all the order is there .... (Log 9: 35 [Kant 2004b: 546])

The Wiener Logik (c. 1780) confirms such a gradual view of obscure representations: representations "are called obscure *in comparison with* ones that have the degree of clarity" (V-Lo/Wiener 24: 840 [Kant 2004b: 295]; emphasis added). However, in the same passage in the Wiener Logik it is stated that "logical obscurity ... is distinct from psychological obscurity, *of which one is not at all conscious*," and that while "[l]ogical obscurity is *comparative, the latter* [i.e., psychological

---

44 However, Jorgensen 2009 makes a plausible case for the view that Leibniz himself espouses a gradual theory of consciousness.
45 See again note 21 above. On the Law of Continuity, see MAN 4: 471, 542 f. and V-Met/Mron 29: 921.

obscurity] *is absolute*" (trans. amended and emphasis added). This would appear to conflict with the view, expressed in the earlier quoted passage in the Metaphysik Vigilantius and the note to B414 in the *Critique* (see again Section 2 above), of the relative degree to which a representation can be psychologically obscure (or clear), as is also suggested in the above-quoted Jäsche passage with regard to the *matter* of consciousness. Given this ambiguity arising from the logic lectures, it is not crystal clear what Kant's definitive stance on psychological obscurity is.

But what is clear is that, in the Critical philosophy, it is the formal consciousness of transcendental apperception which is responsible for the objective *determination*, by means of the categories of quality (specifically, the category of negation), of the qualitative nature of representations, that is, their being conscious states in a psychologically material sense. Transcendental apperception is thus a necessary condition for *determinate*, clear empirical consciousness of objects (including oneself), but that does not imply that, absent transcendental apperception, it is impossible to have obscure representations that are conscious to some extent, but fail to be registered in normal, categorially governed experience.[46] There are occurrences of mental states such that when one is in the state one does not have an *experience* in the strict Kantian sense but nonetheless is, in some subcognitive, indeterminate manner, immediately aware of one's environment or oneself, if perhaps in a way that is barely noticeable. For instance, consider the activity of driving a car, where each function required for doing so skillfully is necessarily performed with some degree of consciousness, but obviously not to the extent that one is constantly reflexively aware of (all of) one's actions, on pain of causing an accident. The degree of intensity of one's empirical consciousness (the "distinctness ... as to matter") varies depending on psycho-physiological circumstances. As Kant says, "consciousness has various degrees of clarity, which become ever weaker, e. g., in falling asleep" (V-Met-K2/Heinze 28: 764 [Kant 2001: 404]), which, of course, one surely hopes not to do while driving! In the act of falling asleep, most evidently, the weakening of one's consciousness amounts to a gradual diminution of one's consciousness to a degree that is no longer noticeable by oneself as a putative self-conscious self, and not an absolute change from a state of consciousness to unconsciousness. In conclusion, then, like the *Critique* itself the metaphysics lectures contemporaneous with it reveal that Kant has moved away from the conflationist view of consciousness and self-consciousness that some of his predecessors espoused.

---

[46] On the topic of consciousness and the categories of quality, see further Schulting 2012: 149–72.

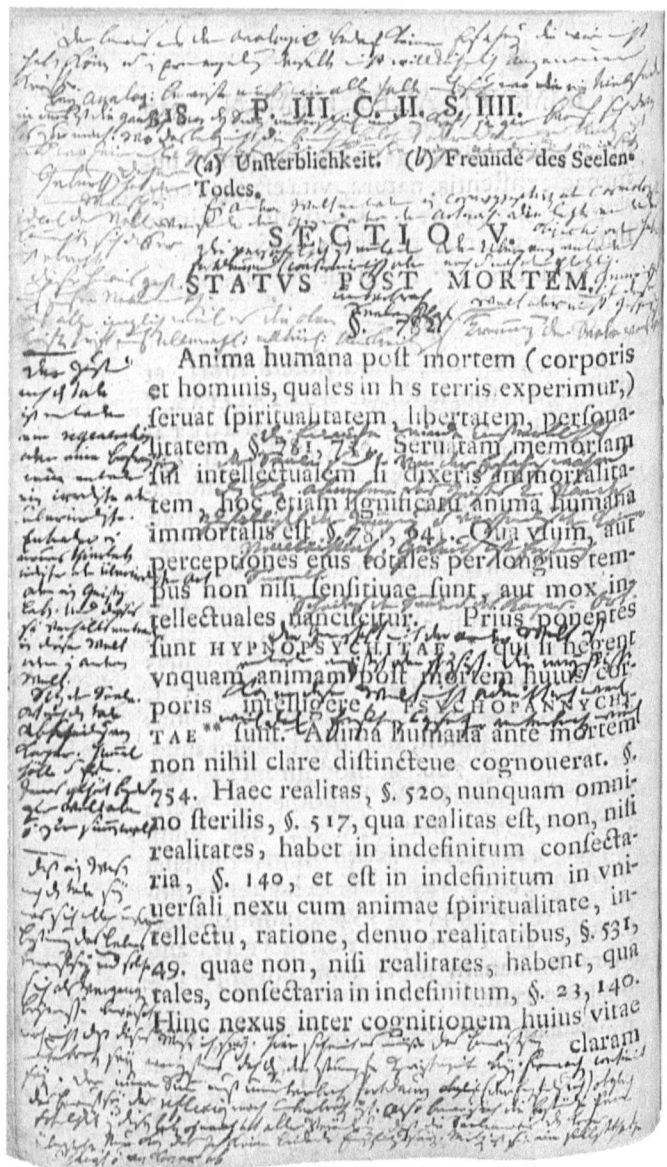

Fig. 4: Reproduction of page 318 ("Status Post Mortem") of Kant's copy of A. G. Baumgarten's *Metaphysica* (Halle, 1757, 4th edn.), with Kant's handwritten notes: Reflections 3631 (AA 17: 151), 4343 (AA 17: 512 f.), 4442 (AA 17: 548), 4559–61 (AA 17: 593 f.), 5478–79 (AA 18: 194). Reproduced with the kind permission of the University of Tartu Library, Estonia. Call number: manuscript 93. Kant's personal copy of Baumgarten's *Metaphysica* is available at the University of Tartu Library website: http://hdl.handle.net/10062/32369. Accessed 22 April 2015.

Chapter 4
Beyond the Paralogisms: The Proofs of Immortality in the Lectures on Metaphysics

Corey W. Dyck

One would expect that the issue of immortality – the proof of the soul's survival of the death of the body and an account of its state in the afterlife – would be a central topic for Kant's criticism of the rational psychologist in the Paralogisms of Pure Reason of the *Critique of Pure Reason*. Indeed, Kant himself would seem to encourage this expectation when he lists immortality as one of the "concepts of the pure doctrine of the soul" at the outset of the chapter (A345/B403). Yet, a look at the Paralogisms chapter itself, in both its original version in the A edition as well as the thoroughly revised B edition version, reveals to the contrary that Kant has little to say expressly about the topic that was arguably the most important for the rational psychologist. So, in the A edition, rather than offering a direct discussion of immortality, Kant focuses his criticism on the claims of the soul's substantiality and simplicity, and then draws the natural consequences from this for the possibility of any cognition of the immortality of the soul (cf. A349, A351, and A356 f.). In the B edition, Kant offers two rather more substantial but still peripheral discussions of immortality, the first in the context of a criticism of Mendelssohn's proof of the perdurance of the soul (B413–15), and the second a concluding section on the warrant for the assumption of the possibility of a future life (B423–6).[1] Considered in light of the reader's expectation of a thoroughgoing criticism of the pretensions of the rational psychologist, and in light of the wealth of discussions available in the broader eighteenth-century context, which includes a variety of proofs that do not explicitly turn on the identification of the soul as a simple substance, Kant's discussion of immortality in the Paralogisms would seem to fall lamentably short.

However, outside of the Paralogisms (and the published works generally), Kant had much more to say about the arguments for the soul's immortality, and he devoted considerable time to the topic throughout his career in his lectures on metaphysics. In fact, the student lecture notes prove to be an indispensable

---

[1] Karl Ameriks also notes that there is "not all that much attention given directly to immortality" in the Paralogisms; see Ameriks 2000b: 177.

supplement to the treatment in the Paralogisms, not only for illuminating Kant's criticism of the rational psychologist's views on the immortality of the soul, but also in reconciling this criticism with Kant's own positive claims regarding certain theoretical proofs of immortality. So, in one of the passages from the B edition referred to above, Kant rather surprisingly identifies the theoretical proof for the soul's immortality which proceeds by "*analogy with the nature* of living beings in this world" (B425) as a "powerful ground of proof, which can never be refuted" (B426), and elsewhere endorses a belief in immortality that is nonetheless not founded upon practical principles (cf. A827/B855). Accordingly, in order to clarify Kant's criticism and to make sense of these otherwise perplexing positive claims, in this chapter I will consider Kant's treatment of the immortality of the soul as presented in the student notes to his lectures on metaphysics. In the first section, I will briefly consider an important piece of the context of Kant's discussion, namely, Baumgarten's treatment of immortality in the *Metaphysica* which served as the template for Kant's own presentation. In the second section, I will present Kant's detailed classification and criticism of the various proofs offered for the soul's immortality as contained in the lecture notes and show how his criticism of a number of these proofs links up with the abbreviated treatment in the *Critique of Pure Reason*. Finally, in the third section, I will turn to Kant's largely sympathetic treatment of one of these proofs (the teleological proof), which as I will show provides an alternative but complementary basis for our belief in the soul's immortality and for a richer conception of the soul's possible state in the afterlife.

1 Baumgarten on the immortality of the soul and its state after death

Before turning to Kant's treatment of the afterlife as recorded in the student lecture notes, it will be useful briefly to present Baumgarten's discussion in the *Metaphysica* which, as is well known, frequently served as the textbook for Kant's metaphysics lectures.[2] Baumgarten's views on the soul's immortality and state after death are presented late in the chapter on rational psychology, in the fourth and fifth sections, respectively, after his discussion of the soul's nature (first section), of the system of explaining the relation between soul and body (second section), and of the soul's origin (third section), which order of presen-

---

[2] English translations of Baumgarten's *Metaphysica* are taken from Baumgarten 2013. In the case of texts by Baumgarten, as well as by Wolff, I refer only to the section number (rather than the page number).

tation Kant largely adheres to in his lectures. Concerning the soul's immortality, Baumgarten understands this rather narrowly as amounting to the "impossibility of dying" (Baumgarten 2013: § 781), although he proceeds to introduce a distinction between absolute and hypothetical immortality. By the former, Baumgarten evidently understands the unconditional impossibility of the soul dying, which is taken to be tantamount to making the soul a necessary being and would therefore exclude even the possibility of annihilation at the hands of God. Yet, as Baumgarten has already shown, the soul is a contingent being (§ 743), one whose non-existence entails no contradiction, and therefore, a being that is capable of destruction by annihilation: "the existence, nature, or life of every human soul is contingent in itself. Therefore, the death of the human soul is possible in itself" (§ 780). However, Baumgarten argues that the human soul can be admitted to be immortal in the hypothetical sense, that is, that the soul cannot naturally perish as the body can and so that it will survive the death of the body *provided that* God does not annihilate it:

> Absolute immortality indeed cannot be attributed to the soul; however, since what is indestructible cannot die in the innumerable ways in which the body can die, the soul possesses a very great hypothetical immortality. No substance of this world is annihilated. Therefore, when the body (such as humans have on this earth) dies, the surviving human soul lives immortally. (Baumgarten 2013: § 781)

While hypothetical immortality is thus contingent on God's preservation of the soul, and so falls short of absolute immortality, there is nonetheless nothing precarious about it as Baumgarten contends that there is good reason to think that God will not annihilate the human soul. This is because the destruction of any substance in the world would entail a loss of harmony and a consequent loss of perfection, which would make the actual world less perfect than that possible world in which the substance is not annihilated (cf. Baumgarten 2013: § 354, § 436).

In addition to attempting to demonstrate the (hypothetical) immortality of the soul, Baumgarten considers what state the soul would find itself in after the death of the body. Here, Baumgarten takes his cue from Christian Wolff's influential treatment in his *Deutsche Metaphysik* and *Psychologia rationalis*, where Wolff argues, against the Cartesians, that the demonstration of the soul's immortality requires not only showing that the soul survives the death of the body but also that the soul retains its distinctive capacities in the afterlife.[3] Following Wolff,

---

3 See Wolff 1983b: § 742 and § 922; and Wolff 1972: § 739–40. For more extended discussion, see Dyck 2014: 142–7.

Baumgarten emphasizes that true immortality requires the preservation of the soul's *spirituality*, or its capacity for distinct cognition (understanding – cf. Baumgarten 2013: § 624, § 754), and *personality*, or its capacity to be conscious that it is the same soul now as it was previously (cf. § 783). To this end, Baumgarten seeks to dispel two spectres with respect to the soul's state in the afterlife: first, that the soul might survive the death of the body but lose its capacity for distinct cognition, which state Baumgarten compares to a condition of sleep (or *psychopannychia*), and second, that the soul will survive the death of the body and retain its understanding but fail to be conscious that it is the same being as it was previously, which Baumgarten relates to the draught of forgetfulness of ancient myth.

Concerning the possibility of the sleep of the soul, Baumgarten argues that the clarity and distinctness of our perceptions should increase rather than decrease after the death of the body. Given that the clear and distinct perceptions that the soul has in this life are realities which, as realities, are pregnant with consequences in the soul, and given that the soul will subsist indefinitely after the death of the body, it is more natural that the perceptions it had in this life will continue to issue in distinct perceptions in the afterlife rather than in something less perfect:

> Before its death, the human soul had clearly or distinctly known something. This reality, which is never completely sterile insofar as it is a reality, has nothing but realities indefinitely as logical consequences, and it is indefinitely in a universal nexus with the spirituality, intellect, and reason of the soul, which again are realities, and which as such have nothing but realities indefinitely as logical consequences. (Baumgarten 2013: § 782)

With respect to the retention of the soul's personality in the afterlife, Baumgarten claims that the soul must be taken to stand in the closest interaction with *some* body in the afterlife (§ 785), and given this, he contends that the soul can be shown to preserve its state of personality:

> The human soul that endures after the death of this body is in the closest interaction with another one [i.e., body]. In its different states, this new body will sometimes be more congruent with the former body, and sometime less so. Therefore, it will have some state in which it will be the most congruent with the body that, in this life, was in the closest connection with the soul, and hence it will be the same. (Baumgarten 2013: § 786)

As Baumgarten argues, inasmuch as the state of the new (spiritual) body will at some point resemble or be congruent with the state of the old one, it follows that the soul will at some point be in the same state that it was previously. Given this, and presumably in accordance with its faculty of imagination, which reproduces a past state given a resembling present one (§ 559), and its memory, which recognizes that a reproduced state has been perceived before (§ 579), the soul will then recall that it is the same soul now as it was previously in this life.[4] As a result, Baumgarten accordingly contends not only that the human soul is (hypothetically) immortal such that it will survive the death of the body, but also that we can be certain that it will retain its distinctive capacities of understanding and personality in the afterlife.

2 Kant's criticism of theoretical proofs of the soul's immortality

Unsurprisingly, Kant's discussion of the soul's immortality, as recorded in the lecture notes, sets out from that of Baumgarten. So, Kant contrasts two questions relating to the soul's future life, the first, "whether the soul *will* live and survive after death" and the second "whether by its nature [the soul] *must* live and survive" (V-Met-L1/Pölitz 28: 284), where the former concerns only the "*contingent* life of the soul" (V-Met-L1/Pölitz 28: 285), or the mere "continuation" of its existence (V-Met-K2/Heinze 28: 763), but the latter concerns true immortality, which is to say, the *necessity* of the soul surviving the death of the body, or the "impossibility of dying" as Baumgarten had understood it. While Kant thus agrees with Baumgarten regarding what is at stake in any proof of the soul's immortality, he nonetheless rejects Baumgarten's proof, which he identifies as a version of what he refers to as a "theological-moral proof" (cf. V-Met/Mron 29: 917). According to Kant, such a proof infers the immortality of the soul from God's moral properties (namely, goodness and justice[5]): given our cognition that God is just, and given that our experience confirms that there is no appropriate reward for virtue or punishment for vice in this life, it follows that there must be an afterlife in which reward and punishment are properly apportioned, or as Kant presents it: "One says: virtue is so little rewarded here in the world, and vice so little punished. If God is just, then a future life is to be hoped for where this disproportion will be removed" (V-Met/Mron 29: 917). Kant likely considered

---

[4] That this produces a recollection of the soul's previous state in connection with the body is suggested by Baumgarten's reference, in his initial account of personality at *Metaphysica* § 641, to his characterization of memory as the perception that "a reproduced representation [is] the same one as one I had formerly produced" (Baumgarten 2013: § 579).
[5] In this context, Kant also mentions a proof for immortality that follows from God's wisdom (cf. V-Met/Mron 29: 917), though this seems to amount to the teleological argument (inasmuch as God's wisdom in endowing human beings with rational capacities would be impugned if the soul did not survive the death of the body).

Baumgarten's argument as a version of the theological-moral proof since, for Baumgarten, God's annihilation of the soul is taken to be inconsistent with God's (presumably moral) perfection.[6] In his criticism of this proof, Kant contends that any proof of the soul's immortality which does not proceed on the basis of the nature of the soul itself can never demonstrate the immortality of the soul in the sense in which both Kant and Baumgarten understand it, namely, as involving the necessity of survival. In this case, because the theological-moral proof turns on features external to the soul (namely, the properties of God), it cannot yield the necessity of the afterlife since "we do not know what [God] will do in accordance with his goodness and justice; it is also audacity to want to determine according to our wisdom what God will do" (V-Met/Volckmann 28: 443; cf. V-Met-K2/Heinze 28: 767).[7] Moreover, Kant argues that this proof fails to guarantee that all will enjoy a lasting afterlife since, on the one hand, there are the blameless few (for instance, those who die very young) for whom an afterlife would be neither required for punishment nor merited as a reward and, on the other hand, the soul might still perish in the afterlife once rewards and punishments have been fully distributed.[8]

The theological-moral proof, then, cannot be taken to furnish a demonstration of the immortality of the soul, as Kant understands it, and Kant further concludes that only proofs founded on the nature of the soul (rather than on the features of something external to the soul) can be taken to demonstrate the immortality of the soul, since otherwise the *universality* of survival and the *eternality* of the afterlife will not necessarily follow as a consequence. Accordingly, Kant proceeds to discuss a wider array of proofs of immortality all of which turn on a consideration of "the nature and the concept" of the soul itself (V-Met-L1/Pölitz 28: 285), and he presents a categorization of the various sorts of arguments that can be offered on this basis. Kant considers, on the one hand, arguments that

---

[6] See, for instance, V-Met-L1/Pölitz 28: 287 f. where Kant's presentation of this proof is prefaced by a consideration of the contingency of the soul (as it also was in Baumgarten's presentation).

[7] Kant's objection here likely draws on that of Baumgarten's student G. F. Meier (whose *Auszug aus der Vernunftlehre* Kant used for his logic lectures) who had contended that we cannot gain insight into the basis for God's decision to preserve the soul after death through the use of reason; see, e. g., Meier 1746: § 5.

[8] For presentations of these criticisms, see V-Met-L1/Pölitz 28: 289–90; V-Met/Mron 29: 917; V-Met/Volckmann 28: 443; V-Met/Dohna 28: 688; V-Met-K2/Heinze 28: 766 f. Significantly, Kant also contends that positing an *eternal* reward (blessedness) or punishment (damnation) would be radically disproportionate to the degree of virtue or vice attained in this world: "no human being's guilt is so great that he should be eternally punished, and no merit so great that it should be eternally rewarded" (V-Met-K2/Heinze 28: 767; cf. V-Met/Mron 29: 917).

argue directly for the soul's immorality, either (1) on the basis of experience or a posteriori (cf. V-Met/Volckmann 28: 441; V-Met/Dohna 28: 686), or (2) a priori (cf. V-Met/Dohna 28: 686; V-Met-Vigil 29: 1038), and on the other hand, arguments which argue indirectly for this conclusion, namely (3) arguments from analogy (cf. V-Met/Volckmann 28: 441; V-Met-L2/Pölitz 28: 591 f.) such as the teleological (or sometimes "cosmological-teleological") argument (cf. V-Met/Dohna 28: 687; V-Met-K2/Heinze 28: 764). Kant's classification is clearly intended to be exhaustive as his aim in his discussion of these proofs in the lectures (at least from the Critical period) is to rule out any possible theoretical cognition of immortality, leaving only his own moral proof for belief in the soul's survival of the body's death; as the notes read: "we can refute all objections to the maintaining of a future life, but can furnish only one proof for it, the moral-teleological" (V-Met/Dohna 28: 688 f.).[9]

Within the first group of arguments, Kant considers proofs that generally proceed a posteriori, such as crude arguments that make use of a presumed analogy between caterpillars and the human soul (inasmuch as the former might be seen to "survive" the death of its former body – V-Met/Mron 29: 912, V-Met/Volckmann 28: 441) or that trade on our observations of elderly people whose bodies are in decline but who maintain their cognitive capacities (which would suggest that the soul can preserve its condition in spite of the decline of the body – V-Met/Mron 29: 912). While such proofs are obviously inadequate, Kant also considers a more promising argument "from empirical psychology" which turns on putative observations of the soul in particular. The argument itself is not actually recorded in the lecture notes,[10] though it can be reconstructed from Kant's criticism of it. So, in the most detailed discussion preserved of such a proof, the notes read:

> We essay, namely, whether we can derive a proof from the experience that we have of the nature of the soul. – We note in experience that the powers of the soul increase just like the powers of the body, and decrease just like the powers of the body. Just as the body decreases, so the soul decreases as well. (V-Met-L1/Pölitz 28: 291)

It is not immediately clear how the observation that bodily and mental states co-vary in this way is intended to yield the conclusion that the soul is immortal. Yet, it is likely that Kant is here trying to draw attention to the fact that, in spite

---

9 For detailed presentations of Kant's own moral proof of immortality (which I will not consider here), see Beck 1960: 267–9 and Suprenant 2008: 88 f.
10 Likely for this reason, Ameriks does not consider this argument in his discussion of the empirical arguments for immortality; see Ameriks 2000b: 181.

of our observations of the agreement between these states, the specific (causal) ground of this agreement is not available to observation. Indeed, Wolff had previously made note of this, appropriately enough, at the conclusion of his empirical psychology, where he writes that we "perceive nothing further than that two things are simultaneous, namely, an alteration that occurs in the organs of the senses, and a thought by means of which the soul is conscious of the external things that cause the alteration" (Wolff 1983b: § 529), and in this he is followed by Kant (see, for instance, V-Met-L1/Pölitz 28: 259 f.). The argument for immortality on this basis would evidently proceed as follows: since we lack any empirical insight into the ground of agreement between states of the soul and states of the body, this constitutes evidence that the soul and body are actually independent of one another such that the former can survive the death of the latter.

For his part, Kant rejects this argument, objecting first that the move from the lack of any insight into the ground of the agreement between respective states of soul and body to the independence of the two is too hasty, even remaining in the context of empirical psychology. As he notes, a proof of genuine metaphysical independence would require that we isolate the soul from the body in life and show, by means of experimentation, that they are capable of alterations in the absence of all connection between them (V-Met-L2/Pölitz 28: 591; V-Met-K2/Heinze 28: 764). Second, Kant contends that even if we have no insight into causal grounds, our experience of the states of the soul is nonetheless limited to the time during which it is connected with the body; thus, this experience cannot license an inference to what might be possible for the soul independently of the body:

> The general reason why we cannot demonstrate the future survival of the soul without the body from the observations and experiences of the human mind, is: because all of these experiences and observations happen *in connection with the body*. We cannot set up any experiences in life other than in connection with the body. Accordingly these experiences cannot prove what we could be *without* the body, for of course they have happened *with* the body. (V-Met-L1/Pölitz 28: 291; cf. V-Met/Mron 29: 911f., V-Met/Volckmann 28: 441; V-Met/Dohna 28: 686; V-Met-K3/Arnoldt 28: 1038)

Aside from these internal criticisms, it would seem clear that a posteriori arguments could be of little use as demonstrations of the immortality of the soul, by which (as we have seen) Kant intends the *necessity* of the soul's survival of the body's death.[11] Nonetheless, and significantly, Kant points out that the foregoing argument performs an important *negative* service for such demonstrations:

---

[11] Here, contrast Ameriks who claims that, in his consideration of empirical arguments, Kant

> But this empirical proof has a *negative* use, namely in that we cannot derive from experience any certain inference *against* the life of the soul; for from that, that the body ceases, it still does not at all follow that the soul will also cease. – Thus no opponent can find an argument *from experience* which would demonstrate the mortality of the soul. (V-Met-L1/Pölitz 29: 291)

Kant here notes that while the observation at the basis of the argument from empirical psychology, namely, that we have no empirical insight into the ground of agreement between the soul and body, cannot be marshalled in support of the soul's immortality, it nonetheless tells against, for instance, the materialist insofar as his claim that the soul dies along with the body might be founded upon an alleged experience of the *dependence* of the soul's states upon those of the body.

Turning to the a priori proof of the soul's immortality, the argument to which Kant devotes the most discussion throughout his career, and even identifies at one point as "the *only* proof that can be given a priori" (V-Met-L1/Pölitz 28: 287; emphasis added), turns upon the identification of the soul as a principle of life inasmuch as it is spontaneous or the source of its own activity. As presented in the L_1 notes, the proof runs as follows:

> Now because all matter is lifeless ..., everything that belongs to life cannot come from matter. The act of spontaneity cannot proceed from an outer principle, i.e., there cannot be outer causes of life, for otherwise spontaneity would not be in life. That lies already in the concept of life, since it is a faculty for determining actions from an *inner* principle. Thus no body can be the cause of life .... The ground of life must rather lie in another substance, namely, in the soul .... Accordingly neither the beginning of the life of the soul, nor the survival of its life will proceed from the body. (V-Met-L1/Pölitz 28: 285 f.)

Given that, for Kant, life involves the capacity for spontaneous action, and given that matter is known to be lifeless,[12] it follows that something non-material must be assumed that contains within it the source of the actions of the body. This non-material ground of activity is identified with the soul, and because the body is not the ground of life, it follows that the separation of the soul from the body cannot result in the death of the soul.[13] In any case, the crucial step in the argument is

---

offers "no proof that in principle such arguments could not be made appealing" (Ameriks 2000b: 181).

12 Kant evidently takes the lifelessness of matter as proven (or at least presupposed) by modern physics; thus, he claims that hylozoism is the "death of all physics" (V-Met/Dohna 28: 687) inasmuch as the postulate of matter that could move itself and not merely be moved by others would contradict the "principle of inertia" (V-Met-K2/Heinze 28: 753).

13 Contrast my presentation of this argument with that of Ameriks (who refers to it as the "prin-

clearly the identification of the soul as spontaneous, and Kant indicates that this is founded merely upon the consciousness of the self, or the I: "[t]he consciousness of the mere I proves that life lies not in the body, but rather in a separate principle" (V-Met-L1/Pölitz 28: 287). Indeed, earlier in the notes on rational psychology, Kant had claimed that our consciousness of the I involves the immediate consciousness of our own activity, either with respect to our thoughts or actions: "When I say: I think, I act, etc., then either the word I is applied falsely, or I am free," which is to say that the I expresses "spontaneity in the transcendental sense" (V-Met-L1/Pölitz 28: 269). It is, then, because we are conscious of ourselves as the subject of the activity involved in thought and (free) actions that we are conscious that the I or soul (cf. 28: 265) is spontaneous.

Strikingly, however, there is no record of Kant's criticism of this a priori argument in the L_1 lecture notes, or indeed any evidence that he rejected the argument in the pre-Critical period. As a matter of fact, Kant himself had at one point explicitly endorsed this proof, which he also calls the proof "from rational psychology," even making use of it himself in the *Dreams of a Spirit-Seer* (which is, otherwise, generally critical of the pretensions of rational psychology):

> That which contains a principle of life in the world seems to be an immaterial nature. All life rests on the inner capacity of determining oneself in accordance with the power of choice. Since, however, the essential mark of matter in the filling of space obtains through a different force that is limited by external opposition [*durch äußere Gegenwirkung*], therefore, the state of all of that which is material is externally dependent and coerced, [whereas] those natures that are spontaneous [*selbst thätig*] and effective on the basis of their internal power are supposed to contain the ground of life. (TG 2: 327n)[14]

It would not, therefore, be surprising if Kant continued to accept this proof barely a decade later (that is, at the time of the lectures recorded in the L_1 notes). It is, in any case, only in the notes from the Critical-period lectures that Kant, drawing on the resources of his mature thought, offers a detailed evaluation of the a priori proof of the soul's immortality. Indeed, Kant's opinion of this proof is made clear when, likely referring to his own previous endorsement in *Dreams*, he is recorded as claiming that this "beautiful" proof is to be rejected since "too much follows from it, [and] one is delivered by it into wild fantasy" (V-Met-L2/Pölitz 28: 592).

---

ciple of life" argument), who takes it to involve a claim about the soul's simplicity in contrast with the compositeness of matter (Ameriks 2000b: 179). While Kant's criticism of this argument parallels, as we will see, his criticism of the extended "unity argument," Kant gives no indication that the argument itself turns on any insight into the soul's simplicity.
14 See also Refl 3855 (AA 17: 313).

This is probably on account of the fact that this proof also suffices to demonstrate the immortality of non-human souls (i. e., those of animals[15]) and that it enforces a rigid distinction between the soul and body which only encourages wild speculation about the ground of their relation.[16] Kant also brings the resources of the Critical philosophy to bear against this proof, claiming for instance that, even if successful, it only serves to distinguish the soul from matter, considered as an external appearance:

> This proof is also not very rigorous. For the lifelessness of matter is merely a property of appearance, namely of the body. But whether the substance underlying the body also has life we do not know. (V-Met/Mron 29: 914; cf. V-Met/Volckmann 28: 441 f.)

Kant's point here, presumably, is that while the spontaneity of the soul might serve to distinguish it from body (taken as an external appearance), it nonetheless does not thereby distinguish it from the *transcendental ground* of matter which remains inaccessible to human cognition and which, accordingly, could be spontaneous in a way similar to the soul. The worry (though Kant does not spell this out) would thus be that simply identifying the soul as spontaneous would not suffice to demonstrate its immortality since we cannot rule out the possibility that the (ground of the) body could be similarly spontaneous and yet can cease to exist; as a result, the soul cannot be taken to be "except[ed] from the perishability to which matter is always subjected" (A356).

3 The teleological proof of immortality and the state of the soul after death

Having ruled out any strict demonstration of the soul's immortality, whether they proceed a posteriori or a priori, Kant proceeds to consider the last class of proofs, namely, those which proceed informally, or by analogy, the primary example of which Kant identifies as the teleological proof. However, Kant's treatment of the teleological proof contrasts starkly with that of the others as Kant had not only long had sympathies with this proof, as is evidenced already by Herder's notes to Kant's lectures from the first half of the 1760s (cf. V-Met-N/Herder 28: 892–4), but as we will see he continues to mine it even in the Critical period for important positive conclusions regarding the afterlife. The proof itself turns on a reflection

---

[15] See V-Met/Mron 29: 916 f. and Ameriks 2000b: 179.
[16] Kant seems to acknowledge this at TG 2: 327 f.

on the general purposiveness of nature with respect to the capacities of living beings, and it sets out from the assumption of a general teleological principle:

> We find in nature a connection of efficient causes, also connection of ends, this connection is indicated in organized beings, and the connection of finality with living beings is the highest principle, from which one cannot depart at all: that no organ is met in living beings that would be superfluous, also that no part would be in a living being that would be useless and not have its determinate purpose. (V-Met-L2/Pölitz 28: 592)

The teleological principle, then, is that we must assume that every organ or, more generally, capacity on the part of a living being has some end or purpose which it is designed to serve. While this principle might seem controversial, it bears noting that Kant frequently endorses it himself, and indeed explicitly with respect to the faculties of the soul, as in the *Critique of Pure Reason* where he asserts that "[e]verything grounded in the nature of our powers must be purposive and consistent with their correct use" (A643 f./B670 f.; cf. B425). The next step of the proof consists in noting that the highest functions of human cognitive and moral powers would seem to be superfluous, or even contra-purposive, considered in the context of the opportunities for their use in this life:

> Now we find in human beings powers, faculties, and talents which, if they were made merely for this world, are really purposeless and superfluous. The talents and equipment of the soul show that it has powers. The moral principles of the will also go much further than we need here. (V-Met-L2/Pölitz 28: 592)

Regarding the soul's higher cognitive powers, Kant frequently refers to the example of astronomy, where the discovery of the laws of attraction that govern the movement of the heavens represent the pinnacle of human scientific achievement and yet apparently serve little use for our ends in this life (cf. V-Met/Mron 29: 915 f.; V-Met/Volckmann 28: 442 and note). With respect to the soul's moral powers, that is, the faculty of will and the higher faculty of desire, Kant echoes a point he makes in his published works on moral philosophy, namely, that morality frequently demands sacrifice of interest and, though rarely, even of our own life: "the moral principles in the reason of a human being intend that he should not attend to the advantages of life and even life itself" (V-Met/Volckmann 28: 442).[17] That our highest faculties should thus appear to be superfluous in this life, or even to work contrary to our worldly interests, is taken to imply that the ultimate ends of their use could only be realized if there is a life to come, which

---

[17] See, for instance, GMS 4: 395 f.

is to say that "it is quite obvious that the soul of the human being is not created for this world alone, but rather also for another future world" (V-Met-L2/Pölitz 28: 592).

It bears noting that the teleological proof had been widely used in Kant's time. Kant himself credits David Fordyce (1711–1751) with its discovery in V-Met/Mron (29: 916), though he later names an unknown "French philosopher" in connection with the proof (V-Met-K2/Heinze 28: 766).[18] In addition to being promoted by Kant in his lectures, the proof was championed by a number of Kant's prominent German contemporaries. So, Hermann Samuel Reimarus presents it in his *Die vornehmste Wahrheiten der natürlichen Religion*,[19] Moses Mendelssohn has Socrates offer a version of the proof in the third dialogue of his famous *Phädon, oder über die Unsterblichkeit der Seele*,[20] and it is well-represented in the work of other authors of the period.[21] Strikingly, Kant himself provides a ringing endorsement of the teleological proof, not only in the lectures, where he lauds the proof as "especially admirable" (V-Met/Mron 29: 916), "the most noble" (V-Met-K2/Heinze 28: 767), and even claims that it "is the best of all that has ever been introduced for the soul" (V-Met-L2/Pölitz 28: 592; cf. V-Met/Volckmann 28: 442), but also in the Paralogisms chapter in the B edition of *Critique of Pure Reason*. There, in a passage referred to previously and which emphasizes the positive contributions of rational psychology, Kant presents a truncated version of the proof "*by analogy with the nature* of living beings in this world" (B425), and continues:

> This powerful ground of proof, which can never be refuted, accompanied by an ever increasing cognition of the purposiveness in everything we see and by a vision of the immensity of creation, hence also by the consciousness of a certain boundlessness in the possible extension of our knowledge, along with a drive commensurable to it, always still remains. (B426)

Yet, it is not obvious, to say the least, how Kant's claim here that this proof "can never be refuted" can be reconciled with his assertion, immediately following this quote, that "we must equally give up insight into the necessary continuation

---

18 For Fordyce's original presentation, see Fordyce 1769: 289–99. Rolf George offers a more detailed consideration of Fordyce's argument and its early uptake by Kant in George (unpublished manuscript).
19 See Reimarus 1766: 691–3.
20 See Mendelssohn 2013: 168 ff.
21 See Beck 1960: 266 n. 18 for a list of other occurrences of this proof among Kant's contemporaries.

of our existence from the merely theoretical cognition of our self" (B426).[22] Fortunately, the student lecture notes provide some additional detail regarding what Kant takes the nature of the positive result of the teleological argument to consist in. In Kant's discussion in the notes, the teleological proof is, like the other proofs for immortality, taken to fall short of demonstrating "the necessary continuation of our existence." This is because the teleological proof might be allowed to demonstrate the necessity of an afterlife, and even to include *only* human souls (rather than extending to the souls of animals – V-Met/Mron 29: 916), though it might be questioned whether it applies to *all* human souls, such as to those who have yet to emerge from a state of animality (cf. V-Met-K2/Heinze 28: 767). Kant argues that it does, however, fail to prove the *eternality* of the afterlife inasmuch as it remains possible that the human soul might simply attain the purpose set for its faculties sometime after the death of the body, at which point the soul could conceivably perish: "Who knows if I do not die once all these predispositions have developed? Granted, that I will live even that long, if I do finally stop then, I would rather wish to have stopped earlier" (V-Met/Mron 29: 917).

While the teleological proof is thus no more successful than the previous proofs in its pretensions to offer theoretical certainty regarding the soul's immortality, it is nonetheless singled out as encouraging a salutary, and indeed, necessary perspective on human action. Along these lines, Kant suggests that the conclusion of the teleological proof can be allowed to hold insofar as it is understood as expressing that we must *assume* that there is an afterlife for the human soul. The conclusion cannot, however, be taken to amount to a cognition that the soul must survive the death of the body, inasmuch as the teleological principle from which it is derived only holds subjectively; thus, in the K_2 notes, Kant is careful to emphasize that the "proper teleological proof is carried out according to the analogy of organized nature, in which we *assume* that nothing is in vain and without purpose" (V-Met-K2/Heinze 28: 766). It is, then, insofar as the teleological proof convincingly establishes a warrant for the *belief* in the afterlife, grounded on the *necessity of assuming* the soul's survival of the death of the body, that Kant continues to make use of and endorse the teleological proof in the Critical period. Kant's surprising claim that this proof "can never be refuted," then, should be taken as an assertion that, while it might not succeed as a proof of immortality, the teleological proof is nonetheless successful in providing another basis for the hope for a future life. Indeed, just this is confirmed by Kant's scattered mentions of this proof in the *Critique of Pure Reason*. So, Kant writes in the Preface to the

---

[22] Ameriks also notes that Kant "does not express precisely what he finds philosophically inadequate in the argument" (Ameriks 2000b: 184 f.).

B edition, in an apparent reference to the teleological argument, that it is that "remarkable predisposition of our nature ... never to be capable of being satisfied by what is temporal" which leads to "the hope of a future life" (Bxxxii).[23] Moreover, Kant claims in the Canon of Pure Reason that the teleological proof discloses another, distinct basis for belief in the immortality of the soul, namely, one founded on a theoretical presupposition of a purposiveness in nature:

> In regard to this same wisdom [regarding the presupposition of the purposiveness of nature], in respect of the magnificent equipment of human nature and the shortness of life which is so ill suited to it, there is likewise to be found sufficient ground for a doctrinal belief in the future life of the human soul. (A827/B855)

Kant here appropriately contrast the resulting belief in the soul's immortality with the more familiar moral belief by characterizing it as *doctrinal* inasmuch as it is grounded on a theoretical rather than a practical presupposition.[24] Yet, in spite of this important distinction, it should be clear that such a doctrinal belief in the soul's immortality can nonetheless be seen to complement the more familiar moral belief inasmuch as it proceeds not on the basis of the recognition of the human being's *distinction*, through freedom, from the natural world, but rather on an understanding of the human being as a part of nature and, as such, likewise governed by "general natural ends" (V-Met/Arnoldt 29: 1035).[25] Despite rejecting the possibility of any *cognition* that the human soul will survive the death of the body, then, Kant's claim that the teleological proof "can never be refuted" should be understood as referring to the fact that this proof nonetheless affords a legitimate and indeed helpful basis for a (doctrinal) *belief* in the soul's immortality.

As the lectures make clear, however, there is more to this belief than simply that the soul survives the death of the body since Kant recognizes that it must also be shown that it is *possible* for the human soul to retain the requisite cognitive and moral capacities. Accordingly, Kant proceeds to consider what can be known about the state, or condition, of the soul in the afterlife. Again following

---

23 See also V-Met/Arnoldt, where Kant is recorded as claiming that from the moral and teleological proofs, "one cannot infer to any necessity of the future life, but rather only that we have cause ... to expect a future life, which is hope of a future life" (29: 1036).

24 Compare L. W. Beck, who contrasts "moral belief" with that "doctrinal belief" for which this proof serves as a basis (Beck 1960: 266 n. 18). For a detailed account of Kant's views on doctrinal belief see Chignell 2007: 345–50.

25 I take it that this is why Kant claims that the "proper teleological proof ... teaches us to study our own nature correctly" (V-Met-K2/Heinze 28: 767).

Baumgarten, Kant claims that with respect to the state of the soul after death "we have three items to prove: (1) the perdurability of the soul as a substance, (2) the survival of this after death, as intelligence, (3) its survival as a person" (V-Met/Mron 29: 912; cf. V-Met/Volckmann 28: 440).[26] Obviously, the perdurability of the soul as substance after the death of the body is a necessary feature of the soul's state after death, but Kant rejects those treatments of immortality that demonstrate *merely* that the soul perdures as a substance since not only does he deny that we can have cognition of the soul as a substance such that it would perdure through the loss of the body (cf. A349), but also because he claims that such accounts do nothing to dispel the spectres of spiritual sleep and the draught of forgetfulness which threaten the loss of the distinctive cognitive and moral capacities required by the human soul if it is to remain possible for it to achieve the ends set for it by nature. As Kant warns, were the soul not to retain its capacities for thought and consciousness of its identity in the afterlife, it would amount to nothing less than a spiritual death (V-Met-L1/Pölitz 28: 296; V-Met/Mron 29: 914) and the death of the person (V-Met/Dohna 28: 688; V-Met-K2/Heinze 28: 769).

As might be expected, Kant will reject the rational psychologist's claim to cognize with any degree of certainty that the soul can retain either its spirituality, that is, its capacity for thought independently of the body (cf. V-Met/Dohna 28: 683 and V-Met-K2/Heinze 28: 755), or its personality, that is, its capacity to be "conscious of being just the same subject as it was previously" (V-Met/Arnoldt 29: 1036) in the afterlife. So, against the rational psychologist's claim that we can know that the soul will be able to think independently of the body and thus will lead a purely spiritual existence in the life to come, Kant points out that not only does experience provide us with little guidance regarding whether the soul can exercise its faculties in the absence of the body, but also that, if anything, the course of experience actually suggests the opposite:

> The spirituality of the soul belongs to the transcendent concepts, i.e., we can attain no cognition of it, because we can give no objective reality to this concept, i.e., no corresponding object in any possible experience. It is not to be decided whether the body is not an indispensable support of the soul for thinking; for we cannot set ourselves outside the body in order to experience this. (V-Met-K2/Heinze 28: 755)[27]

---

[26] Spirituality and personality are also mentioned in the list of the "concepts of the pure doctrine of the soul" in the opening section of the Paralogisms (cf. A345/B403).
[27] See also V-Met-L1/Pölitz 28: 295 f.; V-Met/Mron 29: 914; V-Met/Volckmann 28: 441; and V-Met/Dohna 28: 683 f.

Similarly, experience would suggest that the human soul's faculty of recollection degrades over time and so that it is unlikely that it would retain its memory of itself and past states in the afterlife:

> What concerns ... the identity of the person of the soul, this would be the intellectual memory. To what extent this should belong to it after death, the necessity of that one cannot comprehend at all: one can, of course, assume the possibility, but not prove it, therefore one cannot infer it a priori. Psychologically we rather find that the human being forgets what he previously was. (V-Met/Arnoldt 29: 1038)[28]

While Kant thus rules out any cognition of the soul's state after death on the basis of experience, he nonetheless does not take the soul's preservation of its spirituality and personality in the afterlife to be impossible. So, Kant claims that a complete deficiency of consciousness such that the soul would be unable to think in the afterlife "cannot at all be proven" (V-Met-L1/Pölitz 28: 296), and he contends that even though rational psychology cannot disclose the reality of spirits (and so become a pneumatology, or doctrine of spirit), likewise the materialist cannot disprove the possibility of "the life of the spirit without body" (V-Met/Dohna 28: 688). Regarding personality, Kant is clear in the lectures that it at least remains possible in the absence of the body, as the notes read, "[p]erhaps in the future [the soul] will be able to be self-conscious without body" (V-Met/Mron 29: 914; cf. V-Met-L1/Pölitz 28: 296). Indeed, it is obviously crucial that Kant upholds, at the very least, the *possibility* of the soul retaining these distinctive capacities in the afterlife since otherwise any belief in immortality warranted by the teleological proof will be undermined inasmuch as the soul could not be allowed to retain the very capacities the apparent purpose of which was to be used and developed in the afterlife.

It is not, however, clear *how* Kant can uphold even the possibility of the spirituality and personality of the soul after the death of the body, which he maintains in the Critical-period lectures, in a way consistent with his published Critical views, particularly the doctrine of apperception and emphasis (in the B edition) on the role of external bodies in general as a condition of our cognition, and so consciousness, of ourselves. That it should be possible for the soul to preserve its capacity for thinking in the absence of the body would seem inconsistent with Kant's claim that the activity of thought itself presupposes that a manifold of *sensations* be given to the subject. Kant makes this point, for instance, in a lengthy

---

[28] See also V-Met/Mron 29: 914: "Perhaps in the future it will be able to be self-conscious without body, for I must be conscious of myself through clear representations. But these rest on the body, since they are sensations."

footnote in the B edition Paralogisms, writing that sensation "grounds this existential proposition [i. e., the *I think*]" (B422), and continues:

> Only without any empirical representation, which provides the material for thinking, the act I think would not take place, and the empirical is only the condition of the application, or use, of the pure intellectual faculty. (B423n)

Accordingly, Kant seems to rule out the possibility of any exercise of the soul's cognitive capacity in the absence of the body and its organs of sense through which it is provided with an empirical manifold. In addition, it is not clear how the soul should be understood to preserve a consciousness of its identity, and thus its personality, in the afterlife, given Kant's claim that the experience of myself as existing over time presupposes the existence of (an external) body as a condition of its possibility. In the Refutation of Idealism, Kant sets out from inner experience, understood as the consciousness of "my existence as determined in time" (B275), but concludes that "the existence of outer objects is required for the possibility of a determinate consciousness of our self" (B278). Assuming that the human subject's putative consciousness that it is the same soul in the afterlife as it was previous to the death of the body is just such a case of empirically determined self-consciousness, it is not clear how this consciousness would be possible in the absence of the body and its organs of outer sense by means of which the soul is able to represent external objects. In light of all this, it seems that Kant could not even maintain that it is conceivable that the soul should retain these capacities in the afterlife, thereby undermining the basis for the doctrinal belief in immortality.

While Kant himself does not offer much by way of detail on these points, the beginnings of an adequate solution can be formulated on the basis of the available texts. In claiming that the activity involved in discursive thought is conditioned by a manifold, Kant's point is not that the activity of the *I think* depends on the body but only that it requires that a manifold be given. In the course of *our* lives, obviously, the manifold is only given sensibly, that is, as a result of the affection of the organs of sensation, which is to say that our experience is such that the activity of thought is always conditioned by the body, and so we can hardly claim to know that the soul must be able to exercise its activity independently of it (or indeed of any body whatsoever). Even so, it nonetheless remains *conceivable* that the activity of the soul could occur independently of the body, insofar, namely, as a manifold is not given to us by means of bodily organs of sense but in some other way that does not rely on the body;[29] accordingly, as Kant

---

[29] Along these lines, one might consider the extended discussion contained in the L_1 notes of

notes in his lectures: "it is not necessary that the [activity of the] soul would have to stop with the body" (V-Met/Mron 29: 914; cf. V-Met/Volckmann 28: 441 f.). With respect to the soul's personality, while the empirically determined consciousness of the self undoubtedly requires the presupposition of the existence of body, it is not clear that Kant needs to account for the possibility of such a robust self-consciousness in the afterlife. Rather, insofar as personality is taken to involve only the bare (capacity for the) consciousness that I am the same subject now as I was previously, Kant could contend that this only amounts to the *mere*, as opposed to empirically determined, consciousness of the self, that is, the "*intellectual consciousness*" of the self as the identical subject of consciousness which precedes (as a condition) the thicker consciousness of the self (by means of inner sense – cf. Bxl). This consciousness has a far better claim to being possible in the absence of body, and while it obviously does not amount to the consciousness of my identity as an empirical subject, it nonetheless serves to distinguish the human soul (as an intellectual being) from lesser beings incapable of such complex consciousness which is in any case what is primarily at issue for the rational psychologist in the question of personality.[30] Kant is thus able to shore up the teleological proof by accounting for the conceivability of the soul's preservation of its spirituality and personality after the death of the body. As a result, Kant can contend that by means of this proof we are not only provided with an additional warrant to believe that the human soul will survive the death of the body, but we are also licensed in a belief that the human soul will continue to be outfitted with the capacities required for the realization of its natural purposes in the afterlife.

In the end, then, it should be clear that the discussion of the immortality of the soul as preserved in the student notes to Kant's metaphysics lectures serve as an indispensable supplement to his discussion in the Paralogisms. As we have seen, the account preserved in the notes serves to extend and clarify his devastating criticism of the rational psychologist but, significantly, Kant also makes use of his lectures to elaborate on his positive doctrine of the soul, albeit in a manner that remains fundamentally consistent with Critical strictures. That Kant should take the liberty to explore this territory in the context of his lectures is, perhaps, unsurprising, given that the classroom would have offered him a much

---

a so-called "spiritual intuition [*geistige Anschauung*]" (V-Met-L1/Pölitz 28: 297–9) of which the soul might be capable "when it is liberated from the sensible intuition of the body" (V-Met-L1/Pölitz 28: 298). Even here, however, Kant maintains that it cannot be demonstrated that the soul will receive this kind of intuition after the death of the body, yet Kant allows that it remains a "necessary hypothesis of reason which can be set against opponents" (V-Met-L1/Pölitz 28: 298).
30 See Dyck 2014: 168–71.

more informal venue (and a more receptive audience) for the presentation of these views. Yet, Kant undoubtedly also recognized the transformative potential, for his students' theoretical and practical endeavours, of a belief in the soul's immortality that promotes our investigation of the natural world in terms of its purposive organization (where the human being is no exception), and that continually exhorts us to develop our highest cognitive and moral capacities in this life with an eye towards the life to come.

II **Logic**

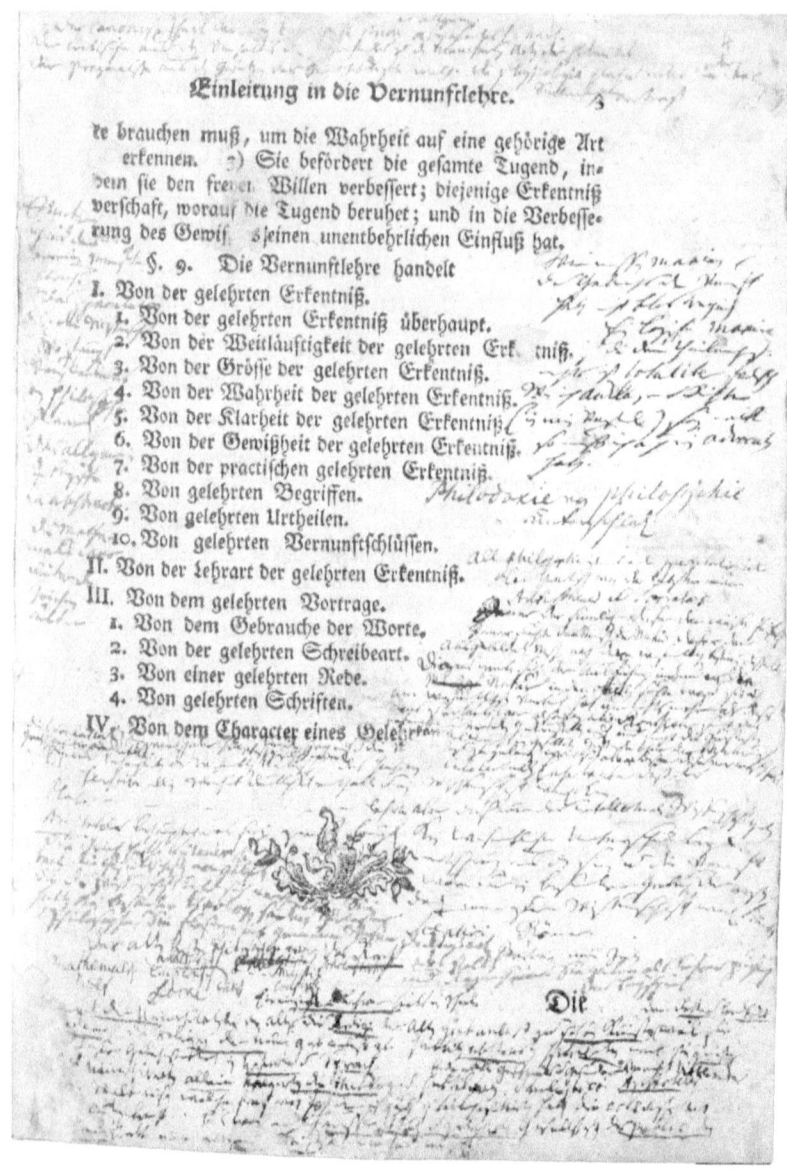

Fig. 5: Reproduction of page 3 ("Einleitung in die Vernunftlehre") of Kant's copy of G. F. Meier's *Auszug aus der Vernunftlehre* (Halle, 1752), with Kant's handwritten notes: Reflections 1616–17 (AA 16: 37 f.), 1635 (AA 16: 58), 1636 (AA 16: 60 f.), 1642–46 (AA 16: 63 f.). Reproduced with the kind permission of the University of Tartu Library, Estonia. Call number: manuscript 92. Kant's personal copy of Meier's *Auszug* is available at the University of Tartu Library website: http://hdl.handle.net/10062/42108. Accessed 22 April 2015.

Chapter 5
Constructing a Demonstration of Logical Rules, or How to Use Kant's Logic Corpus

Huaping Lu-Adler

In this chapter, I discuss some problems of Kant's logic corpus while recognizing its richness and potential value. I propose and explain a methodic way to approach it. I then test the proposal by showing how we may use various materials from the corpus to construct a Kantian demonstration of the formal rules of thinking (or judging) that lie at the base of Kant's Metaphysical Deduction. The same proposal can be iterated with respect to other topics. The said demonstration will have cleared the path for such iterations.

1 Kant's logic corpus:
Some problems and a proposal for its effective use

Kant's logic corpus comprises four sets of materials: (1) items Kant himself prepared for publication, including (though not limited to) the various sections in the *Critique of Pure Reason* that discuss logic, (2) his handwritten notes (*Reflexionen*) on logic, (3) transcripts of his logic lectures, and (4) the *Logic* edited by Gottlob Benjamin Jäsche (Conrad 1994: 43–5). None of these sets of materials can alone represent Kant's views on logic in a way that is at once reliable, precise, and complete.

We may begin with the *Logic*, which was published under the title "Immanuel Kant's Logic: A Manual for Lectures." According to Jäsche, he compiled it at Kant's request and from Kant's original manuscript.

> *Kant* commissioned me to prepare his *Logic* for publication, as he expounded it to his listeners in public lectures, and to transmit it to the public in the form of a *compendious manual*. For this purpose I received from him his own manuscript, which he had used in his lectures, with the expression of special, honorable confidence in me ... that I would not distort or falsify his thoughts, but rather would present them with the required clarity and distinctness and at the same time in the appropriate order. (Log 9: 3; original emphasis)

By the "manuscript," Jäsche was referring to the notes that Kant wrote on the margins and interleaved pages of his copy of Georg Friedrich Meier's *Auszug aus der Vernunftlehre*, which Kant supposedly used as the "guiding thread" for his logic lectures (Log 9: 3 f.). This description is correct. (The notes in question have been published in volume 16 of the *Akademie-Ausgabe* of Kant's works.). So is Jäsche's claim that he compiled the *Logic* at Kant's request (Br 12: 372).

What is problematic, however, is Jäsche's suggestion that he compiled the text *solely* from those handwritten notes. He in fact used a variety of other sources, including transcripts of Kant's logic lectures, which we shall see have their own philological problems. Moreover, as Jäsche himself pointed out, Kant "expanded [the notes] from time to time through new ideas" and "again and again revised anew and improved [them] in regard to various individual materials" (Log 9: 4). As such, the notes are inevitably fragmentary and may not even be compatible with one another, given how Kant's philosophical views changed over time. So, as Terry Boswell puts it, it is possible that

> Jäsche, faced with the problem of putting together one text out of several sources, including fragmentary memoranda by Kant, may have taken the liberty of adding words and phrases of his own to produce a presentable text, and may even have added sentences or passages of his own meant to introduce, summarize, and create transitions between his sources. (Boswell 1988: 199; see also Conrad 1994: 63 f.)

It is certainly understandable that anyone who wishes to compile a presentable text out of fragmentary records has to make many editorial maneuvers. Jäsche made it clear that he was partly responsible for "the *exposition*, the clothing and the execution, the presentation and the ordering of [Kant's] thoughts" (Log 9: 3). It is lamentable, however, that Jäsche failed to say what other sources he might have used to facilitate his editorial efforts or how he might have used them to supplement Kant's notes, and thereby misled the readers into thinking that the *Logic* is, as to content, an accurate presentation of none other than Kant's original views.

This assessment of the *Logic* does not mean that it should be discredited altogether. As Boswell suggests, this text is indispensible – albeit alone insufficient – for our understanding of Kant's views on logic, notwithstanding Jäsche's problematic editorial methods. After all,

> at least in this case we know who prepared the text [which is not the case with most transcripts of Kant's lectures], know that he was a professional philosopher and know that Kant himself thought enough of his competence to assign him the task of editing his logic. What is questionable from a philological point of view would be the exclusive use of this one document. (Boswell 1988: 201)

Hence we may still feel free to use the *Logic* as long as, to follow Michael Young's recommendation, we interpret it with care and appraise it "in light of other available materials" from Kant's logic corpus, namely (1)–(3) listed above (Young 1992: xviii).

It is no easier task, however, to decide exactly how those other materials should be consulted. The available transcripts of Kant's lectures, as many scholars have pointed out, are likewise affected by philological problems (Boswell 1988: 196–200; Young 1992: xxiii–xxvi; Conrad 1994: 52–61). Meanwhile, the direct discussions of logic in the writings Kant himself prepared for publication are sparse and may very well be limited by the specific philosophical concerns attached to those publications. As for the handwritten notes, apart from the fact that they are fragmentary, there is no foolproof way to verify when Kant wrote any given notes or to determine which ones belong to which period of his philosophical developments.[1] Thus, it is impossible to draw from them alone an accurate and complete picture of his Critical views on logic or, for that matter, of how his views might have evolved over time. By Boswell's analysis, it is therefore "unavoidable" to end up with this "circular procedure": to divine the meaning of those notes, we are "generally pressed to take recourse to other materials such as the Jäsche logic itself and the extant students' transcriptions," while "the authenticity of the latter requires verification on the basis of Kant's handwritten notes" (Boswell 1988: 201).

Such a circular procedure, so described, seems unilluminating if not simply problematic. It is unclear how one should move between Kant's notes, on the one hand, and the transcripts of his lectures and Jäsche's *Logic*, on the other, and elucidate individual items from the respective sources in light of each other without running in a vicious circle. In particular, if we want to draw from these sources an accurate and comprehensive account of Kant's Critical views on logic (or of how his views might have changed over time), by what criteria should we decide which items to use from each source? According to Boswell, even if one sets aside the issue of authenticity, Jäsche's *Logic* is still defective in lacking "comprehensiveness and completeness" – for it "present[s] only a limited view both of Kant's logic lecture and of the reflections" (Boswell 1988: 201). How can one be sure, though, that everything in Kant's logic lectures and reflections represents his final views on logic – given that those lectures were freely delivered, that the transcripts thereof might even include materials from other authors (Boswell

---

[1] The dates used in the *Akademie-Ausgabe* of Kant's works came from Erich Adickes. For a well-argued challenge to Adickes's method, see Conrad (1994: 46–51, 65–73), who also discusses the problem with the dating provided by Benno Erdmann before Adickes and concludes that it is in principle impossible to be absolutely certain about the dates of Kant's handwritten notes.

1988: 198; Conrad 1994: 57 f.) and that there is no absolutely certain dating of the reflections?

One can try a different procedure than the one described by Boswell. To begin with, one can simply lump Kant's reflections on logic together with the transcripts of his logic lectures and Jäsche's *Logic*, without privileging one category over another. At this point, as Riccardo Pozzo suggests, in response to some of the aforesaid problems associated with those sources, one may "give up the idea of making recourse to any dating [of the reflections] at all" (Pozzo 1998: 304) and set aside concerns about the authenticity or accuracy of the *Logic* or the transcripts. One can focus instead on identifying a worthwhile *perspective* from which to approach the aggregated materials. To avoid vicious circularity, such a perspective must be formed on independently reliable sources. One obvious source is the few segments in the *Critique* where Kant explicitly discusses logic. One may need more than those segments, though. Jäsche has some insights to offer in this regard. According to him, one must bear at least two things in mind when attempting to figure out precisely what belong to true logic in Kant's view. First, Kant's "explicit pointer" about what should be included in the proper treatment of logic; second, an educated guess as to how Kant – as "the great reformer of philosophy and ... of this part of theoretical philosophy in particular [i.e., logic]" – "would have worked on logic according to *his* architectonic plan" (Log 9: 4 f.). To pinpoint and clarify the relevant "pointer" and "plan," as we shall see, one may have to consult a wide range of Kant's Critical remarks, many of which are not directly about logic. Furthermore, if Kant indeed somehow reformed logic (and it will become clear that he did), his reformative approach to logic was more or less shaped by certain developments in modern logic, which presented him at least with the relevant philosophical problems to consider. Hence, as Pozzo puts it, it may also be instructive to consider "the point of view of the history of the problems" while tackling the interpretative difficulties associated with Kant's logic corpus (Pozzo 1998: 305).

Here, then, is a basic procedure for an effective use of Kant's logic corpus. One begins by describing a philosophical perspective that incorporates two elements: (a) a *philosophical problem* concerning logic that is significant for Kant and probably also for other modern philosophers, and (b) some *general constraints* as to how – given Kant's published views on the related issues – he might address the problem. In the process, one may occasionally cite Kant's notes on logic, transcripts of his lectures, and Jäsche's *Logic*, if the goal is just to articulate fully certain points that are already contained in the writings Kant himself prepared for publication. Having sufficiently explained the perspective, one can then use it to select further materials from those three categories of Kant's logic corpus to construct a full Kantian answer to the identified philosophical problem.

Such a procedure may be iterated. Considering that the corpus contains rich and complex materials on many topics, there is probably no single angle from which to illuminate them all at once. Rather, one might find it more productive to approach the corpus from one perspective at a time, following the basic procedure outlined above. In next section, I try out the procedure with respect to one issue, concerning the source of logical rules, which is pivotal to Kant's Metaphysical Deduction but is not explicitly addressed in the *Critique*.

2 A Kantian demonstration of logical rules

Kant describes Metaphysical Deduction as that by which "the origin a priori of the categories in general was established through their complete coincidence with the universal logical functions of thinking" (B159). The universal logical functions of thinking in turn boil down to the twelve logical forms of judging presented in the Table of Judgments (A70/B95). If the project of Metaphysical Deduction is to succeed, Kant must have a way of explaining how those functions of thinking or forms of judging may themselves be derived independently of the categories (to avoid circularity) (Lu-Adler 2014). They must also be derived in such a way as to prove that "the understanding is completely exhausted and its capacity [*Vermögen*] entirely measured by these functions" (A79/B105). Kant could not simply claim that Aristotle, as "the father of logic," had already sorted them out. For that would amount to committing the fallacy of appealing to authority. Moreover, Aristotle identified more forms than are included in the Table of Judgments, so that Kant would still have to explain why precisely those twelve forms must be included in the table. How else could those forms be derived, then? Kant does not directly address the question in the *Critique*. We will have to use materials from his reflections on logic, together with transcripts of his logic lectures and the *Logic*, to construct a derivation on his behalf. Nonetheless, the *Critique* contains important clues as to which materials from those sources may be used toward the derivation.

In the following, I tease out the relevant clues by examining three propositions in the *Critique*. First, only a general and pure logic is "properly science," which studies the necessary rules for the use of the understanding in general (A54/B79). Second, the presentation of a set of rules is complete just in case they have been systematically demonstrated from a common principle (*Princip*) (A80 f./B106). Third, categories are generated through a sort of "*epigenesis* of pure reason," as what "contain the grounds of the possibility of all experience in general from the side of the understanding" (B167). These propositions are not obviously connected. By my analysis, however, they together point to how Kant would derive the logical forms of judgment or, which amount to the same, the necessary and universal rules governing the act of thinking: find a "principle" of pure reason from which they can be demonstrated a priori, as what constitute the grounds of the possibility of thinking in general. In the following, I spell out the requisite principle, flesh out the demonstration with materials from Kant's logic notes, lecture transcripts, and the *Logic*, and explain what the demonstration reveals about Kant as a reformer of modern logic.

2.1 On logic as a proper science

Kant discusses the nature of logic in two places in the *Critique* – first in "Preface to the second edition" and then in "The idea of a transcendental logic." In the former, he makes three related points about logic. First, logic "exhaustively presents and strictly proves [*beweist*] nothing but the formal rules of thinking" (Bviii–ix). Second, the understanding in logic therefore "has to do with nothing further than itself and its own form" (Bix; cf. GMS 4: 387). Third, it is precisely thanks to such limitation that logic, as a "treatment of the cognitions belonging to the concern of reason," is able to travel "the secure course of a science" (Bvii; cf. Bix). Later in the *Critique*, Kant specifies the logic in question as a science of thinking that is both "pure" and "general." As general logic, it "has to do with nothing but the mere form of thinking" and treats its rules "without regard to the difference of the objects to which it may be directed" (A52/B76; A54/B78). As pure logic, it is "a proven doctrine [*eine demonstrierte Doktrin*]" which "has to do with strictly a priori principles [*Principien*]," "abstract[s] from all empirical conditions under which our understanding is exercised," and therefore "draws nothing from psychology" (A53 f./B77 f.). In these terms, if logic is a "doctrine of the elements of the understanding," (A54/B78) it is properly scientific only insofar as it demonstrates those elements from a priori principles.

Now, a proper science has three key features on Kant's account: it is systematic, namely "a whole of cognition ordered according to principles [*Principien*]"; it "treats its object wholly according to a priori principles"; it has apodictic certainty (MAN 4: 467 f.). A system of cognitions is a "*rational* science" if the cognitions are interconnected as "grounds and consequences." It is not strictly science, however, if "the grounds [*Gründe*] or principles [*Principien*] themselves are still in the end merely empirical," in which case it will not be apodictically certain (MAN 4: 468). A "doctrine of nature," for instance, is properly scientific only in virtue of having a "pure part – namely, that which contains the a priori principles of all other natural explanations" (MAN 4: 469). Scientific logic, as a "doctrine of reason," indeed cannot have any impure (empirical) part at all, but is a "*pure* philosophy" that "sets forth its teachings simply from a priori principles [*Principien*]" (A53 f./B78; GMS 4: 387 f.).

All these remarks about logic qua proper science are reflected in Jäsche's summary of Kant's notion of logic.

> [1] Logic is a science of reason [*Vernunftwissenschaft*], not as to mere form but also as to matter; [2] a science a priori of the necessary laws of thought, not in regard to particular objects, however, but to all objects in general; – hence a science of the correct use of the understanding and of reason in general, [3] not subjectively, however, i. e., not according to empirical (psychological) principles for how the understanding does think, but objectively, i. e., according to principles [*Principien*] a priori for how it ought to think. (Log 9: 16)

Clause [1] captures two senses in which logic is a rational science: as to form, it is a system of cognition ordered by rational principles; respecting matter, it has reason or the understanding per se as the object (V-Lo/Blomberg 24: 24 f.; V-Philippi 24: 315; V-Lo/Dohna 24: 695; V-Lo/Wiener 24: 792; V-Lo/Bauch, LV 1: 10, 13 f.; V-Lo/Hechsel, LV 2: 278, 280).[2] In the latter sense, logic is "a self-cognition [*Selbsterkenntniß*] of the understanding and of reason" (Log 9: 14). Clause [2] presents logic as "general" in the same terms as Kant did in the *Critique*. Clause [3] echoes the claim that logic, as a strict science, investigates the necessary rules of thinking in general according to non-empirical principles. In other words, scientific logic is a "demonstrated theory" that "rests on principles [*Principien*] a priori, from which all its rules can be derived [*abgeleitet*] and proved [*bewiesen*]" (Log 9: 14 f.; cf. V-Lo/Blomberg 24: 24; V-Philippi 24: 317; V-Lo/Dohna 24: 694; V-Lo/Wiener 24: 793; V-Lo/Hechsel, LV 2: 280 f.)

This analysis of Kant's account of logic as a proper science contains, to borrow his expression at A67/B92, some "guiding threads [*Leitfaden*] to the discovery" of all logical forms of judgment or, more generally, all necessary rules of thinking as to form. It suggests that the first step toward a scientific logic is to pinpoint the a priori principles from which those rules of thinking are to be demonstrated. In addition, the notion of logic as "pure philosophy" implies that it is "cognition from pure reason" (A840/B868) and that, accordingly, the requisite principles may be sought in pure reason itself. We need more information in order to figure out what exactly they are, however. For that purpose, we turn to some

---

2 'LV' stands for Kant 1998c (*Logik-Vorlesung: Unveröffentlichte Nachschriften*, ed. Tillmann Pinder). I refer to any lecture transcript from this edition by the name of the transcript, the volume and pagination of LV. The value of Pinder's edition partly lies in the different editorial method that it uses compared to the *Akademie-Ausgabe*. See Pinder in Kant 1998c, ix–xxxvii; Robinson 2000.

of Kant's Critical remarks about the source of categories or pure concepts of the understanding.

2.2 On the origin of categories

Let us first consider Kant's following comment about the completeness of his Table of Categories, with a view to uncovering its connection with the question about the origin of those concepts.

> This classification is systematically generated [*erzeugt*] from a common principle [*Princip*], namely the faculty [*Vermögen*] for judging (which is the same as the faculty for thinking), and has not arisen rhapsodically from a haphazard search for pure concepts, of the completeness [*Vollzähligkeit*] of which one could never be certain[.] (A80 f./B106 f.)

By 'haphazard search', Kant is referring to "Aristotle's search for these fundamental concepts": "since he had no principle [*Principium*], he rounded them up as he stumbled on them" (A81/B107). We already encountered Kant's view that a body of cognitions is systematic just in case the cognitions are organized in accordance with certain principles. Now he reduces its completeness – if we are to be "certain" about this – to the systematic generation of those cognitions from a common principle (A67/B92; A13/B27; GMS 4: 387). In the case of categories, notably, Kant equates the relevant *Principium* (source or ground) with the capacity (*Vermögen*) of the understanding to judge or think, which is essentially its "spontaneity" or "capacity for bringing forth representations itself [*das Vermögen Vorstellungen selbst hervorzubringen*]" (A51/B75; cf. A68 f./B93).

This appeal to the self-generating capacity of the understanding resonates with Kant's remarks about the origin of categories in § 27 of Transcendental Deduction. Here he argues that categories can only arise through "as it were a system of the *epigenesis* of pure reason" (B167). By 'epigenesis', Kant is comparing an epistemic theory of origin to a biological one. To continue with the biological analogy, he likens the empiricist alternative to the biological theory of "spontaneous generation" (*generatio aequivoca*), and the innatist one to the biological theory of "preformationism." He rules out the former for its absurd assumption that one species (a priori concepts) can be generated from an entirely different one (sensible experience),[3] and rejects the latter mainly because it leaves cat-

---

[3] The biological *generatio equivoca* is the view that an organized being is generated "through the mechanism of crude, unorganized matter" (KU 5: 419n). On Kant's objection to the episte-

egories with merely subjective necessity by treating them as predispositions "arbitrarily implanted in us" (B167 f.). On the epigenetic model, by contrast, categories are "self-thought [*selbstgedacht*]" on the part of pure reason (B167).[4] Thus, as Kant later puts it, the origin of categories is traced to the capacity of pure reason for "original acquisition [*ursprüngliche Erwerbung*]," namely acquisition – "a priori, out of itself" – of representations that "did not yet exist at all, and so did not belong to anything prior to this act" (ÜE 8: 221, 223).[5] The "ground" for such acquisition consists solely in "the subjective conditions of the spontaneity of thought" (ÜE 8: 223) – to wit, in the capacity of the understanding to "understand something in the manifold of intuition, i. e., think an object for it" (A80/B106). In that connection, categories are just "different *modi*" by which a given manifold of intuition must be combined to have a determinate relation to some object (A247/B304; cf. B137). As such, they "contain the grounds of the possibility of all experience in general [i. e., all determinate cognition of empirical objects] from the side of the understanding" (B167). The understanding, as "the faculty of *combining* the manifold in general," in fact "prescribes [*vorschreibt*]" these concepts as the necessary rules for the possibility of experience in general (B164). That is why they are "self-thought a priori first principles of our cognition" (B167).

This sketch of how Kant views the origin of categories gives us some helpful hints as to what he may identify as the common *Principium* from which the formal rules of thinking in general are to be generated systematically. Roughly, the *Principium* may be traced to a certain "capacity" of the understanding and reason, from which those rules are to be demonstrated as "the grounds of the possibility" of its exercise. The demonstration must exhibit the self-generating power of pure reason, or the power to bring forth previously non-existent representations a priori out of itself.[6] These points are partly reflected in the following passages.

---

mic version of *generatio equivoca*, see Wubnig 1969: 148 f.; Genova 1974: 264–6; Ingensiep 1994: 382 f., 386–8.

4 In biology, the terms 'preformationism' and 'epigenesis' were used in several ways, of which Kant was aware. On Kant's evolving views about biological preformationism and epigenesis and on how they were reflected in the developments of his Critical philosophy, see Mensch 2013: 1–15, 204 n. 248; Piché 2001; Sloan 2002; Zammito 2003: 80–98; Zöller 1988: 80–90.

5 Here Kant repeats his rejection of innate representations in the *Critique*: "The *Critique* admits absolutely no implanted or innate *representations*. One and all, whether they belong to intuition or to concepts of the understanding, it considers them as *acquired*" (ÜE 8: 221). For discussions about Kant's objection to innatism, see Zöller 1989 and Callanan 2013.

6 Otherwise, one would have to say either that the rules are empirically derived or that we have innate representations of them. Kant would reject the former alternative for the same reason that he dismisses the empiricist account of the origin of categories: what is a priori, as all logical rules are, cannot come from experience. He would reject the latter alternative because innatism con-

> Logic treats of the objective laws of reason, i.e., how it should proceed .... That reason explicates, according to its own laws, the laws according to which it ought to think, means that reason provides [*bedient*] the rules that it will discover first of all. (Refl 3939, 17: 356, translated in Kant 2013: 43)

> Logic is called a science because its rules can be proved by themselves[,] apart from all use[,] a priori ....
> *Logica* will thus have no other grounds or sources than the nature of human understanding. (V-Lo/Blomberg 24: 25)

To these we may add Kant's note that, although logical rules can be proved independently of all use as what "contain the ground of all judgments, namely, their form," logic "does not precede use," insofar as the latter "contains the first acts [*Handlungen*] of the understanding" (Refl 1602, 16: 31 f.). In other words, the use of the understanding provides the *occasion* for reflecting on such use, although the reflection is supposed to bring about an a priori cognition – namely, logic – of the formal conditions for the very possibility of the use in question (V-Lo/Wiener 24: 793).

In these terms, the *Principium* of logical rules has presumably to do with the characteristic act or capacity of the human understanding, i.e., thinking (A69/B94). With respect to categories, Kant treats the understanding in view of its capacity to bring synthetic unity to a given manifold of intuition and thereby relate it to an object a priori. In that connection, categories are just the various "acts [*Handlungen*] of pure thinking" through which the said capacity is exercised (A57/B81). It is in the "expectation" of these pure concepts – and in terms of the "distinction between pure and empirical thinking of objects" (A55/B79 f.) – that we first form the idea of a transcendental logic, as a science that treats "the laws of the understanding and reason ... solely insofar as they are related [*bezogen*] to objects a priori" (A57/B81 f.). By contrast, general logic abstracts from any such relation to objects and "considers only the logical form in the relation [*Verhältnisse*] of cognitions to one another, i.e., the form of thinking in general [*überhaupt*]*.*" That is, it "considers representations ... merely in respect of the laws according to which the understanding brings them into relation to one another when it thinks," no matter how those representations may be related to objects (A55–7/B79–82). In anticipation, then, to demonstrate these laws a priori is to derive them as the various *modi* in which the act of thinking in general – be it pure

---

flicts with the strictly scientific nature of logic. In his view, the hypothesis of innate representations is "very unphilosophical" – for there would be no true "investigation" but only "revelation" of anything inborn (V-Met-L1/Pölitz 28: 233; cf. V-Met/Mron 29: 760–3; V-Met/Vigil 29: 949–52).

or empirical – must take place, much as categories are derived as the different *modi* for relating a manifold of intuition to an object a priori. The demonstrated laws will constitute the grounds of the possibility of thinking in general, just as categories are the grounds of the possibility of experience in general from the side of pure understanding. To spell out the details of such a demonstration, though, we need materials from other parts of Kant's logic corpus.

2.3 Demonstrating logical rules

Both the "Introduction" of the *Logic* and the "Prolegomena" of most transcripts of Kant's logic lectures begin with an account of thinking as the act or capacity of the understanding. On this account, thinking necessarily accords with certain rules.

> Everything in nature ... takes place *according to rules*, ... The whole of nature in general is really nothing but a connection of appearances according to rules; and there is *no absence of rules* anywhere ....
>
> The exercise of our powers [*Kräfte*] also takes place according to certain rules ....
>
> Like all our powers, *the understanding* in particular is bound in its actions [*Handlungen*] to rules, which we can investigate. (Log 9: 11; cf. V-Lo/Philippi 24: 311; V-Lo/Pölitz 24: 502; V-Lo/Busolt 24: 608; V-Lo/Dohna 24: 693; V-Lo/Wiener 24: 790; V-Lo/Bauch, LV 1: 3–6; V-Lo/Hechsel, LV 2: 271 f.; V-Lo/Warschauer, LV 2: 505)

What is special about the understanding is that it is the source of rules and can reflect on the rules that govern its own *Handlungen*.

> Indeed, the understanding is to be regarded in general as the source and the faculty [*Vermögen*] for thinking rules in general .... the question is thus, according to what rules does it itself proceed?
>
> For there can be no doubt at all: we cannot think, we cannot use our understanding, except according to certain rules. But now we can in turn think these rules for themselves, i.e., we can think them *apart from their application* or *in abstracto*. Now what are these rules? (Log 9: 12)

The claim that the understanding investigates the rules of its own act *in abstracto* echoes Kant's characterization of pure logic in the *Critique*, and clarifies the nature of the rules in question: they concern how we *ought* to think, rather than how we do so (Refl 1579, 16: 18, 20 f.; Refl 1599, 16: 30; Log 9: 14; V-Lo/Pölitz 24: 504). In other words, logical rules are the necessary rules of thinking, without which "no use of the understanding would be possible at all" – regardless of any particular objects at which the act of thinking may be directed or any empirical subjective conditions under which it may take place (Log 9: 12; V-Lo/Dohna 24: 694; V-Lo/Hechsel, LV 2: 273). Such rules are to be strictly universal or "universal according to reason" – to which there *could be no* exception – and therefore must be cognized a priori (V-Lo/Dohna 24: 694; cf. B4; Log 9: 12; V-Lo/Wiener 24: 792). Accordingly, logic is bound to be *logica artificialis* rather than *logica naturalis*, proceeding from pure reason rather than from experience (Refl 1579, 16: 18; V-Lo/Philippi 24: 314; V-Lo/Dohna 24: 696–8; V-Lo/Wiener 24: 791, 798; Log 9: 17, 93).

By this analysis of the rule-governed nature of thinking, we can "form for ourselves an idea of the possibility of" logic: it is a "science of the necessary laws of the understanding and of reason in general, or what is one and the same, of the mere form of thought as such [*überhaupt*]" (Log 9: 12 f.; cf. V-Lo/Warschauer, LV 2: 506). Now, on Kant's generic description mentioned above, the form of thinking as such consists in the relation of cognitions to one other. To specify its various *modi*, then, one must begin with an assumption about what kinds of cognition may be properly treated in logic. For Kant, the most basic kind in this regard is concept.

> Logically, all origins [*Anfänge*] in thought are divided thus:
> 1. The cognition is a simple cognition, a *concept*.
> 2. The cognitions are combined in a *judgment*.
> 3. That judgments are combined and that *inferences* arise therefrom.
>
> (V-Lo/Wiener 24: 904; cf. V-Lo/Pölitz 24: 565; V-Lo/Busolt 24: 653; V-Lo/Hechsel, LV 2: 389)

All cognition has matter and form. In logic, one treats the matter of cognition as given and inquires only how any given cognition is possible as far as its form is concerned (V-Lo/Philippi 24: 341; V-Lo/Dohna 24: 764; V-Lo/Wiener 24: 791; V-Lo/Bauch, LV 1: 39). Provided the above division, such inquiry begins with concepts.

By Kant's analysis, every concept as to form originates within the understanding, even though the representations out of which it is made may have to come from without. Since logic deals merely with the form of cognition, it "expects that representations will be given to it from elsewhere, whatever this may be," and asks only how the given representations may be "transform[ed] ... into concepts" through the work of the understanding (A76/B102). The form of a concept is a "universal representation, or a representation of what is common to several objects" (Log 9: 91; cf. V-Lo/Pölitz 24: 567 f.; V-Lo/Wiener 24: 904, 908; V-Lo/Bauch, LV 1: 151 f.; V-Lo/Hechsel, LV 2: 390, 395; V-Lo/Warschauer, LV 2: 609). In that respect, a concept is "always made [*gemacht*]" (Log 9: 93) and "grounded on the spontaneity of thinking" (A68/B93). Thus arises the first question to be addressed in the demonstration of the formal rules of thinking in general: "Which acts [*Hand-*

lungen] of the understanding constitute [*ausmachen*] a concept? or what is the same, Which are involved in the generation [*Erzeugung*] of a concept out of given representations?" (Log 9: 93; cf. V-Lo/Pölitz 24: 566; V-Lo/Wiener 24: 907).

Accordingly, the logical doctrine of the elements of thinking begins with an account of the "logical *actus* of the understanding" – such as comparison, reflection, and abstraction – that "are the essential and universal conditions for generation of every concept whatsoever" (Log 9: 94; cf. V-Lo/Wiener 24: 907–10; V-Lo/Hechsel, LV 2: 393–5; V-Lo/Warschauer, LV 2: 609 f.). The specification of these logical acts does not result from an empirical study of how we actually form concepts, but from an inquiry about the a priori conditions or rules – from the side of the understanding – of concept formation in general. Such rules supposedly follow from the preceding analysis of concept regarding its form, which determines how the understanding *must act* in order to transform a given multitude of singular representations into a universal one, namely into a concept. The resulting account of the relevant logical acts, such as abstraction, in turn determines what kinds of relations concepts, qua universal representations, can stand with one another – e. g., in a series of subordination that can, in principle, have the highest genus but no lowest species (Log 9: 96–8; V-Lo/Pölitz 24: 568–70; V-Lo/Wiener 24: 910–12; V-Lo/Bauch, LV 1: 153 f.; V-Lo/Hechsel, LV 2: 398 f.; V-Lo/Warschauer, LV 2: 611–13).

The demonstration of the logical rules of judging – as the essential and universal conditions for generating judgments – likewise begins with the analysis of judgment regarding its general form. Though the wording of the analysis varies from one text to another, it usually goes as follows: a judgment is a representation of the unity in a relation among many given cognitions; the given cognitions comprise its matter, whereas its form is the manner in which those cognitions are related and united in one representation (Log 9: 101; V-Lo/Pölitz 24: 577; V-Lo/Wiener 24: 928; V-Lo/Hechsel, LV 2: 422; V-Lo/Warschauer, LV 2: 623). Relating and uniting several cognitions in one is an act of the understanding. Accordingly, the logical forms of judgment are often introduced as the various "actions of the understanding [*Verstandeshandlungen*] that appear in a judgment," which "reduce to" quantity, quality, relation, modality (V-Lo/Wiener 24: 929; cf. V-Lo/Pölitz 24: 577; V-Lo/Hechsel, LV 2: 423; V-Lo/Warschauer, LV 2: 623 f.).

Why should all judgments be considered precisely in accordance with those four ways? The modality of a judgment, to begin with, concerns "the relation of the whole judgment to the faculty of cognition," not the way in which several cognitions are related in it. That is, a judgment is either problematic or assertoric or apodictic, given that the act of judging can be accompanied with a consciousness of its mere possibility, actuality, or necessity (Log 9: 108; V-Lo/Pölitz 24: 579; V-Lo/Busolt 24: 662; V-Lo/Wiener 24: 935 f.; V-Lo/Bauch, LV 1: 176 f.; V-Lo/Hechsel,

LV 2: 432 f.; V-Lo/Warschauer, LV 2: 626). As for the way in which multiple cognitions are related and united in a judgment, there are exactly three questions to be asked about it: *quae* (what), *qualis* (of what quality), *quanta* (of what quantity) (V-Lo/Wiener 24: 932; V-Lo/Hechsel, LV 2: 427). These correspond to the relation, quality, and quantity of a judgment. The three moments of relation (categorical, hypothetical, disjunctive) are distinguished by whether the cognitions related in a judgment are concepts or judgments and, if the latter, how the judgments are related with one another "for the unity of consciousness" (through one being subordinated to another) (Log 9: 104–8; V-Lo/Wiener 24: 932 f.; V-Lo/Hechsel, LV 2: 427–9; V-Lo/Warschauer, LV 2: 625 f.). As for quantity and quality, they have to do with the relation between two concepts in a categorical judgment. Kant presents the three moments of quantity (singular, universal, particular) and those of quality (affirmative, negative, infinite) in reference to his account of concept as a universal representation in form. Every concept, as such, is treated in logic as capable of representing many objects, which constitute its logical extension or sphere. (I explain Kant's notion of logical extension – which is needed to understand his logical theory of judgment properly – in Lu-Adler 2012.) The quantity of a categorical judgment concerns what is represented by the subject-concept – as to whether the concept is used to signify one object or a multitude of objects and, if the latter, whether the multitude is taken as a whole or only in part in relation to the extension of the predicate (Log 9: 102; V-Lo/Philippi 24: 463; V-Lo/Busolt 24: 664 f.; V-Lo/Wiener 24: 931; V-Lo/Hechsel, LV 2: 426 f.; cf. Lu-Adler 2014). The quality of the judgment lies in how the extension of the predicate is posited with respect to that of the subject, i.e., whether the former is placed inside or outside the latter or, otherwise, in the infinite extension that lies outside the latter (Log 9: 103 f.; V-Lo/Pölitz 24: 577 f.; V-Lo/Wiener 24: 930 f.; V-Lo/Hechsel, LV 2: 424–6; V-Lo/Warschauer, LV 2: 624 f.).

The demonstration of the rules of inference likewise proceeds from a general analysis of the nature of inference, as that by which one judgment is derived from another in virtue of form, either with or without a mediating judgment (Log 9: 114–30; V-Lo/Pölitz 24: 583–93; V-Lo/Busolt 24: 670–8; V-Lo/Bauch, LV 1: 181–203; V-Lo/Hechsel, LV 2: 439–73; V-Lo/Warschauer, LV 2: 632–47). It is not necessary to elaborate such a demonstration here, since my primary aim in the current section is to demonstrate the logical forms of judgment on which Metaphysical Deduction depends.[7] Still, enough has been said to support Jäsche's following claim.

---

[7] I have not mentioned the law of contradiction either. Kant seems to distinguish two kinds of logical rules. Some rules, such as the ones demonstrated here, specify the various *ways to relate* multiple representations and combining them in one. Other rules, such as the law of contra-

> I would put forth the great man's ideas and principles most fittingly if ... I held myself to his express explanation, according to which nothing more may be taken up in the proper treatment of logic, and in particular in its *Doctrine of Elements*, than the theory of the three essential principal functions of thought: *concepts, judgments,* and *inferences.* (Log 9: 4)

Although Jäsche failed to specify – with textual evidence – the "express explanation" in question or to be fully transparent about the exact materials from which he "put forth" the Doctrine of Elements, he was right about what, according to Kant, strictly belongs to a logical treatment of the "principal functions of thought." In comparison, I have been more straightforward about how I have proceeded in constructing a Kantian account of those functions.

To recapitulate the procedure, we began with a specific philosophical problem: how would Kant demonstrate all the basic logical forms of judgment, a demonstration that is required for the success of Metaphysical Deduction? To fix the parameters for constructing a likely demonstration on Kant's behalf, we examined his Critical account of logic as a proper science, of the sense in which a science is complete, and of the origin of such pure cognitions as categories. We were thereby led to anticipate that the demonstration would proceed from a general analysis of thinking – as the act or capacity of the understanding – and eventually arrive at the logical forms of judgment as the various *modi* in which such an act must take place and therefore as what constitute the grounds of the possibility of thinking as such. To spell all that out, we then selected the relevant materials from Jäsche's *Logic* in conjunction with Kant's handwritten notes on logic and the available transcripts of his logic lectures. Progressing in such an order was meant to minimize, if not entirely cancel out, any negative effect from the philological problems of those texts.

2.4 Kant: A "great reformer" of modern logic?

Earlier I speculated that it might be instructive to approach Kant's logic corpus in light of certain philosophical problems that he inherited from the history of logic. More often than not, however, we may not get a full grasp of such problems until after we have sorted out Kant's own views as are contained in his logic corpus. Indeed, the above construction of a Kantian demonstration of logical

---

diction, determine the formal-logical conditions for the resulting relation *to represent something* (viz., an object, or a true thought). This is a distinction within general logic. I explain some of its implications in Lu-Adler 2013.

rules foregrounded many aspects of Kant's conception of logic that not only set it apart from all the other major developments in modern logic, but also offered us a perspective to identify, articulate, and evaluate the philosophical issues raised by those developments. Jäsche described Kant as "the great reformer" of philosophy in general and of logic in particular (Log 9: 5). In light of post-Kantian, and in particular Fregean, innovations in logic, this characterization may strike readers today as peculiar or even unwarranted. But the reformative nature of Kant's approach to logic, as I shall explain next, is clearly reflected in the demonstration of logical rules presented above.

By tracing the source of the formal rules of thinking to the understanding, the demonstration in question can be seen as a way to determine the domain and validity or legitimate use of those rules, much as Kant means transcendental logic to "determine the origin, the domain [*Umfang*], and the objective validity [*Gültigkeit*]" of the categories (A57/B81). In this regard, Kant is reacting to two developments in modern logic, which pertain to the domain of logic and the validity of its rules, respectively. Apropos of the domain of logic, he observes that

> some moderns have thought to enlarge it by interpolating *psychological* chapters about our different cognitive powers (about imagination, wit), or *metaphysical* chapters about the origin of cognition or the different kinds of certainty in accordance with the diversity of objects (about idealism, skepticism, etc.), or *anthropological* chapters about our prejudices (about their causes and remedies). (Bviii)[8]

By Kant's analysis, such attempts at expanding the domain of logic not only reveal an "ignorance of the peculiar nature of this science," but also threaten its prospect as a science: "It is not an improvement but a deformation of the sciences when their boundaries [*Grenzen*] are allowed to run over into one another" (Bviii). On Kant's account, as we have seen, logic – qua proper science – treats thinking in such a way that totally disregards "whether this thinking be empirical or a priori, whatever origin or object it may have, and whatever contingent or natural obstacles it may meet with in our minds." The boundary of logic is precisely delineated thereby, leaving no room for the afore-mentioned psychological, metaphysical, or anthropological chapters (Bix).

Meanwhile, Kant notes that logic "has been [mistakenly] used as if it were an organon for the actual production of at least the semblance of objective assertions," when in essence it is only a "canon for the assessment [*Beurtheilung*]"

---

[8] When Kant claims that origin of cognition is a topic of metaphysics as opposed to logic, he presumably has in mind origin as to *matter*. So construed, the claim is compatible with his treating the origin of concepts regarding *form* as a properly logical issue.

of cognitions as to form. In other words, logic "teaches us nothing at all about the content of cognition, but only the formal conditions of agreement with the understanding, which are entirely indifferent with regard to the objects" (A61/B85 f.). That is because, in order to present strictly universal and necessary laws of thinking, logic is "obliged to abstract from all objects of cognition and all the distinctions between them," so that in it "the understanding has to do with nothing further than itself and its own form." Accordingly, logical rules have valid use only for the formal assessment of cognitions, not for their "acquisition [*Erwerbung*]" (as regards content) (Bix). Nor is logic "a universal art of discovery" or "an algebra, with whose help hidden truths can be discovered" (Log 9: 20; cf. Log 9: 13, 16; V-Lo/Wiener 24: 793).

When we look at other parts of Kant's logic corpus, it becomes more obvious that, in thus clarifying the domain of logic and the valid use of its rules, he is partly responding to specific developments in modern logic. His lectures often included a brief commentary on the history of logic with references to particular philosophers. The following excerpt from the Wiener Logik, for instance, tells us whom Kant might have in mind when he claimed that some moderns had mistaken views about logic.

> After [Aristotle and Ramus] come Malebranche and Locke. This last wrote a treatise *de intellectu humano*. But both writings deal not only with the form of the understanding but with content. They are preparatory exercises for metaphysics. Among the moderns, Leibniz and Wolff are to be noted. The logic of Wolffius is the best to be found. It was subsequently condensed by Baumgarten, and the latter was again extended by Meier…. The logic of Crusius is crammed full of things that are drawn from other sciences, and it contains metaphysical and theological principles. Lambert wrote an organon of pure reason. (V-Lo/Wiener 24: 796; cf. Refl 1629, 16: 48; Log 9: 21; V-Lo/Blomberg 24: 37; V-Lo/Philippi 24: 337 f.; V-Lo/Pölitz 24: 509; V-Lo/Busolt 24: 613; V-Lo/Dohna 24: 701; V-Lo/Hechsel, LV 2: 288–90)

In a historical review like this, Kant is not just enumerating names. He is assessing the philosophical merits and shortcomings of different approaches as well. In particular, given that he views logic as a sort of philosophical cognition, a general reflection on the method of philosophy is directly relevant. We shall see how such a reflection gives Kant the framework within which to position his own conception of logic vis-à-vis the alternatives.

To begin, it is worth noting that when Kant praised the Wolffian logic as "the best to be found" he was referring only to its formal features such as being *demonstrative*, *distinct*, and *orderly* (Refl 1629, 16: 48; Refl 1641, 16: 62; V-Lo/Philippi 24: 337 f.). From Kant's perspective (given his account of science as a demonstrated system of cognitions), Wolff's contribution to logic lies in having identified some conditions for turning logic into proper science – insofar as its form is concerned.

At the same time, however, Kant would see Wolff – due to his dogmatic philosophical method – as having failed to examine the true *ground* of such a science. In this respect, Kant finds a promising alternative – namely, a critical method – in Locke's *An Essay Concerning Human Understanding*. The contrast is clear from the following passages.

> All the efforts of our philosophy are
> 1. dogmatic
> 2. critical.
> Among critical philosophers Locke deserves priority. Wolff, however, and the Germans generally, have a methodical philosophy ….

> Locke's book *de intellectu humano* is the ground of all true *logica*. (V-Lo/Blomberg 24: 37; cf. Refl 1636, 16: 60; V-Lo/Philippi 24: 338; V-Lo/Bauch, LV 1: 29)

> Leibniz and Locke are to be reckoned among the greatest and most meritorious reformers of philosophy in our times. The latter sought to analyze the human understanding … As for what concerns the special dogmatic method of philosophizing peculiar to Leibniz and Wolff, it was quite mistaken. Also, there is so much in it that is deceptive that it is in fact necessary to suspend the whole procedure and instead to set in motion another, *the method of critical philosophizing*, which consists in investigating the procedure of reason itself, in analyzing the whole human faculty of cognition. (Log 9: 32; cf. V-Lo/Wiener 24: 804; V-Lo/Hechsel, LV 2: 301)

In so many words, Wolff (together with Leibniz) proceeded dogmatically in that he constructed a logical system without premising it on an analysis of the human understanding or reason.[9] Locke's method in the *Essay* is "critical" by doing the exact opposite. The point, from Kant's perspective, is that "the logic of universal human reason" must be founded on an examination of the faculty in question (V-Lo/Wiener 24: 794). Kant rejects Locke's "physiological" approach to the subject, though, which focuses on how the faculty of reason operates under empirical-psychological conditions, when it should really be studied in abstraction from all such conditions (Refl 4851, 18: 8 f.; Refl 4866, 18: 14; Refl 4893, 18: 21).

Kant's attitude toward the Wolffian and Lockean treatments of logic is comparable to how he reviews the history of metaphysics and thereby articulates his

---

[9] Kant was apparently never exposed to any of Leibniz's writings that were specifically on logic. Nevertheless, he saw Leibniz as having laid the philosophical basis for Wolff's logical system (presumably through the *New Essays on the Human Understanding*): "Although actually having written no logic, [Leibniz] nonetheless did much to illuminate concepts (he wrote in defense of his countrymen against the Englishman Locke). In his works he expressed ideas which subsequently moved Wolff to his system" (V-Lo/Dohna 24: 701).

own conception of metaphysics in the *Critique*. In his view future metaphysics, as a strict science, must exhibit the "dogmatic procedure of pure reason" – as has been superbly exemplified by Wolff's system – without the Wolffian "dogmatism," but rather with "an antecedent critique of its own capacity" (Bxxxv). More specifically,

> in the future system of metaphysics, we will have to follow the strict method of the famous Wolff, the greatest among all dogmatic philosophers, who gave us the first example ... of the way in which the secure course of a science is to be taken, through the regular ascertainment of the principles [*Principien*], the clear determination of concepts, the attempt at strictness in the proofs, and the prevention of audacious leaps in inferences; for these reasons he had the skills for moving a science such as metaphysics into this condition. (Bxxxvi)

In brief, a properly scientific metaphysics "must necessarily be dogmatic, carried out systematically, ... hence with scholastic correctness [*schulgerecht*]."[10] This condition was fully satisfied by Wolff's metaphysics. Wolff, however, failed "to prepare the field for [metaphysics] by a critique of ... pure reason itself," which critique is "the preparatory activity necessary for the advancement of metaphysics as a well-grounded science [*Beförderung einer gründlichen Metaphysik als Wissenschaft*]" (Bxxxvi). As for the Lockean approach, which attempted to determine the "lawfulness" of all metaphysical claims through an inquiry about the human understanding, its promise to end all controversies of metaphysics turned out to be illusory. For, by basing metaphysics on a "physiology of the human understanding" and tracing its origin to "the rabble of common experience," Locke attributed to it a false genealogy (Aix). From these critical assessments emerges Kant's own proposal for steering metaphysics onto the secure course of a science. He shares the Lockean insight that metaphysics must be preceded by a study of the human understanding, but contends that such a study must be true critique rather than physiology: "The study ... of the subject is either physiological or critical. Critique separates 1. the pure from the empirical faculty of cognition, 2. sensibility from the understanding" (Refl 4951, 18: 9). The requisite critique boils down to a "self-cognition [*selbsterkenntnis*]" a priori on the part of pure reason,

---

10 By 'dogmatic', Kant means different things in different contexts. When he distinguished dogmatic and critical approaches and disapproved of the former, he was referring to the practice of asserting something without examining the ground of its legitimacy (V-Lo/Dohna 24: 744; V-Lo/Wiener 24: 885; Refl 2667, 16: 459; Refl 5645, 18: 293 f.). The dogmatic procedure he now recommends is meant as what ensures the strict universality and apriority of a science. Dogmatic cognition in this case – as cognition of reason from concepts alone – is contrasted with "historical" or "mathematical" cognition (V-Lo/Blomberg 24: 99; V-Lo/Dohna 24: 723 f.; V-Lo/Wiener 24: 830 f.; Refl 5645, 18: 290 f.).

through which it may "secure its rightful claims while dismissing all its groundless pretensions, and this not by mere decrees but according to its own eternal and unchangeable laws." Only then can there be a "decision about the possibility or impossibility of a metaphysics in general, and the determination of its sources, as well as its extent and boundaries" (Axi f.).

Kant's account of a true or properly scientific logic can be reformulated in similar terms: it must contain a dogmatic presentation of the rules of thinking in general without dogmatism, but preceded by an examination of the human understanding *in abstracto* and a priori. More specifically, as pure logic, it is "the scholastically correct [*schulgerecht*] presentation of a doctrine of the elements of the understanding" (A54/B78; on "scholastic" as opposed to "popular" presentation, see Log 9: 19, 47, 148; Refl 6358, 18: 683; V-Lo/Dohna 24: 779; V-Lo/Wiener 24: 795 f., 820 f.). This requires a dogmatic procedure in the sense depicted above, whereby all those elements are systematically demonstrated from ascertained principles (*Principien*) a priori. Such a procedure boils down to a self-cognition of pure reason as regards the laws in accordance with which the act of thinking ought to take place. These laws are necessary not by decrees, but in virtue of being self-prescribed on the part of pure reason as the universal, a priori conditions of thinking with respect to its form. The self-prescriptive nature of logical rules at the same time limits their validity: they can be legitimately used only for the assessment of cognitions merely as to form, not for the discovery of material truths. From Kant's standpoint, then, it is by tracing all logical rules to their origin a priori in pure reason – which was achieved by the demonstration presented in this chapter – that one establishes the possibility of logic as a proper science and determines its extent and boundaries (Axi f.).

It is hence clear that the Kantian demonstration of logical rules constructed above is significant not only because it is required for the success of Metaphysical Deduction, but also because it touches the deepest point at which Kant connects with the history of logic. In this respect, the demonstration in addition gives us an angle to appreciate what Kant really means by claiming that logic since Aristotle "seems to all appearance to be finished and complete [*vollendet*]" (Bviii). To some readers this claim might suggest that Kant simply held an "invincible belief in the adequacy and finality" of Aristotle's logic thanks to its time-tested "prestige" (Kemp Smith 1918: 184; cf. Kneale and Kneale 1962: 355 f.). On my reading, Kant would take Aristotle's logic – that is, logic as Aristotle presented it – to be complete at most in the loose sense of having not omitted any formal rules of thinking, but not in the strict sense of being a systematically demonstrated science from principles a priori. In fact, even to prove that Aristotle's logic is complete in the first sense, Kant would have to explain precisely what rules *must* be included in logic, which explanation would essentially be the kind of demonstration constructed in this chapter.

3 Conclusion

I began this chapter by discussing the exegetical challenges posed by Kant's logic corpus. In particular, I pointed out that there is no foolproof way to determine the dates of Kant's handwritten notes, that the transcripts of his lectures can be very imprecise and may include many things not presented in the lectures, and that Jäsche failed to explain how he might have used a variety of sources to compile the *Logic*. Meanwhile, I acknowledged that these texts contain potentially valuable materials to enrich our understanding of Kant's views on many topics concerning logic, when the writings he himself prepared for publication contain only sparse discussions of them. Accordingly, I proposed the following way to use Kant's logic corpus as effectively as possible. First, identify a philosophical problem, and outline the parameters for a possible Kantian answer based on the writings that Kant himself prepared for publication. Second, with the perspective resulted from the previous step, find materials from Kant's notes, lecture transcripts as well as the *Logic* to flesh out the anticipated answer. In the process, one may also consider the relevant historical developments and see if Kant's views relate to them in philosophically interesting ways. I tried out such a procedure with the question raised by Metaphysical Deduction, as to how Kant would demonstrate the logical rules of thinking or judging in general from which the categories are supposedly deduced. The resulting demonstration turned out also to reveal the most fundamental point – concerning the ground of logic and the validity of its rules – at which Kant's conception of logic departed from but still deeply connected with what in his view were two key philosophical moves in modern logic, represented by Locke and Wolff respectively.

The same procedure may be iterated in reference to other topics discussed in Kant's logic corpus. In a sense, the above demonstration of logical rules has cleared the path for such iterations. In particular, by clarifying the notion of logic qua proper science and sharpening its boundary, Kant signaled a general direction for how we may handle the parts of his logic corpus that deal with such issues as imagination, provisional judgment (in contrast with prejudice), error (as opposed to merely false cognition). These topics belong to empirical psychology and anthropology, not to the strictly scientific logic as Kant defines it. Nonetheless, Kant's characterization of logic as a proper science in the *Critique* already suggested the possibility of a comprehensive course on logic that would include two parts of general logic, understood as "the science [in the broad sense of the term] of the rules of the understanding in general" (A52/B76).[11] It is just that the relation of the two parts – pure logic and applied logic – must be elucidated first: the pure "part" must be explicated in entire separation from the applied part, and yet is also related to the latter in a non-trivial way – much as how pure morality relates to the doctrine of virtue (A53–5/B78 f.). Hence, if Kant's logic corpus in fact covers all the topics that were commonly treated in modern logic texts, it is his account of the strictly scientific logic and of how it relates to other subject matters that separates his logic corpus from all the other texts. As Jäsche puts it,

> however much many of the older manuals on [logic] may stand out for scientific strictness of method; for clarity, determinateness, and precision of explanations; and for conciseness and evidence in proofs; still there is scarcely a one of them in which the limits [*Grenzen*] of the various spheres that belong to universal logic in its broader extension – the merely *propaedeutic*, the *dogmatic* and *technical*, the *pure* and the *empirical* – do not run into and through each other, so that the one cannot be determinately distinguished from the other. (Log 9: 6)

In these terms, such topics as error and prejudice have a legitimate but determinately marked place in logic broadly construed. Having sufficiently clarified this point, we should then feel free to use the rich materials contained in Kant's logic corpus to sort out his views on any of those topics. The procedure proposed and tested in this chapter thus offers a *methodical* way to approach the materials, with a view to counteracting the various exegetical challenges posed by the corpus, and might thereby open up new lines of research on Kant's logic.[12]

---

[11] If by 'science' in the narrow or strict sense Kant means a system of cognitions grounded on a priori principles, 'science' in the broad sense refers to any system of cognitions arranged by certain principles, *whatever they may be*. This dual use of the same term is reflected in Kant's assessment of empirical psychology: he both denies that it is science in the strict sense – for not being based on a priori principles (MAN 4: 471) – and treats it as one among many sciences (Log 9: 18; Refl 1579, 16: 18; V-Lo/Blomberg 24: 25; V-Lo/Wiener 24: 791 f.). For discussions of metaphysics and chemistry as possible sciences, see the chapters by Courtney Fugate and Henny Blomme, respectively, in this volume.

[12] I thank the editor of this volume, Robert R. Clewis, for his careful reading of and helpful comments on the first version of the chapter. I am also indebted to the participants in the first DC-Baltimore Kant Workshop (March 2014, Georgetown) – Mavis Biss, Sonny Elizondo, Michael Nance, Laura Papish, Michael Rohlf, and Oliver Thorndike – for an insightful discussion of the chapter. Any infelicities that may remain are purely my own.

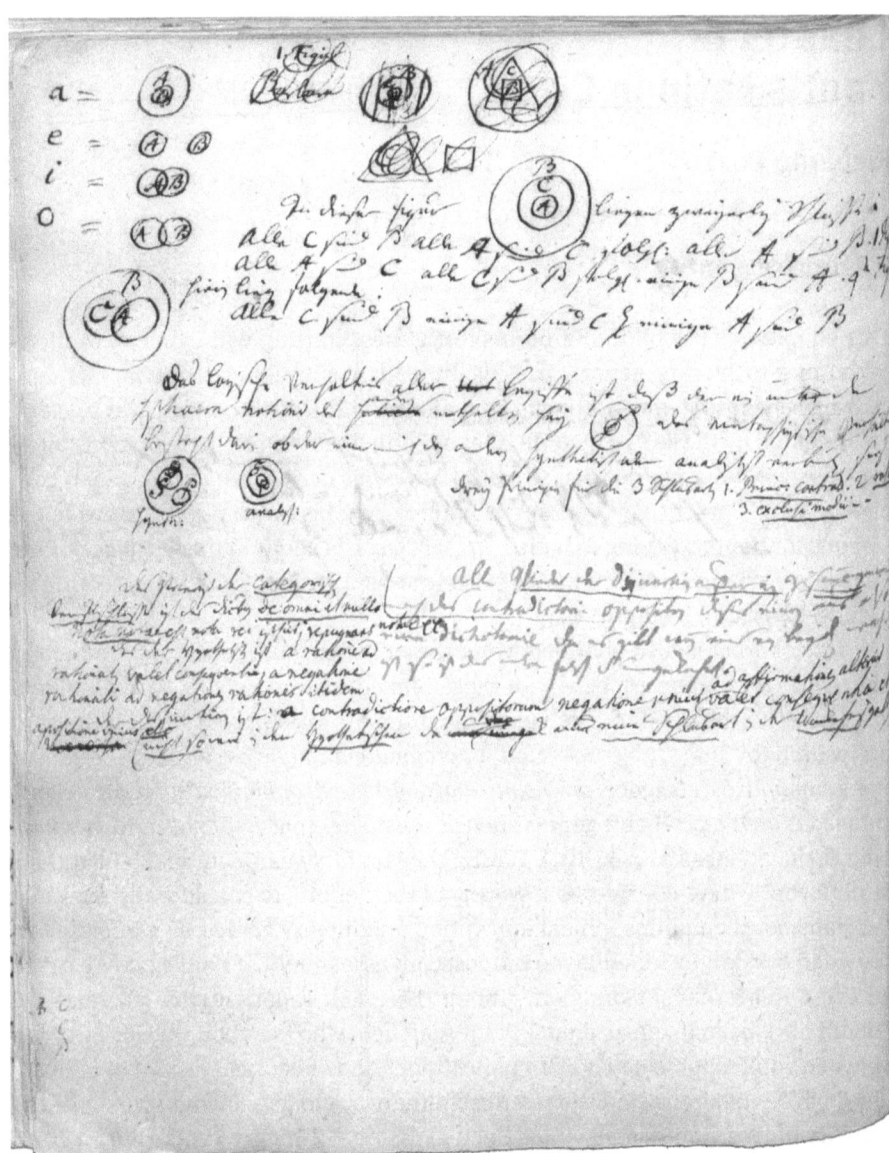

Fig. 6: Reproduction of sheet 101' (verso) inserted between printed pages 100 and 101 of G. F. Meier's *Auszug aus der Vernunftlehre* (Halle, 1752), displaying logic diagrams drawn by Kant: Reflections 3215–16 (AA 16: 715–17), 3218–19 (AA 16: 717), 3221 (AA 16: 718). Reproduced with the kind permission of the University of Tartu Library, Estonia. Call number: manuscript 92. Kant's personal copy of Meier's *Auszug* is available at the University of Tartu Library website: http://hdl.handle.net/10062/42108. Accessed 22 April 2015.

Chapter 6
Kant's Latin in Class

Riccardo Pozzo

1 Literary genres

This chapter shall look into a number of issues, starting with some definitions pertaining to literary genres, passing through institutional requirements concerning scheduling and textbooks, and ending with Kant's use of Latin in class, documented by the substantial number of Latin lines written by Kant in his interleaved copy of Georg Friedrich Meier's *Auszug aus der Vernunftlehre*, which goes back to Kant's practice of dictating in Latin during his *repetitoria*. What were the reasons for Kant's keeping to Latin? The last issue is about Kant's *Critique of Pure Reason* as having been originally conceived as a textbook for lectures on aesthetics, logic, and metaphysics.

This chapter is also about showing the influence on intellectual production of literary genres and especially of those related to academic teaching. Philologists point to the need to keep apart the different roles played, e. g., in ancient philosophy by literary genres such as *pragmateía, dialogos, lógos protreptikós, lógos sumpotikós, eisagogé, próblema, diatribé, chreía, aphorismós, apophthegma, gnóme*, as well as by Latin genres such as *epistulae, consolationes*, and *memorabilia* (Untersteiner 1980: 51–101). During the last fifty years, not many historians of philosophy have considered it worthy of their efforts to consider the manifold relations between philosophical innovation and literary genres. The information provided by Giorgio Tonelli, who proposed an assessment of Kant's oeuvre based on titles and formats, stands out (Tonelli 1955: 55). Today, studies like those of Tonelli have been taken as models by researchers who are about to close the gap between "philosophical history of philosophy" and "historical history of philosophy," while elaborating on the interdisciplinary approach of what used to be the "history of ideas" and is now "intellectual history" (Gregory 2006; Hotson 2007; Sgarbi 2010). As regards the hope of eventually achieving an effectively pragmatic consideration of philosophy within intellectual history, Donald Kelley has made it clear that: "intellectual history need not (or need no longer) be identified with the canon of philosophy .... Rather it should be seen as an approach or range of approaches, to historical investigation and interpretation in general .... The subjects of intellectual historians are texts, or their cultural analogues; the 'intelligible field of study' more generally is language, or languages; and the history of philosophy is not the model of but rather a province in this larger realm of interpretation" (Schneider 1996: 8). One could go as far as to accentuate the sociological aspect against the purely theoretical aspects of many of Kant's writings; however, a skeptical reader might question whether such an approach helps to explain exegetical and philosophical issues. These very doubts were raised by Jürgen Mittelstrass, who pointed out that it is fallacious to presuppose that the "forms of organization of the scientific understanding" are more important than "the scientific results themselves" (Mittelstrass 1999: 7 f.). Keeping the skeptics in mind, one might say that the main contribution of this chapter appears from the point of view of the history of the sources.

The literary genre of lecture-notes (*praelectiones*, *Vorlesungen*) defines itself on the basis of the following requirements: they were (1) connected with a course; (2) circulated as manuscripts; and (3) printed only years later (AA 24: 955–88). Gerhard Lehmann has found in Borowski's biography a reference to Kant having delivered a Latin speech "on an easier and more fundamental exposition of philosophy [*vom leichtern und gründlichern Vortrage der Philosophie*]" at the onset of his teaching career, namely in the winter term 1755/56, when he gave his first lecture, which was, by the way, a lecture on logic (Lehmann, in AA 24: 955). Connected to lectures are two other textual genres: academic programs (*orationes programmaticae*, *Programmschriften*, *Einladungssschriften*) and lecture announcements (*catalogi praelectionum*, *Vorlesungsankündigungen*). The former defines itself on the basis of the following requirements: *Programmschriften* were (1) connected with a course; (2) printed on one or more (also in fractions of half) signatures *in quarto* or *in octavo*; and (3) distributed unbound free of charge at the expenses of the professor (Lee and Sgarbi 2012); *Vorlesungsankündigungen* were instead (1) short texts of a few lines printed in Latin in the *catalogi praelectionum* of the University on the basis of what professors had communicated to the deans; (2) connected with all courses offered at a university; (3) posted free of charge; and (4) eventually translated and printed in German in the local papers, in the case of Königsberg in the *Königsbergische Gelehrten-Anzeigen* (Oberhausen and Pozzo 1999). Two *Programmschriften* have direct bearing to Kant's *Logikvorlesungen*: (1) *Die falsche Spitzfindigkeit der vier syllogistischen Figuren*, 35, [1] pages on two signatures and a half *in octavo* (A to B8 C2), of 1762; and (2) the *Nachricht von der Einrichtung seiner Vorlesungen in dem Winterhalbjahre 1765–1766*, set *in octavo* 5, [3] sheets in 1765.[1] The stakes are high, if only one

---

1 Following librarian cataloguing convention, unnumbered pages are put into square brackets when they are counted, and they are referred to by indicating rectus-versus (r-v) of the letter/sign and number located at the left, under the text's bottom line.

considers that once we have defined the precise contours of the literary genre, we can evaluate more fully the *intentio auctoris*. In fact, Kowalewski (in Kant 2000a: 139 f.) listed only six Kantian *Programm-* or *Einladungsschriften*. It is not easy to explain why, but Kowalewski left out both the *Falsche Spitzfindigkeit* and the *Negativen Größen*, apparently because their frontispieces indeed contain no indicators, although faculty records are clear in attributing to both writings the function of advertisement (*Werbung*) for students. Steve Naragon considers on the whole seven Kantian *Programmschriften*, accepting the *Entwurf eines Collegii der physischen Geographie* but excluding the *Allgemeine Naturgeschichte* and the *Negativen Größen* (Naragon 2015d). This might be the place, by the way, to note that Naragon uses for Kant's *Programmschriften* the English syntagm, "lecture announcement," which translates the German *Vorlesungsankündigung*, whose meaning I have explained above.

It remains to be said that in 1770 Minister Carl Joseph Maximilian von Fürst und Cupferberg – then the *Obercurator sämtlicher preußischer Universitäten* – issued for Königsberg students a guide, the *Methodologische Anweisungen für die Studirenden in allen 4 Facultaeten* (AA 25: lxxx–lxxxii; Oberhausen and Pozzo 1999: xxix–xxxiii), according to which all courses of the philosophical faculty were prerequisites for advancing to any other faculty, although one could also obtain an M. A. and, later, the *venia legendi* in any discipline taught in that faculty. In the guide, each of the four faculties of philosophy, medicine, law, and theology received an overview followed by details about the courses to be taken. Kant adapted to the prescribed "Partition of the Sciences during the Academic Years." He taught philosophical encyclopedia, logic, and aesthetics (in the sense of space and time in the *Dissertatio* and the first *Critique* – Pozzo 2001: 233) for students of the very first term, while metaphysics was planned in the second term of the freshman year.[2]

1° semester.
  I. Linguae, ancient and living.
     α) Latin, Greek, Oriental languages together with elementary courses and hermeneutical exercises.
     β) Living languages: German, French, Italian.
  II. Philosophy
     a) Philosophical and general encyclopedia.
     b) Logic.

---

[2] On Kant's understanding of aesthetics before 1781, see Hohenegger 2004: 185 and Hohenegger 2014: 538.

c) Aesthetics.
III. Mathesis.
   a) Mathematical encyclopedia.
   b) Mathesis pura.
IV. Historia.
   a) Theory of history and biography.
   b) Historia litteraria.
   c) Historia universalis.
V. Economics and political science.
   a) Encyclopedia of all economic, political, and financial sciences.
   b) System of these sciences.

2° semester.
   I. Philology, languages, and beautiful sciences.
      a) Theory of beautiful sciences and arts.
      b) Archeology and knowledge of the ancient world.
   II. Philosophy.
      a) Metaphysica.
   III. Mathesis.
      a) Analysis finitorum et infinitorum.
   IV. History.
      a) History of European empires and states.
      b) Diplomatics.
   V. Economical-political sciences.
      a) Theory of agriculture in its completeness.[3]

2 Kant's *durchschossenes Exemplar*

In his logic lectures, Kant used an interleaved desk-copy of Georg Friedrich Meier's *Auszug aus der Vernunftlehre* (Meier 1752b). In fact, Kant adopted Meier for his logic lectures for about forty years. From the summer term 1756 to the summer term of 1796, Kant used his copy of the *Auszug*, in which he wrote the *Reflexionen über die Logik* that were transcribed and edited by Erich Adickes in volume 16 of *Kant's gesammelte Schriften*. In the summer term 1755 and in the winter term 1755/56, however, Kant used Meier's unabridged *Vernunftlehre* (Meier 1752a; Conrad

---
[3] Oberhausen and Pozzo 1999: xxxii–xxxiii.

1994: 46–8). Establishing timelines represents a major task. Elfriede Conrad for instance, has proven that the whole system constructed by Adickes on the basis of "position identifiers" for the dating of every reflection noted by Kant in the pages of his copy of Meier's *Auszug aus der Vernunftlehre* should be postponed by about twelve months (Conrad 1994: 71, 146–54). In fact, Kant began to read Meier's *Auszug* in the winter term of 1756/57 and not, as assumed by Adickes, in the winter term of 1755/56. For many years Norbert Hinske has been pointing out the considerable problems connected to Kant's logic corpus, divided as it is into reflections, notebooks, a few short publications (*Nachricht* and *Spitzfindigkeit*) and the printed handbook edited by Gottlob Benjamin Jäsche, *Immanuel Kants Logik* (Jäsche 1800), together with the corresponding sections of the *Critique of Pure Reason* (Hinske 1995: xcii).

It is not at all surprising, then, that Kant's own logic writings as well as the *Critique* were influenced by Meier, which is evident already from the terminology (Hinske 1998; Vázquez-Lobeiras 1998; Pozzo 2000; Vázquez-Lobeiras 2001). So too, one finds in Kant's *Reflexionen über die Logik* and *Logiknachschriften* elaborations of some of the fundamental issues addressed by Meier, such as the analysis of prejudices and the articulation of the conditions for the constitution of a horizon. Of course, other philosophers of the *Aufklärung* also discussed such matters, but it is Meier's texts that provide the point of departure for Kant. In this context, Locke's philosophy plays an especially important role, for Meier did indeed serve as mediator between Locke and Kant. Meier not only knew Locke well and appealed to his theories in his writings. He went as far as to acknowledge his debt to Locke's "logic" (*Vernunftlehre*) in the preface to the *Vernunftlehre* (Meier 1752a: *2v). The question is open, however, about what exactly Meier understood under "Logic," which could have been both the *Essay concerning Human Understanding* and *Of the Conduct of the Understanding* (Pozzo 2000: 90, 106). Meier also helped to introduce Lockean issues such as the "extent of human knowledge" and the "degrees of assent" (*Essay*, Book IV, Chapters 3 and 16) to the teaching of logic in the German universities; and, most importantly, he made such issues salient for the philosophy of Kant (Boswell and Pozzo in Locke 1996b: xvi–xxiii). What is peculiar to Meier's approach is that instead of limiting himself to formal truth, he includes in his logic all kinds of epistemic truths. Meier deals not only with "dogmatic" and "historical" truths, but also with "merely aesthetic," "merely philosophical," and even "aesthetic-philosophical" truths, which explains Meier's interest for "prejudices" and "horizons" as epistemic tools. Meier's logic is not only inclusive of aesthetics, it is at the same time rhetoric: it is a "science, which deals with the rules of learned cognition and of learned exposition" (AA 16: 1).

There was, in any case, no "overcoming" of Meier by Kant, just as there was no "double life" (Hinske 1998: 30) of Kant as a teacher in Königsberg and as a scientist within the *république des lettres*. There was instead a genuine connection between teaching and research. In fact, if one examines the logic lectures together with the *Critique of Pure Reason*, one sees that many terms adopted or introduced by Meier played a decisive role in shaping the terminology of the first *Critique*. Kant gradually put together a new philosophical language by drawing upon traditional Greek-Latin or Latin terms and recent Germanizations. Both sorts of terms were available to Kant from Meier in great number. One thinks first and foremost of *Vernunftlehre, Egoismus, Genius, Horizont, Logik, logisch, Partei, populär, Vorurteil,* and *rein* (Hinske 1998: 30–39). In moving from an initial adherence to Wolff's mathematical method to his own formulation in the *Critique of Pure Reason*, Kant passes through his remarks upon Meier's notion of a "system" as a connected set of "dogmatic truths" (AA 16: 275 f.).

With regard to the development of eighteenth-century philosophical terminology, one cannot fail to notice a methodological error first committed by the brothers Jakob and Wilhelm Grimm in the *Deutsches Wörterbuch* and kept by the group entrusted with its new elaboration (Grimm 1961). The error consists in attributing to Kant every first occurrence of a German philosophical term, with the consequence of compressing the whole of the eighteenth century to its end, while ignoring the mid-century contribution of the *Aufklärer* and especially of Meier. One example may suffice: when Kant uses the distinction between the "artist of reason" (*Vernunftkünstler*) and the "legislator of reason" (*Gesetzgeber der Vernunft*), he is entirely dependent on Meier. In fact, in the *Nachricht* Kant notes that Meier's effective explanation of the interaction between the "critique and precept of the common understanding" and the "critique and precept of true science" was the reason he adopted his textbooks. Meier makes it possible, says Kant, to cultivate the "more refined and philosophical reason" together with the "common, but active and healthy understanding, the former for contemplative life, the latter for active and civil life" (NEV 2: 310 f.).

Meier's *Vernunftlehre* is usually placed within the tradition of Wolffianism. There is some truth to this view; however, it cannot explain the most striking traits of Meier's *Vernunftlehre*, beginning with its division into *inventio, dispositio, elocutio,* and *exercitatio*, which was part of the rhetorical canon ever since the time of Cicero's apocryphal *Rhetorica ad Herennium*. Meier's logic consists of the following four parts: "Of Philosophical Cognition" (*Von der gelehrten Erkenntnis*); "Of Philosophical Method" (*Von der gelehrten Lehrart*); "Of Philosophical Speech" (*Von dem gelehrten Vortrage*); and "Of the Character of a Philosopher"

(*Von dem Character eines Gelehrten*), *Auszug*, § 7, 2 (AA 16: 72 f.).[4] The model for Meier's revival of Cicero was most probably Johann Heinrich Zopf's *Logica enucleata* (Zopf 1731:)()(1r-v ; Pozzo 2000: 92–7, 187–91).[5]

In his *Logikvorlesungen*, Kant tried to cover the whole of Meier's logic. It is true that he dedicated most of his exposition to the first two parts, which deal respectively with the "invention" and the "method of philosophical cognition," i. e., with what the rhetorical canon called *inventio* and *dispositio*; but it is also true that he never failed to add some remarks on the third and the fourth part, dedicated respectively to "philosophical exposition" and the "character of a philosopher," which correspond to the rhetorical *elocutio* and *exercitatio*. The group of *Reflexionen* 3398a–3488 deals with the third and fourth part (AA 16: 814–69); and it is interesting to see that while these reflections were conspicuously transcribed in the *Logiknachschriften* of the 1770s (AA 24: 294–301, 484–96), their presence progressively decreases in the 1780s and 90s (AA 24: 685–86, 780–4). This is evidently due to Kant's rejection of rhetorical strategies in the *Critique of Pure Reason*, which culminates in the remark that "sophistical assertions ... open up a dialectical battlefield, where each party will keep the upper hand as long as it is allowed to attack, and will certainly defeat that which is compelled to conduct itself merely defensively" (KrV A422 f./B450), Kant's final word on rhetoric came in 1790 with the *Critique of the Power of Judgment*. It was a rejection without appeal:

> Eloquence and well-spokenness (together, rhetoric) belong to beautiful art; but the art of the orator (*ars oratoria*), as the art of using the weakness of people for one's own purposes (however well intentioned or even really good these may be) is not worthy of any **respect** at all. Further, both in Athens and in Rome it reached its highest level only at a time when the state was rushing toward its ruin and a truly patriotic way of thinking had been extinguished. He who has at his command, along with clear insight into the facts, language in all its richness and purity, and who, along with a fruitful imagination capable of presenting his ideas, feels a lively sympathy for the true good, is the *vir bonus dicendi peritus* [the good man, powerful in speech], the speaker without art but full of vigor, as **Cicero** would have him, though he did not himself always remain true to this ideal. (KU 5: 328n)[6]

It remains to be said that Kant also considered issues from the last two parts of Meier's *Vernunftlehre* in other writings. Meier's thoughts on learning and the formation of character are addressed in the *Vorlesung über philosophische Enzyklo-*

---

4 See the correspondence of this division in *Rhetorica ad Herennium* (Book I, Chapter 2).
5 On this reference to Zopf's unnumbered page with sign)()(, see footnote 1 above.
6 For a discussion of Kant's views of oratory, see also Paul Guyer's chapter in this volume.

pädie (PhilEnz 29: 28–30) as well as in the *Anthropology from a Pragmatic Point of View* (Anth 7: 125–229, 283–333). It is also interesting that *Reflexion* 3444 (AA 16: 840), which Kant dedicates to Meier's exposition of *persuasio malo significatu* (AA 16: 473–75) is one of the sources for the already mentioned condemnation of rhetoric in § 53 of the *Critique of the Power of Judgment*.

3 Logic in the modern age

How did a German philosopher writing on logic during the Age of the Enlightenment, in sum, Immanuel Kant, place himself within the tradition of modern logic? Which tradition would he have envisaged? In fact, it was the tradition of both modern Aristotelianism and modern Ciceronianism combined with Ramism, Cartesianism, and Wolffianism. One must refer especially to the renewed apodictic interpretation of Aristotle's prior and posterior *Analytica* as proposed by Jacopo Zabarella. In Protestant Germany, Zabarella's position was considered in opposition to the doxastic understanding of Aristotle's *Topica* disseminated by Rudolf Agricola, Philipp Melanchthon, and Petrus Ramus, while taking into account, of course, the modernization of the theory of ideas, reintroduced by Marsilius Ficinus and developed further by Descartes, Locke, Leibniz, Wolff, Baumgarten, and obviously Meier.

After the rationalistic beginnings of the 1740s and 50s, when he appeared to follow Martin Knutzen and Johann Gottfried Teske in discussing Newton, Leibniz, Wolff, and Crusius, Kant in the 1760s appeared to have turned to empiricism by considering Locke; by reading Rousseau he could have perceived the depths of the human feelings and eventually, having perceived the great light spreading from Hume's writings, after 1769, he would have seen the need of going to work on the project of that "completely new science" he called transcendental philosophy (Prol 4: 279). Returning to Kant within the tradition of modern logic, several approaches are available, each one, however, having advantages and disadvantages. Tonelli took up the problem of finding out motivations and sources from the history of concepts such as organon, canon, discipline, and doctrine which caused Kant to incline for the rather peculiar partitioning of his masterpiece of theoretical philosophy (Tonelli 1994). One could also give up the idea of making recourse to any dating at all, confining oneself to the interpretation of a relevant problematic context of Kant's logic and attacking it with some crucial questions related to us by the tradition of modern logic. The history of the problems (*Problemgeschichte*) justifies some approximation concerning the history of the development (*Entwicklungsgeschichte*), which means it is legitimate to look in Kant's lectures for logic answers to all four questions (*de natura, de subjecto, de fine, de divisione*) asked by Zabarella in his famous tract of 1575, *De natura logicae* (Zabarella 1578). Obviously, this is in no way a neutral procedure, for it means working *per synthesin* rather than *per analysin* (Pozzo 1989; Pozzo 2015).

The notion of "cognitive horizon" (*horizon cognitionis*) is considered by Kant as part of what Meier had called the cognitive perfection of "amplitude" (*vastitas*, *ubertas*), on the assumption that cognition can be measured according to its "wealth" or "poverty" (AA 16: 170–90). Meier prepares the way for Kant's new understanding of this concept with respect to the major critical task of determining the extent and the limits of philosophical cognition. Both begin by considering the whole spectrum of the *angustia eruditae cognitionis*, which originates either from ignorance or from cognitive deficiency of things and their grounds (AA 16: 170 f.) and continues until the end of philosophical cognition is achieved (AA 16: 202). Meier considers ignorance, on the one hand, as complete deficiency of cognition and, on the other hand, as mere availability of historical cognition (AA 16: 171). Relying on Locke, Meier here has in mind exactly the spectrum of experience that, four decades later, Kant thematizes in the "Dialectic of Pure Reason." Significantly, Kant did not write anything on practical, i.e., epistemic logic, but he wrote the "Transcendental Dialectic," which entails a reflection on the *endoxa*. The doctrine of horizon, or of the "circle of vision" (AA 16: 173), first appears as an invitation to exercise a certain caution in the sense of adopting a criterion with respect not only to (1) what we cannot know, but also to (2) what we do not need to know. After a closer inspection, though, the rhetorical context of this theory becomes distinct. In fact, the outer reach of one's horizon has to be in proportion (what the Greeks called *prépon* and the Latins *aptum*) with one's faculties and one's dignity as a human being (Aristotle, *Rhetorica* 1404b2–3).

Kant follows Meier in outlining the four stances one might take with respect to our cognitive horizon. The first, above the horizon (*supra horizontem eruditae cognitionis humanae*), refers to the limits of human cognition (AA 16: 174). However, one should notice that Meier considers the limits of knowledge in general, not the limits of knowledge of experience. One should think especially of religion and cosmology. Not only Kant's distinction between "empirical" and "logical illusion," but also his definition of a "transcendental illusion" (KrV A296 f./B353), which comes out naturally and which, in defiance of "all the warnings of criticism, carries us away beyond the empirical use of the categories, and holds out to us the semblance of extending the *pure understanding*" (KrV A295/B352) are relevant to the history of the impact of this theory. The second stance, beneath the horizon (*infra horizontem eruditae cognitionis humanae*), concerns those rules of scientific ethos, nowadays obvious, that direct our mind when setting up a research project (AA 16: 175 f.). Meier pleads with particular insistence for their respect. He laments the many sins against this rule, the many treatises concerned with trifles. He gives as an imaginative example a philosophical treatise on shoemaking, an enterprise that costs much labor to a scientist yet yields little or no practical results. The third stance, beyond the horizon (*extra horizontem eruditae cognitionis humanae*), centers on the knowing subject (AA 16: 177 f.). This perspective originates from purely pragmatic observations. Granted that not all subjects are equal, the limits of their cognition are likewise unequal. The "professional scholar" (*Gelehrter von Profession*), as opposed to ordinary citizens such as girls, soldiers, and noblemen, are the examples that Meier gives. The analysis of the subject's cognitive ability becomes central in order to determine one's epistemic range. The fourth stance, within the horizon (*intra horizontem eruditae cognitionis humanae*), is the proper one for a philosopher and its goal consists in the legitimation of the research field chosen by the scientist (AA 17: 177).

4 Latin in class

Frederick the Great was a man of clear words. In 1779 he declared Latin was a priority:

> Young people must absolutely learn Latin, I am accepting no excuses. It should only be refined to the most easy and effective method for teaching it to the young people. Even if they become merchants or if they dedicate themselves to something else, whatever their genius might decide, it shall nonetheless always be useful and a time will soon come when they can make good use of it. (Frederick King of Prussia 1913, vol. 8: 313–16; my trans.)

> [Lateinisch müssen die jungen Leute auch absolut lernen, davon gehe ich nicht ab; es muß nur darauf *raffini*ret werden, auf die leichteste und beste Methode, wie es den jungen Leuten am leichtesten beizubringen. Wenn sie auch Kaufleute werden, oder sich zu was andrem widmen, wie es auf das Genie immer ankommt, so ist ihnen doch das allezeit nützlich, und kommt schon eine Zeit, wo sie es anwenden können.]

Let us now look into a number of case studies regarding Kant's use of Latin. The idea is to come up with conclusions about the conditions under which the original and attributed textual flow of Kant's logical lectures was produced.

At the Albertina, as at many universities at the time, it was usual to give the *exercitia disputatoria sive repetitoria* in Latin (Pozzo 1991). Kant was aware of the necessity of using Latin terms in order to give clarity and rigor to his lectures. It was mainly a practical necessity:

> During the eighteenth century, due to often-discussed reasons, a good knowledge of Latin was more necessary than it is today. The bureaucratic German of civil servants contained so

many Latin elements that even educated people would not understand it without knowing this language. (Langel 1909: 43; my trans.)

[Allerdings war im 18. Jahrhundert eine gründliche Kenntnis des Lateinischen aus oft erörterten Gründen nötiger als heute. Selbst das Amtsdeutsch der Behörden etc. enthielt so viele lateinische Elemente, dass der Gebildete nicht ohne diese Sprache auskommen konnte.]

But it was a necessity that nonetheless involved some theoretical aspects, first and foremost because eighteenth-century German philosophical terminology was developed both in German and Latin (Hinske 1986b). One can look also at another interleaved exemplar of Meier's *Auszug aus der Vernunftlehre*, the one originally preserved at the library of the Gymnasium in Stargard, in which the greatest part of the insertions are carefully worded literal translations of Meier into Latin.[7] The *Vorlesungsverzeichnisse* state quite clearly that Kant announced four *repetitoria*, which were to be given in Latin: summer term 1781 "Repetitorium Logices *publice* latino sermone instituet P. Kant"; winter term 1781/82 "Exercitationem disputatorio-repetitoriam latine *publice* h. VII-VIII. instituet P. Kant"; summer term 1782 "Repetitorium Logices latinum *publice* instituet Idem [= P. Kant]"; summer term 1783 "... dd. Merc. et Sat. examinatorium Logices latine instituet Prof. Log. et Metaph. Ord. Kant" (Oberhausen and Pozzo 1999: 458, 466, 472, 486). Apparently, Kant really gave these courses (Arnoldt 1909: 259, 263 f., 268).

Notwithstanding the fact that the usage of offering at least one Latin course stopped as early as winter term 1783/84, the relevance of Kant's Latin terminology is quite clear. The fact is that Kant was not alone in giving Latin courses. We see from the *catalogi* that many other professors taught in Latin. The reason for this behavior was a letter of 4 December 1780 from the *Etats-Ministerium*, i.e., from Minister Karl Abraham von Zedlitz und Leipe, requiring all professors at Königsberg to teach at least one Latin course per term (Arnoldt 1909: 262). This did not remain without consequences for Kant. Any reader of his *Kollegnachschriften* will have noticed that Kant often felt the need to translate his German speech into Latin. Let us just consider Meier's definition of logic in the *Auszug* "Logic is a science that deals with the rules of learned cognition and of learned exposition [*Die Vernunftlehre ist eine Wissenschaft, welche die Regeln der gelehrten Erkentniß und des gelehrten Vortrages abhandelt*]" (AA 16: 1), which Kant takes up in *Reflexion* 1584 as "the science of the general rules of the understanding [*die Wissenschaft von den allgemeinen Regeln des Verstandes*]" (AA 16: 25), and again in the *Critique of Pure Reason* (A53/B77). The interesting thing is that in the Logik Pölitz (dated around 1780–81) Kant himself translates the following into Latin:

---

7 Call number: Biblioteka Narodowa, Warszawa. XVIII.2.17684/Starg.

"logic is about the universal rules of the understanding and of reason [*Logica est regularum vniversalium vsus intellectus et rationis*]" (V-Lo/Pölitz 24: 505). He did this because he was thinking of providing lines to dictate during a *repetitorium*.

When sitting in a *repetitorium*, students usually took notes. The notebook was either their own *Mitschrift* recording the lectures of the *Vorlesung* or an *Abschrift* or a *Nachschrift*, which they might have bought on the market and which was related to a past *Vorlesung*. The idea was to enrich the value of the notebook by adding the new definitions dictated and discussed by the professor during the *repetitorium* "grösstenteils lateinisch," for the most part in Latin (Pozzo 1991: 180 f.). A number of marginalia of the Logik Philippi (to be dated 1770–72) have apparently been added after sitting in a *repetitorium*. One sees, e. g., on page 67 of the manuscript two additions, the second of which is in Latin: "Congruence of cognition with human perfection [*Congruentia cognitionis cum perfectione humana*]" (V-Lo/Philippi 24: 375). In the Logik Busolt (dated around 1789) we do not find marginalia anymore, but we do find a number of passages such as the following one on page 30 of the manuscript. "A horizon is generally a circle that confines all objects, which we can see. Here the horizon is: congruence of cognition with the limits of human cognition [*Ein Horizont ist ueberhaupt ein Kreis, welcher alle Gegenstände begränzt, die wir sehen können. Hier ist der Horizont: Congruentia cognitionis cum terminis perfectionis humanae*]" (V-Lo/Busolt 24: 623). What is interesting is that the same phrase that was a marginalium in the Logik Philippi becomes part of the text in the Logik Busolt. Another example for this procedure of enriching *Nachschriften* by means of *repetitoria* is in the Latin enunciation of the table of the categories in the Logik Pölitz (V-Lo/Pölitz 24: 517; see Hinske 1995).

Zedlitz's letter of 4 December 1780 had intimated professors in Königsberger that from then on "each instructor shall indicate in *Catalogo Lectionum* which of his courses he shall give in Latin [*ein jeder Docens im* Catalogo Lectionum *anzeigen, welche von seinen Collegien er in lateinischer Sprache halten werde*]" (Arnoldt 1909: 262). It was a negative response to the request of being exempted from teaching in Latin that had been submitted by the professors on 20 October 1780:

> The value of the [Latin] language, its necessity for those who want to drink from the sources of the sciences continues under these conditions; and we would find it conscienceless not to push for its *Cultur*, not to praise its utility, not to make it noticeable everywhere; but Latin will become more and more dispensable in comparison to what it was, when we think that then all sciences remained a mystery for the ones who had not learned it. (Arnoldt 1909: 261; my trans.)

> [Der Werth der Sprache, die Nothwendigkeit derselben für denjenigen der aus den Quellen seiner Wißenschaften schöpfen will, dauret unter diesen Umständen zwar fort; und wir würden es für gewißenlos halten, nicht auf *Cultur* derselben zu dringen, den Nutzen davon anzupreisen, und überall merklich zu machen; sie wird aber doch dem größeren Theil entbehrlicher als sie es ehemals war, da Wißenschaften allen denen ein Geheimniß blieben, die die Sprache nicht erlernt hatten.]

Zedlitz's annotation amounts to a rebuttal:

> The excuse about not offering Latin courses is of little value. It instead makes it clear as ever, that young people are being dismissed from high school without Latin and are admitted to the university the way they are. As long as we do not close this impure source, and as long as students, and not instructors, are in command of the method of teaching, and as long as the academic senate makes itself comfortable and good-willing to the wishes of the students while not obeying the orders of the students' government, which it does at its own peril, it then cannot fail to happen that the dignity of the academic senate will be weakened and the academy itself will gradually fall into decline. (Arnoldt 1909: 261; my trans.)

> [Die Entschuldigung wegen Unterbleibens der *Lateini*schen Vorlesungen ist von geringem Werthe. Daraus erhellet deutlicher als jemals, daß die jungen Leuthe ohne *Latein* aus denen Schulen *dimitti*ret, und so wie sie sind angenommen werden. Solang diese unreine Quelle nicht zugestopft wird, und solange nicht die *Docenten* sondern die *Discenten* den Ton der Lehr-Art bestimmen, und der *Academ*ische *Senat* nicht denen Befehlen der Regierung gehorsamen, sondern dem Willen der Studenten sich bequemen und gefällig bezeigen wird, und zu ihrem eigenen Schaden, so kann es nicht fehlen, daß das Ansehen des *Academ*ischen *Senats* muß geschwächt werden und die *Academie* selbst nach und nach in noch mehreren Verfall gerathe.][8]

Kant accepted the prescription, thus implementing a few years in advance the famous passage of the *Aufklärungsschrift* of 1784, in which he paraphrased the will of the King, "Reason as much as you will and about what you will; only obey! [*räsonnirt so viel ihr wollt, und worüber ihr wollt, nur gehorcht!*]" (WA 8: 41), which he was however to counterbalance two years later in *Was heißt, sich im Denken zu orientieren?* (1786), when he called upon his colleagues for a full display in class of their freedom of thought:

> Men of intellectual ability and broadminded disposition! I honor your talents and love your feeling for humanity. But have you thought about what you are doing, and where your attacks on reason will lead? Without doubt you want to preserve inviolate the *freedom to think*; for without that even your own free flights of genius would soon come to an end. Let

---

8 The original document, *Brief des akademischen Senats an das Etats-Ministerium vom 20. Oktober 1780*, is found at Geheimes Staatsarchiv Preußischer Kulturbesitz (GStAPK) Berlin, with the call number: XX. EM 139 b 25 Bd. 9, sheet 112r–166v.

us see what would naturally become of this freedom of thought if a procedure such as you are adopting should get the upper hand. (WDO 8: 144)

One final question: How about Kant losing control of what the compilators of the *Nachschriften* did? How did Latin lines end up into the *Nachschriften*? In the Logik Pölitz, the Latin thesaurus makes up about 1,500 words (Hinske 1995: 577–601). For instance, the following passage from the Logik Dohna-Wundlacken:

> If we consider philosophy as the sum of several sciences, then we want first to view it in terms of the so-called 7 liberal arts: 1. grammar, 2. rhetoric, 3. dialectic, 4. arithmetic, 5. music, 6. geometry, 7. astronomy. It was Rabanus Maurus who (at the time of Charles the Great) made this partition, to the benefit of theology. – At that time, all sciences were divided into a) higher faculty: 1. preservation of blessedness, 2. of freedom and of property, 3. life and health, in general, being; and into b) being better, the lower faculty. (V-Lo/Dohna 24: 699 f.)

> [Wenn wir die Philosophie als Inbegriff mehrerer Wissenschaften ansehen, so wollen wir sie erst auf die sogenannten 7 freien Künste sehen: 1. Grammatik, 2. Rhetorik, 3. Dialektik, 4. Arithmetik, 5. Musik, 6. Geometrie, 7. Astronomie. Diese Einteilung machte Hrabanus Maurus (zur Zeit Karls des Großen) zum Behuf der Theologie. – Man teilte damals alle Wissenschaften in a) obere Fakultät: 1. Erhaltung der Seligkeit, 2. der Freiheit und des Eigentums, 3. Leben und Gesundheit, überhaupt das *esse*; b) *melius esse*, die untere.]

Given Kant's otherwise nonexistent interest in medieval philosophy, it is quite likely for the quote above to be an editorial insertion. For it was quite common that professional scribes enriched the text of lectures with quotes from learned books, when they were sure there was some demand on the part of the buyers. For another example of Kant losing control of the text of his lectures, one might consider the discrepancy between the appreciative remarks on China and Japan being secluded from all contacts with Europeans in *Toward Perpetual Peace* (ZeF 5: 359) and his apparent endorsement of the plan of La Pérouse of displaying European power against China and Japan by invading Taiwan, which had been placed into one of the *Nachschriften* edited and published by Johann Jakob Wilhelm Vollmer in his *Kants physische Geographie* (1801) (Pozzo 1988).

5 Conclusion

Let me conclude by raising a rather crude question. When Kant started to work on the *Critique of Pure Reason*, did he want to write a textbook for logic, or one for metaphysics? The correct answer to this question lies probably in the middle. One could say that he might have wanted to write a textbook that could be used in both logic and metaphysical courses. Unlike Conrad (1994: 29 f.), I think there is no evidence that can exclude the hypothesis that Kant thought of reading from (a version of) the *Critique* at his own university. My conviction is based on the following argument:

(1) According to the *Studienführer* of 1770 quoted above, the program for the first semester included philosophical and general encyclopedia, logic, and aesthetics, while that for the second semester included only metaphysics. Given that Kant used Feder's *Grundriss der philosophischen Wissenschaften* (Feder 1769a) for the first part of a course on philosophical and general encyclopedia, it is amazing that every one of the remaining courses, namely aesthetics (as theory of space and time), logic, and metaphysics finds a corresponding, ample, exposition in the *Critique*.

(2) Although Kant never referred to the *Critique* as a handbook for aesthetics, logic, and metaphysics, at a certain point things actually took that direction. Despite the fact that the aged Kant no longer seemed interested in the enterprise, his disciple Karl Ludwig Poerschke actually used the *Critique* as a textbook for aesthetics, logic, and metaphysics. An examination of the *Vorlesungsverzeichnisse*, shows that three times, in the summer of 1788, in the winter of 1788/89 and in the summer of 1795, Poerschke announced courses upon "Librum Viri Excellentissimi Kant, Critic der reinen Vernunft" (Oberhausen and Pozzo 1999: 547, 554, 630).

(3) Considering finally the "Introduction: Idea of a Transcendental Logic" (KrV A50–64/B74–88), one can argue that on the basis of the number of its pages, its objective, its propaedeutic argumentation level, and especially its being "externally tacked on" to the "Analytic" (Kemp Smith 1962: 167) this section fulfills all the requirements that a *Programmschrift* needs to meet. In fact, the "Introduction" counts a total of 19,799 strokes. One sees, then, its being in the middle of the *Optimismus*, which counts 15,728 strokes and the *Nachricht*, which counts 21,646 strokes (Lee and Sgarbi 2012: xv–xvi). This matter of fact is the further proof of the process of composition of the *Critique* as a set of layers. Especially, it gives the quite substantial information that in the 1770s Kant had indeed thought of lecturing at Königsberg on the book he was working on, namely the *Critique* itself, which apparently was originally structured in close proximity to circulating textbooks on logic and metaphysics such as, e. g., Feder's *Logik und Metaphysik* (Feder 1769b), which Kant knew well.

Things eventually did not take this course, and the "Introduction" did not appear first as a *Programmschrift*. It is important to consider, however, that for a certain number of years Kant's intention was that of writing the *Critique of Pure Reason* as an aesthetics, logic, and metaphysics textbook for students (Pozzo 1998). Things did not go that way either. It is apparent, however, that Kant continued to toy with the idea, for the *Prolegomena* is very much concerned with the issue, and the notion of a textbook on metaphysics continued to be in the works during the 1790s.

The place of science in a setting profoundly dominated by institutional constraints such as Königsberg during the 148 semesters documented by the *Vorlesungsverzeichnisse* (Oberhausen and Pozzo 1999), i.e., between summer term 1720 and winter term 1803/04, is impressive, indeed at times surprising; it is likewise surprising that most scholars have overlooked this fact. The framework might seem obsolete, but it nonetheless corresponds to the peculiar approach of the *Aufklärung*, whose impact would never have materialized without the network of regional universities such as Königsberg. Kant's *Logikvorlesungen* did not come just out of the blue. The question that is left is, then, what was the relation between a university's institutional constraints, which gave the framework for what Kant called the "private" use of reason, and the "public" creativity of its professors? Such a question is not rhetorical, and the answers that cite scholasticism, pedantism, or servilism are unsatisfactory. This chapter has given an initial answer to this question on the basis of sources that to date scholars have hardly considered.

III Moral Philosophy

Chapter 7
The Supreme Principle of Morality

Oliver Sensen

How do Kant's lectures on moral philosophy cast light on his ethical views and their development? Readers of the lectures enjoy their accessible style, Kant's more elaborate explanations, references to the context which informed Kant's discussions, as well as his views on topics that he does not discuss in his published writings (Naragon 2015a). In addition, the lectures also help us trace the development of his ethics. Starting in the 1760s, Kant used Baumgarten's *Initia* and *Ethica* as the textbooks for his lectures (Stark 2004: 386–9). While Kant's discussions of the topics that relate to the *Ethica* change less dramatically over time, his views on the *Initia* part undergo a radical transformation. In the lectures before the *Groundwork* – the Herder notes as well as a set of thirteen notes, such as Collins and Kaehler – Kant does not yet display the concept of autonomy, which makes it doubtful that he had found the solution to his long-standing problem of moral obligation, and he did not yet have the conception of respect for the moral law as the proper moral motivation.

In this chapter I shall focus on the development of Kant's views on the supreme principle of morality. I shall argue that Kant held some of the positions very early on, while he displays others only starting with the *Groundwork* in 1785. In order to distinguish what changed, and what stayed the same, I shall look at three different aspects of the supreme principle: the content of the moral principle (Section 2), its source (Section 3), and the proper motivation to follow it (Section 4). But I shall start with a brief characterization of the lectures on ethics themselves (Section 1).

1 Kant's lectures on ethics

Kant lectured from 1755 to 1796 (Stark 2004: 380–5), and frequently about moral philosophy (for a list, see Arnoldt 1909: 173 ff. and Naragon 2015b). One can trace basic information of about 25 sets of lecture notes in moral philosophy (Stark 2004: 376–9; Naragon 2015c). These are notes handwritten by students. The fluency with which they are written, and the dates by which they are signed, suggest that they were mostly composed after the lecture, at home (Lehmann 1979: 1050; Stark 2004: 392, 400 f.). One exception might be the Herder notes on moral philosophy. Many of these notes were not taken by the students themselves, but merely copied from a prepared booklet one could buy (Stark 2004: 392–401).

The lecture notes were therefore not written by Kant himself, and have to be treated with caution if one wants to ascribe one of their statements to Kant (for a list of mistakes in the Mrongovius II notes, see Timmermann 2015). It is also not fully clear how carefully Kant himself prepared these lectures, and how he delivered them. There is some indication that he delivered the ethics lectures freely, merely from an outline on a small piece of paper (Jachmann 1993: 116 f.). But he might also have used a specially prepared booklet (Stark 2004: 389–92; see also Lehmann 1979: 1040 n. 9). So there is much that we do not know about these lecture notes, and one should treat them with caution as an authoritative statement of Kant's views. But with this in mind they give us a larger picture of Kant's views (the longer notes record around 80 lectures of 45 minutes length; see Stark 2004: 398), Kant as a person,[1] and especially the development of his moral philosophy.

The lectures are valuable for understanding the development of Kant's moral philosophy because Kant used the same textbooks for his classes from the early 1760s to 1794 (Lehmann 1979: 1047; Stark 2004: 388 f.): Alexander Gottlieb Baumgarten's (1714–1762) *Initia philosophiae practicae primae* (*Introduction to Practical First Philosophy*), and *Ethica philosophica* (*Philosophical Ethics*). The lectures therefore record Kant's different reactions to the same context over time.

In addition, some of the lectures are from a period in which Kant did not publish on moral philosophy. The sets of notes, which are still accessible, roughly fall into four groups. The notes by Johann Gottfried Herder were recorded some time between the summer of 1762 and November 1764 (Schwaiger 2000: 180–3). They are so invaluable because they are the only notes on moral philosophy from the time before Kant became a professor (Stark 2004: 375 f.).[2] The second group consists of about thirteen sets of notes which are largely identical, and might be copies of one and the same text (Lehmann 1979: 1041; Stark 2004: 392–401). Part of this group are the notes by Collins and Kaehler, but also the three sets of notes by Brauer, Kutzner, and Mrongovius I, which became the basis for Paul Menzer's 1924 edition of the lectures, and which were later translated into English by Louis Infield. The notes fall roughly in the time between 1775 and 1785. The Kaehler notes are now considered to be the most authentic representation of Kant's

---

[1] Descriptions of what Kant was like as a lecturer can be found in Jachmann 1993: 116–20; Stark 1995; Schneewind 1997; and Kuehn 2001a: 105–10, 125, 129–34, 158–63, 204–18.
[2] On the Herder notes, see Lehmann 1979: 1046–50; Stark 2004: 375 f.; and Frierson 2015.

lectures during that time, but this does not mean that they are not copies of an earlier text (Stark 2004: 392–401).³

A third period of Kant's lecturing is recorded by the Mrongovius II notes (AA 29: 597–642). Christoph Coelestin Mrongovius wrote these in 1784/85, the time when the *Groundwork* was already in print (on the notes, see Timmermann 2015). Finally, notes by Johann Friedrich Vigilantius, a member of Kant's social circle, and his legal advisor, give insight into Kant's position around 1793/94, the time between the *Critique of Practical Reason* (1788), and the *Metaphysics of Morals* (1797).

I shall focus on the Herder and Collins notes in particular, in order to compare Kant's views on the supreme principle of morality with his mature philosophy as it is stated in the *Groundwork* and *Critique of Practical Reason*.

2 The content of the supreme principle

The main question regarding the development of Kant's moral philosophy is: since when did he think of the supreme principle of morality as a categorical imperative? I shall argue that one will get very different answers if one looks at (1) the content of the moral law or what the law demands, (2) its source or where it comes from, and (3) the proper moral motivation, or what impels one to follow it. These changes take place in the part of Kant's lectures that relate to Baumgarten's *Initia*. There is less change over time in the parts of Kant's lectures that relate to Baumgarten's *Ethica* (Kuehn 2015). I shall start with the content of the moral law.

2.1 The mature view on the content of the law

What is the mature view of the moral principle we are tracking here? In the *Groundwork* Kant introduces the Categorical Imperative as the "supreme principle of morality" (GMS 4: 392). The imperative runs: "*act only in accordance with that maxim through which you can at the same time will that it become a universal law*" (GMS 4: 421). In morality, there are two requirements connected with following the law. On the one hand, one should act in accordance with the law, or do what is right. In addition, one should follow the law not out of self-interest, advantage, or because it would yield a pleasant sensation. Instead one should do the right

---

[3] I here leave out the Powalski notes, which might be from the early 1770s; see Lehmann 1979: 1043 f.; and Schwaiger 2000: 185–8.

thing simply because it is right, out of respect for the moral law: "For, in the case of what is to be morally good it is not enough that it *conform* with the moral law but it must also be done *for the sake of the law*" (GMS 4: 390).

These two requirements are separate. If one just conforms to the moral law, but out of self-interested reasons, the action would have legality, but not morality (KpV 5: 71 f.). But the two requirements are united in the Formula of Autonomy, which runs: "act only *so that the will could regard itself as at the same time giving universal law through its maxim*" (GMS 4: 434). The purpose of this formula is "to indicate in the imperative itself the renunciation of all interest, in volition from duty, by means of some determination the imperative contains" (GMS 4: 431). The formula states the motivational requirement in the content of what one should do, "just because of the idea of giving universal law *it is based on no interest* and therefore, among all possible imperatives, can alone be *unconditional*" (GMS 4: 432). The content of the moral law is therefore that one should be able to will that one's maxim could become a universal law.

This claim admits of different interpretations, and is often rejected as unworkable. What is the idea Kant wants to express? He explains that the moral law wants to rule out cases in which one makes an exception *to a rule one holds to be objectively necessary*: "we would find a contradiction in our own will, namely that a certain principle be objectively necessary as a universal law and yet subjectively not hold universally but allow exceptions" (GMS 4: 424). It is not a contradiction as such that is immoral – otherwise a mistake on a math test would be immoral. Rather the contradiction is supposed to be a way of finding out whether one wants to make an exception for oneself. The immoral quality is trying to be a free-rider. However, it is also not any exception that will be immoral. Otherwise it would be immoral to play tennis at 10 AM on Sundays while one's neighbors are at church (Herman 1993: 138). Here too one tries to make an exception. Rather what is immoral, is if one tries to be a free-rider to a rule one recognizes as 'objectively necessary'.

How can one find out which rules are objectively necessary? Kant distinguishes two kinds of contradiction in order to establish which rules are morally necessary: a contradiction in the will, and a contradiction in conception (GMS 4: 424). I shall focus on duties towards others. A contradiction in the will depends, on the one hand, on the nature of willing as such: "Whoever wills the end also wills (insofar as reason has decisive influence on his actions) the indispensably necessary means to it that are within his power" (GMS 4: 417). But, on the other, each derivation of concrete duties also depends on anthropological knowledge (GMS 4: 412). If human beings were autarkic and indestructible, there would be no need to help others. But since human beings are finite, and will need help at some point, there would be a contradiction in one's will if not-helping were to become a universal law. One wills help and would not get help. As a result, one recognizes helping others as an objectively necessary law, given anthropological knowledge.

Similarly, one does not hold killing, stealing, and lying to be objectively necessary, but its opposite. This is based on anthropological knowledge and a contradiction in conception. As a vulnerable being, one needs to be alive to do anything at all, and any state that can guarantee justice and culture is based on contracts. If these negative conditions were not met, and people were killed and lied to, they would be living in the state of nature (MS 6: 306–12), and one could not hope to achieve anything at all. One recognizes laws of not killing, stealing, lying, etc. as objectively necessary, given the kind of beings we are. To make an exception to these rules without overriding reason would be immoral. (For a defense of this interpretation, see Sensen 2014.)

An idea related to universality is the Formula of Humanity and its demand: "*So act that you use humanity, whether in your own person or in the person of any other, always at the same time as an end, never merely as a means*" (GMS 4: 429). Kant holds this formula to be "tantamount" and "at bottom the same" (GMS 4: 437 f.) as the main formulation of the moral law. The reason is that refraining from making an exception for oneself means to regard others as equally important (KpV 5: 87). In not making an exception but following universal law one thereby does not adopt a maxim of "exalting oneself above others" (MS 6: 450), which is the main requirement of respecting others and not treating them as mere means.

In sum: in his mature moral theory, Kant believes that there is one supreme moral principle. Its content is universality, i. e., that one does not make an exception to a rule one recognizes as objectively necessary for beings like us. Following this requirement is the same as not exalting oneself above others, not thinking of oneself as something better, but as respecting others as equals. We will see that the main idea was there all along, but that Kant clarified and sharpened it over time.

2.2 The content of the moral law in Kant's early ethics

It is not clear that we have a text that fully represents Kant's early view on ethics. The Herder lecture notes are elliptical, and only seem to record what was of interest to Herder himself (Lehmann 1979: 1046, 1048). Therefore I will supplement the discussion in Herder with three other texts. The earliest text on moral philosophy is a brief section in the prize essay (UD) that raises the moral question. Kant's first fuller answer seems to be in the *Observations on the Feeling of the Beautiful and Sublime*. However, there Kant seems to address morality from an aesthetic perspective (Schmucker 1961: 9). Kant later made notes on his *Observations*, but these are not one coherent text, and the exact order in which the notes were taken is not known (Guyer 2012: 78 n. 3). As always, the lectures seem more elaborate and explain more fully Kant's views, so I will try to paint a picture on the content of morality in these early sources.

From his early writings onwards Kant looks out for one supreme principle: "the supreme law of morality is: act according to your moral nature" (V-PP/Herder 27: 8), or "Act according to *your moral feeling!*" (V-PP/Herder 27: 16). Kant specifies this feeling as the **"feeling of the beauty and the dignity of human nature"** (GSE 2: 217).[4] This feeling has two parts:

> The first is a ground of universal affection, the second of universal respect, and if this feeling had the greatest perfection in any human heart then this human being would certainly love and value even himself, but only in so far as he is one among all to whom his widespread and noble feeling extends itself. (GSE 2: 217)

The first part refers to positive duties of beneficence. One has a direct feeling for the well-being of others:

> Do I have, not merely a self-interested feeling, but also a disinterested feeling of concern for others? Yes – the weal and woe of another touches us directly: the mere happiness of another pleases us in the telling: even that of fictional persons whose tale we know of, or in distant ages .... (V-PP/Herder 27: 3)

Already in his early ethics, Kant understands morality as being centrally opposed to self-interested feelings. Morality combats selfishness (KpV 5: 72). And already in his early ethics does he think this is possible because of a more impartial standpoint: "only in so far as he is one among all" (GSE 2: 217). In addition, as these quotes also bring out, Kant aims for a universality, that ideally one should be concerned about the well-being of *all* others (see also Frierson 2012). This early conception of ethics is not the same as the mature conception, especially since Kant grounds morality in feelings and not in reason, but he is aiming at a similar content.

The similarities become stronger if one looks at the second aspect of the moral principle, the feeling for the dignity of human nature, or the respect one should have for others. In his early conception, morality is by no means

---

[4] In the Herder notes Kant talks about moral feelings that are "beautiful or sublime" (V-PP/Herder 27: 5), albeit in a slightly different meaning. On Kant's pre-Critical and Critical notions of the sublime, see Clewis 2009: 32–55 and 56–125.

exhausted by the disinterested feeling for another's well-being: "The universal affection is a ground for participating in his ill-fortune, but at the same time it is also a ground of justice" (GSE 2: 216). Examples of these are telling the truth and respecting property: "truthfulness does ... depend ... on the sense of justice" (BGSE 20: 156), and "in society all mine and thine depends on contracts, yet these on keeping one's word" (BGSE 20: 153). In some passages this sense of justice is said to depend on a feeling, but in others the formulation comes very close to Kant's mature views. For the first, consider the following passage: "This sense ... through which one judges what is categorically good (not useful) ... through supposing the same action in others; if a contradiction and contrast then arises, it displeases; if harmony and unison arise, they please" (BGSE 20: 156). In this passage one's moral judgment depends on a feeling of approval or disapproval. But in another note on property Kant comes much closer to the mature formulation: "That will must be good which does not cancel itself out if it is taken universally and reciprocally" (BGSE 20: 67; Guyer 2012: 80–5). This formulation sounds almost like Kant's contradiction in conception test. The point that Kant uses this formulation in relation to property suggests that he developed his moral formula from legal philosophy.[5]

The previous shows how Kant's early views are already very close to the mature philosophy with regard to the content of the moral principle. But there are of course important differences. I have not said anything about duties towards self, but even in regard to lying Kant does not have his full mature view. For instance, he does not have the absolute prohibition on lying for which he argues later (MS 6: 429). "A white lie ... breaches no *obligation*" and even a regular lie might be excusable if one can avoid great evil (V-PP/Herder 27: 62). In addition, Kant presents many justifications next to each other, and he does not seem to have settled on the one mature view:

> Lying is simply too restricted, as an injury to the other; as untruth, it already has an immediately abhorrent quality, for (a) this most *trenchantly* separates human society, of which truth is the bond; *truth* is simply lost, and with it, all the happiness of mankind; everything puts on a mask, and every indication of civility becomes a deceit; we make use of other men to *our own* best advantage. (V-PP/Herder 27: 59)

Lying provokes an immediate disapproval, it is against the happiness of mankind, and one uses others as mere means. Kant can be read as a sentimentalist, utilitarian, and the mature Kant in one sentence. Nonetheless, one finds the views that there is one supreme principle, that one should not be self-interested, but act on a

---

5 In a different context, this view has been suggested to me by Reinhard Brandt.

universal law, and (thereby) not treat others as mere means at the very beginning of Kant's ethical writings. Therefore it is not surprising, that the content can also be found, now more pronounced, in the Collins lectures.

2.3 The content of the moral law in Collins

Given that Kant had envisioned the content of morality early on, it is not surprising that one can find an even closer formulation of the moral principle in the lectures since 1775. Kant now states more emphatically that there can only be one moral principle (V-Mo/Collins 27: 266), and he states the requirement in that "laws ought to be valid universally" (V-Mo/Collins 27: 263). He also presents the derivation of duties in almost the same terms as he will later give in the *Groundwork*. In examining whether one's proposed action is morally permissible, "I examine by the understanding whether the intention[6] of the action is so constituted that it could be a universal rule" (V-Mo/Mron 27: 1427). The question therefore is: "What becomes of the action if it is taken universally?" (V-Mo/Mron 27: 1428). Kant presents a version of the contradiction in conception test, when he says that "lying, in order to obtain a large estate, becomes impossible to achieve if practiced universally, since everyone knows the aim already" (V-Mo/Mron 27: 1428). And he formulates it more explicitly in saying: "An immoral action, therefore, is one whose intention abolishes and destroys itself if it is made into a universal rule" (V-Mo/Mron 27: 1428). Kant also gives a parallel to the contradiction in the will test when he talks about a duty of benevolence. There one examines "whether it would also be my choice [*Willkür*], in such need, that another should be equally indifferent to me; if I then find that it does not accord with my choice, then the action itself is not moral" (V-Mo/Mron 27: 1427). If one replaces the more subjective sounding "choice" with the more objective "will," one gets an early version of the contradiction in the will test.

In one sense, the formulation of the moral test might even be more explicit and helpful than it is in the *Groundwork*. The mature formulation gives the impression that one should take any maxim, attribute it to everyone else, and see if a contradiction would occur. It is then, however, not clear how specific the maxim can be. If the maxim is to play tennis at 10 AM on Sunday mornings, the test would rule out too much. It is also not clear what would be *morally* wrong about a failed maxim: Is it problematic that a contradiction would occur, or that an institution

---

[6] Kant does not yet formulate the test in terms of maxims. A maxim at this stage is a subjective law one wants to hide from others (V-Mo/Mron 27: 1427); see Kuehn 2015.

would vanish? In the first case, a contradiction on a logic test would be immoral, on the second it would be immoral – to use Brentano's example – to refuse a bribe, since then the institution of bribery would vanish (Brentano 2009: 50).

All of these problems can be avoided, and Kant's test can be made to work, if one includes that it is not any contradiction that counts, but only the ones that appear if one tries to make an exception to a rule one recognizes as *objectively necessary* (GMS 4: 424). But this requires that one has a way of identifying which rules are objectively necessary, and Kant points to anthropological knowledge for that. In the lecture notes from 1775 onwards, Kant is more explicit that this additional step is required. There he says that "rules whereby my actions hold good universally" are "derived from the universal ends of mankind" (V-Mo/Collins 27: 258). One needs anthropological knowledge to see which rules – such as telling the truth and helping others – should hold universally. It is immoral to make an exception to *those* rules, and the contradiction tests are supposed to detect whether one aims to make that exception.

In these lecture notes Kant is also closer to his mature philosophy by stating that moral rules command unconditionally, and he now regards not-lying as such a demand without exception. A moral law "commands categorically and absolutely 'You shall not lie'" (V-Mo/Collins 27: 247). Kant also employs the idea of respect for humanity, when, for instance, he rules out suicide and harming oneself for profit. In that case one "dishonors humanity in one's own person" in that "humanity is subordinated to animal nature" (V-Mo/Mron 27: 1427 f.). Here too, Kant is more explicit than in his mature philosophy in that he rules out this kind of intention because it would be a *contradiction* (MS 6: 420). Instead of governing itself, "my understanding is under the sway of animal impulse; and if so, I contradict myself when I demand to have rights of humanity" (V-Mo/Mron 27: 1428).

To sum up: Regarding the content of the moral principle, Kant's moral philosophy did not change drastically. From his earliest writings, Kant held that there is one supreme moral principle, that the essence of morality lies in not being self-interested, and he even formulates it in terms of universality and contradictions that would occur if an immoral intention were held by everyone. While at the beginning these thoughts were also mixed with others, Kant's formulations become more focused and specific over time. The real development in his moral philosophy took place regarding the source of the moral principle as well as moral motivation.

3 The source of the moral principle

While much of the content of Kant's mature ethical thought can be found early on, there is a drastic change in his views on the source of the moral law. In his earliest writings Kant is still under the influence of "Hutcheson and others" (UD 2: 300), and he regards morality as grounded in feeling. Kant radically changes his view with the Inaugural Dissertation of 1770, when he proclaims that first moral principles are "only cognized by the pure understanding" (MSI 2: 396). The mature view can already be found in the Collins lectures.

3.1 The mature view on the source of the moral principle

Kant argues that the Categorical Imperative must have its origin in pure reason. This is because as a *categorical* imperative, the demand is necessarily and universally valid: "This principle … is not borrowed from experience; … because of its universality … so that the principle must arise from pure reason" (GMS 4: 431). Experience can never yield necessity or strict universality. Only an a priori rule can have these features: "Necessity and strict universality are … secure indications of an *a priori* cognition" (KrV B4). The claim that the moral law must originate in one's own reason does not mean that it is a product of one's reasoning as one is aware in introspection. For otherwise "the one imposing obligation … could always release the one put under obligation …, so that (if both are one and the same subject) he would not be bound at all to a duty he lays upon himself" (MS 6: 417). Rather the moral law is a pre-conscious demand of one's own pure reason: "Pure reason … gives (to the human being) a universal law which we call the *moral law*" (KpV 5: 31). The moral law is therefore constitutive of pure reason. It describes how reason necessarily functions. (For a fuller defense of this interpretation, see Sensen 2013.)

Kant does not believe that the principle is innate, in the sense that it is given by God, nor – one might add – a product of evolution. Because in that case the law would not be strictly necessary, but a different law could have become innate (KrV B167 f.). Instead, the law is "initially acquired" (ÜE 8: 222), which means that "reason … with complete spontaneity … makes its own order according to ideas … according to which it even declares actions to be necessary" (KrV A548/B576). Kant calls this origin of the moral law "autonomy" and defines it as the "*lawgiving of its own* on the part of pure and, as such, practical reason" (KpV 5: 33).

3.2 The source of the moral law in Kant's early writings

In his early writings on moral philosophy, Kant argues that morality is based on a feeling. He even goes so far to argue that it is "a surer guide in morality than reason is, and the good man's feeling [is] more reliable than the reason that makes palpable errors in its inferences" (V-PP/Herder 27: 45). This feeling is a pleasure or displeasure one feels in anticipating an action: "Pleasure in free actions directly is called moral feeling" (V-PP/Herder 27: 4). The feeling is "unanalyzable, basic, the ground of conscience" (V-PP/Herder 27: 5). Everyone has this feeling, and it pushes in the same direction for everyone: "We have a moral feeling, which is (1) universal (2) unequivocal." (V-PP/Herder 27: 4) The feeling is, however, not the same as compassion and sympathy, which are "weak and ... always blind" (GSE 2: 215 f.). For instance, one might be moved to help someone in need, but this can make one blind for one's stricter duty of justice. Or one could be moved by the immediate suffering of a child, but indifferent to the much larger number of casualties in a distant war. The proper moral feeling regards a higher standpoint, which is more universal, but also colder (GSE 2: 216), and refers to an immediate approval or disapproval out of a feeling of pleasure or displeasure.

As such the moral feeling is a natural feeling and contrasted with artificial feelings such as shame which differ from society to society and are caused by education. "The natural feeling here is opposed to the artificial" (V-PP/Herder 27: 8). If one can distinguish those two feelings, one's moral feeling is a sure guide: "My reason can err; my moral feeling, only when I uphold custom before natural feeling; but in that case it is merely implicit reason; and my final yardstick still remains moral feeling" (V-PP/Herder 27: 8).

From the perspective of the agent, this feeling is all there is. It might have a deeper source, e. g., it might be implanted by God, but the agent must rely on his feeling: "It is probable that, since God by His *arbitrium*, is the ground of all things, this is also the case here" (V-PP/Herder 27: 9). But one has to "derive all obligations from within" and "from the nature of the case" (V-PP/Herder 27: 8). Kant rejects voluntarism, according to which God can change morality at will: "In Him there is already morality, therefore, and so His choice is not the ground" (V-PP/Herder 27: 10). The individual has to rely on his moral feeling. But although Kant holds that feeling is more reliable than reason, he notices problems that later lead to arguments against feelings as the foundation of morality. He admits, for instance, that "not all have it in the same degree" and that it is "seldom so great that it inspires active exertions" (V-PP/Herder 27: 3). Different people have this feeling to a different degree. For some it is stronger, and for others weaker, but it is hardly so great that people act on it. That different individuals have this feeling in varying degrees is one especially important reason why Kant later came to reject it as the ground of morality.

3.3 The source of the moral law in the Collins notes

By the 1770s Kant radically changes his view. He does not ground morality in a feeling any longer, and even argues that it cannot be based on a feeling. Instead, he grounds morality on pure reason, in accordance with his mature views: "the principle of morality has a ground in the understanding, and can be apprehended completely *a priori*" (V-Mo/Collins 27: 254). I shall look at three points: (1) Morality cannot be based on feeling, (2) it must be discovered by the understanding, but (3) it must also originate in one's own reason.

(1) In arguing against his former view that morality is based on feeling, Kant cites some of the same features he had acknowledged earlier. Feelings differ in content and strength. If morality were based on feeling, then different things would be morally right for different people, and not everyone would be obligated to the same extent. If someone had a stronger feeling, he would be more obliged than someone with a weaker emotion. However, we believe morality to be necessary and universal, and this can only be achieved through an a priori moral law.

Let us examine his argument in more detail: morality, according to Kant, rests on universal rules: "For example: You are not to lie" (V-Mo/Collins 27: 254). But since our feelings differ, anyone who does not have this feeling, would not be obligated to tell the truth: "If it rested on the moral feeling, then anyone not possessed of a moral feeling so fine as to produce in him an aversion to lying would be permitted to lie." In order to account for universal laws, therefore, morality cannot rest on feelings, but must reside in reason: "But if it rests on a principle that resides in the understanding, then the injunction is absolute: You are not to lie, whatever the circumstances may be" (V-Mo/Collins 27: 254). The reason is the same as in his mature philosophy (GMS 4: 389; KrV B3 f.). We hold morality to be necessary and universal, and experience cannot deliver that: "those principles which are supposed to be everywhere, always and necessarily valid, cannot be derived from experience, but only from pure reason." Necessity and strict universality are sure signs of an a priori law: "All necessary rules must hold good *a priori*, and hence the principles are intellectual" (V-Mo/Collins 27: 254).

But even if everyone had the same feeling, and the feeling had the same strength, this still would not ground moral laws: "And even if it were possible that we should have a sensation for morality, no rules could be established on this principle" (V-Mo/Collins 27: 275). The reasons are that morality would still be conditioned (KpV 5: 26), and not universal but private: "The moral law, however, commands categorically; so morality cannot be based on a ... moral feeling .... Any feeling has a private validity only" (V-Mo/Collins 27: 275 f.).

(2) But if morality is not based on feelings, this still leaves other options. It could be, for instance, that morality is merely judged, discovered, by the understanding, but that one uses reason[7] to discover a separate moral realm or God's will. Kant holds that the morality must be judged by the understanding: "morality is immediately known through the understanding" (V-Mo/Collins 27: 276; cf. 263). But does this mean that reason merely discovers something that exists independently of reason and feeling, or does it originate in one's reason?[8] For instance, it could be – as Kant said in the Herder notes (cf. V-PP/Herder 27: 9) – that ultimately everything has its ground in God, and therefore also morality. This does not mean that morality would be grounded in an *arbitrary* will. If morality were based on an arbitrary will, then something else could be moral the day after, and morality would not be necessary or universal: "not even the deity is the originator of moral laws, since they have not arisen from choice, but are practically necessary; if they were not so, it might even be the case that lying is a virtue" (V-Mo/Collins 27: 283). On Kant's account, God will act morally because he is perfectly moral, not because he arbitrarily set up morality, "just as God is no originator of the fact that a triangle has three corners" (V-Mo/Collins 27: 283). Instead: "God has commanded it because it is a moral law, and His will coincides with the moral law" (V-Mo/Collins 27: 277).

(3) But it seems to me that Kant wants to hold a stronger view in Collins. It is not just that the understanding discovers morality, but also that it originates in one's own reason. For he also says: "It is thus an utterly pure intellectual principle of pure reason" (V-Mo/Collins 27: 276). One reason for attributing this view to Kant is that already in the Inaugural Dissertation of 1770 he says that morality "is only cognized by the pure understanding and itself belongs to pure philosophy" (MSI, 2: 396), and he had specified this as meaning that "such concepts ... are given by the very nature of the understanding" (MSI, 2: 394). This indicates that reason does not merely discover, but also brings forth morality. In Collins Kant expresses this by saying that morality is internal, "emanating [*fließet*] from the ground of our will" (V-Mo/Collins 27: 252). Kant does say that one does not need God in order to discover moral laws, for "then all peoples would first have to know God before they could have the notion of duties; and thus it would have to follow that all people having no proper conception of God would also have no duties, which

---

[7] In the Collins notes, Kant does not yet draw on his later distinction between reason and understanding; see Kuehn 2015.
[8] I thank Marcus Willaschek for pressing me on this point.

is, however, false. Peoples … recognized the odiousness of lying, without having any proper notion of God" (V-Mo/Collins 27: 277). But he does not merely seem to hold that we discover moral laws, but also that we *make* them: "for the making of moral judgments we have no need for any third being" (V-Mo/Collins 27: 277).

The second reason I believe Kant holds a stronger view in Collins is related to moral obligation. If morality would exist independently of human reason, and reason *merely* discovers it, then one would think that one is obligated because of this external morality. However, Kant argues explicitly that morality is not external. This seems to mean that laws originate in one's own will, "emanating from our own will" (V-Mo/Collins 27: 252):

> Crusius believes that all obligation is related to the will of another … It may indeed seem that in an obligation we are necessitated *per arbitrium alterius*; but in fact I am necessitated by an *arbitrium internum*, not *externum*, and thus by the necessary condition of universal will; hence there is also a universal obligation. (V-Mo/Collins 27: 262; cf. 278)

So, moral obligation originates from one's own pure reason, not an external reality: "The principle of morality is *intellectual internum* [internal to the mind]" (V-Mo/Mron 27: 1426).

The puzzle my reading gives rise to, though, is why Kant does not yet speak about autonomy in the Collins notes. It seems that a view where the moral law has the source in one's own reason, and obliges one, is exactly what Kant means by autonomy (see again, KpV 5: 33). Is it because he does not use the word 'autonomy' yet, or does not think in terms of this notion? Is it that he implicitly believes that there is an external moral reality (e. g., created by God), and our reason merely obliges us to act in accordance with it? Or is it because he does not yet have his mature concept of moral motivation, and that motivation is part of the concept of autonomy? My view is that he includes an aspect of moral motivation within his views on autonomy, and that he did not have his mature view on moral motivation yet. What is Kant's view on moral motivation?

4 Moral motivation

If one can find the elements of the *content* of the supreme moral principle from the very beginning of Kant's writings on ethics, and if one can find key elements of the *source* of the moral principle by the 1770s, one can find his complete mature views on moral *motivation* only from the time of the *Groundwork* (1785) onwards. Kant introduces something new. I shall start with his mature views.

4.1 The mature view on moral motivation

Morality, on Kant's account, does not merely demand that one's action could be willed as a universal law, but also that one perform it from the right moral motivation. "For, in the case of what is to be morally good it is not enough that it *conform* with the moral law but it must also be done *for the sake of the law*" (GMS 4: 390). If one's action were in accordance with the law, but not done simply because it is right, the action would have legality but not morality (KpV 5: 71). The central idea is that pure reason, by itself, can be practical, i.e., bring about actions (KpV 5: 15). It does so by striking down the claims of the inclinations, and by removing this hindrance to action in accordance with the moral law (KpV 5: 73), it is at the same time a positive furthering of the influence of this law (KpV 5: 75). There is a debate whether this is meant that reason has of itself a causal power (Zinkin 2006), or whether the humiliation of the inclination causes a positively felt emotional quality, a feeling of respect, which is needed to counter the inclinations (Goy 2007). Here I shall leave this issue open (but for a suggestion of a compromise, see Sensen 2012). Whether one sees the moral feeling as the influence of reason on one's inclinations, or as itself a distinct positive feeling, both parties can agree that this feeling is caused by reason (KpV 5: 73). More important, from the perspective of the agent, is that he should not have a feeling in mind when he acts – this would be moral fanaticism [*Schwärmerei*] (KpV 5: 84–6) – but rather perform the action simply because it is the morally right thing to do: "What is essential to any moral worth of actions is *that the moral law determine the will immediately*" (KpV 5: 71; cf. GMS 4: 390).

4.2 The early view on moral motivation

It might seem as if Kant had already found his position on moral motivation in the earliest writings on moral philosophy. Even early on Kant distinguishes between actions that are good in virtue of their consequences and those that are good in virtue of their intention, and holds for moral actions "that their value is not to be measured by the results" but ought to be "immediately good (give pleasure)" (V-PP/Herder 27: 4; cf. UD 2: 298). In his *Bemerkungen* or notes in the *Observations* Kant even calls this immediate goodness "categorical" and says that the "categorical necessity of an action does not require so much effort, but merely the application of the matter to the moral feeling" (BGSE 20: 155). So, one might think that all the important elements of Kant's views on moral motivation are there early on. A good will does not weigh the consequences, but has an intention that aims to act on the immediate goodness of an action out of a moral feeling.

Even on this point, there are, of course, already important differences. In his mature philosophy, the moral feeling is not a feeling of pleasure (KpV 5: 77), and is "produced solely by reason" (KpV 5: 76). Inasmuch as it is a feeling at all, it is an esteem for the moral law of one's own reason, and these are important differences which are – despite the similar language – not yet there in the early philosophy. It should also be noted that Kant's early view is not anything special or unusual. Even the sentimentalists, who hold that every action is motivated by a desire, would also hold that the agent should not have this desire (or one's own advantage) in mind when acting. This way, the sentimentalist can make a distinction between selfish and altruistic actions (e. g., Butler 1729, Sermon XI). The important difference is the intention of the agent. Did he have his own pleasure or reward in mind when helping others, or was his intention only to alleviate the suffering of others? Just the fact that helping was (subconsciously) his own desire does not make the action selfish. Although an ocean liner burned coal on its voyage, it does not mean that the purpose or intention of the journey was to burn coal (Feinberg 2008: 522 f.). Kant is not specific enough to clarify whether one could have in mind one's own moral feeling, a certain kind of pleasure and approval of an agent from a universal, impartial standpoint.

However, the crucial difference between his early and mature views on moral motivation is that God and religion play a much larger role in his earlier ethics. Even early on Kant separates between the proper moral motivation and religious motivation:

> Supposing the *arbitrium* of God to be known to me, where is the necessity that I should do it, if I have not already derived the obligation from the nature of the case? God wills it – why should I? He will punish me; ... that is how we obey a despot; in that case the act is no sin, in the strict sense, but politically imprudent; and why does God will it? ... Because I am obligated to it. (V-PP/Herder 27: 9)

One should do the morally right action, simply because it is right (GMS 4: 390). However, as we have seen above, Kant believes that the moral feeling itself is not very efficacious: It is "seldom so great that it inspires active exertions" (V-PP/Herder 27: 3). Kant believes that the moral motive has to be supplemented by religion (Frierson 2015).

> For one who has not wholly fulfilled his obligation, morality is incomplete, if all grounds of obligation are not included, and in that case, the *arbitrium divinum* is a ground of external obligation for our morality. So the *arbitrium divinum* should never be left out, as an external obligating ground; thus our moral perfection becomes incomplete, if it arises solely from inner morality, and is considered without reference to God's *arbitrium*. (V-PP/Herder 27: 10)

On the one hand, religion is part of a whole without which motivation would be incomplete. In addition, religion can help to bring about the moral motive. Kant holds that "a person does not actively *love* another *until he is himself in a state of well-being*" (V-PP/Herder 27: 64).[9] Religion can help one getting into a state in which the moral motive would be strong enough. To bring this about: "consider especially that God loves you (the very remark already inspires love)" (V-PP/Herder 27: 25). Furthermore, the thought of a providential God can put one "completely at ease," and thereby "*religion* alone may be completely reassuring" (V-PP/Herder 27: 25). This strong emphasis on religion is still there in the Collins lecture notes.

4.3 Moral motivation in the Collins notes

The Collins notes give a very rich and sophisticated account of moral motivation that is an important transition between the view in Kant's early writings on moral philosophy, and his mature view. It has the following steps: (1) One should do a morally good action for its own sake. (2) An insight of reason does have a moving force of its own, (3) but by itself reason is not strong enough to overcome inclinations. One can try to form a habit, but (4) ultimately it needs religion to motivate. (5) However – and this is a final twist – one should not do a morally good action while having a reward in mind, rather one follows God's command if one does his bidding gladly, and for its own sake. One obeys God in acting morally. The Collins notes are therefore an important transition in that they give greater power to reason and restrict religion, even though religion plays a larger role than in his mature writings.

(1) Consistent with his earliest writings, Kant emphasizes that the proper moral motivation amounts to doing the right thing simply because it is right:

> All morality, however, rests on the fact that the action is performed because of the inner nature of the act itself; so it is not the action that makes for morality, but the disposition from which I do it. If I do a thing because it ... brings advantage ... that is not a moral disposition. But if I do it because it is absolutely good in itself, that is a moral disposition. (V-Mo/Collins 27: 262; cf. KpV 5: 71)

Kant has not changed his views. In acting morally, one should not have one's own advantage in mind, but the inner moral quality of an intended action. In the lectures from 1775 onwards, Kant specifies the inner quality of one's intended

---

9 Compare this to the findings of Isen and Levin 1972.

actions as their ability to become a "universal rule, ... and then they have motivating grounds in the understanding" (V-Mo/Mron 27: 1428).

(2) Kant presents a complicated picture of human action. Human beings are under the influence of sensible stimuli, but they also have motives, which the understanding provides:

> So the *causae impulsivae*, insofar as they are drawn from the good, come from the understanding, and one who is moved to action by them is necessitated *per motiva*; but so far as they are drawn from the pleasant, they come from the senses, and one who is moved to action by them is necessitated *per stimulos*. (V-Mo/Collins 27: 257; cf. 267)

Motives can be of two kinds. If the understanding recommends an action for one's happiness, these are pragmatic motives, if the understanding cognizes the morality of an action, it provides a moral motive: "The motives are drawn either from pragmatic grounds, or from moral grounds of inner goodness" (V-Mo/Collins 27: 257).

How exactly the understanding could move an agent, the mechanism so to speak, is "somewhat difficult to see," and Kant calls it "the philosopher's stone" (V-Mo/Mron 27: 1428). But he does offer a picture, where he refers to the moral feeling: "This motive is the moral feeling" (V-Mo/Collins 27: 274). But by feeling he no longer has a pleasure in mind, an immediate approval or disapproval. Instead, the "moral feeling is a capacity for being affected by moral judgment" (V-Mo/Mron 27: 1428). The feeling is not a separate emotional quality in addition to the judgment, but "if this judgment moves me to do the action, that is the moral feeling" (V-Mo/Mron 27: 1428). The moral feeling is not so much a separate motivation, but the state of being motivated (Stratton-Lake 2001: 29–44). This comes about in the following way: "The understanding ... opposes itself to everything that is contrary to that rule ... Hence, in virtue of its nature there resides in the understanding a moving force" (V-Mo/Mron 27: 1428). The moral feeling occurs when one's natural feelings are in accord with what reason demands: "A sensibility in accordance with the motive power of the understanding would be the moral feeling ... When, therefore, sensibility abhors what the understanding considers abhorrent, this is the moral feeling" (V-Mo/Mron 27: 1429). Reason has moving power in that it frustrates inclinations that go against the moral law. It moves by having an influence on the inclinations, but here this moral feeling is not an additional positive quality, but merely one's sensibility as it is in accord with reason.

(3) However, the problem is that Kant does not consider reason to be strong enough to overcome sensibility: "The will is depraved when the motive power of the understanding is outweighed by sensibility. The understanding has no *ela-*

teres animi, albeit it has the power to move, or *motiva*; but the latter are not able to outweigh the *elateres* of sensibility" (V-Mo/Mron 27: 1429). So, one cannot, for instance, make another feel the abhorrence of an action who is not so inclined: "I can tell him what my understanding perceives, and I do indeed bring him also to the point of perceiving it; but the he should feel the abhorrence ... is impossible" (V-Mo/Mron 27: 1429). One solution is to form a habit: "we can indeed produce a *habitus*" whereby following reason "becomes habitual through imitation and frequent exercise" (V-Mo/Mron 27: 1429).

(4) But this is only a preliminary solution, as one first would have to be convinced that following morality is more important than following one's inclinations. For his ultimate answer of how one can overcome inclinations, Kant turns to religion. Whereas in his early writings on moral philosophy, both judgment and motive were based on a feeling, Kant now distinguishes sharply between two grounds of moral actions: "(1) The principle of appraisal of obligation, and (2) the principle of its performance or execution" (V-Mo/Collins 27: 274). The first, the *principium diiudicationis*, answers the question: "What is morally good or not?" By this one can distinguish what is right and wrong. The second, the *principium executionis*, answers a different question: "What moves me to live according to this law?" (V-Mo/Collins 27: 274). The answer to this second principle is the motive.

The initial answer to the motivational question is the moral feeling, as outlined above. As in his earliest writings, Kant does not hold that one first needs to know God in order to discover what is morally right (*principium diiudiactionis*), but he holds that one needs God for the motivational issue (*principium executionis*):

> In performance, to be sure, there must indeed be a third being, who constrains us to do what is morally good. But for the making of moral judgments we have no need for any third being. All moral laws are correct without such a being. But in execution they would be empty if no third being could constrain us to them. It has therefore been rightly perceived that without a supreme judge all moral laws would be without effect, since in that case there would be no inner motive, no reward and punishment. (V-Mo/Collins 27: 278)

When the question is: 'What moves me to live according to the moral law?' Kant's answer seems to be that it is the reward and punishment one can expect because it is commanded by God.

(5) Kant is quick to point out that this does not mean that one should have the reward or punishment in mind, or aim at it, when one acts. If one acts in order "to obtain rewards from God thereafter, I have not done the action from any moral disposition" (V-Mo/Collins 27: 283). Instead one is worthy of the reward, if one forgets about it, and does one's duty gladly, simply because it is commanded:

> If, however, the act has arisen from an inner principle, and if I do it, and do it gladly, because it is absolutely good in itself, then it is truly pleasing in the sight of God. God wishes to have dispositions, and they must come from an inner principle, for if we do a thing gladly, we do it also from a good disposition. (V-Mo/Mron 27: 1426)

Whether this view is already his mature view, depends on how one reads Kant on the highest good in the 'Dialectic' of the *Critique of Practical Reason*. There Kant repeats that one must hope to be rewarded for a morally good life. Is this the same view? My impression is that religion is much more pronounced in Collins than in his later writings (see also Kuehn 2015). Whereas Kant more strongly endorses religion in Collins, it becomes less important in his mature writings. The hope to be rewarded is not a pleasure, but merely an easing of uncomfortable feelings (KpV 5: 88). It is nothing one can be sure of, and therefore aim at, but merely something one can *hope* for (KpV 5: 130). One should not have it in mind while acting (KpV 5: 88), and, as a result, it is merely for *consolation*, and not motivation (KpV 5: 88). But however one reads Kant on this point, the important difference is that in the *Groundwork* Kant takes back the separation between the *principium diiudicationis* and *executionis* (similarly Kuehn 2015). The Formula of Autonomy combines the criterion of what is morally right, and of the proper moral motive (see again GMS 4: 431 f.).

In sum: there is a break between the Collins notes and Kant mature writings regarding moral motivation. Whereas Kant had sharply distinguished the *principium diiudicationis* and *executionis* in the Collins lectures, he now combines them in the Formula of Autonomy, which runs: "act only *so that the will could regard itself as at the same time giving universal law through its maxim*" (GMS 4: 434). The purpose of this formula is "to indicate in the imperative itself the renunciation of all interest, in volition from duty, by means of some determination the imperative contains" (GMS 4: 431). The formula states the motivational requirement in the content of what one should do, "just because of the idea of giving universal law *it is based on no interest* and therefore, among all possible imperatives, can alone be *unconditional*" (GMS 4: 432). Since he titles the explicit combination of the two *principia* "the principle of the autonomy of the will" (GMS 4: 433), I take it that his earlier separation of the two *principia* is the reason why he does not refer to autonomy in the Collins lectures.

5 Conclusion

Kant's lectures on ethics are an invaluable resource for studying the development of his moral philosophy. In particular, they shed light on Kant's formulation of the supreme principle of morality. If one compares the Herder and the Collins notes to his mature published writings, it seems that Kant endorsed different aspects of the supreme principle at different stages. I have argued that he envisioned the main elements of the *content* of the principle in the Herder lectures. However, between Herder and Collins he drastically changed his views on the *source* of the supreme principle. Lastly, it is only in his mature writings that he formulated his final views on moral *motivation*, and refers to the concept of autonomy. It therefore seems that Dieter Henrich sums up the development of Kant's views well, noting their historical trajectory: "The path by which, in *Groundwork of the Metaphysics of Morals*, the purely good will leads to the formula of the categorical imperative, and further to the doctrine of autonomy of reason, was also the historical course of Kantian ethics" (Henrich 2012: 14 f.; trans. modified).[10]

---

[10] I would like to thank Robert R. Clewis for his helpful comments on the first version of this paper.

Chapter 8
Kant's Concept of Moral *Imputatio*

Faustino Fabbianelli

1 Introduction

In this chapter, I examine Kant's concept of moral *imputatio* as presented in both his published writings and his lectures. By means of a comparative study of the relevant texts, I will show that Kant's remarkable doctrine is subject to oscillations and developments.

In order to bring to light the variety of speculative options, I begin by presenting the different models of *imputatio* that Kant himself pursues as different solutions to the moral phenomenon of imputation. In the second half of my chapter, I turn my attention to the discussion of Kant's contemporaries over problems relating to imputation. We will see that the theoretical gaps characteristic of Kant's doctrine of moral *imputatio* are closely connected to the implications of the theory he proposes. Due to the inferences drawn by several of the acute thinkers (Stattler, Ulrich, Schmid, Reinhold) in various ways either affiliated with or opposed to him, Kant saw that several points of his speculative proposal were no longer defensible, or at least required further explanation.[1]

2 The concept of *imputatio*

By *imputatio*, Kant understands two distinct phenomena of moral life: the ascription (*Zuschreibung*) and the imputation (*Zurechnung*) of a determinate deed (*Tat*). The key feature is whether someone is a free, or unfree, author of an action. Kant expresses the difference in Latin this way: *causa actionis alicuis per libertatem* (the free cause of an action) is not the same as *aliquem iudicare ut causam cuius actionis per libertatem* (judging that someone is the free cause of an action). When a surgeon operates on a patient, both the action and the scar resulting from the operation can be *ascribed* to the surgeon, but not imputed to him (V-PP/Powalski 27: 153). Imputation implies that the surgeon can be blamed for the scar, something we cannot justly do. In other words, the surgeon's action cannot be

---

[1] This aspect of Kant's doctrine of imputation is usually overlooked; see, e. g., Fischer 1988.

judged in terms of the pair of concepts, merit/demerit (*meritum/demeritum*). He is no doubt the cause of the scar. Thus we see him as the cause of the action. But the action that is performed to this end cannot, as a result, be regarded as meritorious or blameworthy, because causing the scar was not the end of the doctor's action. In order to perform his operation, he could not do otherwise; a natural relationship exists between the operating and the scar. As such, he was not free with regard to the causation of the scar. Furthermore, the surgeon's action did not stand under a law that forbade him from causing the scar. Another example: we cannot impute the action of a drunkard to him, but only ascribe it to him. Since he has had too much to drink, he can no longer be regarded as the originator of his deeds. He is no longer free – the drunkenness marks the state (*Zustand*) that causes the deeds themselves. This means that only the drunkenness of a drunkard can be imputed to him (V-Mo/Collins 27: 288 [Kant 1997a: 80 f.]).

The definition from the *Metaphysics of Morals* nicely sums up all of the components that are necessary for imputing an action to an agent: "*Imputation* (*imputatio*) in the moral sense is the *judgment* by which someone is regarded as the author (*causa libera*) of an action, which is then called a *deed* (*factum*) and stands under laws" (MS/RL 6: 227 [Kant 1996a: 381 f.]). Imputation demands that the person who has caused something be free; only then can the imputed action be considered a deed (*Tat*). The action is not physical, i.e., it does not follow from natural causes, but is, on the contrary, "chosen with free will, from the law of freedom," we likewise find in the Metaphysics of Morals Vigilantius lecture notes (1793/94) (V-MS/Vigil 27: 561 [Kant 1997a: 316]). As long as the imputed doing (*factum*) is a free action, i.e., a deed, we speak of "*imputatio facti*." Thus "*imputatio facti*" demands that the human being be free; if the action is coerced, it happens contrary to the person's will, and can no longer be imputed. Besides, when we relate the doing, i.e., the action, to the moral law, we concern ourselves with "*imputatio legis*": the law is applied to the deed in order to determine whether it must be judged as meritorious or blameworthy, Kant claims according to the Practical Philosophy Powalski lecture transcriptions (1782/83) (V-PP/Powalski 27: 154).

3 Models of *imputatio*

Now a question arises. When, for Kant, is someone considered the originator of an action, i.e., what, for him, qualifies one as the free cause of a deed? Different models of moral imputation are discernible in Kant's reflection on this question. I would first like to explain it according to the opposition, "absolute/relative." An imputation can be regarded as *absolute* when there are no constraints that could mitigate the imputation or 'excuse' the agent, as it were. In contrast, it can be considered *relative* when arguments that put limits on the subject's accountability can be adduced.

3.1 Absolute *imputatio*

Kant presents an absolute model of *imputatio* in both the *Critique of Pure Reason* and the *Critique of Practical Reason*. I begin with his presentation of the model in the former work. The resolution of the Third Antinomy shows that freedom and natural necessity can co-exist. According to Kant, this compatibilism[2] can only be defended if we accept the doctrine of transcendental idealism, according to which appearances cannot be viewed as things in themselves. If they were the same thing, it would be impossible to find an effect that does not stand under the law of nature. The connection of all the givens of the world of sense, thoroughly regulated by the unchanging laws of nature, would be the only available series. Thus if appearances that stand under the causality of nature were things in themselves, freedom could no longer be saved. Nature would be the only cause of every given, because it would be sufficient to explain the ultimate. "If, on the other hand, appearances do not count for any more than they are in fact, namely, not for things in themselves but only for mere representations connected in accordance with empirical laws, then they themselves must have grounds that are not appearances" (KrV A536 f./B564 f. [Kant 1998a: 535]). This compatibility of appearance and thing in itself makes it possible for the same acting subject to be seen in two ways, namely, according to its intelligible character and according to its empirical character. In the first case, the person stands under no causality of nature. The law that regulates his actions is not a natural law. What he does constitutes no member of a series of the order of nature. The person is free insofar as he is the only originator of his deeds, a noumenon that is able to begin something by itself in the world of sense. But now the same person also has an empirical character, on the basis of which his actions are appearances, which "would stand through and through in connection with other appearances, [and] constitute members of a single series of the natural order" (KrV A539/B567 [Kant 1998a: 536]). On Kant's view, the compatibility of appearance and thing in itself can also

---

[2] Kant's doctrine presents a compatibilism only insofar as it regards both forms of causality as compatible. Bojanowski (2006: 15) rightly shows, however, that the true compatibilist only argues for a relative concept of freedom that Kant's Critical writings do not defend. On Kant's position, see Wood 1984.

be extended to include the two kinds of character. This implies that a determinate action is seen not only as a given (i.e., a natural effect), but also as the effect of a non-empirical causality. A causality through (*aus*) freedom stands alongside a causality of nature. We can "at least represent" the latter on the basis of the concept of an *ought*, that "expresses a species of necessity and a connection with grounds which does not occur anywhere else in the whole of nature" (KrV A547/B575 [Kant 1998a: 540]). Kant has recourse to the moral imperative here without, however, philosophically proving the reality of freedom. The proof occurs in the *Critique of Practical Reason* with the theory of the fact of reason (*Faktum der Vernunft*). In the theoretico-cognitive framework of the first *Critique*, it suffices for us to speak of an *ought* that has nothing to do with the course of nature. We cannot ask "what ought to happen in nature, any more than we can ask what properties a circle ought to have; but we must rather ask what happens in nature, or what properties the circle has" (KrV A547/B575 [Kant 1998a: 540]). A human being can to his extent be judged for his actions in two ways: first, according to his empirical character – and in this case we will say that all his actions are determined by the order of nature – and, second, according to his intelligible character, and we will thus maintain that the same actions stand under noumenal, i.e., free, causality. If we want to pass a judgment on a human deed, we can have recourse to the two worlds, the intelligible and the phenomenal, within each of which the deed can be evaluated. Kant gives the example of a malicious lie, and considers the extent to which it "and its consequences" can be imputed to a human being (KrV A554/B582 [Kant 1998a: 544]). On account of its empirical character, we have to evoke reasons like a bad upbringing or an ill society in which the human being grows up for it. In this way, the malicious lie finds a natural explanation; it marks an effect that is inserted into the chain of the empirical world. Since it is the result of a law of nature, the lie cannot be judged morally; the lying person cannot be held accountable. However, things look different when we adopt the noumenal perspective: the lie now displays no member of the natural chain; it is now appropriate to criticize the doer for it. From this perspective, the agent was free and could have conducted himself otherwise. The causality of his reason stood under no necessity, and, to this extent, his lie constitutes and counts as a fault.

Kant's solution of the Third Antinomy argues for a model of absolute imputation. Every deed can be viewed in a dual aspect, i.e., can be thought to be simultaneously necessary and free (though for different reasons). This absolute accountability apparently goes along with the compatibilism of the two worlds that brings with it a perfect parallelism between the two series of actions: the empirical and the noumenal. Upon an intelligible determination, a phenomenal effect follows. The unconditionality of the imputing judgment is in no way mitigated. According to this model of *imputatio*, we are not allowed to appeal to any obstacles that explain the immoral deed and could be used as an excuse for it.

Two observations are of great significance. First, for Kant, there is no possible explanation of why an acting subject's intellectual character is determined the way it is.

> For another intelligible character would have given another empirical one; and if we say that regardless of the entire course of life he has led up to that point, the agent could still have refrained from the lie, then this signifies only that it stands immediately under the power of reason, and in its causality reason is not subject to any conditions of appearance or of the temporal series. (KrV A556/B584 [Kant 1998a: 545])

Second, this agnostic position entails that the only proper imputation that can be admitted from the theoretico-cognitive standpoint is exclusively related to the empirical character. Since the morality of the actions remain hidden such that we can only be acquainted with their empirical side, our moral judgment can only extend as far we can see or observe. The lie can only be theoretico-cognitively imputed according to the empirical character of the liar; thus we can only claim that he can be judged on the basis of what we know of his history. Of course, this does not mean that the moral *imputatio* can only be explained by means of the empirical character – the entire argument of the part of the Transcendental Dialectic I have analyzed indicates otherwise. It only means that a fair imputation can be related only to what we actually know. In accordance with the empirical character, we are certainly able to think of the intelligible character "just as in general we must ground appearances in thought through a transcendental object, even though we know nothing about it as it is in itself" (KrV A540/B568 [Kant 1998a: 536]). We still cannot determine in what measure what we see is an effect of freedom or of nature, or, therefore, whether it is to be ascribed to a free decision or to a natural temperament (KrV A551/B579n [Kant 1998a: 542n]).

The second *Critique*'s Critical Elucidation of the Analytic of Pure Practical Reason takes over this model of absolute "imputation" and applies it to the new problem of the practical causality of reason. Whereas from the theoretical heights of the *Critique of Pure Reason* we can only speak of freedom as an idea, Kant thinks that it is now possible to assume freedom as a *ratio essendi* of the moral law. As a fact of reason, the moral law postulates freedom as the condition of the possibility of its existence (KpV 5: 94 [Kant 1996a: 215]). The concept of freedom thereby possesses a reality that is given to it by the apodictic law of practical reason. Kant thinks that freedom is now not only possible – that was the result of the first *Critique*'s Transcendental Dialectic – but also objectively real. We cannot give a theoretico-cognitive explanation of it, but in the practical relation we can claim that reality is furnished "to a supersensible object of the category of causality, namely to *freedom*" (KpV 5: 6 [Kant 1996a: 141]). What before could only be thought in the speculative regard is now confirmed "by means of a fact" – the fact of the moral law (ibid.). Whereas the unconditioned causality of a human being was on the earlier account only the object of a non-contradictory thought – we can only *think* it – this "can" (*Können*) is now "changed into is" in the second *Critique* (KpV 5: 104 [Kant 1996a: 223]). The fact of the moral law shows that pure reason is practical, but it also proves simultaneously that freedom can be construed as a reality in the practical regard. Nonetheless, the doctrine of transcendental idealism presents the foundation of the possibility of the concept of freedom. If we take the conditions of things in time as conditions of things in themselves, "then the necessity in the causal relation can in no way be united with freedom; instead they are opposed to each other as contradictory" (KpV 5: 94 [Kant 1996a: 215 f.]). The compatibilist doctrine of the *Critique of Practical Reason* highlights once again the parallelism between natural causality and the causality through freedom: whereas the law of nature is the law of one kind of causality, the law of morality is the law of the other sort. Kant believes that the freedom that is proven to be real through the law of morality underlies the practical phenomenon of imputation. If a human being were only free by virtue of his inner representations and so only psychologically free, we could regard him as a turnspit "which, when once it is wound up, also accomplishes its movements of itself" (KpV 5: 97 [Kant 1996a: 218]). Thus, for Kant, it is not a question of ascertaining whether the determining grounds of an action are found in the active subject or outside it; imputation according to the moral law can then only occur, if the determining grounds of its action are in its power, i. e., outside time. Kant's argument concerning moral *imputatio* in the *Critique of Practical Reason* and the first *Critique* is based on the theoretical impossibility of knowing the way of thinking (*Denkungsart*), i. e., the intelligible character, of a human being. Now the fact that we do not possess an intellectual intuition of the acting subject no longer serves here as it functions in the *Critique of Pure Reason*, that is, to maintain that moral imputation only pertains to empirical character. Since the whole argument no longer takes place from within a theoretico-cognitive framework, but a practical one, the reason to bring into play the right of a moral judgment informed by mitigating insights or circumstances also falls away. Kant no longer seems interested in showing that knowledge that is confined to the empirical can be adduced as a reason for declaring the real morality of human conduct to be hidden and as a result that a moral imputation can never be made "with complete justice" (KrV A551/B579 [Kant 1998a: 542]). On the contrary, the recognition of the difference between the intelligible and the empirical world within the *Critique of Practical Reason* proves to be functional for the repudiation of every form of practical excuse. Each of us could refer to his own past in order to try to justify why he has done something morally unlawful. The latter "is sufficiently determined in the past and, so far, is inevitably necessary," but one is by no means freed from the appraisal "that he could have omitted it" (KpV 5: 98 [Kant 1996a: 218]). While in the *Critique of Pure Reason* Kant still concedes that no one is in a position to fathom how much of an empirical character can be ascribed to nature and how much to freedom, he now maintains that an immoral action can be imputed to us as absolutely free. Despite being determined by the past, the unlawful conduct of a human being nonetheless belongs "to a single phenomenon of his character, which he gives himself, as a cause independent of all sensibility, the causality of those appearances" (KpV 5: 98 [Kant 1996a: 218]). Here Kant stresses that what counts in practical reflection is the accountability that is connected to the intelligible character. The concept that is used in the practical regard shows us an *uncompromising* account, as it were: conscience is the wonderful capacity in us that makes it impossible for a human being "to excuse his unlawful conduct." He can invoke his entire past to excuse his own conduct, but he knows well that "the advocate who speaks in his favor can by no means reduce to silence the prosecutor within him" (KpV 5: 98 [Kant 1996a: 218]). In this connection, remorse constitutes a painful sentiment (*Empfindung*) induced by means of the moral disposition. Now Kant views this kind of pain as "quite legitimate," because reason only aims at determining whether the immoral given belongs to the person (agent) or not (KpV 5: 99 [Kant 1996a: 219]). While in the *Critique of Pure Reason* the impossibility of noumenal knowledge is still a reason to limit a fair imputation to the empirical character, the "lack of this intuition" is now substituted by the voice of the moral law which justifies the latter judgments, that, "though made in all conscientiousness, yet seem at first glance quite contrary to equity" (KpV 5: 99 [Kant 1996a: 219]). Whether a human being receives a bad upbringing or grows up in a society that is unfavorable to him, all of these are insufficient to free him from blame: this is still impossible because the human being is free, Kant holds.

This different emphasis does not change the fundamental distinguishing mark of the speculative approach at work with respect to imputation. In both the first and the second *Critiques*, Kant argues for a model of absolute moral imputation that rests on the compatibilism of nature and freedom, as well as a perfect parallelism between the two series of actions. In the published writings, viz., the first two *Critiques*, there is no talk of obstacles of the deed.

3.2 Relative *imputatio*

To introduce the new model of imputation, we can refer back to the above-discussed remark of the *Critique of Pure Reason*, where, on the basis of the impossibility of knowing the noumenal, Kant asserts that the real morality of an action remains completely hidden. For him, this means that no one can fathom "[h]ow much of it is to be ascribed to mere nature and innocent defects of temperament or to its happy constitution (*merito fortunae*)" (KrV A551/B579 [Kant 1998a: 542]). It could now seem that Kant subscribes to a different model of moral imputation here because he accepts the possibility of the same action being both the result of a temporal past and a noumenal, i.e., supra-temporal, decision.[3] Insofar as the two series of actions overlap, a perfect compatibilism of the phenomenal and the noumenal worlds would no longer be valid. Indeed, in a note Kant brings to light the idea that an influence of the intelligible on the sensible is possible. It seems to me that this thesis poses no difficulty, and can be incorporated without objection into what I refer to as the *absolute* model of imputation. Such an influence does not call into question at all the perfect parallelism of the two series of actions. One and the same member of the empirical series thereby acquires two different explanations; but this does not rule out the fact that a human being is accountable for his actions insofar as he is absolutely free. But if the action of a human being is the result of his "free" decision, and factors like a bad upbringing or a hardly controllable nature operate on this decision, then it cannot be imputed absolutely to him. Insofar as it stands under empirical conditions, the action is no longer absolutely free.

This model is the one found in the lectures on moral philosophy that Kant held over the years at Albertina University of Königsberg. It marks the chronologically older model that Kant developed on the basis of his lectures in which he used Baumgarten's *Initia Philosophiae Practicae* and *Ethica Philosophica*.[4] It could, therefore, count as pre-Critical, because, by directly bypassing the central motif of transcendental idealism, it finds its theoretical justification within *applied* philosophy. This model of moral imputation ultimately concerns empirical psychology. But this does not mean that it must be considered non-Kantian.[5] The inner connection it implies between the doctrine of relative *imputatio* and applied philosophy shows that another approach can be found that – as Kant himself insists – "must be combined but never confused" (KrV A848/B876 [Kant 1998a: 700]) with Critical thinking.

---

[3] For this position, see Landucci 1994: 256 f.
[4] See also Oliver Sensen's chapter in this volume.
[5] However, Bojanowski (2006: 19, 189 f.) draws just this conclusion and claims that the lectures do not reflect Kant's true position, and that instead of occupying ourselves with the relative sense of freedom presented in the notes, we should confine ourselves to Kant's Critical writings.

Let me illustrate this approach to moral imputation by citing some of the key passages from the lecture notes. According to Kant, only a doing that can be regarded as a deed can be imputed. This is the case when the action has freedom for its practical condition. "All attributions [*Imputationes*], insofar as they are understood as imputation [*Zurechnung*], are a judgment [*Judicium*] on free actions, insofar as they are viewed as merit or demerit, as credit or blame" (V-PP/Powalski 27: 153). To explain when the conditions of the possibility of imputation are not present, Kant himself proposes the example of a child who has not yet come of age. Children who "destroy something useful," cannot be called to moral account "because they know not what they do," he reportedly claims in Moral Philosophy Collins notes (V-Mo/Collins 27: 291 [Kant 1997a: 83]). The children's ignorance is considered an obstacle to imputation. In this connection, he speaks of degrees of imputation that should be taken into account when we pass a moral judgment on someone. Both the degree of morality and the degree of freedom correspond to the degree of imputation. If someone kills a human being because he has an angry temperament, he can be judged in a different way from someone who executes his action in cold blood. The first agent, according to Kant, "has not incurred so much evil as" the second (V-Mo/Collins 27: 291 [Kant 1997a: 84]). The angry temperament has abetted the deed, whereas the cold-blooded nature has not. Natural obstacles justify either a smaller or greater imputation. Kant explains this point by means of the difference between human beings and angels. On his view there is less to impute to the latter, because they have fewer obstacles in the way of their behaving morally correctly (V-Mo/Collins 27: 292 [Kant 1997a: 84]). The picture suggested here is that of a battleground on which good and evil, the moral law and its obstacles, compete against each other. A relation of forces underlies this model of moral imputation. In this regard, the Metaphysics of Morals Vigilantius explains that the moral fact in relation to which a moral judgment is passed contains essential and inessential moments important for imputation. The so-called "circumstances" (*circumstantiae*) of the fact deserve to become the object of an appraisal. They contribute to different ways of construing the deed itself. Hence Kant claims: "*duo cum faciunt idem, non est idem* [when two do the same, it is not the same]" (V-MS/Vigil 27: 563 [Kant 1997a: 317]). No two human beings ever do the same thing – even when they appear to do so – because the circumstances of their actions are never the same. If a physical obstacle (for example, a natural drive) is greater for one human being than for another, the moral imputation must turn out differently. Kant's examples are clear and striking. Consider: "if a man has by nature a choleric temperament, and yet restrains himself in face of an insult, it would be a merit on comparing him to a cold-blooded man, who did not have to overcome the physical hindrance" (V-MS/Vigil 27: 567 f. [Kant 1997a: 321]).

This example nicely illustrates the sense in which this model of imputation can be called relative. Kant describes a relativization of freedom and of the imputation connected with it. The applied concepts – degrees of freedom, obstacles and hindrances – indicate a conception of the practical that is only valid for, and can only be justified by, an empirical-psychological reflection. The unyieldingness that Kant expresses in the first two *Critiques* makes room for a more accommodating or milder view of human actions. Nature and freedom do not run parallel to each other here, according to the lecture notes. Rather, they cross each other's path over and over again.

A clear counterexample to the distance that separates the two models of imputation can be found when we want to determine how far duty extends. In the *Critique of Practical Reason*, Kant considers the case of a human being who has committed a theft. If this deed were the necessary result of the determining grounds of the preceding time, it would have been impossible for it *not* to have happened. As a fact of reason, the moral law presents the *ratio cognoscendi* of freedom here; by virtue of it, we know that it was *possible* for the immoral deed not to happen, because it *ought* not to have been done (KpV 5: 95 [Kant 1996a: 216]). Kant believes that all must be disregarded in the face of the holiness of duty; one must therefore be conscious "that one *can* do it because our own reason recognizes this as its command and says that one *ought* to do it: this is, as it were, to raise oneself altogether above the sensible world" (KpV 5: 159 [Kant 1996a: 267]). According to this position, there is no circumstance that can mitigate the severe face of duty. In contrast to a morality that knows no compromise, Kant presents his students with the thesis that no one is obligated to do something he cannot bring about: "*ultra posse nemo obligatur*" [nobody is obligated beyond what he can do] (V-MS/Vigil 27: 563 [Kant 1997a: 317]). In fact, he deals with unavoidable events or the so-called "*delicta fortunae*" – crimes or offenses where chance plays a major role, and which, as such, go beyond the forces of a human being. The human being could neither foresee nor, accordingly, prevent them (V-MS/Vigil 27: 563). But now the same dictum that 'ought implies can' applies in all moral situations, including those that go beyond human forces and knowledge. Someone could neither foresee nor prevent receiving a bad upbringing or a certain temper or being brought up in bad company. In this sense, such circumstances also go beyond the forces of a human being and count as "*nemo obligatur*" for him. Kant does not say that explicitly, but his lecture's doctrine of physical and moral obstacles (V-MS/Vigil 27: 567 f. [Kant 1997a: 320 f.]) seems to imply a commitment to this claim.

4 A third model of moral *imputatio*?

The models discussed above – the absolute and the relative *imputatio* – can be readily separated from each other. Their difference ultimately lies in the relation between the noumenal and the phenomenal, or rather in the lack thereof, for practical reflection is merely empirical. According to the absolute model, these two levels run parallel, insofar as an unbounded free action can be thought of as producing a determinate effect within the causality of nature, so that the same natural event can be seen as a result of the free action and a member of the necessary chain that is regulated by the law of nature. On the relative model, it is considered to be possible for the empirical character to limit a decision that should nonetheless be defined as free. Accordingly, freedom becomes *gradual*. As already mentioned, there are physical or moral obstacles that, depending on whether they can be simply or strenuously overcome by a human being, make the action more or less meritorious. In this sense, jealousy, anger, and cold-bloodedness are three affects (or lack thereof) that can be regarded as mitigating (or, for cold-bloodedness, aggravating) circumstances, when they are seen as *physical* obstacles for murder. Similarly, in the case of, say, the assistance a human being ought to offer another person, *moral* obstacles can arise that make the same action more, or less, meritorious. For example, suppose a son gives financial assistance to his parents; the kinship presents a support for the action. The moral obstacle is greater when the agent considers it a great duty for him to help his kin: he feels compelled to do it and in this sense has less degree of freedom. Hence the performance of the action is less meritorious. (Kant's use of "obstacle" may of course sound counter-intuitive, since the presence of the kinship-based duty actually *inclines* the agent to perform the action.) Now the human being has "no difficulty to overcome the obstacles and determine himself by free choice in accordance with the law; so the smaller the degree of freedom that is present, the less the merit in the action ... If, on the other hand, with no obligating grounds, he acts well towards the other, simply because he wanted to, then the duty is smaller, and more merit is accounted to the act" (V-MS/Vigil 27: 568 [Kant 1997a: 321]). The *moral* obstacles are smaller when the kinship is missing, and the action thus obtains a higher worth.

Now, a third model of *imputatio* can be recognized in Kant's doctrine of moral imputation, which, given Kant's theoretical resources, could be seen as necessary because it alone would explain the immoral actions that would otherwise remain inexplicable. In other words, Kant should concede this model at least if his thought is to be coherent and without contradiction. This doctrine of *imputatio* can, therefore, be regarded as a hybrid form of the models already considered. On the one hand, it conforms to the absolute approach, and hence rules out the possibility of appealing to some physical obstacle as the reason for an excuse – a human being is and remains noumenally free – but on the other, it implies a relativization of human imputation on the basis of another kind of obstacle. To anticipate what follows: Kant did not explicitly argue for such a doctrine. Against the critics who accused him of appropriating it (or rather, demand that he acknowledge it), he had always maintained that they misunderstood him. Nevertheless, I would suggest that a problem does in fact exist.

In the *Groundwork to the Metaphysics of Morals* and the *Critique of Practical Reason*, Kant defines freedom by its inner connection with both reason and the moral law. A human being is conscious "of himself as an intelligence and consequently as a rational cause active by means of reason, that is, operating freely" (GMS 4: 458 [Kant 1996a: 104]). But now "the moral law expresses nothing other than the *autonomy* of pure practical reason, i.e., freedom" (KpV 5: 33 [Kant 1996a: 166]). In addition, Kant says that "the will [is] nothing other than practical reason" (GMS 4: 412 [Kant 1996a: 66]), thus asserting the equivalence of pure practical reason and freedom. The pure will at issue here "is not merely subject to the law but subject to it in such a way that it must be viewed also *as itself lawgiving* [*als selbstgesetzgebend*] and just because of this as first subject to the law (of which it can regard itself as the author)" (GMS 4: 431 [Kant 1996a: 81]; emphasis added). But now the principle of autonomy stated here presents the positive concept of freedom (KpV 5: 33 [Kant 1996a: 166]). Kant thinks he is entitled to now argue: just as the pure will is autonomous, it is also free; but since it is itself like pure practical reason, the latter must also be considered to be free.

On the basis of these premises, Kant seems to come to the conclusion that freedom consists in the moral fulfillment of the moral law. In this regard, a well-known passage from the *Groundwork to the Metaphysics of Morals* is relevant: "a free will and a will under moral laws are one and the same" (GMS 4: 447 [Kant 1996a: 95]). Now if the will is free because it is autonomous, then the provocative question arises as to whether a heteronomous will, a will that does not stand under the moral law, is therefore unfree. With respect to the topic of moral imputation, this means that a deed can be imputed, because it is the accomplishment of a free action; but since, according to this doctrine, only moral actions are free, they alone stand under the principle of imputation. According to this model, we are only dealing with a relative concept of *imputatio*, where the sphere of actions that can be imputed is exclusively limited to meritorious actions. Contrary to the above-discussed imputation models of Kant's lectures, the absoluteness of a free action remains untouched according to this version. In other words, we are dealing with a transcendental, noumenal freedom, as in the *Critique of Pure Reason*. Moreover, there are now neither physical obstacles nor degrees of freedom resulting from them. The *imputatio* is merely relativized in that it cannot be extended to include immoral actions, since the physical obstacles have been replaced by hyperphysical, or intelligible, obstacles.

5 The contemporary discussion

Benedikt Stattler, author of *Anti-Kant* (1788), demonstrated remarkable insight into the above-illustrated situation. In a penetrating analysis of the *Groundwork to the Metaphysics of Morals*, he raised the following objection against Kant: "Kant posits the idea of freedom here merely on the side of the practical law of reason, and explains it by means of an activity that is independent of the determinations of the world of sense." According to Stattler, it follows from this identification of freedom with autonomy:

> that only the will that is good and in accord with the moral law would be free, but by no means that which would be subordinated to the practical law of nature and sensibility. And now there would be no freedom when rational beings did evil, i.e., *there would be nothing morally evil at all*, as that which cannot be thought without freedom. (Stattler 1788: 269)

A similar criticism of Kant's doctrine of freedom as formulated in the *Critique of Pure Reason* was made public by Johann August Heinrich Ulrich in the same year as Stattler's *Anti-Kant*. Ulrich's thesis was that, contrary to Kant's attempt to argue for the compatibility between freedom and the necessity of nature, there is no middle path between necessity and chance. Ulrich translated Kant's solution of the Third Antinomy into a conceptual scheme of determinism and indeterminism that thereby entered into the contemporary discussion. Kant himself would take over the scheme at a later point. Ulrich saw the main problem of Kant's doctrine of freedom to be the idea of the possibility of a cause *"the effect of which begins in time, but the causality of which does not*, [and] is consequently also not subordinated through other preceding grounds to the law of determination" (Ulrich 1788: § 12). For him, Kant would be right only if we conceded to him what the *proton pseudos* of his approach in fact asserts, namely, that time is merely a subjective form of appearances. This entails that no change occurs at the intelligible level; the absolute power of freedom of which Kant speaks refers to an application or omission of it. But how can we maintain this, if the power is outside time? "The application of a power whose application can be omitted, and the omission of an application which yet occurs at times, cannot possibly be thought without temporal determination, without an arising and beginning" (Ulrich 1788: § 12). Ulrich admitted his inability to understand why the power of freedom is actually applied in certain actions though not in others. "Either something which is once the reason for the application, [and which] contains the reason for the omission at some other time, is present, or it is not. The first case is one of necessity, and the other is one of chance" (Ulrich 1788: § 12). Ulrich's objection soon appeared to be quite dramatic with respect to the issue of immoral actions. He suggested a thesis as a possible solution to the problem he had highlighted – a thesis that would then be taken over by many of Kant's contemporaries in order to cope with the issue of immorality while employing a transcendental-philosophical approach. He did this in the form of a question: "Is omission of reason perhaps an *original* and *unchangeable* lack of the activity of reason, a weakness in the intelligible character, and the application of reason an *original* and n. b. [nota bene] *unchangeable state of a* higher activity and efficacy?" (Ulrich 1788: § 12). Ulrich conceded Kant's thesis that a human being can act in different ways when confronted with the same circumstances. Yet while Kant had used it in order to argue that this is only possible on the basis of transcendental freedom and that the problem of imputation could only thereby be solved – we could accordingly impute a certain deed to someone because he is transcendentally free – Ulrich insisted that the different conduct of the same human being in the same circumstances could not be explained through chance, to which, he thought, Kant's doctrine was ultimately reduced.

In this way, two points that gained increasing significance in the contemporary discussion were defined – the issue of determinism and indeterminism, and the need for an explanation of immoral actions. The difference between the proponents of the absolute freedom that is supposed to be realized in both moral and immoral actions and those of the absolute necessity of all human deeds was brought to a head in the opposition of two approaches: *intelligible fatalism*, which Carl Christian Erhard Schmid, in particular, strongly advocated, and *absolute freedom of choice* (*Freiheit der Willkür*) that Karl Leonhard Reinhold promoted as the core concept of his practical philosophy.

Schmid took over Ulrich's main objection in his *Attempt at a Moral Philosophy* (1790), and came to the conclusion that determinism is the only theory that is in keeping with morality. Concerning the question of a possible unification of the opposed assertions of speculative and practical reason, through which the I is viewed, on the one hand, as an object of experience and, on the other, as a thing in itself, there is only one answer: absolute necessity. "*If we will admit no (irrational) chance, nothing other than necessity remains; for there is simply no middle path between the two*" (Schmid 1975: 249). The necessity in question cannot indeed be explained on the basis of the operation of an appearance on the intelligible I. But although the sensible can by no means determine and constrain the rational, it does not follow that that which underlies sensibility is incapable of constraining the effects of reason in appearances. For Schmid, this was a matter of speculative coherence: if we want to exclude chance in the explanation of immorality, we must be ready to concede determinism in a human being's practical life. Only then could we explain why I *video meliora proboque, deteriora sequor* [I see and approve of the better, yet I follow the worse]. His position, intelligible fatalism, held that there were hyperphysical, i.e., noumenal, obstacles that could explain why a human being decided in favor of an immoral action.

> Reason is thus free with regard to all that happens in time, but constrained by that which determines the given in time. It is free and has received no influence with regard to all that it actually does, as well as to all of its judgments, formally considered; but [it is] dependent and constrained with regard to that which it does not do. It *cannot operate* in this case. (Schmid 1975: 249)

The possibility of moral imputation thus seemed to disappear. If there are intelligible obstacles that, when regarded theoretically, explain why a human being acts immorally, such a solution cannot satisfy the question of imputation from the practical standpoint. And the response that Karl Leonhard Reinhold brought to light in the second volume of his *Letters on the Kantian Philosophy* was aimed precisely at improving Kant's moral philosophy as a foil against Schmid's intelligible fatalism.[6] Reinhold's newly defined concept of the freedom of the will was contrived to explain the problem of immoral yet free actions more plausibly than Kant's theoretical resources allowed. His new definition of the freedom of the will was: "the power of the person to determine himself for the satisfaction or non-satisfaction of a desiring either according to the practical law or against it" (Reinhold 2008: 188). According to Reinhold, freedom is not only the will's independence from the force of sense, not only the independence of practical reason from all that it is not, but also the independence of a person from the necessitation of practical reason. However, these meanings of freedom are only negative. There is also a positive meaning that consists in the "power of self-determination for or against the practical law through the power of choice [*Willkür*]" (Reinhold 2008: 188). For Reinhold, the inner connection between freedom and the power of choice thus established should serve to distinguish the absolute self-sufficiency of a person from the autonomy of the pure will. Whereas, as we have seen, Kant highlighted the identity of practical reason and the will, Reinhold without reservation protested against the so-called "friends of the Kantian philosophy" (and in fact against Kant himself) that practical reason is *not* the will. The action of the former is involuntary – reason decides nothing at all, it simply exhibits the moral

---

[6] For Reinhold's concept of freedom, see Fabbianelli 1998–99; Fabbianelli 2000; Ameriks 2000a: 154–9; Lazzari 2004.

law – while the action of the will alone is voluntary. But if it were not the will, but practical reason, that acted, we would be dealing with a new form of necessity, according to which both moral and immoral actions are effects of practical reason. All these actions only seem to be different, because they only come about when certain obstacles to the activity of reason are present. "The moral action follows inevitably from a completely involuntary operation of practical reason, *once there was no obstacle*; and both the moral and the immoral action must thus be imputed to the presence or absence of the latter" (Reinhold 2008: 200). Even though not overtly – he spoke only of a friend of the Critical philosophy who was consistent enough to draw certain conclusions from its premises – Reinhold disputes Schmid's intelligible fatalism here. The moral imputation of human actions stands at the center-stage of the entire discussion. This would become clear two years later, when in a letter to Schmid Reinhold emphasized precisely this point: only by understanding freedom as freedom of the power of choice, i.e., as freedom of choice, could one speak of "accountability, merit, or blame" (Reinhold 2004: 156). Reinhold followed Ulrich and Schmid in connecting the issue of *imputatio* with determinism insofar as he viewed his own doctrine of freedom as the only one able to overcome the necessity that arises from sensible desiring, without lapsing into the necessity of practical reason.

6 Kant's reaction

Kant's reaction to the contemporary discussion took two different forms: first, the rethinking and redefinition of the relationship between *necessity* and *freedom*, and second, the new systematic formulation of the *power of choice* and its relation to the *pure will*. Both of them involve theoretical revisions that Kant was compelled to recognize when confronted by inferences drawn by thinkers more (or less) affiliated with him. Both find their formal expressions in the published writings as well as in the lecture transcriptions.

The solution of the Third Antinomy was supposed to have established that necessity and freedom are compatible with each other because they are related to different kinds of causality. The causality of nature is one that stands under the conditions of time, while the causality through freedom is regulated by a law that is valid outside of time, namely, the moral law. It is impossible to begin a series of actions unconditionally (*schlechthin*) within appearances, because every action as appearance, that is, "insofar as it produces a given," itself constitutes an event that "presupposes another state…. Thus in the temporal succession all actions of natural causes are themselves in turn effects, which likewise presuppose their causes in the time-series"; there is thus no original action in phenomenal nature, because the latter is constituted through the causal connection of appearances (KrV A543 f./B571 f. [Kant 1998a: 538]). This is not true of a *"causa noumenon"* that is free from the necessary chain of nature.

Whereas writers like Ulrich, Schmid, and Reinhold spelled out their doctrine of the compossibility of necessity and freedom using the conceptual pair, determinism/indeterminism, in the first part of his *Religionsschrift*, or *Religion within the Boundaries of Mere Reason* (1792), Kant held that this was not the correct theoretical opposition. Determinism and freedom might well be unified; the human power of choice can be determined through sufficient inner grounds and nonetheless be free. Every action has its ground, and as such is always determined. The question is whether this determination is natural, i.e., occurs on the basis of the temporal causality of nature, or instead according to the law of freedom independent of time. In other words,

> how can *pre-determinism* co-exist with freedom, when according to pre-determinism freely chosen actions, as occurrences, have their determining grounds *in antecedent time* (which, together with what is contained therein, no longer lies in our control), whereas according to freedom the action, as well as its contrary, must be in the control of the subject at the moment of its happening [?] (RGV 6: 49n [Kant 1998b: 94n])

As far as the question of moral imputation goes, this means that a human being can only be regarded as accountable when his actions are determined, not predetermined. Among all the transcriptions of Kant's lectures on moral philosophy, the Metaphysics of Morals Vigilantius (1793/94) is the first to express the newly formulated relation between determinism and indeterminism. It holds that the actions of a human being that follow as effects completely lack spontaneity, and to this extent, the human being cannot avoid the action. If a human being murders someone to take his money, and we regard the agent as a human being in nature, his action is nothing more than an effect. Pivotal to his deed is the end that he seeks to reach by it, e. g., the victim's money. The reasons for the action can also be seen as causes from which he cannot dissociate. The empirical character with which the resolution of the Third Antinomy is concerned is brought into play here once again, even if not explicitly; need, hot temper, poverty, bad (or rather, defective) upbringing now present reasons that explain the deed of a human being. In view of all these elements, "we see that, already from the agent's youth onward, there begin the causes that have produced their effects, and that the latter have in turn become causes of subsequent effects, right up to the final deed" (V-MS/Vigil 27: 502 [Kant 1997a: 269]). The human being is not accountable according to his empirical character, for his deed was predetermined. From this standpoint, the deed can be taken to be a given of nature that has its determinate cause in time. For Kant, it is important to repudiate a theory that is not able to deliver sufficient reasons for determinate events or facts. Indeterminism is such a doctrine because it entertains the possibility of accepting the uncertain as the explanatory ground of occurrences. On Kant's view, this is "impossible"; the Transcendental Analytic has conclusively shown that there is no chance in nature. But for those actions that are not effects of nature and so stand under the moral bond, they are necessarily determined. Thus though they are not predetermined because they have no ground in the preceding time, they stand "under the principle of determinism" (V-MS/Vigil 27: 504 [Kant 1997a: 270]). The determining grounds do not, in this latter case, present the natural causes of the empirical character; the doer is, on the contrary, "the originator and complete cause of his act" (ibid.). In other words, we are dealing here with a self-determination whose law is not the law of nature, but the law of morality.

Now, a human being is free insofar as he is noumenally self-determined. Nevertheless, the power to which the granted self-activity can be attached remains unspecified. This is not just a question of formulation. We have seen how in the contemporary discussion moral imputation was justified by means of the distinction between practical reason (i.e., the pure will) and the free power of choice. Reinhold, in particular, presented a case for connecting the problem of blame and merit to that of the free power of choice on the basis of which a human being can decide for or against the moral law. Thus, for Reinhold, the freedom of choice (*Willkürfreiheit*) is the same as the freedom to choose (*Wahlfreiheit*). And so I come to the second of the aforementioned topics. With this regard, it is meaningful to observe the difference between Kant's published writings and his university lectures. The dispute between Kant and his contemporaries seems to leave no trace in the lectures. The lectures employ a loose terminology when it turns to this topic. In the Moral Philosophy Collins, we read, for example, that the human power of choice is an *arbitrium liberum*, because it is "not necessitated *per stimulos*" (V-Mo/Collins 27: 267 [Kant 1997a: 59]). Freedom is spoken of here both in connection with the will and with the power of choice. The Practical Philosophy Powalski transcription claims that the moral law stands under no restriction of temperament, "since they are laws of the free power of choice" (V-PP/Powalski 27: 158). The moral law is meant here to be the law of the human power of choice, i.e., the human will. And the later Metaphysics of Morals Vigilantius also makes no clear distinction between the freedom of the will and the freedom of choice.

In contrast, the distinction occurs in the published writings, namely, the *Religion* and the *Metaphysics of Morals*. In the former, Kant claims that a human deed can only be morally imputed when the maxim that underlies it is adopted by the free power of choice. For this adoption, there is no knowable cause; it presents the ultimate ground of the deed. Now if we want to explain the sense in which a human being can be regarded as morally evil, we must take our departure from the fact that the human power of choice is free when its concept "is not empirical" (RGV 6: 35 [Kant 1998b: 58]). Kant apparently speaks here of a noumenal sense of the freedom of choice. The moral judgment of a human being only occurs insofar as the human being is himself the originator of his action; but he is the only author of it because he has decided by his freedom of choice to establish a determinate order between sensible incentives and the moral law. "The human being must make or have made *himself* into whatever he is or should become in a moral sense, good or evil. These two [characters] must be an effect of his free power of choice, for otherwise they could not be imputed to him and, consequently, he could be neither *morally* good nor evil" (RGV 6: 44 [Kant 1998b: 65]). In the *Religion*, imputation is thus grounded on what is emphasized by Reinhold: free human choice that rests on the intelligible, not empirical, concept of the freedom of choice.

When we turn to the Introduction to the *Metaphysics of Morals*, we notice that this is no longer the case. Kant distinguishes explicitly here between the faculty of the will and the faculty of the power of choice: the will describes the faculty of desire insofar as it is considered "in relation to the ground determining choice to action," whereas the power of choice has to do with the production of the action (MS/RL 6: 213 [Kant 1996a: 375]). Whereas Kant had maintained in the *Religion* that the freedom of choice, understood as the freedom to choose, is not empirical – the free adoption of a determinate incentive stood in connection with the concept of free choice (RGV 6: 44 [Kant 1998b: 65]) – he now believes that the free power of choice, insofar as it is construed as a power to choose, is an appearance (MS/RL 6: 226 [Kant 1996a: 380]). The will is now seen (as it is already seen in the *Groundwork* and *Critique of Practical Reason*) as practical reason, from which the laws issue. On the contrary, the power of choice has to do with the maxims of actions. Although different examples can be provided of the free power of choice as a faculty to choose to act for or against the moral law, this only pertains to it considered as a phenomenon. A human being, considered as a being of sense, reveals the faculty to conduct himself in accordance with or contrary to the moral law. Yet intelligible freedom is not defined by it. Whereas Kant explains the freedom of choice in the *Religion* in a positive way – i.e., as the adoption (or nonadoption) of an incentive in the maxims of action – in the *Metaphysics of Morals* he claims that the freedom is only knowable through a negative property, "namely that of not being *necessitated* to act through any sensible determining grounds"

(MS/RL 6: 226 [Kant 1996a: 380]). In addition, while Kant spoke of freedom of the will in both his published writings and his lectures, he now declares that the will "cannot be called either free or unfree" (ibid.).[7]

7 Conclusion

With the statement of 1797, the problem of moral imputation reaches a new climax within the Kantian philosophy. According to this view, all free actions can be imputed; but an action is free if it can be regarded as the first of an intelligible series. The absolute self-determination that is thus implied should not be understood as a freedom to choose on the basis of which a human being can decide both for and against the moral law. Accordingly, we can say that by renouncing Reinhold's definition of the freedom of the will as a freedom to choose, Kant seems to address the question of moral imputation by means of a theoretico-cognitive argument that had earlier been applied in the *Critique of Pure Reason*. We could sum up Kant's views as follows: what we see phenomenally does not allow us to draw conclusions about the noumenal. However, this is *not* to say that the valid model of imputation is the absolute model of the first *Critique*. What the text of the *Metaphysics of Morals* maintains in this regard seems to be the model of moral imputation I referred to as the *relative*. Kant also comments on this issue here in connection with physical and moral obstacles. We find the claim that the greater the physical hindrances are, and the smaller the moral duties, then the greater is the merit: "for example, at considerable self-sacrifice I rescue a complete stranger from great distress." Accordingly, "[t]he greater the natural obstacles (of sensibility) and the less the moral obstacle (of duty), so much the more merit is to be accounted for a *good deed*" (MS/RL 6: 228; Kant 1996a: 382). In any case, unlike Schmid, Kant does not here speak of intelligible obstacles.

We should thus see the differences between the models of moral imputation spelled out above as systematically defined options, even if not always rigidly applied. They are a function of whether human life is viewed merely from a transcendental perspective that admits of nothing empirical, or from the perspective of an applied philosophy devoted mainly to the temporal life of human beings. They reveal essentially different conceptions of human life. To this extent, Kant seems to pursue different needs on the basis of which he approaches human accountability from a variety of perspectives. Sometimes it is important for him

---

[7] In 1797, Reinhold replied to Kant's comment from the *Metaphysics of Morals*. On the dispute between Kant and Reinhold, see Allison 1990: 129–36; Baum 2012; Bondeli 2012.

to stress the circumstances that contribute to passing a milder or more generous moral judgment, sometimes not. Theoretical tensions thus remain rife throughout.

IV Anthropology

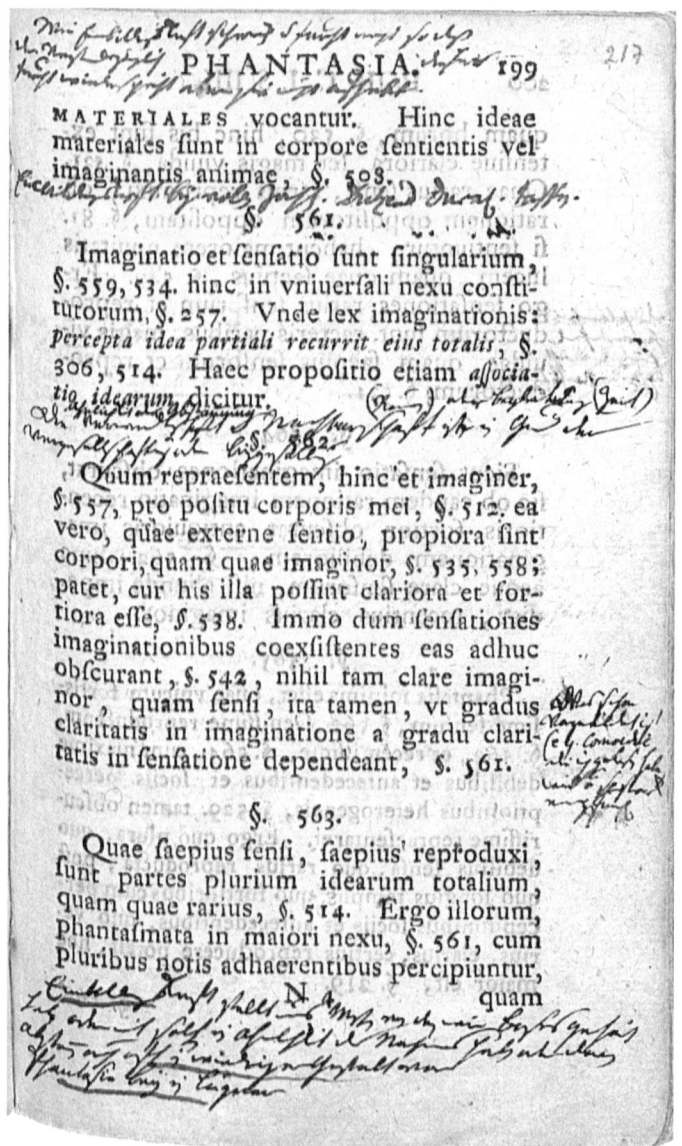

Fig. 7: Reproduction of page 199 ("Phantasia") of Kant's copy of A. G. Baumgarten's *Metaphysica* (Halle, 1757, 4th edn.), with Kant's handwritten notes: Reflections 345 (AA 15: 135), 349 (AA 15: 137), 355 (AA 15: 139), 358 (AA 15: 140). Reproduced with the kind permission of the University of Tartu Library, Estonia. Call number: manuscript 93. Kant's personal copy of Baumgarten's *Metaphysica* is available at the University of Tartu Library website: http://hdl.handle.net/10062/32369. Accessed 22 April 2015.

Chapter 9
Play and Society in the Lectures on Anthropology

Paul Guyer

1 Introduction

In a previous paper, I argued that Kant's lectures on anthropology show that the core of his aesthetic theory – his analysis of the claim of a judgment of taste to speak with a universal voice and his argument that such a claim could be grounded only in a state of our cognitive powers that is harmonious but not governed by rules, the state that Kant typically calls the free play of imagination and understanding – was in place long before the publication of the *Critique of the Power of Judgment* in 1790 and even before Kant's decision in 1787 to write such a book, but that what is missing from Kant's earlier treatment of aesthetics is the connection between aesthetics and morality – including the notions of the ideal of beauty, of intellectual interest in the beautiful, of aesthetic ideas as the spirit of fine art, of the beautiful as the symbol of the morally good, and of the sublime – and that it was Kant's discovery of the various ways in which the aesthetic could be connected to the moral without loosing its own freedom that moved Kant to publish a third *Critique* and to connect aesthetics to teleology within it (Guyer 2003: 135–63; reprinted in Guyer 2005: 163–89). In this paper, I want to focus more closely on what we can learn about Kant's concept of free play from the lectures on anthropology, and in particular that we can see clearly from the lectures that Kant actually uses the concept of play in two different ways. In a much earlier paper, I argued that a certain confusion in Kant's "key to the critique of taste" in §9, a confusion between the universal validity or communicability of aesthetic experience as what grounds the judgment of taste and as what makes aesthetic experience pleasurable in the first place, was the trace of an earlier position in which he expressly maintained that it is indeed the shareability of aesthetic experience that makes it pleasurable (Guyer 1982: 21–54). At that time, long before the publication of Kant's lectures on anthropology in 1997, I based that argument on evidence from Kant's handwritten notes on anthropology, that is, notes on the chapter on empirical psychology in his copy of Alexander Gottlieb Baumgarten's *Metaphysica* that was the text for his lectures, notes that had been published in the *Akademie-Ausgabe*[1] of Kant's works decades before it included the lectures on anthropology. In a second part of this paper, I will argue that this earlier theory is indeed to be found in the earliest lectures on anthropology, but that in subsequent lectures Kant had refined this earlier theory in precisely the way I had argued it should be refined. Hence the two parts of my title, "play" and "society."

2 Kant's concept of play in the lectures on anthropology

The concept of the free play of our cognitive powers, in the first instance the free play of imagination and understanding, in subsequent instances free play among those two and pure reason, especially pure practical reason, as well, is the central concept of Kant's aesthetics. Kant's analysis of judgments of taste and their objects in the "Analytic of the Beautiful" in the "Critique of the Aesthetic Power of Judgment," the first half of the third *Critique*, begins with the theses that judgments of taste are disinterested and not grounded in any determinate concepts of their objects that could ground an interest in them, but that such judgments are nevertheless "subjectively" if not "objectively" universally valid, that is, valid for all subjects experiencing their object, at least under optimal circumstances, but not valid for all objects in any class picked out by any determinate concept applied to the object,[2] and that they have "exemplary necessity," that is, if one subject properly judges an object beautiful, then it follows that others ought to do so as well.[3] Kant then argues that the state of free play between the cognitive powers of imagination and understanding is the only response to objects that could ground such judgments, since as free it is not necessitated by any deter-

---

[1] *Kant's gesammelte Schriften* (1900–). Quotations from Kant's *Critique of the Power of Judgment* will be from the edition by Paul Guyer (Kant 2000b), which will also be located by the relevant section number; quotations from the lectures on anthropology will be from Kant's *Lectures on Anthropology* (Kant 2012a), and will also be identified by the name given to the course of lectures from which they are drawn in the *Akademie-Ausgabe* and the translation.

[2] The trivial exception to this claim would be the concept *beautiful* itself: all objects properly called beautiful are members of the class of beautiful objects. But although, on Kant's theory, the concept *beautiful* does have an analysis, namely the one that Kant gives (so is not a Moorean "unanalyzable" concept), the terms of this analysis are not "marks" immediately applicable to objects the possession of which by objects would directly lead to the application of the predicate "beautiful" to them.

[3] I argued years ago that there is no real difference between Kant's "moments" of the subjectively universal validity and exemplary necessity of judgments of taste, and have never seen a good argument for changing my mind on this. See Guyer 1979 and (second edition) Guyer 1997, especially chapter 4, pp. 142–8, in the second edition.

minate concepts applied to objects, *a fortiori* by interests in them, for interests connect the prospect of pleasure to all objects in a class picked out by a determinate concept, but as involving cognitive powers common to all human beings the state of free play in the representation of a particular object can nevertheless be imputed to all of them, at least under optimal conditions. Kant famously argues that it is only the form of objects, for example the design rather than coloration in the case of an object of visual art (KU §14, 5: 225), that can trigger this state, but whether or not he is justified in making this claim in the first place it turns out that he relaxes it as he continues his argument, for his initial analysis of judgments of taste is just an analysis of a special and simple case of them, judgments of the "free" beauty of objects, paradigmatically natural objects such as birds and flowers and perhaps some special cases of fine or even decorative art, such as wallpaper borders and musical fantasias without words (KU §16, 5: 229), and most other aesthetic objects and our responses to them turn out to be more complicated. Thus, we respond to the beauty of human beings as a non-rule governed expression of human morality (KU §17), to the sublime as the revelation of the powers of human theoretical and practical reason by vast or powerful objects in nature (KU §§ 23–9), and to the beauty of art and in the end even of nature itself as the expression of moral ideas by objects that nevertheless do not fall under determinate concepts (KU §§ 49 and 51). In all of these cases, the aesthetic response can be regarded as a free play between the form of objects – in the case of the sublime, the formlessness of vast or powerful objects or vistas in nature on which Kant insists is itself a kind of form – perhaps their materials as well, and ideas of reason, and thus as free play involving the faculty of reason as well as those of imagination and understanding. What is crucial is that in all these cases our response to the object is aesthetic and grounds an aesthetic judgment because it is at bottom a form of free play, no matter how many higher faculties of mind it turns out to involve and no matter whether it turns out to involve concepts or ideas that we find to fit harmoniously with our perceptions of form, as long as we do not feel that the form of the object or the relation between form and matter or form and concept that we find in it is itself dictated by any determinate concept that applies to it.

But in the *Critique of the Power of Judgment* Kant characterizes the fundamental idea of free play itself only in the most abstract and obscure terms. In the first draft of the Introduction, Kant describes the relation between the two faculties of imagination and understanding in the state of aesthetic response (the basis of what he there calls "aesthetic reflecting judgment") as a "merely subjective" relation in which "one helps or hinders the other in the very same representation and thereby affects the **state of mind**," or one in which the power of judgment, which has no concept ready for the given intuition, holds the imagination (merely in the apprehension of the object) together with the understanding (in the presentation of a concept in general) and perceives a relation of the two faculties of cognition which constitutes the subjective, merely sensitive use of the objective use of the power of judgment in general (namely the agreement of those two faculties with each other). (EEKU, section VIII, 20: 223 f.)[4]

Kant also says that "since a merely subjective condition of a judgment does not permit a determinate concept of that judgment's determining ground, this can only be given in the feeling of pleasure" (EEKU, section VIIII, 20: 225), establishing that the relation between imagination and understanding he is trying to describe is not only caused by but is also the only consciously manifest evidence of the occurrence of this condition. But what exactly this relation is can hardly be made very clear by these highly abstract descriptions. The same is true of Kant's main descriptions of this fundamental concept of his entire theory in the published version of the Introduction and in the body of the work. The key passage in the published Introduction is that "the pleasure" that we take in a beautiful object "can express nothing but its suitability to the cognitive faculties that are in play in the reflecting power of judgment, insofar as they are in play, and thus merely a subjective formal purposiveness of the object" (note that Kant does not say here a subjective purposiveness of form in the object!). Kant then tries to describe this state of play further by saying that "if in this comparison the imagination (as the faculty of a priori intuitions) is unintentionally [*unabsichtlich*] brought into accord with the understanding, as the faculty of concepts, through a given representation and a feeling of pleasure is thereby aroused, then the object must be regarded as purposive for the reflecting power of judgment" (KU, section VII, 5: 189 f.). This tells us that in some way the two faculties are brought into accord or harmony (*Einstimmung*) with each other by or in the representation or reflection on the representation of an object, and that this is "unintentional," but it does not tell us very much about either what such a harmony is like or in what sense it or the activity that leads to it is unintentional. We will see later that the lectures on anthropology suggest two ways in which we might take this state to be unintentional and thus two senses in which it may be play or a product of play.

---

4 The so-called First Introduction is the draft of the Introduction that Kant wrote sometime during the composition of the third *Critique*, most likely earlier in 1789, and then replaced with the somewhat shorter version that was written in January, 1790, after the completion of the work, and published with the whole at the Easter book fair in spring, 1790. The published Introduction places more emphasis on the underlying connection between aesthetics (and teleology) and morality than does the earlier draft, supporting my contention that it was Kant's increasing awareness of the possibility of making this connection that moved him to write a third *Critique*.

In the body of the "Critique of the Aesthetic Power of Judgment," Kant makes two further attempts at stating his central idea. In the section that is supposed to provide the "key to the critique of taste," he describes the state grounding the judgment of taste as "The animation [*Belebung*] of both faculties (the imagination and the understanding) to an activity that is indeterminate but yet, through the stimulus of the given representation, in unison [*einhelliger*], namely that which belongs to a cognition in general," and the feeling of pleasure in the beautiful object as the "sensation of the effect that consists in the facilitated play of both powers of the mind (imagination and understanding), enlivened [*belebt*] through mutual agreement [*Zusammenstimmung*]" (KU §9, 5: 219). In addition to telling us that in the state of aesthetic response the imagination and understanding are in some sort of harmony (*Einstimmung* or *Zusammenstimmung*) that is the condition of the possibility of "a cognition in general," both of which characteristics have been suggested in the Introduction(s) but which remain entirely abstract, Kant now also tells us that this state is one of the "animation" of both cognitive powers, but he offers no explanation of what this means. So we have the general idea that somehow the condition of aesthetic response is a state of the cognitive faculties in which it seems as if the general conditions of cognition, whatever exactly those might be, are satisfied, though without the application of any determinate concept, which surely must ordinarily be a condition of the possibility of cognition, and that this state is in some sense lively and therefore pleasant, but that is all we know.

Finally, in the preparation for the "deduction of judgments of taste" that he offers after he has completed the Analytics of Beautiful and the Sublime (§§ 30–40), Kant not only repeats the idea of animation – "the judgment of taste must rest on a mere sensation of the reciprocally animating imagination in its **freedom** and the understanding with its **lawfulness**" – but also uses some terminology from general logic and his own "transcendental logic" to characterize the relation he has in mind: a judgment of taste, unlike an ordinary cognitive ("logical") judgment, does not "subsume" its object "under a concept at all," but nevertheless is grounded "in the subsumption of the imagination itself (in the case of a representation by means of which an object is given) under the condition that the understanding in general advance from intuitions to concepts"; and further, "the freedom of the imagination consists precisely in the fact that it schematizes without a concept" (KU § 35, 5: 286 f.). But since both subsumption and schematization in the only senses in which Kant has previously defined them properly apply only to determinate concepts – subsumption is the subordination of a more particular determinate concept to a more general one that contains it, as when the concept *tiger* is subsumed under the concept *feline* and that in turn under the concept *mammal*, and it is a concept that is schematized when it is furnished with a rule for its application to intuition, above all a category that is schematized when its purely logical content is accompanied with a rule for its application to intuition, as when the logical concept of substance as that in which properties inhere is associated with the temporal concept of that which endures through change (KrV A137 f./B176 f., A144/B183) – and what Kant has stressed above all about his idea of the harmonious play of the cognitive powers in aesthetic response is that it does not involve the application of a determinate concept to its object, we cannot tell what these logical concepts are supposed to mean here. They are being used metaphorically.

Thus we are left to conjecture about what Kant means by his central concept of the free play of imagination and understanding, or of the cognitive powers more generally, and there have been many such conjectures. My own proposal has been that what Kant has in mind is that the harmony or free play of the faculties is a state in which it seems that the main aim of cognition, namely the unification of our manifolds of sensibility, has been achieved, but not through the application of any determinate concept to the object, and that this state pleases us, all the more noticeably because in the absence of the application of a determinate concept to the object we do not expect it.[5] Others have interpreted Kant's idea in other ways.[6] What I now want to argue is that Kant's comments on aes-

---

[5] I initially presented this interpretation in Guyer 1979 (second edition, 1997), chapter 3. In "The Harmony of the Faculties Revisited" (Guyer 2005: 77–109), I suggested that because any object of representation is both obviously and according to Kant's epistemology in the first *Critique* necessarily subjected to some determinate concept or other, indeed to numerous ones (e. g., "work of music," "work of classical music," "work of the first Austrian school," "string quartet," "Hayden string quartet," and so on), Kant's position must be that in the case of work that we find beautiful – not every string quartet, perhaps not even (hard as this might be to believe!) not every Haydn string quartet – we feel it to be unified or harmonious in some way that goes beyond any and all of the determinate concepts that we do apply to it or that is not explained by those. For this reason I there called my interpretation a "meta-cognitive approach" to Kant's idea: his idea is not that the state of aesthetic response is one that *precedes* ordinary cognition (a "pre-cognitive approach") or one that involves alternation among several different cognitions of an object (a "multi-cognitive approach"), but that it is one that involves a feeling of a degree of unity (or perhaps other cognitive desiderata) in the experience of an object that goes beyond anything entailed by any of the determinate concepts that are applied to it.

[6] In "The Harmony of the Faculties Revisited" (2005), I classified a number of the other main interpretations of Kant's central idea in aesthetics under the rubrics of "pre-cognitive" and "multi-cognitive" approaches. I do not want to repeat that discussion here, but will only add that Henry Allison's argument that we must distinguish between the free play of the faculties and a harmonious play between them because there can also be unharmonious free play, as in the experience of the ugly, is belied by Kant's equation of the state of play between imagination and understanding as one of accord (*Einstimmung*) between them in the Introduction to the third

thetics over the series of lectures on anthropology confirm my approach while at the same time casting light on what he means by "animation," but also make clear that Kant invokes two different kinds of play in his aesthetic theory, and that we would do well to notice this distinction.

Kant did not treat aesthetics as a distinct topic in the lectures on anthropology, but followed his text by Baumgarten, who had of course initiated the treatment of aesthetics as a distinct academic discipline, in touching on issues in aesthetics in the course of his discussion of the faculties of cognition, feeling of pleasure and displeasure, and desire, which constituted the first half of his course. The matters he considered included the nature of taste, imagination, and genius or poetic invention (*Dichtung*), which in turn led to a contrast between poetry and eloquence that survived into the third *Critique*. I will focus on Kant's conception of play in the remainder of this section and on the social nature of taste in the next without attending further to the context in which these topics are broached. And although Kant touched upon these topics in all of the recorded anthropology lectures, I will focus on material from the first version of the course in 1772/73, designated as "Collins,"[7] the "Friedländer" transcription from 1775/76, and the "Mrongovius" transcription from 1784/85, as these not only mark the main stages in the development of Kant's ideas but are also readily accessible in the Cambridge volume of *Lectures on Anthropology* (Kant 2012a).

The 1772/73 course already characterizes judgments of taste as independent of considerations of utility and thus what Kant would subsequently call disinterested or "without interest" ("A choice is to be made without reflecting on utility," V-Anth/Collins 25: 177); as nevertheless universally valid ("What is supposed to be in accordance with taste must please universally, " V-Anth/Collins 25: 179) as in some way made a priori ("In regard to real taste, I must make the judgment about what pleases universally from experience, while in regard to ideal taste one can make it a priori," V-Anth/Collins 25: 179); and as grounded in play and animation of our cognitive powers. Although beauty can be "united with utility," in which case "the liking for it becomes more well-grounded and enduring" (something

---

Critique. There is no room for a *disharmonious* state of play in this dispositive statement. See Allison 2001, chapter 5, especially on 116 f. See also my extended argument in "Kant on the Purity of the Ugly" (Guyer 2005: 141–62).

7 Georg Ludwig Collins (1763–1814) matriculated at Königsberg only in 1784 and his transcription of the lectures is dated 1786. But although it is used as evidence of Kant's lectures in 1772/73 because of its similarity to other manuscripts originating from that course, it must have been a copy made for Collins (it is not in his own hand; see AA 25: cxlv) when he was a student a decade later from a source dating back to the original course.

that should be kept in mind when considering the contrast between "free" and "adherent" beauty in the eventual third *Critique*),

> Just the same, pure beauty, which is only for taste and furnishes a certain pure gratification [*Vergnügen*], remains void of all utility. It pleases us whenever it sets our collective living power [*Lebhafftigkeit*] into activity; but it is a gratification apart only if one sets an activity into play [*Spiel*]. (V-Anth/Collins 25: 176 f.)

Continuing the discussion, Kant makes it clear that he does not mean that a beautiful object has to lack utility objectively, so to speak, indeed if it did then beauty could never be combined with utility, but rather that in responding, subjectively, to an object as beautiful, we set aside consideration of its utility, or "investigate, strain out, and refine" our response to its utility. Indeed he says that our development of the ability to do so "contributes much to the perfection of a human being" (V-Anth/Collins 25: 177); one might want to read into this remark an anticipation of Kant's later claim that the development of our taste for beauty is conducive to the development of our morality because it prepares us to love something disinterestedly (KU, General Remark following § 29, 5: 267). All of these ideas will remain constant in Kant's aesthetic theory. What is most important for our present purposes is that Kant does say a little more or at least a little more that is concrete about what he means by play. He says:

> All human beings have certain harmonious laws through which they form objects: those are the laws of representation. What makes sensible intuition easier pleases and is beautiful; that is in accord with the subjective laws of sensibility, and it promotes the inner life, since it sets the power of cognition into activity. This facilitation happens through space and time. Alteration in space is the figure, in time is merely the play. The play of alteration is facilitated through proportion in the parts. Symmetry facilitates comprehensibility and is a relation of sensibility. In the case of a disproportioned house I can see the whole only with difficulty; by contrast in the case of a well-built house I see the equality of the two sides. Equality of parts promotes my sensible representation, facilitates the intuition, increases the life of activity and favors it; hence the whole must please me; but for that reason also it must please all, for this rule grounds all of them. Alteration in time is called play. – In music the chief factor is the tempo, or the determination of the equality of time .... Between the sounds there must be a proportion and symmetry, if it is to please and this is the *accorde*. This facilitates sensible comprehensibility. – ... In a garden I find beauty through comprehensibility; if there is no order in it, then I can make no image of it; I see too much at once. If I look at a garden, then I am serious at first sight and seek proportion and symmetry, it pleases only because it is usual for me to represent it thus. (V-Anth/Collins 25: 181 f.)

We can learn a great deal from this string of claims. First, what Kant means by "life" or in his later term "animation" is activity or unrestricted or facilitated activity itself. This can be activity of specific powers, as it is here, or, presumably, the activity of the person as a whole – the two different senses of play that Kant will subsequently distinguish might be distinguished along these lines. Although Kant does not repeat it here, he has earlier said that activity or life as such is a source of pleasure or "gratification"; thus a basic part of his theory will always be that the free activity of our cognitive powers in aesthetic experience is a fundamental source of its pleasurableness. Second, Kant also suggests that aesthetic experience culminates in a sort of comprehensibility (*Begreiflichkeit*) that is facilitated by symmetry or proportion among the parts of the representation or object of representation that triggers such response. He does not say this yet here, but of course it is explicit in his later theory that aesthetic experience is independent from the application of determinate concepts, so it must be an experience of comprehensibility independent from concepts, *Begreiflichkeit* without *Begriffe*. This would still just be a metaphor were it not that Kant here gives us some examples of what he means: being able to represent a whole house easily without applying the concept of a house or to form the image (*Bild*) of a garden on the basis of the symmetry and proportion of its elements is what it is to experience comprehensibility without concepts. So in addition to being pleasurable in its own right, mental activity is also pleasurable when it results in an image or sense of the unity of a manifold of representations, the grasp of it as a whole, independently from the application of any determinate concept or concepts to that manifold. We can take this as an explication of what Kant means in his later, more metaphorical terminology such as satisfying the subjective conditions of cognition independently of the usual objective conditions, or of satisfying the conditions for a cognition in general without any particular cognition.

However, it will also have been noted that in this passage Kant uses the term "play" restrictively: he uses it to refer to our mental activity in apprehending and finding comprehensible a temporal manifold, such as we are given in the experience of music, but not a spatial one, such as we are given in the experience of a house or a garden or, presumably, a painting or sculpture. As Kant says, "Alteration in time is called play," or, more precisely, we should think, the experience of alteration in time. This restriction is not present in Kant's initial reference to play in the Collins notes (V-Anth/Collins 25: 177), where he speaks simply of setting "an activity into play," but his subsequent explication of the concept of play seems to be restricted. Yet there may be less to this restriction than meets the eye. For on Kant's own theory that time is the former of all inner sense, a theory in place since the inaugural dissertation of 1770 and thus in place when he is first giving the anthropology lectures, although a spatial manifold itself might not be temporal, *our experience* of it, as of everything else, is necessarily temporal; thus, even though the parts of the house or garden may all exist at once, our experience of them is temporally extended, and thus the activity of apprehending them and then finding comprehensibility in them and being able to grasp them as a whole without the use of a concept but facilitated by proportion and symmetry ought to count as play. And this is precisely what we find Kant saying in the next iteration of the anthropology course, recorded in the Friedländer notes from 1775/76.

Aesthetic issues are broached very quickly in the Friedländer notes. Early in this discussion of the cognitive faculty, under the title "On the Obscure Representations of the soul," Kant states that

> We take pleasure in letting our minds wander about in obscurity, which the hidden and oblique modes of speech prove. Every obscurity which is suddenly clarified provides amenity and delights much. The art of an author consists in concealing his ideas in such a way that the reader can immediately resolve them on his own ... Clarity, however, is soon wearying. Yet, we not only play with such obscure representations, rather we are also ourselves a play of obscure representations .... Every inspiration which is a riddle in the beginning, but which is immediately followed by elucidation, is also a translation and a detour in the mind, and the mind is pleased to have resolved a difficulty. (V-Anth/Fried 25: 481)

Here the concept of play is being used quite generally, not restricted to one medium; indeed, Kant uses it so generally that he also claims that we ourselves are nothing but a play of obscure representations, a Leibnizian-sounding claim that plays no role in his mature aesthetics and which I will thus not attempt to interpret. What is important about this passage is that it suggests that play requires a manifold from which comprehensibility does not emerge immediately, but that we enjoy both letting the mind wander freely *and* then finding clarity or resolution, or in terms of the previous discussion comprehensibility or a sense of wholeness, out of the obscurity. Both elements are part of play. This is the reason why Kant subsequently distinguishes between beauty and mere novelty: if all we have is novelty, a puzzle or something unfamiliar, our pleasure ceases as soon as the novelty wears off, while genuine beauty endures, and therefore must sustain our mental activity, perhaps our sense of obscurity, even while also allowing a grasp of wholeness. "Novelty, which is opposed to uniformity," Kant writes, "is required to put the mind in [a state of] clarity by means of variety" (V-Anth/Fried 25: 507), but at the same time "There exist delights with which, upon their prolongation, one gets fed up; for example, magic, [or] witty ideas," although "On the other hand there exist enjoyments with which one does not get fed up upon their prolongation, and through whose repetition one does not get weary" (V-Anth/Fried 25: 571). Kant illustrates the latter with "intellectual enjoyments ... for example [taking pleasure] in the sciences," but he could also put here true beauty as opposed to mere novelty. True beauty must involve sufficient variety to keep the mind wandering, which is one aspect of the play of the cognitive powers, while at the same time allowing it to reach a sense of comprehensibility, which is the other.

Second, in the Friedländer notes Kant makes it clear that we can play with all kinds of sensible manifolds, because whatever the content of the manifold, our experience of it is always temporally extended. Here is the key passage, which starts off by applying the concept of play to (the arts of) sight as well as to (the arts of) sound:

> Hearing is a play of sensation, and sight a play of shape. Variousness in accordance with time is a play, hence music is a play of sensation. Variousness in accordance with space is shape, hence dancing is a play of shape. It may be called a play to the extent that it occurs gradually, thus in relation to time. Play affects more than shape, because it is sensation. If play buoys up the whole human being, then the individual is animated. (V-Anth/Fried 25: 496)

To be sure, a dance and not only the representation of a dance takes time, so it is reasonable to call the experience of it a form of play (if it meets the other condition for this, namely variety or obscurity leading to comprehensibility through order and proportion) even if play is an essentially temporal notion. But Kant's claim is more general than his example, for he says simply that "sight is a play of shape." This must apply to our sight or our experience of a painting or sculpture as well as a dance, for even though a painting or sculpture is before us all at once in a way that the complete dance is not, the experience of the former takes time as well as that of the latter.[8]

Interestingly, in this passage Kant explicitly includes color among the proper objects of aesthetic response, about which he seems at best conflicted in the later *Critique of the Power of Judgment*. Here Kant says that "Shape is only the form, but color is a play of sensation. One already has the thought of producing consonances and dissonances through colors, in the way that it happens through the tones in hearing, and of making a play of sensation through the eyes." He then continues that "if a complete color results" from such a play of sensations, "then it is becoming," while

---

[8] In *Laocoön*, Gotthold Ephraim Lessing had famously argued that because poetry is an essentially temporal art, the poet (Homer) effectively depicts the beauty of an object (the shield of Achilles, the magnificent dress of a goddess), by describing the *making* of the object or the *act* of dressing (Lessing, *Laocoön: An Essay on the Limits of Painting and Poetry*, [1766] 1984, chapter XVI). Kant makes no allusion to Lessing here, nor is he committed to the thesis that an object, for example a work of art, has to have a specifically temporal content in order for our experience of it to be temporal. All experience is temporal.

> If a complete color does not result, then it does not please. For example, if there is a lot of blue and little yellow, then a complete color, namely green, results. Hence a blue jacket with a yellow vest is becoming, but when a lot of yellow and little blue are intermingled, then a dirty color results. Hence, too, a yellow jacket with a blue vest is not becoming. (V-Anth/Fried 25: 497)

Here Kant does not suggest, as he does in the third *Critique*, that if we are to have a genuinely aesthetic response to color then it must be because we are somehow subconsciously aware of the play of the vibrations of light that, according to Euler, cause our experience of color (KU § 14, 5: 224); his appeal is more straightforwardly phenomenological, the relevant factor simply being whether we have a feeling of completeness or not. Thus his position on color here illustrates his general claim that play is an experience of variety that culminates in a sense of unity or wholeness.

Kant also illustrates his idea of what makes play pleasing in a definition of a poem. This may be taken as an implicit riposte to Baumgarten's famous definition of a poem as *oratio sensitiva perfecta*, or a "perfect sensory discourse," where that in turn is defined as *cuius varia tendunt ad cognitionem repraesentationum sensitivarum*, or "one whose parts tend toward cognition of sensory representations."[9] In the lectures on anthropology given fifteen years before the publication of the third *Critique*, Kant does not yet evince his later hostility to what he considers to be Baumgarten's perfectionism,[10] but he nevertheless substitutes his own concept of play in his definition of a poem for Baumgarten's definition of the perfection of cognition. Kant writes:

> The harmonious play of thoughts and sensations is the poem. The play of thoughts and sensations is the agreement of subjective laws; if the thoughts agree with my subject, then this is a play of the same. Two different things should be noticed about thoughts, that they stand in relation to objects, and hence the thoughts must be true, and that the course of thoughts agrees with the nature of the powers of the mind [*Gemüths Kräfte*], thus with the subject, and therefore the succession of thoughts [must agree] with the powers of mind. This harmonious play of thoughts and sensations is the poem. (V-Anth/Fried 25: 525 f.)

---

9 Alexander Gottlieb Baumgarten, *Meditationes philosophicae de nonnullis ad poema pertinentibus* (1735), edited with a German translation by Heinz Paetzold, §§ix, vii (Baumgarten 1983a: 10 f.)

10 See EEKU, Remark in Section VIII, especially 20: 226–30, and, in the published text, KU § 15, 5: 226–9.

Here Kant brings out both aspects of his concept of play, that it involves a successive experience of variety – a course or train of thoughts[11] – but also harmony, or the realization of a sense of wholeness, completion, or comprehensibility in the manifold or course of thoughts, although without the application of a determinate concept. Now, this last requirement might seem to be undermined in the case of a poem, which has conceptual content, but Kant's statement makes it clear that our pleasure in a poem lies not in the straightforward recognition of the truth that it conveys but rather in the harmonious play between its thoughts or content and its sensations or the ones it stimulates – and that harmony is not itself dictated by the concepts that are the content of the poem. This is the theory that Kant will later present as the theory of aesthetic ideas as constituting the content of successful art, art with "spirit" and produced by "genius." At this early stage Kant thus makes clear that a work of art and our experience of it can contain concepts as parts of their content without those contents dictating our response to the work, thus leaving room for free play of our mental powers with the content of the work and its form and all the sensations it stimulates.

Kant's discussion of poetry in the Friedländer notes also sheds light on his concept of life or animation (*Belebung*), a term used, as we saw, in the "key to the critique of taste" but without explanation. Here Kant says that "To enliven [*beleben*] means to give the thoughts intensity, clarity, intuition," and that the poet, for example, does this through the use of meter and rhyme. Here one also cannot but think of Baumgarten, although the Baumgarten of the later *Aesthetica* rather than the earlier *Meditationes*, for whom characteristics such as *claritas, lux,* and *vita cognitionis* are markers of the aesthetic. For Kant, what these terms seem to mean is that aesthetic qualities make sensations and ideas stand out from the train of thoughts and impress themselves upon us. Combining this with what

---

[11] Just as Kant does not name Baumgarten as his target, so he also does not name a possible source for his alternative view; but it is hard to read his reference to the "course" or "succession" of thoughts and the necessity that they agree with the nature of the mental powers and not to think of the opening chapter of Kames's *Elements of Criticism*, which argues that all thought consists in "a continued train of perceptions and ideas passing in [the] mind," that "we are framed by nature to relish order and connection" in such trains, and that "Every work of art that is conformable to the natural course of our ideas," and to our natural preference for order and connection in such trains, "is so far agreeable"; Henry Home, Lord Kames, *Elements of Criticism* (1762), sixth edition, 1785, chapter I (in Home 2005: 21, 26, 27). The *Elements of Criticism* had been immediately translated into German and there is no doubt that Kant was familiar with it. His aesthetic theory was clearly deeply influenced by Kames and by Alexander Gerard, whose *Essay on Taste* was published in 1759 and *Essay on Genius* in 1774 (although Kant argues with the latter rather than appropriating it).

Kant suggested about animation in the Collins notes, we might conclude that just as play has two sides, the variety of the course of ideas on the one side and the comprehensibility that emerges from that on the other, so does animation: on one side it is sheer activity, pleasurable as such, on the other it lies in the fact that sensations and ideas stand out from that activity, leave an image or even sear themselves into our minds, and it is enjoyable for that reason too.

Kant's discussion of poetry in the Friedländer notes also leads to what I suggested at the outset would be a second sense of play in his aesthetic theory. While play in the first sense is characteristic of mental activity in response to a beautiful object, the activity of both exploring manifolds of sensations and ideas and of finding comprehensibility in them, an activity that according to the third *Critique* itself is manifest to consciousness through the feeling of pleasure that it produces and thus might itself be regarded as playing out below the level of consciousness or at least below the level of intentionality – I may go to the museum intentionally, but what happens in my mind in front of the paintings is a response, in a way unintentional (as Kant himself suggested in the Introduction to the third *Critique* with his term *unabsichtlich*) – of course there is an element of intentionality in the creation of works of art, a conscious exploration and expression of the results of that exploration in some medium or other. Kant characterizes the activity of the poet as a form of play, more precisely he contrasts the activity of the poet and that of the orator in terms of the degree of play that each is allowed, and this seems to refer to the intentional activity of the whole person of the poet (or orator) and not to the play of their mental faculties. Thus Kant continues the passage on poetry we have been discussing as follows. What we previously quoted ended with the remark that "This harmonious play of thoughts and sensations is the poem." But Kant continues:

> Poetry and eloquence are in this differentiated. The poem is a harmonious play in which the thoughts conform to the play of sensations, eloquence is also a harmonious play, but here sensation must conform to the thoughts. The sensations must promote and enliven the thoughts. To enliven means to give the thoughts intensity, clarity, intuition. The poet carries on the play of thoughts, to the extent that they conform to the sensations …. There is always a steady play, which is a matter of expression, and that is the main thing in poetry …. In the art of poetry, the poet has great freedom in thoughts and words, but with regard to the harmony of the play, he has no freedom. (V-Anth/Fried 25: 526)

Kant goes on with the contrast between the degree of freedom of play in poetry and in eloquence, the point being that the orator is allowed a degree of play but is beholden to truth in a way that the poet is not; this is the thought that shows up in the third *Critique* itself in the more exaggerated claim that "**Rhetoric** is the art of conducting a business of the understanding as a free play of the imagination; **poetry** that of carrying out a free play of the imagination as a business of the understanding" (KU § 51, 5: 321), a contrast that seems to imply a certain degree of disingenuousness at least on the side of the orator, which is not any part of Kant's position in the lectures. Kant also makes clear that poems or genres of poetry may differ in their involvement of ideas at all; thus, "Many poems are mere plays of sensation, for example, love poems .... However, to bring virtue and its sensations into a harmonious play is meritorious, for it is something intellectual, and to make this intuitable is truly meritorious, for example Pope's *Essay on Man*" (V-Anth/Fried 25: 527). But the point that I want to emphasize is just that Kant is using the concept of play to characterize the conscious and at least to some degree intentional activity of the *person*, namely the artist, in creating art, as well as using it to characterize the unintended and perhaps not even always conscious activity of the *mind* that goes in the response to aesthetic objects in general and even within the mind of the artist as the audience for his own work as he is creating it. I say "at least to some degree intentional" because it is the gist of Kant's theory of genius that the artist's intention does not completely govern the production of a successful work of art, or is not a sufficient condition for it; that is why genius is or also requires a gift of nature. That an intention cannot completely govern the *creation* of a work of art is the mirror image of the fact that no determinate concept can completely determine the *response* to a successful work of art or other aesthetic object. But my larger point here is that once we recognize that Kant is using the concept of play in two different ways, in one way to characterize the activity of the mental powers or cognitive faculties in aesthetic response and in another although of course related way to characterize the conscious activity of the person in the creation of art, we can also see better how the two halves of Kant's theory, his theory of aesthetic response and his theory of artistic production, fit together without collapsing into each other.[12]

This issue could be pursued further, but at this point I will turn to my second topic, Kant's treatment of the relation between taste and society in the lectures on anthropology.

3 Taste and society in the lectures on anthropology

The "key to the critique of taste" that Kant offers in § 9 of the third *Critique* contains a puzzle. Everything that Kant has said in the first "moment" and in the

---

[12] Kant returns to his contrast between poetry and eloquence in the Pillau lectures (V-Anth/Pillau 25: 760) and the Mrongovius lectures (V-Anth/Mron 25: 1279).

second "moment" of the Analytic of the Beautiful up to that point implies that a judgment of taste asserts the subjective universal validity *of a feeling of pleasure* that has been felt in response to an object independently of the predication of any determinate concept of it or interest in it, or to speak with a "universal voice" (KU § 8, 5: 216) *about that pleasure*, and that the object is called beautiful on that account. But in § 9, although Kant begins by asking under what condition "universal communicability" can be "attributed in the judgment of taste to the representation of the object," he suddenly states that "it is the universal capacity for the communication of the state of mind in the given representation which, as the subjective condition of the judgment of taste, must serve as its ground and *have the pleasure in the object as its consequence*," (KU § 9, 5: 217; emphasis added) and that the "subjective universal communicability of the kind of representation in a judgment of taste, since it is supposed to occur without presupposing a determinate concept, can be nothing other than the state of mind in the free play of the imagination and understanding" and that "this merely subjective (aesthetic) judging of the object ... *precedes the pleasure in it*" (KU § 9, 5: 218; emphasis added). It seems incoherent for Kant to argue that it is the universal validity or communicability *of* a feeling of pleasure that *causes* that same feeling of pleasure. I have argued that in order to avoid this confusion, Kant needs to distinguish two sorts of judging, the harmonious free play of imagination and understanding in response to an object that leads to the feeling of pleasure in it and the judgment of taste proper, the product of reflection *on that feeling of pleasure* that leads to the claim (if it is actually made) that the pleasure is universally communicable. I have also argued that what may have led Kant into this confusion in the first place was an earlier theory according to which the pleasure of sharing our responses with fellow human beings is indeed the sole feeling of pleasure involved in aesthetic experience. The series of lectures on anthropology confirm Kant's early attraction to a so to speak purely social theory of aesthetic experience, but then show how he refined it in a way that recognizes the social source of much of our pleasure in aesthetic objects without a paradox: the opportunity to share our pleasure in a beautiful object *adds* to our pleasure in it, indeed creates an *interest* in beauty, but is not the original or sole source of pleasure in it. This is the same position that David Hume had reached in the *Treatise of Human Nature*,[13] and not only free

---

13 Hume [1739–40] 2007, see especially Book II, Part II, Section V, and Book III, Part III, Section I. See also "The Standard of Taste and the 'Most Ardent Desire of Society'" (Guyer 1993; reprinted in Guyer 2005: 37–74). Kant would not have been familiar with most of the *Treatise* at the time of the Collins lectures, but could have been by the time he gave the Mrongovius lectures, since a complete translation of the *Treatise* had by then appeared.

from paradox but also perfectly sensible. The original theory can be found in its raw form in a few remarks in the Collins lectures:

> A human being in the wilderness is not concerned about taste. Everything beautiful one loves and seeks only for society. It is very probable that the man would choose a woman not in regard to her beauty but according to her health and strength. That one now chooses from beauty, one does this from love for society, for one has a particular gratification when one possesses something that pleases others. (V-Anth/Collins 25: 179)

Even here there is as much overstatement as genuine theory, for this passage follows Kant's initial account of activity or play as the source of our pleasure in beauty, which does not require society, and also his explanation of the "particular gratification" in beauty that we can enjoy in society actually presupposes that there is an antecedent pleasure in beauty independent of society: we experience this gratification when we possess something that *pleases others*, and we will end up with a vicious regress if their pleasure too is one that arises only from sharing pleasure. It would be perfectly reasonable for Kant to say that we are concerned about *taste* only in society, that is, that it is only if we live with others (as of course we humans always start out doing and normally continue to do) that we will *care* whether our pleasures are idiosyncratic or shareable, and only in society that we will make the effort to develop the ability to discriminate between the two. And it would also be perfectly reasonable for him to say that being able to share our pleasure with others *adds* to our original pleasure, which can happen only in the case of genuinely shareable rather than idiosyncratic pleasures. But Kant does not make either of these refinements in the first course on anthropology.

A decade later, however, in the Mrongovius lectures, Kant makes the refinements necessary to avoid paradox and to confirm common sense. The passage is worth quoting at length:

> Taste is thus the ability to choose socially. One must confirm the rules of taste out of experience, otherwise one is uncertain about whether one can immediately know them already beforehand. They also tolerate exceptions, for they are borrowed from experience. It is always possible to dispute taste; one cannot demonstrate it. Taste becomes more universal the more cultivated the nation becomes.... The beautiful conveys with it a comfort; but it is not for this reason beautiful, but rather because it pleases universally. A judgment of taste should be distinguished from an inclination of taste. The latter is the interest I take in taste. When I am on a deserted island, it is true that I will find this or that beautiful, but I will find no interest in it. The useful will outweigh the beautiful. The inclination of taste grows in accordance with the degree of the inclination to sociability. (V-Anth/Mron 25: 1326)

Kant then talks about how the normal social inclination to beauty can easily lead to an excessive desire for luxury and to vanity, but concludes that there is nevertheless a normal and healthy pleasure in being able to share our pleasure in beauty: "We enjoy something twice as much when we see that others like it and that we are good company," and therefore enjoy a social gathering more in an orderly garden than in a forest (V-Anth/Mron 25: 1328). Of course, we can only enjoy something twice as much if we already enjoy it once. And people can be vain about their gardens, too, so there is always the risk that "Vanity [will have] a large share in our pleasure in" our garden and that we will not just enjoy doubling our solitary pleasure in its beauty when we can share it.

This passage makes a number of crucial points. First, it is clear that from the outset Kant is distinguishing the complex phenomenon of *taste* from pleasure in *beauty* as such. Pleasure in beauty can be a relation between a single subject and object, but taste concerns the universal validity or shareability of such a pleasure. It refers to the possibility of society and also, Kant implies, properly develops only in society. Society can confirm our judgments about what is truly beautiful, that is, shareably enjoyable, and even lead to the formation of rules for taste. Kant will later disallow such rules (KU § 33, 5: 284 f.), but Kant's remark here that such rules allow exceptions suggests that they are no more than rules of thumb. He does not spell out an explanation for this suggestion, but it seems natural to suppose that this is because our aesthetic response, our free play of imagination and understanding, is highly context-dependent, sensitive to every nuance of the manifold of representations before us rather than being settled by the few marks included in any determinate concept, and therefore generalizations, though they have their place, are always hostage to actual experience. This would not be incompatible with Kant's mature view.

Second, Kant makes it clear that there is a difference between merely being pleased with a beautiful object and having an inclination toward or taking an interest in beauty. The difference is presumably based precisely on the distinction between the original pleasure in beauty, which anyone can take anytime and anywhere, and the further pleasure that one has when one can share one's pleasure with others. As long as these two pleasures are – theoretically if not phenomenologically – distinct, there is no danger of paradox. The pleasure in beauty as such may be relatively slight, easily outweighed by pleasure in utility in a solitary state (in which survival would probably be precarious and there would be a premium on utility), and the pleasure in sharing our pleasures may be very great, easily obscuring the primary pleasure in beauty and leading to mere fad and fashion.[14] We all know that to be true, and hardly an objection to Kant's distinction. But once we have distinguished between the pleasure in beauty which is due simply

---

[14] Kant discusses fashion further in the Mrongovius lectures, at V-Anth/Mron 25: 1328 f.

to the free and disinterested play of our cognitive powers with the representation of an object and which could in principle take place even on a desert island, on the one hand, and the pleasure in sharing experiences that can be enjoyed only in society and that can lead to an interest in beauty and beyond that to vanity in owning beautiful or just fashionable objects and all the rest, the paradox of Kant's §9 can be avoided.

In conclusion, Kant's discussions of aesthetics in the lectures on anthropology shed light on the central concepts of his mature aesthetic theory, those of the free play of our cognitive powers as the underlying source of our pleasure in beauty on the one hand and of the judgment of taste on the other as an assessment of the universal validity, communicability, or shareability of such pleasure and as the basis of a further social pleasure and interest in beauty. As is so often the case with Kant's lectures, especially the popular courses such as the lectures on ethics as well as the lectures on anthropology, which were addressed to a broader audience than some of his other courses and therefore strove for accessibility, they help make concrete what is often so abstract in Kant's main published works, such as the three *Critiques*.

EXSISTENTIA ANIMAE. 179

§. 517.

Quo plures notas perceptio complectitur, hoc est fortior, §. 23, 515. Hinc obscura perceptio plures notas comprehendens, quam clara, est eadem fortior, confusa plures notas comprehendens, quam distincta, est eadem fortior. PERCEPTIONES plures in se continentes PRAEGNANTES,* vocantur. Ergo perceptiones praegnantes fortiores sunt. Hinc ideae habent magnum robur, §. 148. Termini, significatus praegnantis, sunt EMPHATICI ** (emphases). Horum scientia EMPHASEOLOGIA est. Nominum propriorum non parua vis est.

   * vielsagende Vorstellungen.   ** ein Nachdruck.

§. 518.

Status animae, in quo perceptiones dominantes obscurae sunt, est REGNVM TENEBRARVM, * in quo clarae regnant, REGNVM LVCIS ** est.

   * das Reich der Finsternis.   ** das Reich des Lichtes in der Seele.

SECTIO II.
FACVLTAS COGNOSCITIVA
INFERIOR.

§. 519.

Anima mea cognoscit quaedam, §. 506. Ergo

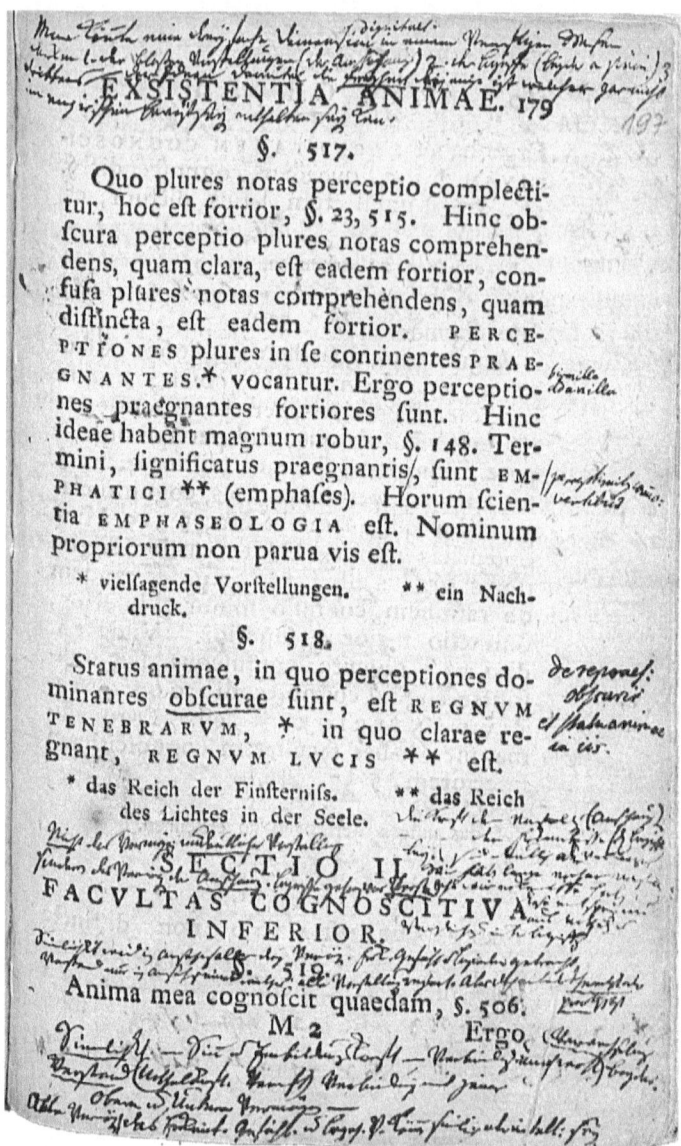

Fig. 8: Reproduction of page 179 ("Sectio II. Facultas Cognoscitiva Inferior") of Kant's copy of A. G. Baumgarten's *Metaphysica* (Halle, 1757, 4th edn.), with Kant's handwritten notes: Reflections 112–13 (AA 15: 7 f.), 209 (AA 15: 80), 221–23 (AA 15: 84 f.), 226 (AA 15: 86). Reproduced with the kind permission of the University of Tartu Library, Estonia. Call number: manuscript 93. Kant's personal copy of Baumgarten's *Metaphysica* is available at the University of Tartu Library website: http://hdl.handle.net/10062/32369. Accessed 22 April 2015.

Chapter 10
From Faking It to Making It: The Feeling of Love of Honor as an Aid to Morality

Alix Cohen

1 Introduction

Until recently, Kant's ethics had been portrayed as unequivocal on one issue: natural drives, including feelings, passions and inclinations, are intrinsically at odds with morality (see, e.g., GMS 4: 398; KpV 5: 151; and MS 6: 392f.). Following a surge of attention to Kant's anthropological works in the last ten years or so, including his lectures on anthropology, a number of exceptions to this claim have been uncovered, most notably the feelings of sympathy and love.[1] By enabling an emotional and epistemic openness to others, these feelings play a facilitating role for moral agency. For instance, regarding our capacity for sympathy, Kant writes:

> [W]hile it is not in itself a duty to share the sufferings (as well the joys) of others, it is a duty to sympathize actively in their fate; and to this end it is therefore an indirect duty to cultivate the compassionate natural (aesthetic) feelings in us, and to make use of them as so many

---

[1] The publication of *Vorlesungen über Anthropologie* in the *Akademie-Ausgabe* of *Kant's gesammelte Schriften* (1997) has been followed by the new English translation of *Anthropology from a Pragmatic Point of View* (Kant 2006), and the publication of the volumes *Anthropology, History, and Education* (Kant 2007) and *Lectures on Anthropology* (Kant 2012a), both in The Cambridge Edition of the Works of Immanuel Kant. In the Anglo-American tradition, the first substantial works dedicated to Kant's anthropology date from 2000 with Robert Louden's *Kant's Impure Ethics*, 2002 with John Zammito's *Kant, Herder, and the Birth of Anthropology*, and 2003 with Patrick Frierson's *Freedom and Anthropology in Kant's Moral Philosophy* as well as Brian Jacobs and Patrick Kain's *Essays on Kant's Anthropology*. Since then, studies have multiplied, including Wilson (2006), Cohen (2009) and Sturm (2009). The *Critical Guide: Kant's Lectures on Anthropology* (Cohen 2014) offers the first comprehensive assessment of Kant's lectures on anthropology, their philosophical importance, their evolution, and their relationship to his Critical philosophy. I am grateful to Robert Clewis for his insightful comments on earlier drafts of this paper. I would also like to thank Pablo Muchnik for his invitation to take part in a North American Kant Society session at the 2014 Eastern Division Meeting of the APA in Philadelphia, which prompted some of the ideas developed in this chapter.

means to sympathy based on moral principles and the feelings appropriate to them. (MS 6: 456 f.)²

We do not have a duty that commands having certain feelings since it would be impossible to act on such a command, just as it is not possible "to love someone merely on command" (KpV 5: 83). Rather, the duty is to cultivate the capacity for having a variety of helpful feelings and to strengthen the ones we already have.³

While a lot of headway has been made with respect to positive feelings such as love and sympathy, the role of negative feelings remains to be explored.⁴ On the basis of his account of the role of positive feelings, one may expect Kant to recommend annihilating negative ones, or at least striving to weaken them as much as possible. Yet it does not seem true of at least one of them, namely the feeling of love of honor: "the inclinations to be honored ... are to be preserved as far as possible" (Päd 9: 482). By encouraging the development of the feeling of the love of honor, not only does Kant go against traditional portrayals of his ethics as antiemotions, he approves of a feeling that is literally self-centered since it consists in desiring that one's self be valued. The aim of this chapter is to make sense of this claim by providing a unified account of the feeling of love of honor.

I will begin by examining the natural function of the feeling of love of honor. Like all natural drives, it has been implanted by nature to secure the survival and progress of the human species. However, mechanically, through the interplay of social forces, it soon turns into a competitive drive for superiority, what Kant calls "love of honor in a bad sense" (V-MS/Vigil 27: 695). Although it enables the progress of human civilization, this drive brings with it all the "vices of culture" (RGV 6: 27). However, from this "glittering misery" (IaG 8: 26) can emerge "something quite serious" (Anth 7: 153), for even the worst forms of love of honor contain a nugget of virtue. A shift thereby transforms its natural function from an inclination to fake virtue to an inclination that aids it, thereby going from generating the mere appearance of worth to generating genuine moral worthiness. The feeling of the love of honor thus has a dual nature, as a means to preserve the species and as an aid to morality. As I will show, these two functions converge in the role of culture, at once anchored in natural predispositions and oriented towards morality, at once an end of civilization and a means to moralization. In this sense, as part of human culture, the feeling love of honor can be seen as the locus of

---

2 All the translations of Kant's works are from The Cambridge Edition of the Works of Immanuel Kant published by Cambridge University Press.
3 For discussions of the feeling of sympathy, see Grenberg 2001. For discussions of the feeling of love, see Baron 2002. For my account of the function of these feelings, see Cohen 2009: 89–105.
4 For a helpful discussion of negative feelings, see, e. g., Solomon and Stone 2002.

the convergence, if not the reconciliation, of the perspective of nature and that of morality.

2 The natural function of the feeling of love of honor

According to Kant, the feeling of love of honor is "a drive constantly to perfect oneself in comparison with others" (V-MS/Vigil 27: 680; see also V-Mo/Collins 27: 408). What he sometimes calls the "urge to *honor*" belongs to the predisposition to humanity "as a living and at the same time *rational* being" (RGV 6: 26). It arises from the urge to equality:

> [I]f the other would take power over me, he must be made to think that I am equal to him. That is *honor*, and it takes two forms: 1. to preserve myself; to have *strength*, and to show it, in order not to become a serf. 2. to preserve one's kind. (V-Mo/Herder 27: 63; see also RGV 6: 26 f.)

Like all natural drives, the feeling of love of honor has been implanted by nature to preserve human beings. It is part of the natural mechanism that aims at the survival of both ourselves and our species, as one of the means to the development and progress of our natural predispositions: "This inclination prompts the activity of making oneself equal to the other in every respect; nature has implanted this emulation in us" (V-MS/Vigil 27: 695). To understand the mechanism behind the feeling of love of honor, we need to look at its function from the perspective of nature's intentions for the human species.

Whilst Kant's account of moral teleology is familiar, what is less so is that in his anthropological works, he also portrays nature as aiming at the preservation of the human species and the full development of its capacities: "Nature has also stored into her economy such a rich treasure of arrangements for her particular purpose, which is nothing less than the maintenance of the species" (Anth 7: 310).[5] The feeling of love of honor is one of nature's means to realize its plan, its initial function being that of a straightforward drive to activity.

---

5 "From various circumstances, however, we can discover certain predispositions from time to time and infer from them what nature's goal for humanity is" (V-Anth/Pillau 25: 839). See also "in nature everything is designed to achieve its greatest possible perfection" (V-Anth/Fried 25: 694). For a detailed discussion of Kant's account of nature's intentions for the human species, see Cohen 2009: 110–22.

> [Nature] has very wisely and beneficently simulated objects for the naturally lazy human being, which according to his imagination are real ends (ways of acquiring honor, control, and money). These objects give the person who is reluctant to undertake any *work* enough *to keep him occupied* and *busy doing nothing*, so that the interest which he takes in them is an interest of mere delusion. And nature therefore really is playing with the human being and spurring him (the subject) to its ends; while he stands convinced (objectively) that he has set his own end. (Anth 7: 275)

By making human beings desire honor through their love of it, nature motivates them to do whatever is necessary to ensure that they are worthy of it, whether it is in terms of possessions, status, power, or strength. Without this drive, their predispositions would remain dormant, like the Arcadian shepherd or the South Sea Islander who live "a life full of laziness with the best attitudes, whereby the human being would never be perfected or cultivated and would not be more esteemed than any other animal species" (V-Anth/Mron 25: 1422).[6] Whilst the love of honor is a beneficial drive, the worth of honor it gives rise to is an illusion, at least from nature's perspective. It is nothing but a means to realize its own purpose for human beings. They believe that they are setting their own ends, whilst nature is really setting its aims for them.

> Honor only has value as a means, but who seeks to attain it without purpose, seeks the means as the purpose itself, and then it is an inclination of delusion. Obsessive ambition and greed are inclinations of delusion. Delusion is false representation, when one takes what has value only as a means, to be the thing itself. (V-Anth/Fried 25: 587)

Through the competition human beings create for each other, they are forced to work and develop their talents, thereby realizing nature's purpose for them, the development of their natural predispositions. The feeling of love of honor is thus a decisive driving force in the process of civilization of the human species, and as part of nature's plans for us, it "must absolutely be cultivated" (V-MS/Vigil 27: 695).

However, whilst the feeling of love of honor begins as the desire to make oneself "equal to the other in every respect" (V-MS/Vigil 27: 695), it does not remain so for very long. The interaction of each and everyone's love of honor turns the initial feeling into the desire to outdo others in an on-going and never-ending quest for recognition. Mechanically, through the interplay of social forces, it soon becomes a competitive drive for superiority, a force akin to what Kant

---

[6] Note that although the feeling of love of honor is my focus here, it is not the only drive to activity in this context.

calls "unsociable sociability" (IaG 8: 20 f.).[7] Through a mechanism reminiscent of Rousseau's portrayal of the degeneration of *amour de soi* into *amour-propre* (Rousseau 1973: 84–6), the feeling of love of honor turns into "the love of honor in a bad sense":

> [I]n judging himself and his inner worth, man founds and measures it instead on a merely comparative estimate of his person and condition against the worth and condition of other men. Hence arises the love of honor in a bad sense; if he finds himself lowered by comparison with the other, that arouses in him dislike of the other's person, and instead of actively exerting himself to become equal in value with the other, he succumbs to resentment at the latter's worth and merit, or tries to diminish him. (V-MS/Vigil 27: 695)

Thus, we need to distinguish the original form of the feeling of love of honor with its degenerate forms, whether it is mania of honor (Anth 7: 272), lust for honor (GSE 2: 227), craving for honor (V-Mo/Collins 27: 412), or greed for honor (V-Mo/Collins 27: 407). The bad forms of love of honor are not a given in human nature; they have evolved from the natural drive to compare each other.

> Out of this self-love originates the inclination *to gain worth in the opinion of others*, originally, of course, merely *equal worth*: not allowing anyone superiority over oneself, bound up with the constant anxiety that others might be striving for ascendancy; but from this arises gradually an unjust desire to acquire superiority for oneself over others. (RGV 6: 27)[8]

Following this shift, human beings soon realize that their degenerate love of honor does not necessarily require real worth. The mere appearance of worth can achieve the same result but at a lesser cost: "it is striving after the *reputation of honor*, where semblance suffices" (Anth 7: 272). Whether they are actually worthy of honor is indifferent to them as long as they appear to be so, and even if they know it is undeserved. Of course, in accordance with nature's plan for them, this "simulacrum of virtue" (GSE 2: 218) nevertheless enables the development of their natural predispositions. But by leading them to fake worthiness, it also gives rise to all the "vices of *culture*" (RGV 6: 27).

Recall Kant's remark about the human capacity "to explore the thoughts of others but to withhold one's own; a neat quality which then does not fail to progress gradually from *dissimulation* to intentional *deception*, and finally to *lying*"

---

[7] Cf. V-Anth/Fried 25: 586 f., and: "The means nature employs in order to bring about the development of human beings' natural predispositions is their antagonism in society" (IaG 8: 20). For a compelling account of the concept of unsociable sociability, see Wood 1991.

[8] As Allen Wood has noted, "honor is sought fundamentally for the sake of achieving a real superiority of one's self-worth over that of others" (Wood 1999: 290).

(Anth 7: 332). The capacity to conceal one's thoughts plays a crucial role in the deterioration of the feeling of love of honor, as Rousseau noted in his second *Discourse*: "It now became the interest of men to appear what they really were not" (Rousseau 1973: 86).[9] In this sense, the degeneration of the feeling of love of honor gives rise to a society where appearances, reputation, and semblances take the place of true desert and worthiness. Amongst this glittering misery, there is, however, a glimmer of hope. As I will show in the following section, Kant believes that even the worst forms of love of honor contain a nugget of virtue.

3 From faking virtue to the virtue of self-mastery

On Kant's account, the mechanism behind the inclination to fake virtue goes from generating the appearance of worth to generating moral worthiness. For, paradoxically perhaps, someone who pretends virtue in order to hide his vices and receive undeserved honor from his peers is, unbeknownst to him, walking on the path towards virtue.

> In society everyone is well-behaved, [but] everything is appearance, the desires of the citizens against each other are there; in acting everyone burns with wickedness ..., and yet he is as composed and indifferent as if this did not stir him at all. Truly this betrays a self-mastery and is the beginning of conquering oneself. It is a step towards virtue or at least a capacity thereto. (V-Anth/Mensch 25: 930)

In this respect, the function of the feeling of love of honor is akin to that of propriety.

> [P]ropriety, an inclination by good conduct to influence others to respect for us ..., as the genuine foundation of all true sociability, gave the first hint toward the formation of the human being as a moral creature. – A small beginning, which, however, is epoch-making, in that it gives an entirely new direction to the mode of thought – and is more important than the entire immeasurable series of extensions of culture that followed upon it. (MAM 8: 113)

Inclinations such as the love of honor and propriety value appearances over substance, and in this respect, they remain at a superficial level. However, whilst they are not virtues, they constitute a step towards it, a step that exercises and

---

9 For Rousseau's criticism of politeness as a source of evil and a social veil on vice, see Rousseau 1973: 6.

strengthens self-mastery, and helps one to overcome – or at least control and refine – one's passions.

> [T]hese signs of benevolence and respect, though empty at first, gradually lead to real dispositions of this sort.... [I]t is still better to have small change in circulation than no funds at all, and eventually they can be converted into genuine gold, though at considerable loss. (Anth 7: 152)

How can empty signs of moral worthiness gradually lead to the real thing? First, by faking worthiness in order to command others' respect, human beings foster polite society and peaceful companionship, albeit in appearance only.[10] The antagonism between all the honor-seekers is thereby regulated. It is the means to this regulation, civilized social intercourse, that allows them to secure their survival in a way that is compatible with their ongoing competitive drive for honor. Second, whilst everyone may be burning with wickedness underneath a veil of politeness, by doing so they exhibit an incredible capacity for self-control. Although this capacity is merely applied to "the manners one is obliged to show in social intercourse" (MS 6: 473),

> Even the illusion of good in others must have worth for us, for out of this play with pretenses, which acquires respect without perhaps earning it, something quite serious can finally develop. (Anth 7: 153)

To make sense of this cryptic remark, recall that for Kant, human beings have a duty to cultivate their capacity for self-mastery by developing the power to control their inclinations. Natural inclinations form obstacles to the performance of duty: "Impulses of nature, accordingly, involve obstacles within the human being's mind to his fulfillment of duty and (sometimes powerful) forces opposing it" (MS 6: 380). So much so that anything that strengthens our self-mastery, even if it is for immoral, vicious, or prudential purposes, is a step towards virtue: "Ethical gymnastics, therefore, consists only in combating natural impulses sufficiently to be able to master them when a situation comes up in which they threaten morality" (MS 6: 485). By becoming better able to overcome – or at least control and refine – our passions so that we can behave according to the rules of propriety and social intercourse, we thereby become more civilized.

---

[10] For an interesting analysis of politeness, see Frierson 2005: 115–17. On the basis of the lectures on anthropology (V-Anth/Fried 25: 502 f.), he argues that since the illusion does not depend on making another believe in falsehood, it is not morally wrong.

> In regard to the inclinations, the human being must be brought under control, just as in regard to the sensations, he must be refined. The propriety which one observes in society does not come of itself and by chance, but much time must be spent on it, so that our natural unruliness can be brought under control, until we attain propriety. (V-Anth/Fried 25: 623)

Crucially, this civilizing process is not purely superficial, although it begins at the superficial level of social appearances. The capacity to appear civilized necessitates our being civilized to the point that we are able to fake the virtues of sociability, thereby turning ourselves into sociable, and thus truly civilized, beings.

Of course, we are still a long way away from true virtue. However, Kant's point is, I believe, that with the feeling of love of honor, we are closer to it than first thought.

> [N]othing except honor can deter the individual from meanness. If an individual thus has no conscience, then a spark of honor can still be in him, which can check him. But if he is without honor, then all is lost with him, then there is nothing more on which one can base the good. (V-Anth/Fried 25: 652 f.)

The loss of the love of honor entails the loss of any hope for virtue, and even its worst forms retain a nugget of virtue in their core. This section has shown that negatively, the feeling of love of honor is one of the means of combating and controlling inclinations through civilized social intercourse, which cultivates the capacity for self-mastery. As I will show in the following section, it also fulfills two positive roles in the moral development of human beings: an epistemic role and an emotional role.

4 From the appearance of worth to moral worthiness

According to Kant, "One must excite the inclinations that most closely agree with morality" (Refl 6619, 19: 113), and the first inclination he lists is the love of honor.[11] Whilst this claim may seem surprising, it shows that the feeling of love of honor is not, as first thought, a negative, self-centered inclination that consists essentially in valuing oneself over others. In fact, nothing said so far gives us a reason to think of the love of honor as necessarily selfish. It can be but it does not have to be.

---

[11] The other two inclinations that most closely agree with morality are sociability and freedom (Refl 6619, 19: 113).

> Man has an impulse towards honor, which is quite unselfish; the craving for honor is often selfish, to wit, when it seeks honor to better its condition, to procure an office or a wife thereby; but he who seeks honor, without any ulterior motive, merely in the approval of others, is truly a lover of honor. (V-Mo/Collins 27: 410)

As I will argue, the love of honor is, at least in its best form, an aid to morality: first in the form of a care for the judgment of others; and second in the form of a care for my inner worth.

The first function of the feeling of love of honor is its epistemic contribution to human beings' moral development.

> Our judgment, on its own, corrupts these [our] actions, whence the need that others should also be able to judge them .... We have, therefore, an honor-loving urge to refer our knowledge to the judgment of others. (V-Mo/Collins 27: 408, 411)

The feeling of love of honor makes us care about others' judgment in such a way that we cannot help but take it into consideration. Thereby, it takes us out of ourselves and broadens our way of thinking. As early as the *Observations on the Feeling of the Beautiful and Sublime*, the feeling of love of honor is depicted as providing hidden incentives to adopt a standpoint outside oneself in order to judge the propriety and demeanor that one presents to others (GSE 2: 226 f.).[12] This function is akin to the second principle of the *sensus communis*, "Thinking in the place of another" (V-Anth/Busolt 25: 1480), which allows "broad-minded" thinking (KU 5: 293 f.).

> [P]rovidence has instilled the inclination [to honor] in us, and hence no man, even a great one, is indifferent to the opinion of others .... The intent of providence, in implanting this desire for respect from others, is that we should assess our actions by the judgment of others, so that such acts may not proceed solely from motives of self-love. (V-Mo/Collins 27: 408)[13]

Thinking in the position of everyone else enables us to escape the subjective, private conditions of judgment, which include my desires, my idiosyncratic tendencies, my temperament, my personal preferences, my history, that is to say

---

12 For an account of the feeling of love of honor in the *Observations*, see Makkreel 2012 and Cohen 2012.
13 Note that there seems to be an interesting shift that occurs from the *Observations* to Kant's later anthropological works. In the former, the feeling of the love of honor merely compensates for the lack of virtue in order to secure the survival of the human species in spite of the moral shortcomings of its parts. In the latter, this feeling prepares us for morality.

everything that makes me who I am qua individual rather than qua rational cognizer and agent.[14] Of course, the feeling of love of honor does not ensure that I do not act from self-love. But minimally, it makes me care about others' points of view insofar as I desire their respect. If I do so for selfish reasons, it is at worst a self-centered openness to others. But at its best, it is a legitimate care for others' recognition of our inner worth.

Second, the motivational function of the feeling of love of honor appears most clearly in moral education. According to Kant, the most effective means to motivate a child to become morally worthy is not to harm him physically but to harm his love of honor instead. Not only does it fulfill the retributive aspect of punishment, more importantly it motivates him to become worthy of honor:

> With regard to the love of honor, the instruction is negative; he must only learn to be sensible of the worth of his person. Through [his] merits, however, he must seek to become worthy of honor. (V-Anth/Fried 25: 728)[15]

More generally, the love of honor prompts and strengthens our sense of "inner worth" (V-Mo/Collins 27: 357). Our conception of self-esteem as autonomous agents, the feeling of "esteem that the human being is permitted to expect from others because of his inner (moral) worth" (Anth 7: 272), yields a desire to become worthy of it and avoid demeaning it. The natural function of the feeling of love of honor is thereby redirected towards true moral character rather than the mere appearance of it. It makes us aspire to be truly deserving of honor now that we come to appreciate its unconditional worth.

Therefore, Kant's claim in the *Anthropology* that "love of honor is the constant companion of virtue" (Anth 7: 257) can be reinterpreted in light of the two moral functions just discussed. First, it enables an openness to others and their judgment, and second, it motivates us to become worthy of honor. It is in this sense that, for Kant, the feeling of love of honor is one of the "aids to morality" (Päd 9: 482).

---

14 Through this principle, one "sets himself apart from the subjective private conditions of the judgment ... and reflects on his own judgment from a universal standpoint (which he can only determine by putting himself into the standpoint of others)" (KU 5: 295).
15 Note that this feeling should only be used in the later stages of education: the love of honor "should not occur in the first stage of education" (Päd 9: 465). A certain level of development is necessary for the child's conception of worth to be operative.

5 The dual nature of the feeling of love of honor

If we review what has been argued, according to Kant nature aims at the preservation of the human species and the full development of its capacities, and the feeling of love of honor is one of nature's means to realize this purpose. It also generates, as an unintended consequence, a shift that seems to transform its natural function from an inclination to fake virtue to an inclination that aids it, thereby going from generating the mere appearance of worth to generating, or at least enabling, true moral worthiness. However, this shift seems in tension with some key passages of Kant's works, and in particular the following:

> We are *cultivated* in a high degree by art and science. We are *civilized*, perhaps to the point of being overburdened, by all sorts of social decorum and propriety. But very much is still lacking before we can be held to be already *moralized*. For the idea of morality still belongs to culture; but the use of this idea, which comes down only to a resemblance of morals in love of honor and in external propriety, constitutes only being civilized.... But everything good that is not grafted onto a morally good disposition, is nothing but mere semblance and glittering misery. (IaG 8: 26)

If this is the case, how are we to understand the passages where Kant seems to suggest that a shift from civilization to moralization takes place through the development of the feeling of love of honor? The aim of this section is to make sense of it by showing that its dual role converges in the role of culture understood as the end of civilization and the means to moralization.

What the interpretation put forward in this chapter suggests is that not only does the feeling of love of honor help develop human predispositions, it makes possible true honor and moral self-esteem. Through its beneficial psychological and social consequences, it opens up the notion of unselfish goodness.

> Since everyone in the civil constitution stands in relation to the other, every human being thus becomes [a matter] of great importance to the other one. The judgment of others has a great influence on him, and from this arises the concept of honor; he becomes inspired to undertake a great deal, not only with regard to his needs, but with regard to the common good of life. (V-Anth/Fried 25: 680)[16]

---

[16] See also "in the civil state, there exists not only the constraint of the authorities, but also an artificial constraint of the parents, of the circumstances of making a living, of propriety, of honor, and through this arises such diverse activity whereby the human being produces much positive good, which would not at all have existed in the savage state" (V-Anth/Fried 25: 690).

Recall that Kant writes that the inclination to honor "serves merely to extend our animal nature and make it adequate to humanity, or the intellectual being within us, and to its laws." (V-MS/Vigil 27: 695) It is intended to help us navigate our dual nature as moral animals. The function of the love of honor is thus twofold: at once anchored in human natural predispositions and oriented towards morality. And far from putting pressure on Kant's account, I believe that this dual nature can be accounted for if we interpret it in light of the role of culture in the development of the human species. To support this claim, let me sketch in what sense the feeling of love of honor is at once part of what Kant calls the ultimate and the final purposes of nature.

According to Kant, the ultimate (*letzte*) purpose of nature is the development of human natural dispositions through civilization. It involves the way in which human beings make use of nature, which includes the capacity to utilize natural products for their ends as well as the ability to free their will from the determination of sensuous impulses (KU 5: 429–31). The final purpose (*Endzweck*) of nature, on the other hand, is their moral progress. It presupposes a conception of human beings as having an intelligible power of acting (freedom), an unconditioned law (the moral law) and a moral object (the highest good):

> [O]nly in the human being, although in him only as a subject of morality, is unconditional legislation with regards to ends to be found, which therefore makes him alone capable of being a final end, to which the whole of nature is teleologically subordinated. (KU 5: 435 f.)

Human beings alone have a final purpose in themselves, and on this basis, nature can be thought of as being subordinated to this purpose by reference to the wisdom of a providence that made them the only natural beings capable of freedom. And conversely, as beings capable of setting ends according to a law that is "unconditioned and independent of natural conditions," human beings "need not hold himself to be subjected by any influence from nature" (KU 5: 435).[17] So depending on whether we consider them as ultimate or final purposes of nature, our understanding of their development takes the form of either a process of civilization or a process of moralization.

The dual nature of the feeling of love of honor can be reinterpreted in light of the distinction between the ultimate and the final purpose of nature. Depending on whether we adopt the standpoint of the former or the latter, it becomes either the means of a process of civilization that is directed towards the development of human natural predispositions, or the means of a process of moralization, which

---

[17] For an analysis of Kant's account of Providence, see Kleingeld 2001.

cannot effect any direct change in moral character but has a decisive impact on the moral development of human agents. Therefore, we can now unify the two functions of the feeling of love of honor. As a means to preserve the species and as an aid to morality, it converges in the role of culture, at once anchored in the natural predispositions and oriented towards morality, at once an end of civilization and a means to moralization.[18] In this sense, as part of human culture, the feeling love of honor can be seen as the locus of the convergence, if not the reconciliation, of the perspective of nature and that of morality.[19]

6 Conclusion

What this chapter has set out to show is that by encouraging the development of the feeling of the love of honor, not only do Kant's lectures on anthropology go against traditional portrayals of his ethics as anti-emotions, they approve of a feeling that is literally self-centered since it consists in desiring that one's self be valued. Instead of recapitulating the arguments I have developed, I would like to conclude by drawing the implications of my account for our understanding of the lectures on anthropology and their contribution to Kant's ethics.

Far from portraying human beings as disembodied pure minds, Kant's lectures on anthropology, and his anthropological works in general, take into account their empirical, contingent, and messy features. The feeling of love of honor is a case in point. As I have shown, it evolves, it degenerates, it seems to cause the worst in us and yet also to enable the realization of our full potential; it can be in turn feeling, mania, inclination, or craving. In other words, the love of honor, as human feelings more generally, is messy, and Kant's lectures on anthropology not only portray this messiness, they embrace it and make allowance for it in their pragmatic recommendations.

---

18 Of course, whilst this is sufficient to make sense of the dual function of the feeling of love of honor, it is only the beginning of Kant's account of the moral role of love of honor. For in his lectures on ethics, Kant claims that love of honor is the object of "a duty" (V-MS/Vigil 27: 635), "the highest duty of humanity toward oneself" (V-MS /Vigil 27: 664). However, this paper is limited to the discussion of the feeling of love of honor. For a discussion of it as a duty, see Denis 2014, especially 204 f.
19 For a slightly different formulation of this claim, see Makkreel who notes that "Kant considers the inclination to gain worth in the opinion of others an incentive to culture (*Triebfeder zur Cultur*) .... Our love of honor can then be said to be not only a social gauge but a cultural means to attain moral dignity. It is by implanting in us a love of honor that nature prepares us to choose our own dignity" (Makkreel 2012: 109).

Therefore, the perspective of the lectures on anthropology differs in important and meaningful ways from Kant's Critical position, for the lectures are not concerned with rationality in general, but rather with the embodied human agent. To understand this claim, we need to recall that Kant's ethics as a whole consists of three parts that are equally essential. First, the project that produces an a priori system of duties for *rational* agents: by focusing on pure practical rationality alone, it is completely independent of any empirical knowledge of human nature (*Groundwork, Critique of Practical Reason*); second, the project that generates an a priori system of the duties that are binding upon a particular type of agent, namely *human* agents: by presupposing certain empirical features of human nature and the human world more generally, it is not completely independent of our empirical knowledge of human nature (*Metaphysics of Morals*); and third, the project that spells out the worldly helps and hindrances for *embodied* human moral agents – what Kant calls "the subjective conditions in human nature" (MS 6: 217) (*Anthropology* and *Lectures on Anthropology*). As Kant writes in the *Groundwork*, "the whole of morals ... needs anthropology for its application to human beings" (GMS 4: 412). By examining the empirical helps and hindrances to moral agency, anthropology provides the empirical knowledge of the world (and in particular of the human being, his capacities, and his inner workings) that is necessary to identify the features that can help or hinder the performance of duty.

> It would deal with the development, spreading, and strengthening of moral principles (in education in schools and in popular instruction), and with other similar teachings and precepts based on experience. It cannot be dispensed with. (MS 6: 217)

Kant's familiar transcendental account, which expounds the a priori rules of morality for human agents, needs to be supplemented by a pragmatic part that expounds the empirical dimension of morality for human agents. Whilst the former refers to our transcendental, objective moral condition (e. g., we have a sensibility, a finite will, etc.), the latter refers to our empirical, subjective moral condition (e. g., we have emotions, temperaments, histories, and cultures, sets of relationships, etc.). On my interpretation of Kant's account, we need not only a metaphysics of morals, but also an anthropology of morals: a pragmatic account of how we can, should, and ought to act insofar as we are embodied human beings.

V **Pedagogy**

Chapter 11
Immanuel Kant's *On Pedagogy*: A Lecture Like Any Other?

Werner Stark
Translated by Robert R. Clewis

The following article explores the origin and structure of the text edited by F. T. Rink in 1803, *Immanuel Kant: On Pedagogy*. Uncertainties associated with the text, doubtless present and legitimate, should be put into better order if not completely eliminated.[1]

1 What do we know?

Strictly speaking, we have no clear information beyond the printed text of the book: a separate manuscript tradition does not exist; the external condition of the manuscripts that were the basis for the printing is unknown. The editor's reports concerning the circumstances of the book's origin offer little insight. From the perspective of a historian or biographer, they are also fundamentally dubious and far from certain.

Friedrich Theodor Rink's preface puts the text in a genetic relation with a *collegio scholastico practicum* that since the mid-1770s was held at regular intervals by the professors of the Faculty of Philosophy at Albertina University.[2] Rink

---

[1] The present article is the result of a lecture held on 7 December 2010 in Arras at the invitation of Jean-François Goubet; it was published as Stark 2012, here translated with permission. [Passages from *Lectures on Pedagogy* are taken from Robert Louden's translation in The Cambridge Edition of the Works of Immanuel Kant (Kant 2007: 437–85), based on Paul Natorp's edition in the *Akademie-Ausgabe* (Päd 9: 437–99). Translations of Kant's works are from The Cambridge Edition of the Works of Immanuel Kant. Translations of other texts are by Robert R. Clewis, who thanks Werner Stark and Franz-Alois Fischer for comments, and accepts responsibility for any errors. – Editor/Translator]

[2] Kant fulfilled this obligation four times (see Stark 2000: 95 f.): winter semester 1776/77, summer semester 1780, winter semester 1783/84, winter semester 1786/87. See Oberhausen and Pozzo 1999: 395, 444, 493, 530, respectively. According to the lecture announcements, starting in the summer of 1780 a textbook was explicitly used as a basis for the course. The author was Friedrich

is explicitly of the opinion that the text he edited was not composed by Kant "of his own accord" (AA 9: 439.25 f.). Rather, the "remarks on the education" (AA 9: 439.10 f.) owe their creation to the fact that Kant did *not* base his teaching on the textbook he used in the course "either in the development of the investigation or in the principles" (AA 9: 439.09 f.). – Until the appearance of the investigation by Traugott Weisskopf (1970), researchers and editors have naturally assumed[3] that the text submitted by Kant was composed and used for a single lecture on pedagogy, newly introduced in Königsberg. – Years ago I stated that in my opinion the doubts expressed by Weisskopf were in principle justified.[4] I would like to add another reason: the idea developed by Rink that the text should be regarded as Kant's outline or concept for a lecture (*Konzept zur Vorlesung*), created after and in opposition to Bock, goes against everything we know about what Kant did in other lectures: all of the lectures – with the exception of the "physical geography"[5] – followed the structure of a principal textbook. Kant's lecture is always structured as a commentary. – The question, *What exactly is the text published by Rink in 1803?*, is still missing a conclusive answer.

1.1 Who was Rink?

It seems advisable first to turn to the person of the editor,[6] to allow a preliminary assessment of his work as editor of Kant's writings. Friedrich *Theodor* Rink was born in Schlawe (Pomerania, southwest Stolp) on 8 April 1770, the younger of two sons of the local pastor, John *Gottlieb* Rink (born 1732). His mother, Gotthilf Christina Rink (1744–1770), a daughter of the Königsberg theology professor Joachim Justus Rau (Berlin: 11 April 1713 – 19 August 1745: Königsberg) died

---

Samuel Bock (1716–1785), Königsberg theologian and professor of Greek in the Faculty of Philosophy at Albertina University, and it was called *Lehrbuch der Erziehungskunst, zum Gebrauch für christliche Eltern und künftige Jugendlehrer* (1780). Bock placed in the work a dedication to the Prussian Minister of Culture von Zedlitz, dated 8 October 1779. Bock himself had already used it for the same purpose in the winter of 1779/80 (Oberhausen and Pozzo: 437). After that it was also cited by other professors; cf. Oberhausen and Pozzo: 451 (Reusch); 459 (Kreutzfeld); 479 (Bock); 486 (Buck); 500 (Reusch). The book was therefore used a total of nine times.

3 Representative and exemplary of these is Paul Natorp (1923): "The origin of the text is known" (AA 9: 569).
4 Weisskopf 1970 and (critically) Stark 2000; on both, see dos Santos 2007: 25–39 and 58–62.
5 For the origins, structure, and development of this very special lecture, see my Introduction to AA 26.1 (2009).
6 The following significantly goes beyond the account of information given in Stark 1993: 23–7.

shortly after his birth. After the early death of his father (1773), Theodor was taken in in Königsberg by the family of his maternal grandmother, Maria Horn, born Schiffert.[7] Until his matriculation[8] at Albertus-Universität (1 April 1786) he was educated at the Collegium Fridericianum.[9] Via his grandmother he stands in relation to the theologian Johann August [von] Starck (1741–1816) who intermittently taught at the Albertina, and who, still in Königsberg in 1774, married the daughter Albertine (1745–1818) of the influential Pietist and school reformer Franz Albert Schultz (1692–1763): the adolescent's background and environment were clearly influenced by the Pietism of the Königsberg sort.[10]

Rink completed his academic apprenticeship in Königsberg very quickly; on 16 April 1789, three years after matriculation, he held a *pro receptione* disputation on the Old Testament prophet Hosea (Osee), under the supervision of the orientalist Johann Gottfried Hasse (1759–1806) in the Faculty of Philosophy. The University of Königsberg awarded him the due Master's degree as early as March.[11] – Although detailed accounts of his course of study are unknown,[12] based on the printed disputations of the Faculty of Philosophy[13] and other sources it can be said that in order to dedicate himself completely to oriental philology, Rink

---

[7] Daughter of the inspector at the Fridericianum, Christian Schiffert (1688–1765); since 1742 (in a second marriage) married to George Martin Horn, one of the teachers at the Fridericianum, having a "matriculation" in Königsberg on (1) 12 March 1727 and (2) 27 June 1737: "Horn, Geo. Martin., Regiomonte-Boruss., Ienae h[oc] a[nno] in Magistrum promotus, redux ius Academicum, quod die 12. Martii 1727. obtinuit repetiit" (Erler and Joachim 1910–17).
[8] "Matriculation" in Königsberg: "Rinck Frdr. Theodor., Slava-Pomer., theol. cult" (Erler and Joachim 1910–17).
[9] See *Memoria virii [...]* (Rink 1811b: 5), and the diary of Puttlich (Warda 1905). The lists of graduates published by Ellendt in 1898 have a gap in the years 1786–1788. "Rink" is not to be found there.
[10] We can perhaps see here the basis for his brief apology for a Collegium Fridericianum chided by other contemporaries; cf. Rink 1805: 128–31.
[11] *Preußische Monatsschrift*, vol. 2 (June 1789), page 205, states: "In March the Faculty of Philosophy issued the master's degree to two candidates, Herr Fried. Theod. Rink, from Pomerania, and Herr Jer. Benj. Richter from Silesia."
[12] Geheimes Staatsarchiv Preußischer Kulturbesitz (Berlin), HA XX [formerly Staatsarchiv Königsberg], EM 139b No. 25. Notably, in their commemorative volume *Memoria virii [...]*, Danzig colleagues name, among Rink's Königsberg academic teachers, predominantly professors of the Faculty of Philosophy (Rink 1811b: 6 f.): Hasse, Mangelsdorf, Kant, Kraus, Schultz. Among these was the pharmacist and chemist Karl Gottfried Hagen, who still belonged to the Faculty of Medicine. As of the summer of 1788 Hasse was also a member of the Faculty of Theology.
[13] See http://staff-www.uni-marburg.de/~stark/albert.ine/al_phil.htm. Accessed 10 October 2014.

very quickly dropped his initial plan[14] to study theology to become a pastor or teacher.[15] In addition, he became a member (probably in 1788)[16] of the "Royal German Society" founded in Königsberg in 1743.

In a sense, Rink got his interest in oriental languages in the cradle, for at the end of the 1730s his maternal grandfather, theologian Joachim Justus Rau,[17] was temporarily professor *extraordinarius* of these languages in the Faculty of Philosophy. His father, Johann Gottlieb Rink, had also been active in this respect: in 1755 he played the role of student respondent at the disputation[18] "pro loco professionis ordinarii linguarum orientalium" of George David Kypke (1723–1779). Earlier at the Fridericianum, Kypke was a classmate of Kant's, and from 1746 on he officiated as professor *extraordinarius* at Albertina University in the said discipline. Even Johann August [von][19] Starck, connected to Rink as kin, and possessing this *Extraordinariat* between 1770 and 1774, perhaps could in this respect have still had a direct effect on the young Theodor Rink before Starck's departure to Mitau in Kurland in 1777. Yet it is more likely that Starck acted as an example later, and from a distance. The fact that Rink dedicated his first single-authored, thematically relevant work to his great-uncle can be interpreted as evidence in this respect. Measured by the academic practices of the day, Rink must of course be considered to be above all a student of the orientalist Hasse, who at the end of 1786 moved from Jena to Königsberg, for the title pages of both of his 1787 disputations (*pro receptione* and *pro loco*) required for the professorship at the Albertina name Rink as one of the three student opponents.[20]

---

14 On the front page of the *pro loco* disputation (19 June 1787) by J. G. Hasse it states, among other things: "th. cand. opponentibus Frid. Theod. Rinck, Slava pomer." – Among the opposing students is: "Friedrich Theodor Rink, from Sławno in Pomerania, Candidate of Theology."
15 Title page of the disputation of Hasse and Rink, 15 May 1788; with dedication to J. A. Starck; Copy: Toruń UB: 266.090; previously at Stadtbibliothek Königsberg.
16 Title page of the disputation of Hasse and Rink, 15 May 1788; Copy: Toruń UB: 266.090.
17 Rau authored only a few publications, including the "*Kurzgefaßten Anfangsgründe der hebräischen Grammatic: Welche nach den Lehrsätzen des D. Danz eingerichtet,* [...]" (Königsberg, 1738), which appeared in Königsberg in 1780 expanded by George David Kypke; cf. Pisanski 1886: 638.
18 *Kypke, Georg David* (1755): Commentatio philologica de apparatu convivii regis persarum ad Esth. I. v. 6 et de vino Chalybonio ad Ezech. 27 v. 18. Quam deo auspice amplissimi senatus pro loco professionis ordinarii linguarum orientalium defendet Georgius David Kypke, linguar. orient. prof. ord. et synagoge iudaicae inspector, respondente Iohanne Gottlieb Rinck, Lycca borussi S. S. theol. stud. opponentibus Friderico Bernhard Stein, Cremitta borusso th. stud. et Davide Henrico Arnoldt, Regiomontano phil. et th. stud. die 22. iulii [without year], horis locoque solitis (Königsberg: Hartung). Copy in Olsztyn, Ośrodek Badań Naukowych.
19 Ennobled in 1811 by the Grand Duke of Hesse and the Rhine, Ludwig I (1753–1830).
20 *Hasse, Johann Gottfried*; Woltersdorf, Jacob Friedrich (Resp.); Manitius, Karl Ludwig (Opp.);

For our purposes it seems sufficient to list his major life events as follows:

October 1789 – September 1790: Studies in Leyden, including meeting with Rhunken
October 1790 – Autumn 1791 and Winter 1791/92: Stay in Darmstadt and return to Königsberg
Summer 1792 – Winter 1792/93: Gives lectures as a *Privatdozent* in Königsberg
Summer 1793 – Fall 1794: Private tutor in Courland (Nogallen)
November 1794: Appointed Associate (*außerordentlich*) Professor at the Faculty of Philosophy in Königsberg. Marriage in the same year
Summer 1795 on: Gives lectures in Königsberg
September 1797: Inspector of Kypke's Institute
October 1799: Dr. and Professor of Theology in Königsberg
August / September 1801: Moves to Danzig (Gdańsk)
15 September 1801: Ordination as preacher
20 September 1801: Installation as pastor at Holy Trinity Church
27 September 1801: Inaugural sermon
13 October 1801: Professor of Theology at the academic Gymnasium
15 October 1801: Public exam of Gymnasium students
August 1802: Takes over Morgenstern's Latin course
August 1810: Rector, Successor to Daniel Gralath (1739–1809)
27 April 1811: Death

1.2 Rink and Kant

Documents or certificates immediately giving information about the relations between Kant and Rink as a student are unknown. We must rely on Rink himself. In his *Ansichten aus Kant's Leben*, it reads:

Rink, Friedrich Theodor (Opp.); Meyer, Johann Christ/ (Opp.) (1787a): De orthographiae hebraeorum indagandiae via ac ratione dissertatio philologica quam pro eo quod in amplissimum philosophorum ordinem recipiebatur consensu eiusdem ordinis benevolo ab oppositionibus iuvenem optimae spei atque indolis [...] fridie calendar. febr. orient. prof. design. respondente [...] [16 pages]. Königsberg: Hartung. / Hasse, Johann Gottfried (Praeses); Broscheit, Johann Wilhelm (Resp.); Rink, Friedrich Theodor (Opp.); Woltersdorf, Jacob Friedrich (Opp.); Schulz, Karl (Opp. (1787b): De dialectis linguae syriacae dissertatio philologica-historica. Quam pro loco professionis ordinariae rite obtinendo A. D. xix jun. MDCC LXXXVII horis ante- et pomeridianis publice defendet [...] [18 pages]. Königsberg: Hartung. See also Warda 1905: 295 and *Preußische Monatsschrift*, vol. 1 (1788): 57, 117 f.

> What I have here said of and about Kant is perfectly true and accords with my beliefs. I was his student between the years 1786 and 1789. After returning from my trip to Holland and Germany, I was his dinner guest in 1792 and 1793, just as I was his dinner guest, usually twice a week, in the years between 1795 and 1801, after my return from Courland until about the time of my transfer to my current location [Danzig]. (Rink 1805: 120)

In the absence of adequate sources, exactly when and in what context Rink began a closer relationship with Kant, and under which circumstances a possible handover of manuscripts, edited later, could become a topic of discussion, likewise remains generally unclear.[21]

The chronologically first statement on the matter, comprehensive in terms of content and at the same time made in public, is found in a work printed by Nicolovius in Königsberg in 1800: *Mancherley zur Geschichte der metacritischen Invasion von Johann Georg Hamann genannt Magnus in Norden, und einige Aufsätze die kantische Philosophie betreffend. Nebst einem Fragment einer älteren Metakritik.*[22] – Pages xix and xx of the preface signed by Rink on 9 February 1800 read:

> Finally, I can here give to the friends and admirers of the Critical philosophy the news, probably not uninteresting, that Herr M. Jähsche[23] and I, are by the kindness of Herr Professor Kant, our revered teacher, placed in a position to promise with certainty the gradual appearance of his metaphysics, – [...] – his logic, natural theology, physical geography, and other interesting writings. (Rink and Jäsche 1800: xix–xx)

Kant lectured on the four aforementioned disciplines; we may therefore assume that Jäsche and Rink received manuscripts that arose in direct connection with these lectures by Kant. After Kant retired from active teaching in summer of

---

21 Rink is not present in Abegg's diary from the summer of 1798, while Gensichen and Poerschke are mentioned several times in connection and commerce with Kant; see the name index in Abegg (1977). – In Kant's correspondence Rink is *possibly* first mentioned in December 1798; see the "Ringkische Sache" (Br 12: 271.17).

22 On the inception and content of the text, see Reicke 1881 and Stark 1993: 22 f. See also the reference in Scheffner's correspondence (Scheffner 1918–38, vol. 1: 90).

23 In other words, based on the Jäsche biography by Morgenstern (1843), it can be said that a somewhat closer relationship to Kant is possible for Jäsche only in the course of the year 1799. Pages 26 f.: in winter 1791/92, Jäsche goes to Königsberg for the first time. Pages 28–30: from April 1792 to early 1799, Jäsche lives in Courland as an educator, and then returns to Königsberg. Page 31: "He could enjoy the splendid fortune of having frequent access to his fatherly friend and great teacher, whose philosophy actually drew him to Königsberg, and in particular, of being, along with with Professor Rink, Kant's dinner guest one or two times a week." – I would conjecture that the friendship between Jäsche and Rink began in Courland, hence in the years 1793 and 1794.

1796, modern textbooks that were suitable for academic instruction were to be produced. – What came of this plan? What about the *Pedagogy* which is unnamed above?

As is well known, toward the end of 1800 Jäsche began to work on *Immanuel Kant's Logik. Ein Handbuch zu Vorlesungen*. Subsequent research has shown that for the production of the text, recourse was made to a student transcription (*Nachschrift*) of the logic lecture, as well as to personal notes from Kant himself.[24] As we know,[25] the textbook on metaphysics announced by Jäsche never appeared. It was to be edited and published "in the same manner" (Log 9: 10.05) as the logic lecture.

Various circumstances – which are not important here – delayed until spring 1802 the work on the physical geography Rink had undertaken.[26] Thanks to the research of Erich Adickes (1866–1928) we have known for over a hundred years that a student transcription and an outline for the lecture (*Konzept zur Vorlesung*) written by Kant himself in the 1750s were combined in the published text.[27] The title was: *Immanuel Kant's physische Geographie. Auf Verlangen des Verfassers, aus seiner Handschrift herausgegeben und zum Theil bearbeitet von D[oktor]. Friedrich Theodor Rink*.

What remains is the lecture on natural theology, which Rink did not see to press, although, as the auction of his library in 1811 reveals,[28] he possessed such a manuscript. In the auction catalog, one finds among the books in quarto the following entry, under number 315: "I. Kants Vorlesungen über die natürliche Theologie, Mspt. Ppbd" [I. Kant's lectures on natural theology, manuscript paperback]. As we have known since 1830,[29] this copy was acquired by Karl Heinrich

---

24 Cf. in particular Hinske 2000.
25 Morgenstern 1821: 485.
26 Stark, forthcoming: chapter 4, on the editions of Rink and Vollmer. See the same work for support for the foregoing biographical sketch.
27 Adickes 1911.
28 *Verzeichniß der hinterlassenen Bibliothek des wohlseligen Herrn F. T. Rink, der Philosophie u. Theol. Doktors, des Danziger Gymnasii Rektors, der S. Trinitatis-Kirche Pastors, der Theologie, der griech. u. der morgenländischen Sprachen Professors, welche 1811, den 23. Septbr. durch öffentlichen Ausruf, in der Holzgasse Nro. 26 verkauft wird*. [91 pages] (Rink 1811a). This reference came from Reinhard Markner (Halle), gratefully acknowledged here.
29 "The fact that the first edition of this *Lectures* had after thirteen years gone out of stock, and that a second edition was necessary, was for me gratifying evidence that Kant's everlasting contributions to philosophy are still appreciated and duly acknowledged. I did not hesitate, after the request of several reviewers of the first edition of this book, to name myself as the editor of the same, whose manuscript I had purchased, during my lectureship at Wittenberg, from the books of the auction of Dr. Rink, who died in Danzig. As is well known, Rink was once Kant's colleague

Ludwig Pölitz (1772–1832) and was first published in 1817 under the title *Immanuel Kants Vorlesungen über die philosophische Religionslehre*. In the 1930s a student of Paul Menzer's, Kurt Beyer, compared and examined both of its editions (1817, 1830) and two other student transcriptions, transmitted by writing and based on a lecture that Kant held in the 1780s. The result is clear: the text published by Pölitz, too, is a student transcription.[30] – I myself could not find any positive evidence confirming the natural assumption that Rink produced this manuscript as a student in Kant's lecture. To the contrary, the fact that the text goes back to the winter semester 1783/84[31] goes against this, for Rink first matriculated as a student only on 1 April 1786.

Between 1802 and 1804 Rink acted as editor of Kant's manuscripts three times: *Physical Geography* (1802, in two volumes), *Pedagogy* (1803), and the answer to the question, "What real progress has metaphysics made in Germany since the time of Leibniz and Wolff?" (1804). From a mainly editorial perspective, prefaces and additional notes reveal a gradually increasing awareness of the essential role of an editor of handwritten documents. In 1804 Rink explicitly identifies three different "manuscripts" (AA 20: 257 f.) and he describes the approach he used in the edition. In 1803 Rink refers to his remarks as merely "incidental" (AA 9: 439 f.); in the text these are almost all[32] designated with a note on the authorship such as "d. H." [*der Herausgeber*: the editor] or "A. d. H." [*Anmerkung des Herausgebers*: editor's note]. The preface to the *Physical Geography* (1802) directly shows that as he worked, Rink altered his original intention of implicitly or explicitly adding to, deleting, and re-working the texts given to him, and that in Part Two he wanted to restrict himself to a mere imprint (*Abdruck*) (AA 9: 153 f.). Adickes's *Untersuchungen* confirms Rink's reports about himself to the full extent. From this I would infer that, in the case of *Pedagogy* examined here, Rink was reluctant to proceed with interventions and stylistic changes. One may thus assume that this text that he published follows a design that was established by, or with, the manuscript(s).[33] If right, *Pedagogy* would then be a truly posthumous work of Immanuel Kant.

---

at Königsberg, and, when Kant was in the stage of life of an old man, edited his aphoristic lectures on pedagogy. Rink followed the great thinker in death, dying prematurely (27 April 1811); otherwise these lectures probably would have been edited by him, for they definitely have more inner value than the aphorisms on pedagogy" (Kant 1830: x f. [edited by Pölitz]).

30 Beyer 1937: ix f., 214–26.
31 Beyer 1937: 229, 269.
32 Exceptions are: AA 9: 450 (crossreference); 461; 473.
33 Weisskopf (1970: 240) explicitly claims otherwise: "The result ... is the testing of a hypothesis about the structure and origin of the text. In the course of our work, the certainty that the text

2 What information can we get from the text of *Pedagogy*?

2.1 The title

The noun "pedagogy" (*Pädagogik*) is used in the first Division (*Abteilung*) of the *Akademie-Ausgabe* (AA) only in volume 9, namely, in the context of the text in question.[34] Even the *Nachlaß* (unpublished remains) volumes 14 to 23 in the *Akademie-Ausgabe* do not contain the word. One likewise finds the word in vain in the student transcriptions of lectures on anthropology (starting from 1772/73) and on moral philosophy (Ms Kaehler, 1774–75). The adjective "pedagogical" (*pädagogisch*) occurs only once, namely in 1777, when giving the title of *Pädagogischen Unterhandlungen* edited by Basedow and Campe in Dessau in 1777–1779.[35] Meanwhile, "teachers" (*Pädagogen*) is mentioned once in the first Part of *Religion within the Boundaries of Mere Reason*, published in 1793 (RGV 6: 19.23). This gives rise to the assumption that the title of the text goes back to Rink. He knows that Kant used a textbook published in 1780 by Friedrich Samuel Bock. He also should have known the wording of the nine announcements in the Latin course catalogue (*Vorlesungsverzeichnis*) explicitly making reference to this book. "Pedagogy" is typically used there as an adjective to *Praelectiones* or *Lectiones*, or simply to *Collegio*.[36] Bock's textbook (1780) defined its object at the outset:

> (§ 1): The instruction in it [the art of education], in its whole extent, is named pedagogy, and the special part that develops the means and method of teaching, for the development of the mind, is called didactics.[37]

Turning to Kant, even if we changed the language and replaced "pedagogy" (*Pädagogik*) with "art of education" (*Erziehungskunst*) or "educational theory" (*Erziehungslehre*), the result would not significantly change. These terms, too, occur in the first Division of the *Akademie-Ausgabe* only in the *Pedagogy* text.[38]

Immanuel Kant: On Pedagogy represents a compilation from various parts, created at different times and created for different purposes, gradually increased."
34 AA 9: (preface) 437.03; 439.04; 439.10; 439.16; (text) 447.20; 447.23; 455.02; 480.24; 493.13 (= 9 times).
35 AA 2: 451.21.
36 Cf. the pages in Oberhausen and Pozzo 1999 mentioned in footnote 2 above.
37 Bock 1780: 3.
38 AA 9: 439.07; 446.30; 447.15; 447.17; 447.19; 447.25; 447.29; 455.02; 455.30. For the anthropology lecture, see AA 25: 1145.34 f. ([Menschenkunde] / Petersburg from 1781/82); 1437.17 (Busolt from 1788/89).

2.2 The structure[39]

The text takes up just under 60 pages of the *Akademie-Ausgabe*. Considered from a merely external viewpoint, the untitled Introduction (Päd 9: 441–54) breaks down into three large parts (*Stücke*). The boundaries between these are typographically marked by two long dashes[40] continuing over a whole line of print (Päd 9: 450.14–15; 451.16). If we take two short dashes (*Gedankenstriche*) located at the end of a paragraph (Päd 9: 444.26; 446.11), then the first large part breaks down into three smaller ones. The explicitly named "Treatise" (*Abhandlung*) states some definitions in advance (Päd 9: 455) and following these definitions consists of two complementary parts (*Teilen*), given the headings "On physical education" (Päd 9: 456) and "On practical education" (Päd 9: 486).

In the *first Part*, three more of the already observed long dashes appear (Päd 9: 466; 469; 475). Just after the first of these dashes it reads:

> The positive part of physical education is culture. In this respect the human being differs from the animal. (Päd 9: 466)

This "positive" corresponds to this earlier statement that seemed out of place:

> In general it should be observed that the first stage of education must be merely negative, i.e., one should not add some new provision to that of nature, but merely leave nature undisturbed. (Päd 9: 459)

At the outset of giving his lectures on anthropology (1772/73) Kant connected such a "negative" outlook with Jean-Jacques Rousseau:

> We call certain practices negative, namely, when we do not bring something authentic to our aim, but just remove an obstacle that opposes our aims. Rousseau's education plan is like this, namely, negative. He is not looking so much to arm the youth with knowledge,

---

39 In accordance with the strictly historical-philological approach of the present chapter, I will dispense with a discussion of the proposals, positions, and arguments contained in the literature; for overviews of the literature and topic, see the discussions in Burger 1889, Weisskopf 1970, and dos Santos 2007. Equally passed over are numerous stimulating and insightful attempts to trace the systematic relationships between *Pedagogy* and other writings of the Königsberg philosopher (e. g., Vogel 1990). – The carefully discussed and convincingly argued exposition of Kauder (1999: 35–83) has a similar aim, yet it is carried out using a different method and remains within the limits of a "collegio scholastico practicum" context that is predetermined by Rink.
40 Burger (1889: 8 f.) already noted the relevance of these lines.

as instead to prevent evil habits from taking up posts, or errors from settling in. (V-Anth/Collins 25: 33.15–21)⁴¹

Approximately the same phrasing is used in two other places in *Pedagogy* (9: 452.02; 462.03). In printed writings, a corresponding statement is found only in *Anthropology from a Pragmatic Point of View*, published in 1798. Here, however, with a sharp theoretical point:

> Rousseau did not really want the human being to go back to the state of nature, but rather to look back at it from the stage where he now stands. He assumed that the human being is good by nature (as far as nature allows good to be transmitted), but good in a negative way; that is, he is not evil of his own accord and on purpose, but only in danger of being infected and ruined by evil or inept leaders and examples. Since, however, good human beings, who must themselves have been educated for this purpose, are necessary for moral education, and since there is probably not one among them who has no (innate or acquired) corruption in himself, *the problem of moral education for our species remains unsolved* even in the quality of the principle, not merely in degree, because an innate evil tendency in our species may be censured by common human reason, and perhaps also restrained, but it will thereby still not have been eradicated. (Anth 7: 326 f.; emphasis by Werner Stark)⁴²

This shift is a result of Kant's teaching, published in 1792,⁴³ of a "radical evil in human nature" (RGV 6: 15.04). *Pedagogy* also refers to it.⁴⁴

Back to the structure of the text: the *second* of these long dashes is found on page 475, followed by the sentence: "But now we must also give a systematic concept of the entire purpose of education and the means by which it can be attained" (Päd 9: 475). After some preparatory remarks, interest is taken in "moral education," which is to be based on maxims:

> For the entire moral worth of actions consists in the maxims concerning the good. (Päd 9: 475.28 f.)⁴⁵

---

41 Manuscript Collins, page 21; cf. Parow, page 18 (1772/73); Friedländer Manuscript 399, pages 764 f.; Manuscript 400, pages 826 f. (1775/76); Menschenkunde, page 45 (1781/82); Mrongovius, page 131 (1784/85); Dohna, pages 18, 45, 365 (1791/92). – It is quite similar, too, in the Manuscript Kaehler ethics lecture from the mid-1770s; see (ed. Stark) Kant 2004a: 15–17 and 286, 443, 446.
42 On the references to Rousseau in the passage (Anth 7: 326.14 ff.), see Brandt 1999: 489–93. See also Refl 1521, especially AA 15: 890.5–7; and Stark 2014a.
43 First appeared in the April 1792 issue of the *Berlinische Monatsschrift*. Cf. AA 6: 501. – The anthropology lecture transcription Mrongovius attributes, already in winter 1784/85, a positive, productive function to "evil" (V-Anth/Mron 25: 1333.32).
44 Päd 9: 446.12 ff.; 448.14 ff.; 451.10; 470.02; 492.24.
45 Without a doubt the central question of the first section of *Groundwork of the Metaphysics*

> Moral culture must be based on maxims, not on discipline. (Päd 9: 480.07 f.)

From this perspective, three individual points are then listed and explained:

> The first effort in moral education is the grounding of character. (Päd 9: 481.08 f.)
>
> A second principal feature in the grounding of character in children is truthfulness. (Päd 9: 484.04 f.)
>
> A third feature in the character of a child must be sociability. (Päd 9: 484.27)

The *third and final* long dash (Päd 9: 485) separates a passage in which are formulated two isolated recommendations concerning the raising of children.

In the *second*, much shorter part, "On practical education" (Päd 9: 486), there are two of these dashes as well, thereby forming three sections.

The first section (Päd 9: 486–93) again takes up the definitions given at the beginning of the *Treatise* (Päd 9: 455): skill, worldly prudence, and morality[46] (*Geschicklichkeit, Weltklugheit, Sittlichkeit*) as the three objective targets of the practical education of the child, i.e., of the human being. This objective trio (trias) is faced, on the subjective side, with these: talent, temperament, and character.[47] In moral education directed at character, "duties to oneself" (Päd 9: 488.30) are distinguished from "duties to others" (Päd 9: 489.16).[48] Common to both is an orientation toward the "dignity of humanity" (Päd 9: 488.36; 489.01; 489.06 f.; 489.08; 489.34; 490.01). Interrupted by critical remarks of others and explanations of its own position, the first section concludes with further definitions (Päd 9: 492) – of desires, vices, and virtues.

The *second section* (Päd 9: 493–6) is devoted to the "education of children with a view to religion"; the terms "religion" and "conscience" are defined.

---

of Morals (1785) is taken up: What does the moral worth of an *action* consist in? – See GMS 4: 401.03, 407.14, and 440.07 f. – In contrast, the ethics lecture from the mid-1770s links the "moral worth" of the *person* directly to the fulfillment of "duties to oneself"; see Manuscript Kaehler: 220 f. and 281.

46 The same trio is found in the imperatives of the *Groundwork* (1785) (GMS 4: 415 f.) and even in the Kaehler transcription of the mid-1770s ethics lecture. See Manuscript Kaehler, pages 8–10 and (ed. Stark) Kant 2004a: 7 f.

47 See *Anthropology from a Pragmatic Point of View* (1798), at Anth 7: 285.17–19 and 292.15–25; it is similar already in the anthropology transcription Friedländer (1775/76) at V-Anth/Fried 25: 625–36; as well as Menschenkunde (1781/82) at V-Anth/Mensch 25: 1156–8; and Mrongovius (1784/85) at V-Anth/Mron 25: 1385.

48 This distinction belongs, among others, to the body of doctrine in A. G. Baumgarten's *Ethica*.

The *last section* (Päd 9: 496–9) examines the transition from "childhood" to "youth." The child (adolescent human) is confronted with two essential differences: that of sex (male/female) and social inequality among human beings. The border between the two stages, sexual maturity, is set around thirteen or fourteen years of age (Päd 9: 497.10); it is just a little before the limit for education in general, specified in the so-called "Introduction" as "until about the sixteenth year" (Päd 9: 453.16 f.). – Because of these time designations, it is clear that the text's subject matter does *not* extend to the age of university education.[49]

To summarize: the text follows a uniform plan.[50] However, from a literary perspective it is not all well formed. Interruptions and digressions can be explained by the fact that remarks or self-referring comments might have been incorporated into the running text without indication. As noted above, the editor offered no information about the external composition of the underlying manuscripts or how he proceeded with them.

2.3 Dating

The text contains many implicit and explicit allusions to its contemporary literary environment. In my view, there are still considerable gaps in the research here.[51]

---

[49] The university matriculation age at the time was around seventeen years old (Stark 1995: 68). Kant himself had completed his sixteenth year by the time of his enrollment in September 1740. – That Kant recognized this age as the beginning of a maturity is evident from a long footnote in his 1786 essay on the "conjectural beginning of the human species" (MAM 8: 116 ff.), as well as from the ethics lecture from the mid-1770s (Kant 2004a: 358 f., 363 f.).

[50] The alleged uniformity is supported by exact philological arguments: the explicit cross-references. 1) At the end of the "Introduction" (Päd 9: 454.27), a content is referred to that is discussed in more detail at the end of the second part, devoted to practical education. 2) The first part is bracketed in by two *broad* references back to earlier passages: a) "sense of proportion" (476.01); b) "will of children" (478.29). For further details, see Stark 2000: 105. There are also two other passages: the first "as already said" (489.33) refers back only briefly and is negligible; the second (496.06) refers to "negative" education. The latter is mentioned in the "Introduction" (442.06; 452.02) as well as in the first part (459.01; 462.03; 465.30; 477.29) and third part (495.16). We are dealing with a remark that is likewise negligible and refers back only briefly. – The second part of Refl 1501 (AA 15: 791 f.) shows agreement on this matter.

[51] Stark 2000: 99 f. See also some references at AA 25: 1612. – Relevant to the hitherto neglected relation of the text to the debate about educational science in the final third of the eighteenth century is the fact that in 1800 Rink also published a text of his own (1800b) which is directly and substantially relevant: *Aphorismen über Volkserziehung und das Landschulwesen insbesondre: mit Hinsicht auf die vorgeschlagenen Verbesserungen des letztern in den Preußischen Staaten* [110

The apparatus of the *Akademie-Ausgabe* offers only two pieces of information directly relevant for dating:

The paper by Lichtenberg (mentioned at AA 9: 470.17 f.) appeared in issue 4, year 3, of the *Göttingischen Magazin*. This reference could not have been written before the end of 1783.

The mention of "Crugott" (Päd 9: 489.32) is identified as a reference to Martin Crugot (1725–1790); yet the sermons to which the text apparently refers were already published in 1759, not 1790.

Like any work composed using words, the text at hand also includes information about the time of its origin which is internal, i.e., in its language. Just as different actors within a linguistic community can be distinguished by their terminology, so each speaker over time develops various idiosyncrasies or mere preferences. If a speaker or author has left a sufficient number of dated examples of his or her linguistic use, it is relatively simple to check[52] if characteristic differences can be established, and if so, according to which distinguishing marks. An arbitrary or merely statistical linguistic accumulation of such individual observations about terminology opens up a very wide and hardly manageable field. It is therefore advisable to limit the field of view to considerations of terms that are fundamentally connected with the theme of the text examined. The theme of the present text, *On Pedagogy*, is without question the education of human beings.

In the passage I am calling the "Introduction," we find the following definition:

> Education is an art, the practice of which must be perfected over the course of many generations. Each generation, provided with the knowledge of the preceding ones, is ever more able to bring about an education which develops all of the human being's natural predispositions proportionally and purposively, thus leading the whole human species towards its vocation. (Päd 9: 446.01–06)

Unlike most animals – with the exception of songbirds – human beings are able to transmit acquired knowledge and abilities from one generation to the next. Such a transmission is no mere work of nature:

> Since the development of the natural predispositions in the human being does not take place by itself, all education is – an art. – Nature has placed no instinct in him for this. (Päd 9: 447.11 f.)

---

pages]. See also the 19 November 1789 letter from Johann G. C. C. Kiesewetter (Br 11: 107 f.) and the intended "review of schools" (*Schulrevision*).

52 The first three Divisions of the *Akademie-Ausgabe* have been electronically digitized and have been available for years. See http://www.korpora.org/kant. Accessed 11 January 2015.

For a concept outlined in this manner, the notion of a "generation" (*Generation*) is essential.⁵³ From today's perspective, the latter may appear trivial. This is indeed because, and ever since, Charles Darwin, in the middle of the nineteenth century opened up a historical perspective that examined the succession of various generations, in a way that also included the animal and plant kingdoms. Yet the periods of time and objects considered by Kant and Darwin are quite different. Darwin is interested in processes that slowly and gradually take effect, the origin of various species. In contrast, Kant looks only at generations that are few in number, near to each other, and exclusively human.

The following result, for the word "generation," is found in the first Division of the Kant Edition of the (Berlin) Academy works of the Königsberg philosopher. The term "generation," adopted by the German language as a "foreign word," appears (singular or plural) for the first time in volume 8, which contains "Treatises after 1781." The first occurrence is found in *Idea for a Universal History with a Cosmopolitan Aim*, published in 1784 (IaG 8: 20.13).⁵⁴ Now we know that Kant discussed this text's subject matter before this, i. e., in his lectures on anthropology.⁵⁵ Indeed, the body of texts written by students confirms this chronological observation. In the Petersburg Manuscript (winter semester 1781/82) it states (page 19) for the first time: the human being is "the only creature where the species becomes more perfect [*vollkommener*] from generation [*Generation*] to generation."⁵⁶ A glance at the *Nachlaß* Division (volumes 14–23) of the Kant Edition corroborates this result.⁵⁷

In the first Division of the Kant Edition – outside of volume 9 – "generation" is used only in two other places: rather in passing in the 1796 *Rechtslehre* (RL 6: 324.23), and in the *Anthropology* published in 1798, where it reads:

> First of all, it must be noted that with all other animals left to themselves, each individual reaches its complete destiny; however with the human being only the species, at best,

---

53 That is, it concerns a *terminus technicus*.
54 The others are: AA 8: 64.27; 117.25; 117.26; 117.32; 172.14; 172.19; 173.12; 174.39; 175.04. – In all of the discussions, the theme is the historical development of the human species.
55 Cf. Stark 1993: 231–4; and comment number 225 on Manuscript Kaehler, in Kant 2004a: 437 (ed. Stark).
56 The *Menschenkunde*, published in 1831, is linguistically modified: "It is the only creature where the species becomes more perfect from genus [*Geschlecht*] to genus" (V-Anth/Mensch 25: 877). The foreign word is used in Manuscript Petersburg, page 118; and Menschenkunde: 179. – For the later lectures, cf. Manuscript Mrongovius (1784/85), page 125 f. (V-Anth/Mron 25: 1417 f.); Manuscript Dingelstädt, page 128; Manuscript Dohna, pages 62, 101, 358, 360; and Manuscript anonymous-Berlin, page 222.
57 Cf. Refl 1521, 1524, 6102, 6155, 6302, 8023; and volumes 20–23: – – [nothing found].

reaches it; so that the human race can work its way up to its destiny only through progress in a series of innumerably many generations. (Anth 7: 324.04 ff.)

In *Pedagogy* the term is used eight times, and exclusively in the "Introduction."[58] Always evident is a substantial connection with "education" (*Erziehung*) or the transmission ("*Tradition*," "*Überlieferung*") of experience and knowledge. The fact that the *Physical Geography* also uses the term[59] does not alter this situation, for there it is always about the transfer of a naturally given, external feature: human skin color. The talk is just as little of a cultural progress[60] supported by education as it is as of reaching the destiny or perfection of the human species.

As for the dating: it would seem that the provisional result is that the text, in the form presently before us (the Rink edition), was written at the very earliest in the middle of the 1780s (*terminus a quo*).

3 What are we looking for?

I come to a final consideration about the intended purpose of the text, *On Pedagogy*. First, on the negative side: (1) evidently it is *not* a (hitherto unrecognized as such) student transcription of a lecture given by Kant in the 1780s. (2) For the opinion stated by Rink in his Foreword, viz., that the text consists of Kant's personal notes written down for the purposes of his lecture, *no compelling* evidence can be found. (3) The depiction presented by Weisskopf, viz., that the text consists of a collection, essentially attributable to Rink, of heterogeneous fragments (*Bestandstücken*), is *not sufficiently* justified. – And on the positive side? Can we determine or state a context of origin differing from this, based on something else? – My answer is clear: Yes!

From different research, not undertaken in the context of the *Akademie-Ausgabe* of *Kant's gesammelten Schriften*, we know that at the University of Königsberg in the 1780s and 90s – in particular in the lower Faculty, the Faculty of

---

58 AA 9: 441.26; 443.17; 444.17; 446.01; 446.02; 446.21; 446.28; 447.27.
59 AA 9: 313.02; 313.06; 314.07. Correspondingly, in the early outline of the lecture (Manuscript Holstein from 1757–59): pages 117, 118, 119; in the student transcriptions: Messina, page 191; Pillau, pages 211–13, 216; Dönhoff, folio 83'; Volckmann, page 68 f.; Dohna, page 121; F. C. Starke's *Betrachtungen* (Starke 1833): 275, 277.
60 On *Fortschritt* (progress) and *fortschreiten*, see note 240 in Kant 2004a (ed. Stark). – In AA volumes 1–8, the following passages are directly relevant: 6: 19 f.; 6: 48.04; 6: 446.19; 7: 14.04; 7: 79.01; 7: 119.02; 7: 324.07; 7: 333.03; 8: 39.11; 8: 65.31; 8: 115.17; 8: 177.34. See also (1972) AA 28: 1187.23 ff.

Philosophy – two effectively pedagogical topics were discussed. And we know further that Kant was actively involved in these discussions.⁶¹ It concerns:

(1) The introduction of the high school graduate exam (*Abiturientenexamen*) in Prussia (1788) and the testing requirement tied to the respective Dean of the Faculty of Philosophy in Königsberg. In the summer of 1791, it was Kant's turn.

(2) The variable "plans for a pedagogical seminar in Königsberg 1788–1793."⁶² Both reform efforts were aimed primarily at school education. It was intended to improve the abilities and knowledge of the students moving to the university or to control this process using state authorities. On the one hand, the level of high schools (*Gymnasien*) was supposed to be raised, while on the other hand, attention was supposed to be given to the university formation of teachers in these schools. Seen in this way, the text was also a counter-proposal to the Latin school that Kant himself attended before 1740: the pietistically oriented Collegium Fridericianum.⁶³

In light of the present task of finding an orientation, I would like, in concluding, to formulate three clues that render plausible such an explanation of the existence and aim of the text, *On Pedagogy*. In fact, these have been already indicated:

(1) In its factual statements, the text extends over the period of a "higher" school formation.

(2) The philosopher, and not the experienced teacher, school teacher, and instructor, doubtless speaks in the "Introduction." It calls for a "theory of education" (Päd 9: 444.27): "The mechanism in the art of education must be transformed into science [*Wissenschaft*]" (Päd 9: 447.25 f.). In implementing this, recourse is to be made to the essential concepts and structures of his own anthropology⁶⁴ and moral philosophy.

(3) Undoubtedly the text – according to the programmatic "Introduction" – is bolstered by an educational optimism:

> It is delightful to imagine that human nature will be developed better and better by means of education, and that the latter can be brought into a form appropriate for humanity. This opens to us the prospect of a future happier human species. (Päd 9: 444.22 ff.)

---

61 Paul Schwartz 1910–12, 1925, 1931; and Werner Euler 1994, 1999.
62 This is the title of a filing report by Forstreuter 1969; see also Schwartz 1925: 405 ff.
63 Cf. Klemme 1994.
64 And indeed only to its first Part, which in turn is based on the empirical psychology of A. G. Baumgarten.

This "education euphoria" can be documented starting from the mid-1770s.⁶⁵ Gradually, however, skeptical moments,⁶⁶ which would eventually take the following form in the middle Part of the *Conflict of the Faculties* (1798), mix with this positive mood:

> In what order alone can progress toward the better be expected? The answer is: not by the movement of things *from bottom to top*, but *from top to bottom*. – To expect not simply to train good citizens but good human beings who can improve and take care of themselves; to expect that this will eventually happen by means of education of youth in the home, then in schools on both the lowest and highest level, in intellectual and moral culture fortified by religious doctrine – that is desirable, but its success is hardly to be hoped for. (SF 7: 92.15 ff.)

Due to the extant preparations for this teaching⁶⁷ we know that, especially in view of the events of the French Revolution (from 1789 on), Kant essentially tied the "progress of the human species" to political and legal transformations.

Finally, taking a view of the work's genesis, we may therefore also assume that the text *On Pedagogy* in substance belongs to the broad context preceding *The Conflict of the Faculties*,⁶⁸ and that in it positions are adopted that are put *ad acta* no later than 1798 (*terminus ad quem*).

---

65 Brandt 2007: 184 ff.
66 See the "Common Saying" (1793) (TP 8: 310.14 ff.) and prior to this (1792) the first Part of "Philosophical Doctrine of Religion" (RGV 6: 19.21–20.17).
67 Stark 2003. Cf. already the anthropology transcription Mrongovius (1784/85) at AA V-Anth/ Mron 25: 1427.08 f.: "Now what are the means of improving the civil society and constitution? 1. education 2. legislation 3. religion."
68 Brandt 2003: 119–40. – The proposed explanation of *Pedagogy*'s own coming into being implies an option, hitherto overlooked, for the interpretation of a widely discussed passage from an October 1797 letter. The *Pedagogy* becomes a candidate for a reference found in Kant's letter (AA No. 784) to Johann Heinrich Tieftrunk from Halle, viz., that there are "two essays [lying] in my dresser," "one completely finished and the other almost finished" (Br 12: 208.14 f.) [*In diesem Falle würde unser Herr Professor Gensichen zwei Abhandlungen in meiner Commode antreffen, deren eine ganz, die andere beinahe ganz fertig liegt (und zwar seit mehr als zwei Jahren)* – Editor/ Translator]. The said writings could have been the manuscripts of the two "works" (*Werke*) published by Rink in 1803 and 1804 from the unpublished remains (*Nachlaß*). Such an interpretation avoids the chronological difficulties surrounding the relation to the Parts of the three-part *Conflict of the Faculties* which has been hitherto accepted (see note 2 in Stark 1993: 39).

Chapter 12
Reading Kant's *Lectures on Pedagogy*

Susan Meld Shell

The text that has come down to us as Kant's *Lectures on Pedagogy* has had a famously checkered career. Originally published in 1803 by Friedrich Theodor Rink, Kant's young colleague and former student, it was evidently neither read nor edited by Kant, who gave over his lecture notes to Rink with the request that he select from them the ones "most useful for the public," according to the co-editor of the first edition of Kant's collected works.[1] Despite the doubtful status of the text, it was among Kant's more popular works until the early twentieth century, especially among progressive educators.[2] With some important recent exceptions,[3] later scholars have given it a wider berth.[4]

Despite these defects, the text is of greater philosophic interest, I will argue, than has sometimes been acknowledged. Read with care, and against the backdrop of Kant's shifting political setting, the *Pedagogy* echoes major themes of Kant's published writings during the late 1780s and 1790s, suggesting that the notes he handed over to Rink were something other than stale fragments. On the contrary, the long-festering contest over popular education in Prussia had reached a state of crisis during Kant's final professionally active decade, with serious, and potentially fatal, implications for his own life work. The *Pedagogy* lectures as they have come down to us obliquely address that crisis while also reflecting Kant's ongoing concern to reconcile freedom and lawful necessity, a concern that reaches back to his earliest reading of Rousseau's *Emile*.

1 Background and context

State interest in popular education in Prussia began around the time of Luther, who deemed popular education vital to the success of the Reformation, and urged

---
[1] For a more detailed account of the status and history of the text, see the essay by Werner Stark in this volume.
[2] See for example Buchner 1904.
[3] Noteworthy recent exceptions include Moran 2012; Munzel 2012; and Roth and Suprenant 2012.
[4] Cf. Kuehn 2001a: 408 f.; but see also Kuehn 2012.

princes to establish schools of elementary religious instruction. By 1600 parish schools offering elementary religious education to both boys and girls were common in most major Protestant German cities. Although popular religious education suffered during and immediately after the Thirty Years War, it underwent a significant revival beginning in the late seventeenth century, largely owing to the emergence of Pietism, which stressed the importance of individual literacy with a view to furthering the goal of inner religious conviction as distinguished from mere outward ritualistic observance (Melton 1988). Pietist emphasis on religious education for all, including the poorest, was balanced, however, by acceptance of the external social hierarchy as divinely ordained. Its intended effect was not to challenge such authority but render it less coercive by encouraging obedience from Christian love rather than fear of external harm. These goals were reflected in Pietist approaches to teaching. August Hermann Franke, the driving force behind the sect's advocacy for popular schooling, strongly discouraged the use of corporeal punishment except in the most recalcitrant cases. In this as in other matters, Franke was influenced by the Czech educator Jan Comenius, a Bishop of the Moravian Brotherhood and pioneer among Reformation educators.

Comenius circulated among the most advanced scientific circles of the seventeenth century, and combined the religious ideals of the Reformation with the methods of the new science (Murphy 1995). His magnum opus, the *Pansophiæ Prodromus*, aimed at the organization of all human knowledge along roughly Baconian lines; his pedagogical works attempted to bring that order, in outline form, within the grasp of children. Comenius's *Orbis Pictus*, which taught multilingual literacy to young children through simple, sensibly accessible pictures, set the stage for later educational experiments along related lines. (The *Orbis Pictus* would later be favorably cited by John Locke, and adapted for his own use by J. B. Basedow, as discussed below.) Comenius also championed establishment of *Realenschulen*, popular schools devoted to such "practical" subjects as geography and natural history, and taught in German rather than Latin, and promoted universal education at the primary level for girls as well as boys.[5]

At the same time, Franke understood education to involve "breaking a child's natural willfulness," with a view to helping to transform the child into a self-abnegating tool of God's own purposes. Pietist emphasis on inward obedience to the powers that be, along with the hostility of a Lutheran Orthodoxy that tended to support members of the Prussian nobility in their struggle against the centralizing efforts of the Crown, led to a seemingly unlikely alliance between Pietist

---

[5] Comenius was apparently invited to become president of Harvard College (by John Winthrop the Younger), but chose instead to accept an invitation to Sweden.

educational reformers and Frederick William I, who saw in inwardly docile subjects both tractable and loyal soldiers, and steady and willing laborers. Frederick William I initiated a number of policies, including a compulsory school edict of 1717 (which advanced the goal of school reform in principle, if not in fact), and a "Lithuanian Seminar" at the University of Königsberg, as well as sponsoring the publication of the first Lithuanian-German catechism in 1721 to counter a reported lack of familiarity with the basic propositions of Christianity in the Lithuanian-Prussian countryside.

The young Kant, who attended Pietist schools before matriculating to the University of Königsberg, was himself strongly affected by these efforts, for both good and ill, as he would later report. On the one hand, despite his relatively impoverished family circumstances, Kant received a strong education in Latin and some modern science that would later stand him in good stead. On the other hand, he described his years there as a kind of slavery, and particularly objected to his schoolings' efforts to inculcate a gloomy and hypocritical self-scrutiny, one that stands in polar opposition, in his later ethical theory, to the sense of personal dignity and inward "cheer" that signals possession of disposition that is genuinely moral.

Whatever his intentions, Frederick William I's funding of such efforts was sporadic, a pattern that continued under Frederick the Great, leaving much of the initiative for popular education in private hands. Frederick the Great's reformist efforts were mainly concentrated in the period from 1763 to 1786, when the throne passed to his nephew, Frederick William II. Although its initial effects were dampened by state financial difficulties, Frederick the Great's *General-Landschul-Reglement* aimed to establish compulsory elementary education along Pietist lines for all children between the ages of five and thirteen. It was only in the 1770s, however, that Frederick was able to fund education on any large scale. These efforts included the establishment of new teacher-training institutes in East Prussia along with expansion of rural schooling, and installation, in 1771, of Carl Abraham von Zedlitz as Minister of Justice and head of the Ecclesiastical Department that supervised Lutheran schools and churches in the monarchy (Kuehn 2001a: 215). Von Zedlitz, to whom Kant's *Critique of Pure Reason* was dedicated, held this important position until two years after the death of Frederick the Great, when he was replaced by J. C. Wöllner, with whom Kant would subsequently come into painful conflict. A strong champion of Kant's thought (within limits), von Zedlitz represented, one might say, the best that the regime of Frederick had to offer from Kant's own point of view. One suspects that Kant's fluctuating views on whether progress in education was to be expected from "above" or from "below" tracked reasonably closely with the waxing and waning fortunes of von Zedlitz's enlightened policies both during and after Frederick's reign.

Among private efforts at reform the Philanthropin movement, founded by Johann Bernard Basedow on both Lockean and Rousseauian principles, was especially influential. Basedow's *Vorstellung an Menschenfreunde für Schulen, nebst dem Plan eines Elementarbuches der menschlichen Erkenntnisse* (1768) borrowed eclectically from both Locke's *Thoughts on Education* and Rousseau's *Emile*. Basedow's copiously illustrated *Elementarwerk* (1774), which was partly modeled on Comenius's *Orbis Pictus*, circulated widely in Germany, along with a companion *Methodenbuch* for parents and teachers (which Kant himself assigned in his first lecture course on pedagogy). Basedow established a school in Dessau in 1774 with the specific aim of training teachers in the new method. Kant was for a time an ardent champion of the school, which closed in 1793, owing both to the difficult personality of its founder (who resigned in 1778), and political sponsorship that proved unreliable (Louden 2012b). The Institute, which enlisted support from a number of important intellectual figures including Goethe, attracted some noteworthy young teachers, including Christian Heinrich Wolke, Joachim Heinrich Campe and Friedrich Rehburg (Garber 2008). As Kant's *Pedagogy* would sum things up:

> [Because] no one generation can present a complete plan of education, experiments matter. The only experimental school [*Experimentalschule*] which in some measure made a start in breaking a path was the Dessau Institute. One must let it keep this fame despite the many errors for which one might reproach it, errors that one finds in all conclusions drawn from experiments [*Versuchen*], and that require new experiments in turn. It was in a certain way the only school in which teachers had the freedom to work according to their own methods and plans, and in which they stood in connection with one another and with all learned persons in Germany. (Päd 9: 451)

At the same time, the *Pedagogy* particularly faults "Basedow and others" for relying on "the assistance of princes" who are almost bound for the foreseeable future to remain unenlightened (Päd 9: 448 f.),[6] a lesson Kant had by then learned only too well.

In sum: the education of children and youths was a major site of political and intellectual contest throughout Kant's life, and not least in its highly charged final decade. For four Prussian monarchs, from Frederick William I through Frederick William III, universal elementary education was official policy (albeit often more honored in the breach than the observance), and state expansion in popular

---

[6] Basedow specifically calls for a state "council of education and studies" with jurisdiction over all orphans' homes, common schools, universities, theaters, and libraries, and direct control over primary and secondary schools. At the time, authority over education was largely in the hands of the church and local institutions (Lang 1891: 22).

education was an important means of extracting newly vital economic and military resources, often in the face of a recalcitrant nobility and their orthodox religious allies. Cameralist theory, which urged precisely the sort of state "paternalism" Kant was later to decry, made universal primary education (with a view to turning subjects into pliant workers and obedient soldiers) a central theme. Prussian state support for popular education was thus always, from Kant's own point of view, a two-edged sword: at once promising, so long as the state educational apparatus remained personally friendly, and threatening – furthering a process of mere "civilization" that without "moralization" would amount to nothing more than "glittering misery" (IaG 8: 26).

Under Frederick the Great, it remained possible for Kant to emphasize the bright side, at least in public (cf. Anth 7: 333n). Frederick, after all, allowed his subjects to "argue" as much as they liked, about whatever they liked, so long as they "obey[ed]" (WA 8: 41). Indeed, Kant was happy to concede that the republican "spirit" was better served, in the short run, by an "enlightened" monarchy of Frederick's sort than by premature resort to a republican form of government. Events in France following upon Frederick's death raised hope that the people's way of thinking might be transformed by a more direct, political route. But such hopes were challenged by the efforts of Frederick William II to reverse his uncle's course, culminating in the new religious edicts of 1788, and with it, the infamous demand that Kant refrain from all future publication on the subject of religion, a move that threatened to undo Kant's efforts to reform the machinery of state education from within (Shell 2009).

One obstacle to taking the *Lectures* seriously is its alleged similarity to Basedow's *Methodenbuch*, suggesting that even if it reflects Kant's own thinking on early education, those views are largely derivative from a figure of little ongoing intellectual standing and thus hardly deserving of careful analysis in their own right. The case for Kant's reliance on Basedow was put forward most forcefully by Traugott Weisskopf (1970), in a lengthy volume that claims to document frequent parallels in content or wording. A few such parallels are undeniable – e. g., the negative example cited in each of forcing a child to kiss the switch with which he has just been punished (Päd 9: 461; cf. Basedow 1965: 87). But others are little more than truisms (Päd 9: 482; Basedow 1965: 84), and/or reflect a common Rousseauian source in which Weisskopf himself shows little interest.[7]

---

[7] On details concerning Kant's reliance on, as well as significant departures from, Rousseau's *Emile*, see Reisert 2012: 12–24. For an enlightening discussion of Basedow and his project, see Munzel 1999: 254–333.

The more likely scenario, as Joseph Reisert (2012) has recently argued, is that Kant's enthusiasm for Basedow's project was based upon its promise to provide the mass application of Rousseauian educational methods that Kant had called for a decade earlier. As is well known, Rousseau, by Kant's own account, inspired a "revolution" in his thinking, teaching him to recognize "the dignity of common [moral] understanding," and to put "establishing the rights of mankind" above all else (BGSE 20: 44). That Rousseau's portrait remained the sole adornment on Kant's walls in later years testifies to the former's life-long significance for Kant.

Rousseau's aim was never, in Kant's view, to "return to the forests." The "main intention of Rousseau," as Kant wrote in notes from the mid-1760s known as the *Remarks*, "is that education ... make a free human being" (BGSE 20: 167). At the same time, Kant objected from the start to Rousseau's "unseemly" sacrifice, according to that author's scheme, of a tutor's life to the education of a single student. "Schools," Kant concluded, "are therefore necessary. One must erect/cultivate [*ziehen*] Emile. Would that Rousseau would show how schools can arise from this" (BGSE 20: 29).

To be sure, the demand for schools ran counter to Rousseau's own insistence in *Emile* on the impossibility of anything but private or domestic education under modern (Christian and post-Christian) circumstances. Still, even Rousseau had there offered tantalizing hints that more might be possible by way of popular or mass education than he explicitly allowed, especially where prospects of genuine republicanism remained alive. A passage in Book Five made the striking suggestion that modern courtship, suitably revised, might provide the needed antidote to modern public decadence, offering a collective solution to the problem of reconciling nature and freedom superior to that of Greece and Rome. The "romance," as Rousseau puts it, of Emile and Sophie "ought to be the history of my species."[8] Expanding on that hint, Kant declares Rousseau better than the ancients (BGSE 20: 11), not least, in his treatment of the society of men and women as a potential vehicle of civil and moral transformation.

Judging by his early lectures on anthropology, Kant for a time seems to have regarded such society as a crucial means of transforming a merely external "*Achtung* for the law," as he puts it in the Friedländer Anthropology of 1775/76 (V-Anth/Fried 25: 675), into genuine morality. By the late 1770s, the importance of sexual propriety to man's moral transformation has shrunk considerably. With

---

[8] Rousseau 2010: 599. The full passage reads as follows: "If I have said what must be done, I have said what I ought to have said. It makes very little difference to me if I have written a romance. A fair romance it is indeed, the romance of human nature. If it is to be found only in this writing, is this my fault? This ought to be the history of my species."

his discovery of the principle of autonomy, and the new meaning of "*Achtung* for the law" accompanying it, the importance of women to the moral education (of men) diminishes even more sharply. Henceforth, women's "refusal" is merely the "first artifice" for "leading men from merely sensed stimulus over to ideal ones" and "the first hint toward the formation of the human being as a moral creature" – in short, the "propriety" in matters sexual on which Kant's earlier program of moral education had hinged, is now only a "second step of reason," which must be followed by prudent "expectation of the future," and, finally, recognition of man as an "end in himself," before human beings can be "released from nature's womb" (MAM 8: 115).

There is further change in Kant's understanding of human progress that proves pertinent to an understanding of the *Pedagogy* lectures. Kant's progress narrative, which is relatively straightforward and linear in the history writings of the early 1780s, grows more twisted following the death of Frederick the Great and the advent of the French Revolution. In 1786, Kant could still write that whether the human race has "gained or lost" by its release from nature's womb "can no longer be" a "question" (MAM 8: 115). By the early 1790s such a conclusion could evidently no longer be taken for granted, as Kant makes clear in the very title of the *Conflict of the Faculties*, Part Two ("A question renewed: whether the human race is constantly progressing toward the better?" [1797]; SF 7: 79). In both *The Conflict of the Faculties* and *Religion within the Boundaries of Mere Reason* (1792), the issue in question boils down to whether or not rulers will forever successfully co-opt institutions of religious education, perverting what ought to be a means of civil and moral transformation into tools of an ever more powerful statecraft.[9]

In *Religion* "Part One" ("On Radical Evil"), Kant tackles that issue practically: what is the right way to "represent" the problem of human evil (as manifested, above all, in human rulers), with a view to reversing that perverse historical tendency? The tack he chooses is to engage the relation of religion and morality directly, through an "authentic" reinterpretation of the doctrine of "original sin" that reconciles it with "heroic opinion" of certain "philosophers" and, "especially in our day, pedagogues" according to which "the world steadfastly ... forges ahead ... from bad to better," or, that there is at least "the predisposition [*Anlage*] in the human being to move in this direction" (RGV 6: 19 f.).

To be sure, experience counts against this happy view, especially if one has "moral" improvement in mind. Still "moralists, from Seneca to Rousseau"

---

[9] The *Pedagogy* lectures betray a similar concern with the education of princes, absent which the problem of educating the human race appears to be (nearly) insoluble (Päd 9: 442 f.), a position echoed in the published *Anthropology* (1798) at Anth 7: 327.

have proposed it, Kant suggests, to "give impetus to" our "unflagging cultivation [*Anbau*]" of "a seed of goodness that perhaps lies in us" – "could one only reckon upon any such natural foundation [*Grundlage*] of goodness in the human race" (RGV 6: 20). Seneca's accompanying assurance (repeated at the beginning of *Emile*) that "we are naturally born to health" (RGV 6: 20) does not only not address the question of *moral* good (or evil) – i.e., one that may be imputed to us as our own free act or "deed"; it seems to contradict the very possibility of our moral goodness, which must, as such, be grounded in "the free power of choice" (RGV 6: 22) rather than in nature.

In order to more adequately elicit unflagging moral effort, Kant proceeds to use the term "human nature" in a peculiar way: namely, to refer to the "subjective first ground" (RGV 6: 22) of the imputable adoption of this or that maxim in relation to the moral law. Inasmuch as such a ground, on which depends the very possibility of moral choice, must be the same for every accountable (human) agent, such a ground is characteristic of the human race as such and can in this specific sense be deemed "innate." Such a "posited ground" of "every use of freedom" can thus be represented as present "from the moment of birth" albeit without "birth itself" being "its cause" (RGV 6: 22).

The question thus becomes how to try to give impetus to moral cultivation without (unwittingly) subverting it – either by presenting man as incorrigibly evil (so that human effort at moral improvement seems pointless), as with many orthodox Christians, or by presenting nature's curative powers as adequate in themselves (so that human effort at moral improvement seems needless), as with some "well-intentioned moralists," including, it would seem, Rousseau himself.

Kant's complex answer, which is presented more fully in *Religion within the Boundaries of Mere Reason*, and *Conflict of the Faculties*, sets an "original predisposition to the good in human nature" against a co-existing "propensity [*Hang*]" to evil, *both* of which must be posited as innate in order to "represent" (for purposes of "moral discipline") the "inner possibility" of our own moral freedom. The "thesis of innate evil," moreover, is of no use to "moral *dogmatics*," whose precepts gain nothing in either content or force from it, but *only* to "moral *ascetic*,"[10] by which Kant means only this:

> In the moral cultivation [*Ausbildung*] of the inherent [*anerschaffenen*] predisposition to the good one cannot begin from natural innocence/lack of indebtedness [*Unschuld*] but from the presupposition of a depravity of our power of choice [*Bösartigkeit der Willkür*] in accepting maxims contrary to the innate moral predisposition, and because the propensity thereto is ineradicable, with unremitting counteraction against it. (RGV 6: 50 f.)

---

10 See also *Metaphysics of Morals* (MS 6: 484 f.).

We must begin moral training not with the presumption of human innocence (as if the germ of goodness needed nothing more than positive encouragement) but rather by working against an innate tendency (*Hang*)[11] to depravity, an innate tendency absent which, as Kant had earlier shown, we could not "represent" the possibility of moral choice at all. Moral improvement, in other words, necessarily begins both with the assumption that a human being is naturally predisposed toward the good (otherwise failure to obey the law would not be one's fault) *and* with the assumption that something in us resists obeying the law (otherwise the law would not be encountered as a *duty*). Counteracting that resistance, however, consists not in penance (analogous to mortification of the flesh), as orthodox Christians wrongly think, but what Kant calls "moral gymnastics" (analogous to working one's muscles with a view to strengthening them).[12]

Kant's accompanying "representation," in *Religion*, presents a kind of schema of that subjectively elusive moral gymnasium. According to that schema, human beings' three-fold predisposition to the good, i.e., to "animality," "humanity," and "personality," is accompanied by an innate tendency to evil, which takes the triple form of weakness, perversity, and depravity. The predispositions to "animality" and "humanity" (but not that to "personality") permit "engraftment" onto them of corresponding "vices" – in the former case, vices of "savagery" (*Wildheit*), in the latter, those of "culture" (*Cultur*) (RGV 6: 26). Vices of brutishness consist in gluttony, lust, and "savage lawlessness" in "relation to other human beings" – i.e., deviations from the natural ends of nutrition, reproduction, and (animal) sociability, respectively. Vices of culture consist in "open or secret hostility to those whom we consider foreign" – i.e., deviations from the end for which nature "wishes to use" the "idea of competitiveness," namely, "as an incentive to culture." Such vices are "engrafted" onto inclinations of "jealousy" and "rivalry" along with an "unjust desire for superiority over others," a desire that "gradually arises" from a concern, not itself irrational, to prevent others from gaining the upper hand over oneself (RGV 6: 27).

---

[11] Kant defines "propensity" as "the subjective ground of the possibility of an inclination" (or "habitual desire") that is "contingent for humanity in general." That is to say, humanity is at least thinkable as altogether lacking in personality, and hence incapable either of obedience to the moral law or an inclination to resist such obedience. Such, at least, is my reading of Kant's accompanying claim that the most "rational being of this world" might still lack all awareness of the moral law as binding and thus lack all genuine moral accountability (RGV 6: 28–29n). It is the ongoing assumption of Kant's argument that we human beings are not rational beings of such a conceptually possible sort, rational beings who would altogether lack a moral life.

[12] See also *Metaphysics of Morals* (MS 6: 484 f.).

As we shall see, the *Pedagogy* systematically addresses the vices of brutishness and/or savagery, and that of civilization (to which young and older children are respectively prone), both "negatively" (through "discipline") and "positively" (through "instruction," "cultivation," and "formation").

The thesis of innate evil reemerges in the final sections of Kant's last major published work, the *Anthropology* (1798/1800) in the form of a race against time (Anth 7: 329).[13]

> [Rousseau] assumed that man is good *by nature* (to the extent that it allows itself to be thus transmitted), but only in a negative way, namely that he is not evil [*böse*] from himself and intentionally, but only in danger of becoming infected and corrupted by evil and unskillful leaders and examples. Since, however, *good* human beings, who must themselves have been educated for this, are demanded for moral education, and since it is likely that none exist who are not corrupt in themselves (either innately or by acquisition), it follows that the problem of moral education *for our species* remains unsolved according to the quality of the principle and not merely the degree, because an inborn evil tendency [*Hang*] may well be reproved by universal human reason, and also, in all events [*allenfalls*][14] contained, but not extirpated. (Anth 7: 326 f.)

The central difficulty, as Kant makes abundantly clear in these final sections of the *Anthropology*, is the moral unreliability of rulers in particular, owing to the temporal preponderance of our natural demand for freedom, a demand that "always presses to be master over other human beings," and that "one is aware of even in the youngest child":[15]

---

[13] The "prospect" of men's bringing about, by their own activity, "good out of evil," if nature does not one day cut this activity short, can be expected with "sufficient certainty for the duty of working toward this end." Kant here leaves up in the air whether our knowledge that natural revolutions *might* prevent man from realizing his destiny modifies this moral certainty, maximizing our own moral incentive to speed things up to the best of our ability rather than passively waiting for human "nature" in the form of a purposive "tendency" (*Tendenz*) to work its way gradually: a practical rhetorical strategy Kant employs throughout the 1790s.

[14] This is the term Kant also uses in the crucial passage of *Religion within the Boundaries of Mere Reason*, describing the reasoning through which (to the extent that we can render this transformation in the form of a practically useful narrative representation) human reason is corrupted (RGV 6: 42). For a detailed discussion of this passage, see Shell 2009: 195–9.

[15] In drawing attention here "even to the youngest child," Kant calls to mind a famous passage in *Emile*, Book One (echoing an at least equally famous passage in Augustine's *Confessions*), which poses the question of whether man is wicked by nature, or only due to bad institutions. The upshot of Rousseau's discussion is that unlike a sense of justice and injustice, which is inborn, the "spirit of domination" (*pace* Augustine) enters a child only owing to the ignorance and/or *malfaisance* of its caretakers (Rousseau 2010: 195 f.).

> In a civil constitution, which is the highest grade of artful heightening of the good predispositions [*Anlage*] in the human species to the final end of its *Bestimmung*, *animality* always manifests itself sooner and fundamentally [*im Grunde*] more mightily than pure *humanity*, and the tame cow is only made more useful than the wild to human beings through *weakening*. The human being's own will [*eigene Wille*] is always ready to break out against his fellow human being, and always presses [*streben*] his claim to unconditioned freedom, to be not merely independent but also to command other beings [who are by nature equal to him][16]…: because nature in him strives [*strebt*] to lead him from culture to morality and not (as reason prescribes) from morality and its laws to a culture purposively commensurate with it. (Anth 7: 327 f.)

The basic difficulty, in other words, is connected with the chronological order in which (human) nature necessarily proceeds, i.e. from culture to morality rather than from morality to culture. The result is an "inevitably perverse, counter-purposive tendency" (*Tendenz*), as with (today's) "religious education," which "ought to be a *moral culture*," but which instead "begins with *historical* culture," or "the culture of memory," and then "vainly attempts to draw morality out of it" (Anth 7: 328).

In sum: Rousseau's conclusion that man is good by nature, albeit only in a "negative way," does not gainsay the fact that our positive moral development has a natural tendency to strive (*streben*) counter-purposively, as shown by "religious education" in particular as a key expression of rulers' ineluctable pressing (*streben*) to dominate those who are their natural equals. If the point were not already clear enough, Kant closes the *Anthropology* with a decidedly negative note on Frederick the Great, whose "republican spirit" he had once famously praised, that bears directly on this theme:

> Frederick II once asked the excellent Sulzer … whom he had entrusted with the direction of educational institutions in Silesia, how things were going there. Sulzer replied "They have begun to go better since one has built on the principle (of Rousseau) that man is good by nature." Ah, said the King: "my dear Sulzer, you do not sufficiently know the wicked race that we belong to." – It also belongs to the character of our species that in striving [*streben*] toward a civil constitution, it also needs a discipline through religion, so that what cannot be achieved through *external* compulsion can be effected through *inner* compulsion (conscience); for the moral predisposition [*Anlage*] of the human being is used politically by lawgivers, a tendency that belongs to the character of the species. But when morality does not precede religion in this discipline of the people, the latter makes itself master over the former, and statutory religion becomes a tool of state authority [*Staatsgewalt*] (politics) under *despots of faith* [*Glaubensdespoten*], an evil [*Übel*] that unavoidably puts character out of tune and misleads it [*den Character unvermeidlich verstimmt and veleitet*] by ruling

---

16 Bracketed phrase not in H manuscript.

through *deception* [*Betrug*] (called state prudence); from whence that great monarch, while *publicly* professing to be merely the highest servant of the state, could not hide the opposite in his inwardly sighing [*seufzend in sich*][17] private confession, though with the excuse in the case of his own person of holding the whole race, called the human species, accountable for this corruption. (Anth 7: 332n)[18]

In the face of this impasse, Kant holds out a sole hope: that human beings, although "malicious" (*bösartig*), are also "ingenious" (*erfindungsreich*) rational beings – beings who – as nature's counter-purposive tendency becomes ever more mutually burdensome "with the advance of culture" – at last become willing to "subjugate themselves, however reluctantly," to the "discipline" of civil restraint. And yet precisely in so doing:

> they subjugate themselves only to laws given by themselves, and feel themselves ennobled through this consciousness – consciousness, that is to say, of belonging to a species that measures up to the human *Bestimmung* that reason represents to them as an ideal. (Anth 7: 329 f.)

The key to moral education lies not in the idealization of sexual desire (as Kant had once supposed), nor in the freedom to "argue but obey" under the "enlightened" rule of an absolute monarch (as Kant had allowed himself to publicly aver in the mid-1780s), but in the "conscientiousness," as he now puts it, that accompanies inner acceptance, however "reluctant," of lawful constraint.

A similar thought is nicely captured by the contrast, and implicit transition, in the *Metaphysics of Morals* (1797), i.e., between the "universal principle of right" as such, and the "ethical demand" that one make it one's incentive. As we shall see, the youth who accepts that universal principle as binding on himself,

---

17 The term *seufzen* rarely occurs in Kant's work. See, however, *Conjectural Beginnings* (MAM 8: 118n), which educes, as a "third example" of "nature [having] grounded two predispositions in us for different ends [i.e., man as an animal species and as a moral species]," Rousseau's complaint as to inequality of right, an inequality which cannot be overcome, as Kant here insists, so long as culture proceeds "planlessly." As Kant concludes, "The human being was to work himself up from the crudeness of his natural predispositions by himself, and yet he was to take care not to offend against them even as he lifts himself above them, a skill he can expect to acquire only late and after many miscarrying attempts, while in the between time humanity sighs [*seufzt*] under the ills it does itself out of inexperience." By the 1790s, the "plan" in question has come to specifically involve reversing nature's own "counter-purposive tendency" as manifested, above all, by rulers such as Frederick II, who pretended to be the servant of the people, while privately betraying a misanthropy that revealed by their "sighing" tone his own bad faith.

18 In this and other passages, I have occasionally modified the Cambridge University Press translation.

even if he does so (at first) for merely prudential reasons, becomes conscious of a capacity for self-legislation that is morally transformative (or "ennobling") and at the same time specifically counters the "counter-purposive tendency [*Tendenz*] of human nature" to which the final pages of the *Anthropology* draw attention.

2 Kant's *Lectures on Pedagogy*

Kant's *Pedagogy* addresses itself to the education of the child from early infancy to around sixteen, the age at which students ordinarily matriculated to the university.[19] As Joseph Reisert (2012) notes, the general plan loosely follows that outlined in Rousseau's *Emile*, childhood (Books One and Two), youth (Book Three) and puberty (Book Four), up to but not including sexual maturity, along with its related opportunities and dangers (Book Five). Like Rousseau, Kant assumes that all our natural "predispositions" are good, and that vice arises only from their perversion or corruption. And like Rousseau, Kant claims that the human faculties come into operation in a certain natural order that is generally conducive to our physical well-being and to the survival of the species, but is more problematic when it comes to achieving the higher (moral) end to which we are also somehow directed. For both thinkers as well, education has both a negative and a positive aim: both preventing the corruption of our faculties (by not allowing "unnatural" tendencies to take root), and encouraging them to flourish and gain strength (Kant calls the former "discipline," and the latter "culture," "formation," and "instruction").

At the same time, whereas Rousseau famously holds society alone responsible for man's corruption, Kant blames a certain "propensity" in man toward lawless freedom. The "ground of evil" does not lie in man's "natural predispositions" (which are good); but in a tendency to "deviate" from his "destiny," namely "humanity," which lies in "[bringing] nature under rules" (Päd 9: 448). The "natural desire for freedom" (or the impulse toward activity unrestrained by natural instinct) must be disciplined by law, "the means by which man's tendency to savagery [*Wildheit*] is taken away" (Päd 9: 442). Accordingly, Kant takes explicit issue with Rousseau's portrait of the savage, setting the tone for what will follow:

---

[19] Education proper ends at puberty, the time at which the youth can become a father and is thus called upon by nature itself to both lead himself and educate others (Päd 9: 454). University instruction is in this respect merely "auxiliary," and its discipline can only be "hidden" – a reversal of Rousseau's procedure, which was to begin with "hidden" discipline and bring it into the open only at the time of puberty.

> By nature man has such a great propensity [*Hang*] for freedom, that when he has grown accustomed to it for a long time, he sacrifices everything for it. Hence discipline must be applied very early, for if this does not happen, it is difficult to change the human being later on. He then follows every whim. It is also observable in savage nations that, though they may be in service to Europeans for a long time, they can never grow accustomed to the European way of life. But with them this is not a noble propensity toward freedom, as *Rousseau* and other believe; rather, it is a certain raw state in that the animal in this case has so to speak not yet developed the humanity inside itself. (Päd 9: 442)

In his earliest responses to Rousseau (in the 1760s) Kant had viewed the savage's willingness to "sacrifice everything" for freedom in a more positive light: to one who has not yet been habituated to deferring to the will of others, as Kant remarked in his notes in the *Observations*, nothing is more "terrible" – nothing more in contradiction with man's status as a "self-conscious" and hence "complete" being – than the prospect of such "enslavement" (BGSE 20: 92).

The contrast between Kant's earlier and later views of savage independence proves instructive in understanding other ways in which the pedagogy lectures deviate from its Rousseauian model and predecessor. Rousseau, showing greater confidence in unregenerate nature, had urged the educator to build a "fence" or "enclosure" around the child's soul in order to remove it from the "highway" and accompanying "impact of human opinions" (Rousseau 2010: 161–3). Such artificial growths are at best like espaliered pear trees, formally suited to civil life of a particularly restrictive sort (e. g., Sparta) but lacking the full vigor of the natural specimen. Negative education, for Rousseau, means holding back the stunting forces of society, whose impact directs growth in an unnatural and haphazard fashion; it consists "not in teaching virtue or truth," but in "securing the heart from vice and the mind from error" (Rousseau 2010: 226).

For Kant, by contrast, what must be restrained lies within the child himself. Accordingly, his preferred model of education is not the fenced enclosure but the forest, in which "trees grow straight and tall," owing to rather than despite their proximity:

> A tree which stands alone in the field grows crooked and spreads its branches wide. By contrast, a tree which stands in the middle of the forest grows straight toward the sun and air above it, because the trees next to it offer opposition. It is the same with princes. (Päd 9: 448)

One is here reminded of a famous parallel passage from the "Fifth Proposition" of Kant's *Idea for a Universal History*, which evokes the same metaphor to similar effect:

> *The greatest problem for the human species, to which nature compels him, is the achievement of a civil society of universally administering right* .... Human beings, who are otherwise so

taken with unconstrained freedom, are compelled by need to enter into [a] condition of coercion, ... given that their own inclinations make it so that they cannot long subsist next to one another in savage freedom. Yet in such a precinct as a civil union is, these same inclinations have afterward their best effect; just as trees that grow in a forest – precisely because each of them seeks to take air and sun from the other – are constrained to look for them above themselves and thereby achieve a beautiful straight growth; whereas those in freedom and separated from one another, putting forth their branches as they like, grow stunted, crooked and awry. (IaG 8: 22; Kant's emphasis)

The need to attend to each child's "particular genius," which for Rousseau dictated an education in social isolation (Rousseau 2010: 227), gives way to efficiencies of scale, suggested by the course of human history, where culture, no less than civil order, results en masse from man's "unsocial sociability."

To (re)educate the human species, it is first necessary to recreate the conditions of man's "asocial sociability" within the confines of the classroom. Schools, for Kant, are thus not just a necessary evil – an imperfect version of an education that is perfectible only domestically (as Rousseau himself insisted) – but the best possible environment for enabling the child to "bring out [his] natural predispositions" "by his own effort" (Päd 9: 441).

Initially, Kant places the emphasis mainly on physical restraint. Children are first sent to school, he notes, "not with the intention that they should learn something there," but in order that "they should there grow accustomed to sitting still and observing punctually what they are told, so that in the future they not put each notion that strikes them actually and instantly into practice."

Kant's insistence on accustoming the child to "sitting still" (and other forms of passive obedience) is certainly inconsistent with the early training of Emile (though not, suggestively enough, with that of Sophie, Emile's female counterpart [Rousseau: 2010: 544–7]).[20] But it is in keeping with Kant's understanding of savage freedom as a propensity that must be forcibly restrained by others until the child's reason is sufficiently developed to assume that role itself. And it is also in keeping with a certain republican spirit that recognizes in the undisciplined child the makings of the willful prince (Päd 9: 443).

The task of education thus conceived is highly problematic, as Kant admits. Indeed a perfect solution has not yet been found: "One of the greatest problems

---

20 Similarly, both Sophie and Kant's young student are exposed to a practical "catechism" at an earlier stage than Rousseau seems to deem most appropriate in the case of a rightly educated young man (Päd 9: 490; cf. Rousseau 2010: 556 f.). It is almost as if Kant consciously incorporates aspects of the ideal female education, as Rousseau understands it, into the education of young men, making possible a "completeness" that Rousseau himself reserves to heterosexual couples (Rousseau 2010: 566).

of education is how one can unite submission under lawful constraint with the capacity to use one's freedom. For constraint is necessary! How do I cultivate freedom under constraint?" (Päd 9: 453). Kant's provisional answer lies in a "judicious" application of resistance that accustoms the child to submitting to rules whose "reasonable[ness] and good[ness]" he progressively becomes able to grasp and thereby internalize. To summarize: in early childhood, the child is "left free" in all matters that do not pose a physical risk or impinge upon the freedom of others. In middle childhood, he learns "that he can reach his goal only by letting others reach theirs." In late childhood and early adolescence he is brought to recognize that restraint is "laid on him only so that ... he may one day be free," i. e., able to use his freedom to support himself without depending "on the support of others" (Päd 9: 454). Kant accordingly divides education into the "physical" (which man has in common with other animals) and the "practical" or "moral," which is "education of a freely acting being who can support himself and be a member of society" and who can also have "inner value." The accompanying order of a child's formation is, respectively, "didactic" (the job of the instructor), "pragmatic," (the job of the tutor), and "moral," for which no external guide, in the strict sense, is possible (Päd 9: 455; cf. 446).

In this final regard especially, public education shows its advantage, by providing an arena for constructive competition ("not incompatible with mutual love" as Kant elsewhere puts it), competition that not only stimulates students to cultivate their powers but also provides "the best model [*Vorbild*] for future citizenship."

> By means of [a public education] one learns to measure one's powers, one learns limitations through the rights of others. Here no one enjoys his [class] advantages, because one feels resistance everywhere, and because one can only make oneself noticed by distinguishing oneself through merit. (Päd 9: 454)

The *physical* culture of the mind is based on "exercise and discipline" brought about by the child's passive obedience to others "who think for him" – a familiar theme of earlier Prussian educational reform, designed to produce obedient subjects and soldiers. The *moral* culture of the mind, by way of contrast, has no "discipline," its place taken by the child's own "maxims," the capacity for which can first be actively cultivated only in later childhood.[21]

---

[21] For a particularly lucid account of the stages of a child's moral education for Kant, see Formosa 2012: 165–75. See also Funke 1985: 102–9.

The question thus becomes how to instill passive obedience without "breaking the child's will" – the goal of certain Pietist practices (like the shaming of young children) that Kant specifically prescribes.[22] His answer – submission to the "law of necessity" – would appear to be adapted from the following famous passage from Rousseau's *Emile*:

> Dependence on things, since it has no morality, is in no way detrimental to freedom, and engenders no vices. Dependence on men, since it is without order, engenders all the vices, and by it master and slave are both corrupted. If the laws of nations could, like those of nature, have an inflexibility that no human force could ever conquer, dependence on men would become dependence on things again; in the Republic, all of the advantages of the natural state would be united with those of the civil state, and freedom which keeps men exempt from vices would be joined to morality which raises him to virtue. (Rousseau 2010: 217)

This propensity toward lawless freedom must first be countered by a law whose "reasonableness and goodness" the child cannot yet grasp. Kant's remedy is not the improbably elaborate theater of illusory necessity that surrounds the young Emile (who regards "his sister as he does his watch"), but an almost ordinary schoolhouse, where students "must follow the rules exactly," without yet knowing, or even asking, what the rules are good for (Päd 9: 472).[23]

The physical disciplining of the mind makes possible, in turn, its positive culture, which Kant divides into "free" culture, which consists in "play," and "scholastic" or "compulsory" culture, which consists in "work." Of the two, work should receive the greater emphasis, owing to man's "unfortunate" inclination toward "inactivity" (Päd 9: 470). Hence (*pace* Rousseau), children must "learn to work" well before they are in a position to understand its usefulness (Päd 9: 772).

"Compulsory culture" consists in cultivation of the lower forces of the mind in the face of man's natural propensity toward laziness. Such compulsory culture is supplemented and gradually superseded by cultivation of the mind's higher forces, including the power of judgment (without which the lower forces of the

---

[22] Shaming is appropriate only in the case of lying, for which children feel an innate shame (as they betray by blushing) (Päd 9: 484). The contrast with *Emile* is here striking; Rousseau there explicitly denies that children can be taught that lying is intrinsically wrong, which, like all other strictly moral lessons, falls on deaf ears prior to puberty. The *Pedagogy* lectures are themselves ambiguous as to the age at which expressions of contempt become an appropriate penalty for childish infractions (Päd 9: 484, 478).

[23] Cf. *Emile* (Rousseau 2010: 325) where the question "What is it good for?" becomes the "sacred word" once the child is capable of distinguishing "work" from "play" or activity that is immediately agreeable.

mind have "no value" [Päd 9: 474]) and the power of understanding. Cultivation of the understanding involves discovery and application of rules "in everything" so that understanding may proceed with "consciousness" rather than "mechanically" (Päd 9: 475), so that the child is himself able to give a "reason" for his own activity (Päd 9: 474).

With a view to this ultimate end, external compulsion must be imposed upon the child with an unwavering impartiality.

> To the character of a child, especially a pupil, there belongs above all things obedience. This is two-fold; first, obedience to a leader's *will* [*Wille*] that is *absolute*; but also, second, obedience to a will that is recognized as *reasonable and good*. Obedience can be derived from constraint, and then it is absolute; or it can be derived from confidence [*Zutrauen*], and then it is obedience of another sort. (Päd 9: 481; my trans.)

In insisting, then, that the child "stand under a certain law of necessity," Kant does not mean that the teacher's directives should seem indistinguishable from acts of nature (as Rousseau sometimes appears to suggest); he means, rather, that they be "universal" in the sense of applying to every student equally: "As soon the child sees that not all the others must submit to the same law, it becomes rebellious (Päd 9: 482). Impartially administered, even "artificial" punishment – i.e., punishment the child does not directly bring upon himself – is useful, so long as it draws on the child's inclination to be loved and honored (which later aids morality), rather than on his aversion to physical pain (which only serves to strengthen a child's "obstinacy" [Päd 9: 483]).

Moral education, by way of contrast, "is based not on discipline," but on "maxims." Here threats and punishments "spoil everything." Instead, the pupil must act on "his own maxims," in full comprehension of his action's "ground" and derivation from "concepts of duty" (Päd 9: 475). Where discipline "prevents bad habits," moral culture "forms the way of thinking [*Denkungsart*]." The child must not only habituate himself to acting upon maxims rather than "certain incentives," but also upon rules whose fairness into which he himself has "insight" (Päd 9: 480). Unlike the obedience of the child, in other words, that of the adolescent consists in "submission to the rules of duty" and hence "obedience to reason" (Päd 9: 483).

The first "effort in moral education" is "the grounding of character," i.e., cultivation of the child's "capacity [*Fertigkeit*] to act on maxims" (Päd 9: 481). To form the character of *children* (as distinguished from *citizens*), one must draw children's attention to a "certain plan in all things, certain laws, known to them, which they must follow exactly." Though they may in indifferent matters choose the time, in having thus "made their law" they must then follow it unswervingly (Päd 9: 481). A second, and even more important ground of character is "truthfulness," lacking which one has "no character at all," but at best a good "temperament" (Päd 9: 484). A third step lies in cultivating sociability by promoting friendship among the students (Päd 9: 484), with due diligence (as adolescence approaches) that inclinations not "turn into passions" (Päd 9: 484–7). And moral cultivation culminates in the pupil's "firm resolution" to carry out what he resolves on, without excuses of exception or delay that especially mark unenlightened religious practice (Päd 9: 487 f.).[24]

In turning to specific duties, Kant draws particular attention to duty to oneself – one that "many writers," such as Crugott,[25] "explain falsely" or "entirely omit." For it is only the "duty to preserve the dignity of humanity in one's own person" that can restrain a youth at the "critical" moment in which sexual inclination "begins to stir." The discrepancy between man's sexual and civic maturity, or between the time in which he is physically capable of reproducing his own kind and the time in which he is prepared to be a self-supporting citizen and father makes moral education necessary well before the time that Rousseau regarded it as possible (Päd 9: 493, 489).[26] And it puts a special premium on the duty to oneself rightly understood if that gap is to be negotiated successfully.

Kant's subsequent treatment of specific moral duties, and of the relation of morality to religion, are consistent with his published views, including works of the 1790s. Its themes include, to name only a few, the priority of duties of right to those of benevolence (Päd 9: 490), the temporal priority of morality to religion (Päd 9: 494), and restriction of religion's role to making moral "conscientiousness" effective without rendering morality mercenary (Päd 9: 495).[27]

---

[24] Kant's criticism here of so-called bed-conversions, along with forms of penitential self-castigation that are themselves morally indifferent, calls to mind his detailed treatment of these topics in *Religion within the Boundaries of Mere Reason*. As the *Pedagogy* notes, religious instruction should ideally be delayed until moral instruction is virtually complete (as in *Emile*), although in the "present situation" this is impossible (Päd 9: 493) – an allusion perhaps to darkening prospects for religious freedom at the time.

[25] Martin Crugott (1725–1790), whose *Predigten* (Breslau, 1790) contained a sermon, "On the Moral Example of Christ with Respect to Mediate Positive Virtue or Duties to Oneself." See the note in the Cambridge translation of the *Pedagogy* (Kant 2007: 527 n. 36).

[26] For Rousseau, by way of contrast, true moral education begins only with the advent of puberty. Emile is restrained not by the "idea of humanity," but by that of an ideal woman that is the product of his imagination.

[27] Kant's specific instructions concerning religion echo many arguments more fully developed in *Religion within the Boundaries of Mere Reason*, including the suggestion, which makes its first published appearance in *On the Failure of all Philosophical Attempts at Theodicy*, that "striving for conscientiousness" is the most that can be expected of man without divine assistance. Cf. Päd 9: 497, 499 and MpVT 8: 268.

At the same time, the lessons thereby conveyed are no less civic than they are moral: benevolence toward the poor is not "meritorious," inasmuch as inequality of wealth "comes only from accidental circumstances": wealth comes from the "seizing of circumstances" that have turned out well for one or for one's predecessor, and for which one cannot claim any special moral credit (Päd 9: 491). Inequality of wealth is a concession to the necessary role of accident in human affairs, not (except, perhaps, in the ideal case) a tribute to superior industry or cunning. The civic attitude Kant wishes to impart avoids the twin perils of pride and envy. One must never let one child shame another, or take pride in advantages flowing from good fortune. Instead, Kant would cultivate a modest confidence (*Zutrauen*) in oneself, one that puts one in a position to show one's talents in a seemly way, and without "indifference" toward the "judgment of others" (Päd 9: 492). Kant's emphasis on securing a well-founded self-confidence in the child calls to mind a related passage in *Religion*, which urged the need for confidence in the sufficiency of one's own moral capital if one is to overcome the "moral hesitation" in which "radical" human evil essentially consists.[28] And it calls to mind another crucial passage, from *Religion within the Boundaries of Mere Reason*, in which the vices of civilization arise, precisely, from a rivalry and competition that is unrestrained by "reciprocal love" (RGV 6: 27). One can easily imagine Kant here presenting an idealized version of his own experience as an impoverished young scholar, competing confidently against, while also frequently befriending, young men who were far superior in wealth and social standing.

As with the discipline of physical compulsion that earlier countered engraftment in the young child of the vices related to the savage state, friendly classroom rivalry now counters the engraftment in the older child of the main vices of civilization. Education, so conceived, promises to reverse the course of human history – finally, and not least, by wresting religion from what Kant elsewhere calls "dominion of the evil principle."[29] As Kant himself summarizes the ultimate goal:

> Everything in education depends on establishing the right principles throughout and making them conceivable and acceptable to children. They must learn to replace abhorrence stemming from hatred for one stemming from disgust and absurdity; they must learn to have inner aversion replace the outward aversion to human beings or divine punishment, to have self-estimation and inner worth replace the opinion of human beings, to have the inner value of actions and deeds replace words and emotions, understanding replace

---

[28] RGV 6: 51–6, 65–8. See Shell 2009: 200–210.
[29] On the moralizing capacity of the "discipline" of civil restraint with respect to the human race in general, see also Anth 7: 329 f.

feeling, and joy and piety with good humor replace morose, timid, and gloomy devotion. (Päd 9: 492 f.)

The extraordinary burdens and expectations that Kant lays upon education in the *Lectures* are thus entirely consistent with the view of history he elaborates from the mid-1780s onward, both with respect to dealing with the primary seats of human vice (both savage and civil), and with a view to overturning an official theology in thrall to rulers who are not (yet) enlightened. Tonally as well, the *Lectures on Pedagogy* resembles Kant's works from the mid-1780s onward, tempering hope with an undercurrent of mordant irony. The problem of education, as he here puts it, is "the greatest and most difficult that can be given to the human being" – i.e., to a being charged with bringing about within himself "all predispositions toward the good," including, above all, the predisposition to morality. Accordingly, the art of education, along with that of government, is "probably the most important human invention," one whose concept arises only "very late" with imperfect clarity, and whose "idea" yet remains controversial (Päd 9: 446). Still, an idea of education that develops "all men's natural predispositions" is a "truthful" one – a "noble ideal," even if one is not yet in a position to realize it. And yet – and here's the rub – it is impossible to know beforehand how far men's predispositions can be developed and the "germs" of humanity thereby unfolded (Päd 9: 445).

> Parents care for the home, princes for the state. Neither has as final end the world best and the perfection to which humanity is destined, and for which he has the predisposition [*Anlage*]. However, the predisposition [*Anlage*] for a plan of education must be made in a cosmopolitan manner [*muss aber kosmopolitisch gemacht werden*]. (Päd 9: 448; my trans.)

As the curious double use of *Anlage* here brings out, the *Anlage* for a plan of education – a predisposition, as it were, to develop all our predispositions – must itself be "made" by man, however paradoxical the charge, guided by the idea of a cosmopolitan community not yet (fully) realized. Men must be *disciplined*, so that animality does not do damage to humanity, and then *cultured* in skillfulness, *civilized* by prudence, and, finally, *moralized* – that is to say, acquire "the disposition to choose only those ends that everyone necessarily finds fair [*von Jedermann gebilligt werden*]" and that can simultaneously be the ends of everyone.

It follows that no single generation can present a complete plan of education – including Kant's own generation, in which "the happiness of states grows simultaneously with the misery of human beings" (Päd 9: 451). The best hope lies with schools set up not by governments but by "enlightened knowers" with the freedom to experiment and communicate their findings – abetted, were it possible, by a "political economy" [*Staatsökonomie*] that extended more favorable terms of credit than at present, when schools are required to pay interest before enjoying the principle (Päd 9: 449; cf. ZeF 8: 345 f.) In this respect as well, Kant's pedagogy, like the education of the human race more generally, remains a "game" of confidence,[30] dependent on a willingness to risk one's capital on the promise of an "unforeseeable" end.

---

30 Compare *Conflict of the Faculties* (SF 7: 85). On moral risk-taking more generally in Kant, see Shell 2009: 141 f.

VI Philosophical Encyclopedia

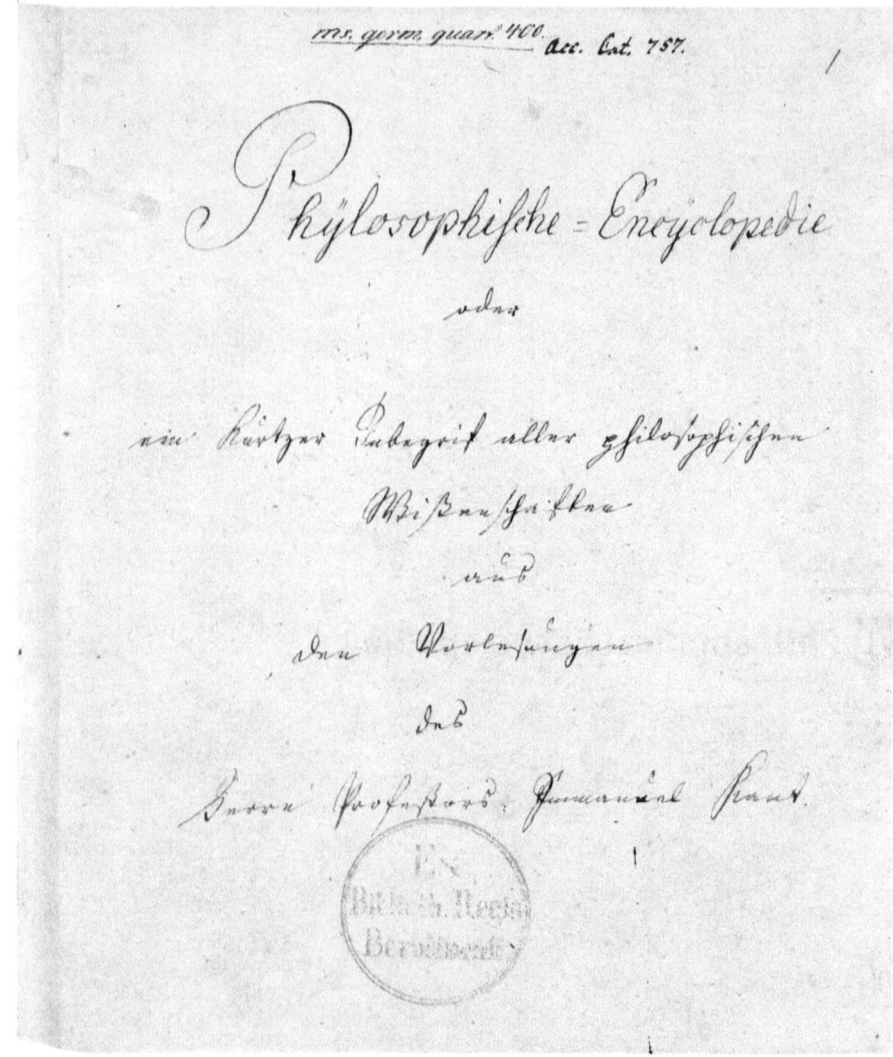

Fig. 9: Reproduction of the title page from the handwritten student notes from Kant's course on philosophical encyclopedia. Reproduced with the kind permission of Stiftung Preußischer Kulturbesitz, Berlin, Germany. Call number: Ms. germ. quart. 400.1. The page states: "Philosophische-Encyclopedie / oder / ein kurtzer Inbegrif aller philosophischen / Wißenschaften / aus den Vorlesungen / des / Herrn Profeßoris Immanuel Kant." ("Philosophical encyclopedia, or a short summation of all philosophical sciences. From the lectures of Herr Professor Immanuel Kant.")

Chapter 13
Philosophy for Everyman: Kant's Encyclopedia Course

John Zammito

In 1767/68, Kant suddenly inaugurated a new course, the *Vorlesungen über Philosophische Enzyklopädie*, a rather remarkable development in his pedagogy which has not received nearly enough attention.[1] We know that Kant offered the course again in 1768/69, 1769, 1770, 1770/71 and 1771/72. For three years the course was not offered, then it resumed in 1775 (for which we have the only surviving, but incomplete lecture notes), 1777/78, 1779/80 and 1781/82, never to be taught again (Arnoldt 1909; Kuehn 1983).[2] No one seems to have asked why Kant decided to offer this new course, why he would have done so in 1767, how the course might relate to the monumental changes going on in his thought at the time, or why it would have been interrupted from 1772–1775, years crucial from the vantage of both the Critical turn and another new course, in anthropology, which began in 1772 but went through a significant mutation shortly thereafter, reflected in surviving student notes from 1775, Anthropology Friedländer (V-Anth/Fried). Emil Arnoldt, who knew more about Kant's university teaching than anyone, bluntly claimed he knew *nothing* about the content or motivation of this course (Arnoldt

---

[1] All translations not taken from The Cambridge Edition of the Works of Immanuel Kant are my own.
[2] We have two modern editions of the course notes, both edited by Gerhard Lehmann: Immanuel Kant, *Vorlesungen über Enzyklopädische Philosophie* (Berlin: Akademie, 1961) and Immanuel Kant, *Vorlesungen über Philosophische Enzyklopädie* (PhilEnz 29.1,1) in the *Akademie-Ausgabe* (AA). Not only are the surviving lecture notes obviously incomplete, breaking off as the course turns to the question of empirical psychology, but they are also bound together with a complete set of notes from Kant's anthropology course and a substantial segment of physics lecture notes. This may betoken that the collector of these materials (all of the same ink and paper) collated together notes from three separate courses to generate what the collector took to be a complete representation of Kant's teachings. Along these lines, one might conjecture the anthropology notes would present a far more thorough articulation of empirical psychology in the wider context of a general "science of man," superseding whatever Kant might have presented based on the Feder text in the Encyclopedia course. Just for this reason, a more complete version from the earlier years of the course might have contributed substantially to our historical reconstruction of the genesis of Kant's anthropology course itself.

1909: 5). He was able to report only the external details of when Kant offered the course and what text he used as his basis (Arnoldt 1909: 214 ff.).

The one point he insisted upon was that the designated textbook appeared useless in establishing any insight into Kant's intentions. The text for the course was from a soon-to-be star in German academic philosophy, Johann G. H. Feder (1740–1821). That text had only just appeared in 1767. Feder composed it while he was still *Hofmeister* and it would be more than a year before he received the *venia legendi* at Göttingen. He was, in a word, a young and relatively unknown figure in the German academic world. What was Kant doing adopting Feder's brand-new textbook for his course? What was this textbook designed to provide to the academic market, in the first place? What sort of course did it imply? Why would Kant, still a *Magister* who needed to attract students to provide for his slender economic wherewithal, undertake such a course? These are questions that no one has seen fit to ask. At least Lehmann offered some conjectures on why it stopped in 1782 (Lehmann 1961: 73n). The acrimony over the Garve-Feder review of Kant's *Critique of Pure Reason* (1781), reflected in Kant's appendix to the *Prolegomena* (1783), Lehmann suggests, may well have motivated Kant to abandon the course.

Lehmann finds fault with Arnoldt's dismissal of the Feder textbook as an indicator of what Kant may have taught (AA 29.1,1: 662). He thinks there *is* something we can learn from it. I agree; indeed, I wish to fault Lehmann himself for a dismissiveness on this score little short of Arnoldt's own. Lehmann writes, for example, "That for Kant what mattered was not so much the coherent text but rather its headings [*Stichworte*] goes without saying" (AA 29.1,1: 663). Or: "[Feder's text was] so wooden and poorly thought-through that it could at the very most have been useful for Kant only in making associations" (AA 29.1,1: 666). Lehmann concedes notwithstanding that from the existing lecture notes it does appear that "for all the differences in level between Kant and the young Feder, Kant nonetheless followed his 'author'" (AA 29.1,1: 666). All the more reason to wonder why Kant should have felt this new course necessary, or Feder's compendium appropriate for it.

If hostility to Feder motivated Kant to abandon the course, might sympathy for Feder's position have motivated its inception? I suggest Feder is indeed the key to the course's origin. What *was* Feder's position in 1767/68? "I sought to develop *applicable* philosophy from the most natural forms of representation, those not sensibly to be doubted, to anchor what the true and the good entailed by whatever rational grounds I could find" (Feder 1825: 81n). Born in 1740, Feder had completed his dissertation in 1765 at Erlangen under Suckow. The dissertation was a defense of man as a social animal, against Rousseau's paradoxical primitivism. Indeed, hostility to Rousseau was one of the prime movers of Feder's early work. In 1768, anonymously, he published *Der neue Emil*, offering a far more conventional idea of education over against Rousseau's radical original. The first volume went through a second edition and was soon joined by a second volume in 1774. Reinhard Brandt writes: "Rousseau led Kant to the critique, but Feder to the defense of contemporary society" (1989: 250 f.). In any event, Feder's textbook entitled *Grundriß der philosophischen Wissenschaft nebst der nöthigen Geschichte zum Gebrauch seiner Zuhörer* (1767) sufficed to win him a *venia legendi* to Göttingen one year later.

What was the nature of Feder's textbook? Actually, that question turns out to be a bit more complex because Feder published *two* textbooks. For his original course, Kant could only have used Feder's *Grundriß* (1767). In 1769, that was joined in print by a second and far more successful compendium from Feder's pen. As newly installed *Ordinarius* at Göttingen, Feder published his *Logik und Metaphysik, nebst der Philosophischen Geschichte im Grundrisse* (1769), which achieved wide acclaim throughout Germany. His fame rested considerably on this work. Lehmann suggests that Kant in all likelihood switched from the first to the second compendium in 1769, since "there are between the two compendia many factual concordances" (Lehmann 1961: 73n).

When Feder released his original compendium, he resisted his publisher's pressure to use the word *encyclopedia* in the title, choosing instead the less explicit term *sketch* (*Grundriß*). Yet he clearly followed the same agenda as his mighty French predecessors, Diderot and D'Alembert – i.e., to create a vehicle for enlightenment, to serve "philosophy for the world" – in short, to propagate "[P]opular philosophy" (Diderot 1956; D'Alembert 1995; Holzhey 1977; Zimmerli 1978; Zande 1992, 1998). The first two parts of his original textbook – "Introduction to the History of Philosophy" and "Outline of the Most Important Parts of Philosophy" – accordingly suffered Lehmann's contemptuous summation: they "contained too many commonplaces and polemics along the lines of the 'enlightenment' of the time" (AA 29.1,1: 663).

I would like to hold out the prospect that Kant had a far more positive view of Feder's effort, especially in 1767. Kant, after all, had received a very enthusiastic review of his *Dreams of a Spirit-Seer* from Feder. It appeared on 23 September 1766 in the *Erlangen Gelehrten Zeitung*. Feder took a highly congenial stance toward Kant at this time and the two actually became correspondents, though little of their correspondence has survived. In his autobiography, Feder noted:

> For Kant I had the highest respect from the time that I read *Dreams of a Spirit-Seer*, while I was still in Coburg. Even though I did not yet know who the author was, in the *Erlangen Gelehrten Zeitung* I praised in the strongest terms this comic-skeptical piece of writing, which all the same revealed the most profound insights, for it coincided very well with the dispositions of my own mind at the time. (Feder 1825: 117)

In the review, Feder's praise clearly pointed to their common agenda: "But in philosophy in general and in particular in psychology to be able to keep oneself from useless questions, from prejudices, from fraudulent propositions and overhasty contradictions – that is the greatest advantage that one can derive from [this book]. To conduct philosophy with an academic tone: *that* the author is unwilling to do" (Feder 1976).

I contend Kant adopted Feder's text and designed his new course in 1767 as a part of his own commitment to Popular philosophy. Manfred Kuehn makes the key observation concerning Kant's *Enzyklopädievorlesungen*: "in comparison with the very negative strictures of the first *Critique* and the *Prolegomena* Kant is almost a common sense philosopher" (Kuehn 1983: 306n). Kuehn argues elsewhere that this commitment to common sense was characteristic of Kant's pre-Critical posture: "during the early states of his development, he thought just as highly of common sense as did his contemporaries. In fact, it appears that, at least for a time, he considered critique to be the business of common sense" (Kuehn 1987: 194). The lectures on Philosophical Encyclopedia – even in their fragmentary 1775 form – offer us insight into the transition from the Kant of the 1760s, the Kant of Popular philosophy, to the Kant of the Critical philosophy (Zammito 2002). My contention is that the Encyclopedia course was an expression of Kant's transient interest in Popular philosophy and a casualty of his Critical turn. Had we course notes from the earlier phase of the course, 1767–1772, this might well be more obvious.

1 "Philosophy for the Schools" and "Philosophy for the World"

Perhaps the most pervasive feature of the middle of the eighteenth century in Germany was the rise of a "public sphere" (Melton 2001; Zammito 2012b). This was the special concern of some new social congeries, the *gebildenten Stände*, in the terms of Hans Erich Bödeker (1992). Frank Kopitzsch notes that while "academic schools and universities were of substantial importance for the propagation of enlightenment ideas," over the course of the eighteenth century "the enlightenment expanded in all ways – in thematic terms as well as in recruitment – turning from a matter of 'scholars' [*Gelehrten*] to a concern of the 'educated' [*Gebildeten*]" (1983: 3 f.). The ideal of sociability (*Umgang; Geselligkeit*) was of immeasurable importance for the emergent *gebildeten Stände* (Mauser 1989). Character-formation (*Bildung*), in that distinctively pragmatic-moral sense central to the pedagogical undertakings of Kant, involved the effectiveness (*Geschicklichkeit*) and the cleverness (*Klugheit*) to cope and indeed prosper in this world, but also the (moral) wisdom (*Weisheit*) to do so with integrity (Kant to

Herz, end of 1773, Br 10: 145 f.) The cultivation of these capabilities stressed observation (*Beobachtung*), a keen notation of particular instances, hence a process of learning that built upon empirical and historical accrual (Moravia 1973). The cardinal value of *Selbstdenken* was a matter of the cultivation of individual judgment (*Urteilskraft*), personal knowledge, drawing upon all of one's own life experience (Hinske 1986a, 1990).

For a social group that needed to define itself and its progressive aspirations around education, the university and its creation and propagation of "human capital" could not be a matter of indifference. The struggle for self-definition and eventual public recognition of the emergent *gebildeten Stände* found expression in a sharply negative attitude toward university scholarship and the model of enculturation it offered. By the middle of the eighteenth century there emerged a contest between the new *gebildeten Stände* and the established *Gelehrtenstand*. R. Steven Turner elaborates: "In the name of Aufklärung critics denounced the universities for their outmoded, medieval constitutions and their pedantic curriculum still mired in Wolffian philosophy, theological dogmatism, and the Latin *imitatis*" (1974: 501). Conceptualization of the tension between academic esotericism, no matter how "rigorous," and practical efficacy and career success can be traced back to a vivid controversy at the main Prussian University of Halle at the turn to the eighteenth century, between the *Klugheitslehre* of Christian Thomasius and the *Gründlichkeit* propounded by Christian Wolff. These two thinkers posed for their age the vital question: what should philosophy be for? It is this which gave sharpness to the challenge of *Popularphilosophie* to Wolffian *Schulphilosophie* at the middle of the eighteenth century (Holzhey 1977; Zimmerli 1978, 1981). Gunter Grimm observes: "Wolff's new concept of science caused a shift in the traditional canon of instruction ... the elimination of the humanistic disciplines ... The system of the liberal arts had no claim with him." As a result, the traditional humanities suffered at Halle (Grimm 1987: 30, 33). Systematicity, rigorous closure, was a hallmark of rationality for Wolff, requiring demonstrative proofs of all propositions. Grounding – *begründen* – was what distinguished philosophy, drawing it close to the lucidity of mathematics (Hinske 1983). To enter the higher realm of truth, Wolff and his school maintained, one had to get beyond mere empirical knowledge (*cognitio historica*) to the autonomous realm of the a priori, i. e., to *cognitio philosophica* (Seifert 1976; Albrecht 1982).

Popular philosophy proposed to turn the tables on Wolffianism. In the words of Werner Schneiders, "school philosophy became conscious of its open flank to the world" (1983: 13). It needed to transform itself into the vanguard articulation of a new public's aspirations to practical success and happiness in the world. A core consideration was the conflict in the purposes of higher education as between individual self-fashioning (*Bildung*) and professional training (*Brodwissenschaft*).

These issues were altogether alive for Kant from the outset of his teaching career in Königsberg. In 1778 the Prussian minister of culture, von Zedlitz, sent Kant a semiofficial request to use his influence "to hold back students at the university from the bread courses [*Brodt-Collegiis*] and to help them understand that the little bit of legal – indeed even theological and medical – learning [they pursued] would be vastly easier and more certain in application if the student had more philosophical knowledge" (Zedlitz to Kant, Br 10: 236; see Stark 1995; Bien 1974; Hardtwig 1985). This had its concomitant in Kant's later argument for the preeminence of the philosophy faculty in the conflict of the faculties within the German universities.

This is the larger context in which Kant designed the new course in 1767 for which he used the term *Encyclopedia*. Kant designed his curriculum to be both pragmatic and academic:

> not just created to achieve a reputation among one's fellow guild members of the academy but rather ... stretching knowledge [*Wissen*, not *Kenntnis*] beyond the school, in the endeavor to propagate one's insights [*Kenntnisse*] for general use: that is what study for the world is. A science is academically proper which is appropriate to the school and to the professional requirements; this is not a perfection to be despised, for all sciences must first become academically proper; thereafter they can also become popular, and available to amateurs for their appropriation and use. (V-Anth/Mensch 25.2: 853)

The academic needed to become a "man of the world" – the opposite of a pedant – by learning how to make his knowledge applicable in a popular context, so that the unschooled could appreciate and understand what he had to offer (Grimm 1987). The word Kant used for this pedagogy was *Weltkenntnis*.

The contrast between "philosophy, according to the academic concept," and "philosophy, according to the world concept," developed by Kant early in his logic lectures and replicated virtually verbatim in the first *Critique*, stood at the core of Kant's sense of his pedagogical mission (Log 9: 21–4; KrV A838 f./B866 f.) Kant was already quite clear about *Weltkenntnis* from the outset of his teaching career, as revealed by the 1757 announcement of his course in physical geography, *Entwurf und Ankündigung eines Collegii der physischen Geographie* (EACG). He generalized his pedagogical point: "An education is still seriously lacking if it does not teach a person how to apply his acquired knowledge and bring about a useful employment of these [acquisitions] in accordance with his understanding and the situation in which he stands, or [in other words] to make our knowledge *practical*. And that is what knowledge of the world is" (PG 9: 157 f.) *Weltkenntnis* had to be systematic. It should begin with the universal: "General knowledge always precedes *local* knowledge if the latter is to be ordered and directed through philosophy: in the absence of which all acquired knowledge can yield nothing more than fragmentary groping around and no science" (Anth 7: 121). Kant argued that only from the vantage of the whole could particular observations have any weight. To be sure, such systematic organization served the *usefulness* of the knowledge "for the world." Yet he remained adamant that there was need for *systematic study*. The task was first to learn the field, and this had as its criterial standards Kant's clearly *academic* notions of rigor (*Gründlichkeit*) and system.

At the same time, Kant's general pedagogical view, presented in *Announcement of the Organization of His Lectures in the Winter Semester 1765/66*, maintained that education should try to avoid burdening students with ideas that "outstrip their years" and "can only be understood by minds which are more practiced and experienced" (NEV 2: 305). Both in his logic and in his metaphysics courses, he clearly privileged accessibility for students. His plan for the core logic course distinguished between common sense (*gesunden Verstand*) and real learning (*eigentlichen Gelehrsamkeit*) (NEV 2: 311). While the latter might serve as the goal in a capstone class at the close of a course of philosophical studies, the former was a more sensible place for students to start. Along similar lines, Kant indicated that he would teach empirical psychology at the outset of his metaphysics class. He offered two sorts of pedagogical reasons: first, on the optimistic basis that students would stay the course, they would be able to use the concrete examples of the early phase to grasp the abstract formulations of the later stages; but, second, on the pessimistic basis that students might well drop out, Kant averred, even for them this bit of empirical psychology would be a good thing. What he construed as his "canon for common sense" would provide a starting point for all learning, one especially serviceable for his students' subsequent "life of action and society" (NEV 2: 311).

Kant also suggested that he planned to adjust his physical geography course "by condensing that part of the subject which is concerned with the physical features of the earth, to gain the time necessary ... to include the other parts of the subject, which are of even greater general utility ... a *physical, moral* and *political* geography" (NEV 2: 312). This "other part of knowledge of the world encompasses knowledge of man." It would "consider *man*, throughout the world[,] from the point of view of the variety of his natural properties." Kant elaborated: "Unless these matters are considered, general judgments about man would scarcely be possible. The comparison of human beings with each other, and the comparison of man today with the moral state of man in earlier times, furnishes us with a comprehensive map of the human species" (NEV 2: 312 f.).

The title of the new course of 1767 needs our attention: "Encyclopedia of Philosophy as a Whole with an abridged History of Philosophy based on Feder's Sketch" (Arnoldt 1909). The idea of a philosophical encyclopedia in 1767 would of necessity have evoked associations with the great French endeavor of Diderot and D'Alembert, launched more than a decade before, only recently renewed, and widely esteemed as the most important project of the French (if not the entire European) Enlightenment. In that light, it is well to recall the ambition of the original *Encyclopédie*: not only to make all knowledge *accessible* to the widest public but to act to *transform the world* in a progressive direction (Diderot 1956; D'Alembert 1995). That is, the *Encyclopédie* was the fulfillment of Diderot's call, "*Hâtons-nous a rendre la philosophie populaire!*" (Diderot 1999; Mortier 1974).

2 Philosophy and the humanities (*schöne Wissenschaften*): the Göttingen program

In the very years Kant offered the Encyclopedia course, Feder and his close ally at the key University of Göttingen, Christoph Meiners (1747–1810), launched the most aggressive program for *Popularphilosophie* in the German *Hochaufklärung* (Zimmerli 1983). These philosophers propagated a critical-empirical eclecticism "not without an enlightenment pathos for thinking for oneself," colored by a (moderate) skepticism of British provenance and an enthusiasm for physiological psychology drawn heavily from Charles Bonnet (Zimmerli 1983: 59). From the calls to Feder in 1768 and to Meiners in 1770, this "Göttingen program" dominated German philosophical discourse up until its infamous and catastrophic tangle with Kant's Critical philosophy and his denunciation in the *Prolegomena* of 1783 (Schulz 1960; Petrus 1994). The program had a "prelude" in the more than fifty-year tenure of Samuel Hollmann (1696–1787), the first professor of philosophy at Göttingen and a strong anti-Wolffian (Cramer 1988). Hollmann and his good friend Albrecht von Haller (1708–1777) dominated the university culture of Göttingen from its founding in 1734 until well past mid-century, and they promoted a tone distinctly hostile to school philosophy. By the time Feder arrived in 1768, though, Haller had been gone for more than a decade and Hollmann was, in Feder's words, "perhaps a bit too learned for the younger people, perhaps too old and too dry for the aesthetic tone that had come to dominance by that time" (Feder 1825: 71).

Feder quickly took over. But, as Zimmerli has it, "When he came to Göttingen in 1768 Feder had no powerfully developed systematic or methodological standpoint." The *Grundriß* was "an opportunistic and an embarrassing book [*ein Ge- und Verlegenheitsbuch*]" (Zimmerli 1983: 61, 64). Feder himself admitted he was "not yet ready for Göttingen. Without a fixed system, I waffled between Wolffian dogmatism and a skepticism produced by natural inclinations and readings[;] deeper insights had not yet been distilled, and proper bounds had not yet been established. These traits must have been discernible to any expert" (Feder 1825: 71). His inaugural lecture was entitled *De sensu interno* and it appealed to Locke and the Scottish Enlightenment for a new approach to philosophy (Brandt 1989: 252). Immediately he plunged into the production of a textbook more in keeping with the avant-garde status he had suddenly attained.

In the Preface to this second textbook, *Logik und Metaphysik* (1769b), Feder proclaimed the book he had published only two years before, and which had earned him the call to Göttingen, "unusable," assuring his readers that he had applied himself "to prepare a more appropriate [textbook] for my current lectures" (Feder 1769b: unpaginated Preface). A striking feature of the opening section, "Preliminary Report on Philosophy and the Philosophical Sciences in General," is that it sets out with an epigraph from Johann Gottfried Herder's *Fragments on Recent German Literature: Third Collection*. The text, cited without acknowledgment, gave expression to a sense for philosophy to which Feder felt an obvious kinship: "That philosophy [*Weltweisheit*] is the goddess of my heart which to begin presents sensible understanding, deigns to speak its language, goes along with it and then finally appears to it in the sphere of reason with all the brilliance of distinctness, then disappears" (Feder 1769b: 2). Just this manner, Feder argued, seemed to him the best way to present philosophy to his students (1769b: 6).

At the outset of *Logik und Metaphysik* Feder proclaimed, "it is my intention to advance knowledge that is of general utility" (1769b: unpaginated Preface). In his earlier book, he explained he wished to provide "the beginners in philosophy a foretaste, so that they would be placed in a position to learn a little bit of [that science] with a greater reward, even if they only had a preliminary notion of it, or if for some circumstances did not permit hearing lectures about all the parts of philosophical knowledge, still they would not be totally ignorant of any part of it" (1767: unpaginated Preface). Feder carried virtually unchanged from his earlier book into the new one a defense of the *schönen Wissenschaften* as the "daily physicians" of philosophical taste (1769b: 12f.; Strube 1990). In his 1767 textbook, Feder had written, "Nothing is more unjust than when one urges that philosophy have nothing to do with the *schönen Wissenschaften* and nothing is more foolish than when one imagines that philosophy can do without them" (1767: 50). In the new text Feder wrote: "Who could doubt that the *schönen Wissenschaften* must be the tenderest friends, the most constant playmates of philosophy?" (1769b: 13). One of the central features of Popular philosophy, as I have tried to reconstruct it historically, is its insistence on the importance of the humanistic disciplines for the pursuit of philosophy, not only in terms of the *tone* of its presentation but in terms of the educative and humanizing burden of its content (Zammito 2002). The popular "philosophers for the world" raised empirical psychology or anthropology "into the central science of the time and into the more or less radical science of enlightenment" (Schings 1977: 13). Wolfgang Riedel minces no words: "One does not overstate to say that the German late Enlightenment stood out as an epoch of empirical psychology" (1992: 26). Accordingly, anthropology became "the royal science of the second half of the century" (Pfotenauer 1987: 4). With regard to this empirical psychology, no boundary could be set between science and literature. This was particularly vivid in the sibling nature of the domains of anthropology and aesthetics (Käuser 1990: 197). Wolfgang Riedel writes of a "triangle" formed by psychology, moral philosophy, and literature (1992: 24). As Helmut Pfotenauer has argued, literature was utterly embroiled, both as instigator and as executor, in the ascendancy of anthropology as "the new, popular science of the eighteenth century" (1987: 1). The psychological novel became a vehicle, indeed a school, for moral judgment in the eighteenth century. In 1770 an astute observer of the times, Christian Garve (1742–1798), came to the conclusion that "the turn to psychology, that optic for analyzing the soul, was the real point of differentiation between ancient and modern literature" (cited in Riedel 1992: 32). Christian Heinrich Blanckenburg (1744–1796) recognized literary authors, especially novelists, as *authorities* on psychology, working in parallel and in competition with physiological psychologists (Riedel 1992: 33–35). All of them aimed at a grasp of the "whole man" (Schings 1994).

The most important endeavor of Feder's new textbook, which became a bestseller in Germany and made him one of the most prominent philosophers of the decade, was to advance a starkly psychological reinterpretation of logic, deriving it from common sense. The origins of this notion lay unequivocally in John Locke. In *Logik und Metaphysik,* Feder made that clear in the crucial section on the "History of Logic." John Locke's *Essay Concerning Human Understanding*, he wrote, "without doubt marked the most important epoch in the history of logic since that of Aristotle" (Feder 1769b: 90). In addition to Locke, the origin of this notion lay in the Scottish Enlightenment, and especially in the "common sense" school (Kuehn 1987: 81). But Feder was not nearly so rigorous as Reid or Beattie in his theory of knowledge. He opted for what Zimmerli calls a "quasi-empiricist basis" which he could never clarify (Zimmerli 1983). The resulting criterion of truth was utterly subjective: "what for all men cannot be thought otherwise, that, therefore, is true" (Feder 1769b: 158). According to the Blomberg Logic student notes (1771), Kant blasted a very similar subjective formulation, which he associated with Crusius, but which he may well have known Feder shared.

Klaus Petrus argues that the idea of a "psychologistic grounding of *logic* in the sense of tracing logical thought back to healthy common sense" was the core idea of the Göttingen program. Feder inaugurated it, albeit imprecisely, and it was "carried to completion in a radical manner by Meiners with his distinction of exoteric from esoteric logic" (Petrus 1994: 290). Zimmerli agrees, noting that not only

Meiners but Feder's student Michael Hißmann (1752–1784), before his untimely death, carried out this program with great rigor (Zimmerli 1983). The upshot was to find metaphysics completely pointless, a conclusion Hißmann drew explicitly in *Briefe über Gegenstände der Philosophie* (1778b). Hißmann produced a survey of literature in philosophy in 1778, *Anleitung zur Kenntnis der auserlesenen Literatur in allen Theilen der Philosophie*, which the review in the *Allgemeine Deutsche Bibliothek* recognized as one of the most discerning assessments of the trends in thought in the decade, having made it clear that metaphysics was obsolete and "as an independent discipline should be allowed to disappear entirely" (Anonymous 1779: 245). In its place, Hißmann presented a rich characterization of the emergent fields of anthropology and history of philosophy. The reviewer agreed completely: "That history is the main repertory of philosophy is correctly observed" (Anonymous 1779: 248).

The most persuasive formulation of the Göttingen program, entitled *Revision der Philosophie*, appeared anonymously in 1772. The author, an open secret, was Christoph Meiners. It was greeted with an enthusiastic review (also anonymous) in the *Göttingische Anzeigen von Gelehrten Sachen*. The reviewer was not really secret either: it was Feder (1772). Meiners, like Feder before him, took a Protagorean view of philosophy: "I believe that knowledge of man in this sense not only encompasses all the objects worthy of investigation by a philosopher, but also that it determines the boundaries [of philosophy] and its kinship with other sciences, and finally that it determines the differing order of importance for the presentation of its parts" (Meiners 1772: 52).

Meiners was an outright Lockean. The core of his book was the argument that logic be reduced to psychology. "Psychology and logic are related to one another," his famous simile went, "like an Aesopian fable to the attached moral" (Meiners 1772: 53). Thus he proposed to discriminate two ideas of logic, the esoteric and the exoteric. While the former was a matter for abstruse thought, it was also not immediately accessible and not for the uninitiated. Meiners argued that novices needed to go through the preparation of "exoteric logic." That entailed first, familiarization with a complete ("encyclopedic") scheme of the disciplines; second, a study of general theoretical-scientific prejudices; third, an investigation of what was fashionable in the current culture; and fourth, practical guidelines for (a) how to be a scholar, (b) what to read, and (c) the "art of observation" (Meiners 1772: 23). Meiners laid out his schema for this exoteric logic in great detail. As to esoteric logic, Meiners thanked Locke and Sextus Empiricus for keeping him from getting lost in all the nonsense of false precision (1772: 161). At the conclusion of his inquiry, Meiners averred, "I perceived that it was not possible to divide psychology from logic, and still less to allow the first to derive from the second" (1772: 164).

Meiners developed his argument that "psychology and logic are one and the same science" in *Kurzer Abriß der Psychologie zum Gebrauche seiner Vorlesungen* (1773: Preface). He opined in that work that "in psychology and the sciences that derive from it is contained the entire theory of man and of philosophy" (Meiners 1773: 8). As his main sources for an adequate psychology, Meiners pointed to Condillac and Bonnet. But he appreciated most David Hume's radical dichotomization of philosophy into two camps – philosophy of ordinary life and esoteric metaphysics – the better to debunk the latter. In Germany it was hard to grasp Hume because "in Germany hardly anyone knows the first kind, because we still have too few writers who have made true philosophy available in the language of the beautiful world" (Meiners 1772: 202). To accomplish this, Meiners contended, philosophy needed support from the *schönen Wissenschaften*.

> History of mankind has filled the gap which lay between the general doctrines of philosophy and the particular facts of history. Before the long separated sisters were reunited, philosophy had lost herself in useless and indeterminate general propositions which had no fixity, no ground on which they were built; the historical inquirer on the other hand was bereft of principles and illuminating ideas through which the formless givens of history could be properly taken up. (Meiners 1772: 139)

It would be wonderful, Meiners professed, "if aesthetics and the history of the human mind and heart would be regarded as sciences which an ordinary professor of philosophy could not do without" (1772: 144). Unfortunately, metaphysics, "as soon as she elevates herself to queen of the sciences, contemplates beautiful literature, history and classical scholarship as unworthy slaves" (Meiners 1772: 214). He concluded that the "great advantage of … transforming all of philosophy into mere philosophical stories would be without question the healthiest imposition which one could make upon one's audience to think for themselves" (Meiners 1772: 82). The challenge of *cognitio historica*, of *a posteriori* knowledge, to philosophy could not be stated more explicitly. More than anything Feder composed, I suspect, *Revision der Philosophie* must have presented itself as a fundamental challenge to Kant's conception of philosophy, especially after his Critical turn.

3 Kant's lectures on Philosophical Encyclopedia

Kant introduced the course by explaining what he meant by *encyclopedia*. It was a "short excerpt from a whole science" aimed to "provide an overview of the whole" (PhilEnz 29.1,1: 6). The implication is that in this endeavor, a *historical* approach might be taken even to *philosophy*. Indeed, Kant spent much more time on the history of the various branches of philosophy in this set of course lectures than in his other courses. That suggests that the historical approach to philosophy seemed to Kant more viable at this moment than typically. In general, this is problematic for Kant, and for two major reasons.

First, Kant made a crucial category distinction between historical knowledge (*cognitio historica*) and philosophical knowledge (*cognitio philosophica*) (KrV A835–7/B863–6). He was entirely Wolffian in this regard (Albrecht 1982). The important question for us is what exactly Kant thought in the Encyclopedia lectures context. Especially in his "pre-Critical" period, Kant distinguished between the "dogmatic" and the "critical" schools, identifying Locke as the paradigm critical philosopher, and Wolff as his dogmatic counterpart. Whether he felt closer to Locke or to Wolff when he elaborated this distinction is not entirely clear. Though Kant took pride in Wolff's German nationality, he was also clear that Wolff and the German dogmatic approach had become beleaguered: "now, finally, the critical philosophy thrives most, and in this the English have the greatest merit." Indeed, "for the most part the dogmatic method has fallen into disuse in all sciences; even morals is not expounded dogmatically any more, but more often critically" (V-Lo/Blom 24: 37). At just this moment, then, Kant's attunement to this English style of "criticism" and to this more popular form of philosophical expression *and mission* (associated with Hume and Rousseau but also Lawrence Sterne and Alexander Pope) was at its height.

Second, *the* fundamental pedagogical idea in Kant was that philosophy is not a body of knowledge to be learned but rather a form of thinking to be cultivated (KrV A836–9/B864–6). Thus it comes as no surprise that in his lectures Kant should admonish: "One must think for oneself," but then he added: "and indeed a priori" (PhilEnz 29.1,1: 7). This elaboration should draw our attention. The insistence on a priori thinking is a departure from the many similar passages where Kant stressed thinking for oneself, and this alerts us to the possibility that *in 1775* Kant was particularly concerned to uphold this aspect of philosophy. Certainly, Feder's textbook made no similar claim. In any event, Kant spelled out the mission of philosophy for his students: "Philosophy has as its domain all human knowledge of matters of whatever origin [*von Sachen, die sich befinden mögen wo sie wollen*]. It is at the same time the highest tribunal of reason" (PhilEnz 29.1,1: 7). Thus Kant maintained for philosophy both a universality of breadth and an authority of judgment that made it, in effect, the "Queen of all the sciences" (KrV Aiii). The difference between these two sorts of claims for philosophy is that the first claim was a stipulation of authority; the second was a characterization of methodology. More precisely, "philosophy is really about the rules for the proper use of understanding and reason" (PhilEnz 29.1,1: 7).

What is crucial is the next discrimination, in which Kant distinguished the "artist of reason," a merely *speculative* philosopher, from the "leader [or lawgiver] of reason," who "leads mankind to their destiny [*Bestimmung*]. His cognitions have to do accordingly with the vocation of man [*Bestimmung des Menschen*]" (PhilEnz 29.1,1: 8). Kant was clearly inserting his argument into the ongoing discourse under this rubric, which dominated the *Hochaufklärung* (Spalding 1908; D'Alessandrio 1999). But the point here is that he was accepting one of the crucial claims of Popular philosophy in so doing: "Science is really not our vocation" (PhilEnz 29.1,1: 8; Zammito 2012a). There was a difference between science and wisdom, he asserted, and "the use of reason in consideration of purposes is its most noble application" (PhilEnz 29.1,1: 8). Only when the philosopher brought all his science to the service of the vocation of man could he be a teacher of wisdom. Thus Kant criticized Christian Wolff by name as *merely* speculative, "a great artist serving the curiosity of mankind" (PhilEnz 29.1,1: 8). This, it must be noted, is a long way from Kant's praise for Wolff in the first *Critique*, as the great bastion of rigor in German philosophy (KrV Bxxxvi). Kant here stood very much on the side of Popular philosophy against the school philosophy personified in Wolff. "One must seek to be wise and not simply to accumulate speculative knowledge, for [such] knowledge leaves a vast emptiness [*Wißen läßt eine große Leere*]" (PhilEnz 29.1,1: 13). And that is Kant as late as 1775; we are free to conjecture how much more emphatic his judgment might have been earlier. Kant maintained that certain ancient philosophers – and among the moderns, Rousseau – came closest to the ideal of a philosopher who was a teacher of wisdom, a leader of mankind in its grand vocation. Socrates, Kant pointed out, was often acclaimed as the one who brought philosophy down from heaven to earth by distinguishing between speculation and wisdom (PhilEnz 29.1,1: 9). To invoke Socrates in this manner was a key trope of the eighteenth-century effort to foster "philosophy for the world," most famously articulated by Joseph Addison (Addison 1961). Thus, of a philosopher in his own time Kant made two demands: first that he oppose superstition, for this was the arch-enemy of enlightenment; and second that he think for himself: "philosophy and taste require genius and not imitation" (PhilEnz 29.1,1: 10). Norbert Hinske has noted that Kant was very fond, in his early years, up through 1772, of identifying philosophy with (artistic) genius and creativity – indeed, the phrase "artist of reason" is a prime example. But that language, which resonated in his logic lectures into the early 1770s, for example, came to be purged utterly from Kant's characterizations of philosophy as a rigorous science in the phase of *Kritizismus* (Hinske 1986a). Associating philosophy with genius was, one can surmise, a part of his transient identification with Popular philosophy. He would be quite ironic about this notion of genius, for example, in his third *Critique* (KU 5: 309 f.; Zammito 1992: 136–42).

Kant expounded philosophy as a speculative science from three vantages in his Encyclopedia lectures: the faculties of man, principles, and the objects of knowledge (PhilEnz 29.1,1: 10). Philosophy, he proposed, considered either objects of pure reason or objects of the senses. "The science which has as its topic an object of pure reason is called transcendental philosophy." More specifically, psychology, the "science of thinking nature," could be either rational or empirical. Rational psychology "considers the soul not at all via experience, but rather through principles of pure reason, for example, whether it is a spirit, material, simple, etc. etc. If one considers the soul empirically, the science is called anthropology" (PhilEnz 29.1,1: 11).

Kant then took up the question of self-cultivation [*Bildung*], starting with what one should read. He distinguished books that provided cultivation along with entertainment from those that were merely entertaining. Novels he was inclined to consign to the latter category, especially if they "make the heart soft" or "awaken passions." But he admitted that "those that are written with wit [*Laune*] are good, and travelogues are the best for entertainment and cultivation." Especially "whatever is written with genius is worth thinking through." Thus, "only novels where one finds sentiments, and comedies in the manner of Shakespeare, where the author has discovered a hidden aspect of man, represents character traits, etc., are useful" (PhilEnz 29.1,1: 29). Here Kant stood in the thick of Popular philosophizing, but a few pages later we find him embroiled in his great transcendental argument about the necessity of binding understanding and sensibility together for a valid cognition. Kant used the phrase "*Titel des Denkens*" – title to a thought, as in legal title – to characterize what he thought transcendental philosophy should explain: "The research into the origin of the action of reason is the [proper] pursuit of metaphysics" (PhilEnz 29.1,1: 35). What needed further investigation was "whether perhaps we are caught up in a confusion in which we take subjective conditions of thought for objective ones" (PhilEnz 29.1,1: 36). Here we stand at the very threshold of the first *Critique*.

The text as we have it breaks off just as Kant began to introduce the theme of empirical psychology. How he did so is very interesting, for it gives us insight into precisely how Kant viewed the project of anthropology in 1775:

> Empirical psychology or anthropology is of such great utility that one can certainly believe that education would remain faulty so long as this science is not treated *ex professo*, it will never come to perfection until it is taught in academies after the manner of the guild [*sie wird nicht eher zu ihrer Vollkommenheit kommen, woferne sie nicht gleichsam zunftmäßig auf Academien gelehret wird*]. (PhilEnz 29.1,1: 44)

I submit that this is a remarkable assertion. It is remarkable first for its guild affirmation. Second, it is remarkable in that Kant clearly conceived anthropology as an independent, empirical science that required systematic formulation.

4 Kant's abandonment of Philosophical Encyclopedia

What Kant feared above all was the intrusion of aesthetic criteria into the domain of rigorous inquiry, the collapse of *cognitio philosophica* not merely into *cognitio historica* but into "beautiful science," a mannerism without warrant or worth (Zammito 1998). This is clearly discernible in the admonitions in his letter to Johann Gottfried Herder of 1768 (Kant to Herder, 9 May 1768, Br 10: 73 f.). The intrusion of such a "beautiful science" (KU 5: 304 f.) – literally *schöne Wissenschaft* – into philosophy was highly deleterious, Kant maintained. "Much, e. g., that now is actually accounted as lastingly beautiful in our writing style is nonetheless nothing but the fashion of our time. Very many learned men and beautiful souls [*schöndenkender Geister*] are actually often more harmful than useful to the learned world. A *Young*, a *Klopstock*, a *Gleim*, etc., have, e. g., really spoiled a multitude of weak minds" (V-Lo/Blomberg 24: 192). These are the pioneer authors associated with what in Germany came to be called *Sturm und Drang*. Kant's distaste for Herder's dominant role in *Sturm und Drang* would become blatant in his *Reflexionen* of the mid-1770s (Zammito 1992: 37–44).

With the publication of the logic lectures, among other sources, we can trace the rise of Kant's anxiety and even attach to it a systematic significance. Especially in the Blomberg transcription of Kant's logic lectures we can see Kant wrestling with the question of whether aesthetic perfection and discursive perfection could be brought into synthesis. He still acknowledged that ideal, but he began to shift it beyond human capacity. Of course, Hume and Rousseau stood out as exemplars of just such an approach, but Kant was now turning to the view that their literary brilliance was detrimental to their philosophical reception, if not even to their philosophical insight. "What prevails in our current age," Kant lectured at the outset of the 1770s, "is not an addiction to demonstrating but instead a certain shallowness, a kind of gallantry even in learned cognitions" (V-Lo/Blomberg 24: 335). He elaborated elsewhere:

> It is absurd to mix feelings [*Empfindungen*] with appearances [*Erscheinungen*] in philosophy. Meier and Feder have this flaw. If the author [Meier] says such judgments are very practical what he should be saying is that they are very moving and exciting [*rührend und reizend*]. Many authors have compromised the esteem for their philosophy because they allowed themselves to be misled into mixing feeling [*Gefühl*] and taste in with it. Rousseau is one of the greatest geniuses. But he mixes into his writings something novelistic [*romanhaftes*], and therefore his sharp mind is not really recognized by everyone and the power of his arguments remains unknown to a portion of his readership. Hume, because he mixes a great deal of novelty into his writings, is considered by many a rhetorician [*ein beredeter Mann*] more than the acute philosopher that we have really come to recognize. (V-Lo/Philippi 24: 465)

Already in a *Reflexion* from the mid-1770s, Kant has made his choice:

> Even if like Hume I had all the decorative skills [*alle Verschönerung*] in my power, I would still have reservations about making use of them. It is true that some readers will be frightened off by dryness. But is it not necessary to frighten some off, since otherwise what matters would fall into the wrong hands? (Refl 5040, 18: 70)

Here we perceive the origin of what would become Kant's blatant estrangement from popular currents of *Aufklärung* by the time his first *Critique* appeared. In just this light, the organization and execution of the Encyclopedia course came to seem incongruous with the Critical project.

In the lectures on Philosophical Encyclopedia, Kant insisted that "the canon of logic is not derived from experience. The universal conduct of reason can be demonstrated a priori, it is thus not derived from psychology" (PhilEnz 29.1,1: 14). That is an utter rejection of the Feder program, as enunciated in the course textbook! Kant maintained transcendental philosophy pursued a different course: "The objects that are given through utterly pure reason [*die pure reine Vernunft*] belong to ontology. But are they also actual things? No, but rather a mere thinking [*ein bloßes Denken*]. Ontology contains no objects, but rather only concepts, laws and principles of pure thought" (PhilEnz 29.1,1: 11 f.). In the Encyclopedia lectures Kant offered two definitions of truth that are in some seeming tension in his logic lectures. "Truth," he said at one point, "is the agreement of a cognition with its object." A bit later he said, "All truth consists in the agreement of a cognition with the laws of understanding and of reason." Kant explained the need for the second characterization because "the statement that [truth] is the agreement of a cognition with its object is insufficiently determined" (PhilEnz 29.1,1: 20 f.). The question of truth for Kant was always a question of the validity of a judgment. The procedural soundness of judgment did not come under question; hence it could err only in misapplication. "In order to secure ourselves from error, we must (1) investigate the influence of the senses on the understanding, [and] (2) isolate our understanding from sensibility" (PhilEnz 29.1,1: 22). Thus Kant here placed the full burden of the folly of judgment at the feet of "subreption." It was a question not so much of refuting error as discovering illusion. To be sure, Kant maintained that philosophy should seek out the "limits of human understanding," an enormously difficult undertaking since "self knowledge is the most difficult [sort], for here understanding must judge its own conduct" (PhilEnz 29.1,1: 23). Yet there is no sign that he recognized the possibility of internal difficulties *in pure reason itself*, the key principle of his antinomy notion in the first *Critique*. Isolation, purity in a priori reasoning, appeared to suffice. This stance was embodied above all in his *Inaugural Dissertation*, the most important publication by Kant preceding the interlude when he suspended offering his Encyclopedia course.

Kant felt confident that "the dogmatic method can be used in philosophy if the cognitions are apodictically certain." Dogmatic cognitions, he explained, were "general (or rational) cognitions that are apodictically certain," as contrasted with "experiential cognitions [*Erfahrungs Erkenntniße*] which are also apodictically certain but which are not rational cognitions (Apodictically certain really means a priori certain.)" (PhilEnz 29.1,1: 27). That experiential cognitions could be a priori certain (apodictic) would prove very problematic in the Critical period, e. g., in the context of empirical "laws."

Kant contrasted the dogmatic method with a skeptical method that wished first to *establish whether* a knowledge-claim really was apodictic. "In metaphysics, where our reasoning concerning the vocation of man goes beyond the bounds of the world and experience, where we have nothing to guide us, the skeptical method is appropriate" (PhilEnz 29.1,1: 28). Skeptical method was a good thing "provided only that one does not have the constant resolve to doubt everything forever, and to leave everything undecided ... The withholding of approval ... with the intentional inclination never to decide anything is really nothing but a lazy doubt, a lazy addiction to doubt [*faule Zweifelsucht*]," and "no more miserable condition for man can be thought ... than the condition that leaves us undecided ... particularly ... when it affects our interests" (V-Lo/Blomberg 24: 126 f., 160).

> The *naturalist* of pure reason adopts as his principle that through common reason, without science, that is, through what he calls sound reason, he is able, in regard to those most sublime questions which form the problem of metaphysics, to achieve more than is possible through speculation ... This is mere misology, reduced to principles; and what is most absurd of all, the neglect of all artificial means is eulogised as a special *method* for extending our knowledge. (KrV A835/B883)

Kant's target here was Popular philosophy, especially as it endeavored an empirical anthropology. His contempt was blatant. The question is, how long had he been of this view? Lewis Beck holds that Kant had never had any patience with "naturalism" in this sense (Beck 1978). Kant, in his view, could never have taken common sense seriously. But in his commentary on Kant's lectures on Philosophical Encyclopedia, Manfred Kuehn suggests something quite different: "Kant sounds like a common sense philosopher" as late as his lecture series of 1775 (Kuehn 1983: 306n). Kant was working through a lot of this in the 1770s, increasingly convinced that Hume and Popular philosophy – the whole ensemble he would label "indifferentism" in the first *Critique* – fell distinctly short of both his *practical* and his *theoretical* concerns. Philosophy, accordingly, had to be rescued from psychological and empirical reduction. Anthropology could not presume to displace or explain philosophy. Popular philosophy needed the discipline of criticism, and in that light, the Encyclopedia approach to philosophy was counterproductive. That is why Kant abandoned the course.

VII **Natural Law/Right**

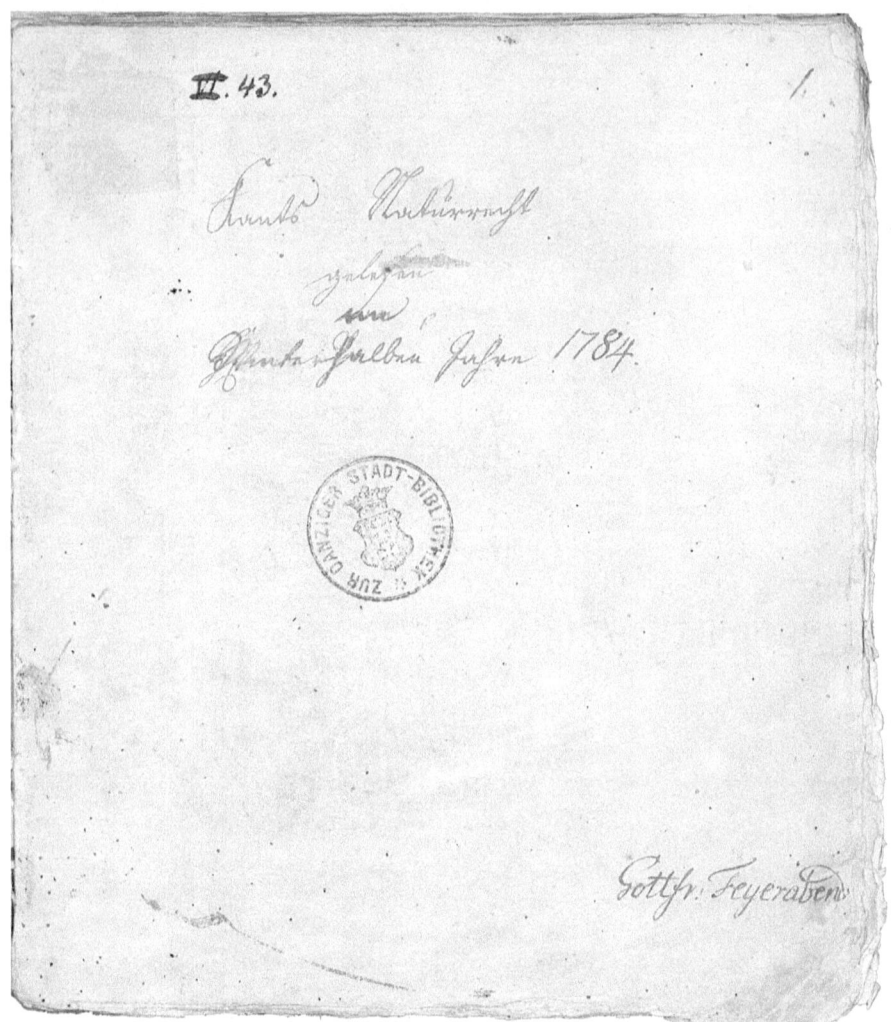

Fig. 10: Reproduction of the title page from the manuscript "Naturrecht Feyerabend" (cf. AA 27: 1317; Delfosse et al. 2010: 3). Reproduced with the kind permission of PAN Biblioteka Gdańska (Danzig), Poland. Call number: manuscript 2215. The title page states: "Kants Naturrecht gelesen im Winterhalben Jahre 1784. Gottfr: Feyerabend." ("Kant's *Naturrecht* read in the winter semester of year 1784. Gottfr. Feyerabend.") Note: the course was actually given during the summer semester of 1784.

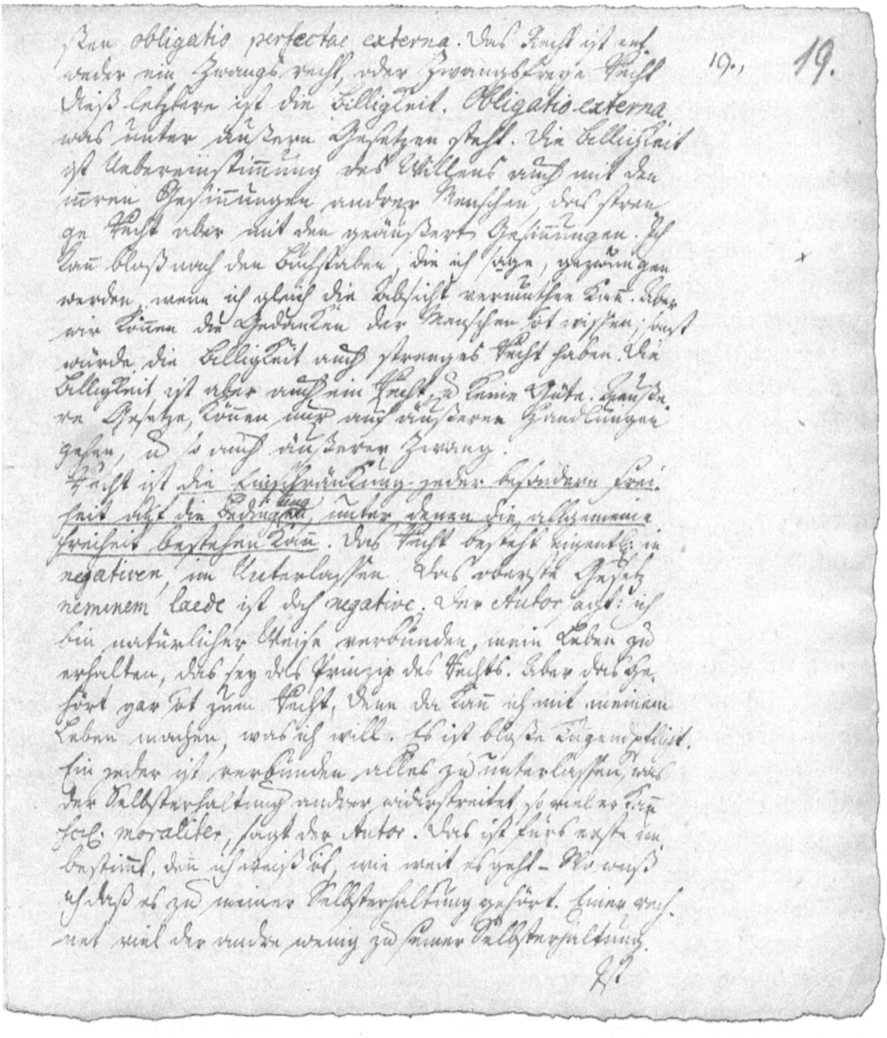

Fig. 11: Reproduction of page 35 (sheet 19 recto) from the manuscript "Naturrecht Feyerabend" (cf. AA 27: 1334; Delfosse et al. 2014: 22). Note the underlined definition of *Recht*. Reproduced with the kind permission of PAN Biblioteka Gdańska (Danzig), Poland. Call number: manuscript 2215. Frederick Rauscher's translation of the text follows; the German text is also given.

Transcription of the Text in Fig. 11

[… Es sollte hei]ßen *obligation perfecta externa*. Das Recht ist entweder ein Zwangsrecht, oder Zwangsfreyes Recht. Dies letztere ist die Billigkeit. *Obligatio externa*, was unter äußern Gesetzen steht. Die Billigkeit ist Uebereinstimmung des Willens auch mit den innern Gesinnungen andrer Menschen; das strenge Recht aber mit den geäußerten Gesinnungen. Ich kann bloß nach den Buchstaben, die ich sage, gezwungen werden, wenn ich gleich die Absicht vermuthen kann. Aber wir können die Gedanken der Menschen nicht wissen; sonst würde die Billigkeit auch strenges Recht haben. Die Billigkeit ist aber auch ein Recht, und keine Güte. Äußere Gesetze können nur auf äußere Handlungen gehen, und so auch äußerer Zwang.

Recht ist <u>die Einschränkung jeder besondern Freiheit auf die Bedingungen, unter denen die allgemeine Freiheit bestehen kann</u>. Das Recht besteht eigentlich in *negativen*, im Unterlassen. Das oberste Gesetz *neminem laede* ist doch *negative*. Der *Autor* sagt: ich bin natürlicher Weise verbunden, mein Leben zu erhalten, das sey das Prinzip des Rechts. Aber das gehört gar nicht zum Recht, denn da kann ich mit meinem Leben machen, was ich will. Es ist bloße Tugendpflicht. Ein jeder ist verbunden, alles zu unterlassen, was der Selbsterhaltung andrer widerstreitet, so viel er kann, *scil. moraliter*, sagt der *Autor*. Das ist fürs erste unbestimmt, denn ich weiß nicht, wie weit es geht. – Wo weiß ich daß es zu meiner Selbsterhaltung gehört. Einer rechnet viel der andre wenig zu seiner Selbsterhaltung.

English Translation
[... It should be called] *obligatio perfecta externa* [perfect external obligation]. Right is either a coercive right or a non-coercive right. This latter is equity. *Obligatio externa* [external obligation], what stands under outer laws. Equity is agreement of the will also with the inner disposition of another human being; the strong right however with the expressed state of mind. I can be coerced only in accordance with the literal meaning of what I said even if I can guess the intention. But we cannot know the thoughts of a human being; otherwise equity would also be a strong right. Equity is, however, also a right and not a good. Outer laws can refer only to outer actions and so also to outer coercion.

Right is <u>the limitation of the particular freedom of each by the conditions under which universal freedom can exist</u>. Right properly consists in *negative*, in omission. The supreme law *neminem laede* [wrong no one] is of course *negative*. The author says I am bound by my nature to preserve my life; this would be the principle of right. But that does not belong to right at all, for in right I can do with my life whatever I will. It is solely a duty of virtue. Each is obligated, as far as he is able, to omit anything that interferes with the self-preservation of others, *scil. moraliter* [namely morality], says the author. This is indeterminate from the start, for I do not know how far it goes. – How do I know that something belongs to my own self-preservation. One may figure upon a lot, another a little, for his self-preservation.

Chapter 14
Did Kant Justify the French Revolution Ex Post Facto?

Frederick Rauscher

Kant had a reputation as a strong supporter of the French Revolution. He was said to have exclaimed after the initial success of the French Revolution, "Lord, now let your servant go in peace, for I have seen the glory of the world."[1] But Kant was also opposed in general to any revolution. In *Theory and Practice*, his first published response to debate about the French Revolution, he writes, "Any resistance to the supreme legislative power, any incitement to have the subjects' dissatisfaction become active, any insurrection that breaks out in rebellion, is the highest and most punishable crime within a commonwealth because it destroys its foundation" (TP 8: 299).

He was also skeptical of others' defenses of revolutions in general. In *Theory and Practice*, when he specifically mentions uprisings in Switzerland, the Netherlands, and Great Britain, Kant also notes that had they failed, the instigators of those revolutions would certainly have been regarded as criminals. He implies that even his readers who now support the results of those revolutions would have likely regarded the revolutionaries as criminals if the revolution failed. Only because these revolutions were successful and resulted in better states than the ones they replaced are these revolutionaries now regarded well. The success of those revolutions in setting up worthy constitutions colors the judgment of those who look back on the events. "For the outcome usually mingles in our appraisal of the rightful grounds, though the former was uncertain and the latter certain" (TP 8: 301).

This last claim might also apply to Kant himself. For Kant did defend the legitimacy of the initial crucial step in the French Revolution, the assumption of sovereign legislative authority by the National Assembly in the summer of 1789, nearly eight years after the fact in the *Doctrine of Right* (RL 6: 342f.). Could it be that Kant's own "appraisal of the rightful grounds" of the French Revolution is partly the result of his approval of the outcome rather than purely a result of

---

[1] This quotation is from an anecdote recorded by Karl August Varnhagen von Ense and not directly from Kant's writings (Malter 1990: 348).

considerations of right? Or do his specific philosophical defenses of the legitimacy of the French Revolution stem from long-held positions about right? Certainly Kant's overall political philosophy changed little from the 1780s through the 1790s.[2] But did he modify it to fit the circumstances of the French Revolution?

We can judge whether Kant might have been guilty of retrospective rationalizing, or to put it more sympathetically, whether the French Revolution triggered a change in his thought, by examining his detailed views on sovereign authority prior to the French Revolution to see whether they fit his later claims. And although Kant published almost nothing on political right and certainly nothing directly on the nature of sovereign authority prior to the 1790s, we have a record of the views he presented in his course lectures on Natural Right (or Natural Law[3])

---

[2] Frederick Beiser claims that "There is indeed little in the 1796 *Rechtslehre* that is not already sketched, if only vaguely, in the *Reflexionen*" (Beiser 1992: 33). Because his focus is on the nature of freedom in relation to the state he overlooks the lack of discussion of the nature and justification of property in the Reflections, largely because the first volume of Achenwall's text that contained his discussion of property, and therefore Kant's corresponding notes, was lost. Bernd Ludwig notes that Kant's detailed theory of property does not appear in his surviving writings until after 1796, and even in the Vorarbeiten to the *Rechtslehre* Kant does not present his developed conception of the postulate of practical reason with regard to rights (Ludwig 1988: 120–25). Philipp-Alexander Hirsch has shown that the core of Kant's philosophy of right as presented in the Introduction to the *Rechtslehre*, hence including the principle of right, the authorization of coercion, and the innate right to freedom, is already present in *Naturrecht Feyerabend* and the Mrongovius Ethics lectures of 1784/85 (Hirsch 2012). Regarding the whole of Kant's doctrine of right, Sharon Byrd and Joachim Hruschka argue that Kant changed his philosophy or right in its details during the 1780s and 90s and published its final form as a system only in the *Doctrine of Right* (Byrd and Hruschka 2010: 13). There is also some debate about whether Kant's philosophy of right is consistent between the 1780s and Kant's earlier, pre-Critical period. Christian Ritter argues that Kant's philosophy of right is substantially formed and fully consistent from the 1760s through the 1790s, in the first book-length study of the subject (Ritter 1971). In contrast, Werner Busch argued that there is a substantial difference between Kant's pre-Critical and Critical philosophy of right based on the development of Kant's conception of freedom as self-legislation (Busch 1979). Both agree, however, that Kant's philosophy of right is essentially developed before the time of *Naturrecht Feyerabend*.

[3] The term *Naturrecht*, which will remain untranslated in this paper, is as difficult to translate into English as is the core term *Recht* itself. *Recht* can be rendered as "law," "justice," or "right," each of which captures part but not all of the meaning of the term. *Naturrecht* is the German term used for the tradition generally known in English as "natural law." But other considerations strongly favored using "natural right" when referring to Kant's usage. If "natural law" is used for *Naturrecht*, then the connections to terms related to *Recht* are lost, specifically the use of *ein Recht* for "a right" and *rechtlich* for "rightful," the latter carrying a normative force missing in "legal." The standard Cambridge Edition of the Works of Immanuel Kant translation of Kant's *Rechtslehre*, translated by Mary Gregor, uniformly uses "right" for *Recht* (and for the Latin *jus* as well), "Natural Right" for *Naturrecht*, and "Doctrine of Right" for *Rechtslehre*. My translation of

in 1784, the *Naturrecht Feyerabend*.⁴ Fully five years before the events in Paris and Versailles Kant laid out for his students his assessments of the nature of sovereign authority, the possibility of transfer of sovereign authority, the prohibition against revolution, and even the nature of monarchy as an institution embodying right. These lectures, along with Kant's notes for them recorded in his copy of the textbook, provide the only source of Kant's views on the nature of sovereignty prior to the French Revolution itself. By assessing Kant's justification of the legitimacy of the French Revolution in light of these earlier views, I will show that Kant did modify his view after the Revolution and used that modification in defense of it.

1

In the *Doctrine of Right* Kant presents two different philosophical arguments that defend the legitimacy of the French Revolution.⁵ One defends the *existence* of the new regime, the other the *process* by which the new regime gained sovereignty. I will look at each but focus on the second.

The first defense is that after the revolution, the French Republic ought to be recognized and considered the rightful authority in France simply because it actually functioned as the state in the post-revolution period. In the *Doctrine of Right* he argues that, since the legitimacy of a particular supreme authority is based on a priori justification and not empirical historical facts, the people must not only always recognize the current governing authority, it would also be dangerous for them to question that authority's origin (RL 6: 318). A "practical principle of reason" is that "the presently existing legislative authority ought to be obeyed whatever its origin" (RL 6: 319). Kant later applies this principle directly to any revolution that overthrows and replaces one governing authority with another. Revolution is always wrong, but if a revolution is successful then the people of that country must recognize the new governing authority as lawfully sovereign (RL 6: 323). Although Kant presents this position in reference to a

---

Naturrecht Feyerabend and other of Kant's unpublished writings in the Cambridge series volume *Lectures and Drafts on Political Philosophy* uses "right" and "natural right" for consistency with Gregor's volume.
4 For details concerning the course and transcript, see the beginning of the second section.
5 In *Conflict of the Faculties*, Kant provides a philosophical defense of sorts when he ascribes proof of the progress of humanity the positive reaction that many had to the French Revolution, but this defense is teleological rather than related to political legitimacy (SF 7: 85).

post-revolutionary government only in the *Doctrine of Right*, the argument does not represent any departure from his published views earlier in the decade.⁶

Kant also defended the French state as legitimate with a second defense, an independent argument that the actual transition of authority that resulted in the new French state was legitimate. This defense would show that the individuals responsible for creating the new French state were never rebelling against legitimate authority and could not ever have been considered as criminals. Indeed, if Kant's analysis is successful one would not even call the process a revolution, in the sense of an extra-legal action to replace one governing authority with another.⁷ One might wonder whether Kant wished to take extra steps to defend the legitimacy of the new French state – not only its mere existence but also its process of coming-into-being – because he was so supportive of the results.

In § 52 of the *Doctrine of Right*, he argues that the process of transfer of sovereign legislative authority from the king to the National Assembly was a legitimate act rather than any unjust seizure of power or act of rebellion on the part of the French people. There is an additional, nearly parallel argument in Reflection 8055 that Kant wrote sometime between the events in France and the publication of the *Doctrine of Right*.⁸ This earlier explanation is found in Kant's copy of the

---

6 Reidar Maliks argues that the claim that the people must obey any newly constituted state authority resulting from a revolution, regardless of the illegality and even injustice of that revolution, is "a new argument in the *Metaphysics of Morals*" although it was implied by Kant's earlier doctrine of absolute obedience and the rejection of resistance that characterized his earlier work (Maliks 2012: 669). Alessandro Pinzani also notes this argument but implies that Kant had presented this claim earlier in *Theory and Practice* (Pinzani 2008: 212, referring to TP 8: 301). There is also a passage in *Toward Perpetual Peace* that likewise claims that after a revolution – Kant uses the term *Revolution* in *Sperrdruck* for emphasis – that instituted "a constitution more in conformity with law" it would be impermissible to "lead the people back to the old one" (ZeF 8: 372).
7 This point is also made by Maliks (2012: 669).
8 Refl 8055 was clearly written before Kant's published *Doctrine of Right* but is not identified as a draft of that work in *Kant's gesammelte Schriften*. Friedrich Berger, who brought Kant's Reflections on *Naturrecht* to publication after the death of Erich Adickes and using Adickes's dating for the material, lists the range of dates for Refl 8055 as approximately 1788–95. Given that the French Revolution did not occur until 1789, it must be no earlier than the latter half of 1789. Maliks (2012) and Pinzani (2008) treat Refl 8055 as a draft for the *Doctrine of Right*, implying that it was written closer to 1795 than to 1789. Complicating matters is that unlike other fragments that have been assumed to be drafts for the *Doctrine of Right* and are collected in *Kant's gesammelte Schriften* volume 23, this Reflection was written not on a loose sheet of paper but in Kant's copy of Gottfried Achenwall's *Jus Naturae*, the text Kant used for his courses on *Naturrecht*. At least one other Reflection, Refl 8078, was also clearly written in the Achenwall book after the events of 1789; in it Kant rejects the definition of freedom given in the August 1789 "Declaration and Determination of the Rights of Man" because it limits freedom to lack of harm of others, a definition that Kant rejects because one could interfere with another's actions in a way that one thinks will profit the

textbook by Gottfried Achenwall, *Jus Naturae*, that he used for his course lectures on *Naturrecht*. While the main argument is present in the *Doctrine of Right* version, some subtle variations from Refl 8055 reveal more of Kant's thinking. I will examine the published version first and then note the relevant differences in Refl 8055 when discussing the details.

In § 52 of the *Doctrine of Right*, Kant provided his justification with a direct application to the events in France (he mentions the National Assembly, although not King Louis XVI by name). In this section he first presents his justification of the transition from monarchy to a republic in light of his conception of representation of the people in any state. He defines "true republic" as "a system representing the people, in order to protect its rights in its name, by all the citizens united and acting through their delegates" (RL 6: 341). The crucial part of this definition is "representing the people" since Kant claims that a king can relinquish this representational relation through an act of subsuming himself under it:

> As soon as a person who is head of state (whether it be a king, nobility, or the whole of the population, the democratic union) also lets itself be represented, then the united people does not merely *represent* the sovereign: it *is* the sovereign itself. For in it (the people) is originally found the supreme authority from which all rights of individuals as mere subjects (and in any event as officials of the state) must be derived; and a republic, once established, no longer has to let the reins of government out of its hands and give them over again to those who previously held them and could again nullify all new institutions by their absolute choice. (RL 6: 341)

Kant's argument works in this way: the king normally represents the people. But should the king – or any particular entity holding sovereign power – relinquish

---

other yet nonetheless not receive the consent of the other (HN 19: 612). Adickes dates Refl 8078 as 1790–95, but it could be in 1789 after August. Alessandro Pinzani dates Refl 8055 to sometime after September 1791 because it begins with a reference to an alteration of the constitution in France in the past tense, and since a constitution was promulgated in September 1791, he concludes that Refl 8055 cannot have been written any earlier (Pinzani 2008: 204, and private correspondence). This point is well taken and gives some reason to prefer a later date, but still inconclusive, since Kant's claim is that "the National Assembly was able to *alter*" rather than "promulgate" the constitution, and Kant could have been referring to the National Assembly's 1789 declaration that it, rather than the Estates General, was the legitimate representative body and that it had full legislative powers, a change from the earlier constitutional framework in France. One might also ask why Kant would write these notes in his textbook rather than on loose sheets as he did other drafts for the *Doctrine of Right*. No Reflections in the Achenwall book except Refl 8078 (already mentioned) are exclusively dated by Adickes as later than 1789, implying that Kant did not make drafts for any of his political works of the 1790s in his textbook. I thus find it more likely that these Reflections were written by Kant in the Achenwall book in preparation for an announced 1789/90 offering of his course on *Naturrecht*, as discussed in the final section of this paper.

that role to the extent that he himself is subsumed into that which is represented, then there is no particular entity representing the whole people other than the people itself. And the people do not *represent* the united people, they *are* the united people and have sovereignty. Kant's use of the term "united people" here is important but requires disambiguation.

The claim that the united will of the people is the ultimate legislative sovereign in any legitimate state (RL 6: 313) lies at the heart of his understanding of the nature of an original contract. In accordance with the idea of an original contract, the superior above all is "the united people itself." The subjects of that superior are the "multitude of the people." The original contract is the idea of the act by which a people forms itself into a state (RL 6: 315). Once a people is formed into a state, they are regarded as "united under a general legislative will ... as the present head of state" (RL 6: 318); that is, the united people is united only in and through the state. The "pure idea of a head of state" is, however, itself an idea or "thought-entity" only actualized through some physical person who represents the supreme authority in the state (Kant is clear that this includes the legislative authority). This person can be either one or several in command of the rest, or all in command of each and every one, so over themselves as well (RL 6: 338). Hence the legislative entity is a single person (autocrat[9]), a collection of individuals (aristocracy) or all the people (democracy) (RL 6: 338 f., cf. TP 8: 297). Each of these three equally embodies the united will of the people and represents the people when ruled well. Each of these three types of rulers is obligated to try to make the government harmonize "*in its effect* with ... a pure republic" (RL 6: 340; Kant's emphasis).

Now there are two ways in which this conception of "united people" can be understood.[10] First one can understand a united people in terms of a united *will* of the people, which is "derived a priori from reason" (RL 6: 338) and is the basis of

---

9 While Kant differentiates between an *autocrat* as a single ruler holding all power and a *monarch* holding executive authority, or at least authority only as representative of the people (RL 6: 338 and V-NR/Feyerabend 27: 1388), he allows in the latter passage that the French king held all sovereign power. To refer to Louis XVI qua holder of sovereign legislative power, I will use "monarch" and "king" instead of "autocrat."

10 Kant derived this approach from Rousseau's distinction between the general will and the will of all but transformed the distinction to reflect his own philosophical commitments. I owe a great deal of my understanding of Kant's approach to Pinzani 2008. He equates the first sense of "united people" with the people as noumenon and the second sense with the people as phenomenon. This is helpful in emphasizing the way that the first sense is merely an idea derived a priori from reason used by Kant in his justifications and assessment of actual political entities, the phenomena.

the authority of the state as such. One might say that to the extent that the people possess rational wills that are able to provide them with the basic principles of right, the people are united in willing a state in accord with those principles. This sense makes the "united people" a kind of abstract entity that lies behind the authority of a state to the extent that the state accords with principles of reason.

The second sense in which one might use the term "the united people" is in understanding a united people as the set of all actual people acting in harmony. In this sense, the people may be understood as potentially existing in every kind of state but only actually existing in a situation that allows for all people to act together. The actual decisions made by the people acting in harmony may be products of their wills, to be sure, but may also be products of their particular powers of choice. In the latter case these decisions made by the people are not based a priori on reason but are the actual empirical choices of existing individuals. This sense makes the "united people" an existing entity that is able to act as such only under certain conditions that allow the individuals to act together in accordance with their choices.

In his political philosophy Kant uses both of these senses. Most clearly he uses the first sense when he talks about the people with regard to the original contract instituting a state in order to actualize right (e. g., RL 6: 256, 6: 315), and he uses the second sense when discussing the presence of the people representing themselves in a democracy or republic in which the citizens act through their delegates (e. g., RL 6: 341).[11] Both senses appear in the arguments Kant gives about the French Revolution, as I will show below.

But first I will show how Kant applies this more general reasoning to the particular circumstances in France in the summer of 1789. In the paragraph immediately following the argument regarding how the united people does not merely represent the sovereign but instead is the sovereign in a true republic, Kant provides this application to the French situation:

---

[11] Sharon Byrd and Joachim Hruschka read Kant's *Doctrine of Right* in a way that combines these two senses. They hold that Kant takes *actual* consent to a law to be required in order for it to be legitimate as a law that one gives oneself, so that in the ideal state the united will of the people is behind every particular law. (In an actual, non-ideal state, they say, Kant resorts to majority rule, even though Kant does not state this in the *Doctrine of Right* and they resort to referring back to *Theory and Practice* to support their claim [Byrd and Hruschka 2010: 143–45].) Clearly every particular law would involve not merely the rational will but also the individual ends of particular citizens and hence their choices. Their claim entails that Kant abandoned his view of the idea of the social contract as one in which the legislative authority must make laws that a people *could* consent to (TP 8: 297). Later in this paper I discuss the kind of consent at issue.

> A powerful ruler in our time therefore made a very serious error in judgment when, to extricate himself from the embarrassment of large state debts, he left it to the people to take this burden on itself and distribute it as it saw fit; for then the legislative authority naturally came into the people's hands not only with regard to the taxation of subjects but also with regard to the government, namely to prevent it from incurring new debts by extravagance or war. The consequence was that the monarch's sovereignty wholly disappeared (it was not merely suspended) and passed to the people, to whose legislative will the belongings of every subject became subjected. (RL 6: 341)

This argument is presented as an application of the previous, more general argument. The entity holding sovereign power, King Louis XVI, gave legislative authority to the people regarding the state budget. But through this act, Kant implies, the king subsumed himself under the legislative authority of the people in this matter, and so was himself among those represented by the Assembly. In doing so he surrendered sovereignty, and thus the French people as a united people assumed the sovereign power that he had earlier held only as representative of the united people.

Certainly the arguments Kant gives reflect some longstanding elements of his theory. These particular arguments, however, depend on more specific elements including the following important claims, which I group into two sets. The first set concerns the indivisibility and transferability of sovereign legislative power. Corresponding more to Kant's general argument, these elements largely work on the assumption that the transfer of sovereign power is a deliberate act by the king. The second set concerns a claim that the actual people are the default sovereign equivalent to the united will of the people. These elements play a larger role in Kant's specific application of his general argument to the situation in France, where one can say that the king did not intend to transfer sovereign power.

1. *The indivisibility and transferability of sovereign legislative authority.* Kant requires that the king is authorized to transfer sovereign legislative power and is unable to retain any sovereign authority once he does. Regarding transferring sovereign power, Kant's argument requires the following specific aspects:

1a. *The king as monarch shifts from representing the people to being one who is represented when calling a legislature to order.* Kant implies in the *Doctrine of Right* that the king can do this simply when calling a legislative assembly into order under which the king also wishes to be represented when he says "as soon as a person who is head of state ... also lets itself be represented" (RL 6: 341). In order for the sovereign legislative power to be transferred in this situation, the king must be deliberately transferring his legislative powers to the other set of representatives. This claim entails that the king qua individual person is the same as the king qua sovereign. If the king qua individual desires to be represented qua individual, one might hold that he can do so without being represented qua sovereign. That is, the king might reserve his own powers qua sovereign legislator when asking to be represented qua individual in an assembly much in the way in the United States the President votes for representation in Congress qua citizen.[12]

1b. *The sovereign has the authority to voluntarily transfer sovereign power and thus the authority to alter the constitution unilaterally.* The action of the king asking to be among those represented by the assembly in Kant's more general argument appears to be an act of voluntary surrender of sovereign authority by the monarch. Hence the king must have the authority to change the constitution by unilateral act. Kant does not rely on this voluntary surrender of legislative authority by the king in Refl 8055, where instead he says that the king normally represented the people but "here he was negated because the people themselves were present" (HN 19: 595 f.). Further, he argues there that simply by allowing the whole to represent itself, the king "becomes nothing" because he had represented the whole that is now representing itself. Refl 8055, then, does not rely on any voluntary explicit act on the king's part of declaring that he will personally allow himself to be represented by the whole people and thus change the constitution.

1c. *The legislative sovereign authority is indivisible.* Only in this case could it be that the king had transferred all sovereign legislative authority when transferring the limited amount of authority over the state budget. In Refl 8055, Kant relies on a claim that Louis XVI had given "indeterminate authority" to make decrees to the National Assembly (HN 19: 595). Kant's argument relies on a claim that by providing the assembly with some powers, the king has transferred all powers.

2. *The people as default sovereign*: Kant holds that in the summer of 1789 in France, since the actual people were present in the National Assembly, and the actual people are either equivalent metaphysically to the whole united people (the stronger version) or the natural or best representatives of the whole people (the weaker version), sovereign authority automatically passed to the "united people." This involves specific claims that can be understood only after a more detailed look at the idea of sovereignty and representation in Kant.

---

12 The U.S. President, qua office holder, can be understood to have some legislative power through possession of a veto power over bills passed by Congress. (Kant implies that veto power is a legislative power [V-NR/Feyerabend 27: 1388].) This legislative power, not any executive power, is at issue. Yet the President is also, qua individual human being, able to vote for members of the House of Representatives and the Senate. In so voting, the President does not transfer veto power to any one member of Congress or the whole of the Congress. The President does not ask to be represented qua President but qua citizen.

Kant held that the people have ultimate sovereignty. The people can be represented in one of three types of sovereign legislative authority as noted above: through an autocracy, an aristocracy, or a democracy. Alessandro Pinzani usefully labels these two types of sovereignty the "real" and the "actual" sovereigns (Pinzani 2008: 206 f.). At all times the united people are the real sovereign, but only in the abstract, their sovereign power is always yielded by an actual entity holding that power – a single individual in an autocracy, a small group in an aristocracy, or whole of the people in a democracy. These three entities that can have actual sovereignty do so as representatives of the united people.

This scheme is at work in Kant's arguments in § 52 and Refl 8055. Kant's point is that when an assembly of the people is officially called, the resulting assembly does not merely *represent* the people but *is* the people and thus has real sovereignty. In this interpretation of the argument, when the king called the assembly into order he did not need to transfer sovereignty to it because the assembly itself automatically had sovereignty as the actually present united people.

This can be understood in two ways:

2a. *The actual people who elect a representative assembly are this "united people."* Kant's claim is that when an entity that has legislative authority places himself or itself as represented by the people, then the whole *united* people is present. The set of actual individuals, or totality of citizens, is equated with the more abstract united people that possesses a common united will grounding the state.

2b. *The default representative of the people (as a whole general will) is the elected representation of the actual people.* A weaker version of this argument could avoid a metaphysical identity of the two but still claim that the actual people are the default sovereign for other reasons. Kant's claim that the actual people are the united people can, alternatively, be understood as a claim that whenever the entire actual people is assembled, the closest thing to the whole united people is present, so actual sovereign power will automatically be vested in the actual people. Kant could be interpreted to be making this point when he says that "the legislative authority naturally came into the people's hands" (RL 6: 341) when the King called the assembly.

To sum up this review of Kant's philosophical defenses of the French Revolution: Kant has two main arguments. The first is relatively unproblematic, namely that after the revolution the people are obligated to follow the new regime simply because it now possesses state power, and whoever possesses state power at a given time possesses it rightfully. The second is more complicated, namely that the transfer of sovereignty from the king to the National Assembly was legitimate. I identified five claims in two different areas that lie behind Kant's defense of the transfer of sovereign legislative authority from King Louis XVI to the National Assembly. The two areas are the claim that sovereign legislative power is indivisible and transferable, and that the set of actual people is the proper possessor of actual sovereign legislative power.

1a. The king qua office holder can shift from being the representative of the people to being one who is represented when calling an assembly into order.
1b. The king has the authority to voluntarily transfer sovereignty from himself to another entity.
1c. Legislative sovereign power is indivisible.
2a. The set of actual individuals electing a legislature is the same as the united will of the people as a whole.
2b. The default representative of the whole united people is the people as set of actual individuals.

The next section examines the main source for Kant's political philosophy prior to the French Revolution in order to see whether any of these claims are stated or can be grounded in that text. If not, then there is some evidence that the French Revolution did change Kant's mind in these matters, possibly because he was so enamored with the outcome.

2

The *Naturrecht Feyerabend* is the sole surviving set of notes from Kant's course lectures on *Naturrecht*. Kant lectured on the topic at least a dozen times between 1767 and 1790 and by the late 1770s settled into a pattern of offering the course summer semesters of even numbered years. Gottfried Feyerabend's notes from summer 1784 are one of only two sets that have been identified; the other, taken by Friedrich von Gentz, was lost well before it could be published, leaving the *Naturrecht Feyerabend* as the single available lecture on the topic.[13]

---

[13] The original *Naturrecht Feyerabend* manuscript now sits in the main library in Gdansk, Poland, and was discovered there along with the 1784/85 Moral Mrongovius as Gerhard Lehmann was completing volume 27 of *Kant's gesammelte Schriften*. Lehmann realized the importance of these sets of notes and included them in 27.2.2 as "Anhang" to the lectures on ethics published in 27.1 and 27.2.1, but without any editorial apparatuses to note variant readings or other matters. A comparison of this published version against the original manuscript reveals many misreadings. Accordingly, a new critical edition drawn from the original manuscript has recently been undertaken (Delfosse et al. 2010 and 2014) and should be used as the standard edition (it includes

Kant used Gottfried Achenwall's textbook *Jus Naturae* (1763) for these lectures. Kant's notes in volume two of Achenwall are included in the *Akademie-Ausgabe*'s *Kant's gesammelte Schriften* (volume 19). Unfortunately, Kant's copy of volume one of Achenwall was lost, so no Reflections from Kant on the topics in that volume – most importantly on right in general, property, and contract – survived to be included in volume 19. *Naturrecht Feyerabend* is the only source of Kant's thoughts on these latter topics prior to the published *Doctrine of Right*. *Naturrecht Feyerabend* fills this gap well in part because most of the lecture corresponds to material that would have appeared in the first volume of Achenwall's text.[14] The full text of Achenwall's second volume is included at 19: 332–442. Achenwall's book has not been translated into either German or English.[15]

In late spring and summer 1784 Kant was composing the *Groundwork of the Metaphysics of Morals*. Fully one fifth of *Naturrecht Feyerabend* consists of a general introduction discussing Kant's conception of right and its relation to ethics that only loosely corresponds to Achenwall's Introduction. This material provides insight into the way that Kant conceived of the *Groundwork* as the basis for both right and virtue. Much of the rest of the lecture follows the order of Achenwall's text closely. Kant follows Achenwall's topics more closely when discussing particular legal issues such as inheritance or sale of property but broadens his focus when discussing issues such as the principle of right, innate right, the nature and use of property, contract, public right and the state of nature, and punishment. Toward the end of the semester Kant apparently ran low on time and told his students that he would skip the right of nations except for the right of war. He does spend a reasonable amount of time expressing his own views on the topics related to sovereignty and representation at stake in this paper.

---

the *Kant's Schriften* pagination for ease of reference). I provide more information about the two versions of *Feyerabend* in Rauscher 2012.

14 One can examine the full table of contents of Achenwall in *Kant's gesammelte Schriften* volume 19 (AA 19: 325–32). The missing volume included the material in Achenwall's general introduction and "Liber I: Ius Naturale strictissime dictum" on natural right in the narrowest sense of the term; the extant volume begins at "Liber II: Ius Sociale Universale" on universal social right, followed by the discussion of domestic right (marriage, parents, heads of the household).

15 An ancestor to this book published in 1750 and written by Achenwall together with Johann Stephan Pütter has been translated into German by Jan Schröder (Achenwall and Pütter 1995), but the differences between the editions make this translation an unreliable source for Achenwall's own views in the volume Kant used. For more discussion of Achenwall's text, see Byrd and Hruschka 2010: 15–19. They also refer to Achenwall's views occasionally in the course of their commentary on the *Doctrine of Right*. For a detailed survey of Achenwall's career and thought, see Streidl 2003.

In 1784 Kant was relatively content with the rule of Frederick in Prussia, as evidenced by his praise of King Frederick in "What is Enlightenment?" as one who "is himself enlightened and deserves to be praised by a grateful world and by posterity as the one who first released the human race from minority, at least from the side of government, and left each free to make use of his own reason in all matters of conscience" (WA 8: 40). In *Naturrecht Feyerabend*, Kant echoes that essay when he refers to the right of a scholar to express his views on religion even though as a clergyman he must conceal them; the ruler's duty regarding enlightenment is to prevent interference by established religion (V-NR/Feyerabend 27: 1386). He says nothing about the recent revolution in Geneva in 1782 or the older revolution in England. His discussions of rebellion, despotism, republics, and sovereignty are presented without reference to any specific instances, and one senses that Kant had no particular instances in mind.

Naturrecht Feyerabend thus presents a source in which Kant's views on rebellion and sovereignty are presented in detail in a way that would reflect his theoretical commitments prior to the French Revolution. Given the assessment of the two arguments in support of the French Revolution and the new French state that Kant gives in the *Doctrine of Right*, we can now determine whether the necessary positions are either stated in *Naturrecht Feyerabend*, implied by the claims in *Naturrecht Feyerabend*, or in contradiction with the claims in *Naturrecht Feyerabend*. I spent most of the space above assessing the premises for the argument that Kant makes regarding the transfer of legislative authority in the *Doctrine of Right*, and will do so here as well. First, however, I will briefly review Kant's other argument used to defend the legitimacy of the post-Revolutionary French state.

The simpler of Kant's justifications of the new French regime in the *Doctrine of Right* is the general claim that after any rebellion, or even more broadly any kind of change of regime, the new state authority must be treated as legitimate. Does *Naturrecht Feyerabend* contain either a direct statement of this claim or the material that implies it? There is no direct statement in *Naturrecht Feyerabend* to the effect that after a change of regime through illegitimate means, the people must now obey the new state authority and treat it as just. Kant does invoke a strong claim about obedience to the state. "If a human being values the right of humanity as the highest priority then he would rather endure all tyranny than defy it …. In the greatest tyranny there is still some justice" (V-NR/Feyerabend 27: 1392). Kant certainly thought that even the worst state should be obeyed, implying that whatever state exists after a rebellion should be obeyed. So although he does not apply this claim to post-revolutionary states in *Naturrecht Feyerabend*, his later use of it in reference to the new French state is not any change in his position.

More important is whether the main argument that Kant gives in the *Doctrine of Right* and in Refl 8055 about the transfer of sovereignty from the French king to the National Assembly is anticipated in *Naturrecht Feyerabend*. Not surprisingly, nowhere in that lecture does Kant describe a situation similar to that in France where a king transfers sovereignty to the people by calling an assembly of the people into being. We have to piece together fragmentary evidence regarding some points although his discussion of the relation of the people to sovereign power and representation is relatively thorough.

I will review in turn each of the assumptions as identified above. These various points are treated in isolation. For Kant's argument to work some combination of them must be true. The first set of assumptions concerns the indivisibility and transferability of sovereign legislative authority.

1a. *The king qua office holder can shift from being the representative of the people to being one who is represented when calling an assembly into order.*
This assumption requires that the individual qua king and the individual qua person or citizen are indistinguishable. If the king calls an assembly that would include him as one who is represented, one might think that he reserves his powers as king and asks to be represented as citizen. In *Naturrecht Feyerabend*, Kant does not treat this topic directly but does distinguish between the sovereign as person and sovereign qua sovereign. When discussing monarchy he says, "*Actus* of a prince are *regii* [royal] and *privati* [private]. Regarding the latter he is to be considered as a private man and thus if he buys something he has to pay for it" (V-NR/Feyerabend 27: 1388). This point does not quite mirror the one in question, but it does show that some acts of the individual are qua king and some qua citizen. If the individual qua king calls an assembly, one would think that he could consider himself represented not qua king but qua citizen. In this way all individuals can be represented in the assembly, but the king does not surrender his own sovereign powers. This would be possible if, as will be discussed below, sovereign legislative power is divisible.

1b. *The king has the authority to voluntarily transfer sovereignty from himself to another entity.*
Naturrecht Feyerabend does not discuss in any detail the transfer of sovereignty from one entity to another. One might be able to get some sense of it in his discussion of monarchy. "Can a *Monarch* abdicate without the consent of the people? No, he stands under the *pactum fundamentale* [the fundamental contract], and because of that has obligations" (V-NR/Feyerabend 27: 1388). In this passage, Kant might just mean that a monarch as executive is contractually obligated to the legislative power, but he might also mean that even a king holding legislative

authority is obligated to "the people" as a whole and cannot unilaterally abdicate. In the same discussion he defines "monarch" as "the head of all executive power" but after that discussion and before the passage I just quoted he notes that in England (meaning Great Britain) the monarch can also be sovereign, defined as "the one who can also legislate," and makes the laws together with the nobility and the people. He also says that the French king is unlimited sovereign. In the following section, Kant seems to deny that the constitutional system of a state can be changed. He mentions that the power of a throne can pass either through heredity or through some selection: "If this is in the fundamental law then no one can alter it" (V-NR/Feyerabend 27: 1388). A king transferring sovereign authority to an elected assembly would be a change in the constitution. A third hint is that the only time in the lecture that Kant talks about a change in the government is not any change in the type of government from monarchy to democracy, or aristocracy to monarchy, but only the corruption of one of those types into their negative counterparts such as a shift from monarchy to despotism (V-NR/Feyerabend 27: 1392) which involves no change in sovereign legislative authority at all. In general, as with point (1a) we have no direct discussion of the possibility of voluntary transfer of sovereign legislative authority and only a few suggestive passages that speak against it.

1c. *Legislative sovereign power is indivisible.*
In *Naturrecht Feyerabend*, it is clear that legislative authority is divisible or shared between entities. I mentioned above that Kant offers England as an example of divided sovereignty with regard to legislative authority: "In England legislative authority rests in the people, the nobility, and the king" (V-NR/Feyerabend 27: 1383). The king, he notes, is also the supreme executor of the law; Kant does not claim that either the king or the two houses of parliament, either individually or both together, have sole legislative authority. Later he cites England when he says that a monarch can have his own share of sovereignty: "The king, the nobility, and the people make the laws. If the king says no then nothing can be made into law" (V-NR/Feyerabend 27: 1388). Veto power, then, is considered part of the legislative authority. Yet elsewhere he seems to limit this arrangement to a mere type of government rather than a type of constitution when he claims that there can be no mixed constitutions: "If one is talking about state constitutions then none can be mixed. But there can be mixed types of governments .... Mixed types of government are good. England is *democratie* mixed with *monarchie* and *aristocratie*" (V-NR/Feyerabend 27: 1389). In saying that legislative authority can be divided he seems to mean only that a very broad sense of legislative authority can be divided into a more narrow legislative authority divided among many persons. He has two ways of explaining this. The first way is less applicable: there is one authority

in making general law and then two subordinate authorities for specifying that law. In his lecture on a section of Achenwall's text "of Legislative, Executive, and Inspection Powers," Kant states that "One can divide *potestas legislatoria* into *rectoria* and *dijudicaria*" (V-NR/Feyerabend 27: 1384). That is, legislative power can be divided into governing power and the power of dijudicating. Kant does not normally consider either governing or judging to be part of the legislative powers but rather to be distinct executive and judicial powers, so this might be an error on the part of the student transcribers, but if the passage is accurate he apparently means that the second two powers include portions of the legislative power. He states that the sovereign has the authorization neither to "determine the law regarding particular citizens" – this would be an administrative matter – nor to judge particular individuals in relation to specifications of the law – this would be a judicial matter (V-NR/Feyerabend 27: 1384). Contemporary legal theory also, of course, considers some judicial decisions to be law making by judges. The second way in which Kant could mean that a single broad legislative authority can be divided into more narrow legislative authorities given to distinct persons is that the united people have ultimate sovereignty at all times but that such sovereignty can be actualized in different, mixed ways. When he says that state constitutions cannot be mixed, he would mean that an indivisible ultimate legislative power must reside in the people as a whole. The particular mixed form of government would be representing the ultimate unified sovereign. In *Naturrecht Feyerabend*, Kant does talk about the people being sovereign at all times (V-NR/Feyerabend 27: 1382). Since this issue concerns the second major topic about sovereignty and representation I will discuss it in detail below.

In *Naturrecht Feyerabend*, Kant does allow for legislative power to be divided between a king and an assembly as in England. In the *Doctrine of Right* there is no discussion of any divided actual legislative authority, and as noted the argument from undivided sovereignty rests upon this claim. So this is one point where Kant apparently changed his mind, perhaps in response to the French Revolution as a way to try to justify its legitimacy.

The second set of assumptions concern the people being default sovereign. Unlike the first assumptions about transferring sovereignty, this second set is covered directly in *Naturrecht Feyerabend* and Kant offers extensive discussions of these issues.

2a. *The set of actual individuals electing a legislature is the same as the united will of the people as a whole.*

There is no doubt that in *Naturrecht Feyerabend* Kant holds that the people are ultimately sovereign. He argues that the whole people is the only possible rightful legislator in his initial section on Public Right in the lecture. The idea of the original contract is that the law is agreed to by those subject to the law. The supreme legislator must be one who can do no wrong. If human beings unite with each other for this universal agreement they can do no wrong, for the agreement of each subject to the law they must obey is possible only in this situation. He concludes that the people are thus the sovereign legislator (V-NR/Feyerabend 27: 1382). This argument places the supreme sovereign power in the people as legislator because only a law that could arise from the agreement of all accords with the original contract. There is thus real sovereign authority in the people.

But Kant insists that this is only an idea and that actual consent by actual people is not required. "Now it is not in question whether human beings have ever come together for this aim and have made their laws this way. Laws given by a despot could be just if they are made so that they could have been made by the whole people" (V-NR/Feyerabend 27: 1382). Kant provides the test case of a law that places a tax on only some of the people. Such a law cannot possibly be just. "It is not necessary that he judges whether the people in this case would have made such a law but whether they could have made such a law" (V-NR/Feyerabend 27: 1382). *Naturrecht Feyerabend* implies that actual consent of the actual people is irrelevant when determining whether a law is just. I think that the touchstone is thus whether a whole people choosing in their rational self-interest under ideal knowledge conditions would have made the law. Clearly actual choices by voters are not always in their rational self-interest and often made in ignorance of the situation. This separation, however, implies a difference between the set of actual people in a society and the abstract set of the whole people, between the actual sovereign has that actual legislative power as representative of the people and the people themselves: "The *summus imperans* [supreme sovereign] is always the people, the individual person who is *summus imperans* is only *repraesentant* of the people" (V-NR/Feyerabend 27: 1382).

And this relation of actual person as representative of the whole people who hold supreme sovereignty holds not only in the stated case of the despot but also in the case of the other possible forms of government. After a discussion in which Kant concludes that only the actual sovereign, not the people, can judge in any disputes between them, Kant continues his argument about representation:

> Genuine *souveraineté* rests in the people. But the government or the exercising of legislative power can be either in the people, and then the state is a *democratie*, or it is in a single person, and then it is *monarchie* and the ruler *monarcha*, or it is in a *collegium* [council], and then it is *aristocratie*. Even here there is no difference in legislative power but only in the governing authority. (V-NR/Feyerabend 27: 1383)

Kant implies that the legislative power is the same whether it is exercised by a single person, a group, or all the individual people. But the exercising or actualization of legislative power, the type of government, can be different. (This claim lies behind the point noted above that that there can be mixed governments, but no mixed constitutions [V-NR/Feyerabend 27: 1389].) This ultimate legislative power cannot, then, be dependent on the individual or set of individuals actually holding that power. The only thing that all have in common is that they are to legislate on behalf of the people as a whole. Thus the legislative power he refers to must be the supreme sovereign authority of the people as a whole exercised by three different types of representatives. This is confirmed when a few sentences later Kant says that democracy must always be representative: "If the people represent themselves then the government is democratic. This is the basis of the idea of the supreme will. Even in *democratie* itself there must be a few who represent the people" (V-NR/Feyerabend 27: 1383).

So Kant does have the distinction between an actual sovereign as representative and a real sovereignty in the people. In the *Doctrine of Right* he argued that these two coincide. I have shown that in *Naturrecht Feyerabend* Kant distinguishes them in general. But Kant hints that it would be possible for the whole people to be actually present when he asks whether a people (Kant switches between *ein Volk* and *das Volk*) can determine whether the ruler has placed their lives in danger to the extent that they could justify using force against him. In his answer to this question Kant insists on his claim that none of the people can validly make this judgment. But he adds an interesting caveat that allows the possibility that the people could in some circumstances make that judgment: "The people must first be the supreme judge and have supreme power, which is however not the case. *It cannot be impossible that a people ought to be allowed that through a law*. For if that is not so then indeed all of humanity is in danger" (V-NR/Feyerabend 27: 1391; my emphasis). This admission that the people could have actual supreme power to make that supreme judgment about an existing governing legislative authority through a law implies that he would allow for some circumstance in which the actual people, as a whole people, can make a judgment about the use of sovereign power by a ruler. Nevertheless, as he continues, Kant appears to relate this possibility to a case of necessity in which no law could possibly prevent persons from acting to save their own lives. "It is clearly a necessity and a duty for the subjects to maintain themselves. No law against that is possible for this would contradict itself since the subjects would be threatened with death" (V-NR/Feyerabend 27: 1392). It is possible, then, that Kant did not have in mind a way in which the people as real sovereign could be present in a way that enabled them as a whole to judge the actual sovereign.

I conclude that in *Naturrecht Feyerabend* Kant does not equate the whole people holding ultimate sovereignty with the set of actual people. The whole people cannot err, but the set of actual people can. The whole people require actual representation even in the case of democracy. Kant's assumption, presented in the *Doctrine of Right*, that when the king called the Estates General into session, the whole people were then not merely represented, but were actually present, cannot be justified by the arguments and positions Kant expressed in his course.

2b. *The default representative of the whole united people is the people as set of actual individuals.*

If the whole people and the set of actual people are not the same in *Naturrecht Feyerabend*, there is still a possible position that the actual people are the default representatives of the whole people. They would take precedence over the other types of representation through a monarch or an aristocracy. In this case if the king called together an assembly of the actual people, and there was then some open question regarding which of the two held actual power, the actual people could assume sovereign power as the default.

Naturrecht Feyerabend does not support this position. As noted already in the assessment of the idea of the social contract, there are some instances in which the actual people might make an actual choice that the whole people, acting rationally, would not make. He goes on to make a pragmatic point about efficiency by suggesting that because of corruption, a mixed type of government appears to be best (V-NR/Feyerabend 27: 1383). Kant also notes that "a people will never be in unanimity," implying that the actual people cannot ever be the same as the whole people whose unanimous consent is required (V-NR/Feyerabend 27: 1392).

Those considerations could be understood as contingent empirical claims. There is a stronger non-empirical basis for a claim that the actual people are not the default sovereign. Kant's stress on representation leads him to conclude that rule by the actual people (democracy) is not any better than rule by one or by a few since all can equally represent the people.

> Types of government are in their basis one and the same. The government is always good where laws are given that the whole people could have given. One type of government is as legitimate as the other. (V-NR/Feyerabend 27: 1383)

He also mentions that mixed types of government are good and provides England as an example (V-NR/Feyerabend 27: 1389).

The *Naturrecht Feyerabend* lecture course, then, does *not* support the claim that the actual people would be the default sovereign authority as the best representatives of the whole united people.

Overall, then, it is clear that Kant's argument in support of the transfer of sovereign legislative power in the French Revolution could not have been made based on the material in *Naturrecht Feyerabend*. Scattered remarks support a claim that Kant did not think that a king could change the constitutional structure of the government unilaterally. He also held that actual legislative authority could be divided, meaning that the king could have transferred only a part of the legislative authority and withheld the rest. Kant did not equate the united people with the actual people, and he allowed that the actual people were no better or worse than a single or aristocratic legislative power at representing the united people. The actual events of 1789 in France appear to have caused Kant to alter his views on these matters in reaction to, and perhaps in order to justify, the French Revolution.

3

There is still one possibility that could prevent this conclusion, namely that Kant developed this position between the time of the *Naturrecht Feyerabend* lecture in summer 1784 and the events in France in summer 1789. In this case the positions would represent the natural development of his thought rather than an ex post facto revision of his position to fit the events in France that he supported.

The only evidence we have for this possibility is in Kant's Reflections. Kant offered his course on *Naturrecht* twice during this time period, in 1786 and 1788. His copy of Achenwall includes pages of Reflections that Adickes dated between 1785 and 1789 that were likely written for the *Naturrecht* course. Among them are several that make points supporting the assumptions I identified in his argument in the *Doctrine of Right*. The most interesting example is Refl 8048[16]:

> Finally the question arises whether, if a *souverän* calls together the whole nation and it is completely represented, he nonetheless retains the rights of a sovereign during this time? He was not more than a placeholder, a steward, with whom the people did not make a contract, but instead one to whom they have merely transferred their right to act as their representative. As long as he does this, he can hinder any movement in the people through which they are planning to constitute themselves as such. But if even once he calls them together and constitutes them as such, then not only is his authority suspended, but it can also be broken off entirely, like the standing of every representative when the one who gave him that power is himself present. (HN 19: 593)

The similarity to Kant's argument in the *Doctrine of Right* is striking. More revealing, however, is the similarity to Refl 8055, assessed in detail earlier in this paper,

---

[16] The other Reflections are Refl 7991, Refl 8018, which Adickes dated 1788–1795, and Refl 8049.

because Refl 8055 is dated after the events in France with certainty since it mentions the National Assembly in France.

I think that it is reasonable to assume that the Reflections that make points such as these stem from the post-revolutionary period, likely in 1789 itself. Their similarity to the actual events in 1789, particularly the way they are described in Refl 8055 and the *Doctrine of Right* that we know are post-revolutionary, makes it unlikely that they were written beforehand.

These notes are all written in Kant's copy of Achenwall as if in preparation for a course. Since no student notes, if there ever were any, of Kant's *Naturrecht* lectures from 1786 and 1788 have survived, we can neither confirm nor deny that Kant wrote and used these Reflections for his courses prior to 1789. There is a further possibility. In late summer 1789, Albertina University's announced course offerings for winter semester 1789/90 included this: "Jus naturae ad Achenwallium h. VIII Prof. Kant" – a reference to Kant's lecture course on *Naturrecht* using Achenwall.[17] There is no evidence that Kant actually taught this course that semester, although there is also no direct evidence that he did not, so it is possible that Kant wrote these notes either in preparation for or during an offering of his course on *Naturrecht* in the immediate wake of the French Revolution.[18] If he did, it is a great loss that no student lecture notes from it exists since it might reveal Kant's earliest public arguments about the French Revolution. This intriguing possibility shows the importance of Kant as lecturer because of the way in which his recurring lectures can change from year to year as Kant works out his thoughts. Unfortunately, the lack of more than one surviving lecture notes in the case of *Naturrecht* does not allow such comparisons among lectures, although of course still allowing comparisons of the lecture to the published material, as seen here. We can value the lectures we do have from Kant while mourning the loss of the ones we do not.[19]

---

[17] Quoted from Arnoldt 1909: 313. Arnoldt himself is skeptical that this announcement is accurate, suspecting that Kant's name was mistakenly used instead of Kraus's. Arnoldt himself notes on the same page, however, that the draft for this catalogue also mentions Kant. Later reports about the actual offerings that semester are missing. I discuss this issue in note 8 as well. I owe this reference as well as much general information about Kant's lecturing activity to Steve Naragon's incomparable, exhaustive website on Kant's lecturing activity (Naragon 2015a).

[18] Both Refl 8055 and Refl 8078 discussed in note 8 might also have been Kant's notes for his lecture course on *Naturrecht* rather than drafts for the *Doctrine of Right*.

[19] I would like to thank Alessandro Pinzani for helpful discussion of these topics, Ken Westphal for useful suggestions, and above all the students in my graduate seminar at Michigan State University Spring 2014 who worked through this material in detail and provided many insightful suggestions, particularly Jennifer Carmichael, John Dombrowski, Eian Kantor, Zachary Piso, Ezgi Sertler, and Aiden Sprague-Rice.

Chapter 15
"Without hope and fear": Kant's *Naturrecht Feyerabend* on Bindingness and Obligation[1]

Günter Zöller

> *Nulla enim vitae pars neque publicis neque privatis ... vacare officio potest ....*[2]

The recent renewal of interest in Kant's lecture activities, as they are recorded in the student transcripts (*Vorlesungsnachschriften*) of the university courses on a whole range of academic subject matters given by Kant over several decades, has added a substantial body of work to the Kantian corpus. In his lectures, Kant expounds the topic at hand by recourse to authorized manuals, occasionally adding a critical perspective on the material to be presented, based on his own views, as they take shape and develop further over the course of his career as an academic teacher. The philosophical interest that resides in Kant the lecturer chiefly consists in the further evidence the lectures provide for the extended emergence of Kant's original and novel views out of the critical reception of received positions and established doctrines. Typically then, analyzing and assessing Kant's lectures will involve both a close consideration of the doctrinal traditions and traditional doctrines involved in the lectures' subject matter and a consideration of Kant's own pertinent philosophical views, as documented in his contemporaneous works, above all the published works, but also the handwritten remains (*Nachlaß*) and correspondence.

The following addition to the ongoing exploration of Kant's lectures seeks to place Kant's Lectures on Natural Law (*Naturrecht*), viz., the lecture transcript *Naturrecht Feyerabend* from the summer semester 1784, into the wider, historical and systematic context of his Critical moral philosophy. The subject of investigation is the conceptual history and the systematic function of two key concepts – bindingness (*Verbindlichkeit*) and obligation (*Verpflichtung*) – from Roman law through early modern natural law to Kant's mature moral philosophy. Through-

---

1 "Without hope and fear" comes from V-NR/Feyerabend 27.2,2: 1331.06: *ohne Hofnung und Furcht*.
2 Cicero 1999: 6 f. (I, 2: "For no part of life, neither in the public nor in the private sphere ... can do without obligation.") English translation by Günter Zöller.

out, the focus is on the relation between law and ethics as featured in the tradition of natural law and its critical continuation in Kant. The particular purpose pursued by the recourse to Kant's Lectures on Natural Law is the comparison of the conception of bindingness found in *Naturrecht Feyerabend* with that of obligation located in the roughly contemporaneous *Groundwork of the Metaphysics of Morals* (1785).

1 Law and morals, ethics and politics

Like other basic concepts of modern moral philosophy, the concept of 'bindingness' (*Verbindlichkeit*), together with its semantic successor 'obligation' (*Verpflichtung*), is derived from the sphere of law, originally from Roman law, in which it occurs as *obligatio*. Its more recent usage can be traced to early modern natural law (*ius naturale, ius naturae*). There are both historical and systematic reasons for the transfer of the concept of bindingness (along with that of obligation) from the sphere of law and politics into that of ethics and morality.

In the beginning there was Plato's approximation of the two spheres in the *Politeia*, a work that in the scholarly tradition had received the descriptive title "On Justice" (*de iustitia*). The modern German translation of the work's title as *Staat* (state) misses the focus of Plato's politico-philosophical *chef d'œuvre* on the lawful constitution of the commonwealth. Other European languages, but also the older German translation tradition that still informs Kant's and Hegel's linguistic practices, render Plato's title more adequately by resorting to the Roman conception of the commonwealth, *res publica*.[3] The dialogic dramatics of the *Politeia* presents it as a prudent device to elucidate the elusive essence of justice in individual, ethical acting by means of the structurally analogous but factually more accessible parallel case of socio-political acting.[4] The pursued psycho-political transfer is justified by appeal to the supposed original identity of the two application spheres of justice, which are said to be based on an identical normative notion ("Form"; *eidos, idea*).

For all his criticism of Plato's theory of Forms, Aristotle continues the twofold understanding of ethics and politics as distinct but also related. For one, he treats ethics and politics in different bodies of work – in the *Eudemian Ethics, Magna Moralia* and *Nicomachean Ethics*, on the one hand, and in the *Politics*, on the

---

[3] For a republican reading of Plato's *Politeia* in the context of classical German political philosophy, see Zöller 2015a.
[4] On the psycho-political analogy in Plato's *Politeia* and its counterpart in Kant, see Zöller 2010.

other hand. But Aristotle also has ethics go over into the politics and regards ethics as an integral part of a comprehensively conceived, complexly structured science of "things political" (*ta politika*).

The earlier intertwined treatment of ethics and politics finds its modified continuation in the theologico-philosophical tradition of natural law, which subordinates positive (juridical) laws to a constant kernel of law that is supposed to be based, in theological terms, on God and, in philosophical terms, on nature or reason. The praeter-positive formation of law has a twofold character, in part juridical, in part ethical. It comprises the God-given or the naturally or rationally based rightful order and includes an ethically binding norm for action for prince and people alike.

It is only with the structural ethico-religious pluralism that results from the West European schismatic movements at the beginning of the modern period that an increasing dissociation of law and morals and hence also of ethics and politics occurs. Still Continental European law in the early modern period continues to be based on natural law and is, to that extent, morally based and ethically dimensioned, and this even where – as in Grotius – natural law is regarded as systematically independent of theology and supposed to be valid even under the counterfactual condition of God's non-existence (*etsi Deus non daretur*). The radical dissociation of law and morals as well as that of politics and ethics is still limited to exceptions, among them Machiavelli's dispensation of the prince from the common moral law and Hobbes's separation of the absolute monarch from political subjection.

It is only with the explicit de-theologization of philosophical thinking about law and politics and about ethics and morals in the eighteenth century that the two spheres, previously distinct but still connected, are separated on principle grounds. Montesquieu replaces the singular source of socio-political norms with the conception of the specifically different character ("spirit"; *esprit*) that rules and regulations ("laws") are said to possess, depending on the culturally and religiously determined communal circumstances, which in turn are considered subject to historical change. Rousseau further reduces what is transhistorical about human beings to a minimal measure of willfulness and freedom that is supposed to be respected by law and politics in accordance with an ideal, outright fictional social contract between beings endowed with will that are equally free. In the process, the former preliminary morals turns into a twofold societal product: the institution of political right (*droit politique*) and the juridico-politically protected and propagated project of the self-moralization of the free citizens.

The independence of law from ethics reaches its full systematic articulation with Kant's mature moral philosophy. In his late *Metaphysics of Morals* (1797), Kant distinguishes the legislation of juridical law, which is always external and based on (external) constraint (*Zwang*) and (physical) force (*Gewalt*), from that of ethics, which is essentially internal and based on conscience and conviction. Yet despite the strict separation of the modes of validation involved in law and ethics – legality (*Legalität*) and morality (*Moralität*), respectively – Kant retains the notion of the original connectedness of juridical law and ethical law. In the *Metaphysics of Morals*, he even transfers the unconditionally commanding character of the principle of morality to the pure doctrine of juridical law or right (*reine Rechtslehre*) by introducing the categorical imperative into public law, especially into criminal justice, and by establishing a categorical imperative to juridico-political progress.[5] Moreover, Kant includes the observance of juridical laws under the ethical duties. [6] To be sure, the moral motivation to observe juridical laws remains outside the sphere of legal requirements and is restricted to a further, specifically ethical, sanction of such laws.

While the early modern critics and reformers of natural law increasingly take back the ancient and medieval moralization of juridical law, Kant goes beyond such strict separation by performing a move that is the very opposite of the former moralization of natural law. In Kant there is to be found an outright juridification of ethics, by means of which concepts and categories that are properly and originally grounded in the sphere of juridical law (or legal right) are carried over into ethics, and especially into the latter's foundation. The point of Kant's articulation of ethical conceptions in juridical terms is not to turn ethics into juridical law, as though the external, constraint-based character of juridical law were to be carried over into ethical matters. Rather than involving doctrinal content, the juridico-ethical transfer undertaken by Kant is concerned with and limited to basic methodological concepts that are imported, *mutatis mutandis*, from *ius* into ethics.

The beginnings of this late-modern development effectuated by Kant, which inverts the earlier, classical transfer from the ethico-moral into the juridico-political to that of the juridical, or rather quasi-juridical, formation of the ethical, can be traced back to Rousseau's juridico-political conception of the general will. By considering the will in political terms – as a kind of willing that does not occur naturally but is due to an artificial consideration of interest, especially interest of a general kind involved in matters that exceed particular preferences and personal predilections – a conception of willing comes into view that seems suitable for and suggestive of being transferred from juridico-political willing to ethical willing and to being applied to the latter's differentiation into the merely selfish and the socially responsible formation of the will.

---

5 See MS 6: 318, 331, 336, 371.
6 See MS 6: 218–21.

The normative linkage of juridico-political laws to a suitably qualified legislation leads to the idea of an analogous understanding of ethico-moral norms as resulting from a suitably qualified genesis, along with the validity so engendered, on the basis of procedural rules. Most importantly, though, the essentially political idea – more precisely, the republican conception – according to which the citizens of a state ought to be subject only to those laws that they could have given themselves and hence to each other, leads to an analogous conception of autonomy qua ethical self-legislation.

It is Kant who draws the ethico-moral consequences from Rousseau's political philosophy of free-willing and rationally informed self-legislation. Kant does so first under the guise of laying the foundation for a future "metaphysics of morals" (*Groundwork of the Metaphysics of Morals*, 1785), then later in the parallel execution of the sum-total of non-empirical principles ("metaphysical first principles"; *metaphysische Anfangsgründe*) of law and ethics in the *Metaphysics of Morals* (1797). In the process, the import of juridical notions into ethics, undertaken by the Critical Kant under inspiration from Rousseau, carries on the Platonic program of the psycho-political analogy between self and state, in which normatively charged political thinking informs and structures the unconditional ethical norms. In Plato, the *intrasubjective* conditions in the ethical sphere, given how hard as they are to ascertain on their own, receive elucidation through their transposition into the *intersubjective* domain of law and politics, with its characteristically larger scale and enhanced intelligibility. Kant in turn transposes originally juridical and political concepts – above all those of the formation of the will (*Willensbestimmung*), of law-giving or legislation (*Gesetzgebung*) and of self-legislation of autonomy (*Selbstgesetzgebung, Autonomie*) – from the sphere of law and politics into that of ethics.

The juridico-ethical transfer of basic practical concepts undertaken by Kant on the basis of the general analogy between (juridical) law and ethics also includes the conception of freedom, so fundamental for Kant's entire practical philosophy, and involves a specifically juridical formation of this ethical category. More specifically, the joining of freedom in its radical understanding as absolute spontaneity to (moral) autonomy takes up the political, specifically republican conjunction of (civic) freedom and (political) self-legislation, according to which freedom does not consist in arbitrary choice but in living under one's own, self-given laws (Machiavelli's *vivere libero*).

To be sure, in the transposition from the juridico-political sphere to the ethico-moral sphere, Kant adapts the originally civic conception of freedom as self-legislation to the different kind of autonomy involved in ethics. Rather than being an externally prescribed self-given law, the law in question – the moral law (*Sittengesetz*) – is an internally issued law. The actual inclusion of all members of a given civic community envisioned in the juridico-political conception of freedom is replaced by the counterfactual extension of a subjective principle of willing and acting (maxim) to all other finite rational beings. Still Kant's mature moral philosophy (practical philosophy) retains the juridico-political idea of the origin of law in self-legislation and retains the normative contrast between a practical, freedom-based legislation through human reason itself and a naturally or supernaturally given lawful order of cosmic or divine origin.

Like jural autonomy as political program of civil self-legislation, moral autonomy – more precisely, ethical autonomy – in Kant is a normative conception, the theoretically possible and practically necessary realization of which presupposes, and therefore requires, the rationally restrained use of freedom. The civic status of being one's own master has its ethical counterpart in the free self-governance of the citizen of an ethical commonwealth ("autocracy").[7] In this regard, too, Kant's thinking stands in the republican ethico-political tradition of self-governance through self-mastery.

2 Shackle or ligament?

One of the basic practical concepts with a juridical origin and an ethical effect is that of bindingness, derived from the Latin *obligatio*. In current German the corresponding term, *Verbindlichkeit*, has an ancient appeal – especially when it is employed for the general, not specifically ethical, designation of a social conduct thereby marked as polite and reliable, in other words, as obliging. The German term *Verbindlichkeit* is still more customary in finance, where it designates a monetary obligation, sometimes even called in German *Obligation*. In the ethical sphere the term by now has been almost completely replaced by the term *Verpflichtung*, customarily translated into English as "obligation." Already Zedler's early eighteenth-century *Universal Lexicon* refers, for the lemma *Verbindlichkeit*, to the entries under *Verpflichtung*.[8] This terminological change in turn is derived from the corresponding shift in Latin, from *obligatio* (obligation) to *officium* (duty). For purposes of terminological differentiation and in view of the different etymologies involved, it is indicated to render the German term *Verbindlichkeit* as "bindingness," and to retain the English "obligation" for the German term *Verpflichtung*.

---

[7] On "autocracy of practical reason," see MS 6: 383. See also Zöller 2010.
[8] Zedler 1732–54, vol. 47: 167.

The specifically juridical concept of bindingness that underlies the latter's later transformation and further extension outside the juridical sphere and into the ethical sphere goes back to Roman law. Like other concepts from the Roman practice and doctrine of law, that of bindingness (*obligatio*) received its codification in late imperial East Rome (Byzantium) and on that basis became decisive for the development of Continental European civil law (*ius civile*).[9] But the Roman legal concept of *obligatio*, eventually rendered in German as *Verbindlichkeit*, is not just one Roman-law concept among others. Rather *obligatio* can be considered a basic concept of Roman legal doctrine and accordingly also as a fundamental category in post-Roman civil law. The Roman jurists employed the term for the general designation of the lawful force and efficacy of a contractual relation. From there stems the continued central significance of *obligatio* or bindingness in civil law, especially in contract law.

As with most concepts of Roman law, the *locus classicus* for the formal fixation and the fundamental function of the Roman jural concept of *obligatio* is the compilation of Roman legal practice and thinking (the later so-called *Corpus Iuris Civilis*) undertaken at the instruction of the East Roman Emperor Justinian in the sixth century C. E. Since its rediscovery in the eleventh century, originating in the faculty of law of the University of Bologna, the *Corpus Iuris Civilis* has shaped the development of legal theory and practice, first in Continental Europe, then later in South America and other legal cultures worldwide. The pertinent passage on *obligatio* reads in the Latin original as follows: *Obligatio est iuris vinculum, quo necessitate adstringimur alicuius rei solvendae secundum iura nostrae civitatis.*[10]

The core of the Justinian definition of *obligatio* is the latter's binding force by means of which legally regulated contractual relations may be realized by forceful means. The definition's marking of *obligatio* as *iuris vinculum* is not merely metaphorical discourse, but brings out the binding character of *obligatio*. The traditional translation of the formula *iuris vinculum* as "law's shackle" (in German, *Fessel des Rechts*), with its connotation of servility and submission, does not adequately capture the metaphorically articulated binding function of *obligatio*. In Roman legal thinking, *obligatio* not only designates what is due, and enforceably so, on the part of the debtor (*debitor*) with regard to the creditor (*creditor*). Rather *obligatio* also, and equally, encompasses the binding force of a contractual relation on the part of the creditor to whom something is owed and who is

---

9 See Schiavone 2005 and 2012.
10 "Obligation is the legal ligature through which we are constrained to render a matter in accordance with the laws of our civil society." (Translation by Günter Zöller). See Justinian's *Institutes*, Book 3, Title 13 (Justinian 1913).

entitled to seek what is so due and to have it rendered by legal means, including legally sanctioned force. Put in modern terms, *obligatio* includes both debtors' obligations and creditors' entitlements, in short: duties and rights. Accordingly, the juridical gist of *obligatio*, its basic function as legal ligature, lies precisely in the binding together of rights and duties, in the tying of duties to rights and in the bonding between the members of a lawfully constituted society (*civitas*) to each other and among each other.

Rather than viewing *obligatio* as a restricting, outright subduing and so to speak enslaving form of constraint, obligation should be regarded as the very mortar that holds civil society together. Like mortar or concrete – the latter incidentally another Roman invention – *obligatio* was designed for and disposed to link together in a fast and lasting manner what previously was different and distinct from each other. Accordingly, in a lawfully constituted society, *obligatio* is as much restricting as it is enabling, and this in an intrinsically connected way: as enabling, it is at once restricting, and as restricting, it is at once enabling. In sum, *obligatio* serves as the basic formative condition for civico-legal relations as such.

Generally speaking, the *iuris vinculum*, when understood as a legal linkage rather than a shackle, stands in a tradition of a philosophical mereology that does not bring together a given manifold externally, additively and belatedly, but maintains the inner, original unity among the manifold, and moreover the unity of the unity and the manifold. At the beginning of those efforts at ascertaining the manifold one and the united manifold stands Plato's concept of the link or tie (*desmon*), first in the *Theaitetos*, then in the *Timaios*.[11] In Leibniz, the concept reappears as the substantial link (*vinculum substantiale*) that comprehends multiple phenomena in a substantial unity.[12] Finally, Kant takes recourse to the old mereology of the linkage or tie when in the first Introduction to the third *Critique* he uses the term "unitary formation" (*Verband*) to designate the systematic unity of the three faculties of reason (understanding, judgment, and reason in the narrow sense), which, while each standing under their own lawful regulation, are thus featured as different as much united – in a word, as bound together.[13]

But the metaphorical import of the Justinian formula of *obligatio* as *iuris vinculum* extends beyond the latter's role as the concrete that binds together civic life. With its verbal root *ligere*, the very term *obligatio* refers to a socially significant semantic field to which belongs, in the first instance, the Latin term *religio*, meaning religion in a socio-cultural sense. In the case of *religio* the civically

---

11 See Platon 1972, vol. 7: 40 f. (Tim. 31c2–32a7).
12 See Leibniz, G 2: 435 (Leibniz to Des Bosses, 5 February 1722).
13 See EEKU 20: 242 (*Verband ... des Verstandes und der Vernunft*).

binding character consists in the linkage established and maintained by religious practices, cults, and rituals between civico-socially constituted human beings and the gods or things divine. The interhuman connectedness conveyed by the jural notion of *obligatio* thus has its counterpart in the bindingness of human beings to divine beings and especially in them being tied back – this in fact being the original meaning of *religio* – to the gods.

The transfer of the Roman legal concept of *obligatio* into Continental European civil law brought with it multiple differentiations of the basic relationship of bindingness, dependent on the parties involved in the binding and the specific modalities of the linkage concerned. Thus early modern *ius civile* distinguished between explicit and implicit, between pure and conditioned, between primary and secondary, between absolute and alternative, between determinate and indeterminate, between divisible and indivisible, between simple and punishable as well as between communal and multiform bindingness. The concept entered modern civil law through its rationally simplified treatment in the *Code Napoléon* (1804).

But at this point the concept of *obligatio* already had been narrowed down to the area of contractual relations and undergone a development that ultimately led to its recent restriction to the contractual transfer of property and of the latter's monetary equivalent. In the late eighteenth century, the comprehensive meaning of *obligatio* as the civico-social binding agent, originally rendered in German by the term *Verbindlichkeit*, had been taken over by another, initially more narrow German term, *Verpflichtung*, derived from the German word for "duty" (*Pflicht*). In contrast with the primarily legal concept of *obligatio* (*Verbindlichkeit*), the German term *Verpflichtung* proved suitable for linking the juridical and the ethical spheres and for conveying a comprehensive and basic conception of obligation or duty encompassing (juridical) law as well as ethics.

An important intermediary step on the way from the civil law concept of *obligatio* qua bindingness (*Verbindlichkeit*) to *obligatio* qua obligation (*Verpflichtung*) as a basic concept of practical philosophy in general – of (juridical) law as well as ethics – was the transposition of the notion of contract from its origin in Roman civil law into the specifically modern sphere of public law (*ius publicum*; *öffentliches Recht*), especially state law and constitutional law.[14] In the process, the contract as juridically framed agreement between private persons became the social pact by means of which a community was thought to constitute itself as a political society (*societas civilis*) – or to regard itself as so constituted. In addition to the contractually regulated private civil rights and duties, there were now pub-

---

14 On the origin and development of *ius publicum*, see Loughlin 2010 and 2003.

licly civil entitlements and obligations that regulated the civico-social relations of the citizens among themselves and with regard to civil law's ultimate authority, the state in its emerging modern shape as sovereign territorial state.

At the center of *ius publicum* in its modern manifestation and development stands not the citizen as a particular, privately interested person, but the citizen of the commonwealth (*res publica*) with a supposed general interest in what concern the citizens communally, viz., the common good or the common wealth (*bonum publicum*). The division entailed by this dual character of the citizen – a division between the private and the public and, by extension, between the personally particular and the publically general – provided a juridico-political model for a corresponding, analogously shaped differentiation in the ethical sphere, viz., between the pursuit of merely personal preferences and the purposive concern and regard for the good of all those that stand in ethical community with each other. It was Kant who undertook the twofold and linked conceptual transition from specifically juridical bindingness (*Verbindlichkeit*) to generic moral obligation (*Verpflichtung*) and from the general validity of public law for all human beings in a political community to the universal validity of ethics for all finite rational beings.

3 *Nec spe nec metu*[15]

The structural parallelism between (juridical) law and ethics and the functional assimilation of ethics to (juridical) law carried out under the related conceptions of bindingness and obligation (*Verbindlichkeit, Verpflichtung*), to be found in Kant's mature moral philosophy, is the result of an extended formative process spanning several decades of philosophical development. Kant's elaborate two-part practical philosophy, comprising a philosophy of law and an ethics ("doctrine of virtue") is published only in the late 1790s, well after the Critical trilogy and close to the end of his philosophical career. The works bears the title *Metaphysics of Morals*, indicating at once the exclusive focus of Kant's pure practical philosophy on non-empirical laws ("metaphysical first principles") and the extensional identification of a philosophy based on the principle of freedom ("practical philosophy") with moral philosophy.[16] The work's original complete

---

[15] "Neither from hope nor from fear." Motto of Isabelle d'Este, Duchess of Mantua, for which a neo-Platonic background is to be assumed, according to which the wise think and act independently of the ordinary incentives or disincentives of hope and fear.
[16] See MS 6: 216–18.

title even indicated its dual systematic structure, announcing "The Metaphysics of Morals in Two Parts" (*Die Metaphysik der Sitten in zwei Teilen*).[17]

But in Kant the position, function, and structure of ethics in relation to (juridical) law and the jural background for the formation of basic ethical concepts and principles is already addressed, well in advance of the late published pure practical philosophy, in the context of his emerging Critical moral philosophy in the early 1780s. A particularly instructive document for the parallel treatment of law and ethics from that period is provided by the preserved lecture transcript of Kant's lecture course on natural law from the summer semester 1784, the so-called *Naturrecht Feyerabend*, named after the author-owner of the transcript. The text of the *Naturrecht Feyerabend* has been available since 1979 in the Academy Edition of Kant's *Collected Writings*, as an appendix in Division (*Abteilung*) IV in the series of Kant's lecture courses (in student transcription) containing the lectures in moral philosophy.[18] Unfortunately, the editor's transcription of the lecture transcript proved somewhat deficient, not unlike other work by the same editor in that Division of the Academy Edition. But a new transcription is being published in the context of the editorial project of preparing comprehensive indices to Kant's lecture transcripts. The volume containing the new transcription of the lengthy and weighty introductory part (*Einleitung*)[19] of the *Naturrecht Feyerbend* is already available.

Kant's *Naturrecht Feyerabend* is of particular interest, and this not only due to the fact that it is the only preserved transcript of Kant's lecture course on natural law, which he offered no less than twelve times between 1767 and 1788. The text is also significant in view of its chronological and philosophical coincidence with the publication of Kant's first foundational writing in Critical moral philosophy, the *Groundwork of the Metaphysics of Morals* of 1785.[20] Unlike the printed text from the following year, which – in spite of the general orientation toward a comprehensive "metaphysics of morals" announced in its title – deals throughout with morality (*Moralität*) rather than legality (*Legalität*), with the moral law (*Sittengesetz*) rather than the law of right (*Rechtsgesetz*), and with motivation rather than action, the quasi-contemporaneous *Naturrecht Feyerabend* addresses, in its introductory section, the methodological and systematic grounding principles of

---

17 See MS 6: 518.
18 V-NR/Feyerabend is found at AA 27.2,2: 1317–94.
19 V-NR/Feyerabend 27.2,2: 1319–38. See Delfosse et al. 2010: 1–15 (text) and 23–9 (explanations and parallel passages).
20 See Hirsch 2012 for an alternatively oriented comparison of the *Naturrecht Feyerabend*, not with the contemporaneous *Groundwork of the Metaphysics of Morals*, but with the late *Metaphysics of Morals*.

law and ethics.²¹ The external occasion for the inclusion of ethical concepts and doctrines into the treatment of the philosophy of right is the basic moral character of traditional modern natural law and the customary extensive involvement of moral and ethical considerations in the development and deployment of basic legal concepts and doctrines in the praeter-positive foundation of juridical law.

To be sure, in the *Naturrecht Feyerabend* Kant sets out to critique the traditional assimilation of right to morals undertaken by natural law, especially in its theological form as a God-given law for human conduct. Rather than basing natural law on a preliminary moral or ethical doctrine, the *Naturrecht Feyerabend* undertakes treating ethics and (juridical) law strictly separately, by building each on its own principal grounds.²² Kant's criterion for the methodological and systematic differentiation between (juridical) law and ethics is the presence (or absence) of "constraint" (*Zwang*), in particular of externally exercised and legally justified coercion, which pertains to the juridical sphere while the ethical sphere eludes any such constraint.²³ According to Kant, juridical constraint is justified – practically possible and even necessary – insofar as it provides the means for the hindrance of any hindrance to (juridically guaranteed) freedom.²⁴

In the *Naturrecht Feyerabend*, the commonality between (juridical) law and ethics that still remains and will eventually be reflected by the generic title for both, "moral philosophy" (*Moralphilosophie*), is no longer to be traced to some ethico-theological origin of law. It is rather grounded in the generic nature of the human being as a free being whose will, in principle, is not determined by laws of nature – not even those of the own, inner nature of the human being.²⁵ In agreement with the contemporaneously published *Groundwork of the Metaphysics of Morals*, the *Naturrecht Feyerabend* ties the origin and the validity of practical laws to the radical freedom of human willing and to the status of human beings as ends in themselves ("inner worth," "dignity"; *innerer Wert, Würde*).²⁶ In complete agreement between the two texts, the basic character of human beings as ends in

---

21 On the relation between juridical law and ethics in the *Naturrecht Feyerabend*, see Zöller 2015b.
22 See V-NR/Feyerabend 27.2,2: 1327.
23 On a specifically ethical form of constraint in Kant's later material ethics ("mutually opposed self-constraint"; *wechselseitig entgegengesetzte[r] Selbstzwang*), see MS 6: 279n. See also Zöller 2010.
24 See V-NR/Feyerabend 27.2,2: 1328.
25 See V-NR/Feyerabend 27.2,2: 1322.
26 See V-NR/Feyerabend 27.2,2: 1319, 1321.

themselves functions as a limiting condition for the use of freedom by placing the latter under the condition of "general freedom" (*allgemeine Freiheit*).[27]

Yet while the *Groundwork* subjects the use of freedom to the "moral law" (*Sittengesetz*) in the latter's guise as the categorical imperative guiding and prescribing the moral qualification of the subjective principles of action (maxims), the *Naturrecht Feyerabend* determines the lawfulness of human actions in a generic and purely formal manner. According to the *Naturrecht Feyerabend*, the freedom of human action is subject to the generic form of "general lawfulness" (*allgemeine Gesetzmäßigkeit*) as such.[28] Moreover, the *Naturrecht Feyerabend* calls the specific, law-based acting instruction characteristic of human free acting ("imperative") quite generally an "imperative of wisdom" (*Imperativ der Weisheit*), contrasting the latter to the merely conditionally valid imperatives oriented toward and motivated by skillfulness and prudence, respectively.[29]

On the basis of the normativity of free acting under the law's form of generality, the *Naturrecht Feyerabend* further distinguishes between ethics and (juridical) law. The distinction is made in terms of the procedure involved in the regulation of the lawful use of freedom in the respective sphere. In the case of (juridical) law, this is "constraint" (*Zwang*), in the case of ethics, it is "bindingness" (*Verbindlichkeit*). In the *Naturrecht Feyerabend* Kant defines "bindingness" (*Verbindlichkeit*) as follows: "Bindingess is moral necessitation of an action, i. e., the dependence of a will that is [not] in itself good on the principle of autonomy, or on objectively necessary practical laws."[30]

Thus bindingness (*Verbindlichkeit*) is separated from juridically justified constraint and from any other external constraint, and identified with purely moral necessitation or "practical necessitation" (*praktische Neceßitation*),[31] which occurs merely by means of the representation or idea (*Vorstellung*) of the lawfulness as such involved. In the *Naturrecht Feyerabend*, Kant occasionally identifies bindingness as a purely formal and narrowly ethical necessitation with "respect"

---

27 See V-NR/Feyerabend 27.2,2: 1334 (with emphasis, in the original). The term "general" in the juridico-political locution "general freedom" employed by Kant indicates not strict, exceptionless generality (universality), but freedom's feature of being "common to all" (*allen gemein*) who are in political community with each other.
28 See V-NR/Feyerabend 27.2,2: 1326.
29 See V-NR/Feyerabend 27.2,2: 1323 f.
30 See V-NR/Feyerabend 27.2,2: 1326: *Verbindlichkeit ist moralische Neceßitation der Handlung, d: i: die Abhängigkeit eines* [nicht] *an sich guten Willens vom Princip der Autonomie, oder objectiv nothwendigen praktischen Gesetzen*. On the conjecturally inserted "not," see Defosse et al.: 12.
31 On the distinction between (objective) practical necessity (*Neceßitaet*) and (subjective) practical necessitation (*Neceßitatio*), see V-NR/Feyerabend 27.2,2: 1323.

(*Achtung*).³² By contrast, he uses the term "duty" (*Pflicht*) to designate the particular action to which an ethical agent is so bound. Accordingly, "duty" is subject to pluralization (*Pflichten*), whereas "bindingness" occurs in the singular. The corresponding term "obligation" (*Verpflichtung*) also occurs, with one exception, in the singular.³³

On Kant's understanding in the *Naturrecht Feyerabend*, bindingness as a specifically ethical, basic deontic modality is opposed to any kind of constraint, including the juridically justified, even required, constraint ("lawful constraint," "right to constrain"; *Zwangsrecht*). Moreover, Kant explicitly excludes, as incompatible with the conception of purely ethical bindingness, the latter's conditioning by means of divine or human promises of reward or threats of punishment, to be found in traditional natural law, including the latter's late version in Achenwall's manual,³⁴ to which Kant's lectures refer by way of summary and critical commentary. Kant states:

> But to oblige someone by means of punishments and rewards is a *contradictio in adjecto*; for in that case I move him to actions which he does not do out of bindingness but from fear and inclination.³⁵

Since ethical action is to occur from no other reason than bindingness (*Verbindlichkeit*) itself and as such, the *Naturrecht Feyerabend* also excludes – in addition to external constraint, including juridical constraint – internally motivating incentives and disincentives from the genuinely moral motivation of ethical conduct. In particular, Kant rules out, with a critical glance at the eudaimonistic reasoning in contemporary natural law, the psychic factors of hope (for reward) and fear (of punishment) from the normative force of ethics – morality, as opposed to legality – and from the specifically ethical modality of bindingness.³⁶

According to the *Naturrecht Feyerabend*, constraint (*Zwang*) and bindingness (*Verbindlichkeit*), each in its respective sphere – law and ethics – are the necessary as well as sufficient conditions for lawful acting and willing under the presupposition of freedom. (Juridical) law does not function without (external) constraint, but also is in need of nothing further than lawfully threatened or exercised

---

32 See V-NR/Feyerabend 27.2,2: 1326, 1330.
33 See V-NR/Feyerabend 27.2,2: 1326.
34 Achenwall and Pütter 1750.
35 See V-NR/Feyerabend 27.2,2: 1326: *Aber durch Poenas und Praemia einen verbinden ist contradictio in adjecto; denn da bewege ich ihn zu Handlungen, die er nicht aus Verbindlichkeit sondern aus Furcht und Neigung thut.*
36 See V-NR/Feyerabend 27.2,2: 1329.

constraint in order to be effective. By contrast, ethical acting rests entirely on acting from bindingness (*aus Verbindlichkeit*).[37] To be sure, objectively speaking, there is also a (moral) obligation (Latin *obligatio*) to what is commanded or prohibited juridically. But acting in accordance with juridical laws from (the motive of) bindingness (*aus Verbindlichkeit*), falls entirely within the sphere of ethics. (Juridical) law as such is not concerned with the reasons and ends for which an action ensues. Its sole concern is with the principal compatibility of the action in question with the freedom of all others involved and capable of free action.[38]

By assigning bindingness as a motivation for action exclusively to the sphere of ethics, Kant in the *Naturrecht Feyerabend* has turned the original, Roman-legal connection of *obligatio* with *jus* into its very opposite. But the *Naturrecht Feyerabend* also contains instances of a reverse procedure, viz., the formal and functional juridification of the sphere of ethics now considered doctrinally independent from (juridical) law. Moreover, the treatment of ethical matters in juridically informed terms and concepts to be found in the *Naturrecht Feyerabend* stands in marked contrast to the ethically cast grounding of morals in the *Groundwork of the Metaphysics of Morals* published the following year, with the morally good will as the systematic point of departure.[39] In contrast, in the *Naturrecht Feyerabend* ethics is introduced by way of the concept of equity (*aequitas*), an originally juridical conception, now applied to actions that are "internally right" (*innerlich recht*) and which therefore are removed from (possible) juridical constraint, given that the latter only concerns what is outwardly or externally right.[40] Most importantly, though, the *Naturrecht Feyerabend* subordinates (juridical) law as well as ethics to a generic conception of what is right (*recht*) – the latter taken as an adjective, corresponding to the Latin word *rectus* and encompassing everything that is in agreement with a given rule or law. Accordingly, (juridical) law and ethics represent the basic alternative forms for the formal lawfulness of free action.[41]

According to the *Naturrecht Feyerabend*, (juridical) law as well as ethics contains practical principles for a free will that are to assure the latter's lawful form. In the case of (juridical) law the sought, law-regulated agreement concerns the *intersubjective* relation of a free-willing rational being to the likes of it in a given civic society. In the case of ethics, the practical laws regulate the *intrasubjective* relation of thoroughgoing agreement of a free-willing rational being with itself:

---

37 See V-NR/Feyerabend 27.2,2: 1327.
38 See V-NR/Feyerabend 27.2,2: 1329.
39 See GMS 4: 393.
40 See V-NR/Feyerabend 27.2,2: 1328 f.
41 See V-NR/Feyerabend 27.2,2: 1328.

> The principles of the free will by way of thoroughgoing agreement according to rules are either with ourselves or with others. Principles of the external and internal use of freedom. To the former we can[not] be forced for they do not hinder the freedom of others.[42]

In the *Groundwork of the Metaphysics of Morals*, the categorical imperative, in its formulation involving the "realm of ends" (*Reich der Zwecke*), relates moral maxims to the (presumed) intersubjectivity of ethical action.[43] By contrast, the *Naturrecht Feyerabend* bases ethical duties on the lawful form of purely individual ethical willing. According to the *Naturrecht Feyerabend*, the systematic consideration of a plurality of freely willing beings in the sphere of law has its counterpart in ethics not in the possible sociality of the ethical formation of the will, but in the compatibility of plural determinations of the will within one and the same ethical subject. While juridical lawfulness is *intersubjectively* shaped, ethical lawfulness is *intrasubjectively* constituted.

According to the *Naturrecht Feyerabend*, then, the generic normativity of moral action involves the requirement of "general lawfulness" (*allgemeine Gesetzmäßigkeit*),[44] which divides into the unconditionally required, external social compatibility of outer action in the sphere of (juridical) law and the unconditionally required, psychic consistency of inner action (willing) in the sphere of ethics. In both basic cases, the possible generality of law concerning (outer or inner) action provides the criterion for the required normative qualification. If one considers the presumed generality of practical laws a defining feature of (juridical) law, then ethics is understood in the *Naturrecht Feyerabend* as a radically introverted and highly individualized modification of the civic-social relation involved in (juridical) law, freed of any (external) constraint and entirely transferred to the *forum internum*. Considered from this perspective, the original affinity of ethics to (juridical) law, based on their common concern with the general form of legislation, therefore amounts to a late, modern retake on the Platonic analogy of the soul and the state, which had configured the ethical domain as a differently dimensioned, but identically structured, parallel case to the politico-legal sphere.

---

42 See V-NR/Feyerabend 27.2,2: 1336: *Die Grundsätze des freyen Willens, durch durchgängige Einstimmung nach Gesetzen, sind entweder mit uns selbst oder andern. Grundsätze des äußeren Gebrauchs und inren Gebrauchs der Freiheit. Zu den erstern können wir* [nicht] *gezwungen werden, denn sie widerstehen nicht der Freiheit anderer*. On the conjecturally inserted negation, see Delfosse et al.: 12.
43 See, e.g., GMS 4: 433: "By a kingdom I understand a systematic union of various rational beings through common laws."
44 See V-NR/Feyerabend 27.2,2: 1326.

VIII Natural Theology

> Vorrede. xix
>
> die der Vernunft unbedenklich den Krieg ankündigt, wird es auf die Dauer gegen sie nicht aushalten. — Ich getraue mir sogar in Vorschlag zu bringen: ob es nicht wohlgethan seyn würde, nach Vollendung der academischen Unterweisung in der biblischen Theologie, jederzeit noch eine besondere Vorlesung über die reine philosophische Religionslehre, (die sich alles, auch die Bibel, zu Nutze macht), nach einem Leitfaden, wie etwa dieses Buch, (oder auch ein anderes, wenn man ein besseres von derselben Art haben kann), als zur vollständigen Ausrüstung des Candidaten erforderlich, zum Beschlusse hinzuzufügen. — Denn die Wissenschaften gewinnen lediglich durch die Absonderung, sofern jede vorerst für sich ein Ganzes ausmacht, und nur dann allererst mit ihnen der Versuch angestellt wird, sie in Vereinigung zu betrachten. Da mag nun der biblische Theolog mit dem Philosophen einig seyn, oder ihn widerlegen zu müssen glauben; wenn er ihn nur hört. Denn so kann er allein wider alle Schwierigkeiten, die ihm dieser machen dürfte, zum voraus bewaffnet seyn. Aber diese zu verheimlichen, auch wohl als ungöttlich zu verrufen, ist ein armseliger Behelf, der nicht Stich hält; beyde aber zu vermischen,
>
> b 2

Fig. 12: Kant's *Religion* as "einem Leitfaden." This photo-reproduction of page xix from the original 1793 publication of Kant's *Die Religion innerhalb der Grenzen der bloßen Vernunft* (AA 6: 10), courtesy of the Universitätsbibliothek at Eberhard Karls Universität Tübingen, features the portion of the first Preface where Kant envisions his book being used as a textbook for a new course on the philosophical study of religion. Between the two dashes, it reads: "I shall even venture a proposal, whether it would not be beneficial, upon completion of the academic instruction in biblical theology, always still to add – by way of conclusion, as required for the candidate to be fully equipped – a special course on pure *philosophical* doctrine of religion (which makes use of everything, even the Bible), in accordance with a [set of] guidelines like, say, this book (or for that matter, a different one, if a better one of the same kind is available)."

Chapter 16
Kant's Lectures on Philosophical Theology – Training-Ground for the Moral Pedagogy of *Religion*?

Stephen R. Palmquist

1 *Religion* as a textbook

Kant maintained a deep interest in theology and religion throughout his life, yet he lectured on philosophical theology only a few times – probably once in the summer semester of 1774 and three times in the mid-1780s: the winter semesters of 1783/84 and 1785/86, and the summer semester of 1787.[1] Perhaps partly for this reason, his decision to devote his publications, during the several years immediately following publication of the third *Critique* (1790), to a series of works relating more explicitly to religion has perplexed many commentators. He wrote an article on the religious experience of suffering (as an existential *anti*-theodicy – in opposition to theological attempts to justify God's goodness in the face of suffering) in 1791 and one on the nature and origin of evil in 1792; then, when the censor rejected the second of his planned series of four articles on the religious implications of the human struggle between good and evil, he hastily collated the four essays, publishing them as *Religion within the Bounds of Bare Reason*[2]

---

1 The only two complete sets of extant lecture notes date from the winter semester of 1783/84, when Kant used the Natural Theology section that concludes Baumgarten 1757 as his primary text, supplementing it with Eberhard 1781 and Meiners 1780. Both sets, together with fragments from three other sets of lecture notes, appear in AA 28; all date from the mid-1780s, overlapping significantly. I shall therefore refer only to the Pölitz notes, translated in The Cambridge Edition of the Works of Immanuel Kant.
2 I adopt the Cambridge Edition for English quotations from Kant's writings or lectures. The only exception is that I use my own, revised version of Pluhar (Kant 2009c) for quotations from *Die Religion innerhalb der Grenzen der bloßen Vernunft*; the complete text of my translation appears in Palmquist 2015b. Where the difference between this translation and the Cambridge Edition is substantive, I provide a brief explanation, beginning here: as I first argued in Palmquist 1992b, Kant's use of "*bloßen*" in *Religion* takes on a technical meaning, alluding to the clothing metaphor that governs the book's overall argument; whereas rational religion is "bare," historical religions "clothe" it with myths, symbols, and rituals whose purpose is to fill the gaps left by rational religion.

in 1793. Confirming that his central concern had shifted to religion during these years, he followed with a significantly revised edition of *Religion*, less than a year later, and an essay on religious eschatology in 1794. Although this turn to religion immediately following the completion of the third *Critique* provides evidence for the claim that the religious and/or theological implications of his philosophical system had been a paramount concern from the outset (see Palmquist 2000, chapter I), it raises the question of why Kant never lectured on the subject of the philosophy of *religion* as such, nor continued lecturing on philosophical *theology* in the 1790s.

Why would Kant turn his attention so explicitly to religious themes in the early 1790s, yet not continue to offer lectures on philosophical theology and/or religion concurrently? One reason might have been that the religious censorship imposed by the new king would have made it quite risky for someone with radical ideas such as Kant's to lecture openly on such topics. Friedrich Wilhelm II had acceded to the throne in August of 1786, one year before Kant completed his last known course of lectures on philosophical theology. This is *certainly* why he did not lecture on the subject after 1794, for in October 1794 Kant "solemnly" declared, in reply to a letter of reprimand from Wöllner (the king's censor, who had warned him that his alleged disparagement of Christianity, in *Religion*, had violated the censorship law), that he would "henceforth refrain altogether from discoursing publicly, in lectures or writings, on religion, whether natural or revealed."[3] Kant was willing to *write* on these contentious themes despite the political risk it obviously posed to him in the early 1790s, so why did he not wish to *lecture* on them as well, between 1787 and 1794?

A clue to answering this question can be found in the Preface to the first edition of *Religion*. After briefly outlining his position on the relation between morality and religion (including a modified version of his argument for the postulate of God as a necessary requirement for belief in the highest good), then defending the philosopher's right to address issues that are also the concern of biblical theologians (especially the proper interpretation of the scriptures they regard as divinely revealed), Kant concludes his prefatory remarks with an expression of hope that could be taken as a prediction (RGV 6: 10): theology degree courses ought to include,

> upon completion of the academic instruction in biblical theology ... – by way of conclusion, as required for the candidate to be fully equipped – a special course on pure *philosophical*

---

[3] See Kant's letter (number 642; in Br 11: 526–30) written sometime after 12 October 1794, which Kant himself published in the Preface of SF (7: 7–10).

doctrine of religion[4] (which makes use of everything, even the Bible), in accordance with a [set of] guidelines like, say, this book (or for that matter a different one, if a better one of the same kind is available).

Kant obviously did not regard the textbooks he used for his own previous lectures on philosophical theology as adequate to serve as the basis for the new kind of course he foresaw. His previous lectures, as we shall see in section 4, dealt primarily with philosophical *theology*, rather than with religion (whether natural or revealed) as such. The radical idea he advances here is that a new course, apparently *supplementing* the existing course on philosophical theology, should include training on how religious leaders should interpret empirical religion, potentially including *any* texts a given tradition regards as divinely revealed. That is, Kant appears to have grown weary of the standard approach to teaching philosophical theology and was formulating his own new approach to such a course; but without an approved textbook, he could not offer the lectures himself. *Religion* is his proposed textbook for that new course.

Having assigned Kant's *Religion* as the textbook for undergraduate Philosophy of Religion courses on numerous occasions, usually with good effect, I am surprised to find little evidence that Kant's immediate successors took his advice seriously. Although his theory of religion influenced the development of modern theology immensely (see, e. g., Dorrien 2012), I know of no theologians and even very few Kantian philosophers who have assigned *Religion* as a textbook for *any* course, much less one aimed at training pastors and/or theologians. After putting this statement – that Kant thought of himself as engaged in the task of writing a textbook – into the context of his philosophical development over the preceding decade, my main goal in the following two sections will be to trace the pedagogical themes that permeate the text of *Religion*. I will then turn my attention in section 4 to a careful analysis of his lectures on philosophical theology, with two questions in mind: (1) Do the student notes to these lectures provide evidence that Kant followed his own, subsequently-articulated theory of moral-religious pedagogy when he lectured on this subject? (2) Do these notes provide evidence that Kant's views on moral pedagogy *within a religious community* were already taking shape in the 1780s? Before examining Kant's lectures, let us look first at the evidence that, even prior to the publication of *Religion*, Kant was keenly aware of the importance of religious pedagogy.

---

[4] The term Kant uses here, "*philosophische Religionslehre*," is identical to the title given to the Pölitz lecture notes. Whoever gave those notes this title probably assumed Kant was referring, here in RGV 6: 10, to his *own* previous lectures. However, as the context clearly indicates, his reference is to a *new* course, quite different from the one he had previously taught.

2 Religious pedagogy as the key to enlightenment

In a much-neglected footnote, tucked away in *Groundwork* II (GMS 4: 411n), Kant refers to an unanswered letter he received from Johann Georg Sulzer (1720–1779), in which Sulzer allegedly asked him why "the teachings of virtue, however much they contain that is convincing to reason, accomplish so little." Kant confesses: "By trying to prepare a complete answer I delayed too long." He is probably referring to Sulzer's letter dated 8 December 1770, written in response to Kant having sent his *Inaugural Dissertation* to him for comment. Sulzer's reply, complimentary but brief, surely disappointed Kant; the penultimate paragraph expresses the hope that Kant's "Metaphysics of Morals" will appear "soon" (Br 10: 112), then describes Sulzer's *own* work as an attempt

> to resolve the question, "What actually is the physical and psychological difference between a soul that we call virtuous and one which is vicious?" I have sought to discover the true dispositions to virtue and vice in the first manifestations of representations and sensations, and I now regard my undertaking of this investigation as less futile, since it has led me to concepts that are simple and easy to grasp, and which one can effortlessly apply to the teaching and raising of children.

Sulzer became the highly influential Director of the Berlin Academy's philosophical division in 1775, but died in 1779.

Although Kant's memory in 1785 appears to have been inaccurate – Sulzer's letter from nearly fifteen years earlier refers not to the *failure* of moral education but to the potential *benefit* that Sulzer's own work in moral philosophy might have for pedagogy – Kant's belated public response tellingly reveals that, at least at this time (during the very period when he lectured most frequently on philosophical theology), Kant was deeply concerned about the role *moral education* plays in an enlightened society. He writes:

> my answer is simply that the teachers themselves have not brought their concepts to purity, but, since they want to do too well by hunting everywhere for motives to moral goodness, in trying to make their medicine really strong they spoil it. For the most ordinary observation shows that if we represent ... an action of integrity done with steadfast soul, apart from every view to advantage of any kind in this world or another and even under the greatest temptations of need or allurement, it leaves far behind and eclipses any similar act that was affected in the least by an extraneous incentive; it elevates the soul and awakens a wish to be able to act in like manner oneself. Even children of moderate age feel this impression, and one should never represent duties to them in any other way. (GMS 4: 411n)

Kant *blames* the failure of moral education to accomplish its task on a strategy Sulzer himself had adopted. Given his influential position, it may not have been accidental that Kant waited until after Sulzer's death to offer this cutting response. Indeed, Kant lectured on the philosophy of education four times from 1776 to 1787; so we must keep in mind throughout this chapter that, during the main period when he lectured on philosophical theology, Kant was at the same time serving as a teacher of *potential future teachers*.

One year before publishing *Groundwork*, Kant had addressed a closely related issue even more explicitly. In "An Answer to the Question: What Is Enlightenment?" Kant states that "the main point of enlightenment" – i.e., the area where people are most in need of "emergence from their self-incurred minority" (i.e., immaturity) – consists "chiefly in *matters of* religion" (WA 8: 41). His argument indicates that he is thinking primarily of religious *education*: in order for enlightenment to occur in any society, the first and foremost step is to *educate the clergy* so that they know how to promote enlightenment through properly educating those laypersons under their care. In WA Kant compares *un*enlightened priests to animal trainers who treat their church congregants as "domesticated animals" (WA 8: 35). The "[p]recepts and formulas" (WA 8: 36) of the typical church education program, he says, "are the ball and chain of an everlasting minority." For (WA 8: 38) "that the guardians of the people (in spiritual matters) should themselves be minors [i.e., immature] is an absurdity that amounts to the perpetuation of absurdities."

What has rarely been noticed by interpreters is that, nine years after publishing his masterpiece on defining enlightenment, Kant was planning to devote another article to the very theme that was foreshadowed by its 1784 precursor: religious education. Perhaps the chief reason the sequel has been so neglected is that, due to the religious censorship in force during the early 1790s, Kant had to publish the follow-up article, initially planned as the *fourth* in his series of articles on religion, as the "Fourth Piece" in *Religion within the Bounds of Bare Reason*. In that position, it has tended to be eclipsed either by the controversial defense of the new theory of the "radical evil" in human nature, advanced by the First Piece (the only one of the four essays that was successfully published in a journal), or by the even more controversial account of how human beings might combat such evil through "practical faith" in the "archetype [*Urbild*]" (RGV 6: 61) of perfect humanity (the essay whose rejection by the censor led Kant to compile all four essays hastily and publish them as *Religion*), or by the enticing depiction of an "ethical community" that might someday develop to such an extent that it could become the vehicle for "the founding of a kingdom of God on earth" (RGV 6: 93), as he argues in the Third Piece. Although Kant's pedagogical intentions for the Fourth Piece (and to some extent, for the whole book) may not be entirely transparent, he does not *hide* them. Rather, the ultimate goal of this new academic discipline, for which *Religion* was to be the first (potential) textbook, is to train future clergy to be philosophically sound in their approach to teaching religion to the masses. Once we recognize this as the chief goal of *Religion*, the widespread neglect of the Fourth Piece, where the pedagogical purpose of the overall project becomes explicit, can be recognized as a serious lacuna in the literature.[5]

In WA Kant had argued that the *primary* reason the masses remain in a perpetual state of "minority" is that their religious "guardians" (i.e., the clergy) hold a false conception of their role. Chief among the problems he exposes is the notion that the clergy are trained to believe the rules of their particular sect provide an unchanging and static set of dogmas that are to be blindly obeyed. Challenging this common assumption, Kant suggests that, while clergy should indeed be required to expound their denomination's received dogmas when they are speaking in their "private" capacity, as employees of the church, they should also be encouraged to think for themselves and to *critique* those same doctrines in their capacity as "scholars" (WA 8: 37 f.). That is, on the assumption that clergy will have had a university education in theology and will therefore maintain some interest in theological scholarship throughout their career, Kant in 1784 was already imagining that they ought to take, as part of their formal training, a course on how to educate the laity so that non-scholars *too* can be liberated to think for themselves. *Religion* in general (particularly its Fourth Piece) is the realization of Kant's dream of designing a textbook for a course that would educate religious educators, since the latter are, according to Kant's own explicit assessment, the most important guardians of enlightenment.

My *Commentary* on *Religion* (Palmquist 2015b) highlights this pedagogical theme, especially as elaborated in the Fourth Piece. Before devoting section 3 to a detailed examination of the latter, let us conclude this section with an overview of how pedagogical themes also permeate the first three Pieces. In the second edition Preface (RGV 6: 12 f.), Kant clarifies that the second of the two "experiments" (*Versuchen*) he conducts throughout *Religion* consists in the examination of a specific religious tradition and its scripture (for which Kant chooses Christianity and the Bible), to assess whether and to what extent its "teachings [*Lehren*]" can be interpreted consistently with the first "experiment," described in the first Preface (RGV 6: 10), of identifying the essential "teachings of bare

---

[5] One of the reasons Kant's focus on religious pedagogy in *Religion* has so often been overlooked is that his frequent use of the word "*Lehre*," best translated as "teaching" in most of its occurrences, has usually been translated as "doctrine" – a word that makes Kant's focus in *Religion* seem more theological than religious. In my Palmquist 2015b translation, I use "doctrine" for "-*lehre*" only when it occurs in compound words, such as "*Religionslehre*" ("doctrine of religion"); in the latter cases the context tends to be more theological and academic than religious and pedagogical.

reason" that constitute a rational (universal, natural) religion that might potentially be united with various historical religions. Kant's focus in both prefaces on interpreting Christian teachings in a way consistent with philosophical teachings is *prima facie* evidence of the book's pedagogical purpose.

The reason this purpose has so often been overlooked may be that the theory of evil defended in the First Piece makes no reference to this goal until the concluding sections, after Kant's *philosophical* (first experiment) argument has been fully elaborated (see Palmquist 2008b). Thus, Section IV warns biblical theologians (i.e., the clergy-in-training whom Kant imagines will be taking this new course) that the Christian doctrine of original sin must be interpreted as referring to the "rational origin" of evil, as set out in the previous three sections, not the "temporal origin" (RGV 6: 39); they must therefore avoid "envision[ing] it as having come to us by *inheritance* from the first parents" (RGV 6: 40). In place of this traditional interpretation, Kant offers a *symbolic* interpretation of the biblical account of the fall. Section V (recast in the second edition as part of a new "General Comment" to the First Piece – possibly due to a printer's error [Palmquist 2015b: 120 n. 74, 144 f.]) then sketches his rational theory of moral reformation. As the argument reaches its climax (RGV 6: 48), Kant (perhaps alluding to Sulzer's position) insists that

> the moral education of the human being must start not from the reformation of mores but from the transformation of the way of thinking and the founding of a character, although it is customary to proceed differently and to fight against vices individually but to leave their universal root untouched.

He then goes on to apply this explicitly to the kind of education clergy must oversee in the context of religious education in churches (RGV 6: 48):

> indeed, children are capable of discovering even the slightest indication that spurious incentives are mixed in, in which case the action instantaneously loses all moral worth for them. This predisposition to the good is cultivated incomparably by adducing the *example* even of good human beings (concerning the lawfulness of the action) and letting one's moral apprentices judge the disingenuousness [*Unlauterkeit*] of some maxims from the real incentives of their actions; and this predisposition passes over into the apprentices' way of thinking, so that *duty* merely by itself starts to obtain in their hearts a noticeable weight.

Kant is encouraging clergy-in-training to take advantage of the natural ability children have to detect unfair situations, by not focusing their religious education on "*admir[ing]* virtuous actions" per se (RGV 6: 48); instead, biblical stories should be used to cultivate a child's innate awareness of the difference between right and wrong *motives*.

The Second Piece follows a similar pattern: after some introductory remarks clarifying how Stoic attempts to cultivate virtue go astray, Kant devotes most of the two main Sections to the elaboration of his philosophical theory of redemption, offering his theology-student readers frequent advice as to how various biblical texts can be interpreted in philosophically respectable ways. When read in light of the book's overall pedagogical theme, the Second Piece can be seen as *affirming* pedagogically sound ways of interpreting numerous traditional Christian doctrines, including divine grace (Palmquist 2010) and even Jesus's divine nature (Palmquist 2013). That Kant's main aim is to influence how clergy-in-training will teach their congregants becomes evident in a lengthy footnote (RGV 6: 69–71) dealing with various "children's questions" (RGV 6: 69n), such as whether it might be most "prudent" to live selfishly with the intention of converting to the good just before death. Kant explicitly rejects the legitimacy of the tendency some ministers have, to delude a dying person who has lived a wretched life into believing that a few magic words uttered just before death can result in salvation; instead, ministers should boldly but lovingly urge the dying to do whatever remains in their power to set right the wrongs they have done. Evidence that this pedagogical application was at the forefront of his mind is that in the second edition Kant adds a second footnote at the end of Section One, urging clergy that a dying person's "conscience should rather be *stirred up* and *sharpened*," and issuing a dire warning to clergy who ignore his advice: "to give, in place of this, opium for the conscience, as it were, is to incur guiltiness against [this person] himself and against others surviving him" (RGV 6: 78n). Similarly, his discussion of miracles in the second General Comment includes an explicit reference to "the rational minister" (RGV 6: 87), who "will certainly take care not to cram the heads of those assigned to his spiritual care with little stories [from books containing extravagant claims] and bewilder [*zu verwildern*] their imagination." On the previous page, he had proposed a specific maxim that "teachers of religion" ought to follow when considering an alleged miracle (RGV 6: 85n) – more evidence of his pedagogical focus. Indeed, Kant's main argument against relying on miracles is that this *paralyzes* reason: it interrupts reason's "familiar laws," yet without instructing reason "by any new law" (RGV 6: 86 f.), thus rendering rational education impossible.

The Third Piece, where Kant introduces his theory of the church as the historical vehicle for ushering in the "kingdom of God on earth" (e. g., RGV 6: 101, 131), is filled with allusions to the need for the "visible church" to be *instructed* by the "invisible" guidance of reason. He thus proposes four "requirements," or "marks, of the true church": "universality"; "integrity [*Lauterkeit*]"; "freedom" (both between church members and between the church and the civil government); and "unchangeability" of these four rational requirements, such that all *other* precepts of one's historical faith must be subject to revision (RGV 6: 101 f.). He then devotes an entire section of Division One to the task of defending a specific approach to biblical interpretation: although most clergy will have been educated in a university, where they will have learned various *theoretical* approaches to textual interpretation, their main focus as *pastors* should be on *moral* interpretation (RGV 6: 109–14).

In Division Two of the Third Piece Kant affirms the Bible's suitability for use in moral instruction within a true church (RGV 6: 132), but laments the stranglehold biblical theologians tend to have on interpretive methods. To solve this problem he introduces a "precept" (*Grundsatz*) of rational faith, whereby instruction in the *historical* content of the Bible "must always be taught and explained as aiming at what is moral" (RGV 6: 132). Kant is not asking clergy to *deny* the legitimacy of sacred history, but to employ it in their church teaching to *illustrate* virtue, thereby motivating their congregants to emulate such virtue in their own lives. To illustrate his respect for the importance of history in moral cultivation, while emphasizing what a weighty responsibility religious educators have, he adds a footnote suggesting that people are typically reluctant to be converted away from their childhood religion because we are, after all, ignorant regarding which religious tradition is ultimately "right" (RGV 6: 132n) – perhaps a hint that he still privately cherished certain core aspects of his childhood Pietism. It should come as no surprise, therefore, that the Fourth Piece places its primary focus on the contrast between clerical religion and a more meditative, quasi-Pietist approach to the teaching of church beliefs and rituals at the interface between godliness and virtue.

3 Kant's guideline for training clerics in religious pedagogy

Given its references to what Kant calls "pseudoservice," the Fourth Piece of *Religion* is often read as an entirely negative, outright rejection of traditional (at least organized, clerical) religion. While exposing pseudoservice is undoubtedly a major concern in this part of *Religion*, it is not the overriding theme. Rather, pseudoservice is the danger that the masses are exposed to *if* religious educators have not themselves been given a proper (philosophical) grounding in rational religion. Kant focuses on the *proper* role of the clergy in any church that retains them. The untitled introduction that opens the Fourth Piece addresses this issue explicitly: an enlightened church will *eventually* do away with clergy altogether (as in many forms of Pietism), for "priestery"[6] is a demeaning tool of domination that frustrates the true purpose of religion by tending to *discourage* people from thinking freely. However, Kant assumes throughout the Fourth Piece that the historical evolution of religion is too young to dispense with clergy in the short term. Similarly, he had argued in WA that a *complete* lack of civil restrictions is not the best way to encourage free thinking in unenlightened people, since this would probably lead to the adoption of a new set of overly restrictive dogmas (i.e., the "medicine" of rules imposed by unenlightened members of a clergy-less church is likely to be worse than the "disease" of priestery that it sets out to cure); instead, the best way to encourage gradual enlightenment is to have a *balanced* set of statutory restrictions that paves the way for the right kind of free thinking (WA 8: 39 f.).

The Fourth Piece depicts the same situation as holding for the true church: having set as the ultimate goal the development of religious communities consisting of free-thinking members, whose mutual adherence to the four marks of the true church convinces them that clergy are *ultimately* dispensable, Kant provides guidelines for how churches that still employ clergy can avoid falling into error. Thus, after the first section of Part One of the Fourth Piece has offered a moral interpretation of the Gospels as containing "a complete [natural] religion,"[7] the second section *defends* the need for historical religious communities to maintain a "scholarly" component to establish basic parameters for teaching the community's traditions. Section Two, entitled "The Christian Religion as a Scholarly Religion," establishes the precept that should guide the influence biblical scholars have on religious matters in a church: while good historical-critical scholarship is crucial for establishing *objective facts* pertaining to the Bible, properly educated clergy will ensure that in their role as pastors such scholarship remains *secondary*: in the true church, scholarly learning always serves only as a *means* to enhance moral religion, never as an end in itself. Particularly dangerous, Kant warns, is the tendency of some theologians (and so also, some clergy) to assume that, because the Bible is believed to consist of revealed propositions, any command found in a biblical text is *ipso facto* an end in itself – i.e., a universal human duty.

---

6 This is Pluhar's translation (Kant 2009c) of the derogatory German term, "*Pfaffenthum*" (e.g., RGV 6: 130, 179), which has no exact English equivalent. The Cambridge Edition (Kant 1998b) uses "priestdom," following Greene and Hudson's translation (Kant 1934).
7 RGV 6: 162. While interpreting the moral core of the Gospels, Kant does not lose sight of his pedagogical goal. At one point he laments that *religious teachers* have failed to take seriously Jesus' prohibition against taking oaths (RGV 6: 159n) – an essential feature of his own moral theory.

Part Two of the Fourth Piece concludes the main text of *Religion* with four numbered sections, each offering a different angle on the nature or application of the foregoing precept, under the general rubric of how to avoid religious delusion. It might seem to any casual readers of *Religion* who have nevertheless been diligent enough to make it all the way through to these concluding pages that Kant is merely letting his mind wander, ending *Religion* with a random set of leftover thoughts.[8] Quite to the contrary, these four reflections on his guiding precept for religious education *accomplish* the main pedagogical purpose Kant set for himself in *Religion*: they defend and justify the requirement that the clergy's power in the church be subordinate to the individual church-goer's *conscience*. Although the title of Part Two of the Fourth Piece, "On the Pseudoservice of God in a Statutory Religion" (RGV 6: 167), admittedly highlights the negative side of Kant's argument, Part Two's four sections are filled with constructive advice and admonitions for clergy charged with the task of educating the laity.

Following an introductory paragraph, §1 argues that all religious delusion rests on a common "subjective basis": humans inevitably tend to think "that by everything that we do solely in order to please the divinity well ... we prove to God our willingness to serve him as obedient ... subjects, and hence we also serve God" (RGV 6: 169). This tendency is unavoidable because, as embodied beings, we cannot think of God without some "anthropomorphism": we *all "make a God for ourselves"* (RGV 6: 168). Probably in response to early criticisms of the first edition (see, e.g., the early book review translated in Palmquist and Otterman 2013), Kant added a footnote at this point in the second edition, explaining that such anthropomorphism "is in no way reprehensible," *provided* one "*makes* a *God* ... according to moral concepts" (RGV 6: 168n). The key to avoiding "*idolatry*" is not to reject all anthropomorphism, but to ensure that people compare all their anthropomorphisms with the moral "ideal" (i.e., the archetype of perfection, provided by reason as the core of natural religion). In communities aspiring to approximate the true church, clergy may openly employ anthropomorphisms in their teaching, provided they discourage people from making the deluded attempt to use such symbolic constructions to manipulate God. Church teaching that encourages the latter, Kant warns, exhibits nothing less than a "hidden inclination to fraud" (RGV 6: 170).

Kant reiterates this point in §2, introducing a generally applicable precept of rational religion that "requir[es] no proof" (RGV 6: 170; original emphasis): "*Apart*

---

[8] For example, Firestone and Jacobs devote less than four pages (2008: 228–31) to the crucial arguments in *Religion*'s concluding 36 pages, passing them off as a mere "catalogue of ... excesses that are of little concern to" the identification and understanding of *Religion*'s main purpose.

from a good lifestyle [Lebenswandels], *anything further which the human being supposes that he can do to become satisfactory* [wohlgefällig] *to God is a bare religious delusion and a pseudoservice of God.*" This precept does not require clergy to *abolish* all religious ritual, but does require them to educate the laity to use rituals and symbols correctly, as historically-conditioned "clothing" for rational religion that empowers people to experience moral reformation. Having been educated in a strict Pietist school, Kant does not mince his words: a "church" (i. e., its clergy) that "proclaim[s] ... a mystery as revealed," daring to claim that merely "*believing* this revelation ... and *confessing* it" *suffices* to make a person "satisfactory to God," is guilty of nothing less than *extortion* (RGV 6: 170). *However*, in line with the oft-overlooked positive pedagogical aim of the Fourth Piece, Kant adds that reason nevertheless offers "comfort" to the people (RGV 6: 171): clergy should be quick to focus on the moral symbolism of scriptural accounts of salvation, and slow to claim any *theoretical* understanding of "what this relation of God to the human being is in itself." Any church – i. e., the clergy who lead it – daring to assert *knowledge* of how "God complements that moral lack in the human race" so confidently as to be willing "to sentence to eternal reprobation all human beings who do not know this means of justification" is, ironically, putting *itself* in the position of "the unbeliever" (RGV 6: 171) by absurdly attempting to use human concepts and rituals as an excuse to avoid "a good lifestyle" (RGV 6: 172). The responsibility of enlightened clergy is to teach people the difference between the delusions of "pious play-acting and do-nothingness" and the "virtuous conviction [that] is occupied with something *real* [and] that by itself is satisfactory to God" (RGV 6: 173). Only thus can clergy avoid promoting the twin dangers of *superstition* and mystical *delirium* (*Schwärmerei*; see note 12), whereby churchgoers claim to be able to identify and even *influence* the mysterious workings of divine grace (RGV 6: 174 f.).

In §3 Kant's polemic against unenlightened religious teachers reaches its climax, as he unhesitatingly rejects any pedagogical strategy that passes off deluded religious concepts as revealed truths. He warns that clergy who fail to heed the subtle but revolutionary pedagogy he is recommending will end up creating churches whose religious practices are not essentially different from those exhibited by primitive tribes – the difference lying only in the sophistication of the methods used in attempting to control God (RGV 6: 175–8). Yet even here Kant's aim is far from being *anti*-religious, for he exclaims (RGV 6: 179; emphasis added): "So much depends, *when one wants to bind two good things*, on the order in which one binds them!" He is not charging unenlightened clergy with deliberately infecting their congregants with *evil*. Rather, their mistake is subtle: instead of teaching people that doing what is right gives us good reason to hope God will be satisfied with us, they reinforce the natural human tendency to believe that doing something *merely* to please God will persuade God to *make us* good, quasi-magically, even if our moral character remains as evil as ever; "true *enlightenment* consists" in reversing this deluded trend in religious pedagogy (RGV 6: 179) – just as Kant had claimed in WA. Borrowing a metaphor from Matthew 11:30, Kant assures his readers that the "yoke" of universal, moral religion is far lighter than that of "statutory law" imposed by the clergy in a typical church: whereas the former *frees* people to obey the moral law, the effect of the latter is "that conscience is burdened" (RGV 6: 179). Kant labels this church structure, whereby the clergy dominates "the multitude" by imposing "revealed" statutes on them, *priestery*. It can dominate even "the national regime" through a form of *mind*-control, by claiming to govern people's *spiritual* destiny (RGV 6: 179 f.). In contrast to such "counter-intuitive" teaching, making "the law of morality" the core of one's religious teaching "is as obvious to every human being ... as if it were literally written in his heart" (RGV 6: 181). *Starting* from the moral rather than the historical in one's pedagogy does not destroy historical religion; rather (RGV 6: 182), "the moral–faithful person is ... also open to the historical faith insofar as he finds it conducive to the animation of his pure religious conviction [*Religionsgesinnung*; see note 14]." Both "in the first instruction of youth and even in the pulpit discourse," it is far more natural and even more prudent "to propound the doctrine of virtue before the doctrine of godliness" (RGV 6: 182). For this enlightened pedagogy instills a "virtue-motivated courage to stand on one's own feet" that will be "strengthened by the subsequent doctrine of propitiation" (e. g., the biblical teaching concerning Jesus' sacrificial death), whereas the old approach to religious pedagogy instills fear, anxiety, and passivity (RGV 6: 183).

The main text of *Religion* concludes in § 4 with Kant's most comprehensive account of the proper role of conscience in religious education. This section might seem particularly out of place to interpreters who think Kant's general goal in *Religion* and/or his specific goal in the Fourth Piece is primarily negative.[9] If the book's goal were to destroy traditional religion, or if the Fourth Piece's goal were to discount the possibility of *any* meaningful religious practices, why would Kant end with such moving reflections on the religious significance of conscience? He ends on this high note because the trajectory of the whole book leads to this singular conclusion: in a congregation that has set itself on the archetypal path whereby it aims to *become* a manifestation of the true church, the clergy will not lull the people to sleep but will serve as a gadfly, pestering the laity to the point of annoyance, if necessary, in hopes of motivating them to look into the depths

---

[9] See, e. g., Pasternack 2014: 215 f.; cf. note 8 above. DiCenso 2012 is one of the few commentators to recognize moral pedagogy in a religious context to be a core feature of *Religion*.

of their hearts and emulate the archetype of perfect humanity, whose nature is best expressed in terms of the *logos*, "the *Word* (the Become!)."¹⁰ In § 4 Kant offers frequent and explicit advice to clergy regarding how they should accomplish this goal – far too much to summarize in an essay of this length. Instead of going into such detail, let it suffice to say that the key to true religion for Kant is to form communities united by the agreement that everyone is free to *consult their own conscience*, with the role of the enlightened clergy being to instill *this skill* in the people; conscience takes priority over any and all claims regarding the priority of historical facts, dogmas, or rituals relating to one's own religious tradition. For the latter exists to serve the former, not vice versa.

Religion concludes with the fourth of a series of General Comments, each of which deals with a specific set of borderline concepts, or "parerga," that inevitably arise for anyone who, like the clergy Kant is hoping to prepare for philosophically-enlightened guidance of religious communities, seeks to explore the interface between rational (moral) religion and their own historical faith. The first three General Comments dealt with religious experiences of being touched by grace, with miracles, and with mysteries of the faith such as the Trinity – all key concerns for any philosophically-minded pastor. The fourth General Comment then explores four examples of rituals that clergy typically encourage the laity to practice: prayer, churchgoing, baptism, and communion. Kant focuses in each case not on denying the legitimacy of the ritual's traditional interpretation, but on showing clergy how to portray the *rational purpose* of each ritual in such a way that it will serve as a tool for *animating* moral convictions rather than stifling them. While some commentators (e.g., Green 1979) complain that Kant poorly reflects the historical richness of these rituals in Christian tradition, his response would be that clergy-in-training do not need a *philosopher* to teach them the details of their own historical tradition! In this concluding section, Kant therefore sticks resolutely to his goal: instilling in his readers, many of whom he hopes will be pastors-in-training, the enlightened need to preserve morality at the core of each ritual.

Before we examine Kant's lectures on philosophical theology, a word of clarification is needed. In *Religion*'s second Preface Kant cautions that the

---

10 The Cambridge Edition (Kant 1998b) follows Greene and Hudson's highly misleading translation of Kant's "*das Werde!*" (RGV 6: 60) – his parenthetical interpretation of the divine *logos* – by rendering it as "the *Fiat!*". Pluhar's "the *Let it be so!*" (Kant 2009c) is closer to the German, but still misses the term's pedagogical thrust: authentic religion, like duty herself, bids us always to strive to *become* the person we are meant to be. I omit the italics, as neither AA nor Kant's two original editions emphasize the parenthetical words.

philosopher's task (even in conducting the second experiment) must not include "the technically practical" consideration "of instructional method as a doctrine of art" (RGV 6: 12). Kant's point here is that the philosopher's task is not to teach clergy the *skill* of teaching well (e. g., *homiletics*); *that* art should be left to biblical theologians within a given religious tradition, for each tradition's idiosyncrasies may require a specific approach to such pragmatic skills. But this warning does not prevent philosophers (like Kant) from offering guidelines for *what* is to be taught and *which element* of one's teaching should be *prioritized* – i. e., from reminding clergy that what *matters most* is the moral impact of their teaching. It matters for reasons that go beyond any *specific* religious tradition; this is why religious pedagogy *is* a legitimate concern of philosophical theologians.

This overview of the religious pedagogy Kant presents in *Religion* has highlighted several key principles. Theology students preparing to enter the ministry should, first, be *open* to the voice of reason as complementing, clarifying, and deepening their understanding of the message of Scripture. Second, in teaching the Bible to laypersons under their care, clergy must never portray assent to historically-contingent facts as being *more important* than (rather than in the service to) moral reformation; for the latter (as Kant argues in the second General Comment) is the true miracle that all genuine religion aims to cultivate. Third, clergy must courageously recognize that their faith in the tradition they have been ordained to promote does not supplant their necessary ignorance of the *ultimate* truth of their tradition's historical truth-claims, so the stories and doctrines upheld by their tradition must be taught with humility, as *symbols* of the moral reality uniting all human beings. Finally, they must never allow their own political power within the church hierarchy to usurp the authority that properly belongs to the sanctity of each person's conscience.

4 The role of Kant's lectures in the development of his religious pedagogy

The foregoing overview of Kant's mature theory of how clergy ought to shape their religious communities into centers for religiously-inspired moral education prepares us to return to the pair of questions posed at the end of section 1. These can be combined and restated as follows: To what extent did Kant's own lectures on philosophical theology serve as a "training-ground," both for Kant himself, to *develop* the pedagogical principles set out in *Religion*, and for his students, to be effectively trained in the ways described above? In order to answer this question, we must take a step back to the lecture notes from the mid-1780s – the very years when Kant was first publicizing his vision of enlightened moral education for and by priests, doctors, and lawyers – to see how and to what extent he was already incorporating these ideas in his lectures on philosophical theology. Answering this question should enable us to determine whether Kant's concern for moral education in religious communities, as argued in *Religion*, marked a sudden change of emphasis or was the fruition of his long-term philosophical goal.

As mentioned in section 1, the text of the Pölitz student notes is based on a course of lectures Kant delivered in the winter semester of 1783/84, using textbooks by Baumgarten, Eberhard, and Meiners. Although the short Appendix relating to Meiners 1780 deals mostly with what we might today call "comparative religion," Kant's brief comments on a variety of non-Christian theological positions and religious traditions are not irrelevant to our discussion. For, although he claims in the second Preface that the focus of his "second experiment" will be on Christianity, *Religion* does contain numerous references to the same non-Christian traditions. Significantly, many points mentioned in the Appendix to his lectures (V-Phil-Th/Pölitz 28: 1122–6) also appear in *Religion*. The latter offers no hint as to Kant's source for these references; but we know that Meiners 1780 was his source for this portion of the lecture notes, and this in turn serves as evidence that when Kant delivered these lectures, he was already formulating the positions later published in *Religion*. Since the Meiners Appendix has no direct impact on the issue of moral *pedagogy* in religious communities, however, I will not comment further on it.

The Pölitz lecture notes begin with an Introduction that sets the stage for a course that was divided into two main parts, covering Natural Theology and Moral Theology. Whereas the content of these two parts is based on Baumgarten 1757, the Introduction consists mostly of Kant's responses to Eberhard 1781. Kant starts the Introduction by alluding to the pedagogical motives he has for teaching his course. After some opening remarks on "an idea of highest perfection" (V-Phil-Th/Pölitz 28: 993), Kant cites "Rousseau's Emile" and "Xenophon's *Cyclopaedia*" to illustrate how an understanding of proper "education" for a given individual "is a true idea of reason" (V-Phil-Th/Pölitz 28: 994). Such ideas are important because they provide human reason with a "maximum" that enables us to measure the degree to which we attain the ideal that is thereby described – a degree that in moral matters is called "virtue" as opposed to the perfection of holiness (V-Phil-Th/Pölitz 28: 994–6). On this basis, Kant explains, the goal of learning about "the concept of God" (V-Phil-Th/Pölitz 28: 997) is to "make use of it as a gauge by which we are to determine the smaller differences in morality." While he admits some "speculative interest" in such inquiries, they are "insignificant" in themselves, and should be regarded as "no more than a means enabling us to represent in a determinate way" the extent of imperfect human virtue. The real reason for engaging in such inquiries is to satisfy "the practical interest which has to do with our making ourselves into better human beings" (V-Phil-Th/ Pölitz 28: 997). All too often, speculative appeals to God are prompted by "a lazy reason"; an attempt to clarify "our cognition of God" can attain "dignity" (V-Phil-Th/Pölitz 28: 997) only "insofar as it has a relation to religion."

Whereas Eberhard's text focused on training "scholars of the divine" (*Gottesgelehrten*), Kant insists that "in natural religion there is no place for scholarship" (V-Phil-Th/Pölitz 28: 998). He continues:

> In general no cognition of reason a priori can be called learning. Learning is the sum total of cognition which must be taught. – The theologian or divine scholar must have true learning, since he must interpret the Bible, and interpretation depends on languages and much else which can be taught.

Here we see Kant formulating what was to be a crucial distinction in *Religion*, between philosophical theologians, who teach a priori truths of reason that lead students to natural religion through a simple process of honest self-reflection, and biblical theologians, who teach historically revealed truths that depend on numerous empirical factors and thus cannot attain universality. Part One of the Fourth Piece must be read in the context of this Introduction, if we are to understand that in pitting "The Christian Religion as a Natural Religion" (the title of Section One of Part One; RGV 6: 157) against "The Christian Religion as a Scholarly [or "Learned"] Religion" (the title of Section Two of Part One; RGV 6: 163), Kant is not implying that historical Christianity should *do away* with the latter (at least in the short term), but only that the clergy who are given the task of teaching their historical tradition to the laity must first be educated in natural religion, if they are to avoid leading the people astray. Section Two repeats the same point quoted above, that insofar as clergy are biblical scholars, they should be trained in ancient languages and other specialist knowledge that, as Kant now points out, cannot be universalized (RGV 6: 113, 166 f.). In other words, Part One of the Fourth Piece is the detailed outworking of the distinction between two types of religious education, which Kant had proposed in the Introduction to his lectures, nearly a decade earlier.

The remainder of the Introduction, like most of the main text of the Pölitz lecture notes, outlines and responds to the analysis of Natural Theology that concludes Baumgarten's *Metaphysica*. Very little of this content relates directly to that of *Religion*, especially its pedagogical goal. However, an understanding of the overall approach provides a helpful propaedeutic to *Religion*. In short, Kant divides "rational theology" into three parts: "transcendental theology" (dealing mainly with the definition of "God" and the ontological argument for God's existence) treats "God as *cause of the world*"; "natural theology" (dealing with themes relevant to the cosmological and physico-theological arguments) treats God "as *author of the world*, i. e., as a living God"; and "moral theology" (dealing with the moral argument that Kant was to refine a few years later, in the second and third *Critiques*) treats "God as *ruler of the world*" (V-Phil-Th/Pölitz 28: 1001). These three types of philosophical theology, taken together, aim to provide the "maximum" (i. e., the most complete) understanding of the concept of God that is possible from a priori principles. Natural *religion*, however, requires only a "minimum" cognition of God, consisting of three features: awareness "that we need a religion"; that this philosophical concept of God "is sufficient for natural religion"; and that this "concept of God is *possible*" (V-Phil-Th/Pölitz 28: 998). Historical religious traditions that appeal to some alleged *revelation* from God attempt to extend this minimum cognition to a confirmation of the maximum rational concept of God – and usually *beyond* that maximum, into the realm that reason can only regard as *mystery*. Other than mentioning this fact at several points, Kant's lectures make very little attempt to address the issue of what happens when revelation is *added* to reason in this way; that is, the inquiry that becomes the focus of the second experiment in *Religion* is virtually absent in the lectures.

The lengthy Introduction to the lectures continues by distinguishing between "[t]he deist" as one who "accepts only transcendental theology" and the "theist" as one who actively believes in "a *living* God" (V-Phil-Th/Pölitz 28: 1001) – a distinction Kant had already made in the first *Critique* (KrV A633/B661). At various points throughout the lectures, Kant clarifies that his own position is that of the *theist* (e. g., V-Phil-Th/Pölitz 28: 1050), even though the position he adopts with regard to our *speculative* cognition of God could be regarded as a form of "skeptical" (as opposed to "dogmatic") *atheism* (V-Phil-Th/Pölitz 28: 1010). Despite appearances to the contrary, skeptical atheism is *consistent* with theism, because the former merely entails the *negative* claim that one can never prove the existence or nonexistence of God; natural and moral theology, by contrast, provide *good reasons* for actively *believing* in a God who (unlike the deist's God) actively participates in the world. Or, as Kant puts it, moral theism "renders superfluous everything that the skeptical atheist attacks" (V-Phil-Th/Pölitz 28: 1012). Thus, as he states at one point: "It is impossible for us to be satisfied with [the "*ontological* predicates that the deist ascribes to God"] alone, for such a God would be of no help to us" (V-Phil-Th/Pölitz 28: 1020; see also 28: 1123). In addition to providing an invaluable summary of the theology presupposed by (but not restated in) *Religion*, these lectures offer readers of *Religion* ample evidence of Kant's position: human beings must believe in God because *we need help with the task of being moral*.

The lectures convey a series of deep insights into Kant's understanding of how God interacts with the world – a position undergirding every argument in *Religion*. Acknowledging this presupposed theory can go a long way in clarifying some of Kant's most perplexing arguments in *Religion*. For example, whereas proponents of the age-old, moral-reductionist interpretation typically assume that "Kant declares that human reason is God,"[11] the lectures explicitly warn against making such an assumption – one that would amount to pantheism and/ or *dogmatic* atheism. After introducing his theory that God's form of cognition is best regarded as "intuitive understanding" (V-Phil-Th/Pölitz 28: 1051), Kant clarifies that this must not be taken as implying the sort of pantheism that Spinoza defended (V-Phil-Th/Pölitz 28: 1052); rather, the whole point of attributing "intuitive understanding" to God is to confirm that God

> has no need for reason; for reason is only a mark of the limits of an understanding and provides it with concepts. But an understanding which receives concepts through itself has no need of reason. Thus the expression "reason" is beneath the dignity of the divine nature. (V-Phil-Th/Pölitz 28: 1053)

Inasmuch as "humanity" consists in the ability "to judge oneself as fortunate or unfortunate only by comparison with others" (RGV 6: 27), human understanding *must* draw its content from sensibility (for our "animality" defines us as beings who can continue to live only by depending on sensible impulses [RGV 6: 26]), deferring to the guiding light of reason in order to glimpse any ultimate truths (e. g., that "personality" consists in the intellectual "idea of humanity" in its perfection [RGV 6: 28]). By contrast, God's understanding immediately *knows* everything and thus has no need for either sensibility *or* reason. Descriptions of God's nature that portray it as sharing a structural *similarity* to human reason (see below) are therefore "to be found only *in our* human representation of God's cognition, and not in this cognition itself" (V-Phil-Th/Pölitz 28: 1054).

When Kant turns his attention to moral theology, in the second main part of the lectures, he clarifies (V-Phil-Th/Pölitz 28: 1072) that "morality not only shows us that we have need of God, but it also teaches us that he is already present in the nature of things and that the order of things leads us to him." This is the essence of what, as I have argued elsewhere (Palmquist 2008a), can be called Kant's "moral pan*en*theism": the element of truth in Spinoza's *pan*theism, making it so

---

11 Pontynen 2006: 132. This popular view, presupposed by those who prefer to view their beloved Kant as *nothing more* than a skeptical atheist, typically treats his "moral theism" as merely an attempt to appease the weak-minded or unphilosophical masses. The most commonly quoted representative of this position is Heinrich Heine, who in 1834 famously quipped (Heine 1959: 119) that the second *Critique*'s moral argument was merely Kant's concession to Lampe; I directly refuted such claims in Palmquist 1992a and Palmquist 1992b (cf. Palmquist 2000: chapters IV and VI).

deceptively attractive, is that God's presence *does* permeate our *moral* nature; yet Kant's God radically transcends the world as we know it, this being the basis of Kant's criticism of Spinoza. Whereas we cannot identify Kant's God with Reason, Kant himself explicitly states that "God is ... the moral law itself, as it were, but thought as personified" (V-Phil-Th/Pölitz 28: 1076; see also 1091). This is why Kant is reluctant to allow any place for miracles within our *understanding* of the natural world (cf. RGV 6: 84–9), yet he openly states that if we wish to believe in a miracle, then "such an effect would have to be *a miracle of the moral world*" (V-Phil-Th/Pölitz 28: 1106 f.; see also 1112) – a position he subsequently defends in *Religion* (RGV 6: 89n). Kant further reveals his tendency toward moral panentheism (or "Critical mysticism," as I called it in Palmquist 2000, Part Four) when he interprets God's "omnipresence" as referring necessarily to "an *inward* presence" (V-Phil-Th/Pölitz 28: 1107) – i.e., a *moral* presence, since God's absolute nature must be conceived as transcending both time and space.

Kant goes on to define "inward presence" as "an action of the duration of the very substance in a thing" (V-Phil-Th/Pölitz 28: 1107). As if to prefigure contemporary theories of non-local causality at the quantum level, he then adds: "God's omnipresence is therefore *immediate* and *inner* but not *local*" (ibid.). That this amounts to a form of panentheism even in a non-moral sense is suggested by Kant's further claim that "space is a phenomenon of God's omnipresence" (V-Phil-Th/Pölitz 28: 1108) – i.e., space exists *in* God and can be regarded as an "appearance" of God, even though (contra Spinoza) it cannot be simply *identified* with God. As usual, and as also occurs repeatedly in *Religion*, Kant cautions his students against interpreting this theory as an un-Critical, *delirious*[12] form of

---

[12] The Cambridge Edition (Kant 1998b) translates "*schwärmerisch*" as "enthusiastic"; Pluhar (Kant 2009c) has "fanatic," and Greene and Hudson (Kant 1934) "fanatical." Yet Kant explicitly distinguishes between "*Schwärmerei*" and "*Enthusiasmus*" ("enthusiasm") in KU 5: 275: the latter "is comparable to *madness* [*Wahnsinn*]," while the former "is comparable to *mania* [*Wahnwitz*]," which Kant goes on to describe as "a disease." Anth 7: 202 defines "mania" as "*mental derangement*," with some variants having "*delirium*" as a synonym for "mania" (Anth 7: 202n). Kant nowhere suggests that "*Schwärmerei*" necessarily expresses itself as an ism-like commitment accompanied by frenzied *zeal* (this being the common meaning of "fanaticism"); rather, it is a *mental derangement* that causes us to believe we are experiencing something that is not actually occurring – as when someone in the throes of infatuation interprets her idol's actions as responses to her, when in fact he remains oblivious to her existence. Indeed, "*Schwärmerei*" in no way refers to an "-ism," a system of belief (as in "capital*ism*" or "de*ism*"), but to a *feature* or *characteristic* of certain ways of believing in such systems. Thus, when Kant refers to "*Schwaermereyen der Fanatiker*" (V-Anth/Mron 25: 1257), he is not merely being redundant ("the fanaticism of the fanatic"), but is citing a *feature* exhibited by many fanatics: "the delirium of the fanatic." In *Religion* Kant distinguishes two distinct types of *Schwärmerei*: either dark and

mysticism, whereby one deludes oneself into believing we can *grasp* this mystical presence of God (V-Phil-Th/Pölitz 28: 1109): "this omnipresence cannot be felt by any of us, nor can any of us be certain for himself that God is operating in him in any particular case." Throughout *Religion* Kant repeats and further develops this warning about the dangers of allowing legitimate religious experience to be usurped by "mystical delirium" (RGV 6: 130), a "supposed inner experience" of "effects of grace" (RGV 6: 53; cf. 83, 201) that can be "sweet or ... fearful" (RGV 6: 68), but risks depriving "the teaching" of "bare morality," as it relates to "the unambiguously moral feeling ..., of its dignity" (RGV 6: 114). The "religious *delirium*" whereby the believer claims to be able to "distinguish effects of grace from those of nature (of virtue), or perhaps even [believes the former] can produce the latter in oneself" (RGV 6: 174), is "a delusion" because human beings do not possess "a receptivity to an intuition" that would enable us to feel "the immediate presence of the highest being" (RGV 6: 174 f.). "Delirious religious delusion ... is the moral death of reason" (RGV 6: 175) because, as the lectures suggest, having such an experience would amount to *being God*; we would require a form of understanding that had no need of sensibility or reason.

Kant's harsh rejection (in *Religion*) of all forms of religious experience that put the believer into a delirious stupor is required by the theory of divine-human interaction developed in the lectures: God is *timeless* and *extramundane*, whereas all products of human reason are and must be bound by spatio-temporality. As such, God must be regarded as "immutable": even though from our limited standpoint God might *appear* to "change," the only way we can depict to ourselves a God who interacts with the world (while remaining God) is to regard God's involvement with the world as "one infinite act" that encompasses the entire manifold of different ways of relating to God that we experience (V-Phil-Th/Pölitz 28: 1096; see also 1110). Kant's explanation of this paradox is worth quoting at length:

> From this highest immutability of God with respect to all his realities it follows that it is anthropomorphic to represent God as able to be gracious after he was previously wrathful. For this would posit an alteration in God. But God is and remains always the same, equally gracious and equally just. It depends only on us whether we will become objects of his grace or of his punitive justice. The alteration, therefore, goes on *within us*; it is the relation in which we stand to God which is altered whenever we improve ourselves, in such a way that, whereas previously our relation to God was that of culpable sinners to a just God,

---

"fearful" or bright and "sweet" (RGV 6: 68). For a more detailed defense of this translation, see the "delirium" entry in the Glossary to Palmquist 2015b: 520 f.

afterward, after our reformation,[13] this relation is removed and the relation of righteous friends of virtue takes its place. (V-Phil-Th/Pölitz 28: 1039)

This passage, read in light of the detailed theory of grace that Kant defends in *Religion*, clarifies two conundrums that have plagued commentators. First, it implies that Kant took seriously the possibility that divine grace is not merely an optional extra supplied by Christian revelation, but that reason (i. e., morally-inspired *natural* religion, the topic of Kant's first "experiment" in *Religion*) also has a place for it. Indeed, we see in this passage (albeit, in embryonic form) the same theory of grace that Kant elaborates in *Religion* as an expression of divine-human *partnership*. In a nutshell, Kant's mature position is that human beings are born with a "predisposition to good" that has a divine aspect (namely, the moral idea within us, otherwise known as the "good will") but that another aspect of that same predisposition (namely, our animality, with its inclination to engage in acts of self-gratification) tempts reason to prioritize self-love over the moral "ought," this choice constituting a "propensity to evil"; the moral character of individual human beings is therefore determined by whether or not their initial evil "conviction"[14] has been *reformed*.[15] Second, this in turn adds significant clarity to Kant's difficult theory of the timeless, noumenal "deed" that determines our moral character (see, e. g., RGV 6: 31); for we can now see that, to the extent that human beings share in God's noumenal nature, we too must be depicted as committing only one act (namely, the act of choosing to be human, and thus necessarily engaged in the lifelong conflict between animality and personality – the latter in its perfect manifestation being the unchanging holiness of divinity); the appearance of a "fall" into evil and of the need for "a return to the good from which [human beings have] deviated" (RGV 6: 44) arises only when we view ourselves in terms of our volition[16] – i. e., in terms of the fact that we always

---

[13] The Cambridge Edition (Kant 1998b) has "improvement" here for "*Besserung*." I use "reformation" because Kant argues in RGV 6: 47 that the change of heart that lies at the basis of this change is a *one-off* "revolution" – a *bettering* that suggests reformation rather than gradual change.

[14] The Cambridge Edition (Kant 1998b) follows Greene and Hudson in translating "*Gesinnung*" as "disposition"; Pluhar (Kant 2009c) uses the more psychological-sounding "attitude." For a thorough defense of my use of "conviction," including a classification and contextual analysis of all 169 uses of "*G/gessin-*" words used in *Religion*, see Palmquist 2015a.

[15] For a detailed account of Kant's theory of moral reformation, see Palmquist 2010.

[16] Pluhar (Kant 2009c) and the Cambridge Edition (Kant 1998b) translate "*Willkür*" as "power of choice," whereas Greene and Hudson (1934) use a superscript "w" (e. g., "will^w" or "choice^w") to distinguish it from "*Wille*." The standard definition of "volition" is "power of choice," and the

remain free to make choices regarding how we will act in every spatio-temporal situation. The perfect grace that God's holiness offers to the world thus always remains constant; "*we* [i.e., authentically religious persons] feel it to be stronger because we no longer resist it; the [divine] influence itself remains the same" (V-Phil-Th/Pölitz 28: 1039 f.).

Conclusion. This section's synopsis of the *religious* themes addressed in the student notes illustrates that Kant's lectures on philosophical theology deal primarily with issues that are more closely related to the *theological* positions defended in the three *Critiques* – most notably, to questions relating to the nature and existence of God – than to the nature and proper implementation of actual religion. Thus, while the lectures serve as a crucial theological propaedeutic to *Religion*, and can therefore aptly be regarded as Kant's *personal* training-ground for his later development of a more thoroughgoing analysis of empirical (revealed) religion as such, they made only a feeble start to the task of training the theology students who attended these lectures (many of whom would go on to become clergy) in the art of religiously-inspired moral pedagogy. Although the Introduction to the lectures begins with a clear statement of Kant's concern for *educating* people in the proper approach to *religion*, the lectures themselves are far from delivering the goods. He does state at one point (V-Phil-Th/Pölitz 28: 1066) that, given God's all-sufficiency, it "would not be suitable to the dignity of the most blessed being" to act "as if God were out for praise or glory." This and the similar warnings made later in the course – that we must not try "to entic[e] [God's] favor by rendering him all sorts of praise" (V-Phil-Th/Pölitz 28: 1102), that "we must never regard our *prayer* as a means of getting something,"[17] and that the use "most peoples" make of "the entire natural concept of God" is "nothing else than ... a superstitious object of ceremonial adoration and hypocritical high praise" (V-Phil-Th/Pölitz 28: 1118) – all hint at the moral pedagogy that Kant obviously wanted the theology students attending his lectures to internalize. As such, they foreshadow the far more detailed discussion of "pseudoservice" and "religious delusion" in *Religion*, concluding as it does, in the fourth General Comment, with

---

former works well as a translation of "*Willkür*," referring to anything subject to human "choosability."

17 V-Phil-Th/Pölitz 28: 1112. As in *Religion*'s fourth General Comment, Kant continues by noting that prayer can also have a good and proper (i.e., morally constructive) use: "as regards corporeal advantages, we ought to offer [prayer] both with a trust in God's wisdom and with submission to this wisdom. The greatest utility of prayer is indisputably a *moral* one, because through prayer both thankfulness and resignation toward God become effective in us." For a thoroughgoing analysis of Kant's philosophy of prayer, see Palmquist 1997 (cf. Palmquist 2000: appendix VIII).

a discussion of the delusion of controlling God through a false understanding of the role of rituals such as prayer. However, in the lectures these warnings appear as merely passing comments, whereas in *Religion*'s Fourth Piece they become the main focus of Kant's argument.

Kant's lectures provide unmistakable evidence that he was already concerned about religious education in the early 1780s. For example, at the outset of his discussion of the problem of evil (V-Phil-Th/Pölitz 28: 1077), he speculates that God "gave the human being senses" – these being the occasion for our reason to choose evil – "to be moderated and overcome through the education of his understanding." However, his solution to the problem of evil follows the theological tradition of seeing it as a "*mere negation* and ... *limitation of the good*" (V-Phil-Th/Pölitz 28: 1078), without referring to anything remotely similar to the radically *religious* "propensity to evil" that dominates the First Piece of *Religion*. For only in *Religion* is Kant concerned with interpreting *revealed doctrines*, such as original sin. Likewise, his brief discussion of immortality depicts it as an occasion for "moral growth": "if in this world [a person] strives to act in a morally good way and gradually attains to moral accomplishment, he may hope to continue his moral education [in the afterlife], too" (V-Phil-Th/Pölitz 28: 1085). While this comment on its own foreshadows the arguments of the second *Critique's* Dialectic, more than any arguments in *Religion*, Kant's next point is that any hope of receiving *rewards* from God must stem not from an appeal to God's *justice* but from an appeal to God's *benevolence* (V-Phil-Th/Pölitz 28: 1085) – a nuanced point that should help readers of *Religion* understand why Kant is so reluctant to *spell out* an explicit theory of divine grace: *justice* corresponds to the theme of the second *Critique* and (as Kant insists both in the lectures and throughout his Critical writings) human beings "can never expect rewards from God's justice" because "we can never do more than is our duty" (V-Phil-Th/Pölitz 28: 1085); yet *benevolence* corresponds to the theme of the third *Critique* (i. e., the "interest" human reason has in fulfilling our desire for "pleasure"[18]) and any hope of ben-

---

[18] Kant associates the third *Critique* with the faculty of "pleasure and displeasure" (*Lust und Unlust*); but its arguments reveal that reason's special interest in this faculty leads it to experiences that offer a higher fulfilment of our natural mental capacity, in terms of "satisfaction" (*Wohlgefallen*). In *Religion* Kant consistently uses the latter term to refer to *God* being (or not being) *satisfied* with human beings. Unfortunately, Pluhar and other translators often translate this term as "liking" or "pleasing," thus making it difficult to distinguish from *Lust*. My translation (in Palmquist 2015b) reserves "pleasing" for forms of *gefallen*, which Kant consistently uses throughout *Religion* to refer to *false* attempts to *ingratiate* God, with *Wohlgefallen* referring to *genuine* satisfaction of God's demands, through adoption of moral convictions. Benevolence is the idea of reason that provides human beings with *hope* that God will indeed be satisfied

efitting from this aspect of God's nature must be based on an appeal to *historical* (revealed) religion.[19]

Probably the only exception to this observation, that the lectures merely *foreshadow* the themes that eventually became the focus of *Religion* rather than working them out in any detail, is that they do present a fairly detailed account of the various *non-Christian* religious traditions that uphold some version of the doctrine of the Trinity: following Meiners' text, Kant depicts this as a nearly universal characteristic of world religions (V-Phil-Th/Pölitz 28: 1074 f.) – comments that were later incorporated in a very similar form in *Religion* (RGV 6: 140 f.). Kant's position (as mentioned in all three *Critiques* and *Religion*, as well as being a key focus of these lectures) is, of course, that our most profound and useful way of thinking of God is in terms of a *moral* Trinity. This is not because Kant seeks to identify God with reason (see footnote 11), but because our a priori cognition of God can be based on nothing other than the structure of human reason. Thus, God as holy lawgiver is how our theoretical reason *must* think of God; God as benevolent ruler is how our (judicial) capacity for pleasure and displeasure requires us to present God to ourselves; and God as righteous judge is how our practical reason (e.g., as manifested in conscience) necessarily shapes philosophical theology (V-Phil-Th/Pölitz 28: 1075). Kant is not saying God necessarily *is* a lawgiving, benevolent Reason that judges us with perfect righteousness, but that we must *conceive* of God in this way, if the idea of God is going to be of any practical use in educating human beings to become better persons. This theme is covered in similar detail in both the lectures and *Religion*, but it has only minimal implications for Kant's moral pedagogy, serving more as a propaedeutic than as instruction in moral pedagogy as such.

We can now answer the two questions posed at the end of section 1. Our analysis of Kant's lectures on philosophical theology here in section 4 provides ample evidence that his lectures were, indeed, a formative step on the way to several of

---

with the latter, even though our attempts to be good are inevitably imperfect – an argument that relates not so much to divine *justice* as to divine *goodness*.

19 Other references to education and/or the cultivation of reason in V-Phil-Th/Pölitz are very brief allusions, with no direct implication for religion. Thus, at V-Phil-Th/Pölitz 28: 1097 Kant mentions that astronomers have "taught us modesty and caution in our estimation of ["the whole world" – i.e., the universe]." He then adds that "the cultivation of our own reason urges us to assume and use" the "necessary maxim of our reason that in every animal and plant there is not the least thing that is useless and without purpose" (V-Phil-Th/Pölitz 28: 1098). While these examples illustrate how natural theology has an *educative* emphasis, they do not concern specifically *moral* or *religious* education. For an excellent account of how Kant affirms the wise use of rhetorical devices in moral and religious education, see Stroud 2014.

the key claims that shape the main arguments in *Religion*; however, the student notes provide very little evidence that in delivering these lectures Kant was attempting to *accomplish the same goal* that he set out to accomplish in *Religion*. Rather, the hints we have picked up from the text suggest that, while delivering these lectures, Kant came to recognize the need for a *radically different* university course, and that he hoped *Religion* might serve as an adequate textbook for that new course. The lectures Kant actually delivered focused on philosophical *theology*: they brought together the essential tenets of the theology that Kant develops in various passages throughout the three *Critiques*; by contrast, the new course Kant formulated in his mind as he was delivering those lectures was to be a sequel to his course on philosophical theology, aimed at *philosophical training for biblical theologians*, especially those training to be clergy. Because the lectures Kant actually delivered were not intended solely for that purpose (e. g., they rarely, if ever, allude to biblical texts, whereas *Religion* does so repeatedly), they cannot be viewed as anything more than *Kant's training-ground* for constructing his own *subsequent* philosophical doctrine of a particular religious tradition (i. e., his philosophy of the Christian religion). Otherwise, we would find much more than a few hints as to how the clergy-in-training who attended his lectures ought to educate people, once they begin pastoring a church. Yet there can be no doubt that certain key aspects of Kant's views on moral pedagogy *within a religious community* were first expressed in seed form in his lectures.

This nuanced way of answering our two questions explains *why* Kant turned to religion in the early 1790s. For the lectures explicitly state the great paradox that lies at the heart of Kant's abstract philosophical theology (which I have described elsewhere, using the label "Critical mysticism"), arguably forming the core of the whole Critical philosophy, an existential paradox that can be resolved only by immersing oneself in a particular religious tradition. Even though our most valiant attempts to understand and emulate the idea of God, imposed upon us by our own reason, may end up as merely "fruitless seeking" (V-Phil-Th/Pölitz 28: 1113), *this very striving* nevertheless "fulfills our great vocation and furthers the cultivation of our reason."

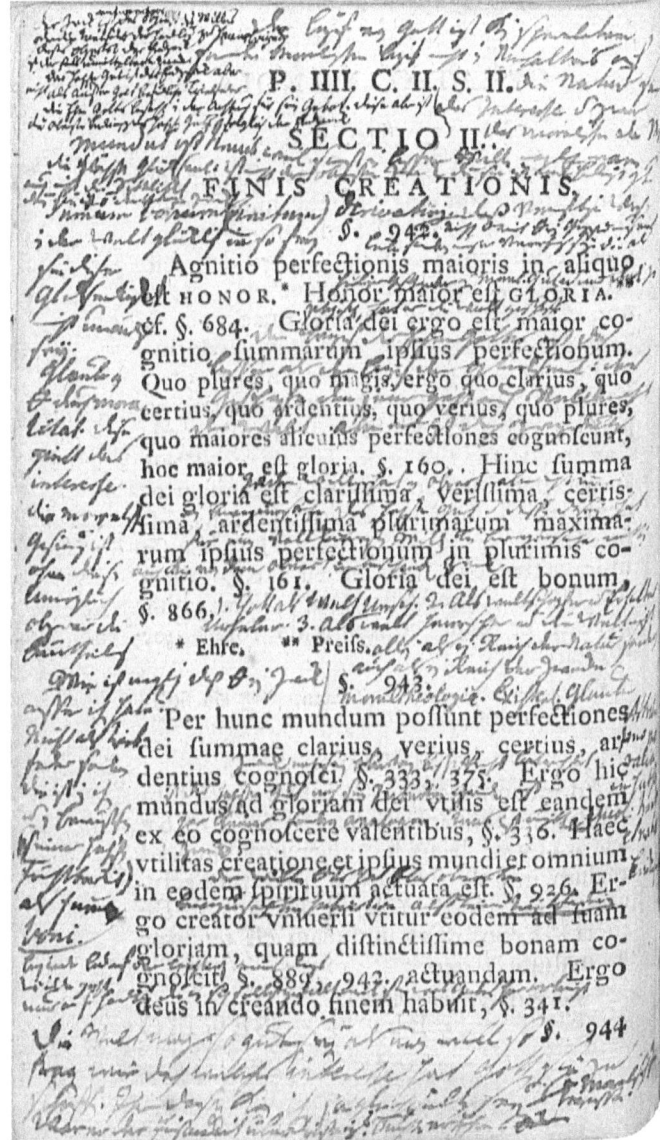

Fig. 13: Reproduction of page 386 ("Sectio II. Finis Creationis") from Kant's copy of A. G. Baumgarten's *Metaphysica* (Halle, 1757, 4th edn.), with Kant's handwritten notes: Reflections 6142–52 (AA 18: 467–69) and 6452 (AA 18: 724). Reproduced with the kind permission of the University of Tartu Library, Estonia. Call number: manuscript 93. Kant's personal copy of Baumgarten's *Metaphysica* is available at the University of Tartu Library website: http://hdl.handle.net/10062/32369. Accessed 22 April 2015.

Chapter 17
Kant as Pastor[1]

Norbert Fischer
Translated by Christian Göbel and Frederick Van Fleteren

> *It is impossible to prove that God is impossible.*[2]

> *To honor and love without flattery a God who has all perfection.*[3]

Is it, as contemporary opinion might suggest, really so unlikely to think that a philosopher could be involved in 'pastoral care'? The notion may seem strange in a milieu stamped with a spirit of the time which scarcely recognizes a rational

---

1 The essay's (translated) subtitle is: "Kant's *Lectures on the Philosophical Doctrine of Religion* in Comparison with His Published Works, with Special Attention to His Teaching on the 'Purpose of Creation'."
2 PR 58=V-Phil-Th/Pölitz 28: 1026. Kant's lecture notes, *Vorlesungen über die philosophische Religionslehre*, were published by Karl Heinrich Ludwig Pölitz (first edition 1817, second edition 1830, reprinted in Kant 1982), and also in AA 28.2.2: 993–1126. References are to the second edition in Kant 1982 (= PR) followed by the AA page numbers in volume 28. Translations are from Allen Wood in *Religion and Rational Theology* in The Cambridge Edition of the Works of Immanuel Kant (Kant 1996b). All other translations of Kant's published works are likewise from The Cambridge Edition volumes. Translations of Kant's lectures and other works (including primary texts and secondary literature) unavailable in English are by Christian Göbel unless otherwise indicated.
3 This quote (PR 221=V-Phil-Th/Pölitz 28: 1117) ties in with a thought Augustine expresses frequently, viz., the idea of "gratis diligere" (e. g., *Sermo* 91,4: "invenitur Iob gratis colere deum, gratis diligere: non quia aliquid dedit, sed quia se ipsum non abstulit"). Kant, too, often sees a connection with Job, most clearly in his 28 April 1775 letter to Johann Caspar Lavater (Br 10: 175–9): "You ask for my opinion of your discussion of faith and prayer. Do you realize whom you are asking? A man who believes that, in the final moment, only the purest candor concerning our most hidden inner convictions can stand the test and who, like Job, takes it to be sin to flatter God and make inner confessions, perhaps forced out by fear, that fail to agree with what we freely think. I distinguish the *teachings of Christ* from the *report* we have of those teachings. In that the former may be seen in their purity, I seek above all to separate out the moral teachings from all the dogmas of the New Testament" (Br 10: 175 f. [Kant 1999: 152]).
The *previous* quote ("It is impossible ...") builds on thoughts expressed in the first *Critique*, and it continues: "Rather, reason does not put the least obstacle in the way of my accepting the possibility of God, if I should feel bound to do so in some other way." With this thesis Kant apparently joins Pascal in making a 'wager', an attitude that is also mirrored in *Critique of Pure Reason* (KrV A825/B853): "If we entertain the thought that we should wager the happiness of our whole

foundation for religion and which has lost an understanding of the deeper sense of words such as 'soul' or 'pastoral care' (i.e., 'care of the soul'). These notions may, at most, be familiar in the form of pastoral care in emergency situations ('emergency pastoral care') or in a context of psychological 'counseling'. If, however, we follow Heidegger's suggestion and think of the human being (*Dasein*) as *Sorge* (care) – having to care for its "authentic potentiality-of-being-a-whole"[4] – we should be able to see a connection with the Socratic-Platonic notion of *autepitaxis* and *epimeleia* (Plato, *Politicus* 260b–261d), a self-ordered care for oneself which all human beings exercise in their temporal existence.[5] If and when *philosophers* consider existential questions, their striving for clarification and 'care for the soul' can also be interpreted as 'pastoral care' – for *themselves*, but also for *others* (with whom they will share their thoughts once they believe they have found clarity for themselves). Even the educated today would not contest the plausibility of a book title such as *Augustine the Pastor*,[6] yet they would not equate it with genuine 'philosophical' thought[7] but with Augustine's role as bishop and Church father; they would suppose that it concerns the Christian tradition. This position may not in the final analysis be false since the 'selfhood' of persons that justifies the use of the word 'soul' appears most clearly in the Bible

---

life on something, our triumphant judgment would quickly disappear, we would become timid and we would suddenly discover that our belief does not extend so far. Thus pragmatic belief has only a degree, which can be large or small according to the difference of the interest that is at stake." See also Vorlesungen über die Metaphysik Pölitz (AA 28: 304): "*The certainty of this presupposition* [viz., the supposition of God's existence] *is subjectively just as strong as any objective mathematical proof*, although it is not as strong objectively. If I have a strong subjective conviction, I will not even read the objections made against it, unless out of curiosity, because there is nothing to dissuade me from this belief. For, even if I cannot immediately prove it, it still is a necessary presupposition of reason. This subjective belief is so strong in me, yea even stronger, than a mathematical demonstration. For I can stake everything on this belief, but I would be hesitant to stake everything on a mathematical demonstration: there could always be something where reason could have erred."

4 In *Sein und Zeit* (1927), the sixth chapter of Part I, "Die Sorge als Sein des Daseins" (Heidegger 1977: 180–230).

5 Cf. Fischer 1990: 34, 36. See *Phaedo* 82d; *Protagoras* 322c.

6 E.g., van der Meer 1951 and May 2003: 95–105.

7 A genuinely *philosophical* reception of Augustine started relatively late. It may have begun with Edmund Husserl; see *Texte zur Phänomenologie des inneren Zeitbewusstseins (1893–1919)* (Husserl 1985); in his "Introduction," editor Rudolf Bernet speaks of "Husserl's 'side-remarks' on Augustine" (XI; cf. XIII, XVII, LXVI). Respect for Augustine grew among 'phenomenologists' such as Max Scheler, Martin Heidegger, Karl Jaspers, and Paul Ricoeur. See, e.g., Heidegger, *Augustinus und der Neuplatonismus. Frühe Freiburger Vorlesung 1921* (Heidegger 1995: 157–299).

– in passages on responsibility and guilt in human beings.⁸ Since philosophers such as Socrates and Plato also support the idea of personal *responsibility*, they could easily be seen as "animae naturaliter christianae."⁹

Inaccurate and misleading, however, are interpretations that either saw Kant's critique as the 'destruction' of metaphysics – and aimed to (re)establish a metaphysics (old or new)¹⁰ – or, on the other hand, which welcomed Kant's philosophy as the beginning of an era without any metaphysics or religion.¹¹ Such views actually result from a desire for 'knowledge' in an area in which according to Kant's philosophical judgment there can only be 'belief'. The works of Fichte, Schelling, and Hegel which laid the foundation of *German Idealism* by overcoming *Critical philosophy* and producing an 'absolute metaphysics' were the *proton pseudos* of the ambiguous reception of Kant's new philosophical approach. Only after metaphysics in general had been put through a fundamentally destructive critique, for example by Feuerbach and Nietzsche (to name only two of the most prominent figures), did a reconsideration of Kant's Critical philosophy begin.¹² Nietzsche seems to have considered the possibility, albeit reluctantly, that with his Critical metaphysics Kant had discovered an 'antidote' to the atheism propa-

---

8 According to Plato, 'selfhood' makes 'self-ordering care' possible (*autepitaxis* and *epimeleia*) which is to be performed by the soul (see *Politicus* 260c, 267a/b, 274d/e, 279a; see also *Republic* 617e). According to Augustine 'selfhood' indicates godliness ("id ipsum," see *Confessiones* 12,7); cf. Aurelius Augustinus, *Suche nach dem wahren Leben. Confessiones* X/*Bekenntnisse* 10, ed. Norbert Fischer, 2006: XXXI, L.
9 Tertullian, *Apologeticum* 17,6. Cf. "Introduction," 16, 31, 47, 51 in Carl Becker's edition (Tertullian 1961); according to Becker this idea refers to a "Stoic theory."
10 Examples can be found in Catholic anti-Kantianism; see Göbel 2005. *German Idealism*, too, interfered with a proper reception of Kant's philosophy, but could not arrest tendencies Kant had fought against (materialism, positivism, and atheism); they emerged even more prominently after the end of the dominance of German Idealism.
11 Cf., for example, Karl Marx's letter to his father (10 November 1837) in *Frühschriften* (Marx 1971: 1–11, especially 3 and 7).
12 Nietzsche thought he had destroyed metaphysics and belief in God by destroying 'Platonism' and 'Christianity' (which Nietzsche saw as 'Platonism for the masses'). But that was based on his inadequate understanding of Platonism (where the highest knowledge is found in the knowledge that the Highest Good cannot be known) and of Christianity (the anti-corporeality Nietzsche saw in Christianity is not supported by scriptural evidence – cf. e. g., Genesis 1–2 or Jesus' healing and waking of the dead – and still less by the belief in the resurrection of the body). The return to Kant was also inspired by the growing influence of positivistic materialism in the nineteenth century, for example in Ludwig Büchner, *Kraft und Stoff oder Grundzüge der natürlichen Weltordnung. Nebst einer darauf gebauten Moral oder Sittenlehre* (1855) (the book had 21 German editions). A different stance, more authentically following Kant's intentions, is taken by Emil Du Bois-Reymond, *Von den Grenzen des Naturerkennens. Die sieben Welträtsel* (1872).

gated by Nietzsche himself.¹³ When the Neo-Kantians revived interest in Kant's work, his (Critical) metaphysics and philosophy of religion did not immediately stand in the foreground, despite the fact that Hermann Cohen and Paul Natorp, the protagonists of the Marburg school, were open to a 'metaphysical' reading of Kant.

A more explicitly 'metaphysical' interpretation of Kant started at the beginning of the twentieth century.¹⁴ Here, Critical philosophy was related to the history of metaphysics, thus liberating it from an apparent hostility to metaphysics. Heidegger's systematic 'metaphysical' interpretation of Kant, too, was based on an intensive reading of Kant's texts; and his understanding of Kant is, to a certain extent, evident in his publications, but more clearly in Heidegger's lectures, and therefore only became known to the wider academic public when these lectures were published in the Heidegger-Gesamtausgabe.¹⁵

Before we can consider exemplary aspects of the relationship between Kant's *Lectures on the Philosophical Doctrine of Religion* and his published works, with special attention to his teaching on the "purpose of creation," I would like to present some general reflections about Kant's intentions based on the published works. Attention to his intentions is paramount if we wish to understand Kant adequately and develop his approach further.¹⁶ Independently of Kant's philosophy, the God-question arose (and arises) in all cultures and 'world-views' on the basis of interior and exterior phenomena in human life (for example contingency, guilt). This question, which has various degrees of significance for the human

---

13 Although Nietzsche expressed a lot of disrespect for Kant, he admitted: "Why all the rejoicing over the appearance of Kant that went through the learned world of Germany, three-fourths of which is made up of the sons of preachers and teachers – why the German conviction still echoing, that with Kant came a change for the *better*? The theological instinct of German scholars made them see clearly just *what* had become possible again." *Der Antichrist. Fluch auf das Christentum* 10 (Nietzsche 1888–89: 176 [Nietzsche 1918: 52 f.]).
14 This school still exists today. Cf. Funke 1979; Heidegger, *Kant und das Problem der Metaphysik* (1929) (Heidegger 1991). Heidegger saw Kant principally as a metaphysician; see also Wundt's *Kant als Metaphysiker* (1924) and Fischer 2004 and 2010.
15 The relationship between an author's publications and his lectures has caused questioning long before Kant and Heidegger, e. g., with regard to Plato and the debates about the *agrapha dogmata*; see Norbert Fischer 1990. According to Heidegger, Kant belongs in the history of Western metaphysics; see, e. g., *Die Grundprobleme der Phänomenologie. Marburger Vorlesung 1927* (Heidegger 1997: 2).
16 This is merely a provisional outline and needs further development. There cannot be any doubt, however, that, in the publication of his works, Kant was convinced that he provided something valid and valuable for philosophy as such. It is primarily in his published works that the philosopher speaks to *others*; it is almost as if, in his works, he spoke to humankind in general.

effort to cope with life – some compatible with one another, others not – is to be differentiated from the 'disinterested' pursuit of absolute and unconditional truth (cf. Hutter 2003). Kant, too, considers both quests – for a solution to human problems on one hand and the search for something absolute and unconditional on the other hand – to be tasks of human thought.

In a preemptive riposte to critical questions regarding the propositions I am about to make, it should be noted that atheistic arguments against religion may be able to uncover failed forms of religious practice but cannot eliminate the existential foundations for the relation to God. In this sense, atheism, which contests God's existence, could actually be understood as an affirmation and positing of the fundamental problem, but in a 'mode of deficiency'.[17] The great thinkers would by no means disagree with the common critique that insists that God is no objectively determined reality.[18] We should keep in mind what is recorded in *Lectures on the Philosophical Doctrine of Religion* about the difference between "skeptical" and "dogmatic" atheism and Kant's belief that "either there never have been such dogmatic atheists, or they have been the most evil of human beings" (PR 31=V-Phil-Th/Pölitz 28: 1010).[19]

Kant's works show his tenacious effort to construct a 'Critical metaphysics' and make the "advantage of the transcendental investigation both comprehensible and interesting to even the dullest and most reluctant student."[20] Kant thus suggested that his readers not be content merely with geometry, mathematics, and natural science – i.e., not limit themselves to "the empirical use" of the

---

[17] An example of this would be the 'protest' we find among humanistic atheists; cf. Fischer 2005a: 201–16.

[18] Cf. the 'classic' passages in Plato, *Republic* 509b; Augustine, *Sermo* 117,5; and Kant, KpV 5: 147 f.

[19] This is also an idea that cannot be found in the published works, but only in lecture notes. Kant continues: "for in them all the incentives of morality have broken down. And it is the atheist of this kind who is to be contrasted with moral theism" (which is the approach Kant himself suggests). Parallels can be found in Metaphysik Volckmann (AA 28: 1257); Religionsphilosophie Volckmann (AA 28: 1151; 1174 f.). See also PR 54 f.=V-Phil-Th/Pölitz 28: 1023 f.: "if the dogmatic atheist denies that there is a God, he takes upon himself the obligation to prove that God is impossible. For all our a priori knowledge is of such a kind that when I presume to prove from pure reason that something does not exist, I can only do it by proving that it is impossible for this thing to exist."

[20] KrV A238/B297. Kant describes this advantage as follows: "the understanding occupied merely with its empirical use, which does not reflect on the sources of its own cognition, may get along very well, but cannot accomplish one thing, namely, determining for itself the boundaries of its use and knowing what may lie within and what without its whole sphere."

understanding – although he himself knew well, and had even felt, the attraction of these sciences.

Proofs for Kant's relation to Christian theology, which can often be called *deconstructive* – and thus has a *constructive* tendency – and sometimes *restorative*, are found in many places in his work. Kant would neither have concerned himself with the destruction of a transcendent God nor with a reduction to an immanent 'God in us', although he does know and mention this *theologoumenon*.[21] Although he sees finite reason related to a divine ideal, the difference between finite reason and what the term "God" should signify is constitutive for him. Job's question remains without a knowable answer because according to Kant there is a gap between finite human reason and what can be thought about God. This topic had already occupied Kant early in his career – and later he became increasingly concerned with it.[22]

In the following, I shall first discuss key elements of Kant's philosophy of religion in his published works (section one), then focus on Kant's analysis of religion in his *Lectures on the Philosophical Doctrine of Religion* (section two); in section three I will offer brief reflections on the approach to some central themes from (the Christian) religion presented in these lectures (where Kant covers them, in part, more deeply than in his published works [cf. PR 31 and 55=V-Phil-Th/Pölitz 28: 1024]) and in other writings.

1 Key elements of Kant's philosophy of religion in his published writings

From the very beginning, Kant's published works are related to the foundation of a philosophical doctrine of religion. The writings dedicated explicitly to religion (above all *Religion within the Boundaries of Mere Reason*) build, on the one hand, on the foundation of a 'Critical metaphysics' in his theoretical works and, on the other hand, they also build on his practical philosophy. The latter does not, as such, presuppose any religion, but, according to Kant's *Religion within the Boundaries of Mere Reason*, "inevitably leads to religion," namely by extending itself "to

---

[21] See KrV A551n/B579n and A633/B661. An anthropomorphic idea of God would make no sense within the 'moral theism' that Kant sets out to develop in his works.

[22] Even when Job is not mentioned explicitly, his way of thinking is still present, e. g., in KpV 5: 147 f.; the maxim 'without hope, without fear' is to be understood in Kant's sense. Cf. KpV 5: 129: "Here again, then, everything remains disinterested and grounded only on duty, and there is no need to base it on incentives of fear and hope, which if they became principles would destroy the whole moral worth of actions."

the idea of a mighty moral lawgiver outside the human being, in whose will the ultimate end (of the creation of the world) is what can and at the same time ought to be the ultimate human end" (RGV 6: 6).[23]

From the outset Kant searched for the *living God*: only in so far as philosophy may have something to say about "God's providence"[24] (referring to God's care for his creatures)[25] does the God-question have a meaning that is of interest to Kant (BDG 2: 67). He is not looking for 'hegemonic knowledge', he is not searching for an abstract 'Absolute' in order to know "what holds the world together in its innermost being" (Goethe, *Faust*).[26] When he states that the goal of his inquiry in the *Critique of Pure Reason* is the possibility of postulating "*God, freedom*, and *immortality*," Kant refers to the "living God" who can be approached not through *knowledge*, but only through *belief*.[27] Kant reduces the tri-partite goal to *two* questions: concerning (1) God and (2) a future life.[28] This approach is close to the idea that it is ultimately *one* fundamental question which calls forth all philosophical thought and which could be phrased as follows: how are human beings, despite all the trials and tribulations life holds, able to accept and embrace thankfully the life into which they come unasked?[29] With regard to this question, we can see

---

[23] Cf. RGV 6: 3, RGV 6: 6–8. See also Dörflinger 2004: 207–23. True, however, is the opposite: "All religion presupposes morality; therefore, morality cannot be deduced from religion" (V-Mo/Collins 27: 307). Cf. Fischer 2013: 195–220.

[24] See PR 215 f., 218=V-Phil-Th/Pölitz 28: 1114–16 and Religionsphilosophie Volckmann, 'On Providence': V-Th/Volckmann 28: 1212–21.

[25] Cf. Plato, *Politicus* 273d (κεδομενος). See also Augustine, *Confessiones* 6,8 ("I always believed in your existence and your care for us, even though I did not know what to think about your essential nature, or conceive what way could lead me, or lead me back, to you") and 11,3 (Augustine 1997: 103).

[26] Thus, Kant is not concerned with any kind of metaphysics that would find its culminating expression in the 'will to power' (as Heidegger insinuated, referring to the essence of all metaphysics since Plato).

[27] For Kant, such "knowledge" would even be harmful; see KrV Bxxx, A633/B661; KpV 5: 147 f.; and PR 30 and 34=V-Phil-Th/Pölitz 28: 1010–12.

[28] For example, KrV A803/B831. Thus Kant comes close to Augustine's fundamental question (*sol.* 1,7).

[29] This question is found in the beginning of Augustine's *Confessiones*, which starts with a praise of God cited from the psalms (1,1). The praise, however, is not a mere citation, but corresponds to the deepest desire of human beings who hope that the life into which they have come without any foreknowledge is a pure and true gift. Close inspection, however, reveals that this gift is full of pitfalls: man notices his insignificance in the whole, his mortality, his many failures in life, and his own arrogance. Based on these facts, the initial praise of God seems untenable. Nevertheless, Augustine adheres to his diagnosis that man wants to praise God: "et tamen te laudare vult homo." And this "nevertheless" inspires our thinking. Augustine only arrives at this

how Kant anticipates Heideggerian motifs: Heidegger says about the *causa sui*, i.e., the 'God' of speculative philosophy: "Man can neither pray nor sacrifice to this god. Before the *causa sui*, man can neither fall to his knees in awe nor can he play music and dance before this god."[30] Kant shows a similar understanding of *praying*: "I know that everything can happen according to God's (1) ordinary or (2) extraordinary good will. Thus do I pray and work. Trust in prayer is lessened when it is tied to a particular result but not with regard to the entire worth of the wish."[31]

In his published works, Kant's reflections on the philosophy of religion seem to follow a pattern and understanding of *time* that he borrows from the theological tradition: (1) creation, or the divine Being as creator of the world (the *beginning of time*), (2) the fall into sin and redemption (existence *in time*), and (3) the eschatological goal of creation which Kant also calls the "final end" (the "kingdom of God" *after time*). We should keep in mind what Kant writes in a letter to Carl Friedrich Stäudlin (and these ideas are mirrored in his works, but even more clearly in *Lectures on the Philosophical Doctrine of Religion*):

> With the enclosed work, *Religion within the Boundaries [of Mere Reason]*, I have tried to complete the third part of my plan. In this book I have proceeded conscientiously and with true respect for the Christian religion but also with a befitting candor, concealing nothing but rather presenting openly the way in which I believe that a possible union of Christianity with the purest practical reason is possible.[32]

---

conclusion by introducing an inversion of activity (*Confessiones* 1,1): "tu excitas, ut laudare te delectet." The idea of an 'inversion of activity' is also found in Kant. His claim that freedom 'reveals' itself in the (awareness of the) 'moral law' is not without a deeper meaning; and the significance of his concept of revelation is particularly evident in the lectures.

30 Heidegger, "The Onto-theo-logical Constitution of Metaphysics" (Heidegger 1969: 72). [Heidegger 1957: 77].

31 Refl 8083 (AA 19: 626); see also Moralphilosophie Collins (AA 27: 323, "Of Prayer"): "It seems to be generally supposed that praying to the supreme being is needless, since He knows our requirements better than we do ourselves ... Objectively, then, prayers are quite unnecessary ... But subjectively prayer is needed, not so that God, who is the recipient of it, should learn anything, and thereby be moved to grant it, but rather for our own sakes." There are numerous passages, especially in the lectures, on God's 'direction' or even 'extraordinary direction'. According to Reiner Wimmer's *Kants kritische Religionsphilosophie*, Kant had little appreciation for other forms of worship: "The autonomous and supra-rational character of living religiosity cannot be grasped within Kant's conceptual framework. That is why it remains questionable and limited" (Wimmer 1990: 13). This thesis, however, calls for a more nuanced judgment. Kant *did* have a sense of the exaltation (*Begeisterung*) and gratitude believers feel with regard to God, but he was convinced of a hiatus between wonder and the possibility of objective knowledge (see Fischer 1993: 170–94).

32 Letter to Stäudlin (4 May 1793), AA Br 11: 429 [Kant 1999: 458]; cf. *Introduction* by G. Wobbermin (AA 6: 497–516, on 497).

In the four Pieces of *Religion within the Boundaries of Mere Reason*, Kant concentrates on questions that concern the existence of the human being *in time* and thus are more accessible to philosophical reflection: the "radical evil of human nature," the "war of the good principle with the evil one," the "the victory of the good principle over the evil principle and the founding of a kingdom of God on earth," and "the service and pseudo-service under the dominion of the good principle." With regard to content, however, these four Pieces are consistent with the doctrine of 'creation' (the origin of the world and of the human being before time) and its eschatological goal (the 'eternal' kingdom of God after time). This consistency is even more obvious in Kant's *lectures*.[33] Elements of his doctrine of a 'kingdom of God' *after time* can already be seen in his published works, although the doctrine is surely subject to larger systematic problems.

The suspicion that, with regard to the origin of morality, philosophy and theology are incompatible (this is a popular idea among both philosophers and theologians and it refers either to the notion of human *autonomy* or to the doctrine of a *divine origin* of the moral law)[34] is, according to Kant, unfounded:

> From this it can also be seen if one asks about *God's final end* in creating the world, one must not name the *happiness* of the rational beings in it but the *highest good*, which adds a condition to that wish of such beings, namely the condition of being worthy of happiness, that is, the *morality* of these same rational beings, which condition alone contains the standard in accordance with which they can hope to participate in the former at the hands of a *wise* author. For, since *wisdom* considered theoretically signifies *cognition of the highest good*, and practically the *fitness of the will for the highest good*, one cannot attribute to a highest independent wisdom an end that would be based merely on *beneficence*. For

---

33 For references to 'creation' in Kant's published works, cf. KrV A206/B251 f., B426, A630/B658. For a theology of creation as a background to his moral philosophy, see KpV 5: 87: "On this origin are based many expressions that indicate the worth of objects according to moral ideas. The moral law is *holy* (inviolable). A human being is indeed unholy enough but the *humanity* in his person must be holy to him. In the whole of creation everything one wants and over which one has any power can also be used *merely as a means*; a human being alone, and with him every rational creature, is an *end in itself*: by virtue of the autonomy of his freedom he is the subject of the moral law, which is holy. Just because of this every will, even every person's own will directed to himself, is restricted to the condition of agreement with the *autonomy* of the rational being, that is to say, such a being is not to be subject to any purpose that is not possible in accordance with a law that could arise from the will of the affected subject himself; hence this subject is to be used never merely as a means but as at the same time an end. We rightly attribute this condition even to the divine will with respect to the rational beings in the world as its creatures, inasmuch as it rests on their *personality*, by which alone they are ends in themselves."

34 See, on the one hand, Wenzel 1992 and, on the other, Sala 2004. Cf. my critique of Sala (Fischer 2004: xx n. 10).

one cannot conceive the effect of this beneficence (with respect to the happiness of rational beings) as befitting highest original good except under the limiting conditions of harmony with the *holiness* of his will. Hence, those who put the end of creation in the glory of God (provided this is not thought anthropomorphically, as inclination to be praised) perhaps hit upon the best expression. (KpV 5: 130 f.)

The idea of the "immortality of the soul" which Kant introduces as a "postulate of pure practical reason" (KpV 5: 122 ff.) requires "an endless progress toward that complete conformity" (i.e., the "complete conformity of the will with the moral law") which Kant calls "holiness," i.e., "a perfection of which no rational being of the sensible world is capable at any moment of his existence." Kant thus introduces a notion of 'eternity'. The striving for "holiness" is unavoidable in Kant's practical philosophy, for "the concept of holiness must necessarily serve as a *model* to which all finite rational beings can only approximate without end" (KpV 5: 32). This notion may be understood as a 'problem', viz., a task that remains speculatively and practically unsolvable, and yet arises inevitably – and calls for an answer that humans may only find in faith.[35] The lack of any reference to God among some modern Kant scholars has no foundation in Kant's own thinking, neither in his published work nor in his lectures. True 'autonomy' will first have to overcome the 'self-will' of a human being, which is only possible – since this process involves "dolor et labor" (Augustine, *Confessiones* 10,39) – if practiced with 'obedience' (in Meister Eckhart's sense) which is capable of overcoming even the "love of life" (KpV 5: 30; see also KU 5: 446 on "*thankfulness, obedience, and humility*" in the "purest moral disposition").

2 Outline of Kant's presentation of religion in *Lectures*

In *Lectures on the Philosophical Doctrine of Religion*, Kant takes handbooks as his models (Waterman 1899), namely Johann August Eberhard's *Vorbereitung zur natürlichen Theologie*,[36] Alexander Gottlieb Baumgarten's *Theologia naturalis* (*Pars quarta* of Baumgarten's *Metaphysica*) and Christophorus Meiners' *Historia*

---

[35] Thus, the definition of the "autonomy of the will" as "the sole principle of all moral laws and of duties in keeping with them" (KpV 5: 33) does not contradict what Meister Eckhart said about "true and perfect obedience" and a person's "self-will." See *Die Rede der Unterscheidungen* (Meister Eckhart 1993, vol. 2: 334–433, especially 334–41). Eckhart's teaching on the will relates to Kant's examples well (KpV 5: 30).
[36] Eberhard, *Vorbereitung zur natürlichen Theologie zum Gebrauch akademischer Vorlesungen* (Halle 1781), reprint in AA 20: 491–606.

doctrinae de vero deo omnium rerum auctore atque rectore.[37] This fact alone, however, solely regards external aspects of the work and does not shed any light on the internal motives that may have driven Kant in the composition of these lectures. What the notes published by Pölitz allow us to grasp about Kant's thoughts does not contradict anything in the published works, but helps us better understand some excessively brief passages in the writings. The lectures shed light on the existential background of several reflections and focus on existential acts that would constitute the connection between Kant's Critical philosophy and its realization in human life. In the *Lectures* it reads: "For the practical interest which we have in the existence of God as a wise ruler of the world is, on the contrary, *the highest* there can ever be, since if we remove this fundamental principle, we renounce at the same time all prudence and honesty, and we have to act against our own reason and our conscience" (PR 160=V-Phil-Th/Pölitz 28: 1083).

Kant's interest in 'pastoral care' – which includes both philosophical care for his own soul and a 'pastoral interest' in the well-being of his students – is evident throughout the entire text of *Lectures*, but especially at the end of the second section of part II ("Moral Theology"), "Of the nature and certainty of moral faith." Kant warns here against fanaticism (*Schwärmerei*), for who dares to "transcend them [the limits of our reason] will be punished by reason itself for his boldness with both pain and error" (PR 174=V-Phil-Th/Pölitz 28: 1091). Aiming to instruct himself and others to avoid pain and error, Kant assumes the role of someone who strives for wisdom and holiness and, at the same time, shows philosophical-pastoral care for others. He recommends modesty in one's demands and instills a human sense for belief in God. "But if we remain within these boundaries, then our reward will be to become wise and good human beings" (PR 174=V-Phil-Th/Pölitz 28: 1091). This recommendation to exercise moderation, however, does not lead – neither in the lectures, nor in the published works – to a surrender of the hope that accompanies faith in God.[38] In *Lectures*, this is evident in various ways. I can, however, only offer a short overview of relevant passages here, focusing on the third section of part II, entitled "Of God, regarding His Causality" (PR 175–219=V-Phil-Th/Pölitz 28: 1091–1104).

---

[37] Meiners' work stands in the background of the appendix (PR 226–235=V-Phil-Th/Pölitz 28: 1112–26).
[38] See, e. g., KpV 5: 114: "If, therefore, the highest good is impossible in accordance with practical rules, then the moral law, which commands us to promote it, must be fantastic and directed to empty imaginary ends and must therefore in itself be false."

It should first be noticed that, in Kant, the patristic understanding of the Old Testament (Genesis) account of creation – as *creatio ex nihilo*[39] – appears *only* in *Lectures*; in his published works, the thought sometimes stands in the background but it is not expressly mentioned or reflected upon at all.

In *Lectures*, however, Kant speaks of "creation" *as* "making actual out of nothing" and accordingly calls the result "a *creature*" (PR 182=V-Phil-Th/Pölitz 28: 1095). He further explains that God creates *only once*, that he as creator acts "freely" and that "the world created by God is the *best* of all possible worlds" (PR 183 f.=V-Phil-Th/Pölitz 28: 1097).[40] These considerations lead Kant to a reflection on the "purpose of creation." He asks: "What kind of incentive, if one may so express it, could move God to create a world?" (PR 188=V-Phil-Th/Pölitz 28: 1099).[41] Although there cannot be an "incentive" if God creates *out of nothing* (i. e., *not* from any given or preceding motives), Kant still recognizes "*absolute* ends" of God's creation, namely the "true perfection of the world-whole [which] has to lie in the use *rational creatures* make of their reason and freedom" (PR 188=V-Phil-Th/Pölitz 28: 1099). Kant sees the *purpose of creation* solely in the possibility of "the moral perfection of the world," which, in his published works, he calls "absolutely good" or 'unconditionally' good, "good without qualification," "good in itself," or "the highest good" (GMS 4: 393 f.; KpV 5: 110 f.). According to *Lectures*, God has created anything at all "merely *because it is good*" (PR 192=V-Phil-Th/Pölitz 28: 1101): "The objective end of God in creation was the perfection of the world and not merely the happiness of creatures" (PR 190=V-Phil-Th/Pölitz 28: 1100). Thus, Kant explains the sole "purpose of creation" – which cannot be determined by needs since God cannot be conceived as a 'needy' being – in the following way: "God's infinite understanding, on the contrary, recognized the *possibility of a highest good* external to himself in which morality would be the supreme principle" (PR 193=V-Phil-Th/Pölitz 28: 1102).

---

39 See for example Augustine, *De libero arbitrio* I,5. This interpretation was developed as a counter-position to Neo-platonic and Manichean teachings (*perilampsis, chysis*; the origin of the world results from a battle between the kingdom of darkness and the kingdom of light) (Fischer 1987: 143).
40 Cf. PR 185=V-Phil-Th/Pölitz 28: 1097: "There is more on this subject in Kant's Attempt at Some Considerations on Optimism." See also PR 185–7=V-Phil-Th/Pölitz 28: 1097–9 where Kant refers, among others, to the insights of astronomers and "beneficial" challenges such as "stinging flies." This confirms a thesis by Friedrich Paulsen (1920: xi–xx), according to which Kant and Leibniz share similar beliefs, but with the proviso that for Kant such belief cannot be presented as 'knowledge'.
41 It is impossible for there to be any 'incentives' in God. "In God no incentive is thinkable except an objective motive" (PR 191=V-Phil-Th/Pölitz 28: 1101).

Kant's notion here is thus close to the Christian explanation of the 'ground of creation' which Augustine sees in 'God's love': *gratis diligere*. Kant teaches that God created the world "for his honor's sake" but not so as to be served in the sense of enticing "his favor by rendering him all sorts of praise" (PR 193=V-Phil-Th/Pölitz 28: 1102).[42] Although Kant does not address God's purpose of creation in a similarly detailed way in *Religion within the Boundaries of Mere Reason*, he still remarks that we can be sure of "God's love for humankind through reason" (RGV 6: 120; cf. KU 5: 434–6). In *Lectures*, Kant mentions in this context traditional theological considerations that refer to God's will to create in the sense of *creatio continua* (PR 197=V-Phil-Th/Pölitz 28: 1104).[43] Kant maintains that a "*concursus* between God and events given in the world" is not impossible, but he rejects heterodox interpretations and interpretations that rely too heavily on a theology of grace.[44]

3 Reflections on the 'Christian' religion in the *Lectures* and published works

Although Kant's *Lectures on the Philosophical Doctrine of Religion* shows a greater proximity in content to the central tenets of Christian theology, in contrast to the published works and to other lectures it contains no explicit references to Christianity.[45] The reason for this may lie in the fact that these lectures presuppose a Christian background as self-evident. This background does not have to be emphasized explicitly, especially since Kant's recognition of the contents of the Christian faith (centering on Augustine's key ideas regarding the concept and purpose of creation, and time and eternity) is almost palpable throughout the

---

42 Cf. Fischer 2009: 169–89.
43 See also: "But I myself may nevertheless always have need of some other being for my own existence. And this being may be the author of my existence and duration without its having to be the author of my actions at the same time. Hence substance and accidents must be carefully distinguished from cause and effect" (PR 198=V-Phil-Th/Pölitz 28: 1105).
44 Kant combats as 'heterodox' Descartes' definition of substance, on which Spinoza's understanding depends (PR 198 f.=V-Phil-Th/Pölitz 28: 1105); according to Kant, God's "innermost presence" does not lead to a "constant influence on substances" or to the recognition of a "*potestas dei absoluta*," which Martin Luther – following Ockham – had believed in; on this topic, see Fischer 2012; cf. RGV 6: 120 f. Kant's critique is directed against some features of the Protestant doctrine of grace.
45 Kant often uses "Christian," "Christianity" and similar words, but not in *Lectures*: there is not a single case where he uses such a term, neither in Pölitz's edition nor in any other version of the lecture notes.

text. Moreover, Kant rejects views about God and religion that contradict fundamental Christian teachings as approached from a philosophical perspective. The fact that Kant's aim is to be understood as a "scientific or, if you will, pastoral service for the educated" (Delekat 1969: 343) is already clear from his published works, but it is even more obvious in *Lectures*, especially in his reflections on the purpose of creation.

Special praise then for the Christian religion (something often expressed in his published works) would have been simply redundant in *Lectures* because his audience would already have been well-acquainted with Kant's commitment to the Christian religion. It would also have been self-evident to Kant and his audience that the 'philosophical' doctrine of religion focuses on the inner of the two "concentric circles" (RGV 6: 12.)[46] Thus, it was not necessary in *Lectures* to emphasize the special approach in a particular way. It is true, though, that Kant expresses misgivings regarding belief in revelation. He says in *Religion within the Boundaries of Mere Reason* (RGV 6: 163): "The acceptance of the principles of a religion is preeminently called faith (*fides sacra*). We shall have to consider Christian faith, therefore, on the one hand as pure rational faith, and on the other as revealed faith (*fides statutaria*). The first may be considered as a faith freely accepted by everyone (*fides elicita*), the second as a commanded faith (*fides imperata*)."

However, Kant also sees his own historical situation as advantageous, since it provides him with insight into the biblical message (for example, he calls the book of Job "the most philosophical book of the Old Testament.)"[47] With respect to the Christian religion Kant sometimes even goes so far as to employ exuberant language. In the third *Critique* (§ 91), he calls Christianity a "wonderful religion" which "in the great simplicity of its expression has enriched morality with far more determinate and pure concepts than morality itself could previously supply" (KU

---

46 See Winter 2005: 37–42.
47 The Danziger Rationaltheologie transcription (that is, a *lecture*) reads: "We further see that it was the purpose of creation to leave our development and self-perfection to ourselves; we have been given the equipment and the capability of doing so. In this regard we find ourselves to be greater than an angel who is already perfect. Now, however, it cannot be avoided that we will have to work our way through a lot of hardship and evil and, of course, some may go astray. Leibniz's theodicy was written with a view to deal with these objections. The book of Job in the Old Testament has this as its purpose, and it is the most philosophical book in the Old Testament" (AA 28: 1287). Kant's references to Job can be found in various writings, e. g., in his 28 April 1775 letter to Johann Caspar Lavater (Br 10: 175 f.) and in his 1791 essay *On the Miscarriage of all Philosophical Trials in Theodicy* (MpVT 8: 265 f.).

5: 471n).⁴⁸ Some Christian practices, however, are the targets of harsh criticism. Yet such criticism could also draw on the very words of Jesus Christ himself and hence does not have to be seen as a critique of Christianity as such.⁴⁹ What Kant says in the Mrongovius ethics lecture sounds like something Christ might have said: "What good are, for instance, all his morning and evening prayers to a merchant if, right after mass, he cheats a customer?" (V-Mo/Mron 27: 1473).⁵⁰

Kant has spoken of the Christian faith with respect, calling it a 'wonderful religion' (KU 5: 471n) whose truth is not impossible (cf. V-Phil-Th/Pölitz 28: 1026),⁵¹ but which must be examined and questioned by reason. Even the following well-known phrase from Kant's *Groundwork of the Metaphysics of Morals* is not rooted in any anti-Christian feelings: "Even the Holy One of the Gospel must first be compared with our ideal of moral perfection before he is cognized as such" (GMS 4: 408). Rather, Kant expressly refers to the New Testament (Mt 19:17): "even he [Christ] says of himself: why do you call me (whom you see) good? None is good (the archetype of the good) but God only (whom you do not see)."⁵² Kant must have been heart-stricken when he received shortsighted critique from individuals who saw themselves as defenders of the 'orthodox faith', e. g., the physician Samuel Collenbusch who on 26 December 1794 wrote to Kant: "My dear Professor! Mr. Kant's rational belief is a very pure belief, totally bare of all hope. Mr. Kant's morality is a very pure morality, totally bare of all love. Now the ques-

---

48 See also *The End Of All Things*: "If, meanwhile, these attempts have for once finally prospered far enough that the community is susceptible and inclined to give a hearing not merely to the received pious doctrines but also to a practical reason which has been illuminated by them (which is also absolutely necessary for a religion)" (EaD 8: 336).
49 For example, Mt 7:21: "Not everyone who says to me, 'Lord, Lord,' will enter the kingdom of heaven, but only he who does the will of my Father."
50 This notion is close to Meister Eckhart who says: "Who were the traders in the temple, and who is like them today? Listen to me exactly: I now want to preach about *good* people only. This time, however, I want to point out who the traders were (and still are), the traders who were driven from the temple by our Lord. He still does this to all those who buy and sell in this temple; he wants none of them in there. See, they are all merchants who try to avoid big sins and would certainly like to be good people and do good works to honor God, such as fasting, waking, praying and so forth, all kinds of good works; and yet they do these only so that our Lord may give them something in return, or that God would do for them something they wish for; these are all traders" (Sermon 1 = Eckhart 1993, vol. 1: 10–22, especially 10–13).
51 Kant does not even reject the possibility of exterior miracles, although he sees them as problematic (PR 200–14=V-Phil-Th/Pölitz 28: 1105–13). "Yet a *concursus* between God and natural occurrences in the world is still not impossible" (PR 200=V-Phil-Th/Pölitz 28: 1106).
52 Cf. Mt 10:18; Lk 18:19.

tion arises: where is the devil's belief different from Mr. Kant's belief? And where is the devil's morality different from Mr. Kant's morality?"

Johann Wolfgang von Goethe, in a harsh review of *Blicke ins Reich der Gnade* (*Views into the Kingdom of Grace*), a collection of sermons by Friedrich Wilhelm Krummacher, called Krummacher's sermons "narcotic."[53] A similar 'self-narcotization' among believers (and the will to 'isolate' religion) can be found in Collenbusch's judgment. Against such criticisms Kant never tires of emphasizing that "a *religion* that rashly declares *war on reason* will not long endure against it" (RGV 6: 10). Thus Kant is in agreement with Augustine, who seems to anticipate Kant's image of the "concentric circles" when he says: "So it is taught and believed as a chief point in man's salvation that philosophy, i. e., the pursuit of wisdom, cannot be quite divorced from religion."[54]

---

[53] Goethe 1989–94, vol. 12: 357. Cf. the editor's note on 721. Krummacher had been a preacher in Barmen-Gemarke (see Gollwitzer 1967: 23), which is in present-day Wuppertal. Collenbusch wrote from nearby Elberfeld: it appears that they came from a similar milieu.

[54] *De vera religione* 8. According to Augustine, the natural striving for wisdom – which is the same in philosophy and faith – is a fundamental condition of the possibility of human salvation; he assumes that philosophy does not lead to the *possession* of truth, but that it entails a never-ending effort (*studium*).

IX Mathematics

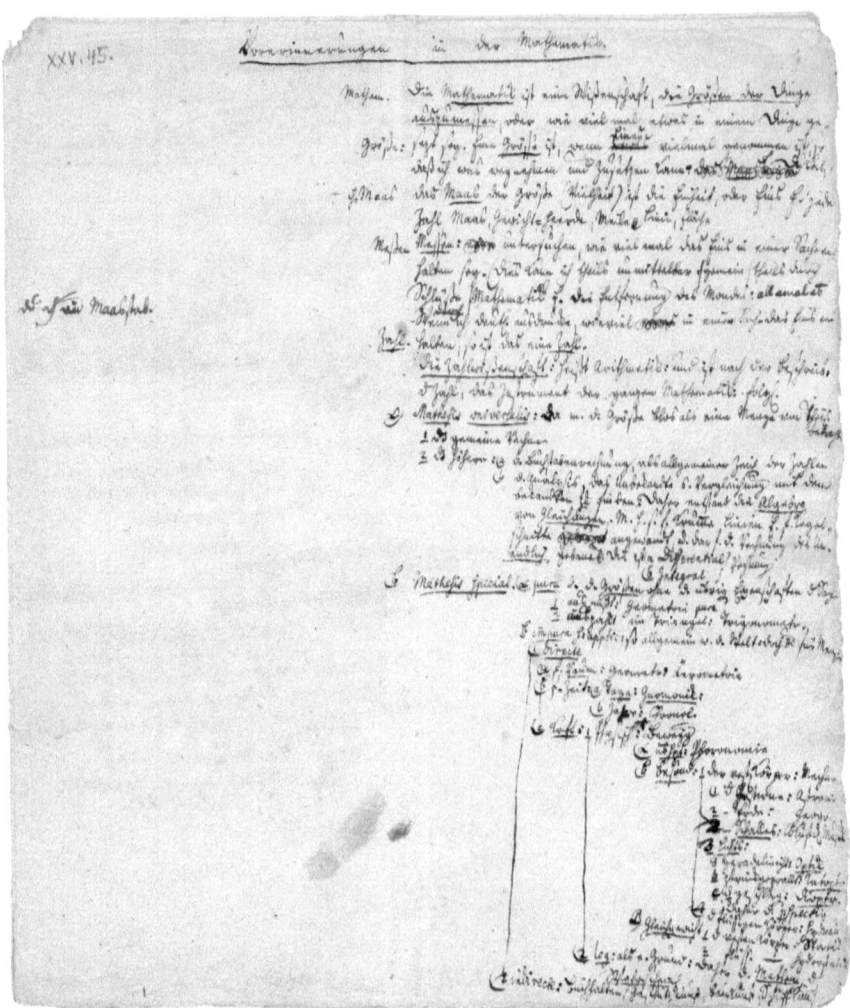

Fig. 14: Reproduction of page 1 from Herder's notes on mathematics, "Mathematik Herder" (cf. Irmscher 1964: 17–19; AA 29: 49 f.). Reproduced with the kind permission of Staatsbibliothek zu Berlin-Preußischer Kulturbesitz, Germany. Call number: NL-Herder XXV. 45. Steve Naragon's translation of the text follows; the German text is also given. (Recall that figures are not necessarily to be seen as objects of commentary by a chapter.)

Transcription of the Text in Fig. 14

[Ms 1]

Vorerinnerungen in der Mathematik

Mathematik. Die Mathematik ist eine Wißenschaft, die Größen der Dinge auszumessen, oder wie viel mal etwas in einem Dinge gesetzt sey.

Größe: Eine Grösse ist, wenn Eines vielmal genommen ist, so daß ich was wegnehmen und zusetzen kann. Exempel: Dukaten

ihr Maas. Das Maas der Größe (Vielheit) ist die Einheit, oder Eins. Exempel: jede Zahl, Maas, Gewicht = Heerde, Meile etc. Linie, Fläche

Meßen Messen: untersuchen, wie viel mal das Eins in einer Sache enthalten sey. (Dies kann ich theils unmittelbar (gemein) theils durch Schlüße) Mathematik Exempel: die Entfernung des Mondes: allemal aber durch [einen Maasstab]. Wenn ich deutlich ausdrucke, wieviel in einer Sache das Eins enthalten, so ist das eine Zahl.

Zahl. Die Zahlwißenschaft: heißt Arithmetik: und ist nach der Beschreibung der Zahl, das Instrument der ganzen Mathematik: folglich

(A) Mathesis vniversalis: Da man die Größe blos als eine Menge von Theilen betrachtet
  (1) das gemeine Rechnen
  (2) das höhere [Rechnen]:
    (a) die Buchstabenrechnung, als allgemeiner Zeichen der Zahlen
    (b) die Analysis, das Unbekandte aus Vergleichung mit dem Bekandten zu finden. Daher entstand die Algebra von Gleichungen. Man hat sie auf krumme Linien, Exempel auf Kegelschnitte angewandt und darauf die Rechnung des Unendlichen gebauet. Die ist
      (a) Differential-
      (b) Integral-Rechnung

(B) Mathesis specialis.
  (a) pura die die Größen ohne die übrigen Eigenschaften der Sachen
    (1) ausmißt: Geometria pura
    (2) auszählt im Triangel: Trigonometrie
  (b) impura sive applicata: so allgemein wie die Welt: doch nicht für Menschen
    (1) directe
      (a) auf Raum: Geometrie, Aerometrie
      (b) auf Zeit:
        (a) Tage: Gnomonik:
        (b) Jahre: Chronologie
  (c) [auf] Kraft:
    (1) Physisch: Bewegung

　　　　　(a) überhaupt: Phoronomie
　　　　　(b) besonders:
　　　　　　　(I) der vesten Körper: Mechanik
　　　　　　　　　(1) der Gestirne: Astronomie
　　　　　　　　　(2) der Erde: Geographie
　　　　　　　(II) des Schalles: Akustik, Musik
　　　　　　　(III) des Lichts:
　　　　　　　　　(a) geradelinicht: Optik
　　　　　　　　　(b) zurückgeprallt: Katoptrik
　　　　　　　　　(c) durchgeschlagen: Dioptrik, daher die Perspective
　　　　　　　(IV) der flüssigen Körper: Hydraulik
　　　　　(B) Gleichgewicht
　　　　　　　(1) der vesten Körper: Statik
　　　　　　　(2) der flüssigen Körper: Hydrostatik
　　　(2) logisch als ein Grund: Daher die Mathematik der Wahrscheinlichkeit.
　(2) indirekte: Buchhalten, Geschützkunst, Baukunst, Schiffkunst

English Translation

[Ms 1]

Preliminary Remarks about Mathematics

Mathematics. Mathematics is a science for measuring the magnitudes of things, or how many times something can be placed in a thing.

Magnitude: A magnitude is when a unit is taken multiple times, so that I can subtract and add something. Example: ducats

its measure: The measure of the magnitude (plurality) is unity, or unit. Example: every number, measure, weight = herd, miles, etc. line, area

To measure: To measure: to investigate how many times a unit is contained in a thing. (I can do this in part directly (common), in part through inference) Mathematics example: the distance of the moon: but always through [a standard of measurement]. If I express distinctly how many units are contained in a thing, that is a number.

Number. The science of number is called arithmetic, and is according to the description of number the instrument of the whole of mathematics. Consequently

(A) Mathesis universalis [universal mathematics]: here one considers the magnitude merely as a set of parts.
　　(1) common calculation
　　(2) higher [calculation]
　　　　(a) algebra, as general signs of numbers

(b) analysis, to find the unknown by comparison with the known. Thus arises the algebra of equations. It has been used for curved lines, conic sections for example, and on this is built the calculus of the infinite. It is
　(a) differential-
　(b) integral-calculus
(B) Mathesis specialis [special mathematics]
　(a) pura [pure]: magnitudes without the other properties of the things,
　　(1) are measured: geometria pura [pure geometry]
　　(2) are triangulated: trigonometry
　(b) impura sive applicata [impure or applied]: as general as the world, but not for human beings.
　　(1) direct
　　　(a) to space: geometry, aerometry
　　　(b) to time:
　　　　(a) days: gnomonics
　　　　(b) years: chronology
　(c) [to] power
　　(1) physical: motion
　　　(a) in general: phoronomy
　　　(b) special:
　　　　(I) of solid bodies: mechanics
　　　　　(1) of the stars: astronomy
　　　　　(2) of the earth: geography
　　　　(II) of sound: acoustics, music
　　　　(III) of light
　　　　　(a) straight-lined: optics
　　　　　(b) reflected: catoptrics
　　　　　(c) transmitted: dioptrics, thus perspective
　　　　(IV) of fluid bodies: hydraulics
　　　(B) equilibrium
　　　　(1) of solid bodies: statics
　　　　(2) of fluid bodies: hydrostatics
　　(2) logical as a ground: thus the mathematics of probability
　(2) indirect: accounting, artillery, architecture, shipbuilding.

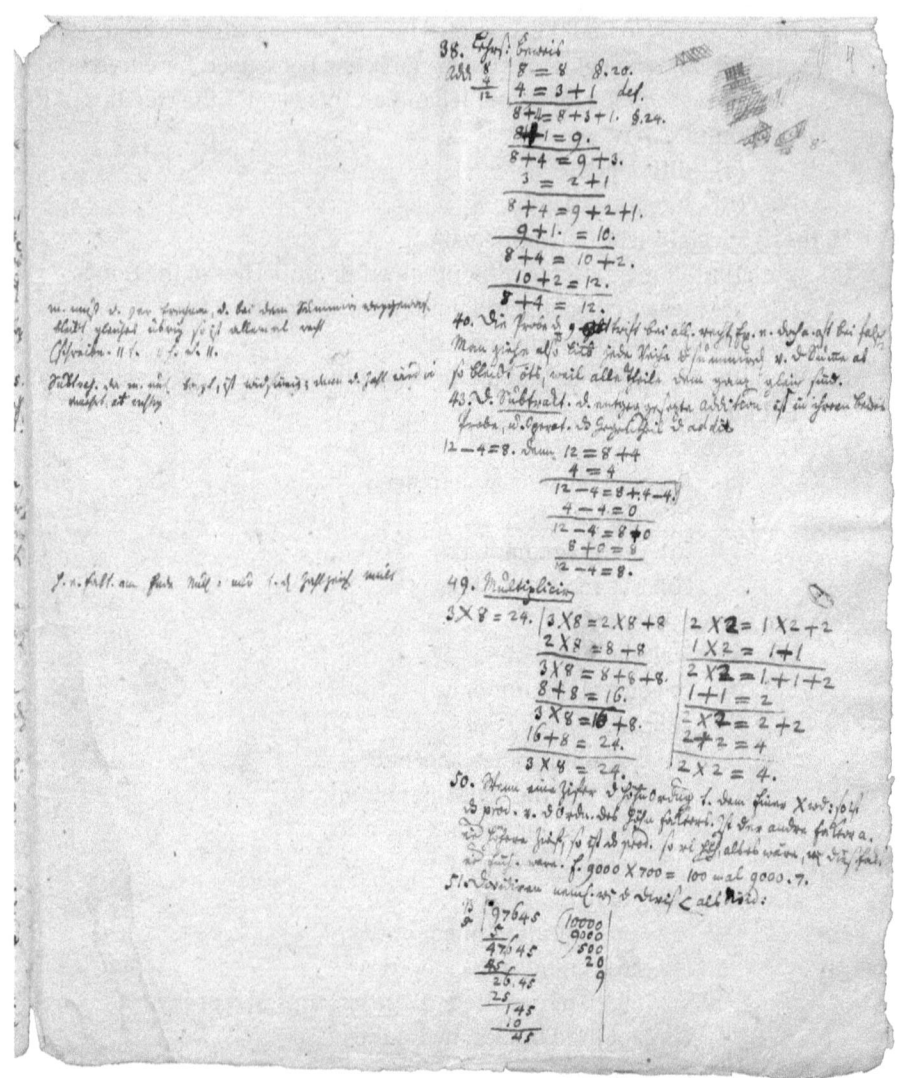

Fig. 15: Reproduction of page 7 from Herder's notes on mathematics, "Mathematik Herder" (cf. Irmscher 1964: 27 f.; AA 29: 57 f.). Reproduced with the kind permission of Staatsbibliothek zu Berlin-Preußischer Kulturbesitz, Germany. Call number: NL-Herder XXV. 45. Steve Naragon's translation of the text follows; the German text is also given.

Transcription and Translation of the Text in Fig. 15
[Ms 7]
38 Lehrsazt: Beweis:

Addition

8	
4	
12	

$8 = 8$ §20.
$4 = 3 + 1$ definition
$8 + 4 = 8 + 3 + 1$ §24.
$\underline{8 + 1 = 9}$
$8 + 4 = 9 + 3$
$\underline{3 = 2 + 1}$
$8 + 4 = 9 + 2 + 1$
$\underline{9 + 1 = 10}$
$8 + 4 = 10 + 2$
$\underline{10 + 2 = 12}$
$8 + 4 = 12$

40. Die Probe durch 9 trift bei allen rechten Exempeln ein, doch auch oft bei falschen. Man ziehe also lieber jede Reihe der summirenden von der Summe ab, so bleibt nichts, weil alle Theile dem ganzen gleich sind.
{Man muß die 9er mitrechnen, die bei dem Summiren weggeworfen, bleibt gleiches übrig so ist allemal recht (schreibe 11 tausend 11 hundert und 11)}

43. Die <u>Subtraktion</u> die entgegen gesete Addition ist in ihren Beweisen, Probe, und Operation das Gegentheil der addition.
{Subtrahiren, da man unten borgt, ist widersinnig; denn die Zahl wird nicht vermehrt: aber richtig}

$12 - 4 = 8$ denn $12 = 8 + 4$
                   $\underline{4 = 4}$
                   $12 - 4 = 8 + 4 - 4$
                   $\underline{4 - 4 = 0}$
                   $12 - 4 = 8 + 0$
                   $\underline{8 + 0 = 8}$
                   $12 - 4 = 8$

49. Multipliciren
{hat ein Faktor am Ende Null: nur mit dem Zahlzeichen multipliciren}

$3 \times 8 = 24$ $3 \times 8 = 2 \times 8 + 8$ $2 \times 2 = 1 \times 2 + 2$
                $\underline{2 \times 8 = 8 + 8}$ $\underline{1 \times 2 = 1 + 1}$
                $3 \times 8 = 8 + 8 + 8$ $2 \times 2 = 1 + 1 + 2$
                $\underline{8 + 8 = 16}$ $\underline{1 + 1 = 2}$
                $3 \times 8 = 16 + 8$ $2 \times 2 = 2 + 2$
                $\underline{16 + 8 = 24}$ $\underline{2 + 2 = 4}$
                $3 \times 8 = 24$ $2 \times 2 = 4$

50. Wenn eine Zifer der höheren Ordnung mit dem Einer malgenommen wird: so ist das produkt von der Ordnung des höheren Faktors. Ist der andere Faktor auch eine höhere Zifer, so ist das produkt so viel höher, als es wäre, wenn dieser Faktor eine Einheit wäre. Exempel: 9000 × 700 = 100 mal 9000 . 7.

51. Dividiren, nemlich wenn der Divisor < als der Dividend

```
B        97645   (10000
5          5     (9000
         47,645    500
          45        20
          26,45      9
          25
          145
           10
           45
```

English Translation
[Ms 7]

38 Theorem:		Proof	
Addition	8	$8 = 8$	§ 20.
	4	$4 = 3 + 1$	definition
	12	$8 + 4 = 8 + 3 + 1$	§ 24.
		$8 + 1 = 9$	
		$8 + 4 = 9 + 3$	
		$3 = 2 + 1$	
		$8 + 4 = 9 + 2 + 1$	
		$9 + 1 = 10$	
		$8 + 4 = 10 + 2$	
		$10 + 2 = 12$	
		$8 + 4 = 12$	

40. The 'casting out nines' test works with all correct examples, but often with false ones as well. Therefore, one should instead take away each row of the summing from the sum, so that nothing remains, because all the parts equal the whole.

{One must take into account the 9s thrown away with the summing; if the same remains then it is correct (write 11 thousand 11 hundred and 11)}

43. Subtraction, as opposed to addition, is the opposite of addition in its proofs, testing, and operation.

{It is peculiar to borrow something when subtracting; for the number is not increased, but correct}

12 − 4 = 8 since 12 = 8 + 4
4 = 4
12 − 4 = 8 + 4 − 4
4 − 4 = 0
12 − 4 = 8 + 0
8 + 0 = 8
12 − 4 = 8

49. Multiplication
{if a factor ends with a zero, multiply only with the numeral}

3 × 8 = 24	3 × 8 = 2 × 8 + 8	2 × 2 = 1 × 2 + 2
	2 × 8 = 8 + 8	1 × 2 = 1 + 1
	3 × 8 = 8 + 8 + 8	2 × 2 = 1 + 1 + 2
	8 + 8 = 16	1 + 1 = 2
	3 × 8 = 16 + 8	2 × 2 = 2 + 2
	16 + 8 = 24	2 + 2 = 4
	3 × 8 = 24	2 × 2 = 4

50. If a number of the higher order is multiplied by one, then the product is of the order of the higher factor. If the other factor is also a higher number, then the product is that much higher than it would be were this factor a unity. Example: 9000 × 700 = 100 times 9000 . 7.

51. Division, namely if the divisor is less than the dividend

```
B     97645   (10000
5     5       (9000
      47,645   500
      45       20
      26,45    9
      25
      145
      10
      45
```

Chapter 18
Herder's Notes on Kant's Mathematics Course

Antonio Moretto
Translated by Giorgio Galbussera

1 Kant's lectures on mathematics and the Russian period – Herder in Königsberg

During the course of the Seven Years' War Russian troops occupied eastern Prussia from January 1758 to July 1762.[1] This, however, did not disrupt local government or the normal functioning of Albertina University. It must be noted that in addition to a rich social life "a part of the officer corps manifested an impulse towards culture," and Kant is said to have given many Russian officers private lessons in mathematics (Vorländer 1977: 89–90).

In "Einführung in Kants Vorlesungen," in *Beiträge zur Geschichte und Interpretation der Philosophie Kants*, Gerhard Lehmann reminds us that Arnoldt divides the *Vorlesungen* into four groups and inserts in the third group (*aus den Dozentenjahren*) the lectures on physics, mathematics, mechanical sciences (mechanics, hydrostatics, hydraulics, aerometry), and mineralogy. Lehmann also adds that during the Russian period (1758–1762) Kant held *Privatissima* on fortification and on pyrotechnics (Lehmann 1969: 75).

According to Gottfried Martin, Kant lectured on mathematics for sixteen consecutive semesters, from the winter semester 1755/56 through the summer semester 1762, and he held lectures (*vorgetragen habe*) on fortification in the presence of Russian officers (Martin 1967: 58–62). It bears keeping in mind that mechanics, hydrostatics, hydraulics, aerometry, fortification, and pyrotechnics rank among mathematical sciences in Wolff's conception, and that Kant's lectures had Wolff's *Auszug aus den Anfangsgründen aller mathematischen Wissenschaften* as reference text. Right at the beginning of the "Russian period," at the end of his essay *Neuer Lehrbegriff der Bewegung und Ruhe* (dated 1 April 1758), in announcing his lectures for the current semester, Kant states that Wolff's *Auszug* will be used (*Die Mathematik wird über Wolffens* Auszug *angefangen werden*)

---

[1] On the invasion of eastern Prussia, see Hasenkamp 1866.

(NLBR 2: 25). Similarly on 7 October 1759, in his *An Attempt at Some Reflections on Optimism*, Kant announces his lectures for the semester, specifying that he will address pure mathematics (*die reine Mathematik*) and the mechanical sciences (*die mechanischen Wissenschaften*) according to Wolff. He then adds: "It is understood that I will complete each of these sciences in one semester and, if that is too short, I will catch up with the rest in a few hours during the following semester [*Man weiß schon daß ich jede dieser Wissenschaften in einem halbe Jahre zu Ende bringe und, wenn dieses zu kurz ist, den Rest in eineigen Stunden des folgenden nachhole*]" (VBO 2: 35).

Kant's *Vorlesung* on mathematics transcribed by Johann Gottfried Herder most likely dates to the years 1762–1763. Herder (Mohrungen 1744 – Weimar 1803) arrived in Königsberg in the summer of 1762. Schwartz-Erla, a regiment doctor at the service of the Russian military (*in russischen Diensten*), had offered to pay for Herder's education in surgery at Königsberg and his later application to study medicine in Petersburg. However, shortly after his arrival, Herder decided to dedicate himself to the study of theology and philosophy, abandoning his original intent. He matriculated on 10 August 1762 at the Faculty of Theology and he entered the "Collegium Friedericianum" the same day. On 22 November 1764 he interrupted his studies and moved to Riga to accept a position as associate at the local Cathedral School. During his stay in Königsberg, Herder attended Lilienthal's lectures on dogmatic theology, Arnold's on the history of the church, Kypke's on philology, Kant's on logic, metaphysics, ethics, mathematics, and geography, and Teske's on physics. He is also likely to have attended Christoph Langhansen and Friedrich Samuel Bock's lectures on the New Testament, and Friedrich Johann Buck's on mathematics (Irmscher 1964: 7–9, 12).

For *Mathematik Herder*, I am using both the 1964 version, edited by Hans Dietrich Irmscher,[2] and the 1980 version, edited by Gerhard Lehmann for the *Akademie-Ausgabe* (AA). For textual citations, I refer to Lehmann, that is, volume 29.1,1 of *Kant's gesammelte Schriften*. According to Irmscher, *Mathematik Herder* consists of two manuscripts (which I designate *A* and *B*), both dating to either the winter semester 1762/63, or the summer semester 1763.[3]

---

2 Irmscher observes that the text of *Mathematik Herder* resumes and continues what had been started by Martin 1936: 294 ff.

3 Such distinction between the two texts does not figure in the edition by Lehmann, who in his *Einleitung*, referring to the two *Stücke* of Irmscher's edition, nonetheless indicates them as I and II (AA 29.1,1: 658). In any case, for the sake of convenience, I use *A* and *B* for the corresponding parts in Lehmann's edition, AA 29.1,1: 49–58 and AA 29.1,1: 59–66, respectively.

The text edited by Lehmann is divided into the following sections. The title *Vorerinnungen in der Mathematik* introduces the articulation of mathematical sciences (*A*: 49–51), which essentially corresponds to Wolff's articulation in *Auszug*. Then comes the presentation of Arithmetic (*Rechen Kunst*), dedicated to the concept of number and to the four fundamental arithmetical operations (*A*: 52–8). The text continues with the *Vorläufige Erinnerungen* (*B*: 59), which partly repeat the *Vorerinnungen*, followed by a section dedicated to *Arithmetik*; after considerations presented at *B*: 60, which mostly correspond to the content of the *Rechen Kunst*, this section examines fractions, power and roots, and ratios and their uses (*B*: 61–64.22). At the end the *Vorlesung* ends with the *Vorläufige Anmerkungen der Geometrie* (*B*: 64.23–66).

Because there is a repetition of topics dealing with the articulation of mathematical sciences and of the part on arithmetic dedicated to number, which appear in both *A* and *B*, in order to avoid a double exposition of the same topics, I will divide the treatment of the subject into three parts. In the first part, I will present the articulation of mathematical sciences, referring to text *A* for the *Vorerinnungen in der Mathematik* and to text *B* for the *Vorläufige Erinnerungen* on page 59; in the second part, I will present Arithmetic (*Rechen Kunst*), referring to text *A* until the end, and to text *B* on page 60, then text *B* from page 61 through page 64.22; in the third part, I will present from page 64.23 through page 66.43 the *Vorläufige Anmerkungen der Geometrie*.

Moreover, I note that Irmscher's edition places in double round parentheses parts of the text which, based on ink color, he thought to be inserted by Herder at a later time, while still belonging to his "student period" (Irmscher 1964: 14). Lehmann's edition does not make this distinction; it inserts the written parts in the same order as Irmscher's edition, with the exception of the concluding part of *Vorlesung* (*B*: 66).

According to Kant's announcements of his lectures, the reference text for the mentioned 1758 and 1759 lectures was *Auszug aus den Anfangsgründen aller mathematischen Wissenschaften*. Based on this indication, I am considering for *Mathematik Herder* the Frankfurt and Leipzig 1755 edition of *Auszug* (first edition, Halle 1713). However, as will become clear later, we cannot exclude the use of additional mathematical and philosophical texts by Wolff (his *Anfangs-Gründe aller mathematischen Wissenschaften, Mathematisches Lexicon, Elementa matheseos universae, Ontologia*, and *Psychologia empirica*), nor texts by other mathematicians.[4]

---

4 On this, I wish to point out that on some occasions the exposition in *Mathematik Herder* corresponds remarkably to Kästner's *Anfangsgründe*, which at times joins or overlaps the reference to Wolff.

Note that Euclid's *Elementa*[5] is often in the background. Finally, let me point out that we cannot exclude additions by Herder.

It must be mentioned that the text of the mathematics *Vorlesung* is not edited with equal care in all its parts. It is generally a very concise draft, at times incomplete both in size and clarity of exposition. On the other hand, Wolff's *Auszug*, despite being his most compact mathematics textbook, could not lend itself to being addressed and commented on by Kant in an exhaustive manner in just two cycles of lectures, due to its size. Nonetheless, it is an important text for understanding Kant's relationship to Wolff's conception of mathematics, and the development of his reflections on this discipline.

I will first focus on the 'architecture' of mathematics, examining a) the importance of the notion of *measuring magnitudes*, which is the fundamental goal of this science,[6] b) *mathesis universalis* and *mathesis specialis*, c) and the mathematical method. After this part dedicated to all of the mathematical disciplines, I will examine some aspects of the treatment of arithmetic and geometry. It must be noted that *Mathematik Herder* considers in particular the disciplines of *mathesis pura*, arithmetic and geometry. Negative magnitudes are not considered, and there is no treatment of trigonometry; mechanics, hydrostatic, hydraulics, and aerometry, which belong to *mathesis applicata*, were meant to be addressed (probably) in the following semester. Therefore, the preliminary part (*Vorerinnungen in der Mathematik*) must be considered as a concise introduction to the whole complex of mathematical sciences. Because the space dedicated to geometry is very limited and its exposition is often only briefly sketched, one can venture the hypothesis that Kant was thinking of dedicating to geometry some more time in the following semester, in accordance with the above-quoted observation in *An Attempt at Some Reflections on Optimism* (VBO 2: 35).

In this essay, due to limited space it is not possible uniformly to address all of the different topics presented in Herder's notes. I consider it sufficient to highlight certain aspects that I find interesting from a mathematical and philosophical point of view, especially if they touch on themes that would eventually develop in Kant's mature philosophy; I do not presume to examine exhaustively the various issues presented by a text of such notable complexity in structure and content.

---

5 It is doubtful that Kant read Euclid in the original; see Erich Adickes's note at AA Refl 14: 24. Yet Kant could have used translations and re-elaborations of *Elementa*.
6 I am using the term "magnitude" in reference to the *theory of mathematical magnitudes* which has a celebrated precedent in the doctrine in Book V of Euclid's *Elements*.

2 The reference to Wolff and Kästner in the measurement of magnitudes

In *Vorerinnungen in der Mathematik* – in text *A* of *Mathematik Herder* – mathematics is defined as the science of measurement: "Die *Mathematik* ist eine Wißenschaft, die *Größen der Dinge auszumessen*" (*A*: 49.1–4; original emphasis). This is in agreement with Wolff's *Lexicon*: "[Mathematics] is a science to measure all things that can be measured [*ist eine Wißenschaft, alles auszumessen, was sich ausmessen last*]" (Wolff 1978: column 863), and with the *Vorerinnungen*[7] to Kästner's *Anfangsgründe* (Kästner 1758: 1–3). Text *B* starts in a similar way with the *Vorläufige Erinnerungen*, succinctly reminding the reader that mathematics (*mathesis*, from the Greek *manthāno*, corresponding to the Latin *disco*), is a science of the measurement (*Ausmessung*) of magnitudes (*Größen*) (*B*: 59.3–4). Based on Wolff's important considerations on measure, *Vorlesung Herder* distinguishes between magnitude (*Größe*), intended as that which can be increased or decreased,[8] unit of measurement of magnitude (*Maas* in abstracto, and *Maasstab* in concreto, e. g., a mile), and the act of measuring (*messen*), i. e., specifying how many times the unit (*das Eins*) is contained within a thing (*in einer Sache*). [Unit of] measurement is intended as a synonym for unity (*Einheit*), and magnitude as a synonym for multiplicity (*Vielheit*). This measurement can be taken directly, through a unit of measurement, or indirectly, through inferences (*Schlüße*), as in the case of the distance between the earth and moon (*A*: 49.5–14).[9]

It is thus stated that number is the distinct (*deutlich*) expression of how many times the unit (*das Eins*) is contained within a thing (*in einer Sache*) (*A*: 49.16–18). In this regard one must note that Wolff, in the entry *Numerus, eine Zahl* of his *Lexicon*, reminds us that Euclid defined number as "a set of unities" (*eine Menge von Einheiten*), and explained only "whole rational numbers" (*die ganzen Rational-Zahlen*).[10] Similarly, in his *Deutschen Anfangs-Gründen der Rechen Kunst*, Wolff limited himself to such explanation, deeming it very clear for beginners and adequate for understanding the foundations of arithmetic, avoiding the discussion of irrational numbers. In *Elementis Arithmeticis*, however, Wolff uses a wider definition of number as something that is to the unit as a segment of a straight

---

[7] The complete title of the Introduction is *Vorerinnungen von der Mathematik überhaupt und ihrer Lehrart*.
[8] See Wolff 1978: column 1143; Kästner 1758: 1.
[9] See Kästner 1758: 2. As Sutherland observes, Euler in his *Algebra* (1770) shares this notion of magnitudes and measurement (Sutherland 2006: 544).
[10] Instead of 'whole numbers', today one uses the synonymous term 'integers' (and not 'integer numbers'). Note that *Mathematik Herder* does not consider 'negative integers'.

line is to another straight line, thus defining number as the relationship between two straight lines.[11] However, it still needs to be clarified what is meant by the relationship between two straight lines, and of two magnitudes in general. The question will be solved in late nineteenth-century mathematical analysis (Dedekind, Cantor) through the definition of real number.[12]

As far as the mathematical problem of measurement is concerned, it is necessary to remember the great importance attributed to this issue by Wolff and, as we will see later, the attention given to it by Kant. This aspect is already present in Wolff's *German Metaphysics* (Wolff 1983b: § 62), but measurement is treated more articulately in his *Ontologia*. Concerning the notion of *mensura/metiri*, Wolff indeed observes that we say we are measuring (*metiri*) a magnitude (*magnitudinem*) if we assume another magnitude as unity (*pro unitate*) and we determine the relationship (*rationem*) that the former has with the latter. The magnitude that is assumed as unity is called [unit of] measurement (*mensuram*), and the magnitude whose relationship with the [unit of] measurement we are investigating is called the measured (*mensuratum*) (Wolff 1977: § 438).[13] Thus Wolff connects the meaning of measurement to the relationship between magnitudes, consistent with Euclid's theory in the fifth Book of *Elementa*, which is probably taking up Eudoxus's proposal.[14] Wolff also observes that "in measuring magnitude, we express it distinctly through numbers," because, in measuring, the relationship between magnitude and the unit of measurement is the same as the relationship between a number and the numerical unity (Wolff 1977: § 440).[15] The philosophical importance of the concept of measurement in Kant is clear from the fact that, in the table of categories in the *Prolegomena* (§ 21), under the class of Quantity, next to the terms *Einheit*, *Vielheit*, and *Allheit*, used in *Critique of Pure Reason*, the corresponding terms from the doctrine of measurement also appear: *das Maß*, *die Größe*, and *das Ganze*. Through this we can more easily understand the connection between the Kantian category of Unity and measure (i.e., unit of measurement), between Plurality and magnitude, and between Totality and the

---

11 Wolff 1978: columns 944–5. See Euclid's *Elementa*, Liber VII, Def. II (Euclides 1970: 103; Euclid 1956b: 280). In Kästner 1758: 21, too, a whole positive number is defined as a set (*Menge*) of things of the same kind. Regarding Wolff, see Moretto 2007: 146–8; Moretto 2008: 26.
12 On the problem of measurement, see Moretto 2012.
13 See Kästner 1758: 2 for similar considerations on the measurement of the distance between two places.
14 See the basic definitions of the theory in Euclid's *Elementa*, Liber V, Def. I–XVIII (Euclides 1970: 1–3; Euclid 1956b: 113–36).
15 On the notion of measurement in Wolff, see Moretto 2007: 148–50; Moretto 2008: 30 f.

whole.¹⁶ In *Mathematik Herder*, as we have seen, such correspondence is established between the concepts of *Einheit*, *Vielheit* and the mathematical notions *das Maß*, *die Größe*. Although the notion of Totality (*Allheit*), corresponding to the whole (*das Ganze*), is missing, on the basis of this text it is possible that at the time Kant was already connecting the concepts of the class of Quantity to the notions of measurement.

3 *Mathesis universalis* and *Mathesis specialis*

3.1 *Mathesis universalis*

The science of numbers is called arithmetic (*Arithmetik*). It is the instrument of all mathematics through the "description of numbers [*Beschreibung der Zahl*]" (*A*: 49.19–20), and it can be divided into *Mathesis universalis* and *Mathesis specialis*. *Mathesis universalis* is divided into common calculus (*das gemeine Rechnen*), and higher calculus (*das höhere Rechnen*), which in turn is divided into literal calculus (*die Buchstabenrechnung*) and analysis, which determines what is unknown by comparing it to what is known. From this derives the discipline called the algebra of equations. It is applied to curves, for example conic sections; for this purpose infinitesimal calculus (*die Rechnung des Unendlichen*) has been developed, which is articulated into differential and integral calculus (*A*: 49.21–33).¹⁷ In text *B* it is stated that *mathesis universalis* "measures magnitude in itself [*die Größe an sich ausmisst*]," and it is arithmetic if it expresses magnitudes through numbers; it is algebra if it represents them through other signs (*B*: 59.6–10). Concerning *Mathesis universalis* and *Mathesis specialis*, the text of *Mathematik Herder* rather faithfully follows the considerations concisely presented by Kästner in the above-mentioned *Vorerinnungen* to his *Anfangsgründe* (§9), at times even adopting the same order of exposition. It must be noted that in his *Auszug*, Wolff defines algebra as the science that, given finite magnitudes, allows one through equations to find other magnitudes that are in a certain relation to the former (Wolff 1755: 698). More concisely, in *Elementa Matheseos Universae*, in § 132 of *Elementa*

---

16 See KrV A80/B106; Prol 4: 303. On the categories of quantity and the theory of measurement, see Moretto 1999: 208–11, 224–7.
17 This part of *Vorlesung* corresponds to the concise exposition on pure mathematics (*reine Mathematik*), in Kästner 1758: 4 f.

Analyseos Mathematicae tam finitorum quam infinitorum, he states that "algebra is the method to solve problems through equations" (Wolff 1968a: 341).[18]

The text of *Mathematik Herder* can be better appreciated if one considers Wolff's indications that *Arithmetica* or *Rechen Kunst* is the science of numbers (Wolff 1978: column 169), and one keeps in mind that *Mathesis universalis* has been considered the art of calculating through letters, or through digits and letters, to be used also in order to show general properties of magnitudes (e. g., direct proportionality between a class of magnitudes and another, inverse proportionality, or square proportionality); one finally gets to Leibniz's *Acta Eruditorum*, who by *Mathesis universalis* means those disciplines that give general rules for measuring all things. However, Leibniz observes that this *mathesis* has not yet been discovered (Wolff 1978: column 869; cf. Leibniz 1691: 446). This in *Lexicon*; but in *Ontologia* (§ 755 note), Wolff also thinks that his conception of *Mathesis universalis* is strengthened by higher mathematics, which, through infinitesimal calculus, made the quantitative evaluation of qualities possible, in order to comprehend the "laws of variation [*variationum leges*]" of phenomena: in other terms, functions[19] that describe phenomena through "curves" (Wolff 1977: 559). It must be added that in *Psychologia Empirica* (§ 522 note), he shows how it is possible to propose even a discipline that deals with "measurement of the psyche," psychometry [*Psycheometria*], through which one can see that, in those areas that pertain to quantity, the human mind too follows mathematical laws, just like the material world. And he goes so far as to propose mathematical laws even for the evaluation of what is pleasant and what is not.[20] Moreover, in *Critique of Pure Reason* and in *Metaphysical Foundations of Natural Science*, one can clearly observe Kant's great attention to quantitative evaluation of qualities and the concept of function (Moretto 1999: 265–74).

Note that in his 1764 essay, "Inquiry concerning the Distinctness of the Principles of Natural Theology and Morality," from the same period as the *Vorlesung Herder*, Kant states that magnitude (*Größe*) constitutes the object of mathematics, which is based on a "general theory of magnitudes [*allgemeine Größenlehre*]," which is properly "general arithmetic [*allgemeine Arithmetik*]" (UD 2: 282). Note that Segner (1756: 262) uses the term *arithmetica universalis* to refer essentially to

---

18 Note that in *Anfangs-Gründe aller mathematischen Wissenschaften* algebra is addressed in the last section (Wolff 1750c: 1549–1798), together with infinitesimal calculus; in *Auszug*, too, it is treated in the last part (Wolff 1755: 698–740).
19 In both Wolff and Kant these notions are presented in relation to intensive magnitudes. On Wolff, see Moretto 2007: 152–6; Moretto 2008: 31–6. On Kant, see Moretto 1999: 265–76.
20 Wolff 1968f: 403 f. See Moretto 2007: 162–5.

literal calculus, and that Segner later (1773: 324 f.) uses in this context the term *allgemeine Arithmetik*. In the later *Metaphysical Foundations of Natural Science*, Kant states that Phoronomy is "the pure theory of magnitude (*mathesis*) of motions [*die reine Größenlehre* (Mathesis) *der Bewegungen*]" (MAN 4: 489).[21]

3.2 *Mathesis specialis*

In *Mathematik Herder*, *mathesis specialis* is divided into *pura* and *impura*. *Mathesis pura* measures magnitudes independently of the rest of the properties of things; examples of it are pure geometry and trigonometry (*A*: 49.34–37). In contrast, according to the *Lexicon*, under the entry *Mathesis pura sive simplex*, *die eigentliche Mathematik*, or mathematics strictly speaking, are included arithmetic, geometry, trigonometry, and algebra (Wolff 1978: column 868).[22] *Mathesis impura* is *mathesis applicata* (applied), which is rendered in German by A. G. Kästner as *die angewandte Mathematik*; it extends to the whole world (parallel to what Kästner states at *Vorerinnerungen*, § 6), excluding humans (*A*: 49.38–39). As we have observed in Wolff's perspective, mathematics can be used in all sciences. In *Metaphysical Foundations of Natural Science*, Kant will claim that a physical doctrine of nature contains as much science properly to the extent that it contains mathematics. Such conviction leads him to exclude chemistry and the empirical doctrine of the soul from the number of veritable sciences (MAN 4: 471).

The claim contained in *Mathematik Herder*, that *mathesis applicata* cannot concern the human being, could anticipate the Kantian exclusion of psychology from the list of sciences; these are considered as such in proportion to the role mathematics played in them, as expressed in *Metaphysical Foundations of Natural Science*. According to Kant, the "empirical doctrine of the soul" (*empirische Seelenlehre*) is susceptible to mathematization to a too limited degree (MAN 4: 471), and in this his point of view diverges from Wolff's, who, as we have seen, was favorable to the mathematical consideration of empirical psychology.

Note that this *angewandte Mathematik*, as it is called in the Kantian *Vorlesung*,[23] is called by Wolff *Mathesis impura sive mixta, die angebrachte Mathema-*

---

[21] See Sutherland 2006: 549.
[22] Note that text *B*, in contrast to text *A*, does not consider a geometry and a trigonometry in which magnitudes (*Größen*) are considered "without the residual properties of things [*ohne die übrigen Eigenschaften der Sachen*]" (*A*: 49.35), but rather "in specific things [*in besondern Dingen*]" (*B*: 59.11).
[23] In MAN, Kant states that the science of nature is either a pure or applied doctrine of motion (*reine oder angewandte Bewegungslehre*) (MAN 4: 477). Note that A. G. Kästner published *An-*

tik, and it includes all of mathematics that is outside of arithmetic, geometry, and algebra (Wolff 1978: columns 866-7; on this see Siegmund-Schultze 2014: 21 f.); trigonometry should be added to these because of what was said above. The other mathematical sciences are only parts derived from other sciences that through mathematics are elaborated or brought to completion. Thus from physics we derive mechanics, statics, hydrostatics, hydraulics, optics, catoptrics, dioptrics, perspective, acoustics, aerometry, astronomy, geography, hydrography; from ontology, chronology and gnomonics; from politics, the art of constructing fortifications and civil construction (Wolff 1978: columns 863-4).[24] Kästner instead uses the term *angewandte Mathematik* in the aforementioned *Vorerinnungen* to his *Anfangsgründe* (§§ 10-20), which, in addition to Wolff's observations, are taken into account in Herder's notes (*A*: 50.1-23).

Mathesis impura is applied directly (*directe*) and indirectly (*indirecte*); directly to the measurement of physical space (geometry and aerometry) and of time, expressed in days (gnomonics) and in years (chronology). In this case, therefore, we are not dealing with pure geometry, but with practical geometry, which describes, measures, and divides lines, surfaces, and solids both on paper and on the ground; it is divided into the disciplines of longimetry, planimetrics, stereometry, and geodesy.[25] Aerometry is defined as the science of measuring certain properties of air on the basis of experimental data (Wolff 1978: columns 29-30).[26] Kästner mentions these two disciplines in *Vorerinnungen*, considering practical geometry in its application to land surveying (*Feldmessung*) (§ 10), and aerometry (§ 12).

Force (*Kraft*) is considered first from a physical point of view, namely, in relation to motion. We therefore have the science of phoronomy, which studies the motion of both solids and fluids from a general point of view (Wolff 1978: column 1054). From a specific point of view, it is mechanics when it deals with the motion of solids (*der vesten Körper*), which is divided into astronomy, for the motion of stars, and geography, for the motion of the earth. It is acoustics when it deals with the motion of sound (*A*: 50.1-23);[27] it is optics, catoptrics, or dioptrics when it deals with the motion of light in its linear, reflected, or refracted

---

fangsgründe der angewandten Mathematik in 1759-1761 (Martin 1985: xxiv).
24 The treatment of the themes pertaining to *Mathesis pura* and *applicata* is contained in sections of *Auszug* (Wolff 1755); sections of *Anfangsgründe* (Wolff 1750a, 1750b, 1750c, 1757); and of *Elementa matheseos universae* (Wolff 1968a, 1968b, 1968c, 1968d, 1968e).
25 See the *Lexicon* entry, *Geometria practica, die ausübende Geometrie* (Wolff 1978: columns 669-71).
26 In certain respects it is similar to the *physics of gas*.
27 Herder's text improperly links acoustics to music; Kästner, in *Vorerinnungen* (§ 10), points

mode, respectively. Perspective (visual) can be linked to these three disciplines.[28] Phoronomy is hydraulics when it deals with the motion of fluids. Statics deals with equilibrium (*Gleichgewicht*) in solids, which is seen as the correspondent to motion; hydrostatics deals with equilibrium in fluids.

Force (*Kraft*) is also considered from a logical point of view "as a ground" (*als ein Grund*) in the mathematics of probability (*Mathematik der Wahrscheinlichkeit*). A link between *probability* and *ground* is attested in *Deutsche Metaphysik*, where in § 399 Wolff states that if we have some ground (*Grund*) for a proposition, but it is not sufficient (*zureichend*), then we call the proposition probable (*wahrscheinlich*), because it has the appearance of being connected to other truths (Wolff 1983b: 242). Wolff deals with the probable in §§ 399–403, observing (§ 402) that Leibniz had often lamented the lack of a logic of the probable (*Vernunfts-Kunst des Wahrscheinlichen*), on which, despite some pioneering work, there is still much to do (Wolff 1983b: 245). In this regard, note that according to the Jäsche *Logic* Kant welcomes a mathematics of probability that would, however, render a *logica probabilium* useless (Log 9: 62).[29]

Referring to Kästner's *Vorerinnungen* (§§ 11, 15, 18, 20), impure and indirectly applied mathematics is categorized in the following manner (A: 50.26–31): accounting (*Buchhaltung*), ballistics (*Geschützkunst*), architecture (*Baukunst*),[30] and navigation (*Schiffkunst*).[31] *Mathesis indirecta* "more remotely flows into [*remotior fließt ... ein*]" many arts, for example into painting (*ins Mahlen*), through drawing (*die Zeichenkunst*) and perspective, into fencing (*Fechten*) through mechanics.[32] Indeed all craftsmen use, next to what is physical (*nebst dem physischen*) something mathematical (*etwas mathematisches*), not derived from principles, but rather only for its practical use (*zum Gebrauch*). Mathematik Herder

---

out that ever since ancient times, music has always been considered a mathematical discipline, given its elaboration of scales.

28 In *Elementa matheseos universae*, vol. 3, Wolff sees perspective in connection with the functioning of the eye. See Wolff 1968c: 6 ff., 105.

29 See Wolff's *Philosophia rationalis sive logica*, Pars II, Sect. I, Cap.III: "De certo, incerto atque probabile" ("On the certain, uncertain, and probable"), in particular §§ 578–95 (Wolff 1983a: 437–43).

30 Kästner's *Vorerinnungen* (§ 15) states: "civilian and military architecture [*die Bürgerliche und die Kriegsbaukunst*]."

31 Kästner's *Vorerinnungen* (§ 10) notes that navigation is connected with geography for the calculation of a ship's course at sea, and with mechanics for steering the ship via the use of its parts.

32 On the relation of fencing with mechanics, see Kästner's *Vorerinnungen* (§ 20). Note that Kant's mention of fencing (*Fechten*) might have been connected to military life during Königsberg's Russian period.

pays attention to the overall architecture of applied mathematical sciences, but in many cases the description of the mentioned discipline, or *techne*, is kept to a minimum or is absent altogether. This happens with artillery and with architecture, which is civilian, but also military (fortification); however, it is possible that Kant treated these disciplines at greater length in private for the Russian officers.[33]

If we look at the corresponding treatment of special mathematics in text *B* (59.11–29), we can observe that it does not contain the distinction between pure mathematics and impure or applied mathematics. Special mathematics is divided up according to the notions of space, time, and force. With reference to space, we have geometry and trigonometry; for time, we have chronology and gnomonics. Force is divided into motive force (*beweg[ende] Kraft*) and latent force (*stillstehende Kraft*). Dynamics (a term that does not appear in *A*) deals with motive force; it is divided into mechanics, which deals with solids in general, and hydrodynamics or hydraulics, which deal with fluids. There is no reference to phoronomy.

The picture of the science of motion presented in *Mathematik Herder* differs greatly from what will be its treatment in *Metaphysical Foundations of Natural Science*, where the mathematical science of nature pertains to *matter*,[34] in relation to motion; according to the four categories of quantity, quality, relation, and modality, it is divided into: phoronomy, which studies motion as pure *quantum*; dynamics, in which motion belongs to the quality of matter under the name of an original motive force; mechanics, which considers matter in reciprocal relation as a consequence of motion; and phenomenology, which considers motion or rest in relation to the modality of representation (MAN 4: 475–7).

4 Method

Vorerinnungen in der Mathematik concludes with some considerations on mathematical method, a theme that is not treated in part *B*. It is stated that concepts in general have marks (*die Begriffe überhaupt haben Merkmale*), going back to the observation in § 26 of Kästner's *Vorerinnungen* (1758: 14). But no examples of marks are provided for the question: "What is virtue [*Tugend*]?" (*A*: 50.40). Such question must not have been random: in the *Logic* edited and published by

---

[33] According to Gottfried Martin's reconstruction, some disciplines of applied mathematics (mechanics, hydrostatics, hydraulics, and aerometry) would have been addressed in the following semester (Martin 1967: 61 f.).
[34] Wolff thinks of matter in Newtonian fashion, namely, as mass (Wolff 1750c: 1914 f.).

Jäsche (Log 9: 35), it states that the concept of virtue contains as marks the concepts of freedom (*Freiheit*), obedience to rules (*Anhänglichkeit an Regeln*), i. e., duty (*Pflicht*), and overpowering the force of inclinations insofar as they oppose rules (*von Überwältigung der Macht der Neigungen wofern sie jenen Regeln widerstreiten*).[35]

After dwelling on the classification of concepts into the clear, obscure, distinct, indistinct, complete, and the incomplete (A: 50.40–51.6), the text introduces the distinction between definitions of a name (*Worterklärungen*), "from which all other words can be distinguished," and definitions of a thing (*Sacherklärungen*), which can be real or genetic (A: 51.10–12). With greater precision in § 3 and § 4 of "Kurzer Unterricht" in *Auszug*, we see that *definitiones nominales* give characteristics (*Kennzeichen*) from which we can recognize the thing that bears that name; *definitiones reales* consist in a clear and distinct concept of the way the thing is possible (Wolff 1755: 2). In *De methodo mathematica brevis commentatio* (§ 17, § 18), it is added that nominal definition of a thing is the enumeration of the marks that are sufficient to distinguish that thing from others, and that real definition is "the distinct notion of the genesis of the thing [*notio distincta rei genesis*]" (Wolff 1968a: 7). Kästner, too, states that *Sacherklärungen* are "definitiones reales vel geneticae" (§ 26, cited above).

According to the transcendental point of view of *Critique of Pure Reason*, to define means "to exhibit originally the exhaustive concept of a thing within its boundaries" (KrV A727/B755); only mathematics possesses definitions, because only concepts "containing an arbitrary synthesis which can be constructed a priori" (KrV A729/B757) lend themselves to definition. In the first *Critique*, Kant states that real definition (*Realerklärung*) "not merely makes distinct a concept, but at the same time its objective reality [*objektive Realität*]," and that "mathematical definitions [*Erklärungen*], which exhibit the object in accordance with the concept in intuition, are of this kind" (KrV A242).[36] This point of view is difficult to accept in mathematics, because definitions are nominal, and it is up to a postulate, an axiom, or a demonstration to show that the object really exists (Moretto 2013: 89).

---

[35] On Wolff's mathematical method, see Shabel 2003: 49–52.
[36] In *Logic* (§ 106), nominal definitions are those that contain the signified assigned arbitrarily to a certain noun; whereas real definitions are those that present the possibility of the object starting from its internal marks; genetic definitions are those that allow the a priori presentation of an object in concreto, and all mathematical definitions (*Definitionen*) are like this (Log 9: 143 f.).

With reference to §§ 16–25 of *Kurzer Unterricht* (Wolff 1755: 4–9), and §§ 27–29 of *Vorerinnungen* (Kästner 1758: 14 f.), *Vorlesung* treats very concisely the classification of mathematical propositions (A: 51.15–30). Thus, after distinguishing between theoretical and practical propositions, it specifies that a theoretical proposition can be a) indemonstrable, and be called a principle or axiom (*Grundsatz, axiom*): these propositions correspond to a great extent to Euclidean *notiones communes*; or it can be b) demonstrable, in which case one can accept the explanation that it is a theorem (*Lehrsatz, theorema*) if it is obtained through several inferences; it is instead unacceptable, and not in accord with Wolff, the explanation that it is a corollary (*Zusatz, corollarium*) if it is obtained through a single inference. A practical proposition can be indemonstrable and it is either a postulate (*Heischesatz, postulat*), or a problem (*Aufgabe, Problem*). In *Kurzer Unterricht* (§ 16) a proposition immediately derived from the content of definitions is called a principle (*Grundsatz*). Principles can be divided into *axiomata*, if they show that something is, and *postulata*, if they show that something can be done (§ 17). A *theorema* is a conclusion obtained using several definitions. A *corollarium* is the application of a proposition to a particular case, or a proposition derived from the first (§ 25). A *problema* (*Aufgabe*) deals with something that needs to be demonstrated or performed (§ 24).

Within the transcendental perspective of *Critique of Pure Reason*, in the Doctrine of Method, axioms are understood as synthetic a priori principles, immediately certain, in which synthesis happens a priori through the construction of concepts in the intuition of the object itself (KrV A732/B760); this occurs through the successive synthesis of productive imagination (KrV A163/B204). A postulate is understood as a practical proposition "that contains nothing except the synthesis through which we first give ourselves an object and generate its concept" (KrV A234/B287). In *Critique of Practical Reason*, Kant writes that these propositions pertain to the *possibility* of an object and have apodictic certainty (KpV 5: 11). Note that in Euclid the propositions that guarantee the existence of a straight line passing through two given points, and of a circle having a given center and a given radius, are *postulates*; for Kant, however, the former is an *axiom*.[37]

Mathematik Herder (A: 51.28–29) deals with demonstrations (*Beweise*), observing that they happen through chains of inferences (*kettenmässige Schlüße*),[38] in which the *majores* are often omitted; in addition to the hypotheses

---

37 See Moretto 2013: 75–8.
38 Kant states that analytical principles are needed "for the chain of method [*zur Kette der Methode*]" (KrV B16), and that the mathematician arrives at the solutions to the problem through a chain of inferences (*durch eine Kette von Schlüßen*) (KrV A717/B745).

contained in the statement of a theorem, other previously demonstrated properties are kept in consideration (axioms, postulates, propositions). Wolff claims that demonstrations consist in an accumulation (*Hauffen*) of connected inferences, according to the rules of logic, pointing out that sometimes *some* (in the text: *one*) of the premises may not be formulated explicitly (*Kurzer Unterricht*, § 23). *Vorlesung* distinguishes thus between synthetic demonstrations, which proceed from fundamental truths up to higher and certain propositions; analytic demonstrations, which start from (complex) propositions[39] and arrive at simple propositions that are the foundations of mathematics; and mixed demonstrations (*A*: 51.31–37). In this *Vorlesung* passage, there is *no* anticipation of the distinction between analytic and synthetic judgments, whereas it considers the distinctions among the analytic, synthetic, and mixed methods. Speaking rather generally, in *Philosophia rationalis sive logica* (§ 885) Wolff states that with *methodus analytica* one presumes to have already found the truths, whereas with *methodus syntetica* one demonstrates a truth by starting from another truth. *Methodus mixta* results from their combination (Wolff 1983a: 633). A bit more concisely and clearly, Georg Friedrich Meier, in *Auszug aus der Vernunftlehre*, writes that in the synthetic method, principles are put before conclusions; in the analytic method, first come the conclusions, and from these one moves to principles.[40]

In *Vorlesung* we find the meaning of hypotheses in mathematical statements,[41] as it can be observed in *Rechen Kunst* (*A*: 54.4–8) with the example of the demonstration (*Beweis*) of the theorem (*Lehrsatz*) that states "from A = C and B = D it follows that A + B = C + D," where the propositions A = C and B = D are specified as hypotheses (*Hypothesen*).[42] However, the *Vorlesung* text states that mathematical hypotheses (*die mathematischen Hypothesen*) are the most probable and, after many confirmations, become almost certain; because of this we understand that it does not refer to the hypotheses contained in the statements of mathematical demonstrations, but rather to the use of hypotheses as propositions introduced to explain a complex of phenomena, and accepted as long as they are confirmed by experimental data, as it is done for example in physical sciences. Note that the *Vorlesung* text reflects the explanation of this notion in § 36 of *Vorerinnungen*

---

39 The text reads "from definitions [*aus Definitionen*]," but that puts it too simply.
40 See AA 16: 786. To write his *Reflexionen* on logic, Kant used his copy of Meier's *Auszug aus der Vernunftlehre* (Halle, 1752), reproduced in AA volume 16.
41 On the distinction between the *hypothesis* and *thesis* of a mathematical statement, see Wolff 1750a: 23 and Wolff 1968a: 12.
42 It is pointed out, at Kästner 1758: 17, that the name *Hypotheses* is also used for arbitrary propositions that define the "state and disposition" (*Beschaffenheit und Einrichtung*) of mathematical objects, for example signs (*Zeichen*) for numbers in arithmetic.

(Kästner 1758: 18 f.). It must be added that under the name *Theorica, Seu Theoriae Planetarum*, in *Lexicon* columns 1382–1385, the planets' *theoricae* are attempts on the part of astronomers to explain the motion of planets, and are also called *hypotheses*: among them the Ptolemaic hypothesis, the Copernican hypothesis, the Tychonian hypothesis, and the Keplerian hypothesis (*Theorica elliptica*); this last theory is amply described under the entry *Theoria planetarum elliptica*, in *Lexicon* columns 1385–1391. In *Elementa matheseos universae*, Tomus II (§ 115), an example of physical hypothesis is the Galilean hypothesis about falling bodies, which is considered acceptable (Wolff 1968b: 28).

The Jäsche *Logic* states correctly that the hypothesis of the Copernican system is particularly appreciated for its power to explain phenomena (Log 9: 85 f.),[43] unlike Tycho Brahe's theory, which needs subsidiary hypotheses (*hypotheses subsidiariae*). In the Doctrine of Method in *Critique of Pure Reason*, in the section called "The Discipline of Pure Reason with Regard to Hypotheses" (*Hypothesen*), Kant claims that a hypothesis is an opinion that, in order not to be groundless, must be connected as a principle of explanation with what is given in reality and therefore is certain (KrV A770/B798).

5 Arithmetic (*Rechen Kunst*)

5.1 History of Arithmetic

The second part of *A* deals with arithmetic (*Rechen Kunst*), opening with a paragraph entitled *Historie*, which contains some references to the history of arithmetic (*A*: 52). Albeit concise, these observations show Kant's attention to arithmetic and algebra, and give some indications of the Kantian view of the history of mathematics. Archimedes is mentioned, as well as Diophantus, the very sharp arithmetician "who knew many things that we do not know [*der vieles, was uns unbekant ist, wußte*]" (*A*: 52.6–8). It is then pointed out that Euclid, in books "7–9" of *Elements*, translated by Tacquet, presented very rigorously (*sehr demonstrativ*) the properties of numbers, which in later editions have been omitted because of their difficulty. There are also brief mentions of Nicomachus's two books on arithmetic, which deal only with the classification of numbers (*nichts als Eintheilung*

---

[43] The text adds appropriately: "as far as what has been presented up to now." Indeed, the Copernican hypothesis, in comparison with Kepler's, has less explanatory power.

der Zahlen), and of Psellus, a 10th-century CE Greek ("Psellus, Seculum 10"), whose *Arithmetic* was translated by Xylander in 1556.[44]

It is worth looking at these limited hints to observe that this historical information could derive from Christian Wolff's texts, in particular *Kurzer Unterricht von den vornehmsten Mathematischen Schriften* (Wolff 1750d), and *De praecipuis scriptis mathematicis brevis commentatio* (Wolff 1968g), which I will refer to as *Von den vornehmsten Mathematischen Schriften* and *De praecipuis scriptis mathematicis*.[45]

Von den vornehmsten Mathematischen Schriften contains some concise information on Archimedes: in § 39, Wolff mentions the Archimedean texts *Measurement of a Circle* and *On the Sphere and Cylinder*, dedicated to metric problems.[46] The former essay on cyclometry (*Kreismessung*) uses regular polygons with 96 sides, inscribed in and circumscribed around a circumference, in order to obtain an approximate evaluation of the measure of the relationship π between a circumference and its diameter: $(3 + 10/71) < \pi < (3 + 1/7)$. Kant would later address this topic in "On a Discovery whereby Any New Critique of Pure Reason Is to Be Made Superfluous by an Older One" (1790) (ÜE 8: 212). As for Archimedes's text on the sphere and the cylinder, see also the observation, from Kant's *Vorarbeiten*, about "the relation of the cone, the sphere, and the cylinder [*das Verhältnis des Kegels der Kugel und der Cylinders*]" (AA 23: 200).[47] In "On a Recently Prominent Tone of Superiority in Philosophy" (1796) (VT 8: 393), Kant refers to Jean Etienne Montucla (1725–1799), author of *Histoire des Mathématiques* (Paris 1758), about some fine properties of the circle.[48]

The information on Diophantus and the translation of his *Arithmetica* by Guilliesmus Xylander (Wilhelm Holtzmann) could derive from *Von den vornehmsten Mathematischen Schriften* (§ 52), where Wolff points out that Diophantus had written thirteen books on algebra, of whom only six were preserved; Guillesmus Xylander translated them from Greek into Latin, and printed them in 1575 (Wolff 1750c: 35).[49] The aforementioned observation, from *Mathematik Herder*, that

---

[44] A: 52.2–14. On this topic, see also Sutherland 2006: 546 f.

[45] The term *Historie* is indeed used by Wolff in the *Vorrede* to *Von den vornehmsten Mathematischen Schriften* (Wolff 1750d: 3): *Historie von den Mathematischen Wissenschaften*.

[46] See Archimède, *De la sphère et du cylindre* and *La mesure du cercle*, or Archimède 1970a and 1970b, and (in English) Archimedes 1953a and 1953b, respectively. See also Moretto 2010: 267 f., 273.

[47] See Lehmann's note to A: 52.6, at AA 29.1,1: 683.

[48] See Lehmann's note to A: 52.2, on Montucla, at AA 29.1,1: 683. With regard to Archimedes on this, see Montucla 1758: 233–5.

[49] See also *De praecipuis scriptis mathematicis*, Caput IV (*De scriptis analyticis*), § 2. In Wolff 1968g: 51.

Diophantus "knew many things that we do not know" might refer to the loss of the remaining seven books of *Arithmetica*. From *Von den vornehmsten Mathematischen Schriften* (§ 3), we can also have an idea of the relation between Psellus and Xylander: Psellus (9th century CE) had written a compendium on ancient arithmetic, which Xylander translated into Latin in 1556 (Wolff 1750c: 5 f.).[50]

As for Euclid, Wolff mentions books VII-X of *Elements* in the *Lexicon* entry *Arithmetica theoretica vel speculativa, die erwegende Rechen Kunst oder Zahl-Wissenschaft*, the science that deals with the properties of numbers (Wolff 1978: column 180).[51] In *Von den vornehmsten Mathematischen Schriften* (§ 6) and in *De praecipuis scriptis mathematicis* (§ 4), he refers to books VII-IX of *Elements*. They are indeed about arithmetic proper, whereas Book X concerns *incommensurable magnitudes*.[52] For Andrea Tacquet's "translation" (*Elementa Geometriae planae et solidae*), the *Vorlesung* text may refer to *Lexicon* (Wolff 1978: column 667), which talks about it in the entry *Geometria elementaris, die gemeine Geometrie*.[53] In *Lexicon* again, Wolff observes that elementary geometry is presented in books I-VI, XI, and XII. Many introductions to *Elements* for beginners are limited to those books. Andreas Tacquet, in his *Elementa Geometriae planae ac solidae*, made demonstrations simpler, without compromising clarity (*Deutlichkeit*), and he also inserted Archimedes's main demonstrations on calculating the circle and the sphere (Wolff 1978: columns 667–8).

De praecipuis scriptis mathematicis brevis commentatio (Wolff 1968g: 33) points out that, because the whole Euclid would have been of little use to beginners, many mathematicians have only printed the first six books of *Elements*, adding at most books XI and XII; and he observes that "Continetur autem in Elemento VII, VIII & IX theoria numerorum, seu Arithmetica elementaris: unde Tacquet tria haec Elementa Arithmeticae suae inseruit" ("The theory of numbers, or elementary arithmetic, is also contained in *Elements* VII, VIII, and IX; therefore, Tacquet included these three books in his arithmetic"). Anyway, the positive tone bestowed upon Euclid's arithmetic work is noteworthy, given that Kant's position towards Euclid's *geometry* is not one of general praise. In particular, he deems the parallel postulate superfluous, as expressed in the *Nachlaß* (Moretto 2013: 86–91).

---

50 See also *De praecipuis scriptis mathematicis*, Caput II (*De Arithmetica*), § 2. In Wolff 1968g: 28.
51 He also mentions Boethius and Nicomachus.
52 For books VII-IX of *Elementa*, see Euclides 1970: 103–227, Euclid 1956b: 277–426. For Book X of *Elementa*, see Euclides 1972, Euclid 1956c: 1–255.
53 Tacquet 1761: 1–112. On Tacquet's *Elementa*, see Irmscher 1964: 21 n. 2.

Wolff, in *Von den vornehmsten Mathematischen Schriften*, § 2 (Wolff 1750c: 5), mentions the two books on arithmetic by Nicomachus of Gerasa (printed in Paris in 1538), and he states that Severinus Boethius's arithmetic derives from Nicomachus. Nichomacus lived between the late first and early second centuries CE; it is therefore necessary to correct Wolff's dating (third century *ab urbe condita*, "from the foundation of Rome"), and also the dating in *Mathematik Herder* (300 BCE), which instead corresponds to the time of Euclid's life. In *De praecipuis scriptis mathematicis*, Caput II (*De Arithmetica*) (§ 1), Wolff observes that ancient arithmetic differs from modern arithmetic because the former only considered "varias numerorum divisiones" (Wolff 1968g: 28). In § 6, Wolff points out that in his 1523 work on arithmetic and geometry, Luca Pacioli also considers the divisions of numbers according to Nicomachus (Wolff 1968g: 29). Wolff also pays attention to Nicomachus's arithmetic in *Ontologia* (Wolff 1977: Notes to §§ 208, 260, 345), recalling the distinctions among different kinds of numbers proposed by Nicomachus and by other ancient authors who followed him.[54]

5.2 Whole numbers and arithmetical operations

After the section dedicated to the history of arithmetic (*A*: 52.2–14), the specific exposition of *Rechen Kunst* begins. It uses the same paragraph numbering adopted by Wolff in §§ 1–51 of *Rechen Kunst* in his *Auszug*, which the text for the most part follows. In this respect it is worth keeping in mind that the axiomatic systemization of arithmetic, with the clarification of the notion of natural number through Peano's axioms, only takes place at the end of the nineteenth century. Therefore, Wolff's *Rechen Kunst* and the closely related considerations in *Mathematik Herder* are vastly unsatisfactory from the point of view of scientific rigor. For that matter, Wolff states in the *Vorrede* to *Auszug* that for didactic reasons he did not consider rigor as a starting point for the exposition of mathematics in *Anfangsgründe* (and in *Auszug*), as it was aimed at beginners (Wolff 1755: iv–v). He adds that he was reserving a more rigorous exposition for his Latin works.

In *Mathematik Herder* (§ 1), *Rechen Kunst* is defined as the science that deals with numbers; in § 3 it states that *number* is a whole that is obtained from multiple things of one kind (homogeneity requirement), expressed in a distinct (*deutlich*) manner. It then specifies that unit, which is used in mathematics as unit of

---

54 On Nicomachus's classifications of numbers, see T. L. Heath's *A History of Greek Mathematics* (Heath 1981: 99 f.).

measurement (*Maas*), is here a known concept (*bekandter Begrif*) (*A*: 52.15–19).[55] In *Auszug*, Wolff more simply states that number is the result of the aggregation of many single things of one kind; in §4 he adds that each number requires a specific unity (*eine gewisse Einheit*); otherwise one cannot make comparisons and combinations (Wolff 1755: 11 f.).

According to Wolff's text, to add means to find a number that is equal to several numbers gathered together (*A*: 52.27–30; Wolff 1755: 13). Although this definition is very generic, in *Auszug*, § 10 of *Rechen Kunst* Wolff clarifies that, because a number results from several units put together, to add two numbers consists in adding subsequently to one the units of the other: *die Einheiten der Andere nach und nach zählet* (Wolff 1755: 13). This consideration is already important in light of the concept of number in Kant's transcendental philosophy, because it contains the notion of adding units in succession. Kant's transcendental philosophy further progresses on this perspective in *Critique of Pure Reason*, where the *pure schema* of quantity (*quantitatis*), as a concept of the understanding, is number, which is "a representation that comprises the successive addition of one unit to another (homogeneous)" (KrV A142f./B182). Similar progress is achieved with the explanation of addition as synthetic a priori proposition – in Kant's example $7 + 5 = 12$ – in which the concept of 12 is obtained by adding subsequently to the concept of 7 the units of number 5 given in intuition (KrV B15).

After some observations on mathematical symbols and on the definition of subtraction, in *Rechen Kunst* (§ 15, *A*: 53.1–17) the multiplication ab of whole positive numbers is defined as the repetition of the amount of the multiplicand a as many times as indicated by the multiplier b.[56] To illustrate this definition, a geometric example is used: given two perpendicular segments AB and AC, whose length is respectively a and b, we have the rectangle ACDB of area ab; in Herder's notes the segments AB and AC are both 3 in length, and in the figure units are represented with dots, so that counting the dots one has $3 \times 3 = 9$.[57]

A ... B
...
C ... D

---

55 Kästner (1758: 1) states that unit of measurement is a magnitude that is considered to be known (*bekannt*).
56 This definition should be amended with the inclusion of the commutative property and with the definitions: $a \times 1 = a$, $a \times 0 = 0$.
57 In order to avoid this overly specific case, it would have been better to use unequal sides, e. g., 4 and 3 in length, obtaining the representation of the product $4 \times 3 = 12$.

Exact division (§ 17, *A*: 53) is understood as the inverse operation of multiplication: from the dividend one subtracts the divisor as many times until nothing is left, and one determines a number (quotient) that is contained in the dividend as many times as 1 is contained in the divisor.[58] For example, in the case of 12 : 4, the operation is done with three subtractions: 12 − 4 = 8; 8 − 4 = 4; 4 − 4 = 0.

Mathematik Herder proposes the case of the operation of exact division, 9 : 3 = 3 (exact quotient).[59]

```
      ... d ...
D ...
      ...
```

The case of approximate division is exemplified through 8 : 3, from which one gets 2 as approximate quotient, given that $8 = 2 \times 3 + 2$. If we had fractions, which are not yet introduced, one could also write 8 : 3 = (2 + 2/3); this is consistent with *A*, where it is pointed out that the quotient falls between 2 and 3, "it is a fraction [*das ist ein Bruch*]" (*A*: 53.32).

```
      ... d ...
D ...
      ..
```

In Refl 13, written in 1790 in the *Mathematik* section of the *Nachlaß* (Refl 14: 55.9), Kant observes that "the concepts of number require likewise pure sensible images [*Zahlbegriffe bedürfen eben so reinsinnlicher Bilder*], e. g., Segner," echoing his considerations in *Prolegomena* (Prol 4: 269) and the first *Critique* (KrV B15). Editor Erick Adickes comments that in his essays Johann Andreas Segner uses sensible images such as dots and dashes (*Punkte und Striche*) in order to make operations with numbers intuitable (*veranschaulichen*) (Refl 14: 55.21–32).[60]

Note that, in order to illustrate multiplication and division of whole positive numbers, *Mathematik Herder* uses figures similar to those presented by Segner,

---

[58] Indicating the dividend with D, the divisor with d, and the quotient with Q, we have Q : D = 1 : d; the text also has d : D = 1 : Q; both are equivalent to d × Q = D.
[59] In the *Nachschrift* text, we find Q instead of d. In this case the divisor d is equal to the quotient Q.
[60] These are the essays as quoted by Adickes: A. Segner, *Cursus matematici pars I: Elementa Arithmeticae, Geometriiae et Calculi Geometrici*. Halle: 1756. New edition 1767; A. Segner, *Anfangsgründe der Arithmetik, Geometrie und der Geometrischen Berechnung*, From the Latin [translated by his son Jh. Wlh. Segner]. Halle 1764. 2nd edition 1773; A. Segner, *Deutliche und vollständige Vorlesungen über die Rechenkunst und Geometrie*. Lemgo. 4°. 1747. 2nd improved edition 1767.

e. g., in *Cursus matematici pars I. Elementa Arithmeticae Geometriae et Calculi geometrici* (1756), in particular Figure 2 of Table 1, and §§ 44–50 (Segner 1756: 19–21). Kästner, in *Rechenkunst* (§§ 7, 13, 17) of *Anfangsründe*, proposes similar illustrations (Kästner 1758: 22–5). It must be added that both texts, in § 49 and § 17 respectively, point out that in approximate division the remainder can be expressed with a fraction.

Regarding sensible images of numbers, let me point out that five aligned dots (. . . . .) constitute an *image* of number 5 already formed, but they do not represent the *generation* of the number 5, which depends on the *schema* of the number, which requires, in time, the successive addition of units. From this perspective, the tables for multiplication and division created by Kant and Herder contain *images* of numbers both in totals and in lines and columns, but they do not touch on the generation of number.

Moreover, next to Segner's and Kästner's graphic representations, one cannot ignore the arithmetic of the *Rechenmeister*, who used the beads of the abacus (*den Korallen des Rechenbretts*) to make their calculations, as Kant points out (KrV A240/B299).[61]

5.3 The principles of equality and inequality

The following paragraphs of *Vorlesung* are dedicated to the *Grundsätze* of the *Auszug*,[62] which deal with the properties of equalities and inequalities, of magnitudes, and of numbers. Some of these principles refer to *Notiones Communes* in Euclides's *Elementa*.[63] For example: I) things that are equal to the same thing, are equal to each other; II) when adding equal things to equal things, the sums are equal; III) when from equal things one subtracts equal things, the results are equal; IV) the whole is greater than the part. These *notiones communes* correspond to § 22, § 24, and § 25 in *Auszug*[64] and in *Vorlesung Herder*. Strangely, there is no mention of *Grundsatz* VIII of *Auszug* (§ 30): the whole is equal to the sum of all its parts, and is therefore greater than each of them;[65] this principle is instead

---

[61] On the abacus, see the *Lexicon* entry *Arithmetica calculatoria, die Rechnung auf den Linien*, columns 170–2 (in reference to Adam Ries, 1550). Kästner's *Rechenkunst* (§ 25) mentions the use of the abacus among Eastern peoples (Kästner 1758: 27).
[62] Respectively, A: 53.35–55.30, and Wolff 1755: 15–17. Note that these *Grundsätze* appear in the *Rechen Kunst* of *Anfangsgründe* under the numbering 20–30.
[63] Euclides 1969: 5 f.; Euclid 1956a: 222–32.
[64] Referring to the above-cited *Grundsätze* I, II, III.
[65] This principle corresponds to the Euclidean notion VIII: the whole is greater than the part.

emphasized in *Critique of Pure Reason*. The following principle, not present among the Euclidean *notiones*, is inserted in §20 (*Grundsatz* I): each number and magnitude is equal to itself. Under the designation of *analytic principles*, these propositions are re-proposed by Kant in *Critique of Pure Reason*. According to Kant, some of the principles assumed by geometricians are indeed analytic, because they are based on the principle of contradiction, "for example, $a = a$, the whole is equal to itself, or $a + b > a$, i.e., whole is greater than its part;" although they are based on mere concepts, they are admitted in mathematics only because they can be exhibited in intuition (KrV B16 f.) (Moretto 2013: 76).

Note that in *Elementa Arithmeticae* Wolff adopts a different exposition, articulated in the definitions of equality: equal things are those that can be substituted with each other *salva quantitate* (§15); in the notion of greater than and less than (§20): *greater than* is that whose part is equal to the whole of another thing, and *less than* is that which is equal to the part of another thing; in the axiom of the reflexive property of equality (§81), corresponding to *Grundsatz* I: *Idem est aequale sibimetipsi*; and in a principle of dichotomy of homogeneous magnitudes (§83), for which two of these magnitudes, however considered, are either equal or unequal (Wolff 1968a: 24, 33). This choice allows Wolff to propose demonstrations for the other *Grundsätze*.[66]

It is interesting to note that *Mathematik Herder* follows *Auszug* in the numbering and enunciation of propositions,[67] but for demonstrations follows *Elementa Arithmeticae* instead, as one can see in the demonstration of theorem 24) a): if $A = B$ and $C = D$, then $A + C = B + D$ (*A*: 54.4–8). It uses the principle of the reflexive property of equality, $A + B = A + B$ (§20 in both *Mathematik Herder* and *Auszug*), then it uses the hypotheses $A = C$ and $B = D$, and it substitutes in the second member A with B, and C with D, based on *Elementa Arithmeticae* (§15), obtaining $A + B = C + D$. The demonstration in Kant's *Nachschrift* faithfully follows Wolff in *Elementa Arithmeticae* (§88), placing on the right margin the sign "§15," on the definition of equality and inequality in *Elementa*.

According to T. L. Heath, the addition "and is therefore greater than each of them" can probably be attributed to Clavius; see Euclid 1956a: 232.

66 By using only principles, one can avoid demonstrations, which can be useful in an exposition for beginners.

67 The same goes for *Anfangsgründe* in the exposition, but with different numbering.

5.4 Representations of numbers

After giving other examples that illustrate the properties of the said relations of equality and inequality, *Vorlesung* turns its attention to the representation of numbers through signs and through the generalized use of decimal positional notation (*A*: 55.31–57.19).[68] Text *A* (56.35–38) claims that the Indian notation of numbers was taken to Spain by the Saracens, and to France by Gerbert of Fleury (who later became Pope Sylvester II, and died in 1003) and from there it spread to the rest of Europe. And text *B* (60.14–15) states that we owe to the Arabs the representation of numerical concepts through digits, which became known in Europe thanks to Gerbert of Fleury.[69]

Considering other representations, *Vorlesung* observes that Leibniz's binary and Weigel's tetradic numeral systems show numerical systems other than the decimal (*A*: 56.17–42). In this respect, in *Lexicon* (column 169), *Arithmetica binaria sive Dyadica* is defined as the science of writing all numbers with digits 1 and 0, and of calculating using these two digits.

Mathematik Herder (*A*: 56.21–22, 56.25–26) points out the advantages of a dyadic (binary) representation of numbers: the possibility 1) of multiplying and dividing numbers without the use of Pythagorean multiplication tables (*Einmaleins*), because the only digits used are 0 and 1; 2) of explaining Chinese characters; 3) of explaining *creatio ex nihilo*, by having *1* represent God, who creates all things from nothing, *0*.[70] It mentions the lengthy representation of the number as a disadvantage (*A*: 56.22–24). As pointed out by Lehmann,[71] an indication can be given by the title of Leibniz's essay, published on 5 May 1703 in Mémoires de l'Académie Royale des Sciences de Paris, cited after the *Nachschrift* with this title: *Explication de l'Arithmétique Binaire qui se sert de seuls Caractères 0 et 1, avec des Remarques sur son utilité, et sur ce qu'elle donne le sens des anciennes figures Chinoises de Fohi, pp. 85–89*.[72]

Arithmetica tetractica is defined in *Lexicon* (Wolff 1978: columns 180–181) as *Rechenkunst* that only uses the digits 1, 2, 3, and 0, discovered and described by *Erhard* Weigel,[73] professor of mathematics in Jena. In *Critique of the Power*

---

68 On decimal notation, see *A*: 56.11–15 and *A*: 57.1–12.
69 A possible source for this historical reference might be (vol. 1) Montucla 1758: 415 f.
70 See Boyer and Merzbach 1989: 452 f.
71 In the note to *A*: 56.17, at AA 29.1,1: 685.
72 The essay is published in Leibniz 1962b: 223–7. In the *Rechenkunst* of *Anfangsgründe* (§ 39), Wolff examines binary and tetradic arithmetic (Wolff 1750a: 46 f.).
73 See the note to *A*: 56.27, at AA 29.1,1: 685, which erroneously mentions the mystic *Valentin* Weigel rather than Erhard Weigel.

of Judgment, Kant claims that in the understanding's estimation of magnitudes (*Größen*) (in arithmetic) one gets equally far whether one pushes the composition (*Zusammenfassung*) of the units up to the number 10 (in the decadic system), or only to 4 (in the tetradic system) (KU 5: 254).

5.5 Decimal representation

As for decimal notation, *Vorlesung* highlights the utility of recurring to superscripts for approaching numbers with a lengthy decimal representation. The example is the number written with equivocal stenography as 25^{42}, where the superscript number 42 means that in the number's decimal notation, the first two digits, 2 and 5, are followed on the right by 42 zeros (*A*: 57.13–16). The same decimal number, with different stenography, is found in Kästner (1758: 29), with the difference that the number 42 is written above the number 25, rather than on its upper right side.

Mathematik Herder proceeds with examples of addition, subtraction, multiplication, and division in the decimal system (§§ 38, 43, 49, 51). From an algorithmic perspective, only the illustration of division requires a certain effort for beginners. In contrast (§ 38), in the example of addition proposed as a theorem, $8 + 4 = 12$, it is interesting to take notice of the sequence of simpler operations offered as its equivalent: $8 + 4 = 8 + 3 + 1 = 9 + 3 = 9 + 2 + 1 = 10 + 2 = 12$. The sequence is incomplete and the use of commutative and associative properties is left unexplained; however, it uses definitions, for example $4 = 3 + 1$, and the principle of the substitution of identicals. The procedure consists in diminishing at each step the second addend of one unit, which is added to the first addend.

From an operational perspective, this is similar to the explanation of $2 + 2 = 4$ proposed by Leibniz in *Nouveaux Essais*,[74] which uses the definitions $2 = 1 + 1$, $3 = 2 + 1$, $4 = 3 + 1$, as Parsons correctly points out (1992a: 51 f.). As for the Critical Kant, there are affinities with the later demonstration of the proposition of addition, $7 + 5 = 12$, offered in *Critique of Pure Reason*. Parsons (1992b: 157) considers *Mathematik Herder* for the demonstration of $8 + 4 = 12$, and $3 \times 8 = 24$ (*A*: 57.20–32, 58.15–21), referring to Leibniz's and Kant's demonstrations. Note that one can find a similar example in Wolff's *Ontologia* (§ 273): $4 = 3 + 1$, but $3 = 2 + 1$, $2 = 1 + 1$, therefore $4 = 1 + 1 + 1 + 1$. Regarding the foundation of arithmetic, *Mathematik*

---

[74] Leibniz 1962a: 413 f.

Herder lacks any mention of *time*, which in *Critique of Pure Reason* is instead presented as necessary (KrV B15; A142 f./B182).[75]

6 Fractions, powers and roots, proportions

6.1 Fractions

Unlike the order of topics followed by Wolff, *Vorlesung* addresses the doctrine of fractions before proportions. In this respect it seems to follow the point of view of Kästner, who had criticized Wolff for founding the doctrine of fractions on the doctrine of proportions, which constitutes a serious mistake against method.[76] In *Mathematik Herder*, fractions (*Brüche*) are defined imprecisely as parts of a whole, and are indicated with the sign a/b, where a is the numerator and b the denominator (a and b are whole numbers, $a \geq 0$, $b > 0$). One says that the former is to the latter as the fractional number is to the unit (*B*: 61.1–4). The definition is in § 60 of *Auszug* (eleventh definition): one has a fraction (*Bruch*) when a whole is divided into equal parts and one takes one or more of those parts (Wolff 1755: 37). Fractions are then divided into *common* (e. g., 2/3) and *decimal* (e. g., 3/100). Six rules for calculating with common fractions follow (*B*: 61.5–20): among them, the most significant are I and II, which express the property of invariance of fractions: when multiplying numerator and denominator of a fraction by the same whole positive number, one obtains an equivalent fraction. Rules I and II correspond to the ones expressed in *Auszug, Rechen Kunst*, § 63. All six rules are present in *Rechenkunst* of Kästner's *Anfangsgründe*, §§ 62–3, 65–7 (Kästner 1758: 47–9). Fractions are further divided into *proper*, when the numerator is less than the denominator, e. g., 3/5; and *improper*, e. g., 7/3, which can be reduced to the *mixed form*, e. g., 7/3 expressed as 2 + 1/3 (*B*: 61.21–24).

6.2 Powers and roots

After focusing on decimal fractions, in which the denominator is a power of 10, Herder's text deals with square and cubic numbers, and square and cubic roots,

---

[75] On the function of time in *Critique of Pure Reason*, see Moretto 1999: 208–13, Parsons 1992b: 147 f.; Friedman 1992b: 200; Shabel 2003: 109–11; Sutherland 2006: 541 f.; Moretto 2004a: 529–36; Moretto 2010: 300–07.
[76] Kästner 1758, in *Vorrede*, page vi (my pagination).

referring to *Auszug*, §§ 72–80 (*B*: 62.1–14).[77] These are rather rushed notes, out of which one can retain the definition of square number (*Quadratzahl*) as the result of the multiplication of a number by itself; and of cubic number (*Würfelzahl*), which results from the multiplication of a number by its square. In the first case, the number that is multiplied by itself is called *square root*; in the second case, the number multiplied by its square is called *cubic root* (*Auszug*, §§ 72–5).

6.3 Relationships between magnitudes

The theory of the relationships between magnitudes is extremely important in view of its applications, in particular if one cannot resort to analytic geometry or infinitesimal calculus, as is the case in Galileo's *Discorsi e dimostrazioni matematiche intorno à due nuove scienze* (*Discourses and Mathematical Demonstrations Relating to Two New Sciences*). Turning to Kant, note that he makes ample use of the doctrine of proportions between magnitudes, as one can see in *Reflexionen zur Mathematik*, i.e., *Reflexion* 1 through *Reflexionen* 5, and *Reflexionen* 12 (Refl 14: 1–22, 52). *Mathematik Herder* deals with relationships between numbers or magnitudes (*Verhältnisse*)[78] in text *B* (62.15–63.10), referring to *Auszug* §§ 52–59. *Vorlesung* proposes the following definition for the relationship between magnitudes (*Verhältnis* = ratio): the distinction (*Unterschied*) between two magnitudes, the *antecedent* α and the *consequent* β, obtained through a third magnitude ρ, called the *exponent* (*B*: 62.17–20). This description is very vague, and is further clarified by a distinction between *arithmetic ratios*, where the exponent indicates how many units one must add to the antecedent to obtain the consequent, and *geometric ratios*, where the antecedent fits into the consequent as many times as expressed by the exponent.[79] See *Auszug* § 52, which mentions *Verhältnisse* between numbers, divided into *arithmetic Verhältnisse*, e.g., between 3 and 5, with exponent 2, being 5 − 3 = 2; and *geometric Verhältnisse*, e.g., between 3 and 12, with exponent 4, being 12 : 3 = 4. Note that the text uses the German *Verhältniß*

---

77 Cf. Wolff 1755: 43–51.
78 Note that for the English translation of the Greek *lógos*, indicating the relationship between magnitudes (translated as *Verhältniß* by Wolff and in *Vorlesung*), in Euclid's *Elements* the editor Heath uses the English term "ratio." See Euclid, 1956b: 114 f. [Note: The rules of spelling – e.g., for *Verhältniß*, *Rechen Kunst* – varied during this period. – Editor]
79 The ancient reference is the theory of relationships and proportions between magnitudes, proposed in Book V of Euclid's *Elements*, with geometric applications in Book VI, and applications relating to relationships between whole numbers in Books VII, VIII, and IX.

in correspondence with the Latin *ratio*, but also the German *Relation*, connected with the Latin *relatio*.

6.4 Proportions

Vorlesung deals then with *zusammengesetze Verhältnisse*, chains of relationships; the first is *proportion*, intended as equality of two relationships. The text distinguishes between *arithmetic* proportions, when a − b = c − d, and *geometric* proportions, when a : b = c : d, pointing out that for the latter, b : a = d : c is also valid, as well as c : d = a : b.[80] A further distinction is made between *continuous geometric proportion* (a : m = m : b), which has three terms, and *discrete geometric proportion* (a : b = c : d), which has four. Lastly, a chain of at least three relationships is called a *progression*, which can be divided into *arithmetic* and *geometric*, depending on the kind of relationships used. On this, see *Auszug*, which in § 53 clarifies that one has *proportions* when two or more *Verhältnisse*, arithmetic or geometric, have the same exponent, e. g., 3 − 5 = 6 − 8, and 3 : 12 = 5 : 20 respectively; § 55 explains that a *continuous proportion* is one in which the middle terms are equal; and § 56 points out that a *progression* is made up of a series of numbers that proceed in a continuous *Verhältniß*, arithmetic or geometric. In § 57 it is noted that if two relationships between quantities are each equal to a third, they are equal to each other. Example: from 1 : 4 = 3 : 12, and from 1 : 4 = 5 : 20, one derives that 3 : 12 = 5 : 20.

Vorlesung (*B*: 63.12–26) then introduces some of the properties of (geometric) proportions between quantities. In the case of proportions between numbers, the fundamental property is emphasized: the product of extremes is equal to the product of means, which in the case of a continuous proportion (when means are equal) becomes: the product of extremes is equal to the square of the mean. Note that some of the properties of numerical proportions are not valid for proportions between magnitudes in general. For example, in the proportion between magnitudes A : B = C : D, it is necessary that A and B be homogeneous, as well as C and D; but if A and B are not homogeneous with C and D, then the means cannot be exchanged to obtain the proportion A : C = B : D, which is instead valid if the magnitudes A, B, C, and D are all homogeneous (*Auszug*, § 83). Properties of composing, (A + B) : B = (C + D) : D, and decomposing, (A − B) : B = (C − D) : D (valid if A > B and C > D), also apply.

---

[80] *Vorlesung* deals mostly with geometric proportions.

6.5 Applications of proportions

As examples of applications (*B*: 63.27–33), the text offers the proportion R : Q = Q : C (the square root is to the square as the square is to the cube, which derives directly from the definitions of square and cube); and the *Regel Detri* (rule of the fourth proportional), used to find a quantity x, fourth proportional after the first three a, b, and c (that is: a : b = c : x), without enunciating the solution in the numerical case, i. e., x = (b × c) : a (*Auszug*, §§ 85, 86). In *Critique of Pure Reason* and *Prolegomena*, Kant uses for proportion the term *analogy* (*Analogie*), from the Greek ἀναλογία, drawing a distinction between analogy in mathematics, which is the equality of two quantitative relationships (a : b = c : d) and allows, given three known terms, the determination of the fourth (*Regel Detri*); and analogy in philosophy, where, given three terms, it is possible to determine only their relationship with the fourth, but not the fourth member itself. These considerations are used in *Prolegomena* to describe the knowledge of *noumena* by analogy.[81]

As for the applications of proportions between magnitudes, which as previously mentioned are equalities between relationships, the text points out that *rational* relationships[82] are those in which the two magnitudes are commensurable; *irrational* are those in which magnitudes are incommensurable (*B*: 63.34–36). The addition of "-- hier Rational" next to "*Irrational*" may refer to the fact that Kant's *Vorlesung*, just like Wolff's *Auszug*, does not deal with the problem of irrationality.

For the applications of proportions to triangles and parallelograms, and keeping in mind Definition I (of similar figures) from Book VI of *Elementa*, the following propositions are given (Euclidean references in parentheses): a) a straight line parallel to the base of a triangle cuts the other two sides in orderly proportional parts (*Elementa*, VI, 2); b) in triangles with orderly equal angles, sides are orderly in proportion, and the triangles are therefore similar (*Elementa*, VI, 4); c) if sides of triangles are in proportion, angles are orderly equal and the triangles are similar (*Elementa*, VI, 5).[83] From here originate methods to find d) the third proportional, e) the fourth proportional, and f) the mean proportional (*Elementa*, VI, 11, 12, 13).[84] It is then pointed out that g) in parallelograms, if heights are equal, surfaces are proportional to bases (*Elementa*, VI, 1); and that h) rectangles

---

[81] See KrV A179 f./B222 and Prol 4: 357–60. On the concept of analogy in Kant, see Moretto 1986: 341–64; Chiereghin 1988: 81–106; Faggiotto 1989; Faggiotto 1996; and Moretto 1999: 197–206.
[82] Not "rational proportions," as one might think based on the text.
[83] *B*: 63.37–40.
[84] *B*: 64.1–4.

are to one another in compounded ratio to their respective bases and heights (*B*: 64.5–7). Proposition h) represents a particular case of proposition 23 in *Elementa*, VI:[85] "parallelograms having correspondingly equal angles have to one another the ratio compounded of the ratios of their sides."

The text then briefly mentions (*B*: 64.8–13) the possibility of useful application of the doctrine of proportions to the solution of problems in several disciplines: a) euthymetry, for measuring straight lines (*Lexicon*, column 609); b) ichnography, for scale reproductions (*Lexicon*, columns 686–7 under the entry *Grund-Riß, Ichnographia*);[86] c) altimetry, for measuring altitude (*Lexicon*, columns 41–2); d) epipedometry, for measuring flat surfaces (*Lexicon*, columns 670 and 1064–5); e) and geodesy, for measuring fields (*Lexicon*, column 670).[87] The list is clearly very concise, presenting rushed notes regarding practical geometry (with topics that had already been touched upon: *Feldmessung*).[88] However, no examples are provided. Even more concise are the considerations on stereometry (*B*: 64.20–22), divided into three titles, which are not explained any further: a) concepts, e.g., parallelepiped; b) relationships and theorems; c) measurement of surfaces and volumes.

7 Geometry

In *Mathematik Herder*, considerations on geometry are mostly presented under the unassuming title, *Provisional Observations on Geometry* (*Vorläufige Anmerkungen der Geometrie*). The text mentions the etymological definition of geometry as the science for measuring the ground (*B*: 64.24–25). In *Auszug*, it is defined as the science of space occupied by physical objects according to their length, width, and depth (Wolff 1755: 65). As for its utility (*Nutzen*), geometry in general as a science, due to its certainty and order, is a logic; in particular, a) in mathematics it is the spirit of arithmetic, the basis for the whole *mathesis applicata*,

---

[85] Euclid introduces "compounded ratio" without having first defined it. Indeed, Definition V of Book VI in *Elements* is considered spurious: see Heath's note at Euclid 1956b: 189 f.
[86] The text reads (B: 64.8–10): "Hieraus Problematik ... b) für die (Ichnographie anmerken)." Incompleteness aside, this might be either Kant's emphasis, or a temporary note by Herder, to be checked later.
[87] See, in *Vorerinnerungen*, Wolff's subdivision of practical geometry.
[88] *Lexicon* states that *Geometria practica, die ausübende Geometrie*, deals with the description, measurement, and division of lines, surfaces, and bodies, both on paper and on the ground; it is divided into the disciplines of longimetry, planimetry, stereometry, and geodesy (Wolff 1978: columns 669–71).

b) outside of mathematics, it is a support to other arts, e. g., music and drawing (*B*: 64.34–41).

As a general overview, the text gives the definitions of the indivisible point as the end (*Ende*) of a line; of line as boundary of a surface; and of surface as boundary of physical space. The reference is to definitions I, III, VI from Book I, and definition II from Book XI of *Elements*: a point is that which has no parts; the ends of a line are points; the boundaries of a surface are lines; the boundary of a solid is a surface.[89] This complex of definitions is connected with the attribution of one dimension (*Abmessung*) to a line, two dimensions to a surface, and three dimensions to physical space (*B*: 65.1–7).[90]

A possible source for these considerations might be Andrea Tacquet, mentioned in *Mathematik Herder* (*A*: 52.9–11) and in *Lexicon* (Wolff 1978: column 667). In *Elementa geometriae planae ac solidae*, Tacquet connects the Euclidean definitions of point, line, and surface, to the notions of dimension and indivisible point. In Book I, one finds the following definitions: 1) *Punctum est signum in magnitudine individuum* ("A point is a sign indivisible in magnitude"). 3) *Lineae termini sunt puncta* ("The ends of a line are points"). 6) *Superficiei extrema sunt lineae* ("The boundaries of a surface are lines"). In Book XI, Definition 2 states that *Solidi extremum est superficies* ("The boundary of a solid is a surface"). A comment after Definition 7 in Book I reads: *Tres igitur dimensiones habet corpus, superficies duas, lineam unam, punctum nullam* ("Therefore a body has three dimensions, a surface two, a line one, and a point none").[91]

This conception of geometric elements is relevant to Kant, who uses it in his 1770 Dissertation, *De mundi sensibilis et intelligibilis forma et principiis*. Here, in the note to § 15 C, Kant writes: *Terminus solidi est* superficies, *superficiei* linea, *lineae* punctum. *Ergo tria sunt terminorum genera in spatio, quemadmodum tres dimensiones* ("The limit of a solid is a *surface*; the limit of a surface is a *line*; the limit of a line is a *point*. There are, therefore, three sorts of limits in space, just as there are three dimensions") (MSI 2: 403). The Latin *terminus* is rendered by Kant with the German *Grenze* in both *Critique of Pure Reason* and *Prolegomena*; the related concept plays an important role in its transcendental use in determining the limit of knowledge, as well as in the important distinction between *Grenzen* (limits) and *Schranken* (the limiting) explained in *Prolegomena* (§§ 57–60), "Conclusion. On Determining the Limit [*Grenzbestimmung*] of Pure Reason." Here it is

---

89 Euclides 1969: 1; Euclides 1973: 1; Euclid 1956a: 153; Euclid 1956c: 260.
90 See also *Elementa Geometriae*, §§ 1, 3, 6, 11, 28, 29, 30, 444 (Wolff 1968a: 121 f., 124, 220).
91 Tacquet 1761: 1 f., 91. In the last quote by Tacquet, I substituted *nullum* with *nullam*.

also pointed out that in all limits (*Grenzen*) there is something positive, unlike the limiting (*Schranken*), which only contain negations (Prol 4: 350–65).[92]

Geometry is then divided into longimetry and planimetry, with no mention of stereometry (*B*: 65.9–66.25). In this case the text refers to pure geometry, linear and flat, not to practical geometry. For longimetry, defined as the discipline that measures lines, the observations are not very significant. I only want to point out the definition of a curved line as a line "of which no part is straight" (*B*: 65.15), which is also mentioned in the Doctrine of Method in *Critique of Pure Reason*.[93] As for planimetry, surfaces are divided into indeterminate (*unbestimmte*), for example the angle, which, consistent with Euclid, is defined as the inclination of two lines (*crurum*); and determinate (*bestimmte*), i. e., contained within a perimeter. The latter are further divided into surfaces whose perimeter is composed of a) segments of a straight line, and b) curved lines.

Point a) introduces, in progressive order according to the number of sides of the perimeter, trilaterals (*B*: 65.33–40),[94] quadrilaterals, and then polygons (with more than four sides). Classifications of polygons follow. As for their properties, it is pointed out that a parallelogram is divided by its diagonal into two [equal] parts, and that parallelograms of equal base and height are equivalent (the text reads "equal") (*B*: 66.11–13). *Vorlesung* refers to the second part of proposition I, 34 and to I, 35 of *Elementa*, which, however, does not mention equal height, but parallelograms positioned between the same parallels.[95]

Among flat figures bounded by curves, the following are mentioned: 1) the circle, with the related notable notions of center, diameter, radius, sector, tangent, and chord;[96] 2) ovals and the ellipse;[97] and 3) the cylinder (although a solid, its lateral surface can be flattened into a rectangle). At this point in the text (*B*: 66.25), after "Cylinder" we find the expression "etc. etc.," which might signal a gap to be completed in a later revision of the text. Then under point "4" we find

---

[92] See Faggiotto 1986: 231–42; Illetterati 1996: 27–35; Moretto 1999: 143–7, 174–82, 188–96; Moretto 2004b: 58–63.
[93] Kant points out that, in the definition of a circle as the curved line whose points are all equidistant from a given point (the center), the specification 'curved' is superfluous (KrV A732/B760).
[94] Right after this, we have their classification as triangles (*B*: 66.1–6).
[95] Euclides 1969: 46–9; Euclid 1956a: 323–7.
[96] See Definitions XV-XVIII of Book I of *Elementa*, and Definitions II, X of Book III of *Elementa*; however, these do not contain direct definitions of radius (*Radius*) and chord (*Saite*). See Euclid, 1956 a: 153 f.; Euclid 1956b: 1 f.; Euclides 1969: 2 f., 93 f.
[97] These figures are merely mentioned. A possible reference could be the entries *Ellipsis* and *Ovalis linea, ein Oval*, in *Lexicon*: Wolff 1978: columns 581–3; Wolff 1978: column 1006.

the editor's note "[*bricht ab*]," in correspondence with the end of the text edited by Irmscher.[98]

Lehmann's edition of *Vorlesung* continues with two more paragraphs, entitled *Polygon* and *Cirkel*, dedicated to regular polygons and the circle (*B*: 66.26–43). The following theorems are mentioned: a) every regular polygon [inscribed in a circumference] is equivalent to a triangle whose base is the perimeter of the polygon, and whose height is the perpendicular from the center to the chord (apothem);[99] b) the side of a [regular] hexagon is equal to the semi-diameter [of the circumscribed circle]; this is the Corollary (*Porism*) to Proposition IV, 15 of *Elementa*. For the circle, the following properties are mentioned: a) equal arcs correspond to equal chords, and vice versa;[100] b) a perpendicular drawn from the center bisects a chord and the diameter, and vice versa;[101] c) an angle at the circumference is half the corresponding central angle (this property is inaccurately expressed in Herder's notes).[102]

These statements follow: 1) A triangle that has the circumference as base and the radius as height is equivalent (the text reads "equal") to the circle (Archimedes, *Measurement of a Circle*, Proposition I).[103] 2) Two triangles are equal if two sides [and the contained angle] are respectively equal (*Elementa*, I, 4). 3) In an isosceles triangle, the angles at the base are equal (*Elementa*, I, 5). 4) The sum of the angles of a triangle equals 180° (*Elementa*, I, 32); this Proposition is used by Kant in the Doctrine of Method of *Critique of Pure Reason* (KrV A713 f./B741 f.), and it must be noted that it is characteristic of Euclidean geometry. 5) Two triangles with equal (*gleich*) base and height are equivalent (*gleich* again, in the text). In *Elementa*, I, 37, one finds: triangles that are on the same base and between the same parallels, are equivalent (equal in the Euclidean text). 6) A triangle is half a parallelogram [with the same base and height] (*Elementa*, I, 41). 7) In a right triangle, the square of the hypotenuse is equivalent to the sum of the squares of the other two sides: *Vorlesung* concludes its part on geometry with this direct formulation of the Pythagorean Theorem (*B*: 66.42–43).[104]

---

98 *B*: 66.25; see Irmscher 1964: 39. In Lehmann's notes, there is no comment on this editorial note.
99 The statement is only approximate. The text states "side" (*Seite*) instead of "perimeter." It is easily demonstrated.
100 See Euclides 1969: 132–4; Euclid 1956b: 59 f.
101 See Euclides 1969: 97 f.; Euclid 1956b: 10.
102 See Euclides 1969: 122 f.; Euclid 1956b: 46 f.
103 Archimedes is quoted at *A*: 52.6.
104 The same proposition and its inverse close Book I of Euclid's *Elements*. Euclides 1969: 63–6; Euclid 1956a: 349–50, 368 f.

It is noted that in this part, the order of the text in Irmscher's edition differs from that of Lehmann. Indeed, a) after considering the classification of triangles based on angles, Irmscher inserts specific propositions about triangles;[105] b) after the considerations of a general character about quadrilaterals, propositions on parallelograms are inserted;[106] c) after considerations of a general nature concerning polygons come propositions about regular polygons;[107] and after general considerations on the circle, propositions on the circle are introduced.[108]

8 Conclusion

We have seen that the topics addressed in texts *A* and *B*, which make up *Mathematik Herder*, at times overlap; this suggests that the two texts were written at different times. The title *Vorerinnungen in der Mathematik*, used for the beginning of part *A*, refers to preliminary notions; but in *Vorläufige Erinnungen*, which opens part *B*, the adjective *vorläufig* seems to indicate the *provisional* nature of the notes; this aspect is even more evident in *Vorläufige Anmerkungen der Geometrie*. Although the two texts overlap, they do not coincide exactly: recall that text *B*, unlike text *A*, does not consider a geometry and a trigonometry in which magnitudes (*Größen*) are considered "without the residual properties of things" (*A*: 49.35), but rather "in specific things" (*B*: 59.11).[109] Undoubtedly these inconsistencies have repercussions on the dating of the manuscripts. A further problem is given by the last part of text *B*, where the exposition of geometry in Lehman's edition, after the indication "4 [*bricht ab*]," continues with two more paragraphs, "Polygon" and "Circle," concerning propositions that in Irmscher's edition were inserted earlier, in paragraphs with specific content.[110]

In this respect, the analysis of *Vorlesung Herder* shows a problem of compatibility between the dating proposed by Irmscher (and by Lehmann), who deems it possible to date both *A* and *B* to either the winter semester 1762/63 or the summer semester 1763; and Martin's research (1967: 61 f.), which dates them to the winter semester 1762/63. But, even accepting the dating theory proposed by Martin, one cannot exclude the hypothesis that part *A* was taught in the winter semester

---

105 Corresponding to *B*: 66.6–7.
106 Corresponding to *B*: 66.16–17.
107 Corresponding to *B*: 66.19–20.
108 Corresponding to *B*: 66.22–23.
109 See 3.2 above.
110 Such a focus does not occur in Lehmann's edition, where under the heading "Circle" we also find, for instance, the statement of the Pythagorean Theorem.

1762/63, and part *B* was reserved for the summer semester 1763, consistent with Kant's announcement in 1759, that if one semester was not enough to complete the course, he would complete it in the following semester.

Referring to Irmscher's great diligence in editing such a text, which presents considerable problems, Lehmann wonders "whether the time spent was worth the effort [*Ob die aufgewendete Mühe sich gelohnt hat, ist eine andere Frage*]" (AA 29.1,1: 659). He thinks that the mathematical content of *Vorlesung Herder* is not on par with the *Reflexionen* on mathematics. However, the comparison is ill conceived, because, according to the dating proposed by Adickes, the *Reflexionen* belong to a later period than the composition of *Vorlesung*. In addition, one must remember that, up to this point in time, this is the only *Nachschrift* on mathematics that we possess, and it does not seem that at a later time Kant gave any other lectures in the discipline. It is therefore an essential reference for gathering further data on Kant's knowledge of mathematics, without having to rely solely on the meager information in his biographies.

Kant's mathematical background is rooted mostly in Wolff's textbooks, as is his understanding of the history of mathematics; but he also shows a regard for Segner's textbooks, and especially for those of Kästner. Examining the structure of the text, we can see that the effort to classify disciplines and their parts is evident in *Vorerinnungen* and in *Vorläufige Anmerkungen*. The treatments of the arithmetic of whole numbers and fractions ≥ 0, and the doctrine of proportions, are consistent with the textbooks of his time. In this chapter I have tried, when possible, to trace Euclid's influence on the arithmetical theory and the propositions of geometry presented in *Mathematik Herder*, given that Euclid was a model for his rigorous mathematical argumentation, before the scientific systemization of arithmetic and geometry in the late nineteenth and early twentieth centuries.

The absence of any consideration of negative magnitudes and infinitesimal calculus could reflect a deliberate choice by Kant, who probably considered them unsuitable for an elementary presentation; in his essay, "Attempt to Introduce the Concept of Negative Magnitudes into Philosophy," published in 1763, around the same time as the *Vorlesung Herder*, he greatly admires the clarity and simplicity with which Kästner had presented the concept of "opposed magnitudes" and calculation with them (NG 2: 170.1–28); he also shows great interest for the notion of the infinitely small, and he hopes that philosophy will bring itself up-to-date on these issues (NG 2: 168.25–169.3).

Based on the findings of this chapter, it seems that the degree of Kant's dependence on Wolff should be somewhat reconsidered: *Vorlesung* can be placed between 1762 and 1763, and Kant's announcements on the use of Wolff's *Auszug* date to the years 1758–1759. But it is precisely from 1758 to 1761 that Abraham Gotthelf Kästner published a series of textbooks covering so-called elementary mathematics (1758), the analysis of finite magnitudes (1759), the analysis of the infinite (1760), and applied mathematics (1761). In the present essay, it has been possible on many occasions to note the presence of Kästner's point of view through his work of 1758; it is also significant to note Kant's above-mentioned appreciation of Kästner in his 1763 essay on negative magnitudes.

Mathematik Herder highlights the utility (*Nutzen*) of mathematics a) for its actual use (*wirklicher Gebrauch*) in the arts, and b) for its capacity to form (for *Bildung*) the mind to persuasion and order, through its certainty and method (*A*: 50.32–35). In this regard it bears keeping in mind the observation that geometry, due to its *certainty* (*Gewißheit*) and its *order* (*Ordnung*), is a logic (*B*: 64.35–36). In *Vorrede* to *Auszug*, Wolff, referring to the point of view of Melanchthon and the Greek philosophers, approves of the Greek philosophers' habit of not letting anybody continue with his studies unless the student had already learned arithmetic and geometry (Wolff 1755: i–ii). According to *Lexicon*, the first of these philosophers was Plato (Wolff 1978: column 667).[111]

In this chapter, I have pointed out some of the content of *Vorlesung* that is also interesting in light of the later development of Kant's thought. Particularly relevant are the overtures towards philosophy: the concept of magnitude connected with the categories of unit and multiplicity; *mathesis universalis* as universal science of magnitudes; the attention to the applied part of mathematics (*mathesis applicata*); the consideration of algorithms that show how natural numbers[112] are reducible to additions of units; and the attention to sensible images in arithmetic. Indeed, *Mathematik Herder* gives insights not only into Kant's activity as a teacher of mathematics, but also into his philosophical reflection.

---

[111] *Vorlesung Herder* refers to these observations imprecisely, stating that *Pythagoras* wanted only geometricians among his students (*A*: 50.34–37).
[112] Excluding zero and one.

X Physics

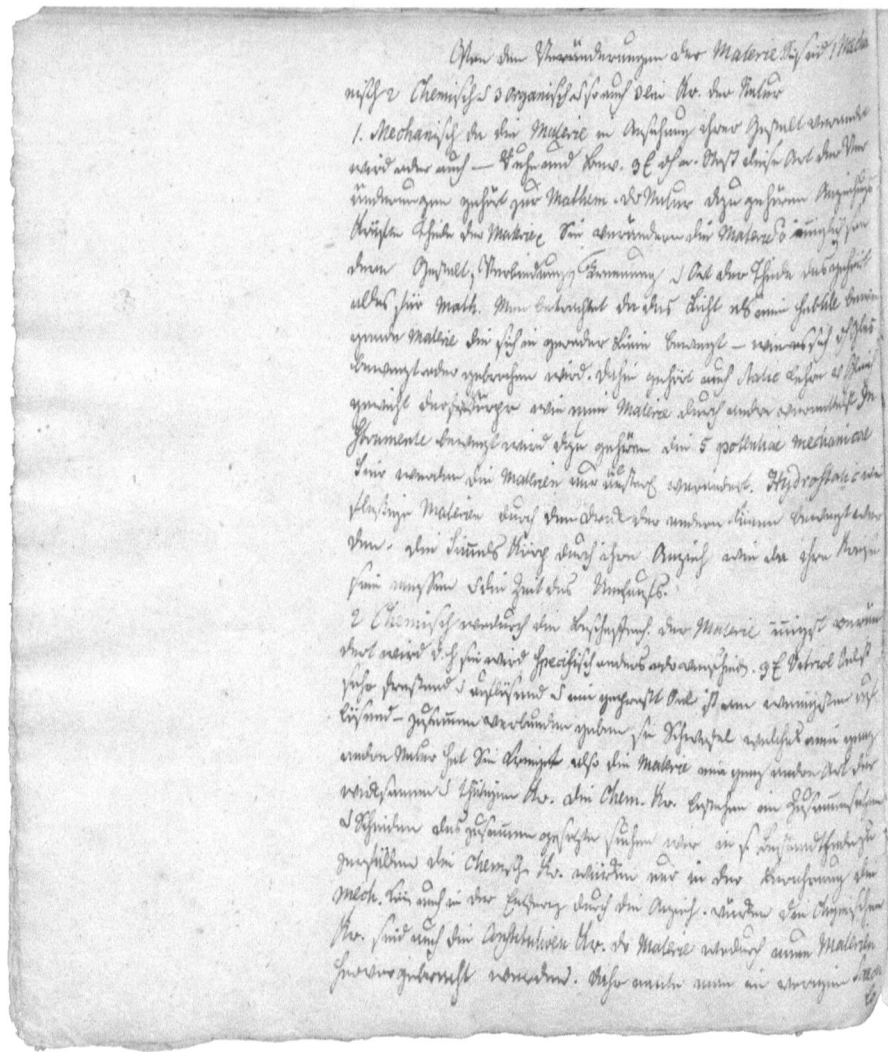

Fig. 16: Reproduction of sheet 14 verso (in Lehmann, AA 29: manuscript page 25) from the "Danziger Physik" manuscript (AA 29: 116 f.). See the next caption for more information.

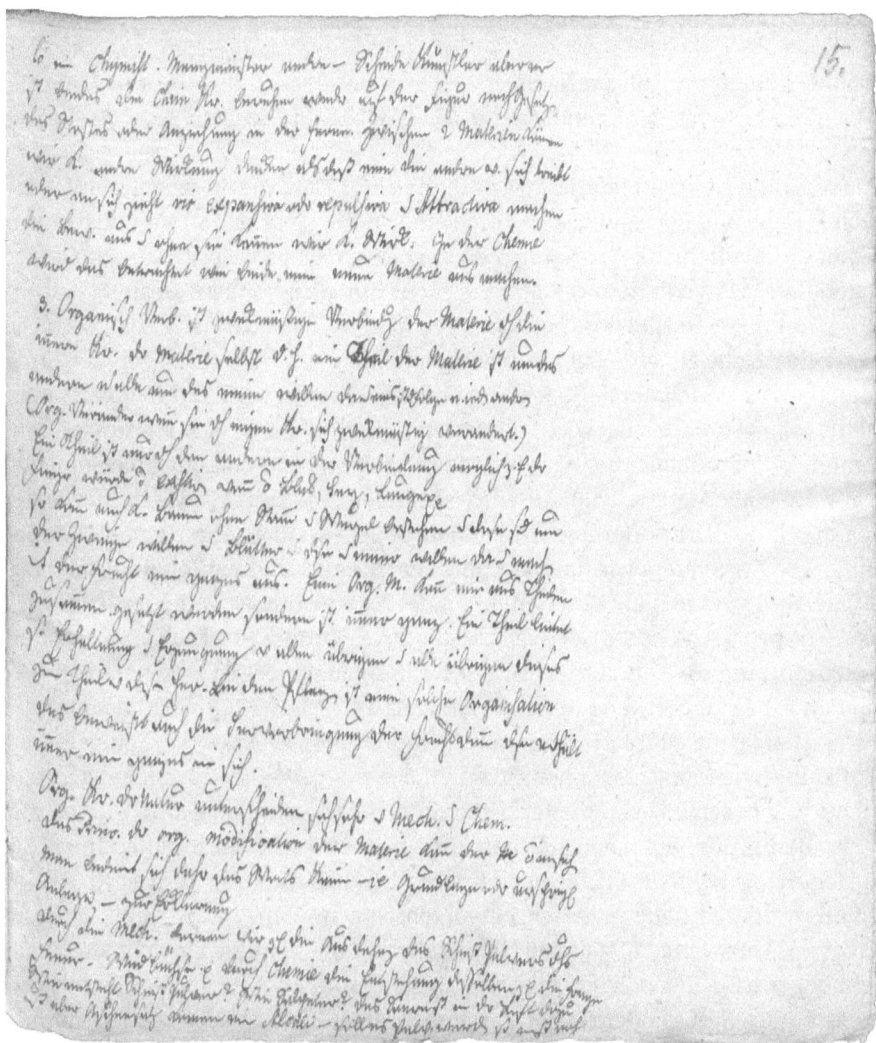

Fig. 17: Reproduction of sheet 15 recto (in Lehmann, AA 29: manuscript page 26) from the "Danziger Physik" manuscript (AA 29: 117 f.). Reproduced with the kind permission of PAN Biblioteka Gdańska (Danzig), Poland. Call number: Ms 2218. Robert Clewis's translation of the text follows; the German text is also given.

Transcription of the Text in Figs. 16 and 17

Von den Veränderungen der Materie.
Sie sind 1 Mechanisch 2 Chemisch und 3 Organisch und so auch 3erlei Kräfte der Natur.
1. Mechanisch da die Materie in Ansehung ihrer Gestalt verwandelt wird oder auch – Ruhe und Bewegung, z. E. durch einen Stoß; diese Art der Veränderungen gehört zur Mathematik der Natur[;] dazu gehören Anziehungskräfte, Theile der Materie etc. Sie verändern die Materie nicht inniglich sondern Gestalt, Verbindung, Trennung und Ort der Theile, das gehört alles für Mathematik. Man betrachtet da das Licht als eine subtile bewegende Materie, die sich in gerader Linie bewegt – wie es sich durch Glas bewegt oder gebrochen wird. Dahin gehört auch Statik, Lehre vom Gleichgewicht der festen Körper, wie eine Materie durch andre vermittelst Instrumente bewegt wird, dazu gehören die 5 potentiae mechanicae. Hier werden die Materien nur äußerlich verändert. Hydrostatic, wie flüßige Materien durch den Druck der andern können bewegt werden. Die Himmels Körper durch ihre Anziehung, wie da ihre Kräfte sein müssen und die Zeit des Umlaufs.
2. Chemisch wodurch die Beschaffenheit der Materie innigst verändert wird d. h. sie wird specifisch anders oder verschieden, z. E. Vitriol Oel ist sehr freßend und auflösend, und ein gepreßt Oel ist am wenigstens auflösend — zusammen verbunden geben sie Schwefel welcher eine ganz andre Natur hat. So kriegt also die Materie eine ganz andre Art der wirksamen und thätigen Kräfte. Die chemischen Kräfte bestehen im Zusammensetzen und Scheiden. Das zusammengesetzte suchen wir in seine Bestandteile zu zerfallen; die chemischen Kräfte würken nur in der Berührung, die mechanischen können auch in der Entfernung durch die Anziehung würken, die chemischen Kräfte sind auch die Constitutiven Kräfte der Materie wodurch neue Materien hervorgebracht werden. Daher nante man im Vorigen Saeculo einen Chymisten Mengmeister andre nannten ihn Scheide Künstler, aber er ist beides; die chemischen Kräfte beruhen weder auf der Figur noch Gesetzen des Stoßes oder Anziehung in der ferne. Zwischen 2 Materien können wir keine andre Wirkung denken als daß eine die andre von sich treibt oder an sich zieht; vis expansiva oder repulsiva und Attractiva machen die Bewegung aus und ohne sie kennen wir keine Wirkung. In der Chemie wird das betrachtet, wie beide eine neue Materie aus machen.
3. Organische Verbindung ist zweckmäßige Verbindung der Materie durch die innern Kräfte der Materie selbst d. h. ein Theil der Materie ist um des andern und alle um des einen willen da und eine ist die Folge eines ieden andern. (Organische Veränderungen wenn sie durch eigne Kräfte sich zwekmäßig verändert.) Ein Theil ist nur durch den andern in der Verbindung möglich z. E. der Finger würde nicht existiren, wenn nicht Blut, Herz, Lunge usw. existirten.

So kann auch kein Baum ohne Stamm und Wurzel bestehen und diese sind um der Zweige willen und Blätter, und diese um iener willen da und machen mit der Frucht ein ganzes aus. Eine Organische Materie kann nie aus Theilen zusammengesetzt werden sondern ist immer ganz. Ein Theil leitet seine Erhaltung und Erzeugung von allen übrigen, und alle übrige dieses zum Theil von diesem her. Bei den Pflanzen ist eine solche Organisation, das beweist auch die Hervorbringung der Frucht denn diese enthält immer ein ganzes in sich.
Organische Kräfte der Natur unterscheiden sich sehr von Mechanischen und Chemischen. Das Princip der organischen modification der Materie kann der Mensch nicht einsehen. Man bedient sich daher des Worts Keim — i. e. Grundlage oder ursprüngliche Anlage — zur Erklärung.
Durch die Mechanik lernen wir z. E. die Ausdehnung des Schieß Pulvers durchs Feuer — Windbüchse usw.; durch Chemie die Entstehung desselben z. E. die Frage: Wie entsteht Schieß Pulver? Wie Salpeter? Das Saure ist in der Luft, dazu muß aber Aschensalz kommen Alcali — soll es Pulver werden so muß noch [... Schwefel und Kohle hinzukommen — aber dies ist bloße Vermischung und nicht chymische Auflösung.]

English Translation
On the Alterations of Matter.
They are 1 mechanical 2 chemical and 3 organic, and so [there are] also three kinds of forces of nature.
1. Mechanical[:] when the matter is transformed with respect to its shape; or also – rest and motion, e. g., through an impact; this kind of alteration belongs to the mathematics of nature; to which belong forces of attraction, parts of matter, etc. It does not alter the matter internally, but rather [its] shape, connection, separation, and location of the parts; all of this belongs to mathematics. Here one considers light as a subtle, moving matter that moves in a straight line – as it moves through or is refracted by glass. Here also belong statics, the theory of the equilibrium of solid bodies, how a matter is moved by another by means of instruments; the 5 mechanical forces [*potentiae mechanicae*] belong to this. Here the matter is altered only externally. Hydrostatics[:] how fluid materials can be moved by the pressure of others. The heavenly bodies [that are moved] by their attraction[:] what their forces must be and the time of their revolution.
2. Chemical[:] by which the constitution of the matter is altered internally, i. e., it becomes different or other in species, e. g., oil of vitriol is very corrosive and dissolving, and a pressed oil is least dissolving – when combined they make sulfur, which has an altogether different nature. So in this way the matter acquires a wholly different kind of effective and active force. The chemical forces consist

of composition and separation. We try to divide the composite into its constituent parts; the chemical forces are effective only by contact, the mechanical ones can also be effective from a distance though attraction; the chemical forces are also the constitutive forces of matter through which new materials are produced. Hence in the past century some called a chemist a "Bulking Master" [while] others called him a "Dividing Artist," but he is both; the chemical forces lie neither in the figure nor in the laws of impulse or attraction at a distance. Between two pieces of matter we can think of no other effect than that the one drives the other away, or else attracts it; *vis expansiva* or *repulsiva* and *attractiva* make up motion, and without the latter we know cannot know any effect. In chemistry one observes how both [materials] constitute a new material.

3. Organic connection is [the] purposive connection of matter through the inner forces of matter itself, i.e., one part of matter is there for the other, and all are there for the sake of the one, and the one is the consequence of each of the others. (Organic alterations[:] when it [i.e., the matter] purposively alters by means of its own forces.) A part is possible only through the others to which it is connected, e.g., the finger would not exist if blood, heart, lungs, etc., did not exist.

In just this way no tree can persist without trunk and root, and these exist for the sake of the branches and leaves, and these are there for the sake of the former and, with the fruit, make up a whole. An organic matter can never be composed from parts; rather, it is always whole. One part derives its preservation and generation from all the others, and all the others in part from this one. Plants have this kind of organization; the production of fruit also proves this, since the latter always contains a whole within it.

Organic forces of nature are quite different from mechanical and chemical [forces]. The human being cannot have insight into the principle of the organic modification of matter. For clarification, one thus employs the word "germ" – i.e., basic structure or original predisposition.

Through mechanics we learn about, e.g., the expansion of gunpowder through the spark – wind rifle, etc.; through chemistry we learn of its origin, e.g., the question: how does gunpowder arise? Like saltpeter? The acid is in the air, but potash must then be added alkali – if it is to become powder, then sulfur and charcoal must still [sheet 15 verso continues:] be added – but this is only mixing and not chemical dissolution.

Chapter 19
Kant's Lectures on Physics and the Development of the Critical Philosophy

Christian Onof

Kant's lectures on physics are collected in volume 29.1,1 of Kant's works as published in the *Akademie-Ausgabe*, and edited by Gerhard Lehmann (see also Kant 1961, with Lehmann's useful introduction, which is also reproduced in AA 29.1,1). There are three sets of lecture notes: the Herder, Friedländer, and the Mrongovius notes. The latter two are given titles in the *Akademie-Ausgabe* which refer to the cities where they were found, namely the Berliner Physik (AA 29.1,1: 75–91) and Danziger Physik (AA 29.1,1: 97–169) respectively, while the first is referred to as the Physik Herder (AA 29.1,1: 69–71).[1] Also noteworthy are the 32 pages of endnotes to the physics lectures (29.1,1: 686–717), which shed light on the historical context of the scientific topics that Kant discusses.

While the Physik Herder are early notes from Kant's 1763 lectures, the Friedländer notes date from 1776, i. e., from the middle of Kant's "silent decade" between the *Dissertation* of 1770 and the first edition of the *Critique of Pure Reason* in 1781. The Mrongovius notes, on the other hand, date back to 1785, i. e., between the two editions of the first *Critique*, and importantly, a year before the publication of the *Metaphysical Foundations of Natural Science* (MAN 4: 466–565).

Kant lectured on physics every year for which we have records from 1755 to 1770, and thereafter somewhat less regularly, with another seven courses, the last of which was in the winter semester 1787/88. At first, Kant gave a winter semester course entitled "Physics," and one in the summer semester on natural science (*Naturwissenschaft*). The titles then changed, with Kant eventually giving his lecture courses the title "Theoretical Physics."

This temporal spread of the lecture notes provides a good basis for an examination of evidence of the development of Kant's Critical philosophy in these lecture notes, and this issue will be the focus of the present chapter. Before examining the content of these lecture notes, a few remarks should be made.

---

[1] There are also notes on physics in the lectures on metaphysics to be found in AA 28: 160–66. In this chapter, all translations from the lecture notes are by the author. Hereafter, "AA" will be omitted in references to the physics lectures.

First, although we can make a nice tri-partite division between pre-Critical, semi-Critical (after the *Dissertation* of 1770), and Critical periods that the Herder, Friedländer, and Mrongovius lecture notes map onto, the material is by no means evenly distributed. The Mrongovius notes are by far the most extensive, and mostly contain well-formed full sentences. The Friedländer notes are also largely composed of very readable sentences, but the short Herder notes are sketchy and piecemeal. So there is little material to enable us to comment upon the pre-*Dissertation* period. Rather, the bulk of the evidence is relevant to understanding the development of Kant's Critical system during the 1770s and 1780s.

Second, there is some uncertainty as to whether Herder's notes are indeed from Kant's lectures. It is known that Herder (who was enrolled as a student at Königsberg University from 1762 to 1764) also attended lectures by Teske and F. J. Buck, and the notes could be from either of these. This provides additional grounds for being cautious about drawing conclusions from Herder's notes.

Third, as with all lecture notes, we are of course dependent upon the filtering of Kant's spoken words through the note-taking by one of his students. This not only means that some content is lost, but also that there is a degree of interpretation involved in what is actually written down by the student, and in some cases, there are errors (possibly due to distraction or the multiple copying of notes from other students). Consequently, there is some uncertainty inherent to the following interpretations of Kant's lectures on physics.

Finally, these are notes from lectures, and Kant used textbooks written by Eberhard (1753), Erxleben (1772) and Karsten (1783) for the Herder, Berliner, and Danziger Physik courses, respectively. The material that is taught is therefore constructed around the content of these textbooks, and should not be treated as straightforward expressions of Kant's views.

This chapter is structured as follows. I first give an overview of the content of three sets of lecture notes (1). I then focus upon key themes which seem particularly relevant to understanding the evolution of Kant's Critical ideas: the next two sections are thus devoted to the place of mathematical physics in natural science (2), and the notion of matter (3), with a detailed examination of the role of the forces of attraction and repulsion (3.1–3.2) and the topic of infinite divisibility (3.3). A fourth section examines Kant's statements about other types of material reality to be found in nature, such as heat and electricity (3.4).

1 Overview of the content of the lecture notes

The notes of the Berliner Physik were taken by David Joachim Friedländer (1750–1834), the son of a Königsberg Jewish silk merchant, who continued in his father's trade and moved to Berlin in 1771, where he became the first Jewish city councilor. Friedländer counted Moses Mendelssohn and Markus Herz among his friends. The Berliner Physik notes start with a brief introduction that sets out the domain of investigation as that of outer sense and stresses the fact that this world is phenomenal and that it is only through movement that we become aware of phenomena of outer sense (29.1,1: 75.13–17). There then follow some results concerning the movement of a point (i. e., kinematics, or as Kant refers to it, "Phoronomy"), both rectilinear and circular (29.1,1: 75–77). In the section entitled "Of the communication of forces" (29.1,1: 77–89), Kant first discusses the fundamental forces of attraction and repulsion, and then the so-called "derivative" forces, whereby Kant distinguishes these fundamental original forces (*ursprüngliche Kraft*) from derivative ones (*abgeleitete Kraft*) (29.1,1: 78.21–37) through which movement is communicated, before defining matter (29.1,1: 79.1–14) as that which occupies space, is a substance, divisible, and with a certain inertia. The definition of bodies (29.1,1: 79.15–25) in terms of the figures defined by matter, is followed by a statement of laws of motion (29.1,1: 79.26–36).

In the following pages, Kant discusses a number of topics, from the infinite divisibility of matter (29.1,1: 80.11–20), to the gravitational force (29.1,1: 80.27–82.25), elasticity (29.1,1: 82.38–83.17), warmth (29.1,1: 83.18–84.9), light (29.1,1: 84.3–29), and sound (29.1,1: 84.25–85.7), and then returns to these themes of elasticity, warmth, sound, and light, comparing them and relating them to one another and to the ether (29.1,1: 84.37–86.31). A discussion of combustion (29.1,1: 86.37–87.35), fermentation (29.1,1: 87.36–88.17), solvability (29.1,1: 88.17–37) concludes this section. The next and last two sections are short and discuss respectively magnetic and electric forces (29.1,1: 89.3–29) and electricity (29.1,1: 89.30–91.29).

The notes of the Danziger Physik were taken by Krzysztof Celestyn Mrongovius (1764–1855), a Polish protestant pastor, philosopher, and linguist known in particular for his translations of classics into Polish (e. g., from the Greek), and for one of the first Polish-German dictionaries. Mrongovius studied at the Cathedral school in Königsberg, from which he graduated in 1782. The notes on Kant's lectures on physics are one out of a set of seven compilations of lecture notes discovered in Danzig.

The Danziger Physik covers themes familiar from the earlier Berliner Physik, but the approach is more structured, and there is a substantial introduction that sets out to systematize the different parts of our knowledge of the natural world. The lectures thus start with an extensive section entitled "Prolegomena" (29.1,1: 97.1–107.20), which distinguishes three parts (29.1,1: 97.1–100.2):
1. physics which uses a conceptual approach, i. e., is essentially metaphysical;

2. physics which is mathematized and has a priori principles;
3. chemistry, which has so far not shown itself to be mathematizable and thus has no a priori principles, and therefore is not part of the doctrine of nature (*Naturkunde*) – rather, it involves an a posteriori description of nature which Kant opposes to the history of nature, which focuses upon the temporal dimension of natural phenomena.

Changing his vocabulary somewhat, Kant then refers to our knowledge of nature as either "pure physiology," which can be a priori – as mathematic of nature (i); or metaphysic of nature (ii); a posteriori principles (iii); or a combination of both (iv) in applied physiology where a posteriori principles are required to complement a priori ones (29.1,1: 101.16). Areas (i), (ii) and (iv) are parts of what Kant describes as "rational physics," and which is to be distinguished from the history of nature (*Natur Geschichte*) which provides the material for rational physics (29.1,1: 102.17–18).

Kant then further distinguishes:
- different types of experience used in our knowledge of nature: simple perception and artificial experiences; the latter are in turn either observations or experiments (29.1,1: 102.25–103.8);
- two types of proofs: dogmatic or hypothetical (29.1,1: 103.17–29);
- between explanations through "contingent" (*zufällig*) and a posteriori causes, and those from "necessary" and a priori causes (29.1,1: 104.1–11);
- types of explanation that are physical (connections between causes and effects) from those that are teleological (connections between means and ends) (29.1,1: 104.33–105.23), whereby the first are either mechanical (in terms of already existing forces), dynamic (in terms of special forces not previously present), or organic (in terms of the receptivity to sensations of a being) (29.1,1: 105.24–106.14);
- between two types of explanation used by the Ancients which are to be avoided, namely the *hypophysical*, where less is explained than could be through experience (e. g., explanations through the mere naming of some unknown cause), and the *hyperphysical*, where supernatural causes are adduced (29.1,1: 106.13–107.20).

A short section on the history of natural science (29.1,1: 107.21–108.4) is followed by a short study (*Abhandlung* – 29.1,1: 108.5–110.9) presenting the key concepts (space, bodies, matter, forces) and some remarks (e. g., basic properties of bodies).

The next section deals with the properties of bodies (29.1,1: 110.18–116.29), namely, the repulsive and attractive forces and the resulting impenetrability of bodies, as well as the issue of infinite divisibility, rigidity, and movement of bodies.

This is followed by a section on the changes of matter, which are classified into three groups: physical, chemical, and organic alterations (29.1,1: 116.30–118.30).

The next section, entitled "Second chapter," deals with certain "materials" (*Materien*) that are widespread in nature, namely fire, light, and air, to which Kant tentatively adds heat ("If we assume that heat is a special material …") (29.1,1: 119.3–4). After introducing them (29.1,1: 118.31–119.22), Kant reviews their various properties, discussing in particular the measurement of heat, e. g., through deformation of materials, phase transitions between states of matter, and with a focus upon thermometry (29.1,1: 120.15–128.26).

A discussion of weight is the focus of the following section (29.1,1: 128.27–132.4), which is presumably the third chapter of the notes. Some of the topics touched upon are the center of gravity, where Kant claims that the center of gravity of the whole universe must be at rest (29.1,1: 129.12–13); hydrostatics; and applications to the measurement of the weight of wines and beers.

The fourth chapter deals with the force of attraction either at a distance or through contact, with a focus upon the latter in such phenomena as surface tension and capillary phenomena in liquids (29.1,1: 132.23–136.6), and the discussion turns towards hydrostatics again, this time with a focus upon the measurement of pressure with barometers and manometers (29.1,1: 136.7–138.32).

A short section on the motion of bodies, presumably chapter five (29.1,1: 139.23–140.19) distinguishes between rotational and linear movement, the latter being either uniform or accelerated/decelerated. The next section, presumably chapter six (29.1,1: 140.20–146.7), has a Latin title announcing a focus upon such accelerated or decelerated movement, but eventually the topic changes towards hydraulics. Noteworthy in this chapter is the discussion of the "idea of absolute movement," which, Kant says, serves the purpose of preventing us from taking anything as absolute movement (29.1,1: 142.37–38), insofar as it is a mere idea.

Chapter seven deals with sound, the wavelike nature of the propagation thereof, acoustics and resonance (29.1,1: 146.8–149.39), while the next section, presumably chapter eight (29.1,1: 150.1–154.10) focuses upon light and color, with a discussion of geometric optics. This is followed by a section on the eye (29.1,1: 154.11–156.26).

Chapter nine examines "electrical matter" (29.1,1: 156.27–160.39), and chapter ten the "elements or materials out of which bodies are composed" (29.1,1: 161.1–169.15), where issues pertaining to chemistry are presented.

2 The place of mathematical physics in the investigation of nature

In the Danziger Physik, Kant sets out very clearly what a mathematical physics involves, by differentiating this approach to the investigation of nature (*Naturkunde*) (29.1,1: 97.19) from one which is merely metaphysical (*blos metaphysisch*) (29.1,1: 97.3). Mathematics is presented, as in the *Critique of Pure Reason*, by its method according to which it "simultaneously constructs the bodies [*Körper*]" that it examines (29.1,1: 97.6). Kant also refers to the "mathematical part of physics" (29.1,1: 97.7) but does not say much more about this in the opening page of the Danziger notes. Rather, he shifts the focus to chemistry and the fact that, "here, one can hardly do anything with mathematics" (29.1,1: 97.22–3). This relegates chemistry to the status of a "description of nature" (*Naturbeschreibung*) (29.1,1: 97.19), although further on, Kant distinguishes it from mere description in that the latter has "no principles", while chemistry does have "a posteriori principles" (29.1,1: 97.26–7).

Here, we find Kant presenting the position he will publish in *Metaphysical Foundations of Natural Science*, that chemistry is not a science, while physics clearly is. While the latter claim is unsurprising, the former is not *prima facie* an obvious one, particularly in the light of the growing body of chemical knowledge in the latter part of the eighteenth century, a growth Kant himself acknowledges: "Chemistry has, in recent times, raised itself to great completeness" (29.1,1: 97.30–1). What chemistry lacks, however, is mathematical explanations, a fact which is hardly surprising since "only the smallest part of natural occurrences can be rendered mathematically" (29.1,1: 97.33–4). And for Kant in his Critical period, it has no a priori principles.

In contrast, Kant claims that the principles of physics are a priori (29.1,1: 97.25). Together with the claim that the mathematical method is at the heart of physics, this presentation of physics might seem to diverge somewhat from that given in the *Prolegomena* (1783), for instance, where Kant distinguishes pure mathematics from the pure science of nature, whereby the former rests upon its own evidence, and the latter, although it springs from the pure understanding, rests upon and is confirmed by experience, "experience being a witness that natural science cannot fully renounce and dispense with" (Prol 4: 327).[2]

---

[2] There are in fact ambiguities in the *Prolegomena*, as Friedman (1992a: 177–210) discusses at length. In section 38, Kant appears to be deriving the inverse-square law governing gravitational attraction, from purely geometrical considerations (without referring to Kepler's laws of planetary motion or Newton's laws of motion). Friedman provides an interesting account of how that

But in fact, Kant has more to say about the exact role of mathematics in physics as, four pages later, the lectures strangely feature a return to the introductory theme of the subdivision of the investigation of nature into different subjects. Starting with a clear statement of the distinction within our "knowledge of nature" (*Naturkenntnis*) between the "doctrine of nature" (*Naturlehre*) and the "description of nature" (*Naturbeschreibung*), the first is then further subdivided into rational physics (*rationale Physic*) which rests on a priori principles (29.1,1: 101.16), while the second is based on a posteriori principles, and although Kant does not repeat it, this presumably includes chemistry.

Indeed, rather than considering the nature of chemistry in opposition to physics as he did at the outset of the notes, Kant here further subdivides rational physics. He distinguishes between a pure form, which he intriguingly calls "pure physiology" (*Physiologia pura*) and an applied form, where a priori and a posteriori grounds are combined (29.1,1: 101.17–21). Notably, he refers to both the principle of action and reaction (Newton's third law of motion) and to a version of the principle of inertia (Newton's first law of motion)[3] under this heading of applied physiology, reflecting on "whether action and reaction are equal or that a body that is in motion remains in the same [motion] until another body pushes it away" (29.1,1: 101.21–24).[4] Here, rather than the one-level subdivision of the doctrine of nature into "mathematical physics, chemistry and the description of nature" (29.1,1: 99.25–26) which summarizes the opening section of the lecture, we now have different levels of distinction which create the space for an applied part of physics ("applied physiology") in line with Kant's writings in the *Metaphysical Foundations of Natural Science* and *Prolegomena*.

Moreover, the whole content of the lectures shows Kant's belief that physics has an important experimental dimension: all the concepts he introduces are immediately illustrated by experiments (mostly real but occasionally also virtual) that show how the concept is instantiated. Thus, for instance, he lists a number of

---

passage is best understood.

[3] This focus upon the first and third Newtonian laws is consistent with *Metaphysical Foundations of Natural Science*. This point is noted by Friedman (1992a: 168 n.6), who shows how Newton's second law "appears to be contained" in Kant's third, and it is discussed in detail by Watkins (2001).

[4] I note that under this understanding of the principle of inertia, it would appear that an actual collision is required to disturb the motion, whereas Kant knows of course that this could be achieved by a force at a distance (e.g., gravitational attraction). But the statement is not the full law, and Kant does not say it is the only way in which the inertial motion can be disturbed. Here, it is therefore important to bear in mind that these are lecture notes: in a lecture, it would be perfectly reasonable to refer to a collision as an obvious way in which a motion might be disturbed.

examples to illustrate the surface tension phenomena[5] characterizing the interface of a liquid with air and solids. Describing the shape of the surface of water in a glass, he observes that:

> When the glass is powdered or smeared, it [the water] stands lower at the edges, insofar as the less dense material is to be viewed, in relation to water, as empty space, and water therefore strives as far as possible to form a spherical shape. The same happens when mercury is poured into a glass because this is lighter than mercury. If I have two empty balls of glass swimming in a glass of water, they will knock vigorously against each other, which happens because the water which surrounds these balls seeks the greatest possible contact, and therefore gathers into a spherical shape and brings the balls closer together. When a capillary tube is immersed in water, water climbs up inside it. (29.1,1: 133.31–134.3)

Kant creates one more level with a distinction, within pure physics, between the mathematics of nature and the metaphysics of nature, a distinction that hinges upon the relation to intuition:

> Pure physiology is either:
> A/ Mathematics of nature; this is the knowledge of nature from mathematical grounds or from the construction of concepts, so that everything can be represented in intuition.
> B/ Metaphysics of nature: this is the knowledge of nature from mere concepts without any intuition. (29.1,1: 101.25–30)

This distinction is reminiscent of Kant's distinction between the method of mathematics and that of philosophy in the *Critique of Pure Reason*: "Philosophical cognition is rational cognition from concepts, mathematical cognition that from the construction of concepts" (KrV A713/B741).

As explained above, with the Critical turn Kant is now clear about the grounding role of metaphysics for physics, and this role is clearly set out in *Metaphysical Foundations of Natural Science* and in the earlier preface to the first edition of the *Critique of Pure Reason* (KrV Axxi). There is a need for this grounding role to be spelled out and clearly delimited:

> This metaphysics of nature … is, however, indispensable to the mathematics thereof, as it grounds the latter. No one has so far presented this metaphysics of nature as completely separate from the mathematical [i. e., the mathematics of nature], although the mathematicians have themselves made use of it. (29.1,1: 102.3–7)

---

[5] These phenomena were soon to be properly described by Young in 1804, and mathematically formalized by Laplace a year later. They had however been investigated since the early eighteenth century.

Kant therefore thinks that there is a pressing need for the kind of work that he undertakes in *Metaphysical Foundations of Natural Science*. Indeed, the *Critique of Pure Reason* defines the bounds of possible knowledge and states very general principles for the application of the categories to experience, the Principles of Pure Understanding (KrV A148–235/B187–294). In the Analogies of Experience, where the relational categories are applied to spatio-temporal manifolds, the category of substance is central, for all causality is then defined in terms of alterations of determinations of substance. What Kant leaves open at this transcendental level is what, in our experience, will play the role of substance and what specific causal laws will hold. In a similar vein, the *Critique of Pure Reason* does not address the issue of the determination of the motion of an object or its parts, namely the issue of how to determine objects in both space *and* time simultaneously.

These issues are addressed in Kant's outline of a metaphysics of nature that serves to ground natural science: in *Metaphysical Foundations of Natural Science*, Kant discusses the empirical concept of matter and its schematization under the four classes of categories. This leads Kant to show in detail how the spatio-temporal determination of objects requires an appeal to principles which amount to Newton's first and third laws (see footnote 3), and how the outcome of this determination will never result in the determination of absolute motion, but only in approximations thereto. As a result, Kant's version of Newton's laws of motion will come to form part of a set of a priori principles of natural science.[6]

Moreover, one can read a hint of criticism in the last sentence of the quote above insofar as the failure to properly investigate the metaphysical foundations of nature has important consequences for the validity of the claims made by the mathematical physicist. This criticism is made explicit for instance in Kant's noting in *Metaphysical Foundations of Natural Science* that Newton was "at variance with himself" in not recognizing that the attractive force of gravity is an essential property of bodies, i.e., of matter (MAN 4: 515): Kant remedies this by taking it as an priori truth that the attractive force is a fundamental property that belongs to the very concept of matter.

Matters are somewhat different after the publication of the *Dissertation*. The *Dissertation* had achieved a clear split between the sensible domain described by the exact sciences such as physics, and the intelligible domain of metaphysics (e.g., as Kant explains in a letter to Lambert from 1770, see Br 10: 98.17–36), a point I shall return to below. There was therefore no role for metaphysics in providing any principles for the sensible domain. It should thus come as no surprise

---

[6] Newton's first and third laws have their Kantian versions in *Metaphysical Foundations of Natural Science* as propositions 3 and 4 respectively.

that the Berliner Physik does not discuss the role of metaphysical principles in physics.

But, more significantly, we find Kant alluding to a clear distinction between the domain of philosophy and that of physics when he states, of the indivisibility of matter, that "This question does not really belong to physics" (29.1,1: 80.11–12), thus emphasizing the distinct domains of natural sciences and metaphysics.

3 Matter

3.1 Characterization of matter

The Danziger Physik states that "the manifold in space is the object of our senses and the epitome thereof is nature, more specifically, corporeal nature" (29.1,1: 108.7–8). Kant then identifies the two essential characteristics of corporeal nature, namely:

> 1. that they [bodies] occupy a space, that is the extension
> 2. the property of an extended being to fill this space. This is the impenetrability (*impenetrabilitas*), i.e., bodies have an ability to prevent that things[7] can be in the same place they are. The concept of matter follows from this. (29.1,1: 108.13–17)

Kant thus defines matter in terms of its occupying space and its being impenetrable. Of particular interest in this period between the two editions of the *Critique of Pure Reason* are Kant's pronouncements on space in relation to matter. Kant argues that prior to the being of matter, we have to represent a space (*Wir müssen uns ... einen Raum denken*), insofar as matter has to be contained (*eingeschlossen*) in a space. He concludes that "space must have been there before matter" (29.1,1: 108.10–11). This claim of a priority of space over matter[8] reminds one of the first argument for the a priority of space in the Transcendental Aesthetic (KrV A23/B38). The main difference lies in the fact that here, Kant is explicitly referring to the a posteriori concept of matter as that which occupies space, and therefore appeals to the notion of containment of matter in space. This "application" of the argument from the Transcendental Aesthetic to a world of appearances in which

---

[7] Mrongovius gets it wrong by negating the next clause, i.e., by saying "cannot" (which would make no sense) instead of "can," but it is an error one can easily imagine happening in the process of taking notes: a double instead of a single negation.

[8] Although the grammar suggests otherwise, this cannot be a claim of temporal priority since what is at stake is what we can represent. The priority is therefore logical.

matter is what occupies space, does not therefore establish the a priority of the representation of space, but the priority of space relatively to matter.

In that proof in the Transcendental Aesthetic, Kant had also claimed that one could conceive of space as empty of objects, and indeed, we find him here applying this possibility to matter by defining a vacuum (29.1,1: 108.20–1) and by adding that there can be "relative" vacua ("comparative" empty space) and "absolute" vacua (29.1,1: 109.14–5 and 110.11–17).

Kant summarizes the dual material-spatial nature of bodies with two spatial and two material properties:

1. All bodies are extended.
2. All bodies are divisible.
3. All matter subsists, even if we destroy its shape or volume.
4. All matter has forces. The force cannot be given to any body if it does not yet have it, but we can determine it: these forces are driving [i. e., expansive]⁹ and attractive. (29.1,1: 110.3–9)

This summary is important in two respects. First, it confirms that matter plays the role of substance for the First Analogy, i. e., that it is that which subsists while its determinations (volume or shape) change. Second, it brings up two properties which were at the heart of Kant's interest in natural philosophy, namely the divisibility of matter, and its being endowed with attractive and repulsive forces, both of which Kant sees as properties that are fundamental to the very definition of matter as something impenetrable that occupies space. It is through knowledge of these fundamental forces that the basic principles underpinning the causal behavior of matter can be understood.

Let us compare the characterization of matter in the Berliner Physik. There, Kant also presents four points:

Matter is:
1. something that occupies a space. It fills a space when both forces [i. e., of attraction and repulsion] which work on it are equal, or it fills a space which is present in it through impenetrability. Matter is
2. a substance. Substance is a *perdurabile subiectum actionum*.
3. All matter is divisible, because it is in space. Everything that is divisible is composite. The last property of matter is:

---

[9] Kant clearly distinguishes attraction and expansion/repulsion in the rest of the lecture, but here, the words *treibende Kraft* are used to describe the latter, i. e., thereby characterizing it, literally, as "driving force." He also uses the word *forttreibende Kraft* (29.1,1: 111.13).

4. Inertia. This inertia consists in lifelessness. This lifelessness of matter consists in the fact that it cannot bring about any movement of itself. (29.1,1: 79.2–14)

Points 1, 2, 3, and 4 match up loosely with points 1, 3, 2, and 4 respectively in the Danziger Physik. But there are differences. First, the property of divisibility is accompanied by the claim that all that is divisible is composite. Second, although the forces of attraction are mentioned as accounting for space's property of occupying space, Kant does not list it as a characteristic of matter that it has these forces. Rather, a property of inertia is mentioned.

I offer two tentative comments about these differences. To understand them, it is worth recalling that at the time of the lectures reported in the Berliner Physik (1776), Kant's metaphysical picture of reality has it that there is an intelligible world, which is accessible to our reason, while what is in space and time is a sensible world of appearances. So the ultimate nature of what appears as matter is something that is not found in space and time. It may therefore be for this reason that Kant emphasizes that matter, as it is found in space, is a composite, which points to the existence of simple parts (see the 1764 *Inquiry concerning the Distinctness of the Principles of Natural Theology and Morality*, UD 2: 286 f.). As to forces, it is worth noting that prior to the *Dissertation*, e. g., in the *Physical Monadology* (1756), repulsive forces were properties of the unobservable monads explaining the impenetrability of matter as we experience it. With the new metaphysics of the *Dissertation*, these forces can no longer characterize the monads, now located in an intelligible world: forces are given by experience (MonPh 1: 417.1). Kant may therefore be reticent to characterize matter in terms of forces, as this would appear to endow it with some essential nature that could only reside in the intelligible domain of monads. And indeed Kant avoids giving any characterization of matter that might appear to define its essence (even inertia is defined purely negatively as lifelessness). Rather, he precedes the spelling out of the four characteristics above by the remark "We want to dissect everything before we define" (29.1,1: 79.1–2). And after the characteristics have been presented, he proceeds to give what is, in effect, a definition of sorts, albeit with an inherent circularity: "What is a body? A matter, insofar as it is coherent and has a figure. *Materia cohaerens figurata est corpus*. Matter is therefore the stuff of bodies" (29.1,1: 79.15–17).

With the Critical system, however, it is clear that there is no essential nature of matter, as appearances are distinct from things in themselves. It is therefore not possible to state fundamental properties of matter such as its having certain internal forces, since it is clear that these cannot define its essence. Rather, the form that the characterization of matter takes in the Danziger Physik (29.1,1: 110) follows from the analysis of the concept of a body two pages earlier, which leads to a definition of the concept of matter: "The concept of matter thus follows [from the preceding analysis]. Matter is an extended impenetrable (*extensum impenetrabile*)" (29.1,1: 108.18–19).

Let us examine more closely the two important characteristics of matter that Kant identifies in the Danziger Physik: its being endowed with two basic forces (repulsive and attractive) and its divisibility.

3.2 Forces

As Kant explains in the Danziger Physik (29.1,1: 112.27–35), the expansive (repulsive, driving)[10] force is that through which a body occupies space, such that the void gets filled through this force, and this accounts for the impenetrability of matter. But, if there were only expansive forces, bodies would occupy an infinite amount of space, and thereby become empty. There is therefore a need for an attractive force to counterbalance it. Such an explanation is also found in the Berliner Physik (29.1,1: 77.21–78.2), where Kant clarifies that the repulsive force is not exerted at a distance, but only through contact (29.1,1: 78.94–95). The need for both repulsive and attractive forces is already claimed in the *Physical Monadology*, and later reiterated in *Metaphysical Foundations of Natural Science* (MAN 4: 508–511).

Additionally, in both the Berliner Physik and Danziger Physik, Kant indicates that the actual figure (*Figur*) of material body, i.e., the limit of the space it occupies, is defined by where the attractive and repulsive forces are identical (29.1,1: 112.36–7 and 29.1,1: 78.3–5).

In the Berliner Physik, Kant adds that the impenetrability of a body, which he derives from the expansive (repulsive) force, is not a fundamental property of matter: "Impenetrability is no characteristic determination [*eigenthümliches*] of matter that could somehow be derived from the law of non-contradiction [*Satz des Widerspruchs*]; rather, a force is needed for that" (29.1,1: 78.5–7). Here, Kant is criticizing the view that impenetrability is a property that is analytically derivable from the very concept of matter. Kant instead proposes an explanation of impenetrability in dynamical terms, i.e., as resulting from a repulsive force. He claims this already in his pre-Critical writings (NG 2: 198.36–199.05), and later in *Metaphysical Foundations* when he criticizes Lambert and others (MAN 4: 497),

---

10 Kant refers to this force using different names: *treibende Kraft* (29.1,1: 77.22), *Kraft der Repulsion* (29.1,1: 78.8), *Expansions Kraft* (29.1,1: 110.34), *expansive Kraft* (29.1,1: 110.36), *via repulsiva* (29.1,1: 78.35).

a group he refers to as the mathematicians of nature (MAN 4: 498). As Warren (2001: 104) explains, one of the main reasons for this criticism is that Lambert's theory amounts to the wrong kind of explanation: "Matter, he says, does not resist penetration with 'absolute necessity' [as it would, were it a matter involving the law of non-contradiction]; rather it rests on a 'physical ground'" (Warren 2001: 104 f., commenting on MAN 4: 502). That is, impenetrability is an effect of some causal relation.

A second issue worth noting is the Berliner Physik's distinction between original (*ursprünglich*) and derivative (*abgeleitet*) forces (29.1,1: 110.36): "An original force is [one] through which a movement or a resistance from immobility arises, while the derived [is one] through which movement is communicated" (29.1,1: 78.17–19). This distinction looks both back to the metaphysical tradition, and forward to *Metaphysical Foundations* in Kant's Critical period. First, Kant reminds his audience of the difference between "living" and "dead" forces.

> The living force is the force that is expressed through an impact or through a real velocity. The dead force is that which happens through pressure, or the inception of velocity, i.e., through [something's] effort to move itself. The living forces are communicated, and let themselves be created only by means of the dead force. (29.1,1: 80.5–9)

The dead forces are therefore manifestations of the original forces, while the living forces are derived forces on Kant's understanding of living and dead forces. This refers to the debate between the Cartesians and Leibnizians about whether the product of a body's volume and its velocity, or rather the product of a body's mass and the square of its velocity, is conserved. The first defined the dead force, and the second, the living force. Kant's definition of these forces in the Berliner Physik therefore distances itself from the terms of this original debate on which he himself had taken a stance in his *Thoughts on the True Estimation of Living Forces* (1747). There, he had argued for a reconciliation between the two positions, claiming that while the dead forces provided a good mathematical description of the phenomena, living forces were required from a metaphysical perspective (Watkins 2001: 140). Since this position was to change radically in the Critical period with *Metaphysical Foundations of Natural Science*'s focus upon the quantity of matter as that which is conserved, it is interesting to have this text from the pre-Critical period to see how Kant made use of the original duality of dead and living forces to integrate it in his distinction of original and derived forces.

Second, this distinction between original and derived forces would ultimately be integrated into the Critical framework through Kant's distinction in *Metaphysical Foundations* between dynamical and mechanical forces. As Kant puts it in the chapter on Mechanics, in mechanics the force of a matter set in motion is regarded as present in order to impart this motion to another matter. But it is clear that the movable would have no moving force through its motion if did not possess original moving forces, whereby it is active in every place where it exists before all proper motion. (MAN 4: 536.14–18)

after which Kant refers to the forces of repulsion and attraction as these original forces required for the possession of moving forces.[11] Although the pre-Critical Kant does not yet have the table of categories in place from which the distinction dynamic/mechanical will arise (as following from the categories of quality and relation respectively), the key distinction of types of forces which will underpin it is already in place in these pre-Critical lecture notes of the Berliner Physik.

A third issue of note concerns Kant's claims about the limits of our understanding of forces. We find in the Berliner Physik that Kant underscores the limits of our grasp of the nature of original forces: "Original forces cannot be recognized through reason of any kind, but only through experience; one can indeed recognize them, but not comprehend them, for instance attraction" (29.1,1: 78.11–13). "No basic or original force is comprehensible, but, for sure, [it is] understandable" (29.1,1: 78.36–7). The first quote helps make sense of "understandable" as "recognizable through their role in experience." This kind of remark is also found in earlier publications (e. g., in the 1763 essay on negative magnitudes, NG 2: 202–04), and re-stated in *Metaphysical Foundations* (MAN 4: 524 f.). As Warren explains (2001: 107–10), this can be understood as an aspect of Kant's criticism of the mechanists' (e. g., Lambert) position, which criticism can best be defended as part of the broader framework of his Critical system. According to the Critical position, we can only know relational features of things, not their inner determinations, for knowing the latter would be tantamount to knowing something about reality in itself. While the mechanists seem to provide accounts appealing to the inner constitution of things and thus going beyond relational properties, even such accounts can only be understood in relational terms, i. e., in terms of fundamental forces (attractive, repulsive) for which no further account can be given.

---

11 Carrier (2001a: 117) discusses the distinction between "dynamic" forces which he characterizes as acting "within matter," while the mechanical forces operate "between parts of matter." While correct, this does not sufficiently bring out the dependence.

3.3 Divisibility

Kant states that the divisibility of matter goes on to infinity (29.1,1: 115.37–116.13). He adds that this cannot be confirmed by experience, but that it is simply based upon the claim that space is infinitely divisible (he opposes this claim to a view of space as made up of points), a view that is for instance already found in the *Physical Monadology*.

Physik Herder suggests that Kant did not, however, always hold these views so unequivocally. On the issue of the infinite divisibility of matter, we find Kant saying in Physik Herder that "The divisibility of matter is real – we never get to simple substances when dividing matter, but we don't know whether the divisibility is infinite" (29.1,1: 69.24–8). This apparent agnosticism vis-à-vis the infinite divisibility of matter contrasts with clear affirmations in the Danziger Physik (see above) and Berliner Physik where we read "Matter is divisible to infinity" (29.1,1: 80.16–17), and where Kant accompanies this statement with the claim that the question of the infinite divisibility of matter "does not really belong to physics" (29.1,1: 80.11–12). This claim can be viewed as echoed in the Danziger Physik with the claim that no experiment will show that matter is infinitely divisible. But there is more to say about these differences between the Physik Herder and the other two texts on these two issues, on the assumption (which I shall make for the purpose of this discussion) that we can trust the Physik Herder as a reliable source. To investigate this further, we need to take a look at the evolution of Kant's views of physics.

The progression of Kant's thought can be largely understood as an attempt to reconcile Newtonian physics with a metaphysics originally derived from Leibnizian monadology. As Kant is clear from the start, Newton's physics, while admirable as a theory of natural science, lacks a proper grounding in metaphysics. Thus, in the *Physical Monadology*, he says:

> For those who only hunt out the phenomena of nature are always that far removed from the deeper understanding of the first causes. Nor will they ever attain knowledge of the very nature itself of bodies, any more than those who persuade themselves that by climbing higher and higher up the pinnacles of a mountain, they will at last be able to reach out and touch the heavens with their hands. (MonPh 1: 475.13–17)

As Friedman points out (1992a: 2 n. 3), Kant holds similar views throughout his career. For instance, in *Metaphysical Foundations of Natural Science* he claims that the problem lies in the fact that "mathematical physicists in no way avoid metaphysical principles" and, insofar as they did not want to erect empirical principles into metaphysical ones, they "preferred to postulate such [principles] without investigating with regard to their a priori sources" (MAN 4: 472.27–35).

The problem faced by Kant was considerable, for Leibniz's account of the natural world involved a clear rejection of the doctrine of physical influx according to which there are causal links between substances, whereby one billiard ball's knocking another is the result of a causal effect of the first upon the second. For Leibniz, there is a harmony between substances and each substance is endowed with its own causality, such that the movement of each billiard ball has its cause in this substance itself.

This follows from Leibniz's views about the monads, or the non-spatial and non-temporal, unextended, ultimate constituents of the world, of which we only have a dim perceptual grasp in space and time. Monads, Leibniz states,

> have no windows, through which anything could come in or go out. And accidents cannot detach themselves and stroll about outside of substances, as the Scholastics sensible species used to; so neither substance nor accident can come into a monad from outside. (*Monadology* §7, vi, 608, Leibniz 1997: 268)

Such a doctrine is hard to reconcile with Newtonian doctrines such as that of action at a distance, or the equality of action and reaction. Much as Kant is brought up in the Leibnizian tradition as it is further developed by Christian Wolff, it is the Newtonian doctrine which shapes his conception of the physical behavior of substances.

It is worth recalling what these laws claim. According to Newton's *Principia*:

> Law I: Every body perseveres in its state of rest, or uniform motion in a right line, unless it is forced to change that state by forces imposed thereon ....
> Law II: The alteration of motion is ever proportional to the motive force impressed; and is made in the direction of the right line in which that force is impressed ....
> Law III: To every action there is always opposed an equal reaction: or the mutual actions of two bodies upon each other are always equal, and directed to contrary parts. (*Principia*, Newton 2010: 19)

As the second law makes clear, Newton's physics involves claims about forces which reflect the doctrine of physical influx. A key consequence of this is that Kant's understanding of space can no longer be the Leibnizian relational theory. While Leibniz held that spatial relations are ideal in that they are only reflections of the real underlying harmony of non-interacting monads, according to the *Physical Monadology* they are real relations that are defined by the mutual interaction of substances from which they derive.

Kant's attempts at a reconciliation of Newtonian physics with Leibnizian metaphysics thus involve apportioning to each a specific explanatory role, with mathematical physics describing the interactions of substances in space. In the

Physical Monadology, a key problem in such a reconciliation lies in the infinite divisibility of space – which Kant takes to be a real divisibility insofar as space defines the real relations between substances – with the fact that there are simple substances, monads, which are not extended and not divisible. Kant's solution consists in arguing that such monads fill space through the sphere of influence they define because of the repulsive force that characterizes them. As a result, while one can indeed endlessly divide space, it is the relations of mutual interaction between monads that are thereby divided, not the monads themselves, which retain their indivisibility (MonPh 1: 480; cf. Friedman 1992a: 8 f.).

This understanding of the progress of Kant's thought on the reconciliation of metaphysics and mathematical physics helps us see why in the 1760s Herder writes down in his notes that we do not know whether the divisibility of matter is actually infinite: the experiment of dividing matter is indeed one that can be repeated, but the nature of the monadic realm that underpins the spatial relations we observe is a metaphysical issue. So although it is true that matter is infinitely divisible, this is only insofar as the monads' sphere of activity through which they fill space by means of their repulsive forces is infinitely divisible, while the monads themselves are ultimate components of matter. This means that, depending on what is understood by divisibility (either the spheres of activity of monads, or the monads themselves), different answers will be given. This suggests a distinction between two different points of view of the issue: that of physics, from which matter is endlessly divisible, as space is; and that of metaphysics, from which unobservable monads are the indivisible constituents of matter.

This division between the scope of metaphysics and that of mathematical physics becomes clear in the period following the publication of the *Dissertation*. One primary motive for this change is the observation that, if space is defined by the relations of interacting substances, geometry would seem to become a science that is dependent on the science of motion, and thereby to lose its apodictic status (Friedman 1992a: 26 f.). As a result, after 1770, Kant makes some important changes. Most importantly, Kant rejects any relational understanding of space. However, already in 1768, in *On the First Ground of the Distinction of Regions of Space*, Kant claims that "absolute space, independently of the existence of all matter and as itself the ultimate foundation of the possibility of the compound character of matter, has a reality of its own" (GUGR 2: 378.9–11; cf. Friedman 1992a: 28). And in the *Dissertation*, this autonomous nature of space (and time) is specified: space and time are the forms of the faculty of sensible intuition. In this autonomous space, infinite divisibility is a given fact, and a fact about spatial reality, so Kant can unequivocally assert the infinite divisibility of matter in the Berliner Physik. But at the same time, Kant points out that the question of infinite divisibility arguably does not belong to physics, and accordingly, "Phenomena cannot be derived through simplicity, nor through endless divisibility" (29.1,1: 80.13–14).

But it is not clear what role, if any, the metaphysics of the monads, which are now understood as reality in itself as grasped by the intellectual faculty, actually plays in explaining nature. This strongly suggests the further move Kant makes in his Critical period in putting reality in-itself beyond our cognitive reach. As a result, in the Danziger Physik, Kant is able to lay out precisely the place of mathematical physics as a body of scientific knowledge and how it relates to the principles of transcendental philosophy of which it provides an instantiation.

But there is more to say about the apparent agnosticism about the infinite divisibility of matter in the Physik Herder. In claiming that space can be endlessly divided, but withholding a clear affirmation of infinite divisibility, Kant is introducing a distinction that will be important in his later work, namely that between potential and actual infinities. In the *Critique of Pure Reason*, Kant comments on the regress of the second antinomy, and the regresses in the first, third, and fourth antinomies: "In neither of these two cases, that of the *regressus in infinitum* as well as in that of the *in indefinitum*, is the series of conditions regarded as being given as infinite in the object" (KrV A514/B542). That is, while these series define endless regresses, this does not amount to exhibiting an actual infinity, but only defines a potential infinity. In the spatio-temporal phenomenal world, there are no actual infinities. An actual infinity would amount to an inner determination, but the Critical Kant does not allow us any access to such properties in the world of appearances, as they can only be features of things in themselves (Warren 2001: 101). As in the *Metaphysical Foundations of Natural Science*, in the *Dissertation* Kant claims that actual infinity cannot be represented in intuition (MSI 2: 388.6–40). But in the language of the pre-*Dissertation* Kant, as discussed above, space had not yet become independent of the underlying metaphysical reality. While it is clear that we can never experience actual infinities, this fact could not yet be related to the distinction between a phenomenal world of appearances and an intelligible world of things in themselves. Rather, it exhibited the limits of the domain of experimental physics.

3.4 Other substances

It is noteworthy that Kant's concept of matter has a greater extension than it does today. Although matter (*Materie*) is, as explained above, defined on the basis of the two essential characterizations of bodies, namely that they are extended and space-filling (impenetrable) (29.1,1: 108.18–19), Mrongovius introduces the second chapter of the notes by saying:

> The author [of the book used in the lecture, Karsten] mentions provisionally certain materials [*Materie*] that seem to be generally widespread in nature. He deals with: 1. Fire as a substance which penetrates all materials but which no body can penetrate.... 2. Light is precisely a similar material to fire. It is similarly spread throughout the whole universe.... If we assume that heat is a particular material, there are then 2 materials which can penetrate everything.... 3. Air. This is certainly not as widespread as the two previous materials.... The author's classification into air, heat, and light is very uncertain. He is merely talking provisionally about them. (29.1,1: 118.22–120.2)

While the last remark reminds us of the fact that, as an account of the content of lectures, these notes do not have the kind of final structure that characterize published works, it is nevertheless noteworthy that such phenomena as fire, heat, and light are grasped under the concept of substance, and therefore as types of "matter" for Kant.[12]

That Kant's philosophy has this flexibility is a feature that distinguishes it from the mechanistic approach of those Kant describes as "mathematicians" (MAN 4: 498), where Lambert is a particular target. On the mechanistic approach, matter is fundamentally characterized as having space-filling properties and any force it may have is to be explained in terms of its fundamental nature (Warren 2001: 104). For Kant in his Critical period, on the contrary, there are no such intrinsic properties of matter,[13] but rather any such properties are to be derived from dynamics (as dynamics deals with the space-filling properties of matter, i.e., the application of the categories of quality) in terms of the interplay of forces of repulsion and attraction. On this picture, it is possible to think of different forms of interplay of such forces that give rise to different notions of what is material, and this explains Kant's particular interest in the properties these materials have to penetrate others or themselves be penetrated by others.

Nevertheless, we must not overlook the uncertainty Mrongovius refers to with respect to these other types of material substances, and this is no doubt in

---

[12] There is in fact a very influential eighteenth-century tradition in natural philosophy which originates in Newton's speculative experimentalism, and which identifies heat and light with an ethereal substance, one which is also at work in electric and magnetic fluids (Massimi 2011).

[13] In the Dynamics in *Metaphysical Foundations*, matter is characterized as endowed with attractive and repulsive forces. These are relational properties of matter. But this does not logically entail that they are extrinsic. Indeed, there are relational properties that are intrinsic, e.g., the property of having a proper part is an intrinsic but relational property of a thing (Weatherson and Marshall 2014). Nevertheless, it seems that insofar as these forces, qua relational properties, are not relations internal to matter, but are described by Kant as relating a matter to another matter (MAN 4: 498), they are therefore extrinsic. Thanks to Michela Massimi for prompting me to think about this issue.

no small part connected with the subjective character of, in particular, heat. In the *Prolegomena*, Kant says: "When we say, 'The room is warm, sugar sweet, and wormwood bitter,' we have only subjectively valid judgments" (Prol 4: 299.10–11). And indeed, in the Danziger Physik, Kant spells out the worry as: "Heat can certainly be detected [*unterschieden*] through sensation, but this is very uncertain, because in this sense warmth is merely relative" (29.1,1: 120.3–5).

The concern is that there is an absolute notion of heat that would enable it to be an objectively valid phenomenon. While the sensation of heat allows it to be determined in terms of the categories of quality, what is needed for a full objective determination, is to bring heat under the categories of quantity, relation, and modality. The text which follows the above quote therefore looks first into heat's causal impact, in particular in terms of its bringing about the dilation, and its absence, the contraction, of solids (29.1,1: 120.15–121.27), as well as phase transitions of matter between solid, liquid, and gas (29.1,1: 121.27–123.2), making explicit the relation between these two phenomena (29.1,1: 123.3–6). Then Kant addresses the issue of the measurement of the quantity of heat with an extensive disquisition on the various forms of thermometry and the different temperature scales in use at the time (29.1,1: 123.9–127.4). Finally, it is arguably a category of the fourth group of categories (modality), namely the category of existence that Kant brings to bear on the notion of heat when he considers the occurrence of typical temperatures in nature, e. g., body temperature, a typical cellar temperature, the temperature needed to boil an egg, etc. (29.1,1: 127.5–128.26).

A category that does not come into play for heat, however, is that of substance. This represents a significant difference from Kant's later views in the *Opus Postumum*, where the existence of the ether or "caloric" changes from having a merely hypothetical to a categorical status. Kant presents this as the solution to the problem of

> whether, indeed, there exists a *material* [*Stoff*], thoroughly distributed throughout cosmic space (and thus also penetrating all bodies), which one might perhaps call caloric [*Wärmestoff*] (without thereby having regard for a particular feeling of warmth, for the latter concerns only what is subjective in a representation, as perception) – whether, as I say, such a material *is* present or *not* as the basis of all the moving forces of matter, or whether its existence be only dubitable; in other words: whether it is to be assumed by the physicists as a merely *hypothetical material* solely for the explanation of certain appearances, or whether it is to be set up *categorically* as a postulate. (OP 22: 550)[14]

---

14 See also the passage at OP 21: 550.

Kant will opt for this categorical status of the ether or caloric (at OP 21: 226, he uses both words) insofar as a "constant *motion* of all matter" is required otherwise there would be "no experience" (OP 22: 551).

Kant's treatment of sound (29.1,1: 146.9–149.39) and light (29.1,1: 150.2–154.10) also involves examining the determinations of their quantity and quality. The quality of these phenomena is defined by the kind of sensations they give rise to, and this includes the diversity of color sensations in the case of light. The quantity of sound is determined by the speed at which it propagates, its amplitude, and the frequency of its oscillatory nature (29.1,1: 146.29–148.13), and the quantity of light is essentially determined by its speed (29.1,1: 150.33–154.10). For both phenomena, Kant also gives plenty of evidence of the existence of different manifestations of sound and light in nature, and devotes sections to the available knowledge about how they impact causally upon the senses of hearing (29.1,1: 148.7–149.29) and seeing (29.1,1: 153.8–156.4).

Towards the end of the Danziger Physik, Kant has only one sentence referring to magnetism (29.1,1: 156.19–21), but devotes an extensive section to electrical "matter" (29.1,1: 156.27–160.39). We see Kant describing electricity both as matter and as a force (29.1,1: 156.32), and this dual description is in line with Kant's understanding of matter as fundamentally characterized in dynamics terms, through the forces that account for its properties. In the case of the electrical force, Kant says that:

> No body is electric in and of itself, but can become so. It [electrical matter][15] consists in [the fact] that a body attracts others and can repel them again and when pulled up to release light or sparks. (29.1,1: 156.29–32)

He then examines how bodies become charged with electricity, how others are conductors of electricity, and, generally, how the quantity of electricity varies and moves about (29.1,1: 156.34–158.29).

It is interesting to draw a comparison with the Berliner Physik: there, Kant refers many times to electricity as a "subtle material" (*subtile Materie*) (e. g., 29.1,1: 89.32). This suggests a much greater sense of ignorance as to its properties, a point Kant confirms: "As yet, little is known about it, and it is for us equally as secret as the magnetic force" (29.1,1: 91.24–26).

This no doubt reflects the progress of the understanding of electricity between the 1760s and 80s. In particular, one can speculate that Benjamin Frank-

---

[15] The German *Sie* here can only refer to the title of the section, as there are no other feminine nouns in the previous sentence.

lin and Joseph Priestley's experiments, which Priestley reported in publications to the Royal Society between 1767 and 1770, and in his 1767 book, *The History and Present Status of Electricity*, were known to Kant. It is also noteworthy that Kant's insight into the phenomenon of electricity is quite prescient. Indeed, in the next sentence, he seems to be anticipating the nineteenth century's discoveries of the interrelations between electricity and magnetism that culminated in Maxwell's theory of electromagnetic fields published in 1884:[16] "There is such a great analogy between the two forces that, with a closer knowledge [of them], one will perhaps be able to derive them from one principle" (29.1,1: 91.27–29).

4 Conclusion

In conclusion, Kant's lecture notes on physics shed light on the transition taking place in his thinking between the pre-*Dissertation* and the Critical periods. This chapter has in particular examined the notes' discussions of key topics that Kant dealt with repeatedly throughout his career, such as the nature of matter, its characteristic basic forces of repulsion and attraction, and its infinite divisibility, and how they relate to Kant's published works. While the aim of this chapter has been to contribute to Kant scholarship, it is noteworthy that these discussions also provide interesting insights into the science of the day, and the accompanying descriptions of experimental protocols should be of great value to historians of experimental physics. This thus makes them important source material for further investigation in both Kant scholarship and the history of science.[17]

---

[16] This insight is, however, closely related with the tradition in natural philosophy mentioned in footnote 12.

[17] Helpful comments from Michaela Massimi and Dennis Schulting are gratefully acknowledged. The author would also like to acknowledge the excellent source of materials about Kant at Naragon 2015b.

Chapter 20
Kant's Conception of Chemistry in the Danziger Physik

Henny Blomme

1 Introduction

In the preface to *Metaphysical Foundations of Natural Science* (1786), Kant famously asserts that chemistry is not likely to ever become a proper science. It must, Kant says, be instead called a 'systematic art' or an 'experimental doctrine' (MAN 4: 470). In this chapter, I will show why, for Kant, chemistry is as it were 'less scientific' than physics. I will refer in particular to the "Danziger Physik" lecture notes, since they offer important complementary claims and are also often more explicit on statements that are a bit obscure in *Metaphysical Foundations*, although strictly speaking the latter could in principle suffice for a reconstruction of Kant's argument.

In the literature, the question why Kant thought that physics is a proper but chemistry an improper science mostly gets a fairly simple answer: whereas mathematics can be applied in physics, in chemistry that is impossible and that is why the latter is not a science in the proper sense. That is indeed what Kant asserts himself in *Metaphysical Foundations*. On the one hand, Kant famously claims there that "in any special doctrine of nature there can only be as much proper science as there is mathematics therein" (MAN 4: 470).[1] On the other hand, he states that "the principles [of chemistry] are merely empirical, and allow of no a priori presentation in intuition, and thus they do not in the least make conceivable the possibility of fundamental laws of chemical appearances, because they are not suitable for the application of mathematics" (MAN 4: 471).

There is a problem with this standard reply, however, for it supposes that we all know that and how mathematics can be applied in physics. Now, with respect to *Metaphysical Foundations*, the claim that it is possible to apply mathematics in physics seems to be based on some kind of proof that the fundamental characteristics of the object of physics can be constructed in a priori intuition. Indeed, Kant writes: "in order to make possible the application of mathematics to the doctrine

---

[1] For Kant, both physics and chemistry are special doctrines of nature (see section 4 below).

of body, which only through this can become natural science, principles for the *construction* of the concepts that belong to the possibility of matter in general must be introduced first" (MAN 4: 472) I think that this rather complex claim has not been well understood in the literature.[2] Note that Kant does not speak about the possibility to construct the concept of matter, but about the possibility to construct "the concepts that belong to the possibility of matter in general." Thus, the task of *Metaphysical Foundations* is to provide evidence for the claim that the concepts that belong to the possibility of matter in general can be constructed, by introducing the principles for such construction. But even then, the quoted passage stays obscure because it is not clear what these "principles for the construction of the concepts belonging to the possibility of matter" should look like. It is also unclear how these principles relate to the fundamental determination of matter, i. e., the concept of motion. And what are the concepts that belong to the possibility of matter in general? So it seems that much has to be explained in order to understand why Kant thought that chemistry is not a proper science.

Because these questions have less to do with history of science than with Kant's philosophical approach to the relation between metaphysics and empirical sciences, I will not discuss in detail the chemical knowledge that is treated in the Danziger Physik, nor will I make an extensive comparison between the lecture notes and the textbook that Kant used for these lectures. This means that I also will not provide an overview of what Kant took in 1785 to be the most important teachings of chemistry. This has been discussed elsewhere: fellow scholars and I have written on that topic, and have included references to the Danziger Physik (e. g., Carrier 1990, 2001b; Friedman 1992a, 2013; Blomme 2015). However, we need a minimum of history of science in order to be able to situate Kant's declarations on chemistry in the scientific context of the seventeenth and eighteenth centuries. In the following sections, I first offer a succinct history of the theories of elements and principles (section 2) and situate the Danziger Physik with regard to contemporaneous chemistry (section 3). Next, I explain what, for Kant, turns a doctrine of nature into a proper science (section 4), whereas in the fifth section I describe Kant's conception of a special metaphysics of corporeal nature. In the sixth section, I ask why it is that Kant needs a fundamental determination of matter. The seventh section then offers a reconstruction of Kant's conception of empirical affection and its role in *Metaphysical Foundations*, which in my view has to take into account Kant's theory on the predicables of change and movement or motion (*Bewegung*) (section 8). In the concluding section, I

---

[2] Plaaß (1965) is perhaps the most ambitious in trying to understand this claim, but I do not follow his analysis or conclusions.

consider whether Kant would have considered modern chemistry to be a proper science.

2 A very short history of chemistry: Elements and principles

The first chemical theories coincide with the ancient Greeks, who searched to determine the basic element(s) of the universe. The oldest theories proposed one element as first principle of everything: Thales (640–546 BCE) water, Anaximenes (550–480 BCE) air, and Heraclitus (576–480 BCE) fire. It was Empedocles (490–435 BCE) who first said that the basis of the universe is constituted of four elements: water, fire, air, and earth. Aristotle later took up this theory of four elements and stated that they form two pairs with contrary characteristics: fire was hot and dry, water was cold and humid, air was hot and humid, and earth was cold and dry.

By taking Aristotle as an authority, the later alchemists could think that all observed transformations of matter only concerned alterations of formal properties, while matter stayed basically the same. Hence there were, e.g., the attempts to transform lead into gold, which were motivated by the conviction that the material essence of these two kinds of metals was the same basic matter. The art of the alchemist was then to manipulate kinds of matter in order to bring about a change of the formal characteristics. The alchemists distinguished between two principles: sulphur and mercury. Sulphur was taken to be 'male', 'active', 'hard', 'hot' and 'stable', whereas mercury was taken to be 'female', 'passive', 'soft' (malleable), 'cold' and 'volatile'. Mercury was defined as the metallic principle and explained why metals can melt. It was supposed to be liquid at normal temperature. Sulphur was defined as the principle of combustibles.

Paracelsus (1493–1541) added a third principle: salt or arsenic. The function of salt was to unite mercury and sulphur and assure their cohesion. When, e.g., salt was applied to meat, Paracelsus took it to block the separation of sulphur and mercury and thus to prevent the meat from rotting. Because salt blocks the separation of the other two principles also in living beings, it was defined as the principle of life as such.

Now the theory of the elements and the theory of principles gave rise to convenient relations of correspondence between them. As the principle of combustibility, sulphur corresponds both to earth, which is solid, and to fire, which is subtle. Water, which is liquid in its normal state, and air, which is gaseous, take on the form of the recipients in which they are stored. This passivity makes them belong to the feminine kinds of matter and thus they correspond to mercury. The third principle, salt, as mediating instance between sulphur and mercury, was associated with a fifth element: the ether or quintessence (literally 'fifth essence'). However, in the alchemic tradition the ether was never given the same importance as the other elements.

As we will see, until 1781 at least, the tradition of the elements survives in Kant's conception of matter and chemistry. He does not take over the doctrine of principles, however. The elements are completed with a number of 'instruments' – Kant thought there were three – which are the media in which chemical reactions take place.

3 The scientific context of the Danziger Physik

For over 30 years Kant lectured on physics: from 1755 until 1788. We know of exactly 21 physics courses that he actually held during this period. For the first 15, held between 1755 and 1770 when he was still a Magister, Kant used as a textbook the *Erste Gründe der Naturlehre* (1753) of the physician Johann Peter Eberhard (not to be confused with Kant's later opponent, Johann August Eberhard). Kant's promotion to *Ordinarius* in 1770 marked the beginning of a pause of six years. Between 1776 and 1788 then, Kant delivered another six courses on physics, for which he used the *Anfangsgründe der Naturlehre* (1772) by Johann Christian Polycarp Erxleben (1744–1777). But there is one exception: for his penultimate physics lecture in the summer semester of 1785, Kant used the recently published *Anleitung zur gemeinnützlichen Kenntniß der Natur, besonders für angehende Aerzte, Cameralisten und Oeconomen* (1783) by Wenceslaus Johann Gustav Karsten (1732–1787). The reason for this textbook change was Kant's interest in chemistry (Lehmann, AA 29.1,1: 650) – a discipline that received indeed a much more extensive and up to date treatment in Karsten's *Anleitung* of 1783 than in Erxleben's *Anfangsgründe* that Kant possessed in its first edition of 1772 (Warda 1922).

In the preface to the second edition of his *Anfangsgründe der Naturgeschichte*, Erxleben had written that he would have preferred to include more chemistry, because he offers a section on mineralogy and cannot "imagine mineralogy without chemistry" (Erxleben 1773). Karsten quotes this passage both to argue for the necessity of his new handbook and to utter a critique of Erxleben's undertaking: in the latter's "little handbook," "mineralogy ... is not at all what it should be. It supposed that the future scientist had first to visit lectures on the history of nature and only then lectures on chemistry" (AA 29.1,1: 175; my trans.). Karsten's *Anleitung* indeed includes discussions of recently made discoveries in chemistry, particularly those concerning the so-called pneumatic chemistry, i. e., the study of the properties of different kinds of air. The most prominent representatives of pneumatic chemistry at the time were, Stephen Hales (1677–1761), Joseph Black

(1728–1799), Joseph Priestley (1733–1804), Henry Cavendish (1731–1810) and Carl Wilhelm Scheele (1742–1786). Although informed by the discoveries of these scientists, and although a century before Boyle had already highlighted the inadequacies of the old theories of the four elements (earth, water, fire, air) and three principles, Karsten's chemical considerations are still based on a theory of four elements (earth, water, salt, phlogiston).

For his last course on physics, held during the winter semester 1787/88, Kant returned to the textbook of Erxleben, though in its third edition. Erxleben had died in 1777, but his famous student Georg Christoph Lichtenberg took care of extending and actualizing his teacher's textbook and published a new edition in 1784. In a passage of the Danziger Physik, Kant refers to this book when he says:

> Some savants have tried to connect chemistry with physics, so for example Erxleben, who started a chapter on chemistry, although it leaves much to desire: because he only speaks about solutions and condensations [*Niederschlägen*]. Lichtenberg has presented it already a bit more extensively. (29.1,1: 98; my trans.)

For Kant, it is Stephen Hales who may have been the most important source of the new discoveries in pneumatic chemistry. Kant owned a German translation of Hales' work *Vegetable Staticks* (1727), in which it is shown that air as such is not an element but that there are different kinds of air, all with their own chemical properties. But in the *Critique of Pure Reason*, Kant writes: "one reduces all materials to earths (mere weight, as it were), to salts and combustibles (as force), and finally to water and air as vehicles (machines, as it were, by means of which the aforementioned operate), in order to explain the chemical effects of materials in accordance with the idea of a mechanism" (A646/B674). This passage indicates that, in 1781, Kant still held on to a chemical theory of three elements and two instruments, which brought him closer to Stahl, van Helmont, and Boyle.[3] Jan Baptista van Helmont (1577–1640) and Robert Boyle (1627–1691) are considered to be at the origin of pneumatic chemistry. Both studied gases and their effects, but still thought of air as an instrument.[4] These indications may suffice to bear in mind that, when Kant states that chemistry will probably never be a proper science, he is not referring to organic chemistry (of which Lavoisier is generally

---

[3] The Danziger Physik proves that, at the time of the publication of the second edition (1787) of the *Critique of Pure Reason*, Kant already knew that air is not an element, but he left the passage as it was in the first edition.
[4] Van Helmont introduced the concept of "gas," following the Dutch pronunciation of the Greek χάος. Kant was perhaps a bit too patriotic when he taught his students that 'gas' was derived from the German *Gescht* (29.1,1: 163).

considered to be the father).⁵ He has in mind the so-called *phlogistic* chemistry, founded by Johann Joachim Becher (1635–1685) and popularized by his much more famous student, Georg Ernst Stahl (1660–1734). In fact, Kant's adoption of three elements and two instruments in the first *Critique* perfectly corresponds to the theory of Stahl (Carrier 2001b).

Now, the Danziger Physik proves that, by 1785, Kant had adopted at least the new conception of air from the pneumatic chemists, perhaps by reading Karsten's handbook. But, in line with the reaction of most chemists of his time (and also with Karsten), this did not turn him away from Stahl. Hence the very telling passage in the lecture notes: "Air is not an element because it seems to be a certain form into which everything can be transformed. Instead of air it is better to put phlogiston [as an element]" (29.1,1: 162; my trans.). A bit later, Kant explains: "Phlogiston or pure elementary fire has been first introduced in chemistry by Stahl, who proved it to be an element that is of the same kind in all combustibles.... As a kind of air, it is called phlogistic air" (29.1,1: 163).

Becher proposed to distinguish between five fundamental substances: air, water, and three kinds of earth – first, the *terra pinguis* (also called "fat" earth or sulphur), second the *terra lapidia* (the principle of sand, stone, and metal), third the *terra mercurialis* (a principle that is present in metals, but not in sand or stones). Becher believed that, during the process of combustion, the *terra pinguis* was expulsed in the form of fire. It is this *terra pinguis* that Stahl would give the name 'phlogiston', derived from the Greek verb φλογίξειν ('phlogidzein'). Stahl managed to gather experimental evidence for the existence of phlogiston by transforming metals into calces⁶ and these calces again into metals. This reversible transformation is explained by phlogiston: when a metal is intensely heated and transformed into metallic calx, the phlogiston that was linked to the metal is expulsed. That is why, when one introduces phlogiston to calx by heating the latter with coal, oil, or other matters from which Stahl asserts that they are rich in phlogiston, the metal reappears. During the process of combustion, the air absorbs the expulsed phlogiston, but no fusion of air and phlogiston can occur. Moreover, the air can only absorb a certain quantity of phlogiston and when that limit is reached, combustion is not longer possible.

---

5 Hence the question whether Kant would have considered Lavoisier's chemistry to be a proper science – which I discuss in the final section.
6 In the terminology of phlogistic chemistry, the calx (plural 'calces' or 'calxes') is what is left of a metal once its phlogiston has been driven off. Lavoisier later discovered oxidation and declared that 'phlogiston' was an unnecessary scientific hypothesis.

It is Stahl's experimental transformation of metals into calces that Kant refers to in a famous passage of the preface to the second edition of the first *Critique*:

> When Galileo rolled balls of a weight chosen by himself down an inclined plane, or when Torricelli made the air bear a weight that he had previously thought to be equal to that of a known column of water, or when in a later time Stahl changed metals into calces and then changed the latter back into metal by first removing something and then putting it back again, a light dawned on all those who study nature. They comprehended that reason has insight only into what it itself produces according to its own design, that it must take the lead with principles for its judgments according to constant laws and compel nature to answer its questions, rather than letting nature guide its movements by keeping reason, as it were, in leading strings; for otherwise accidental observations, made according to no previously designed plan, can never connect up into a necessary law, which is yet what reason seeks and requires. (Bxii f.)

In this passage, praise goes as much to Stahl as to Galileo and Torricelli. One would thus expect that Kant does not make any fundamental distinction between physics and chemistry and that he takes the latter to be a proper science just as much as the former. Yet we know that this is not the case: physics is a proper science, but chemistry is not. What, then, is a 'proper science'?

4 Kant's conception of proper science

Before discussing Kant's conception of proper science, one should know which conditions must be fulfilled, in Kant's view, for a doctrine of nature to be called 'science'. For Kant's conception of what it is to be a science radically differs from our contemporary understanding. In *Metaphysical Foundations of Natural Science*, Kant writes: "Any whole of cognition that is systematic can, for this reason, already be called *science*, and, if the connection of cognition in this system is an interconnection of grounds and consequences, even *rational* science" (MAN 4: 468). Chemistry can be systematic ("a systematic art") and its cognition is built on the interconnection of grounds and consequences that experience (chemical experiments) teaches. But because the principles of this interconnection are merely empirical, chemistry is not a proper science. This is a short answer to the question why, for Kant, chemistry is not a proper science. But it leaves aside the question why the principles of physics would be less empirical then the principles of chemistry; so this reply is unintelligible as long as we do not know more about the deeper reasons for Kant's distinction between physics and chemistry.

In the Danziger Physik, Kant teaches that research concerning nature can be divided into four parts (29.1,1: 97–100; cf. MAN 4: 468–70): mathematical physics, chemistry, description of nature, and history of nature. Below I present a succinct representation of these disciplines and their characteristics, based on what he taught in his physics lecture and completed with claims from the *Metaphysical Foundations* preface.

A. Natural Sciences
1. Mathematical Physics:
– presents the laws of the interaction of bodies (effect of a body on another body)
– has a priori principles; these principles are metaphysical – "presupposes metaphysics of nature" (MAN 4: 469)
– contains proofs that concern only a very little part of nature
– is a proper science

2. Chemistry:
– presents the laws of the interaction of matters (effect of a matter on another matter)
– has a posteriori principles that are adopted during chemical practice: "laws of experience" (MAN 4: 468)
– is an improper science

B. Historical Doctrines of Nature
3. Description of Nature ('natural description'):
– presents the diversity of things in nature, as given together in space
– has no principles: it is built on observation
– provides us with a system of classes on the basis of similarities between species (MAN 4: 468)
– is a historical doctrine of nature – no science

4. History of Nature ('natural history'):
– presents the diversity of things in nature, as the latter are present through time; "presentation of the effects and the many states of things as they follow on each other in different times" (29.1,1: 99; my trans.)
– is a systematic presentation of things of nature, "in different times and different places" (MAN 4: 468)
– is a historical doctrine of nature – no science

The criterion that is important to understand the distinction between physics and chemistry directly concerns the possibility of a metaphysics of corporeal nature. In Kant's view, in order to be called proper science, a scientific doctrine needs an a priori part that serves as the metaphysical foundation of that doctrine. Only then will we be able to attain systematicity and apodicticity. In the following passage, taken from the *Metaphysical Foundations* preface, Kant develops this view and connects it with his distinction between physics and chemistry:

> Natural science would now be either *properly* or *improperly* so-called natural science, where the first treats its object wholly according to a priori principles, the second according to laws of experience. What can be called *proper* science is only that whose certainty is apodictic; cognition that can contain mere empirical certainty is only *knowledge* improperly so-called. Any whole of cognition that is systematic can, for this reason, already be called *science*, and, if the connection of cognition in this system is an interconnection of grounds and consequences, even *rational* science. If, however, the grounds or principles themselves are still in the end merely empirical, as in chemistry, for example, and the laws from which the given facts are explained through reason are mere laws of experience, then they carry with them no consciousness of their *necessity* (they are not apodictically certain), and thus the whole of cognition does not deserve the name of a science in the strict sense; chemistry should therefore be called a systematic art rather than a science. (MAN 4: 468)

This passage gives us the means to say something more about systematicity and apodicticity – criteria of a proper science that can be distinguished yet are interconnected: there is no real or strict systematicity without apodicticity, and vice versa.

So, in order to be called a proper science, a doctrine must first be articulated as a system. Kant uses the concept 'system' in a strict and in a loose way. When taken in the strict sense, to talk of an empirical system would entail a *contradictio in terminis*. Thus, in the strict sense, systematicity is both a necessary and a sufficient condition for a doctrine to be called science proper. But Kant's strict comprehension of the term 'system' was not widely accepted: his contemporaries would use the concept to refer to any well-ordered presentation of knowledge (empirical or not), for example Linnaeus's classification of the species of nature. In *Metaphysical Foundations of Natural Science*, there are instances where Kant also uses this looser meaning, for example when he speaks of the historical doctrine of nature, which contains only "facts of things of nature, ordered systematically" (MAN 4: 468), or when he calls chemistry a "systematic art." When used in this broader sense, systematicity is only a necessary, not a sufficient condition for a doctrine to be called proper science. Now systematicity in the strict sense is the mark of a proper science because, for Kant, a theory of nature in general[7] does not in the first place investigate empirical things. A theory of nature in the

---

[7] 'Theory of nature' is here to be taken in a broad sense: it includes both inner and outer nature, is a priori, and is to be situated at a higher level than 'physics'.

Kantian sense will present us with everything that pertains to the existence of a thing insofar as it can be derived from the internal principle of that thing. As a result, a theory of nature will only be called systematic (in the strict sense of the word) when the connection of the things within this system is known a priori through reason alone.[8]

A second condition of proper scientificity is, for Kant, that the certainty that we (seem to) meet with in a doctrine of nature has to be apodictic. It is this condition that makes that every science proper has to be either totally pure, or contain at least a pure part on which its apodicticity can be grounded. If we take for example geometry, its purity is guaranteed by its exclusive use of the pure intuition of space. Indeed, because geometry tries to give the laws of that which pertains to the essence of concepts that are constructed a priori in pure intuition, it can proceed wholly a priori. But natural science does not seek the laws of what pertains to the *essence* of a concept: it wants to present the laws of that which pertains to the *existence* of a really existing thing. Now, in the first *Critique* Kant's major claim against dogmatic metaphysics is that the existence of a thing cannot be presented in an a priori intuition. In the case of a doctrine of nature, to be called proper science therefore means that it must contain a pure part that gives us a priori the concepts of what pertains to the existence of its object considered in its generality. These fundamental concepts will a priori specify the object of physics, but they will not depend on construction in intuition a priori, i.e., they will not be generated through construction. Nonetheless, these concepts will have to be such that they can in principle be constructed, by showing how they can be presented as instances of the general concept of motion that Kant claims to be the fundamental determination of matter (see section 6). This pure part of physics as natural science proper will be provided by Kant's metaphysics of nature.

5 Metaphysics of corporeal nature

We have to specify what Kant means when he refers to a 'metaphysics of nature'. From the author of the *Critique of Pure Reason*, we cannot of course expect that he would provide us with but another 'dogmatic metaphysics'. So here we will have to speak of a *Critical* metaphysics of nature. But what is that?

---

[8] Kant develops this view of systematicity already in the Architectonic chapter of the first *Critique*. He there claims that systematicity (in the strict sense) is only guaranteed when the system has been constructed following the indications of the idea of the whole of a science. This idea is an idea of reason that commands a priori the systematic divisions that have to be made.

When the concept 'nature' is taken in its purely formal sense, where it refers to the first principle of everything that pertains to the existence and lawfulness of a thing in general, the metaphysics of nature is a part of the system of transcendental philosophy, of which the first *Critique* is the propaedeutic. Indeed, even in Kant, transcendental philosophy is not in the first place concerned with the conditions of the possibility of experience but with the a priori concepts that determine the unity of an object in general. As Kant states, the concept of an object in general is still problematic with regard to its empirical reality and needs further determination to be classified as something rather than nothing (A290/B346). When it is determined as something and the mathematical categories are positively realized, the object in general becomes the thing in general, and this latter concept is the only one that can express a priori the empirical but still undetermined content of appearances (A729/B748). The thing in general thus is the object in general that is positively determined with respect to quantity and quality. Now, a metaphysics of nature in this formal sense has been provided by the first *Critique*, where Kant discussed the synthetic a priori characteristics of the thing in general (see the axioms of intuition and the anticipations of perception).

When one takes the concept 'nature' in its material sense, it refers to the totality of things that constitute the object of our senses (29.1,1: 100). If we talk of metaphysics of nature taken in this sense, it is a particular or special metaphysics, as opposed to the general metaphysics that is concerned with the object in general. Following Kant's indications in the Architectonic chapter of the first *Critique*, the special metaphysics of nature contains two divisions: a metaphysics of corporeal nature that is devoted to the object of the outer senses, and a metaphysics of thinking nature concerned with the object of inner sense (A846/B874). But since the *Critique* has shown that a special metaphysics of thinking nature cannot have objective validity (the so-called rational psychology of the metaphysicians is, for Kant, a doomed project), the Critical philosopher will only need to say more about the special metaphysics of corporeal nature. It is this metaphysics that Kant develops in *Metaphysical Foundations of Natural Science*.

The first task of the special metaphysics of corporeal nature is to provide us a priori with concepts that, on the one hand, can lend themselves to mathematical construction and, on the other hand, are synthetic a priori determinations of the empirical concept of 'matter'. Indeed, "although a pure philosophy of nature in general, that is, that which investigates only what constitutes the concept of a nature in general, may indeed be possible even without mathematics, a pure doctrine of nature concerning *determinate* natural things (doctrine of body or doctrine of soul) is only possible by means of mathematics" (MAN 4: 470). *Metaphysical Foundations* will thus isolate the empirical concept of 'matter' and present us with all concepts and principles that are in fact a priori determinations of the object in general of corporeal nature. In order for this presentation to be complete, *Metaphysical Foundations* will show how the content of the concept of 'matter' ("object of the outer senses") and the intension of the elementary concepts of transcendental philosophy – i.e., metaphysics of nature in its formal sense – specify and determine each other.

6 The fundamental determination of matter

As we have seen, Kant considers 'matter' to be an empirical concept. This means that when we take matter as given to us, we must also presuppose an empirical affection of the outer senses. In the literature, this is seen as the reason why Kant takes *motion* to be the fundamental determination of matter (Carrier 1991; Kötter 1991; Kerszberg 2001; Friedman 2013; McNulty 2014). Although this seems correct, it is not entirely clear why Kant needs such fundamental determination in the first place. Indeed, Kant repeats in the *Metaphysical Foundations* preface that the scheme to obtain completeness of a metaphysical system, whether it concerns nature in general or corporeal nature in particular, is the table of categories, because there are no other pure concepts of the understanding that concern the nature of things (MAN 4: 474). Now the structure of *Metaphysical Foundations* will indeed follow the synthetic order of the categories. But why then the need for a fundamental determination of matter, that has to precede the determinations following quantity, quality, relation, and modality? I think that this problem has not yet received a convincing answer in the literature. It is indeed not enough to state that, since matter is an empirical concept, we need to presuppose empirical affection and thus also motion. I think that the only convincing answer is more complex, and I also think that we need this complex explanation to fully understand why, for Kant, chemistry will probably never be a proper science.

As we saw above, the fact that Kant speaks about matter as an empirical concept means that its objective reality cannot be proved a priori but has to rely on empirical intuition. But it seems better to speak of a metaphysics of material bodies instead of a metaphysics of matter, because matter is not sensed as such: we are not affected by "*the object* of the outer senses"; we are affected by material bodies.[9] Nonetheless, *Metaphysical Foundations* will start with the analysis of

---

9 It is important to distinguish between the general object of outer sense and the general object of the outer *senses*. The general object of the outer senses is 'matter' and it is with this general object that *Metaphysical Foundations* is concerned. The object of outer sense is simply an intuition in space and this can be an a priori or empirical intuition. Only in the second case will the

matter as such, without making a distinction between different material bodies. The reason is that *Metaphysical Foundations* is meant to provide us with a *metaphysics* of corporeal nature and cannot thus be built on experience (empirical cognition). We learn from experience that outside of us there is not only matter, but also several material bodies. Speaking from the start about material bodies would suppose more empirical input than just introducing the empirical concept of matter in metaphysics.[10] Now, just because *Metaphysical Foundations* is concerned with metaphysics and because empirical cognition about matter thus falls outside their scope, the empirical nature of matter must itself be integrated in the complete presentation of synthetic a priori determinations that specify the concept of matter. But metaphysics of corporeal nature is a part of physics and if the latter is to be a science proper, Kant has to find an expression for the empirical nature of matter that is nonetheless constructible in a priori intuition – only then will it be proved that mathematics is not only applicable in physics, but that this application is valid. Finding a fundamental characteristic of matter that fulfils these conditions is thus the first task for *Metaphysical Foundations*, and that explains the importance of its preface. Again, this fundamental characteristic will have to be an integral part of the synthetic a priori content of the concept of matter; it will have to express the empirical nature of the concept of matter and it must be constructible in a priori intuition.

The analytic content of the concept of matter is to be the general object of the outer senses. Thus, the proposition "a material body is an object of the outer senses" is analytic. Now, one of the results of the first *Critique* was the insight that all cognition of empirical outer objects has to be based on an intuition that is delivered by a perception. A perception is the effect of an empirical object that

---

object of outer sense also be an object of the outer senses. This is mostly neglected in the relevant literature, but whether one will be able to understand the project of Kant's *Metaphysical Foundations* as opposed to the section of the *Critique of Pure Reason* that presents the transcendental principles of the understanding depends on grasping that kind of detail in Kant's theory. To give one recent example, McNulty (2014) fails to distinguish between 'object of outer sense' and 'object of the outer senses'.

10 The Danziger Physik states: "the mathematical part of physics presents the laws governing the effects of bodies on bodies and has a priori principles and that is what distinguishes it from chemistry, which presents the laws governing the effects of matter on matter" (29.1,1: 97; my trans.). It seems thus that *Metaphysical Foundations*, as the a priori part of mathematical physics, should be concerned in the first place with material bodies and not with matter as such. Matter is everything that occupies a (portion of) space, whereas a body must have a certain figure. But *Metaphysical Foundations* starts from matter as such and does not presuppose material bodies, because the question how they are generated out of matter is partly a question of empirical research.

affects us. Cognitions that are based on such perceptions are therefore empirical, although any system of empirical cognition will of course also contain realizations of all the elementary concepts (categories) and principles of the understanding. In the following section, I will show that Kant gets at the fundamental determination of matter by analyzing what it means to be affected by an empirical outer object.

7 An analysis of empirical affection

Matter or bodies cannot be sensed as such. We can feel certain effects on our own body, but it is only our understanding that will give us the concept of substance to grasp the unity of a series of sensations. In order for the affection by an empirical object to lead to a perception, the affecting object must be thought of as the cause of changing receptive states in the perceiving subject. It would not be possible to gain knowledge of different external objects if the effect they had on our senses were always the same, just as a quality that pertains to every object cannot be empirically perceived. The fact that the concept of matter is to be linked with empirical affection, i.e., with matter or material bodies affecting our outer senses, means that the change of receptive states in the subject is a change of outer relations. For Kant, every real change has to occur in time and each outer relation is *per definitionem* a relation in space. Empirical affection thus basically means: change (in time) of outer relations (in space). Now the only concept that can express a priori a change of outer relations and is at the same time constructible in a priori intuition is the concept of motion. This is the hidden context behind that seemingly innocent remark of Kant in the preface to *Metaphysical Foundations*, that the fundamental determination of a something that is the object of the outer senses has to be motion, because it is only by motion that these senses can be affected (MAN 4: 476). 'Motion' is thus the only concept that can at once a priori "schematize" empirical affection (and thus also the empirical nature of the concept of matter) and be mathematically constructed (namely, as a description in the a priori intuition of space).

8 The predicables 'change' and 'motion'

For Kant, the logical content of the concept 'motion' can be derived a priori from the predicable 'change', namely, when the latter is brought together with the a priori forms of intuition. On the other hand, Kant holds that we do not need the concepts of space and time to express the logical content of the concept 'change'.

As a predicable, the concept of 'change' is generated by bringing together the relational couple "substance – accident" with the modal couple "existence – non-existence." Although the predicable of change can be defined without reference to the form of time (the analytic content of the concept of change does not include the statement that it occurs in time), Kant also says that we (humans) cannot understand its possibility *without* representing the concept of change as occurring in time (B48 f.). Formal logic does not involve time, and the concept of change there only leads to contradiction. Indeed, the concept of time cannot be realized in formal logic because the conjunction of *opposita* generates analytical impossibility. As a consequence, the concept of change is entirely empty when considered apart from all content of intuition. Time as the form of all representations is thus for us humans an absolute condition of the objective validity of the concept of change. When we speak about change of our inner state, this means that we attribute to our soul (thought as a substance) mutually exclusive predicates and such attribution is only possible when we are in possession of the pure manifold of inner sense that is delivered by its a priori form: time.

Now, as we have seen, when it comes to the analysis of empirical affection, through which alone an object of the outer senses can become an object of cognition, change has to be understood here as occurring in time and in space. When one now links the predicable of change (as realized in time) with space as the a priori form of outer sense, one gets the predicable of motion. But the predicable of motion can be objectively realized in two ways: either as a priori motion or as empirical motion. A priori motion is realized within the manifolds delivered by the forms of intuition and thus takes place in pure space and pure time, without any reference to experience. One can thus realize the predicable of motion when executing a geometrical construction in pure intuition, by moving a point in geometrical space (space as a quasi-object or formal intuition) in order to create a line. The predicable of motion is then a priori realized as geometrical description. But the predicable of motion can also be objectively realized within the empirical manifold delivered by experience: it is then realized as physical motion.

The analytic content of the predicable of motion does not change as a result of its realization as geometrical or physical motion. The analytic content is indifferently characterized through the formula 'real change of outer relations'. Thus all change in the empirical world of physical bodies and all change in geometrical space must be motion if it has to be grasped by the understanding. When Kant states that motion has to be the most fundamental determination of matter, we must take motion as a predicable and thus as meaning 'real change of outer relations'. In the phoronomy chapter, matter is then further determined as the movable in space, and Kant will show how the fundamental determination is specified by the a priori construction of the properties that pertain to it as an extensive magnitude: speed and direction. The motion of the movable in space is then studied without presupposing any quality of the movable. Because of the fundamental determination of matter by the predicable of motion, chemistry will not be a proper science of nature as long as chemical reactions cannot be represented a priori as motions. Only then would mathematics find an objectively valid application in chemistry, and the a posteriori principles of the latter could then be preceded by a pure part on which the necessity of real chemical laws could be grounded. Because chemical reactions cannot be presented as motions in space, they cannot be grounded on the metaphysical principles that *Metaphysical Foundations* provides by taking motion as the fundamental characteristic of matter.

> So long, therefore, as there is still for chemical actions of matters on one another no concept to be discovered that can be constructed, that is, no law of the approach or withdrawal of the parts of matter can be specified according to which, perhaps in proportion to their densities or the like, their motions and all the consequences thereof can be made intuitive and presented a priori in space (a demand that will only with great difficulty ever be fulfilled), then chemistry can be nothing more than a systematic art or experimental doctrine, but never a proper science, because its principles are merely empirical, and allow of no a priori presentation in intuition, and thus they do not in the least make conceivable the possibility of fundamental laws of chemical appearances, because they are not suitable for the application of mathematics. (MAN 4: 470 f.)

If chemical reactions could be grounded on the metaphysical principles of matter, chemistry's basic concepts would be expressible through a priori constructions, because they would then be reducible to a kind of motion that could be presented in intuition. Chemistry would then be a proper science because one could show that the possibility of the application of mathematics in chemistry is very well conceivable, by providing the principles for the construction of the chemical concepts that pertain to the possibility of matter in general. Such principles would be metaphysical principles of chemistry.

9 Conclusion: Post-Stahlian chemistry as science?

We know that Kant was interested in the new discoveries made by British and French chemists and became gradually convinced of Lavoisier's new model. Kant compares the theories of Stahl and Lavoisier in a *Reflexion* that Adickes dates to 1789 or 1790. Kant does not yet express a clear preference for Lavoisier, apparently seeing the two theories as interchangeable:

> Following Lavoisier, when something (following Stahl) is dephlogisticated, then something is added (pure air): if it is phlogisticated, then something (pure air) is taken away, except when it concerns dephlogistication by plants, which is only the removal of combustible air. For him [Lavoisier], the solvents [*Auflösungsmittel*] are themselves replaced. (Refl 14: 489; my trans.)

In the notes associated with Heinrich zu Dohna-Wundlacken, based on a metaphysics lecture that Kant gave in winter semester 1792/93, we find the following passage: "An element is a simple part. Is water an element? No, because it can further be dissolved [*es läßt sich noch auflösen*], it consists of vital air and combustible air and we call something that does not contain species elementary" (V-Met/Dohna 28.2,1: 664). This shows that Kant had definitively rejected Stahl's theory of three elements, but it does not prove that he already adopted Lavoisier's system of chemistry. In a postscript to a letter that Johann Benjamin Erhard sent to Kant on 17 January 1793, we read: "Girtanner still wants to know if you have read his chemistry, and what you think about it" (Br 11: 408). Erhard refers to Girtanner's *Anfangsgründe der antiphlogistischen Chemie*, published in 1792. That Erhard writes 'still' (Girtanner *still* wants to know, etc.) may be an indication that Girtanner sent a copy of his book to Kant and told him in the accompanying letter that he would be happy to know what the sage philosopher thought about it. We know indeed that Kant owned a copy of Girtanner's book (Warda 1922: 34) and given his interest in chemistry, we can at least suppose that he read some of the passages in which the author presents the decomposition of water as one of the most important results of the anti-phlogistic chemistry. In Kant's reply to Sömmering, published in 1796 but written in 1795, we find a passage in which Kant invokes the recent developments in chemistry:

> The pure common water that was until recently considered to be a chemical element is now by means of pneumatic experiments separated in two different kinds of air. Each of these kinds of air contains not only its base, but also the caloric, which perhaps can be in turn decomposed by nature into a light-matter and other matter. (Br 12: 33 f.)

The context of this passage is Kant's argument that chemical division can be done *in indefinitum*. He clearly refers here to Lavoisier's anti-phlogistic chemistry in which it is proven that water consists of hydrogen and oxygen, whereby both gases can be decomposed into their base (respectively hydrogen base and oxygen base) and heat-matter or caloric (see also Friedman 1992a: 288 f.).

With respect to Lavoisier's new systematic model in chemistry, which gave rise to organic chemistry, one can now ask, finally, whether Kant would have considered this to be a proper science. Dussort (1956) takes this to be the case, but I do not agree. As we saw above, in *Metaphysical Foundations* Kant proposed motion as the fundamental determination of matter. We also saw that the ultimate foundation of this determination is an a priori account of empirical affection. Now, following Kant, chemistry is not a proper science because there are no metaphysical principles showing how the fundamental concepts of the actions of matter on matter can be reduced to the concept of motion and thus be presented in a priori intuition. But even in Lavoisier's chemistry, one cannot discover "for the chemical actions of matters on one another" a "concept ... that can be constructed" (MAN 4: 470). Indeed, even after Lavoisier's model has replaced Stahl's, the motions that these matters undergo during a chemical (re)action cannot "be made intuitive and presented a priori in space" (MAN 4: 471).

Elsewhere, I proposed that one could perhaps think of another metaphysical schematization and reduction of empirical affection – one that does not refer to the concept of motion, but to the concept of *force* (Blomme 2011: 166–8). When one abstracts from *Metaphysical Foundations*'s project, there is indeed no reason why empirical affection could not be reduced to force.[11] But this does not change anything with respect to Kant's claim about forces as opposed to motions, namely that "the rules for the connection of motions by means of physical causes, that is, forces, can never be rigorously expounded, until the principles of their composition in general have been previously laid down, purely mathematically, as a basis" (MAN 4: 487). Accordingly, the condition of 'constructability by means of reduction to the concept of motion' is a criterion of a rigorous exposition as such. In other words, it is a criterion of proper science.

---

11 In that same text (Blomme 2011), I argued that Kant tries to develop this alternative conception in his *Opus postumum*. But I see now that that is false. Even if Kant sometimes seems there to oppose the concept of force as the fundamental *dynamical/qualitative* determination of matter to the concept of motion as the fundamental *phoronomic/quantitative* determination of matter (as found in *Metaphysical Foundations*), this is not Kant's point. One should note that, when the *Opus postumum* proposes to anticipate a priori the forces of matter, this concerns far more specific forces than the metaphysical forces of attraction and repulsion that Kant discusses in the dynamics chapter in *Metaphysical Foundations*. Thus, in my opinion the *Opus postumum* does not contain a critique of *Metaphysical Foundations*' phoronomy.

XI Physical Geography

Chapter 21
The Last Frontier: Exploring Kant's Geography

Robert B. Louden

1 Introduction: The neglect of Kant's geography[1]

In 2012, the first complete English translation of Kant's *Physical Geography* (PG) – which first appeared in German back in 1802 (Kant 1802) – was finally published in the *Natural Science* volume of The Cambridge Edition of the Works of Immanuel Kant (Kant 2012c).[2] The text of the *Physical Geography*, which runs 275 pages in the German Academy Edition of Kant's collected writings (*Kant's gesammelte Schriften*)[3] and thus easily qualifies as a "big" book at least in quantitative terms, is the only such work of Kant's never before to be translated into English. This long delay in translation is all the more surprising when one considers the fact – I quote now from the dust jacket for *Natural Science* – that Kant was "instrumental in establishing the newly emerging discipline of physical geography, lecturing on it for almost his entire career." Why wouldn't a text of such significance, written by an author of Kant's stature, warrant a speedier English translation?

---

[1] This essay, previously published in *Society and Space* 32.3 (June 2014): 450–65, began as an invited symposium paper presented at the Eastern Division meeting of the American Philosophical Association, held in Atlanta, Georgia in December 2012. A revised version was also presented as an invited paper at the IV Coloquio Kant Multilateral in Tiradentes, Brazil in August 2013. I would like to thank audience members on both occasions for helpful comments during the discussions following my presentations. I am also grateful to Stuart Elden, Charles Withers, Werner Stark, Dilek Huseyinzadegan, and Robert R. Clewis for their comments and suggestions on an earlier version of the written text.

[2] May (1970: 255–64) includes an English translation of the Introduction of Kant's *Physical Geography*. And Bolin (1968) completed a translation of Part I as part of his M. A. Thesis for Indiana University, Bloomington.

[3] Quotations from Kant's works are cited in the body of the text by volume and page number to this edition (viz., Kant 1900 –), except for quotations from the *Critique of Pure Reason*, which are cited by the customary use of the pagination of its first (A) and second (B) editions. The traditional Academy volume and page numbers (and also the A and B pagination from the *Critique of Pure Reason*) are reprinted in the margins of most recent editions and translations of Kant's writings.

But even though we now finally do have a complete English translation of Kant's *Physical Geography*, fastidious scholars are already complaining that the wrong text was translated. For the work entitled *Physical Geography* is actually a compilation of different materials edited by Kant's colleague and former student Friedrich Theodor Rink, and the quality of Rink's editing work has been uniformly criticized for many years. The main criticism, first made by Erich Adickes over a hundred years ago and still widely accepted today, is that Rink's version of the lecture notes "consists of two parts of entirely different origin" (Adickes 1911: 278; see also Watkins and Reinhardt 2012: 435), a not-so-minor detail that Rink did not inform his readers about.[4] The first half (PG 9: 156–273) comes from lecture notes written in 1775, while the later part (PG 9: 273–436) stems from 1758–59 lectures. As a result, some commentators have concluded that Rink's edition is "hopelessly corrupt, and extremely problematic as the basis for any careful study of Kant" (Elden 2011: 5; see also Elden 2009: 8); and others go so far as to advise that it is "best avoided ... if we want to understand Kant's own thought on the subject" of physical geography (Bernasconi 2011: 298). Even Olaf Reinhardt, the translator of Rink's text, confesses that it "was unsatisfactory from the start and received poor reviews" (Reinhardt 2011: 103)[5] and that "there is no straightforward and unequivocal sense in which it can be taken to represent his [viz., Kant's] actual views" (Watkins and Reinhardt 2012: 436).

One might therefore think that Rink's editorial sloppiness is the explanation for the neglect of Kant's *Physical Geography* – "this text is very untrustworthy, stay away from it." But while it is not my intention to defend Rink, I do not think that he is the primary cause behind the scholarly inattention to Kant's *Geography*. The problem is much larger than Rink. For Rink also edited other works of Kant's, including the *Lectures on Pedagogy*, first published in 1803, one year after the *Geography* (Kant 1803).[6] And (surprise, surprise) scholars have also uniformly

---

[4] Rink does say in his "Editor's Foreword" that "three almost complete notebooks of the physical geography were found, written by him [viz., Kant] at different times, and this edition has been based on these" (PG 9: 155). But he does not give dates for these notebooks, nor does he specify how his own published text relates to the three notebooks.
[5] Reinhardt cites a review published in the *Göttingische Gelehrte Anzeigen* 154 (25 September 1802): 1530, in which the anonymous reviewer claims that Rink's text "contains little that is worthy of distinction" (Reinhardt 2011: 113 n. 2).
[6] Rink also edited a collection of some of Kant's shorter pieces (Rink 1800a), in addition to writing one of the earliest biographies of Kant (Rink 1805). And his scholarship was not limited to Kant – he "was also an industrious collector, editor, translator, and publisher of Arabic manuscripts and of volumes in Abyssinia, the Nigritia, and the Arabic, Syriac, and Ethiopian languages" (Watkins and Reinhardt 2012: 723 n. 4).

criticized the quality of Rink's editing of these lectures (see, e. g., Stark 2012). For it too is a compilation based on Kant's classroom lectures – a fact which led several nineteenth-century German editors of Kant's *Pädagogik* to rearrange the order of Rink's text, based on their own hypotheses about where he went wrong and how the text ought to go. And the first two English translators of the *Pädagogik* (Churton 1899; Buchner 1904) followed these German revisionist efforts (see Louden 2007: 435f.). But my main point here is that Rink's sloppy editing of the *Pädagogik* did not deter later editors, translators, and commentators from jumping in. Two complete English translations of Kant's *Pädagogik* were published over a hundred years ago – one in England by Annette Churton (1899), another in the US by Edward Franklin Buchner (1904). My own translation, which was first published in the *Anthropology, History, and Education* volume of The Cambridge Edition in 2007 (Kant 2007: 434–85; see also Kant 2009a: 253–80 and Kant 2012b: 153–73), is the third English translation of this extremely popular Kantian text. Thus far, Rink's edition of Kant's *Lectures on Pedagogy* has also been translated three times into French, five times into Spanish, and fourteen (!) times into Italian (Zöller 2007: 576–77). The secondary literature on Kant's *Pedagogy* – in English as well as in other languages – is also more extensive than the secondary literature on Kant's *Geography* (see Weisskopf 1979: 445–71; Zöller 2007: 582f.; Roth and Surprenant 2012; Johnston 2013: 248–58). Clearly then, Rink's editorial sloppiness hasn't scared scholars away from Kant's *Pedagogy*. And this fact supports the claim that the comparative indifference to Kant's *Geography* cannot simply be due to Rink alone.

Meanwhile, the German Academy Edition of Kant's collected writings, the preferred edition for serious Kant scholars, has yet to publish some of Kant's most significant work on geography. Rink's edition of the *Geography*, reedited by Paul Gedan, was first published in 1923 in volume 9 of *Kant's gesammelte Schriften* (PG 9: 151–436), along with Rink's edition of the *Pädagogik* and Jäsche's version of Kant's Logic Lectures. Eighty-six years later, in 2009, vol. 26.1 appeared, edited by Werner Stark, but it contains only the early Holstein Geography Lecture (1757–59; AA 26: 1–320). Pages 85–320 of Holstein are quite close – though not exactly identical – to pages 311–436 of Rink's text. A second, longer Academy volume of Geography Lectures (26.2), also edited by Werner Stark, will be published later, and is expected to include the Hesse (1770), Kaehler (1774), Messina (1778), Dönhoff (1782), and Dohna (1792) transcriptions, as well as an extract from a 1791 version of the Geography Lectures first published in 1833 by Friedrich Christian Starke.[7] So on the German side too, it is very difficult to survey the publication history

---

7 For discussion of Starke (a pseudonym for Johann Adam Bergk) see Louden 2012a: 283–7.

without concluding that Kant's Geography Lectures have been unduly neglected. Multiple volumes of Kant's extensive classroom lectures on ethics, logic, metaphysics, theology, and anthropology have been available for many years in the Academy Edition, works that enable scholars to track the development of Kant's thinking in each of these areas. Yet we are still waiting for a comparable publication treatment of Kant's multiple classroom lectures on geography.[8]

In sum, whether one looks at the situation from an English- or a German-language perspective, the conclusion is the same: Kant's geography lectures have not been taken as seriously as the rest of his work. As Elden observes, "Of all of Kant's work, and of all his wide areas of interest, the neglect of geography is perhaps the most glaring" (Elden 2009: 8). Editors, translators, and publishers have proceeded much more slowly with these lectures than with Kant's other lectures. What is the cause of this unequal treatment? My own view is that it is primarily due to the fact that most scholars simply don't believe that Kant's geography is as important as his ethics, logic, metaphysics, theology, anthropology, etc. As David Harvey remarks, "Kant's geography is hardly known at all.... Whenever I have questioned Kantian scholars about it, their response has almost always been the same. It is 'irrelevant', 'not to be taken seriously', or 'there is nothing of interest in it'" (Harvey 2011: 269). Kant's geography is, so to speak, the Rodney Dangerfield of his corpus: "It don't get no respect." Additionally, to a certain extent Kant's geography has simply fallen through the disciplinary cracks. It is viewed as not philosophical enough by philosophers, but also as not geographical enough by geographers. For instance, American geographer Richard Hartshorne (a notable exception to my generalization about geographers' judgments of Kant's geogra-

---

[8] As noted earlier, critics of Rink have also asked why the editors of The Cambridge Edition of the Works of Immanuel Kant decided to publish an English translation of his version of the *Geography*, rather than offer readers a translation of a more reliable geography manuscript. According to Paul Guyer, General Editor (along with Allen Wood) of The Cambridge Edition, there are several reasons: 1) Reinhardt's translation of Rink was one of three items in hand that originally prompted the edition back in the 1980s – the editors could not reasonably ask him to throw it away and translate a new text when the *Natural Science* volume was finally completed in 2012. 2) Rink's text is the one that has been known and referred to for many years, and there is a historical value in having an English translation available. 3) The *Natural Science* volume includes only published texts rather lecture transcriptions (Holstein and all of the other Geography texts that Stark is editing for the Academy Edition are lecture transcriptions). 4) If a text other than Rink's were to be translated, the Cambridge Edition editors would need to first wait until the other versions of the geography lectures had first appeared in the German Academy Edition in order to make a reasonable choice. But most of these texts (with the sole exception of Holstein) have still not been published, and it is not yet known for certain when they will appear (email correspondence to author, 9 July 2013).

phy – see Hartshorne 1939: esp. 35–48) observes that "Kant's work and interest in geography was largely ignored for nearly a century after his death" (Hartshorne 1958: 104; cf. Church 2011: 32). And Livingstone and Harrison push this claim even further, with their remark that "within the geographical community of scholars, Kant's insights have been largely overlooked" (Livingstone and Harrison 1981: 359).

In the remainder of this essay, I shall challenge these judgments, partly by enlisting the support of the contributors to Stuart Elden and Eduardo Mendieta's recent interdisciplinary collection of essays, *Reading Kant's Geography* (Elden and Mendieta 2011). Kant's work on geography forms an important and integral part of his wide-ranging philosophy – it deserves our respect. Granted, Kant does warn readers in his second *Critique* (KpV) that *"respect [Achtung]* is always directed only to persons, never to things" (KpV 5: 76), and he later qualifies this statement by adding that the respect which we show to a person is "strictly speaking to the law [*dem Gesetze*] that his example holds before us" (KpV 5: 78). So when I say that Kant's Geography deserves our respect, I am using the term 'respect' in a non-Kantian sense. But non-Kantian respect is also important.

2 Geographical metaphors

Why then should we pay more attention to Kant's Geography? One reason for doing so is that Kant's philosophical writings are permeated with geographical metaphors (cf. Caygill 1995: 215). Therefore, if you want to understand his philosophy, you need to know something about his geography. Lakoff and Johnson have argued that "our *ordinary* conceptual system, in terms of which we both think and act, is fundamentally metaphorical in nature" (Lakoff and Johnson 1980: 3; my emphasis), but I am claiming now that the conceptual system of Kant's *philosophy* is fundamentally metaphorical in nature, and that the metaphors he lives by are predominantly geographical. Kant's favorite geographical metaphor is undoubtedly his oft-stated concern to map out the boundaries (*Grenzen*) of human reason – reflected, for instance, in the title of his main work in the philosophy of religion, *Religion within the Boundaries of Mere Reason* (RGV 6: 1–202), as well as in his frequent criticisms of enthusiastic (*schwärmerisch*) intellectuals whom he deems guilty of "an overstepping of the boundaries of human reason undertaken on principles" (KpV 5: 85). But Kant's use of geographical metaphors is much more extensive than this. In a famous passage in the first *Critique* where he explains the ground of the distinction of all objects into phenomena and noumena, he writes:

> We have now not only traveled through the land of pure understanding, and carefully inspected each part of it, but we have also surveyed it, and determined the place of each thing in it. This land, however, is an island, and enclosed in unalterable boundaries by nature itself. It is the land of truth, ... surrounded by a broad and stormy ocean, ... where many a fog bank and rapidly melting iceberg pretend to be new lands and, ceaselessly deceiving with empty hopes the voyager looking around for new discoveries, entwine him in adventures from which he can never hope to escape and yet also never bring to an end. (KrV A235 f./B294 f.)

As translators Paul Guyer and Allen Wood remark in their note on this passage, "Kant's geographical imagery goes back a long way" (Guyer and Wood in Kant 1998a: 732 n. 94). For instance, in a *Reflexion* written in 1772, Kant describes metaphysics as "an unknown land of which we intend to take possession;" a land that "lies in the ... hemisphere of **pure reason** ... connected by bridges to the land of experience, ... separated by a deep sea." Even though we are somewhat "acquainted with its geography," Kant continues, "we do not yet know what might be found in this land, which is maintained to be uninhabitable by some people and to be their real domicile by others. We will take the general history of this land of reason into account in accordance with this general geography" (Refl 4458, 17: 559).

Kant is thus a self-described "geographer of human reason" (see KrV A760/B788); one who – unlike the earlier geographer of human reason, David Hume – attempts to locate "not mere **limits** [*bloß Schranken*] but rather determinate **boundaries** [*bestimmten Grenzen*]" of reason, and to provide us not merely with a temporary "resting place [*Ruheplatz*] for human reason," but with "a dwelling place [*Wohnplatz*] for permanent residence" (KrV A761/B789). As Malpas and Thiel note in their contribution to *Reading Kant's Geography*, Kant is "one of the pioneers, perhaps the very first, in the project of a 'philosophical topography' – a project that aims to explore the manner in which space, and also place, figure in human knowledge and experience as both the object of such knowledge and experience, and as part of its very structure" (Malpas and Thiel 2011: 195). Kant's own conception of his philosophical project is determined by a set of geographical metaphors to such an extent that one cannot properly understand this project without a clear sense of the geographic frame within which it is set. And reading Kant's Geography Lectures is the best way to gain an understanding of this geographic frame. Kant's geography informs his philosophy from the start – he began lecturing on geography back in 1756 (nearly thirty years before his most famous philosophical works of the 1780s were published), and it is not an exaggeration to say that his philosophy to a certain extent grows out of and is influenced by his earlier work in geography. Geography and philosophy for Kant are not two independent projects, but rather are deeply intertwined with each other.

Granted, Kant is by no means the only modern philosopher who was fond of geographical metaphors. For instance, Locke in *An Essay Concerning Human Understanding* undertakes "a Survey of our Understandings" in order to discover "the Extent of our Knowledge" and to find the "Horizon ... which sets the Bounds between the enlightened and dark Parts of Things" (Locke 1975: I.1.7), and he describes the understanding as a "little world" (II.2.2) surrounded by "an huge Abyss of Ignorance" (IV.3.24). Similarly, Leibniz in his *New Essays on Human Understanding* compares mathematicians who try to advance without axioms and theorems which are already known to "traveling by sea without a compass, on a dark night when one cannot see the sea-bed or the shore or the stars; or tramping over vast plains where there are no hills or streams" (Leibniz 1996: IV.iv.19), and he compares the totality of human knowledge to "an uninterrupted ocean which is divided into the North Sea, the Atlantic Ocean, the Indian Ocean and the Red Sea only by arbitrary lines" (IV.xxi.5). But while Kant admittedly is at one level simply endorsing a commonplace Enlightenment strategy of employing spatial and cartographical metaphors,[9] it is important to remember that he was also a philosopher who actually taught a university course in geography "at least forty-eight times" (PG 9: 509) between 1756 and 1796. Geography is much more than a source of occasional metaphors for Kant. It was also one of his primary teaching commitments, as well as a focal point for many of his natural science publications.

3 Geography as an essentially contested concept

> Needless to say, geographers never agree completely, and often disagree radically, in defining their subject. (Hartshorne 1959: 8)

A second reason for taking Kant's *Geography* more seriously concerns his influential discussion concerning the nature of geography and its place among the sciences. For 'geography', like many core ideas that intellectuals fixate on, is itself an "essentially contested concept" (Gallie 1956), one whose correct meaning cannot be determined simply by appealing to empirical evidence, linguistic usage, or canons of logic alone. Geography, given the wide diversity of phenomena it studies and the numerous and conflicting methods championed by its practitioners over the years, seems particularly resistant to an uncontested

---

9 For some recent discussions of this strategy, see Mayhew 2010; Withers 2009; and Brewer 2004.

definition, and certainly the history of its development, as others have noted, "is the history of a contested tradition" (Livingstone 1992: 101). But Kant does in some texts defend a distinctive conception of geography as a science of space, a conception that was rediscovered and embraced later by Alexander von Humboldt and Alfred Hettner as well as by the American geographer Richard Hartshorne (Hartshorne 1958), a conception that has also been labeled "a basic tenet of orthodox geography" (Harvey 1969: 70). However, Kant's conception of geography as a spatial or chorological science is by no means universally accepted by contemporary geographers. Harvey, for instance, in his early work *Explanation in Geography* (1969), maintains that "the logical justification for the particular view of geography adopted by Kant, Hettner, and Hartshorne can no longer be maintained" (Harvey 1969: 212), and in a more recent essay he continues to protest against "the Kantian prescription to construe geographical knowledge as mere spatial ordering, kept apart from the narratives of history" (Harvey 2000: 554). Similarly, Schaefer dismisses Kant's description of geography as a science of space as simply an "unfortunate statement" (Schaefer 1953: 233).

There is a huge and contentious literature on this topic,[10] and to analyze and evaluate all of it is beyond the scope of this essay. But I hope to show that there is no need to do so. For my main point here is that Kant himself does not consistently adhere to the view that geography should be defined as a descriptive science of spatial relations (it is at most his *occasional* view of geography). Here I side with May, when he observes that "Kant exhibits considerable ambivalence at times respecting the issue of clearly separating the history of nature from the 'description of nature,' or geography" (May 1970: 121). Additionally, there are strong common sense reasons for skepticism regarding the thesis that geography is exclusively spatial. A geography that is exclusively spatial – that is divorced from temporality – is simply not a very interesting geography, for it would lack explanatory power. It would not be able to tell us why something happened, nor would it be able to predict what will happen in the future. This is primarily why Schaefer fumes so furiously against what he calls Kantian "exceptionalism" in geography. Such a geography, he complains, "does not go beyond mere description" (Schaefer 1953: 228; cf. Harvey 1969; Martin 1989). Regardless of where one stands with regard to the interminable debate about what constitutes 'real' science (another essentially contested concept?), there are many fundamental

---

[10] Part of the problem concerns insufficient attention to Kant's complex (and nonstatic) view(s) of space. Elden offers an appropriate warning here: "we think we know Kant's view of space, [but] the account of space in the work on geography and, more importantly, elsewhere, is at odds with this received wisdom" (Elden 2009: 20).

problems that most people (including Kant himself, in many but admittedly not all texts) expect geography to address that it will not be able to do if it forgoes temporality. As May notes, "since geography requires historical knowledge for explanatory purposes, it is epistemologically dependent on history" (May 1970: 151).[11]

However, I do not by any means think the conclusion to draw from this is that Kant's discussion of the nature of geography and its relation to the other sciences is best avoided. My own view is that his discussion has enduring value – not because of its ultimate accuracy or inaccuracy, but rather because it is a paradigm of systematic and critical reflection on the nature and scientific status of geography. Geography needs to be better theorized. This is not a trivial topic, as evidenced by the sheer volume of critical commentary devoted to it that scores of geographers and philosophers of science since Kant's time have produced.

Kant's influential claim that geography is concerned solely with spatial relations is presented chiefly in the Introduction to Rink's *Geography*, to which Adickes assigns a date of 1775, and here he is fond of contrasting geography to history. Geography categorizes perceived objects spatially; history organizes them temporally: "history and geography extend our knowledge in relation to time and space. **History** concerns the events that have taken place one after another in time. **Geography** concerns phenomena that **occur simultaneously** [*zu gleicher Zeit*] **in space**" (PG 9: 160). Geography thus considers things simply "in terms of the places [*Stellen*] they occupy on earth" (PG 9: 160), and its task is to offer "a report [*Nachricht*] of events that are next to each other in space [*Begebenheiten, die neben einander im Raume*]" (PG 9: 161). Geography, according to this conception, thus lacks a temporal dimension.[12] And since causal analyses also presuppose a temporal dimension (causes normally precede their effects), this kind of Kantian geography also does not investigate causes.

---

11 To the extent that Hartshorne is clear when he maintains that defining geography as the study of areal differentiation by no means excludes causal analysis (see Hartshorne 1939: 92, 98, 240; 1959: 13, 18, 88), the debate between him and Schaefer, Harvey, and others is yet another case of academics talking past one another. But in the case of Kant, who sometimes (but not always) defines geography in a similar manner, the charge of ambiguity and inconsistency is demonstrable and unfortunate.

12 In those passages where Kant does argue for a nontemporal conception of geography, it is possible that he is also signaling a disagreement with an older humanist tradition that defines geography as "the eye of history" – a tradition stretching back at least as far as Flemish geographer Abraham Ortelius (1527–1598; see Mayhew 2010: 612). And it is also worth noting that Kant does occasionally refer to *mathematical* geography (e. g., PG 9: 164; EACG 2: 3). However, he does not develop this alternative nontemporal conception of geography in any detail.

However, here as elsewhere in his writing (see, e. g., Louden 2000: 93–106), Kant is not always consistent. For instance, in the last section of the First Part of Rink's *Geography*, entitled "History of the Great Changes that the Earth Has Undergone and is Still Undergoing" – in part a prescient warning about climate change – Kant does briefly discuss some of the causal changes on the earth's surface initiated "[t]**hrough human beings**. They build dams against the sea and rivers and thus create dry land .... They drain swamps, fell forests and thus change the climate of countries considerably" (PG 9: 298). Similarly, his references to moral, political, mercantile, and theological geographies back in the Introduction all refer to types of geography that involve causal judgments about how the natural environment influences human practices (PG 9: 164). All of these geographies thus assume a temporal dimension.

Kant's strict separation of time and space also leads him to call history a *narrative*, and geography a *description*, and to insist that never the twain shall meet: "every foreign experience [*jede fremde Erfahrung*] is imparted to us either as a **narrative** [*Erzählung*], or as a **description** [*Beschreibung*]. The former is a **history,** the latter a **geography**" (PG 9: 159). "History is a narrative, but geography is a description. Thus we can have a **description of nature** [*Naturbeschreibung*], but not a **natural history** [*Naturgeschichte*]" (PG 9: 161). "The term 'geography'," he adds later, "thus refers to a description of nature, indeed of the whole earth" (PG 9: 162). Geography as Kant conceives it here is thus "a physical description of the earth [*physische Erdbeschreibung*]" (PG 9: 157) and all that one finds on it, where 'earth' is understood as the outer surface (*Oberfläche*) (see PG 9: 184) of the planet – in part to distinguish geography from other spatial sciences such as geology and astronomy.

As noted earlier, this particular concept of geography as a descriptive science of space remains essentially contested. But what I find more interesting in the present context is Kant's own inconsistency regarding this particular conception of geography. For elsewhere in the Introduction to the *Geography* he states: "But we can equally well call both history and geography descriptions. The difference is that the former is a description in terms of *time*, the latter in terms of *space*" (PG 9: 160). Here the alleged differences between history and geography begin to diminish: they are both called *Beschreibungen*. But the differences diminish still further when Kant makes a turnaround regarding the possibility of natural history – viz., a type of empirical knowledge that involves both spatial and temporal relations:

> The history of nature [*Geschichte der Natur*] comprehends the diversity of geography, as it has been at different times, but not how it is now, at a single moment; for the latter would be a description of nature. Only if one were to describe the events of the whole of nature as

it has been through all time, then and only then would one write a real so-called natural history. If, for example, one were to consider how the various breeds of dogs descended from one line, and what changes have befallen them through all time as a result of differences in country, climate, reproduction, etc., then this would constitute a natural history of dogs. Such a history could be compiled for every part of nature – for instance, plants and so forth. (PG 9: 162)

One can almost hear Darwin's footsteps in the background of this amazing passage, and it is unfortunate that Kant's best-known foray into natural history at present (but see also *Universal Natural History and Theory of the Heavens*, NTH 1: 214–368) is his extremely prejudiced and imprudent speculations concerning how the different races of human beings descended from one line. Kant devoted three separate essays to the question of race in the 1770s and 80s, but his race theory too is in part an outgrowth of his earlier work in geography. For instance, in the section entitled "Concerning Human Beings" in Rink's *Geography* (which Adickes believes was written in 1758–59), Kant argues for a climatological account of race.[13] In discussing different human skin colors, he states: "it is obvious that the heat of the climate is the cause of it" (PG 9: 314). But in his later race essays, hereditary factors are combined with climatological factors (see, e. g., VvRM 2: 435). Also, Kant's first race essay was itself an announcement for his geography lecture course of summer 1775 (VvRM 2: 443).

Kant warns his audience in the *Geography* that natural history is fated to remain highly conjectural, in part because it will always suffer from a data problem. It is very hard to know for sure what happened before there were any reliable witnesses to record events. As he puts it: "But there is the problem that it [viz., natural history] has to be guessed [*errathen müßte*], more through experiment than by accurate testimony. For natural history is not one whit shorter than the world itself. But we cannot guarantee the accuracy of our information, even since the invention of writing" (PG 9: 162). Similarly, in his 1788 essay, "On the Use of Teleological Principles in Philosophy," he claims that description of nature and natural history are "entirely *heterogeneous*" disciplines: "one (the description of nature) appears as a science with all the splendor of a great system, the other (natural history) can only point to fragments or shaky hypotheses" (ÜGTP 8: 162). In his three essays on race Kant unfortunately throws caution to the wind and does not heed his own advice carefully enough. (The accuracy of the 'information' he offers readers is far from guaranteed; his hypotheses are often extremely shaky.) But the subsequent immense impact of Darwin's theory of evolution is surely evidence that many people want a natural history, regardless of its inherent data

---

13 See also the following chapter in this volume.

problem. As Kant himself writes in his 1775 essay, *Of the Different Races of Human Beings*: "No matter how much one opposes, and rightly so, the boldness of opinions, one must venture a *history* of nature, which ... could gradually advance from opinions to insights" (VvRM 2: 443). And even in the *Geography* he declares that it is "the task of true philosophy to pursue the differences and diversity of a thing through the whole of time [*durch alle Zeiten*]" (PG 9: 162) – i.e., philosophy's job is to construct a natural history, and to help it advance from opinions to insights.

Max Marcuzzi, one of the French translators of Rink's *Geography* and also a contributor to *Reading Kant's Geography*, writes:

> it seems that we might be in a vicious circle before this hesitation of Kant's with respect to the necessity of linking geography and history .... [Geography] is only complete when it integrates becoming, and in moving into history, which is impossible: it is only complete (as a system) in moving into that which makes it impossible (as a system). (Marcuzzi 2011: 120)

The only way out of this vicious circle is to change the initial definition of geography, which Kant in effect does, albeit not as explicitly as one would like. The implicit conception of geography that he assumes in most of his geographical work is that geography is a type of natural history, one whose job is to describe "the Earth's most important features at different times and places" (Watkins 2012: xvii).

4 Pedagogical aims

A third reason for paying more attention to Kant's geography concerns his multiple pedagogical aims in offering this particular type of course to students. While Kant was certainly not unique among Enlightenment geographers in stressing the instructional value of geography (Withers 2011: 49), the strongly moralistic dimension of some of his pedagogic aims is, as one might suspect, distinctly Kantian. First, Kant sees geography as "a **propaedeutic** for **knowledge of the world**" (PG 9: 157), and here it serves as a preliminary instruction in both science and life (May 1970: 132). Geography serves as a propaedeutic to life insofar as it teaches students about the surface of the earth, which as Kant remarks, "is the foundation and stage on which our ingenious play is performed" (PG 9: 158). Geography, along with anthropology, which Kant began to offer as a separate course in 1772, and which to a large extent grows out of his earlier geography course, together belong to "the preliminary exercise in the *knowledge of the world*" (VvRM 2: 443). "The experiences of **nature** and the **human being** together constitute **knowledge of the world. Anthropology** teaches us **knowledge of the human being**, we owe our **knowledge of nature** to **physical geography**, that is, to a **description of the earth**" (PG 9: 157). In learning about these two essential parts of knowledge of the world (*Weltkenntnis*), the successful student "is introduced to the stage of his destiny [*Bestimmung*], namely, the *world*" (VvRM 2: 443). The German word "Bestimmung" has been called "the controlling center [*das dirigierende Zentrum*] of Kantian philosophy" (Brandt 2007: 7), and it also means *vocation* or *calling*. Part of Kant's point here is that humans need to learn about the world and all that resides on it in order to carry out their vocation successfully. As he remarks in the Introduction to Rink's *Geography*, the world "is the ground on which we obtain and apply our knowledge. But for that to be able to happen which the understanding tells us **ought** to happen, we need to know the nature of the subject, without which this is not possible" (PG 9: 158). In other words, without the fundamental instruction in *Weltkenntnis* that geography provides, we will not be in an empirically informed position to carry out our duty "to contribute everything possible" to the realization of the highest good" (KpV 5: 119) and "to promote with all of our powers what is best in the world [*das Weltbeste*]" (KU 5: 453; cf. KpV 5: 114). Moral ideals cannot become efficacious without knowledge of the world, the stage on which our moral efforts are enacted. Geography thus provides students with a broad, empirically informed orientation toward the world at large – a sense of what to expect after they leave their local communities, and a knowledge base that will enable them to become better informed and more effective cosmopolitan citizens. This is the moral dimension of geography's contribution to *Weltkenntnis*, and it is a decidedly impure, empirical dimension (Louden 2000).

Kant sees geography as a propaedeutic to *science* in at least two senses. First, in his *Lectures on Pedagogy* he recommends repeatedly that science education for children should *begin with* geography: "It is most advantageous to have the first scientific education be concerned with geography.... Maps have something in them which appeals to all children, even the smallest ones. When they are weary of everything else, they still learn something when maps are used.... One could actually begin with geography in teaching children" (Päd 9: 474, 476). Kant views geography as the ideal entrée into science – maps appeal to children's natural curiosity and imagination, but unlike fairy tales, which in Kant's day (EACG 2: 3) as well as our own continue to be a favorite vehicle in children's education – they also introduce children to the importance of structure and order in thinking about the world.

Kant also sees an important role for geography later on in university science education. For instance, in the fourth announcement for his geography course, published in 1765, he bemoans the fact that while university students are taught the art of subtle argumentation, ... they lack any adequate knowledge of historical matters, which could make good their lack of *experience*. Accordingly, I conceived the project of making the history of the present state of the earth, in other words, geography in the widest sense of the term, into an entertaining and easy compendium which might prepare them and serve them for the exercise of practical reason. (NEV 2: 312; cf. PG 9: 158)

Note that here too that in calling geography "the history of the present state of the earth," Kant clearly includes a historical or temporal dimension in his conception of geography, which further supports my earlier claim that he does not consistently adhere to his "geography is a spatial science" conviction. And in claiming that geography prepares students for the exercise of practical reason, he is also reiterating another point stressed earlier: *Weltkenntnis* provides humans with the empirical know-how that is necessary for the efficacious application of moral principles. But he also implies here that geography provides a general and accessible framework for knowledge in which all empirical knowledge of the world can find its place. Geography thus serves as an elementary introduction to all of the other empirical sciences, natural as well as social. (But here too, note that geography is unable to serve this "introduction to the sciences" role if it forswears causal relationships – cf. Richards: 1974: 14 n. 7.) Kantian geography, in other words, is a synoptic discipline: by means of geography "we become acquainted with the objects of our experience **as a whole**" (PG 9: 158). Geography combines the findings of the more specialized sciences into an easily communicable compendium, and it also functions as systematic introduction to empirical science generally. Through exposure to the right kind of geography, we learn that "our knowledge is not an **aggregate** but a **system**" (PG 9: 158). Geography itself helps establish the unity of science, a unity "without which all our knowledge is nothing but a fragmentary patchwork" (NEV 2: 313). Without this necessary systematic preparation to empirical science that geography and anthropology jointly provide, students are lost, and any knowledge that they do manage to acquire "can yield nothing more than fragmentary groping around and no science" (Anth 7: 120; cf. PG 9: 158).

Related to Kant's conviction regarding geography's role as a propaedeutic to empirical science is what I have called its "popular science goal" (Louden 2011a: 140). Kantian geography is designed to be pleasurable and entertaining – it "serves to organize our knowledge for our own pleasure [*Vergnügen*], and provides ample material for social conversations" (PG 9: 165), and, as we saw earlier, is intended to be "an entertaining and easy compendium [*einem angenehmen und leichten Inbegriff*]" (NEV 2: 312). But the entertainment is in effect a hook for the rudiments of a scientific understanding of nature. As Holly Wilson and Olaf Reinhardt both emphasize in their contributions to *Reading Kant's Geography*

(Reinhardt 2011: 110; Wilson 2011: 163–65), when lecturing on geography Kant repeatedly emphasizes causal connections between events in his descriptions of nature, and in doing so he is trying to get students to think about the world from a scientific point of view. As he remarks at the beginning of the first announcement for his geography course, published in 1757, "the rational [*vernünftige*] taste of our enlightened time" has fortunately brought us to the point where we are "no longer in danger of losing ourselves in a world of fables" (EACG 2: 3) but can instead begin to develop an accurate science of nature. "Liberation from superstition is called **enlightenment**," Kant remarks later in third *Critique* (KU 5: 294), and he sees geography as a major means of liberation for overcoming superstition about the natural world we live in.

Here as well, Kant's emphasis on causal analyses of natural events as a central aspect of geographical instruction belies his claim that geography restricts itself to "phenomena that **occur simultaneously in space**" and is a mere "**description of nature**" (PG 9: 160). And we must of course also acknowledge that his causal stories are often glaringly incorrect. "Perspiration that is too great or too little" does not cause "thick, viscous blood" (PG 9: 317), the bite of the Demokalo spider in Ceylon does not cause insanity (PG 9: 395), goiter is not "caused by the water in the Tyrol and Salzburg, which contains calcerous stone" (PG 9: 315), etc. But rather than simply rely on the benefit of hindsight to bemoan "the intellectual and political embarrassment" of Kant's efforts and to snicker at "the incredible mix of materials more likely to generate hilarity than scientific credulity" (Harvey 2011: 275) that we today find in them, we should rather view them as empirical statements that are subject to confirmation or refutation by contact with experience. Kant is trying to teach his students to have the courage to make use of their *own* understanding – this is "the motto of enlightenment" (WA 8: 35), and correcting empirical errors is an integral part of the growth of science and enlightenment. In lecturing on geography Kant intends "to teach students to think for themselves and think critically by being exposed to the scientific understanding of natural causality that occurs in experience…. [P]hysical geography can protect against superstition and fairy tales and this is one of its great advantages" (Wilson 2011: 165).

Granted, Locke too argued that "the child's education should begin with *Geography*" (Bowen 1981: 149). For instance, in *Some Thoughts Concerning Education* (1693), he writes: "*Geography*, I think, should be begun with: for the learning of the figure of the *globe*, the situation and boundaries of the four parts of the world, and that of particular kingdoms and countries, being only an exercise of the eyes and memory, a child with pleasure will learn and retain them" (Locke 1996a: § 179; see also §§ 166, 182). And here as well, Kant may seem to be merely echoing earlier Enlightenment sentiment. But while "the magnitude and principal focus of Kant's debt to [Lockean] empiricism are not in doubt" (Waxman 2006: 93), to the best of my knowledge Kant never read Locke's *Thoughts Concerning Education*.[14] And, as the above citations illustrate, Kant's own views about the importance of geography as a propaedeutic to science are much more detailed and multifaceted than Locke's. Also, as noted earlier, the sage of Königsberg's beliefs concerning the specific importance of geography for *moral* education are distinctively Kantian.

5 Human beings from a geographic point of view

Finally, a fourth reason to take Kant's Geography more seriously is that human beings themselves form an important part of the subject matter of these lectures. The official title of each of Kant's geography lectures is *Physische Geographie*, but in fact there is a good deal of human or cultural geography in all of them. During the time period in which Kant lectured on geography in the late eighteenth century, "there was no definitive distinction made between human geography and physical geography" (Church 2011: 21; cf. Livingstone 1992: 114), and some contemporary geographers continue to fight against "the dualism of physical and human geography" (see, e. g., Hartshorne 1959: 65–80). Kant's decision to begin offering a separate course on anthropology in 1772 and to in effect decouple it from geography – motivated in part by his conviction that the human being is "a free-acting being" rather than simply a product "belonging to the play of nature" (Anth 7: 119, 120) no doubt contributed to the growth of this dualism (see Livingstone and Harrison 1981), in addition to fueling the flames for the more radical conviction that a true science of human nature is impossible. Nevertheless, it is a fundamental mistake to think that one will not learn anything about Kant's views on human beings in his geography lectures (as well as to think that Kant did not believe there could not be a science of human nature). Human beings feature prominently in all extant versions of these lectures. For instance, in both Rink's edition and in the Holstein lecture, there are substantial sections entitled "Concerning the Human Being" (PG 9: 311–20, V-PG 26.1: 85–102), and the concluding Third Part of each text (in effect a regional geography of the world) is devoted to a "Summary Consideration of the Most Important Peculiarities of Nature in All Countries in Geographical Order" (PG 9: 377–436, V-PG 26.1: 197–320). The opening discussion of China in each Third Part includes numerous details about

---

[14] Kant's main debts in his education writings are to Basedow and Rousseau. For discussion, see Louden 2012b and Reisert 2012.

human customs concerning "Eating and Drinking," "Compliments," "Agriculture, Fruits, and Manufacturing," "Sciences, Language, and Laws," "Religion," and "Marriage" (PG 9: 378–82, V-PG 26.1: 200–07).

Furthermore, as the reference to China already suggests, the *kinds* of human beings one hears about in Kant's geography lectures differ substantially from those that one hears about in the anthropology lectures. There is much more discussion of non-European peoples in the geography lectures than in the anthropology lectures. In the latter, Kant's various analyses of "The Character of the Peoples" are very (west) Eurocentric, and focus almost exclusively on the "Big Five" – viz., the French, English, Spanish, Italian, and German peoples. In his discussion in the 1798 *Anthropology*, for instance, he concludes his nine-page analysis of the Big Five with a single paragraph containing dismissive remarks regarding the Russians, Poles, Turks, Greeks, and Armenians (Anth 7: 311–20, see esp. 319 f.). Granted, Kant's (west) Eurocentric bias is less pronounced in some of the earlier anthropology lectures. For instance, in his discussion of national character in Collins (1772/73) we find a brief discussion of the Turkish people (V-Anth/Collins 25: 234); in Parow (1772/73), of Native Americans, Africans, and East Indians (V-Anth/Parow 25: 451), and in Friedländer (1775/76), of Asians (V-Anth/Fried 25: 655 f.). And his 1764 discussion of national character in *Observations on the Feeling of the Beautiful and Sublime* [which despite its title is not primarily a book on aesthetics but rather "a work in what Kant would later call 'anthropology from a pragmatic point of view'" (Guyer 2007: 19)] also includes a fair amount of material on non-European people (GSE 2: 243–56; for discussion, see Louden 2011b: 150–63). But in the geography lectures he sets out to discuss "*all* countries" (PG 9: 377; V-PG 26.1: 197; my emphasis), and he describes the peoples of Asia and Africa before turning to Europe. Furthermore, in both Rink and Holstein, Europe warrants much less space than Asia, Africa, and America,[15] and the discussion of Europe includes positive coverage of Bulgaria, Greece, Hungary, Italy, France, Spain, Portugal, Sweden, Norway, and Russia – but nothing at all on England and Germany (see PG 9: 421–27; V-PG 26.1: 288–99).

In an earlier essay, I argued that there is "no bright, clear line to be drawn between Kant's geography and anthropology lectures, particularly when we use human beings as the intended line of demarcation" (Louden 2011a: 147). Human beings play a prominent role in both sets of lectures, and even the perspectives taken on human beings in these lectures do not vary as much as many

---

15 The page breakdowns in Rink and Holstein respectively are as follows: Asia: 29 (PG 9: 377–406), 66 (V-PG 26.1: 197–263); Africa: 13 (PG 9: 407–20), 25 (V-PG 26.1: 263–88); America: 8 (PG 9: 428–36), 20 (V-PG 26.1: 300–20); Europe: 6 (PG 9: 421–27), 11 (V-PG 26.1: 288–99).

commentators have claimed. It is not the case, for instance, that humans are treated exclusively as free-acting beings in the anthropology lectures, and entirely as products of nature in the geography lectures, or as objects of inner sense in the former and as objects of outer sense in the latter (for examples, see Louden 2011a: 145–7). There is considerable overlap between the two sets of lectures as regards their discussions of human beings (but, again, there are also some important differences – e. g., the less Eurocentric vision of human beings presented in the geography lectures). And this should not come as a surprise, once one takes the time to learn a bit about how Kant understands the interrelations between these two disciplines. They are both overlapping parts of *Weltkenntnis*, through which the student "is introduced to the stage of his destiny, namely, the *world*" (VvRM 2: 443; cf. PG 9: 157).

And because there is a substantial amount of material on human beings in Kant's geography lectures, these lectures are also an important source of information for his views about race. One finds discussions on race in the earliest surviving version of the geography lectures (Holstein, 1757–59)[16] up to the last (Dohna, 1792), and thus one might reasonably infer that these texts would enable us to test the controversial claim of Pauline Kleingeld and others that "during the 1790s, … Kant drops his hierarchical account of the races in a favor of a more genuinely egalitarian and cosmopolitan view" (Kleingeld 2007: 573; see also Muthu 2003: 184 and Shell 1996: 387 n. 23). Bernasconi, for instance, notes that "until Kleingeld's [2007] essay, Kant's lectures on *Physical Geography* played virtually no part in the current debate about Kant's theory of race and racism" (Bernasconi 2011: 296). But (alas) the hoped-for test is inconclusive at best. On the one hand, in the 1792 Dohna Geography lecture, Kant once again (just as he did 28 years earlier in the *Observations* – see GSE 2: 253) endorses Hume's notorious claim that "of the many thousands of Negroes who have gradually been freed, there is no example of one who has distinguished himself with a special skill."[17] This sad statement has led some of us to be skeptical about Kant's alleged second thoughts on race. However, Kleingeld herself acknowledges that while in Dohna "Kant once again endorses Hume's claim that blacks are naturally inferior," "by the *middle* 1790s … he has radically changed his mind on the subject of race"

---

[16] Stark (2011b) argues that the early Holstein lecture presents a less objectionable account of the human races than one finds in Rink's *Geography*. E.g, the notorious claim that "humanity has its highest degree of perfection in the white race" (PG 9: 316) is missing in Holstein (see V-PG 26.1: 93).

[17] Physische Geographie Dohna, 105. (This lecture will be included in Academy volume 26.2). Available online at: http://kant.bbaw.de/base.htm/geo_doh.htm. Accessed 29 July 2014.

(Kleingeld 2012: 111; my emphasis). Unfortunately, even though Kant continued to lecture annually on geography up to and until his retirement from teaching in 1796, no extant versions of his geography lectures after 1792 have yet turned up.

In conclusion, when we examine Kant's geography we learn more about the fundamental metaphors that structure his philosophy, we become aware of the different meanings that he and others assign to the contested concept of geography, we find out about the manifold pedagogical values he assigns to geography – particularly its fundamental role in making morality efficacious, and we discover more about his complex views concerning human beings. These are four fundamental reasons why philosophers, geographers, and all who seek to know the world and its earthly contents (see PG 9: 158) should take a closer look at these important texts. It is well past time to give Kant's geography the respect it deserves.

Fig. 18: Reproduction of the title page of a printed copy of Kant's essay "Von den verschiedenen Racen der Menschen" ("Of the Different Races of Human Beings") (1775), with a decorative engraving of a bird bath. After this follow (bound in the same volume) the handwritten "Kaehler" student notes on physical geography, from a course most likely given during the 1774 summer semester. Reproduced with the kind permission of the Rare Book and Manuscript Library at The University of Pennsylvania, USA. Call number: UPenn Ms. Codex 1120 (previously listed as Ms. German 36). An online facsimile of the essay and Kaehler notes can be found at http://hdl.library.upenn.edu/1017/d/medren/4259941. Accessed 11 February 2015.

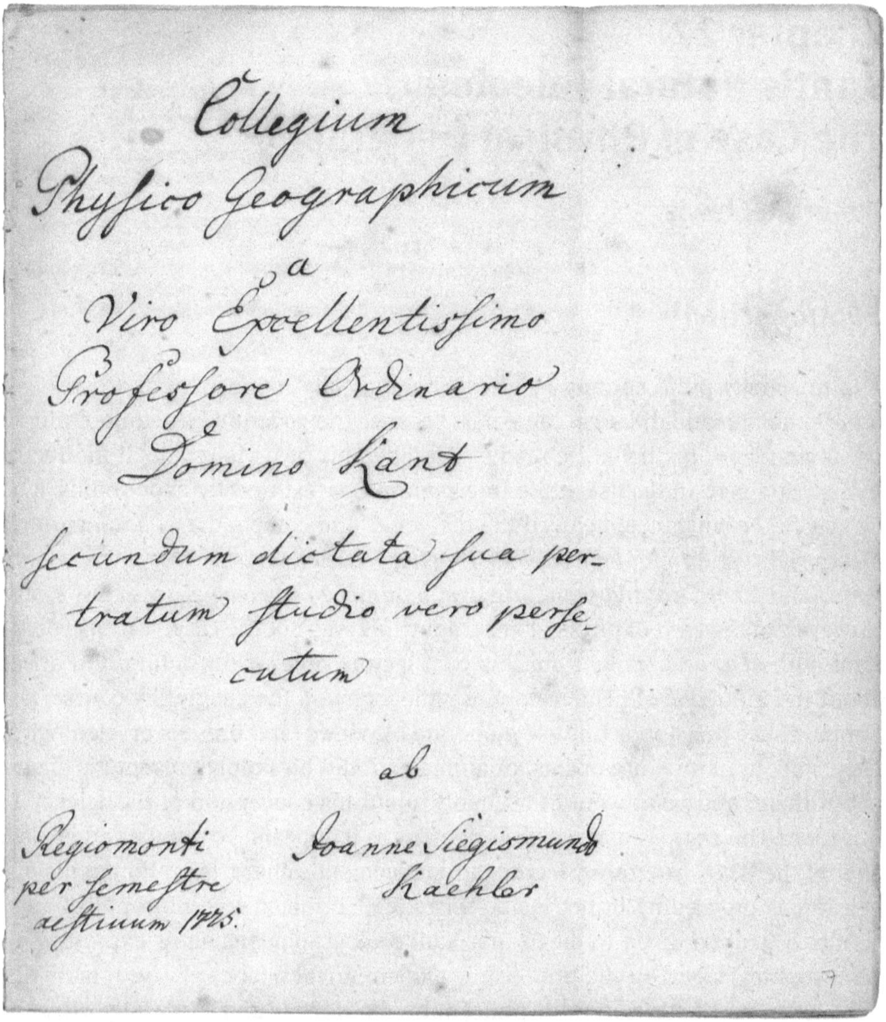

Collegium
Physico Geographicum
a
Viro Excellentissimo
Professore Ordinario
Domino Kant
secundum dictata sua per-
tratum studio vero perse-
cutum
ab
Regiomonti Joanne Siegismundo
per semestre Kaehler
aestivum 1775.

Fig. 19: Reproduction of the title page (7 recto) from the "Kaehler" handwritten notes on physical geography. Reproduced with the kind permission of the Rare Book and Manuscript Library at The University of Pennsylvania, USA. Call number: UPenn Ms. Codex 1120 (previously listed as Ms. German 36). An online facsimile of the Kaehler notes can be found at http://hdl.library.upenn.edu/1017/d/medren/4259941. Accessed 11 February 2015. The page reads: "Collegium / Physico Geographicum / a / Viro Excellentissimo / Professore Ordinario / Domino Kant / secundum dictata sua per- / tratum studio vero perse- / cutum / ab / Joanne Siegismundo / Kaehler / Regiomonti / per semestre aestivum 1775."

Chapter 22
Kant's Natural Teleology?
The Case of Physical Geography

Robert R. Clewis

1 Introduction[1]

As a university professor and lecturer, Kant typically commented on the texts of other scholars, and did so in large part because the government required him to use a manual or textbook. He read or defended his own views, albeit indirectly, by taking a certain license while interpreting the text and by expounding it as he saw fit. For instance, he used the textbooks and compendia of Baumgarten's *Metaphysica* and *Initia Philosophiae Practicae*, Meier's *Auszug aus der Vernunftlehre*, and Eberhard's *Vorbereitung zur natürlichen Theologie*, to name a few. However, in the case of physical geography this was not the case: for this course Kant authored, and spoke from, his own lecture notes. Now, a question arises about the influence of his developing philosophy on the geography course. Did Kant ever use this opportunity to elaborate his views on the *status* of teleological claims about nature, organisms, or animals, or did he simply present his claims about them; and what would that imply about his conception of the science in question? The answer may not be as obvious as it appears. To put it another way: should the (1757) geography lecture announcement's characterization of his discussion as proceeding in not just a "historical" but also a "philosophical" way (EACG 2: 9.16) be taken to mean that Kant's geography somehow expresses his philosophical views, or did philosophy and empirical science always remain distinct, even as Kant's notion of philosophy developed, and especially *after* the

---

[1] Acknowledgements: This chapter is published (in modified format) as an article in *Kant-Studien* (Clewis 2015); it was made possible in part by the Alexander von Humboldt Foundation's Fellowship for Experienced Researchers and the *Journal of the History of Philosophy*'s Kristeller-Popkin Travel Fellowship. For granting access to manuscripts of transcriptions, I am grateful to the Marburger Kant-Archive (especially Werner Stark), Archiv der Berlin-Brandenburgischen Akademie der Wissenschaften, Staatsbibliothek zu Berlin – Preußischer Kulturbesitz, Colombia University, and the University of Pennsylvania. For comments and discussions, I thank Robert Louden, Jennifer Mensch, Steve Naragon, Amanda Pirrone, Dennis Schulting, Susan Meld Shell, Günter Zöller, anonymous reviewers, and Karin de Boer and participants at KU Leuven's first annual Kant conference (2013); I alone am responsible for any errors.

publication of *Kritik der Urtheilskraft* in 1790?[2] In the process of answering this question, we will also ask, concretely: What were his conceptions of animals and organisms in the geography lectures? Did these transcriptions attribute agency to nature? How did the course handle arguments about providence and design?[3]

Given over the course of four decades starting in 1756, the geography lectures discuss living and organized beings, in addition to many other topics such as seas and landmasses. Hence, the lectures offer us a chance to discern whether their characterizations of animals, organisms, design, and natural agency reflect Kant's criticisms of natural teleology or whether he continues to make the same kinds of teleological claims as those of the pre-Critical period. Referring to some passages that are relatively unknown or overlooked, I discuss the relation between the lectures on physical geography and the development and expression of the Critical philosophy, though my focus is mainly on the lectures. This issue is of greater historical and philosophical significance than has generally been recognized, offering us insight into how Kant conducted a course in a natural science (perhaps even to an extent 'engaged' in the science itself), including how he actually employed teleological principles.[4]

Whereas, especially (but not exclusively) since the 1990s, transcriptions in other areas of his teaching – logic, natural theology, metaphysics, ethics, and anthropology – have been increasingly translated into several languages and/or examined by scholars, physical geography has until recently been far less studied. Why? Perhaps it is due to geography's empirical status. Yet the anthropology, likewise an empirical discipline, has been studied far more (especially since the 1997 publication of *Akademie-Ausgabe* volume 25, even if much of that material was already available in the published *Anthropology* of 1798), so one cannot attribute the relative oversight of geography to empirical status alone. Perhaps it is in part due to the known (if not always appreciated) shortcomings of F. T. Rink's edition. Thankfully, publication of the lectures in *Akademie-Ausgabe*

---

[2] Compare the (like geography, 'worldly' and 'pragmatic') anthropology lecture (1798), published *after* the third *Critique*. It employs *KU*'s notion of a merely regulative faculty or principle: "Geschmack ist ein bloßes regulatives Beurtheilungsvermögen" (Anth 7: 246.17); pursuing lasting peace is "nur ein regulatives Princip" (Anth 7: 331.527).

[3] Translations of Kant's geography transcriptions are my own. All translations of Kant's published works are, unless otherwise indicated, from The Cambridge Edition of the Works of Immanuel Kant (1992–): Kant 1992; Kant 2000b; Kant 2007; Kant 2012a; Kant 2012c. My translations typically adopt The Cambridge Edition's glosses.

[4] Mark Fisher (2007: 115 n. 15) claims, plausibly, that the lectures on physical geography are "an especially valuable source" for understanding Kant's "natural scientific and natural historical contexts."

volume 26 is a step toward remedying this. In addition, Robert Louden points out that Kant's geography has simply not been viewed as being as important as his ethics, logic, metaphysics, theology, or anthropology; Louden suggests that such oversight is unwarranted and gives four reasons for taking Kant's *Geography* seriously (Louden 2014: 450–65; reprinted as the previous chapter). Indeed, with the 2012 translation of the (however flawed) Rink edition in The Cambridge Edition and recent articles and books on the topic (notably, Elden and Mendieta 2011), there is a recent increase in interest in Kant's physical geography. With the digitization and publication of Kant's lectures on geography made possible by Werner Stark,[5] we are in a position to pose new questions about Kant's intellectual development in this area.

Although the span of years here covered is quite large, the aim of this developmental-historical article can be expressed simply: to characterize Kant's teleology in the transcriptions and writings on physical geography, focusing on the claims about organisms and animals, apparent design, and nature's agency. For instance, I will look for the application of teleological principles such as 'nothing in an organized being is in vain' (KU 5: 376.28) or related maxims of reason (KrV A666/B694), as well as references to providence's intentions and natural purposiveness in Kant's geographical descriptions of outer nature, at or near the surface of the earth.

A clarification of terms is in order. 'Nature' is here understood not as the sum total of all appearances (B163), but as the part of the world that includes the mineral, plant, and animal kingdoms. A 'purpose' (*Zweck*) is an end or aim, in the tradition of an Aristotelian final cause ('that for the sake of which' an action is done or a being exists). Kant defines *Zweck* (KU 5: 180.32) as the concept of an object insofar as it at the same time contains the ground of the reality of that object. Kant distinguishes a 'purpose' from 'purposiveness of form' (*Zweckmäßigkeit der Form*),[6] or the correspondence of a thing with that constitution of things that is possible only in accordance with ends or purposes (KU 5: 180.34). In the *Critique of Pure Reason*, 'purposiveness of nature' is treated as part of reason's 'regulative' use of the idea of God or a supreme intelligence, which is seen as producing nature according to its wise intentions (e.g., A619f./B647f.; A664/B692; A671/B699; A685f./B712f.). In *KU*, the search for purposes is assigned not to

---

[5] The student transcriptions of Kant's physical geography lectures have been available at the Kant-Arbeitsstelle of the BBAW since 2007: http://kant.bbaw.de/base.htm/geo_base.htm. Accessed 11 November 2014. Access requires username and password, granted upon making an inquiry to the Arbeitsstelle.

[6] I shall not here take into account the undeniable importance of "der Form."

reason but to the 'power of reflective judgment', the capacity to find an appropriate universal concept to fit a given particular (KU 5: 179.26; see Wood 1999: 216–8). A 'teleological' consideration of nature is one that sees nature as having ends or, less strongly, at least as purposive. An 'intention' (*Absicht*) of nature is an aim that it appears to have – or as Kant puts it, has only by analogy – to design or fit an organic being or beings in a certain way. A natural 'organized being' or 'organized product' is one in which everything is an end and reciprocally also a means (KU 5: 376.12)[7]; every part is there for every other one, and ultimately for the sake of the whole organism itself. (Although there may be key differences between 'organisms' and 'organic' or 'organized' beings, I do not explore them here.) Organisms have inner ends; an 'inner end' is a purpose that an organism has within itself or that it gives itself, as when it grows or regenerates. In the Critique of the Teleological Power of Judgment, the second Part of the third *Critique*, Kant discusses, in addition to inner ends, the *relative* ends of nature, which, however, do not require teleological judging since they are not found in one organism, species, or system, but are relations between two organisms or systems.

To my knowledge, despite growing attention to Kant's theory of race and philosophy of biology, the present article's question about teleology and the influence of the developing Critical philosophy has not been adequately addressed with regard to Kant's geography (on anthropology, see Wood 1999: 215 ff.). This precise question is discussed neither by the classical studies by Adickes[8] nor by contemporary scholars, even if both the former and latter have certainly examined and criticized Kant's theory of race in *Von den verschiedenen Racen der Menschen* (1775)[9], *Bestimmung des Begriffs einer Menschenrace* (1785), and *Über den Gebrauch teleologischer Principien in der Philosophie* (1788).[10] Although any discussion of the teleological judgment about the human being will probably refer to Kant's conception of race, my focus is not on his troubling concept of race per se, but how the geography reflects the development of Kant's thinking about beings with purposes. After all, in the 1788 essay he claimed to derive the organization of organic beings (*organischen Wesen*) from laws of the gradual development of

---

[7] Cf. ÜGTP 8: 179.08–10. See even the early (1755) NTH 1: 230.14–26.
[8] Adickes carried out extensive philological and philosophical analyses that are still useful today. See Adickes 1911 and Adickes 1913; see also Adickes 1924–25.
[9] Following the *Akademie-Ausgabe*, from which I cite (VvRM 2: 429–43), I do not here distinguish between the 1775 course announcement and the 1777 published version. Mikkelsen (2013) translates both texts; see also his comment at 2013: 45.
[10] See Adickes 1924–25: 406–59. More recent studies include: Eze 1997; Larrimore 1999; Boxill and Hill 2001; Eigen and Larrimore 2006; Bernasconi 2011; and Kleingeld 2012: 92–123. For a useful overview of the debate, see Mikkelsen's Introduction at Mikkelsen 2013: 1–32.

original predispositions (*ursprünglichen Anlagen*) to be found in the organization of its phylum (*Organisation ihres Stammes*) (ÜGTP 8: 179.18–22). The human animal, alongside plants and other animals, counts as one organism among many to be studied in this way; my discussion should be understood in this context.

The date in which a transcription was composed often differs from the (more important) year (or semester) Kant gave the course. I analyze representative manuscripts (all extant) from each of the four distinct periods[11]; the date ranges for each *group* are given in parentheses.

- "Ms Holstein." From Group A[12] (based on courses from 1757–1772)
- "Ms Kaehler."[13] From Group B (1774–1779)
- "Ms Dönhoff." From Group C (1780s)
- "Ms Dohna." From Group D (1790s)

Since *KU* was composed shortly before 1790 and published in that year, it should be noted that several geography transcriptions were based on courses given after 1790. However, only one manuscript is extant: "Ms Dohna" (from circa 1792). Johann Adam Bergk (1769–1834), under the pseudonym Friedrich Christian Starke, edited *Immanuel Kant's vorzügliche kleine Schriften und Aufsätze*.[14] Its second volume contains a 21-page excerpt (pages 262–83) of a lost student transcript from summer semester 1791 ("anonymous-Starke 4"). Since its content and date of composition are relevant to this article, I discuss Bergk's excerpt; I also briefly mention a manuscript called "Ms 1729" or "anonymous-Königsberg 3" (circa 1791 or 1792),[15] which is related[16] to "Ms Dohna." To provide some context,

---

[11] On the periods and types, see BBAW 2007, at http://kant.bbaw.de/base.htm/geo_typ.htm; and Stark 2011a: 73–5. Although it does not concern us here, in the latter Stark differentiates A_0, A_1, and A_2 (within type A); B_0 and B_1 (within type B); and, within type X (standing for "mixtures"), X_1 and X_2.

[12] "Ms Hesse" (1770), named after Georg Hesse and of Stark's type A_2, is sufficiently reliable and lengthy (at 71,000 words) to merit examination. However, since "Ms Hesse" comes from the A period, discussing it would not have contributed much to answering the present question, even if the Ms is a noteworthy source of Kant's views on geography toward the end of period A.

[13] "Ms Kaehler" is located at the University of Pennsylvania's Rare Book and Manuscript Library (Philadelphia, USA), listed as Ms. Codex 1120 and (formerly) Ms. German 36. An online facsimile is available at: http://hdl.library.upenn.edu/1017/d/medren/4259941. Accessed 11 Febrary 2015. I am grateful to John Pollack for his assistance and for granting access to the manuscript. Mss Holstein, Dönhoff, and Dohna are privately owned (see AA 26.1: lxi).

[14] Starke 1833. See 26.1: lxii.

[15] See BBAW 2007, at http://kant.bbaw.de/base.htm/texte.htm/frg_1729.htm. Accessed 11 November 2014. Adickes labeled it "S."

[16] See BBAW 2007, at http://kant.bbaw.de/base.htm/geo_doh.htm. Accessed 11 November 2014:

I examine the published announcements referring to Kant's geography lectures and the three essays on teleology (1775, 1785, 1788). In examining the representative transcriptions, I proceed chronologically; this seems to be the most straightforward way to discern how the lectures evolved with respect to our question.

My first section examines "Ms Holstein"; section 2 examines the 1775 essay on race and "Ms Kaehler." Section 3 analyzes "Ms Dönhoff"; the fourth section first fills in some gaps by looking at the essays from the 1780s and then turns to the manuscripts from the 1790s, namely, "Ms Dohna," "anonymous-Starke 4," and "Ms 1729."

We do not know beforehand, a priori as it were, that Kant employed his own strict demarcation of the empirical and pure disciplines and that he systematically kept them apart in his lecturing practice: that this was the case must be shown by close examination and citation of the relevant texts. If so, a demonstration that Kant hardly reflected – at least not in any sustained way – on the nature of teleology in his course would appear noteworthy after all. It would allow us to see how Kant conceived of one natural science, geography, namely, as an empirical, pragmatic, worldly, scientific investigation rather than a scholastic discipline. By answering the present question, we can thus better understand how Kant conceived of the boundaries between the transcendental and empirical disciplines, his understanding of natural science, and his lecturing activity and pedagogical practice.

2 Animals and nature's agency in the 1750s

Before we turn to "Ms Holstein," some background is needed.[17] A few years before the lecture associated with "Ms Holstein" was given, Kant published two German essays that, given their topics and themes, can be seen as contributions to physical geography. The first, *Untersuchung der Frage [...]*, published on 8 and 15 June 1754, responds to a prize question posed in 1752 by the Prussian Royal Academy of Sciences. The second treatise, *Die Frage, ob die Erde veralte [...]*, published in 1754, is connected to a dispute that raged throughout Königsberg concerning the earth's aging. Although reading the texts of biblical Christian revelation as directly relevant for claims in natural science was common in Königsberg at the time, as Michael Church (2011: 26) has pointed out, Kant deliberately chooses not to do

---

"verwandt mit Ms 1729."
[17] For a discussion of the natural sciences (including geography) and Kant's intellectual environment at the Collegium Fridericianum and Albertina University, see Stark 2014b.

so. Kant discusses four theories of the earth, three of which are mechanical and the fourth biological, and, since it introduces the notion of a world spirit or soul, even metaphysical. Moreover, in response to the 1755 Lisbon earthquake, Kant published three brief essays on earthquakes the following year. Although Kant also touched on and defended optimism, the tracts were mostly scientific and, indeed, concerned physical geography. He also published two short meteorological essays in 1756 and 1757. *Entwurf und Ankündigung eines Collegii der physischen Geographie*, to which an essay on wind was appended, appeared in 1757. Thus, notwithstanding some exceptions – e. g., the Latin writings, *Gedanken von der wahren Schätzung der lebendigen Kräfte*, and *Neuer Lehrbegriff der Bewegung und Ruhe* – the works from 1754 to 1758, including *Allgemeine Naturgeschichte* (1755), can be considered to be texts pertaining to physical geography. In turn, Kant's course began with some remarks on mathematical geography, on which he also had published. These writings are not solely works in natural science or physics, even if the more Newtonian writings are certainly closer to physics. Hence, at the beginning of his academic career, the *Privatdozent* worked intensely on the themes relevant to or addressed by physical geography.

In a page in *Entwurf und Ankündigung* (EACG 2: 9), Kant briefly advertises some material that he promises to discuss in the early version of the course, although he fails to mention a great deal of what (according to "Ms Holstein") he actually presented to students. In any case, Kant introduces his notion that animals, including human beings, have a natural shape and color that are conditioned by what region they occupy (EACG 2: 9.5–7). He claims that certain tendencies or inclinations of human beings are derived from the zones in which they live (EACG 2: 9.19–20).[18]

Rather than being the result of student note-taking during Kant's class, "Ms Holstein"[19] was copied by anonymous transcribers[20] who produced it, presumably at Kant's own request, from a copy of his own notes or outline for his course given in the late 1750s; Kant added his some marginalia and a dedication to Holstein around 1772. "Ms Holstein" contains no references to or mention of organisms, organized beings, or an end (*Zweck*), even as it devotes the first Section (Holstein, V-PG 26.1: 85–102)[21] to human beings. In addition, "Ms Hol-

---

18 "… die Neigungen der Menschen, die aus dem Himmelsstriche, darin sie leben, herfließen."
19 References to the Holstein are to AA volume 26.1 (Kant 2009b). Adickes (1911: 4) refers to "Ms Holstein" as "B" (see also AA 26.1: lxi) and, at 1911: 31 f., conjectures that "B" is the so-called *Diktat-Text* since it was based on Kant's own lecture notes.
20 According to Stark (2011a: 72): "a copy made by several people." Stark's Introduction reads (AA 26.1: v): "von mehreren unbekannten Schreibern angefertigt."
21 Cf. PG 9: 311–20. I will indicate the parallel passages in Rink's *Physische Geographie* when

stein" never explicitly refers to a germ (*Keim*) or predisposition (*Anlage, Prädisposition*). Hence, it seems that these core elements of Kant's theory appear only *after* 1757–59 and before 1775.[22]

To clarify this, it will first be useful to present Kant's theory in *Von den verschiedenen Racen der Menschen* (1775). One of the key ideas in 1775 is the principle that an animal's natural capacities and *Keime* are developed according to the climatic, hence external, conditions associated with a particular region on the earth – in particular the amount of sun and heat and the air's moisture level. By appealing to both natural, internal 'mechanisms' and to circumstantial and climatic conditions, Kant's theory of variation and differentiation conceives of humans as animals whose characteristics are shaped by naturally given germs and predispositions, in interaction with regional conditions. According to the *autochthonous* principle (from the Greek: 'sons of the soil') (VvRM 2: 432.13) a people adapts to the place where it originally resides, thereby developing its *Keime* and *Anlagen* although it can in principle later migrate to a different region.

"Ms Holstein" reveals that Kant had a climatically determined conception of racial difference *before* he developed the more technical "germs-and-endowments" theory, as Mikkelsen (2013: 44) calls it. Kant starts out with a mainly climatological race theory and gradually adopts a predominantly hereditary one, even though the latter still retains some climatological features. "Ms Holstein" uses the notion of a natural aptitude (*Naturell*) twice (Holstein, V-PG 26.1: 96.06, 97.05),[23] so even here inherent 'factors' may play a role, yet it comes in a single passage, and the latter ultimately suggests that climate has a very strong influence on the form and behavior of animals, including humans. The passage links the temper of the climate with the temperament of the people. (The Cambridge Edition translates the two instances of *Naturell* as "temperament" and "temper," respectively.)

---

relevant. For, starting with § 53 (PG 9: 273.22) and up to the end (PG 9: 436.37), PG was based on a text similar to "Ms Holstein," Kant's own lecture "outline" (*Konzept*) of 1757–59 (see AA 26.1: lxvii). PG's *preceding* part (AA 9: 156–273.21) was based on a student *Nachschrift* from the mid-1770s, very similar to "Ms Kaehler." Rink occasionally but significantly altered these texts for his hurried edition, as Stark also notes (AA 26.1: lxvii).

22 "Anlage" in the relevant sense appears by 1763, in the essay, BDG 2: 126.22–23: "Denn selbst im Baue eines Thieres ist zu vermuthen: daß eine einzige Anlage eine fruchtbare Tauglichkeit zu viel vortheilhaften Folgen haben werde." "Anlage" is also discussed in the Herder metaphysics notes from about the same time (V-Met/Herder 28: 892.2). "Keim" in the relevant sense appears to emerge slightly later. Cf. (1764) VKK 2: 270.34: "der Keim der Krankheit sich unvermerkt entwickelt." Cf. (1771) RezMoscati 2: 425.06: "Keim von Vernunft."

23 Cf. PG 9: 317.23, 318.04.

> If one enquires into the causes of the forms and *Naturell* inherent in a people, then one need only consider the degenerations[24] of animals in relation to their form and behavior, for as soon as they are transported to a different climate, then different air and food, etc., make them to be different from the descendents.[25] ... The Nordic peoples that migrated to Spain not only left behind descendants with bodies that were not nearly as big and strong as they were, but also degenerated into a temperament that is very different from that of a Norwegian or Dane.[26] ... Although a nation will slowly degenerate to accommodate itself to the *Naturell* of the climate to which it has moved, occasionally traces of its previous place of residence can be found for a long while afterward.[27] (Holstein, V-PG 26.1: 96.05–97.07)

In the late 1750s and early 1760s, Kant's geography was known in Königsberg for its views on climate, as two letters from Sebastian Friedrich Trescho (dated 23 January and 5 March 1760) to Ludwig Ernst Borowski attest.[28]

Turning to another theme: Kant writes as if nature were an agent, as if it could have had a part in the formation of objects like stones, though admittedly this may be only a manner of speaking or a largely stylistic use. In The Mineral Kingdom, Kant claims that one often digs up stones that were not shaped by nature but by human beings (Holstein, V-PG 26.1: 192.23–24).[29] In making this contrast, nature is characterized, implicitly at least, as an agent who uses practical intelligence to pursue her own designs. "Ms Holstein" states that nature acts over long periods of preparation: nature works slowly and through the centuries, through a slow "accretion" (*Ansa[t]z*) (Holstein, V-PG 26.1: 195.27).[30]

In short, the lecture does not yet employ the notion of a germ or predisposition; Kant seems to have defended a mostly climatically determined conception of racial difference that preceded his germs-and-predispositions theory. In the early version of his geography course, Kant imputed intention and purpose to natural processes, while at the same time evading explicit natural theology and physico-theology.

---

24 Cf. Kant on "degeneration" with Buffon's complex use of the term. See Mensch 2013; and Sloan 1973. "Buffon" is mentioned already at (1755) NTH 1: 238.16, 277.20, 345.03; and (1757) EACG 2: 8.11, 4.14.
25 Holstein, V-PG 26.1: 96.05–10. Cf. PG 9: 317.22–7.
26 Holstein, V-PG 26.1: 96.12–18. Cf. PG 9: 317.29–33.
27 Holstein, V-PG 26.1: 97.04–07. Cf. PG 9: 318.04–07.
28 Trescho writes (23 January 1760): "Ich glaube auch dass Hr. Kant in einigen Kapiteln der phys. Geographie den Einfluss und das Verhältniss des Klima zu der Gemüths- und Handlungsart der Völker anzeigt." Quoted at AA 26.1: lxii.
29 Cf. PG 9: 374.06–07.
30 Cf. PG 9: 376.01–02.

3 Organisms, animals, and agency in the mid-1770s

I must pass over some key publications from the 1760s. For instance, although the notable pre-Critical essay *Der einzig mögliche Beweisgrund zu einer Demonstration des Daseins Gottes* (1763) examines physico-theological arguments, explores apparent design and agency, and employs the notion of an *Anlage*, there is insufficient space to address it properly here; moreover, my focus is on the lectures and writings more plainly devoted to geography. Even if the popular (1764) *Beobachtungen über das Gefühl des Schönen und Erhabenen* appeals to an intentional plan of nature or providence (*so hat die Vorsehung in uns noch ein gewisses Gefühl gelegt*) (GSE 2: 218.14)[31] and some of the "Ms Holstein" material about human beings is placed into *Beobachtungen*,[32] for the sake of space I must instead focus on more explicitly geographical writings and lectures. The 1765 course announcement, *Nachricht von der Einrichtung [...]*, while noteworthy, contains only two pages on the geography course, though Kant does promise to consider human beings in light of the variety of human natural traits (*nach der Mannigfaltigkeit seiner natürlichen Eigenschaften*) (NEV 2: 312.33–34) and moral characteristics, in order to provide a great map of the human species.

I turn to "Ms Kaehler,"[33] named after Johann Sigismund Kaehler, who writes the year 1775 at the beginning of his manuscript's 530 pages (78,700 words), although the course seems to have taken place during summer semester 1774.[34] This transcription is particularly interesting in that it is the first one that is based on a geography course given *after* Kant began lecturing on anthropology. Indeed, unlike "Ms Holstein," "Ms Kaehler" explicitly refers to the kindred pragmatic discipline, anthropology (Kaehler: 04).[35] Another indication of a consequent change is that in "Ms Kaehler," Europe is not described in Kant's overview of the

---

31 See also GSE 2: 217.28–29.
32 Robert Louden (2011b: 197) asks whether "Ms Holstein" may have been a source of some of the anthropological material in *Beobachtungen*. I think that some of Ms Holstein's claims made it into the *Beobachtungen*, which focuses mostly but not exclusively on European peoples. At the same time, Ms Holstein's discussion of, e.g., the French, Italians, and Spanish is much shorter than the one in *Beobachtungen*, and there are many peoples in Ms Holstein that never make it into *Beobachtungen*.
33 See Malter 1987 for the brief announcement of the discovery of "Ms Kaehler."
34 Adickes did not mention "Ms Kaehler" – which is unsurprising since it was discovered only in the 1980s. Yet Adickes (1911: 32, 182 ff.) reveals that he knew that one of the sources of Rink's edition was material dating around 1775. See also *Ein neu aufgefundenes Kollegheft* (Adickes 1913), on manuscript anonymous-Werner [Ms "W"]. "W" is conjectured to be from around 1774 and, in Stark's typology, is type B_0.
35 Cf. PG 9: 157.03, 157.28. As with the geography transcriptions except for "Ms Holstein" (= AA

continents, whereas in "Ms Holstein," a discussion of Europe comes after Asia and Africa and before America: it examines Bulgaria, Greece, Hungary, Italy, France, Spain, Portugal, Sweden, Norway and the Faroe Islands, and Russia (Holstein, V-PG 26.1: 288.03–299.13).[36] Presumably this change can be attributed to the fact that Kant mentioned nearly all of these countries in the anthropology course, which tended to focus on Europe more than the geography course.

In the contemporaneous course announcement, *Von den verschiedenen Racen der Menschen* (1775), Kant held that there are four fundamental races of human beings: whites (including Moors, Arabs, Turkish-Tatars, and Persians), the Negro race, the Hunish (Mongolian or Kalmuckian) race, and the Hindu or Hindustani race (VvRM 2: 432.05–07).[37] He subscribed to monogeneticism[38]: the four races of human beings originated from a single phylum (*Stamme*) (VvRM 2: 430.30). To explain racial differentiation, Kant maintained that there was an interaction of substantial germs and predispositions with circumstantial causes and environmental influences, as noted in the previous section. Kant distinguished four main types of climate (using the pairs humid/dry and cold/hot) and correlated each of the four human races with one of them. He also made a superficially simple distinction between natural history (*Naturgeschichte*) and natural description (*Naturbeschreibung*) (VvRM 2: 434n), a distinction that was of considerable importance for the history of the life sciences and geography. The essay, at least stylistically, attributes intentions and aims to nature, which is portrayed as if it were as agent.[39] One finds a similar understanding of nature in "Ms Kaehler."

An analysis of "Ms Kaehler" is, moreover, worthwhile since many of the passages examined here do not make it into Rink's *Physische Geographie* and are therefore relatively unknown.

"Ms Kaehler" reveals a developed philosophical awareness in comparison with "Ms Holstein." In the 1770s, after the publication of the "Inaugural Dissertation" (1770), Kant was in the midst of the 'silent decade', as he was formu-

---

26.1), references to "Ms Kaehler" are to the Ms page number, also used in the digitized versions of the aforementioned Kant-Arbeitsstelle.

36 Cf. PG 9: 421.01–427.25.

37 This list changes in the 1777 version (noble blond from northern Europe, copper red from America, black from Senegambia, olive-yellow from Asian India) – a list (white, black, yellow, copper red) retained in anthropology "Reichel" (semester 1793/94, estimated); see Reichel: 146 f. For the dating of the anthropology transcriptions, this chapter follows the editors Brandt and Stark (AA 25.1: xciv).

38 On monogeneticism, see Zammito 2006: 45–8.

39 VvRM 2: 431.32–33: "Natur ungestört ... wirken kann"; 2: 431.28: "weisere Natur"; 2: 436.33–34: "Fürsorge der Natur"; 2: 439.19: "Selbsthülfe der Natur."

lating the Critical philosophy even if not publishing these thoughts, so we might expect the Ms to reveal something resembling Critical reflection. And, indeed, the first three sections reflect the developing Critical philosophy (Kaehler: 01–09).[40] Kant claims that for all of our knowledge, one must first direct attention to its sources or origins (§ 1). He then states that so far as the sources and origins of our knowledge are concerned, we derive it all either from pure reason or from experience, which in turn is instructed by reason, that reason gives us pure rational knowledge, whereas knowledge from experience is attained through our senses; since the senses cannot transcend the world, our knowledge from experience is limited to the present world (§ 2). He adds that we need to become acquainted with the objects of our experience as a whole, so that our knowledge is not an aggregate but a system, where the whole is prior to the parts. The next section begins with the claim that our cognitions originate (*fangen an*) (Kaehler: 07)[41] with the senses, which give us the material while reason merely gives "new forms" (§ 3). Hence, the transcription reflects certain elements of the emerging Critical philosophy.

In "Ms Kaehler," Section II (§ 75), Kant refers to purposive products and distinguishes unorganized creatures from living, organized ones. Kant's use of the distinction between organized and unorganized beings is quite ordinary in many places; for instance, he uses the conventional sense of 'products' to designate what grows in a region (Kaehler: 513 f.). More interestingly, he understands organized beings in terms of purposiveness.

> After we have mentioned the elements from which the earth is composed, it is also appropriate for us to go over its inhabitants and products, and therefore its creatures. Among these, however, we find things in which we can become aware of something purposive as well as things in which this cannot be discovered. Among the former, we find living beings and call these organized, but among the latter, minerals, etc., which we call unorganized creatures. Now because among the living, the rational creatures are the most notable, we will first consider human beings, their bodies, and mental character, for this order is the most convenient for human understanding. (Kaehler: 354)

His claim that "rational creatures" – foremost human beings – are "the most notable" might reflect the emerging Critical ethics, yet Kant does not develop the point.

---

40 Cf. PG 9: 156.01–159.27.
41 Cf. PG 9: 159.02.

Just as Buffon influenced much of Kant's conception of natural history, and is cited in "Ms Kaehler,"[42] Buffon's notion of "varieties" underlies a distinction Kant makes between *race*, which is that subspecies the intermixing of which produces "half-breeds," and *varieties* (within a race) such as blonds and brunettes (Cf. VvRM 2: 430.26).

> Among other living beings, one observes that even if they are different, they nevertheless bring forth such products that can propagate themselves and are exactly like one of the two parents, and these are called *varieties* by Buffon, because the difference of the animals then has no influence on the generative power. (Kaehler: 356)

The text elsewhere speaks of an arrangement according to the maxims of nature (*Maximen der Natur*) (Kaehler: 245) yet does so with no suggestion that this is a merely regulative principle. It states that nature has its own feedback loops whereby it checks itself: since nature does not often create 'harmful' products like the crocodile, the ichneumon or Pharoah's mouse eats crocodile eggs (Kaehler: 412). Nature is depicted as having a kind of agency and a sense that harmful products should be regulated and controlled, but there is no reflection on the ends of nature or of nature as a system.

How did Kant's 1770s lecture handle the notion of divine providence, an issue of obvious political, theological, and philosophical importance in Kant's Königsberg? "Ms Kaehler" does not read the apparent order in the slopes of banks as evidence of divine design, but instead explains the geological formation in naturalistic terms. Such an arrangement is best explained by Dampier's navigational rule that when the land slopes gently, the water is shallow, and when there are steep cliffs the water is deep; it would be seen as foolhardy, it reads, "if we tried to explain this arrangement as the most perfect one" (Kaehler: 60 f.).[43] In *Discours sur l'origine et les fondements de l'inégalité parmi les hommes* (1755), Rousseau, like several other writers, conjectured that humanity's development into its present state required a long period of time, and in similar fashion Kant rejects a literal interpretation of Genesis on the creation of the earth (Kaehler: 201).[44] Nature is described as if it were an agent with intelligence, for it can determine a place to be inhabited or uninhabited, even if humans can overcome this plan and choose to leave an otherwise suitable region. This underlies Kant's distinction

---

[42] Buffon is mentioned at Kaehler: 109, 166, and 356.
[43] "... wenn wir diese Einrichtung für die Vollkommensten erklären wollten."
[44] Cf. PG 9: 267.04–09.

between deserts, which nature rendered unfit for human inhabitation, and isolated regions or wildernesses.

> Some regions, such as those in America near Peru where tribes roam about only rarely and where the American paradise is located, are uninhabited only as a result of the human power of choice, without nature determining them to be uninhabited, and thus are called isolated regions ... Deserts are really places where nature determines and makes it so that human beings cannot live there. (Kaehler: 141)[45]

Shortly after this passage, Kant makes a point that resurfaces in his essays on history, namely, that the human being is made for the whole earth because his body is formed by nature, such that he can become habituated to any climate, which, Kant here adds, is partly the reason for the origin of differences in national character (Kaehler: 145).[46] Nature determines both non-human and human animals (Kaehler: 397 f., 395 f.), even if in different ways. With its long neck and padding, a camel seems to be quite suited for carrying loads (*recht bestimmt zu seyn scheinet*) (Kaehler: 397 f.). Likewise, the rhino has been well equipped (*verliehen*) by nature (Kaehler: 395).

The section "Von dem Nationalcharacter, Sitten und Gebräuchen verschiedener Völker" extends his remarks about mental character and national character[47] in what we might consider a mix of political and cultural geography (Kaehler: 477 ff.). Several of his claims place Kant in an unfavorable light. The Hottentots (today: Khoekhoen), Kant says, are "the most uncouth people in the world [*das unschlachteste Volk in der Welt*]" (Kaehler: 505), a race of Negroes inhabiting a land that nature has well supplied. He uses the existence of the Greenlanders (i.e., Greenlandic Inuit) to distinguish refined and wild conditions (Kaehler: 529). Despite his claim about natural capacities, Kant never explicitly mentions *Naturell*, as if the notion of a germ (*Keim*) were doing most of the work.[48] The Ms states that in certain products (organisms) in general there are germs developing, from a single phylum, according to a region's air and food products (*in gewißen Producten überhaupt solche Keime liegen*) (Kaehler: 401). The example here is the dog, but, as we know, Kant thinks this applies to organic beings in general.

---

45 "... Die Wüsten sind eigentlich Oerter, welche von der Natur dazu bestimmt und eingerichtet sind, daß die Menschen nicht darauf wohnen können." Cf. PG 9: 234.23–33. This passage is significantly different in the Rink edition, which says that nature only *appears* to determine and arrange. PG 9: 234.32–33: "Wüsten sind eigentlich Örter, die von der Natur dazu bestimmt und eingerichtet zu sein scheinen, daß die Menschen nicht darin wohnen können."
46 Cf. PG 9: 236.25–28.
47 On these see Munzel 1999; Louden 2011b; and Kleingeld 2012: 117–23.
48 Ms Kaehler also lacks any mention of *Anlage* or *Prädisposition*.

I conclude this section by citing an example of a passage that forms part of the empirical background of the Critique of the Teleological Power of Judgment,[49] for his physical geography is the source of many of the empirical claims found there.[50] Nature, "Ms Kaehler" reads, provides the Greenlandic Inuit their wood, which they put to good use (*Ihr Holtz, welches sie aus dem Waßer bekommen*) (Kaehler: 530).[51] Although "Ms Kaehler" shows that the geography is the source of some of the empirical claims scrutinized in the Critique of the Teleological Power of Judgment, it contains no sustained analysis of them.

4 Manuscript Dönhoff

Although "Ms Dönhoff," which dates from 1781 or 1782 and hence belongs to the official Critical period, contains no references to *Bestimmung*, *Anlage*, or *Prädisposition*, it does make use of the concepts of natural aptitude (*Naturell*) (Dönhoff: 94') and germ (*Keim*) (Dönhoff: 85–91'), providence (*Vorsehung*) (Dönhoff: 86, 127'), and purpose (*Zwek*) (Dönhoff: 79–79', 93). It again asserts Kant's view that nature unites all its purposes in the human being (Dönhoff: 79'). It continues to characterize human and non-human animals in terms of teleological and purposive[52] notions.

A noteworthy passage on the origin of human beings reveals sensitivity to the limits of reason. Its suggestion that one has warrant to assume a postulated notion after, or if, one has established its possibility, seems to be written in a Critical vein:

> It can first be asked whether the human race was conceived at the very beginning under a single title and whether all humans are of one species, or whether it contains different humans that could not have originated from one phylum, but instead must have had various phyla? Reason cannot determine if they have really all emerged from a single phylum; it

---

49 There are many examples, such as: KU 5: 377.31–378.11.
50 While my interest in this chapter goes in the inverse direction and focuses mainly on the lectures, the Critical works in practical and theoretical philosophy undoubtedly employ concepts and metaphors taken from the geography lectures (e.g, *Keime*, *Anlage*). On the significance of the metaphors, see, e. g., Eigen and Larrimore 2006. On Kant's organic concepts in theoretical philosophy, see (*passim*) Mensch 2013; Zammito 1992: 207; and Sloan 2002. On organic concepts in the Critical ethics, see Mikkelsen 2013: 20–21. On geographic notions and the Critical philosophy, see Malpas and Thiel 2011.
51 Cf. KU 5: 369.11–12: "dem Holze, welches ihnen das Meer zu Wohnungen gleichsam hinflößt."
52 Mikkelsen (2013: 21, 27) rightly discerns, in Kant's theory, a connection between natural purposiveness and black skin color as a purposive adaptation of nature.

can only ask about its possibility, and if the latter becomes apparent, then it already has a reason to assume it. (Dönhoff: 79')

Kant would express similar views on the matter in the 1785 and 1788 essays on race (next section). In its Prolegomena, "Ms Dönhoff" distinguishes "geographic description" from a "system of nature":

> This is either a system of nature, where the things are ordered according to concepts, and constitutes the first part, or is a geographic description. Here we distinguish between worldly and scholastic cognitions, where only proper order is followed. Moreover, whoever aims for worldly cognitions, attempts to use his popular cognitions for all purposes. We distinguish ourselves from natural investigators in that we seek what is noteworthy with the curiosity of a voyager and for each thing assign the place where nature put it, but in fact many natural investigators definitely put many unnatural connections into their system. (Dönhoff: 2')

This distinction between *worldly* cognition, to which anthropology and geography belong, and *scholastic* knowledge, will help explain (see Conclusion) why Kant does not offer much philosophical reflection on teleology in these popular lectures, but employs teleological principles directly or 'naively' (by which I only mean that he applied them without the Critical strictures about their purely regulative character).

The second Part of the course, which concerns the animal kingdom, opens with a noteworthy passage that shows what conception of organisms Kant employed circa 1782.

> If we now go over the three kingdoms of the earth, then the mineral kingdom should perhaps be the first, for the natural creatures from the mineral kingdom are of the simplest structure and at least one sees no inner ends in them. With every single plant, one part is for the sake of the other, and, to an extent, it is even there through the other. The stalk cannot grow without the root, and without the stalk the root cannot exist. It is also like this with human beings. Without the stomach, the hand cannot be, and it is also there because of it. One can cut off somebody's hand without making the human being die, the cause of which is that nature has a means of helping itself and compensating for what was taken from it, so that when one takes something away, nevertheless other [parts] nearby are still there, through which the blood can circulate. But a piece of stone is not there for another piece. (Dönhoff: 79)

Kant then proceeds to lecture on the animal (rather than mineral) kingdom since the former includes what he had called the first[53] purpose of nature (*ersten Zwek der*

---

[53] Recall that "Ms Holstein" contains no reference to a purpose (*Zwek*), let alone to a first purpose.

Natur) (Dönhoff: 19), the human being – perhaps further revealing the influence of the ethics on the geography. Kant here considers organic life to be an object of empirical knowledge and observation; he views the being as a natural product with "inner ends." However, he gives no hint that making such an assertion about purposes consists in applying a 'regulative' principle of reason, to use the *KrV* language that was available to him at this time (A685–8/B712–16).[54] Largely in agreement with my interpretation, Reinhard Brandt comments on this passage that the Critical "restriction" that such claims about organic life would be only for the "reflective power of judgment" is still absent (Brandt 2010: 163).[55] In a similar passage from the "Danziger Physik" (also called "Mrongovius") from 1785, a year before the publication of *Metaphysische Anfangsgründe der Naturwissenschaft*, Kant claims that organic powers of nature are quite different from mechanical and chemical ones, yet he adds the reflective comment that the human being lacks insight into the principle of organic modification of matter (29.1,1: 118.10–11).

When it comes to matters of physico-theology, the 1782 transcription defends a naturalistic archeology and paleontology (cf. KU 5: 419.09, 428n; Anth 7: 193.24, 323n). It claims that there are two ways to propose and defend a theory of the earth, to determine the present form of the earth and the changes it has undergone. The first is the method of the "archive" or "archeology of nature" (*Archiologie Naturalis*) according to which one draws conclusions about earlier causes by looking at the visible effects on or in the earth. Secondly, there is "sacred archeology," whereby one consults religious scriptures. It states that this is not useful since such history goes only as far back as writing (Dönhoff: 67'). "Ms Dönhoff" holds that the creation of the earth took place according to natural laws. It notes that though the religious writings describe the process as one day's work, the current form of the mountains and streams suggests that they developed over long periods. Even the biblical commentators, "Ms Dönhoff" continues, see that these expressions aim only to describe the divine's work, not to make a claim about nature's development. The physicist or natural philosopher must examine natural forces, to see how the earth gradually was formed (Dönhoff: 68). An archeology of nature brings out evidence from the past of human history and is aimed at the history of the earth and its products – animals, plants, and minerals. For this reason, Werner Stark claims that the theory of the earth (*Theorie der Erde*)

---

54 See Wood 1999: 216 f.
55 Although, as scholars have noted, there is an important difference between the *KrV*'s "regulative/constitutive" distinction and the *KU*'s "reflective/determinant" distinction, I cannot take this into consideration here.

(EACG 2: 8.21) that Kant proposed in his 1757 lecture announcement was eventually replaced by 'geology' (Stark 2009: 109).

In short, while supporting a naturalistic archeology, "Ms Dönhoff" makes no explicit mention of the (by then published) *Critique of Pure Reason*'s distinction between regulative and constitutive principles, yet it does insist that human reason is limited, namely, that it does not have insight into whether organisms (humans) emerged from a single phylum – a question Kant would take up about six years later in a controversy with Georg Forster, as we shall see.

5 The 1790s: Ms Dohna, Anonymous-Starke 4, Ms 1729

Like the transcriptions in anthropology, logic, and metaphysics bearing the name, the anonymous geography manuscript "Dohna" belonged to the family of Heinrich Ludwig Adolph Graf zu Dohna-Wundlacken (1777–1834).[56] The anthropology, logic, metaphysics, and geography "Dohna" transcriptions were each written by at least three different, unidentified hands. "Ms Dohna" is relevant to our theme because it was based on a course given about two years after the publication of *KU*. The transcription emphasizes the notions of organism and reproduction, especially in the section On Human Beings, which concerns the cultural, biological, and physical aspects of human beings (Dohna: 98–118).

Between the years in which he taught the courses underlying "Ms Dönhoff" and "Ms Dohna," Kant published several key essays, including *Idee zu einer allgemeinen Geschichte in weltbürgerlicher Absicht* (1784). In its Fourth Proposition, Kant identified "unsociable sociability [*ungesellige Geselligkeit*]" (IaG 8: 20.30) as one of the features of humanity which *nature* used to scatter humans around the globe and populate the earth, a point he also made throughout his anthropology lectures.[57] The Introduction to the Cambridge Edition's translation states, plausibly, that the 1784 essay "anticipates much of the theory of the use of *natural teleology* in the theoretical understanding of nature that Kant was to develop over five years later in the *Critique of the Power of Judgment*" (Kant 2007: 107; emphasis added).

---

[56] Adickes did not mention Dohna. The pages of the Ms indicate the beginning and closing dates of 28 April and 22 September 1792. Kowalewski's "Aus Kants Vorlesungen über physische Geographie nach einem ungedruckten Kollegheft vom Sommersemester 1792" contains eight printed pages from "Ms Dohna" (Kowalewski and Kowalewski 1925: 94–101).

[57] E. g., V-Anth/Fried 25: 586.32; V-Anth/Pillau 25: 844.26; V-Anth/Mensch 25: 1199.18–19; V-Anth/Mron 25: 1416.17–23, 1422.06–19.

Kant also published the second (1785) and third installments (1788) of his trilogy on teleology and race. In *Bestimmung des Begriffs einer Menschenrace*, Kant's principal aim is to determine the concept of race, which he describes as follows: the classificatory difference of the animals of one and the same phylum insofar as this difference is unfailingly hereditary (BBM 8: 100.07–09). The key point is that there is only one common phylum for the four races or subspecies, and that over generations the original germs of the subspecies develop according to the demands of their climates. After one of these predispositions (*Anlagen*) developed in a people, the other predispositions were extinguished (BBM 8: 105.27–28). Although the essay's references to natural agency need not be taken literally, Kant continues to speak of nature as agent – "nature's foresight"[58] (BBM 8: 93.25), "nature has originally given"[59] (BBM 8: 98.27–29), "nature must have organized this skin"[60] (BBM 8: 103.11–12), "an arrangement very wisely made by Nature"[61] (BBM 8: 103.19) – while offering little to no philosophical reflection on such claims. He does, however, warn against assuming different first human phyla as "poor advice for philosophy"[62] (BBM 8: 102.08). He says there is little comfort for philosophy in artificially constructing hypotheses (BBM 8: 104.30–31)[63] and he concludes that it is impossible to guess (*unmöglich zu errathen*) the shape of the original first human phylum (BBM 8: 106.03).

Kant was called, as he himself paraphrased it in *Über den Gebrauch teleologischer Principien in der Philosophie* (1788), a naturalist "of his own kind [*eigner Art*]" (ÜGTP 8: 178.17–18), i. e., a natural philosopher who used teleological rather than theological terms. In the 1788 essay, Kant endorsed the principle (*Grundsatz*) that "everything in natural science must be explained naturally"[64] (ÜGTP 8: 178.12–13). A characterization of Kant as a naturalist is found in Büsching's review of the 1785 essay. Göttingen professor Anton Friedrich Büsching (1724–93) was author of the eleven-volume geographical work, *Neue Erdbeschreibung* (1754), which appeared just two years before Kant's first geography lectures. Kant's (almost exact) contemporary used geography to draw physico-theological conclusions and support the idea of providence, but Kant did not adopt this strategy.

Über den Gebrauch teleologischer Principien in der Philosophie further develops Kant's racial theory, and its introductory and concluding sections operate on "a

---

58 "Vorsorge der Natur."
59 "Die Natur hat ... ursprünglich ... gegeben."
60 "die Natur diese Haut so organisirt haben müsse, daß ...."
61 "eine von der Natur sehr weislich getroffene Anstalt."
62 "der Philosophie wenig gerathen sein ...."
63 "Doch es ist wenig Trost für die Philosophie in Erkünstelung von Hypothesen."
64 "alles in einer Naturwissenschaft natürlich müsse erklärt werden."

much higher level of generality" (Zammito 1992: 208) than the previous essays on race and provide a level of philosophical sophistication arguably not found there. Kant replies to criticisms put forward by Georg Forster (1754–1794). Kant not only clarifies various misunderstandings allegedly made by Forster, but, more importantly, defends an account that takes up certain themes later found in the Critique of the Teleological Power of Judgment,[65] even if his view differs from that of 1790. Kant early on hints that he will discuss to what extent and how we are warranted in using the teleological principle where sources of theoretical cognition are not sufficient[66] (ÜGTP 8: 160.20–22). Later, he defends the idea that the concept of purposiveness should play a role in natural science, even if empirically conditioned. He offers a definition of 'organized being' as matter in which everything is mutually related to each other as end and means, and insists that as far as human reason is concerned, the possibility of an organized being leaves only the teleological mode of explanation:

> Since the concept of an organized being already includes that it is some matter in which everything is mutually related to each other as end and means, which can only be thought as a system of final causes, and since therefore their possibility only leaves the teleological but not the physical-mechanical mode of explanation, at least as far as human reason is concerned, there can be no investigation in physics about the origin of all organization itself. (ÜGTP 8: 179.08–15)

He declares that no one can know a priori that there must be ends in nature (ÜGTP 8: 182.17), so this is not yet the position regarding purposiveness he would adopt in *KU*. Still, whatever his notions were at this stage, one might whether, or to what extent, some of these ideas surfaced in the geography lectures given from the 1780s on.

In any case, "Ms Dohna" comes from a course given circa 1792, hence *after* both the 1788 essay and the first edition of *KU* (1790). What do we find? Although "Ms Dohna" contains no references to *Keim*, *Anlage*, or *Prädisposition*, I see little reason to think Kant gave up on these notions or that of some internal 'factor' or

---

[65] I agree with the Editor's Introduction that in the 1788 essay Kant defends the need and justification for introducing and applying a "principle of purposiveness in the investigation of nature in general and in that of living beings in particular" (see Kant 2007: 193). See also Mikkelsen (2013: 27), who claims that in the 1788 article the development of skin color serves as the primary example of *purposiveness*. Finally, Zammito (1992: 209) claims that the essay argued that it was impossible to conceive of organisms and the process of generation and variation in heredity except in terms of purposiveness.

[66] "... noch nicht genug ins Licht gestellten Befugniß, sich, wo theoretische Erkenntnißquellen nicht zulangen, des teleologischen Princips bedienen zu dürfen ...."

'structure'. "Ms Dohna" speaks of the natural aptitude (*Naturell*) of the Southeast Asian Indian race (Dohna: 106). Kant quotes without criticism Hume's troubling characterization of blacks, employing the notion of a *Naturell* in the section, On Human Beings. On the natural aptitude of blacks, Kant says we should attend to Hume's remark (Dohna: 105).[67] Again, I shall not here enter into the important debate about Kant's race theory; the point here is that Kant's claim that the different races have unique traits that express the purposes of nature reveals his own brand of teleology, the epistemic status of which he never discusses in the course when he could have, post-1790.

"Ms Dohna" attributes purposes to nature, which is characterized as an agent, desiring to preserve diversity among the world's peoples (Dohna: 107f.). It then gives the example of a man who lost his large, deformed nose, had it replaced by a more symmetrical, artificial one, only to realize that the first, natural one looked better – an account Kant told repeatedly (Dohna: 108).[68] Kant thought that one could not improve on nature viewed as a whole, that is, if one allowed the diversity of nature's forms to shine through. Even if the individual nose looks asymmetrical in the singular case, it plays a role in the whole by counter-balancing the sizes and shapes of other human noses. These apparently disparate topics – race and facial figures – both illustrate that nature aims for and even requires diversity of external figures and of characters.[69]

There are more examples. "Ms Dohna" reads that nature has the most to do with the formation (*Ausbildung*) (Dohna: 111) of those human beings whom it placed in the marshes. Unlike the Holstein, Kaehler, and Dönhoff, Ms Dohna employs a structural distinction between a Doctrine of Elements and a Doctrine of Method, but the sense differs from the one in the *Critiques* (and without the preceding word, "Transcendental"). The geography lecture's *Elementarlehre* gives descriptions of the earth's surfaces (seas, mountains, winds), while the *Methodenlehre* contains empirical observations about organized natural products, organisms, and animals, above all, human beings. Nature, it is reported, made the Greenlanders the most skilled and cultured among those nations toward which nature was 'step-motherly'. As evidence for this claim, Kant describes

---

[67] Kant had made a similar remark in (1764) *Beobachtungen* at GSE 2: 253.02–10. For Kant's source, see David Hume's essay "Of National Characters" (Hume 1985: 208 n. 10). For the debate about Kant's intentions and considered views, see Kleingeld 2007; Louden 2011a: 153; Bernasconi 2011: 306f., and Stark 2011b: 93ff.
[68] For Kant's story, cf. V-Anth/Fried 25: 555.24–28, 25: 666.08–19; and V-Anth/Mron 25: 1378.30–35.
[69] Cf. the face/race analogy when discussing diversity at ÜGTP 8: 166.14–21. On diversity, see Kleingeld 2012: 120–3.

how the Inuit put attractive, white, whalebone buttons on their sealskin clothing (Dohna: 93).

Kant continues to appeal to his racial theory and concept of half-breeds (mixed sub-species or races), which he applies to non-human and humans animals alike.

> If we wish to divide the products logically, we divide them into species and kinds; if physically, then into species and races. There one could divide the animal kingdom into birds and mammals. There are different races among human beings. A difference in species would be [e. g.] the one between human beings and apes. Physically, we could derive species from one general phylum; e. g., poodles and greyhounds, etc., etc., reproduce with all other dogs. The word *race* designates only a subspecies, not phyletic difference. The concept of race applies to the plant kingdom and animal kingdom, but not at all to the mineral kingdom, for here there is no generation whatsoever. The wolf and the dog are thus probably from a single race because they copulate, and all of our current apple species thus perhaps descend from the little tree. (Dohna: 99)

Unlike a logical description or taxonomy into genus and species, modelled on Linnaeus's *systema naturae*, a natural history describes the generation and reproduction of living organisms, using the notions of species and races (Dohna: 2).

Like earlier transcriptions, "Ms Dohna" distinguishes between unorganized and organized products of nature (Dohna: 98). But "Ms Dohna" offers no philosophical analysis of its application of teleological notions and no conscious application of *KU*'s distinction between a regulative principle for reflecting power of judgment and a constitutive principle for determining teleological judgment.[70]

I now mention two texts based on courses given after 1790, since they could also appeal to the Critical or *KU* understanding of teleological concepts. "Starke" (Bergk) gives the 6,400-word geography excerpt (from the lost Ms "Anonymous-Starke 4," which belongs to Group D) the heading *Betrachtungen über die Erde und den Menschen*. Starke thus offers considerations on the earth and human beings, probably reflecting either his own interests or Kant's increased attentiveness to human beings. The reference to *Menschen* is noteworthy since the notes were composed around 1791, about two decades after Kant started offering a university course on anthropology. In a footnote, Starke claims that he is excerpting only what he considers to be of general interest (*allgemeinem Interesse*) (Starke 1833: 262'). Starke concludes his excerpt with a paragraph that is reminiscent of the anthropology lectures typical conclusion: a reflection on humanity's propensity

---

[70] See, e. g., First Introduction, EEKU 20: 251; and KU 5: 197.07, 361.01–06, 379.10–20, 416.24–27.

toward evil, inclination for war, three basic predispositions (animality, humanity, and personality), and vocation (Starke 1833: 283).

Betrachtungen makes use of the concepts of species and race rather than the taxonomical or logical terms, genus and species. A section on human beings begins with this passage which reflects the *KU* understanding of organisms in terms of reproduction (KU 5: 371.07–12) as well as individual growth (*Wachsthum*) (KU 5: 371.13–29) and regeneration.

> Descent can occur through generation or propagation of its kind, and one calls this organic generation. Organized beings distinguish themselves by growth internally, but minerals only grow externally by adding something to themselves. By contrast, animals grow according to all sides and in all parts. Growth and the reproduction of its kind is the mark of organized beings, which one can divide into species and races. There are no different human kinds; for otherwise they could not have one phylum. Under species of beings can again be distinguished races or subspecies and racial strains. Degeneration would be a diversity of kinds where the germ in the phylum is not to be found. (Starke 1833: 275 f.)

This noteworthy passage overlaps nicely with the *KU* conception of organisms, but – after we find and examine it – we see that it is not and does not pretend to be a discussion of its biological terminology or the epistemic status of its claims, even though a discussion of possible transcendental-philosophical justification of such terminology or claims would have been possible at this point.

Betrachtungen speaks of nature as an agent that gives and withholds certain capacities to peoples. Relying on the work of Peter Simon Pallas, it cites the Mongolians' lack of beards by nature (*von der Natur*) (Starke 1833: 279).

Finally, the 1,700-word, fragmentary text surviving from "Ms 1729,"[71] whose composition dates from the summer of 1791 or 1792, contains none of the familiar concepts connected with Kant's teleology – e. g., organization, inner ends, natural aptitude, providence, natural design, the whole or system of nature – nor any philosophically oriented reflection on them. This is surely due to its brevity.[72]

---

[71] "Ms 1729," also called "anonymous-Königsberg 3," was from Staats- und Universitätsbibliothek zu Königsberg. Adickes (1911: 4) refers to "Ms 1729" as "S." It was originally 183 pages.

[72] Similarly, the remnants of the now lost "Ms Vigilantius," based on a summer 1793 course, are too brief to warrant discussion here; yet there is a section on the purposiveness (*Zweckmäßigkeit*) of mountains. Before WWII, "Ms Vigilantius" was apparently held at the Staats- und Universitätsbibliothek zu Königsberg. Adickes (1911: 4, 276 ff.) referred to it as "T." Excerpts appear in later publications, e. g., Kant 2000a and Glasenapp 1954.

6 Conclusion

A close examination of core teleological concepts – organisms and animals, design and nature's agency – found in Mss "Holstein," "Kaehler," "Doenhoff," and "Dohna" has revealed that Kant developed a largely climatically based theory of racial differentiation before he developed a mostly hereditary ("germs-and-endowments") one. Shedding light on Kant's conception of natural science, the passages examined show, moreover, that throughout the span of his geography course he continued to attribute agency to nature without, however, seeing nature as a product of divine design. Finally, I have also established that there is little trace of those regulative / constitutive distinctions (or related notions) presented in *KrV* and, in modified form, in *KU*: neither *after* the publication of these works, nor during the so-called silent decade. On the basis of the transcriptions that are now available to us, we can infer from these last two points that the empirical physical geography lectures and works of Critical philosophy had distinct aims and that Kant's goals in the two fields were different. Kant's pedagogical theory distinguished between his technically philosophical courses (in which he introduced discriminations from the Critical philosophy) and a pragmatic, worldly curriculum that included the courses on physical geography and anthropology.

Nonetheless, this result opens up the opportunity to explore more questions, such as to what extent empirical content is actually kept apart and distinct from the transcendental reflections and analyses informed by the Critical philosophy, as Kant arguably wanted it, and what assumptions[73] about what counts as 'empirical' or 'transcendental' enable Kant's philosophical strategy.[74] Kant did not remove all empirical or scientific "facts" (or assertions) from *KU*; he refers to data that he had presented in his geography courses. He cites claims about organisms, animals, humans, etc., in order to explain how we should think of such statements, how such teleological claims could be possible a priori. More importantly, the Critical philosophy makes use of concepts taken from his geography course, and we can better understand Kant's ethical-political, historical, religious, aesthetic, and theoretical writings by paying closer attention to these

---

[73] E. g., for questions concerning the "blatant disjunction" between transcendental philosophy and anthropology (in connection with race), see Zammito 2006: 39.

[74] Mensch (2013) draws attention to the "organicism" at work in Kant's publications and letters from the 1770s, just as the Critical philosophy was emerging. Mensch holds that Kant did *not* intend to 'naturalize' his account of reason, and she suggests that some commentators have not paid sufficient attention to the difference between empirical/natural and transcendental considerations.

notions and metaphors.[75] In contrast – to go in the inverse direction as I have done – the Critical philosophy did not leave a very heavy mark on Kant's lectures in the empirical discipline of geography, which employed teleological principles without the mature Kantian strictures about teleology – although this should not be taken to mean that he thought that the teleological judging of organisms is incompatible with judging them mechanistically[76] (KU 5: 379.16).

One could thus also ask why the Critical philosophy did not leave a more conspicuous print on the physical geography lectures. As a step toward answering this question, in addition to my more principled, theoretical point about the distinct aims of scholastic and worldly philosophy, here are two more reasons. First, Kant's lectures were already firmly established and, as any university instructor knows, it takes a considerable effort to revise a course, assuming that one has permission to do so. And even if it were possible, it may have been pedagogically imprudent to adjust the geography course's contents and claims to reflect the Critical writings.

Second, the lectures were delivered orally: even in the current, post-Darwinian world, scientists who know better speak and write as if nature were in control, guiding evolutionary processes. From this perspective, it is not surprising that the student transcriptions (even if not verbatim recordings) and the writings here examined read as if nature were a designing agent. Indeed, according to developmental psychologists Kelemen (1999) and Piaget (1929), children tend to think teleologically and although informed adults outgrow their belief in teleological explanations, sometimes they speak and write, as Kant probably did, as if the behaviors of non-human animals were intentional and purposeful, as these "agents" exercise their natural, biological functions in interactions with their environments. Indeed, even in a *logic* lecture (the "Vienna" logic), Kant is recorded to have said that providence 'placed' in us the drive to test our judgments on the reason of others, and had 'arranged' it that way (V-Lo/Wiener 24: 874). Kant was after all speaking to students, and in addition to having pedagogical aims, he may have been speaking loosely.

But it is more surprising that, after 1790, this continued to be the case. It is indeed worthy of note – after thoroughly examining the texts rather than remaining content with one's best educated guess (which could after all be wrong) – that Kant's geography employs teleological principles 'naively', not simply in the years Kant was formulating his central philosophical arguments concerning nature and

---

[75] Of four compelling reasons to study Kant's geography lectures, Louden defends this one first. See the previous chapter.
[76] "... doch unbeschadet dem des Mechanisms ihrer Causalität zu erweitern."

his philosophy of nature, but after 1790 as well. Perhaps more than the geography lecture, the *anthropology* course – likewise a pragmatic, worldly lecture sharing the goal of educating students for world-citizenship (Anth 7: 120.05) – reveals the influence of the Critical works, including *KU*.[77] The anthropology course covers ethical-political and religious issues concerning character, disposition, passions, evil, and forms of government; aesthetic topics involving beauty, taste, and imagination; and subjects relevant to theoretical philosophy such as sensibility, perception, and illusion; despite this intersection, even the post-1790 anthropology lecture notes – "Dohna-Wundlacken,"[78] "Matuszewski,"[79] and "Reichel"[80] – typically attribute agency to nature and providence without the mature strictures. By contrast, the student transcriptions on *metaphysics*[81] and *logic*[82] reveal that in the lectures in those disciplines he would refer to his Critical philosophy or its key tenets. Moreover, the metaphysics lecture notes discuss, typically on a more philosophically nuanced level, several of the teleological concepts and principles we have examined.[83]

---

[77] Cf. Anth 7: 246.17 and 331.27 (both quoted in footnote 2). / See also Anthropology Dohna-Wundlacken (from semester 1791/92), Ms. page 125: "Das Schöne* ist der Grund der Lust und Unlust durch die Reflection, (Geschmak). [*Footnote:] Es gefällt nur in der puren reflektirten Anschauung." / A nearly identical statement is found at (1791/92) anthropology Ms "Matuszewski": 271. / See also the discussions of "Reflexion" and "Geschmack" at anthropology Reichel: 72 f., 81.
[78] E. g., anthropology "Dohna-Wundlacken," Ms. page 246: "Die Natur, die immer den sichersten Weg wählt, zu ihrem Zwecke zu gelangen, hat Leidenschaften in uns gelegt." / Page 293: "Doch hat die Vorsicht etwas in die Züge der Menschen gelegt." / Page 317 even offers a maxim: "Alles was in der Natur liegt, ist gut indem es seinen gehörigen Zwek hat." / These three anthropology transcriptions are available at: http://www.online.uni-marburg.de/kant_old/webseitn/gt_ho304.htm#variant2. Accessed 12 December 2014.
[79] "Ms Matuszewski" is from semester 1791/92, the same semester as "Dohna-Wundlacken" (yet both contain some passages that overlap with notes from semester 1772/73). Ms page 297: "Die Vorsehung hat daher sehr weise gesorgt, daß wir ...." / Page 319: "Die Natur hat uns Triebe zur Fortpflanzung unseres Geschlechts ... gegeben." / Page 377: "Die Kunst macht die Keime, die die Natur in die Dinge gelegt hat, erst sichtbar." / Page 404: "Die Vorsicht hat ihn so eingerichtet, daß er ohne andere nicht sein kann." / Page 407: "aus weiser Absicht der Vorsehung."
[80] "Reichel," Ms. page 101: "Die Natur hatt freylich Anlagen zu Affecten geschaffen." / Page 13: "Eine gewisse Eitelkeit ist uns schon von der Natur eingelegt." / Page 131: "Da die Natur in den weiblichen Schooß die Erhaltung ihrer Art gelegt hatt [sic]."
[81] For 'constitutive' as opposed to 'regulative' principles, see V-Met/Mron 29: 859.32–33, 861.12–15. On 'transcendental' or 'Critical' philosophy or method, see, e. g., V-Met/Mron 29: 752.14–19, 779.24–34, and 928.34–38. "Transcendental idealism" occurs at V-Met/Dohna 28: 682.10–11.
[82] On 'transcendental' philosophy and concepts, see, e. g., V-Lo/Blomberg 24: 262.03; V-Lo/Dohna 24: 753.13; V-Lo/Wiener 24: 833.33. On 'constitutive' and 'regulative', see Log 9: 92.25–27. On Critical philosophy, see Log 9: 32.22 and 84.14–18.
[83] For Kant's assessment of an argument for immortality based on the finality of organisms and

Accordingly, operating within an empirically-realist framework, the geography lectures give indication of the development, or existence, of the Critical philosophy only in a limited way. The course had pragmatic goals that included being appealing to beginning students as a propaedeutic to future learning, even life. In an instance of pedagogical judiciousness, Kant may have considered it too difficult, or inappropriate, to introduce geography students to the core doctrines of the Critical philosophy. In conclusion, the foregoing characterization of 'natural teleology' in the physical geography, in addition to giving an account of core biological and teleological notions, can help us appreciate Kant's conception of a natural science, pedagogical practice and aims, and his actual application of the distinction between transcendental philosophy and empirical disciplines.

---

teleological principles of nature, see, e. g., V-Meta/Volckmann 28: 442.6–31 and V-Met-K2/Heinze 28: 765.26–766.12; for discussion, see also Corey Dyck's chapter in this volume. For reflective comments on providence and finality, see V-Met-L2/Pölitz 28: 574.6–30. On the systems of preformation and epigenesis, see, e. g., V-Met/Dohna 28: 684.3–30; V-Met-K2/Heinze 28: 760.12–23 (the discussion continues through 761.31); V-Met/Arnoldt 29: 1031.9–33 (full discussion ends at 1032.26).

References

Abegg, Johann Friedrich ([1976] 1977) *Reisetagebuch von 1798*, ed. Jolanda Abegg et al. 2nd edn. Frankfurt am Main: Insel Verlag.
Achenwall, Gottfried (1763) *Jus naturae*. 5th edn. Göttingen: Bossiegel.
Achenwall, Gottfried, and Johann Stephan Pütter (1750) *Elementa juris naturae*. Göttingen: Johann Wilhelm Schmidt.
— (1995) Jan Schröder, trans. *Anfangsgründe des Naturrechts*. Frankfurt am Main: Insel.
Addison, Joseph (1961) Scott Elledge, ed. *Eighteenth-Century Critical Essays*. Vol. 1. Ithaca: Cornell Univ. Press.
Adickes, Erich (1896). *German Kantian Bibliography*. Boston: Ginn & Company.
— (1911) *Untersuchungen zu Kants physischer Geographie*. Tübingen: J. C. B. Mohr (Paul Siebeck).
— (1913) *Ein neu aufgefundenes Kollegheft nach Kants Vorlesungen über physische Geographie*. Tübingen: J. C. B. Mohr.
— (1924–25) *Kant als Naturforscher*. 2 vols. Berlin: De Gruyter.
Aertsen, Jan A. (2000) "Transcendens – Transcendentalis: The Geneology of a Philosophical Term." In Jacqueline Hamesse and Carlos Steel, eds. *L'Élaboration du Vocabulaire Philosophique au Moyen Âge*. Turnhout: Brepols, 241–55.
Albrecht, Michael (1982) "Kants Kritik der historischen Erkenntnis – ein Bekenntnis zu Wolff?" *Studia Leibnitiana* 14, 1–24.
Allison, Henry E. (1990) *Kant's Theory of Freedom*. Cambridge: Cambridge Univ. Press.
— (2001) *Kant's Theory of Taste: A Reading of the* Critique of Aesthetic Judgment. Cambridge: Cambridge Univ. Press.
Ameriks, Karl (1992) "The Critique of Metaphysics: Kant and Traditional Ontology." In Paul Guyer, ed. *The Cambridge Companion to Kant*. Cambridge: Cambridge Univ. Press, 249–79.
— (2000a) *Kant and the Fate of Autonomy: Problems in the Appropriation of the Critical Philosophy*. Cambridge: Cambridge Univ. Press.
— (2000b) *Kant's Theory of Mind: An Analysis of the Paralogisms of Pure Reason*. 2nd ed. New York: Oxford Univ. Press.
Anonymous (1779) Review of Michael Hißmann, *Anleitung zur Kenntnis der auserlesensten Literatur in allen Theilen der Philosophie* [Göttingen, 1778], *Allgemeine Deutsche Bibliothek* 38, 243–52.
Archimède (1970a) *De la sphère et du cylindre*, in *Archimède*, vol. I, prepared and trans. Charles Mugler. Paris: Les Belles Lettres, 8–131.
— (1970b) *La mesure du cercle*, in *Archimède*, vol. I, prepared and trans. Charles Mugler. Paris: Les Belles Lettres, 138–43.
Archimedes (1953a) *On The Sphere and Cylinder*, Books I, II. In *The Works*, ed. T. L. Heath, with a Supplement, *The Method of Archimedes*. New York: Dover, 1–90.
— (1953b) *Measurement of a Circle*, Books I, II. In *The Works*, ed. T. L. Heath, with a Supplement, *The Method of Archimedes*. New York: Dover, 91–8.
Aristotle (1926) J. H. Freese, trans. *Aristotle, The Art of Rhetoric*. Cambridge, MA: Loeb.

Arnoldt, Emil (1908–09) *Kritische Exkurse im Gebiete der Kant-Forschung*. 2 parts. Reprinted as vol. 4 (1908) and vol. 5 (1909) in Emil Arnoldt, *Gesammelte Schriften*, ed. Otto Schöndörffer. 10 vols. Berlin: Bruno Cassirer, 1906–11.
Augustine (1997) Maria Boulding, trans. *The Confessions*. New York: Vintage.
Aurelius Augustinus (2006) *Suche nach dem wahren Leben. Confessiones X / Bekenntnisse 10*, ed. Norbert Fischer. Hamburg: Meiner.
Baron, Marcia (2002) "Love and Respect in the Doctrine of Virtue." In Mark Timmons, ed. *Kant's 'Metaphysics of Morals': Interpretative Essays*. Oxford: Oxford Univ. Press, 391–407.
Basedow, Johann Bernhard (1965) *Ausgewählte pädagogische Schriften*, ed. A. Reble. Paderborn: Schöningh.
Baum, Manfred (1990) "Herder's Essay on Being." In Kurt Mueller-Vollmer, ed. *Herder Today*. Berlin and New York: De Gruyter, 126–37.
— (2012) "Kants Replik auf Reinhold." In Violetta Stolz, Marion Heinz, and Martin Bondeli, eds. *Wille, Willkür, Freiheit. Reinholds Freiheitskonzeption im Kontext der Philosophie des 18. Jahrhunderts*. Berlin and Boston: De Gruyter, 153–63.
Baumgarten, Alexander Gottlieb (1740) *Ethica philosophica*. Halle: Hemmerde. [3rd edn. 1763].
— (1757) *Metaphysica*. 4th edn. Halle: Hemmerde.
— (1760) *Initia philosophiae practicae primae acroamatice*. 3rd edn. Halle: Hemmerde.
- (1761) *Acroasis logica*. Halle: Hemmerde.
— (1766) *Metaphysik*, trans. G. F. Meier. Halle: Hemmerde.
— (1773) *Acroasis logica*. 2nd ed., Johann Töllner. Halle: Hemmerde.
— ([1735] 1983a) *Meditationes philosophicae de nonnullis ad poema pertinentibus*, ed. Heinz Paetzold. Hamburg: Meiner.
— (1983b) *Texte zur Grundlegung der Ästhetik*, trans. and ed. Hans Rudolf Schweizer. Hamburg: Meiner.
— (2011) *Metaphysica = Metaphysik: historisch-kritische Ausgabe*, trans., ed., and with an introduction by Günter Gawlick and Lothar Kreimendahl. Stuttgart-Bad Cannstatt: Frommann-Holzboog.
— (2013) *Metaphysics. A Critical Translation with Kant's Elucidations, Selected Notes, and Related Materials*, trans. and ed. Courtney Fugate and John Hymers. London: Bloomsbury.
BBAW (2007) Berlin-Brandenburgische Akademie der Wissenschaften. "Immanuel Kant: Vorlesungen über Physische Geographie / Dokumentation." http://kant.bbaw.de/base.htm/geo_base.htm. Accessed 11 February 2015.
Beck, Lewis White (1960) *A Commentary on Kant's* Critique of Practical Reason. Chicago: Chicago Univ. Press.
— (1978) "Kant's Strategy." In *Essays on Kant and Hume*. New Haven: Yale Univ. Press, 3–19.
— (1979) "Kant on Education." In J. D. Browning, ed. *Education in the 18th Century*. New York: Garland, 10–24.
Beiser, Frederick C. (1987) *The Fate of Reason*. Cambridge, MA: Harvard Univ. Press.
— (1992) *Enlightenment, Revolution, and Romanticism: The Genesis of German Political Thought 1790–1800*. Cambridge, MA: Harvard Univ. Press.
Bernasconi, Robert (2011) "Kant's Third Thoughts on Race." In Stuart Elden and Eduardo Mendieta, eds. *Reading Kant's Geography*. Albany: SUNY Press, 291–318.
Beyer, Kurt (1937) *Untersuchungen zu Kants Vorlesungen über die philosophische Religionslehre*. Dissertation. Halle. [Partial print; 64 pages].
Bien, Günther (1974) "Kants Theorie der Universität und ihr geschichtlicher Ort." *Historische Zeitschrift* 219, 551–77.

Blomme, Henny (2011) "Pourquoi la chimie ne peut-elle aspirer au titre de science proprement dite?" In Sophie Grapotte, Mai Lequan, and Margit Ruffing, eds. *Kant et les sciences. Un dialogue philosophique avec la pluralité des savoirs*. Paris: Vrin, 129–38.
— (2015) *Kant et la matière de l'espace*. Hildesheim: Olms.
Bock, Friedrich Samuel (1780) *Lehrbuch der Erziehungskunst, zum Gebrauch für christliche Eltern und künftige Jugendlehrer*. Königsberg and Leipzig: Hartung.
Bock, Karl (1920) *Geschichte des Seminarwesens in Ostpreußen bis zu den Freiheitskriegen*. Dissertation. Königsberg. [Printed only in excerpt; documented in the Berlin Staatsbibliothek].
Bödeker, Hans-Georg (1992) "Die 'gebildeten Stände' im späten 18. und frühen 19. Jahrhundert: Zugehörigkeit und Abgrenzungen. Mentalitäten und Handlungspotentiale." In Jürgen Kocka, ed. *Bildungsbürgertum im 19. Jahrhundert. Teil IV*. Stuttgart: Klett-Cotta, 1–52.
Bojanowski, Jochen (2006) *Kants Theorie der Freiheit. Rekonstruktion und Rehabilitierung*. Berlin and New York: De Gruyter.
Bolin, Ronald L., trans. (1968) *Immanuel Kant's Physical Geography*. MA Thesis. Indiana Univ.
Bondeli, Martin (2012) "Zu Reinholds Auffassung von Willensfreiheit in den *Briefen II*." In Violetta Stolz, Marion Heinz, and Martin Bondeli, eds., *Wille, Willkür, Freiheit. Reinholds Freiheitskonzeption im Kontext der Philosophie des 18. Jahrhunderts*. Berlin and Boston: De Gruyter, 125–52.
Borowski, Ludwig Ernst (1804) *Darstellung des Lebens und Charakters Immanuel Kants, Von Kant selbst genau revidirt und berichtigt*. Königsberg: Friedrich Nicolovius.
Boswell, Terry (1988) "On the Textual Authenticity of Kant's Logic." *History and Philosophy of Logic* 9, 193–203.
Böttiger, Karl August (1838) K. W. Böttiger, ed. *Schilderungen aus Karl Aug. Böttiger's handschriftlichen Nachlasse*. Vol. 1. Leipzig: F. A. Brockhaus.
Bowen, Margarita (1981) *Empiricism and Geographical Thought: From Francis Bacon to Alexander von Humboldt*. Cambridge: Cambridge Univ. Press.
Boxill, Bernard and Thomas E. Hill, Jr. (2001) "Kant and Race." In Bernard Boxhill, ed. *Race and Racism*. Oxford: Oxford Univ. Press, 448–71.
Boyer, Carl B. and Uta C. Merzbach (1989) *A History of Mathematics*. 2nd edn. New York: John Wiley & Sons.
Brandt, Reinhard (1989) "Feder und Kant." *Kant-Studien* 80, 249–64.
— (1994) "Rousseau und Kants 'Ich denke'." In Reinhard Brandt and Werner Stark, eds. *Autographen, Dokumente und Briefe. Zu Edition, Amtsgeschäften und Werk Immanuel Kants*. Kant-Forschungen, vol. 5. Hamburg: Meiner, 1–18.
— (1999) *Kritischer Kommentar zu Kants Anthropologie in pragmatischer Hinsicht (1798)*. Kant-Forschungen, vol. 10. Hamburg: Meiner.
— (2003) *Universität zwischen Selbst- und Fremdbestimmung. Kants Streit der Fakultäten. Mit einem Anhang zu Heideggers Rektoratsrede*. Deutsche Zeitschrift für Philosophie, Sonderband 5. Berlin: Akademie Verlag.
— (2007) *Die Bestimmung des Menschen bei Kant*. Hamburg: Meiner.
— (2010) *Immanuel Kant: Was bleibt?* Hamburg: Meiner.
Brandt, Reinhard, Werner Euler (eds.), and Werner Stark (collaborator) (1999) *Studien zur Entwicklung preußischer Universitäten*. Wolfenbütteler Forschungen, vol. 88. Wiesbaden: Harrasowitz Verlag.
Brentano, Franz (2009) *The Origin of our Knowledge of Right and Wrong*. London: Routledge.
Brewer, Daniel (2004) "Lights in Space." *Eighteenth-Century Studies* 37, 171–86.

Buchner, Edward Franklin (1904) *The Educational Theory of Immanuel Kant*. Philadelphia and London: J. B. Lippincott.
Büchner, Ludwig (1855) *Kraft und Stoff oder Grundzüge der natürlichen Weltordnung. Nebst einer darauf gebauten Moral oder Sittenlehre*. Leipzig: Thomas.
Burger, Anton (1889) *Über die Gliederung der Pädagogik Kants*. Dissertation. Jena.
Busch, Werner (1979) *Die Entstehung der kritischen Rechtsphilosophie Kants 1762–1780*. Berlin and New York: De Gruyter.
Butler, Joseph ([1729] 2002) *Fifteen Sermons and the Dissertation on the Nature of Virtue*. Cambridge: Cambridge Univ. Press.
Byrd, Sharon and Joachim Hruschka (2010) *Kant's Doctrine of Right: A Commentary*. Cambridge: Cambridge Univ. Press.
Callanan, John (2013) "Kant on Nativism, Scepticism and Necessity." *Kantian Review* 18, 1–27.
Carrier, Martin (1990) "Kants Theorie der Materie und ihre Wirkung auf die zeitgenössische Chemie." *Kant-Studien* 81, 170–210.
— (1991) "Kraft und Wirklichkeit. Kants späte Theorie der Materie." In Siegfried Blasche, ed. *Übergang: Untersuchungen zum Spätwerk Immanuel Kants*. Frankfurt am Main: Klostermann, 208–30.
— (2001a) "Kant's Mechanical Determination of Matter in the *Metaphysical Foundations of Natural Science*." In Eric Watkins, ed. *Kant and the Sciences*. Oxford: Oxford Univ. Press, 117–35.
— (2001b) "Kant's Theory of Matter and His Views on Chemistry." In Eric Watkins, ed. *Kant and the Sciences*, 205–30.
Cassirer, Ernst (1918) *Kants Leben und Lehre*. Berlin: Bruno Cassirer.
Caygill, Howard (1995) *A Kant Dictionary*. Cambridge, MA: Blackwell.
Chiereghin, Franco (1988) "La metafisica come scienza e esperienza del limite. Relazione simbolica e autodeterminazione pratica secondo Kant." *Verifiche* 71 (1), 81–106.
Chignell, Andrew (2007) "Belief in Kant." *Philosophical Review* 116, 323–60.
Church, Michael (2011) "Immanuel Kant and the Emergence of Modern Geography." In Stuart Elden and Eduardo Mendieta, eds. *Reading Kant's Geography*. Albany: SUNY Press, 19–46.
Churton, Annette (1899) *Kant on Education*, trans. Annette Churton, with an introduction by C. A. Foley Rhys David. London: Kegan Paul, Trench, Trübner & Co.
Cicero, Marcus Tullius (1999) *De officiis. Vom pflichtgemäßen Handeln* [Latin/German], trans. and ed. Heinz Gunermann. Stuttgart: Buchner.
Cicero [Incertus Auctor] (1954). Harry Caplan, trans. *Rhetorica ad Herennium*. Cambridge, MA: Harvard Univ. Press.
Clasen, Karl-Heinz (1924) *Kant-Bildnisse*. ed. Königsberg Ortsgruppe of the Kant-Gesellschaft. Königsberg: Gräfe & Unzer.
Clewis, Robert R. (2009) *The Kantian Sublime and the Revelation of Freedom*. Cambridge: Cambridge Univ. Press.
— (2014) "Kant's Empiricist Rationalism in the Mid-1760s." *Eighteenth-Century Thought* 5, 179–225.
— (2015) "Kant's Natural Teleology? The Case of Physical Geography." *Kant-Studien*.
Cohen, Alix (2009) *Kant and the Human Sciences: Biology, Anthropology and History*. London: Palgrave Macmillan.
— (2012) "Kant's 'curious catalogue of human frailties': The Great Portrait of Nature." In Susan Shell and Richard Velkley, eds. *Critical Guide to Kant's Observations on the Feeling of the Beautiful and Sublime*. Cambridge: Cambridge Univ. Press, 144–62.

— ed. (2014) *Critical Guide: Kant's Lectures on Anthropology*. Cambridge: Cambridge Univ. Press.
Conrad, Elfriede (1994) *Kants Logikvorlesungen als neuer Schlüssel zur Architektonik der Kritik der reinen Vernunft: Die Ausarbeitung der Gliederungsentwürfe in den Logikvorlesungen als Auseinandersetzung mit der Tradition*. Stuttgart: Frommann-Holzboog.
Cramer, Konrad (1988) "Die Stunde der Philosophie. Über Göttingens ersten Philosophen und die philosophische Theorielage der Gründungszeit." In Jürgen von Stackelberg, ed. *Zur geistigen Situation der Zeit der Göttinger Universitätsgründung 1737*. Göttingen: Göttinger Universitätsschriften [Series A, vol. 12], 101–43.
Crusius, Christian August (1745) *Entwurf der nothwendigen Vernunft-Wahrheiten*. Leipzig: John Friedrich Gleditschens Buchhandlung.
D'Alembert, Jean Le Ronde (1995) *Preliminary Discourse to the Encylcopedia, 1752*. Chicago: Univ. of Chicago Press.
D'Alessandro, Giuseppe (1999) "Die Wiederkehr eines Leitwortes: Die 'Bestimmung des Menschen' als theologische, anthropologische und geschichtsphilosophische Frage der deutschen Spätaufklärung." *Aufklärung* 11, 21–47.
Delekat, Friedrich (1969) *Immanuel Kant. Historisch-kritische Interpretationen seiner Hauptschriften*. Heidelberg: Quelle & Meyer.
Delfosse, Heinrich P., Norbert Hinske, and Gianluca Sadun Bordoni (2010) *Stellenindex und Konkordanz zum "Naturrecht Feyerabend". Einleitung des "Naturrechts Feyerabend"*. Forschungen und Materialien zur deutschen Aufklärung. Division III: *Indices. Kant-Index*. Section 2: *Indices zum Kantschen Ethikcorpus*. Vol. 30.1. Stuttgart-Bad Cannstatt: Frommann-Holzboog.
— (2014) *Stellenindex und Konkordanz zum "Naturrecht Feyerabend". Abhandlung des "Naturrechts Feyerabend": Text und Hauptindex*. Forschungen und Materialien zur deutschen Aufklärung. Division III: *Indices. Kant-Index*. Section 2: *Indices zum Kantschen Ethikcorpus*. Vol. 30.2. Stuttgart-Bad Cannstatt: Frommann-Holzboog.
Denis, Lara (2014) "Love of Honor as a Kantian Virtue." In Alix Cohen, ed. *Kant on Emotions and Value*. Basingstoke: Palgrave Macmillan, 191–209.
Denis, Lara and Oliver Sensen (2015) eds., *Kant's Lectures on Ethics: A Critical Guide*. Cambridge: Cambridge Univ. Press.
DiCenso, James (2012) *Kant's Religion within the Boundaries of Mere Reason: A Commentary*. Cambridge: Cambridge Univ. Press.
Diderot, Denis (1956) "Encyclopedia." In *Rameau's Nephew and Other Works*. Indianapolis: Bobbs-Merrill.
— (1999) *Thoughts on the Interpretation of Nature and Other Philosophical Works*. Manchester: Clinamen.
Dobbek, Wilhelm (1961) *Johann Gottfried Herders Jugendzeit in Mohrungen und Königsberg 1744–1764*. Würzburg: Holzner.
Dolch, Josef (1967) "Immanuel Kant als Dozent der Pädagogik." In Franz-Josef Holtkemper, ed. *Pädagogische Blätter. Heinrich Döpp-Vorwald zum 65. Geburtstag*. Ratingen: A. Henn, 43–57.
Dörflinger, Bernd (2004) "Führt Moral unausbleiblich zur Religion? Überlegungen zu einer These Kants." In Norbert Fischer, ed. *Kants Metaphysik und Religionsphilosophie*. Hamburg: Meiner, 207–23.
Dörflinger, Bernd, Claudio La Rocca, Robert B. Louden, Ubirajara Rancan de Azevedo Marques, eds. (2015) *Kant's Lectures*. Berlin and Boston: De Gruyter.

Dorrien, Gary (2012) *Kantian Reason and Hegelian Spirit: The Idealistic Logic of Modern Theology*. Chichester: Wiley-Blackwell.
Du Bois-Reymond, Emil (1872) *Über die Grenzen des Naturerkennens. Die sieben Welträthsel*. Leipzig: Veit.
Du Prel, Carl, ed. (1889) *Immanuel Kants Vorlesungen über Psychologie*. Leipzig: Ernst Günther.
Dussort, Henri (1956) "Kant et la chimie." *Revue philosophique de la France et de l'étranger* 146, 392–7.
Dyck, Corey (2011) "A Wolff in Kant's Clothing: Christian Wolff's Influence on Kant's Accounts of Consciousness, Self-Consciousness, and Psychology." *Philosophy Compass* 6 (1), 44–53.
— (2014) *Kant and Rational Psychology*. Oxford: Oxford Univ. Press.
Eberhard, Johann August (1781) *Vorbereitung zur natürlichen Theologie*. Halle: Waisenhaus.
Eberhard, Johann Peter (1753) *Erste Gründe der Naturlehre*. Halle: Renger.
Eigen, Sara and Mark Larrimore, eds. (2006) *The German Invention of Race*. Albany: SUNY Press.
Elden, Stuart (2009) "Reassessing Kant's Geography." *Journal of Historical Geography* 35, 3–25.
— (2011) "Reintroducing Kant's Geography." In Stuart Elden and Eduardo Mendieta, eds. *Reading Kant's Geography*. Albany: SUNY Press, 1–15.
Elden, Stuart and Eduardo Mendieta, eds. (2011) *Reading Kant's Geography*. Albany: SUNY Press.
Ellendt, Georg Albrecht (1898) *Lehrer und Abiturienten des Königlichen Friedrichs-Kollegiums zu Königsberg Pr. 1698–1898*. Königsberg. [Reprinted in *Sonderschriften des Vereins für Familienforschung in Ost- und Westpreussen e. V.*, 10. (1969)].
Erdmann, Benno (1880) Review of *Die formale Logik Kants in ihren Beziehungen zur transcendentalen* [by Moritz Steckelmacher (1879)], *Göttingische gelehrte Anzeigen* 20, 609–34.
Erler, Georg and Erich Joachim, eds. (1910–17) *Die Matrikel [und die Promotionsverzeichnisse] der Albertus-Universität zu Königsberg i. Pr.* 3 vols. Leipzig.
Erxleben, Johann Christian Polykarp (1768) *Anfangsgründe der Naturgeschichte*. Göttingen: Johann Christian Dieterich.
— (1772) *Anfangsgründe der Naturlehre*. Göttingen: Johann Christian Dieterich.
— (1773) *Anfangsgründe der Naturgeschichte*. 2nd edn. Göttingen: Johann Christian Dieterich.
— (1777) *Anfangsgründe der Naturlehre*. 2nd edn. Göttingen: Johann Christian Dieterich.
— (1782) *Anfangsgründe der Naturgeschichte. Aufs neue herausgegeben von Johann Friedrich Gmelin*. 3rd edn. Göttingen: Johann Christian Dieterich.
— (1784) *Anfangsgründe der Naturlehre*. 3rd edn., with additions by Georg Christoph Lichtenberg. Göttingen: Johann Christian Dieterich.
Euclid (1956a) *The Thirteen Books of the Elements*. Trans. from the Text of Heiberg with Introduction and Commentary by T. L. Heath. Vol. I, Introduction and Books I, II. New York: Dover.
— (1956b) *The Thirteen Books of the Elements*. Trans. from the Text of Heiberg with Introduction and Commentary by T. L. Heath. Vol. II, Books III-IX. New York: Dover.
— (1956c) *The Thirteen Books of the Elements*. Trans. from the Text of Heiberg with Introduction and Commentary by T. L. Heath. Vol. III, Books X-XIII and Appendix. New York: Dover.
Euclides (1969) *Elementa*. Vol. I, Libri I-IV cum appendicibus. Post I. L. Heiberg edidit E. S. Stamatis. Leipzig: Teubner.

- (1970) *Elementa*. Vol. II, Libri V-IX cum appendice. Post I. L. Heiberg edidit E. S. Stamatis. Leipzig: Teubner.
- (1972) *Elementa*. Vol. III, Liber X cum appendice. Post I. L. Heiberg edidit E. S. Stamatis. Leipzig: Teubner.
- (1973) *Elementa*. Vol. IV, Libri XI-XIII cum appendicibus. Post I. L. Heiberg edidit E. S. Stamatis. Leipzig: Teubner.

Euler, Werner (1994) "Immanuel Kants Amtstätigkeit. Aufgaben und Probleme einer Gesamtdokumentation." In Reinhard Brandt and Werner Stark, eds. *Autographen Dokumente und Berichte*. Kant-Forschungen, vol. 5. Hamburg: Meiner, 58–90.

- (1999) "Kants Beitrag zur Schul- und Universitätsreform im ausgehenden 18. Jahrhundert." In Reinhard Brandt, Werner Euler, and Werner Stark (collaborator), eds. *Studien zur Entwicklung preußischer Universitäten*. Wiesbaden: Harrasowitz Verlag, 203–72.

Eze, Emmanuel Chukwudi (1997) *Postcolonial African Philosophy*, ed. Emmanuel Eze. Oxford: Blackwell, 103–40.

Fabbianelli, Faustino (1998–99) "La concezione della libertà del volere nel 'Versuch einer neuen Theorie des menschlichen Vorstellungsvermögens' di Karl Leonhard Reinhold." *Annali del Dipartimento di Filosofia dell'Università di Firenze*, 39–53.

- (2000) "Die Theorie der Willensfreiheit in den 'Briefen über die Kantische Philosophie' (1790–92) von Karl Leonhard Reinhold." *Philosophisches Jahrbuch* 107 (2), 428–43.

Faggiotto, Pietro (1989) *Introduzione alla metafisica kantiana dell'analogia*. Milan: Massimo.
- (1996) *La metafisica kantiana dell'analogia. Ricerche e discussioni*. Trento: Verifiche.

Falkenstein, Lorne (1995) "The Great Light of 1769 – A Humeian Awakening? Comments on Lothar Kreimendahl's Account of Hume's Influence on Kant." *Archiv für Geschichte der Philosophie* 77, 63–79.

Feder, Johann G. H. (1767) *Grundriß der philosophischen Wissenschaft nebst der nöthigen Geschichte zum Gebrauch seiner Zuhörer*. Coburg: Findeisen.
- (1769a) *Grundriss der philosophischen Wissenschaften*. Coburg: Findeisen.
- (1769b) *Logik und Metaphysik, nebst der Philosophischen Geschichte im Grundrisse*. Göttingen and Gotha: Dieterich.
- (1772) Review of *Revision der Philosophie*, Göttingische Anzeigen von Gelehrten Sachen 15, 113–7.
- (1825) *Johann Georg Heinrich Feder's Leben*. Leipzig [publisher unknown].
- (1976) Review of *Träume eines Geistersehers*. Reprinted in Immanuel Kant, *Träume eines Geistersehers erläutert durch Träume der Metaphysik*, ed. Rudolf Malter. Stuttgart: Reclam, 125–7.

Feinberg, Joel (2008) "Psychological Egoism." In Joel Feinberg and Russ Shafer-Landau, eds. *Reason & Responsibility*. Belmont: Thomson Wadsworth, 520–32.

Firestone, Chris L. and Nathan Jacobs (2008) *In Defense of Kant's Religion*. Bloomington: Indiana Univ. Press.

Fischer, Norbert (1987) *Augustins Philosophie der Endlichkeit. Zur systematischen Entfaltung seines Denkens aus der Geschichte der Chorismos-Problematik*. Bonn: Bouvier.
- (1988) "Der formale Grund der bösen Tat. Das Problem der moralischen Zurechnung in der Praktischen Philosophie Kants." *Zeitschrift für philosophische Forschung* 42, 18–44.
- (1990) "Menschsein als Möglichsein. Platons Menschenbild angesichts der Paradigmendiskussion in der Platonforschung." *Theologische Quartalschrift* 170, 23–41.
- (1993) "Zur neueren Diskussion um Kants Religionsphilosophie." *Theologie und Glaube* 83, 170–94.

- ed. (2004) *Kants Metaphysik und Religionsphilosophie*. Hamburg: Meiner.
- (2005a) *The Philosophical Quest for God. A Journey through its Stations*, trans. Frederick Van Fleteren. Münster: LIT-Verlag.
- ed. (2005b) *Kant und der Katholizismus. Stationen einer wechselhaften Geschichte*. Freiburg: Herder.
- (2009) "Amore amoris tui facio istuc. Zur Bedeutung der Liebe im Leben und Denken Augustins." In Edith Düsing and Hans-Dieter Klein, eds. *Geist, Eros und Agape. Untersuchungen zu Liebesdarstellungen in Philosophie, Religion und Kunst*. Würzburg: Königshausen & Neumann, 169–89.
- ed. (2010) *Kants Grundlegung einer kritischen Metaphysik. Einführung in die "Kritik der reinen Vernunft."* Hamburg: Meiner.
- ed. (2012) *Die Gnadenlehre als "salto mortale" der Vernunft. Natur, Freiheit und Gnade im Spannungsfeld von Augustinus und Kant*. Freiburg: Alber.
- (2013) "Endzweck Mensch. Zum Sinn der Schöpfung nach Immanuel Kant." In Michael Hofer, Christopher Meiller, Hans Schelkshorn, and Kurt Appel, eds. *Der Endzweck der Schöpfung. Zu den Schlussparagraphen (§§ 84–91) in Kants "Kritik der Urteilskraft."* Freiburg: Alber, 193–218.

Fisher, Mark (2007) "Kant's Explanatory Natural History: Generation and Classification of Organisms in Kant's Natural Philosophy." In Philippe Huneman, ed. *Understanding Purpose: Kant and the Philosophy of Biology*. Rochester: Univ. of Rochester Press, 101–21.

Fordyce, David (1769) *The Elements of Moral Philosophy*. 4th ed. London: J. Dodsley.

Formosa, Paul (2012) "From Discipline to Autonomy: Kant's Theory of Moral Development." In Klass Roth and Chris Surprenant, eds. *Kant and Education*. New York and London: Routledge, 163–76.

Forstreuter, Kurt (1969) "Pläne eines pädagogischen Seminars in Königsberg 1788–1793." *Preußenland* 7, 1–8.

Frederick King of Prussia (1913) *Die Werke Friedrichs des Großen in deutscher Übersezung*, ed. G. B. Volz. Berlin: Hobbing.

Friedman, Michael (1992a) *Kant and the Exact Sciences*. Cambridge: Harvard Univ. Press.
- (1992b) "Kant's Theory of Geometry." In Carl Posy, ed. *Kant's Philosophy of Mathematics. Modern Essays*. Dordrecht: Kluwer, 177–219.
- (2001) "Matter and Motion in the *Metaphysical Foundations* and the First *Critique*. The Empirical Concept of Matter and the Categories." In Eric Watkins, ed. *Kant and the Sciences*. Oxford: Oxford Univ. Press, 53–69.
- (2013) *Kant's Construction of Nature*. Cambridge: Cambridge Univ. Press.

Friedrich, Carl J. (1949) *The Philosophy of Kant*. New York: The Modern Library.

Frierson, Patrick (2003) *Freedom and Anthropology in Kant's Moral Philosophy*. Cambridge: Cambridge Univ. Press.
- (2005) "The Moral Importance of Politeness in Kant's Anthropology." *Kantian Review* 9, 105–27.
- (2012) "Two Concepts of Universality in Kant's Moral Theory." In Susan Shell and Richard Velkley, eds. *Kant's "Observations" and "Remarks": A Critical Guide*. Cambridge: Cambridge Univ. Press, 57–76.
- (2015) "Herder: Religion and moral motivation." In Lara Denis and Oliver Sensen, eds. *Kant's Lectures on Ethics: A Critical Guide*. Cambridge: Cambridge Univ. Press, 34–50.

Fugate, Courtney (2014a) "Alexander Baumgarten on the Principle of Sufficient Reason." *Philosophica* 44, 127–47.

- (2014b) *The Teleology of Reason: A Study of the Structure of Kant's Critical Philosophy.* Berlin and Boston: De Gruyter.
Funke, Gerhard (1979) *Die Wendung zur Metaphysik im Neukantianismus des 20. Jahrhunderts.* In Gerhard Funke *Von der Aktualität Kants.* Bonn: Bouvier, 181–216.
- (1985) "Pädagogik im Sinne Kants heute." In Jürgen-Eckardt Pleines, ed. *Kant und die Pädagogik: Pädagogik und pratische Philosophie.* Würzburg: Königshausen & Neumann, 99–110.
Gallie, Walter Bryce (1956) "Essentially Contested Concepts." *Proceedings of the Aristotelian Society* 56, 167–98.
Garber, Jörn, ed. (2008) *"Die Stammutter aller guten Schulen": Das Dessauer Philanthropinum und der deutsche Philanthropismus 1774–1793.* Tübingen: Niemeyer.
Gawlick, Günter and Lothar Kreimendahl (1987) *Hume in der deutschen Aufklärung. Umrisse einer Rezeptionsgeschichte.* Stuttgart-Bad Canstatt: Frommann-Holzboog.
Genova, Anthony C. (1974) "Kant's Epigenesis of Pure Reason." *Kant-Studien* 65, 259–73.
George, Rolf (unpublished manuscript) "An Essay on Kant and Immortality, with Digressions."
Glasenapp, Helmuth von (1954) *Kant und die Religionen des Ostens.* Kitzingen am Main: Holzner.
Göbel, Christian (2005) "Kants Gift. Wie die 'Kritik der reinen Vernunft' auf den 'Index Librorum Prohibitorum' kam." In Norbert Fischer, ed. *Kant und der Katholizismus. Stationen einer wechselhaften Geschichte.* Freiburg: Herder, 91–137.
Goethe, Johann Wolfgang von (1989–94) *Werke.* 14 vols. Munich: Beck.
Gollwitzer, Helmut (1967) *Die marxistische Religionskritik und der christliche Glaube.* Munich and Hamburg: Siebenstern.
Goy, Ina (2007) "Immanuel Kant über das moralische Gefühl der Achtung." *Zeitschrift für Philosophische Forschung* 61, 337–60.
Green, Ronald M. (1979) "Religious Ritual: A Kantian Perspective." *Journal of Religious Ethics* 7 (2), 229–38.
Gregory, Tullio (2006) *Origini della terminologia filosofica moderna: Linee di ricerca.* Florence: Olschki.
Grenberg, Jeanine (2001) "Feeling, Desire and Interest in Kant's Theory of Action." *Kant-Studien* 92, 153–79.
Grimm, Gunter (1987) "Vom Schulfuchs zum Menschheitslehrer: Zum Wandel des Gelehrtentums zwischen Barock und Aufklärung." In Hans Erich Bödeker and Ulrich Herrmann, eds. *Über den Prozess der Aufklärung in Deutschland im 18. Jahrhundert.* Göttingen: Vandenhoeck & Ruprecht, 14–38.
Grimm, Jacob and Wilhelm Grimm (1961) *Deutsches Wörterbuch: Neubearbeitung.* Berlin: Akademie Verlag.
Guyer, Paul (1979) *Kant and the Claims of Taste.* Cambridge: Harvard Univ. Press. [2nd edn., Cambridge: Cambridge Univ. Press, 1997].
- (1982) "Pleasure and Society in Kant's Theory of Taste." In Ted Cohen and Paul Guyer, eds. *Essays in Kant's Aesthetics.* Chicago: Univ. of Chicago Press, 21–54.
- (1993) "The Standard of Taste and the 'Most Ardent Desire of Society'." In Ted Cohen, Paul Guyer, and Hilary Putnam, eds. *Pursuits of Reason: Essays in Honor of Stanley Cavell.* Lubbock: Texas Tech Univ. Press, 37–66.
- (2003) "Beauty, Freedom, and Morality: Kant's *Lectures on Anthropology* and the Development of his Aesthetic Theory." In Brian Jacobs and Patrick Kain, eds. *Essays on Kant's Anthropology.* Cambridge: Cambridge Univ. Press, 135–63.

- (2005) *Values of Beauty: Historical Essays in Aesthetics*. Cambridge: Cambridge Univ. Press.
- (2007) "Translator's Introduction to *Observations on the Feeling of the Beautiful and Sublime*." In Kant, *Anthropology, History, and Education*, ed. Günter Zöller and Robert B. Louden. New York: Cambridge Univ. Press, 18–22.
- (2012) "Freedom as the Foundation of morality: Kant's Early Efforts." In Susan Shell and Richard Velkley, eds. *Kant's "Observations" and "Remarks": A Critical Guide*. Cambridge: Cambridge Univ. Press, 77–98.

Hardtwig, Wolfgang (1985) "Krise der Universität, studentische Reformbewegung (1750–1819) und die Sozialisation der jugendlichen deutschen Bildungsschicht: Aufriß eines Forschungsproblems." *Geschichte und Gesellschaft* 11, 155–76.

Hartshorne, Richard (1939) *The Nature of Geography: A Critical Survey of Current Thought in the Light of the Past*. Lancaster, PA: Association of American Geographers.
- (1958) "The Concept of Geography as a Science of Space, From Kant and Humboldt to Hettner." *Annals of the Association of American Geographers* 48, 97–108.
- (1959) *Perspective on the Nature of Geography*. Chicago: Rand McNally.

Harvey, David (1969) *Explanation in Geography*. New York: St Martin's Press.
- (2000) "Cosmopolitanism and the Banality of Geographical Evils." *Public Culture* 12, 529–64.
- (2011) "Cosmopolitanism in the *Anthropology* and *Geography*." In Stuart Elden and Eduardo Mendieta, eds. *Reading Kant's Geography*. Albany: SUNY Press, 267–84.

Hasenkamp, Xaver von (1866) *Ostpreußen unter dem Doppelaar: Historische Skizze der russischen Invasion in den Tagen des siebenjährigen Krieges (Aus den Neuen Preußischen Provinzialblättern 3. Folge Bd. VI – XI.)*. Königsberg: Verlag der Th. Theile'schen Buchhandlung [F. Beyer].

Heath, Thomas (1981) *A History of Greek Mathematics*. New York: Dover.

Heidegger, Martin (1957) "Die ontotheologische Verfassung der Metaphysik." In *Gesamtausgabe*, vol. 11. Frankfurt am Main: Klostermann.
- (1969) Joan Stambaugh, trans. "The Onto-theo-logical Constitution of Metaphysics." In *Identity and Difference*. New York, Evanston, and London: Harper & Row, 42–74.
- (1977) *Sein und Zeit*. In *Gesamtausgabe*, vol. 2. Frankfurt am Main: Klostermann.
- (1991) *Kant und das Problem der Metaphysik*. In *Gesamtausgabe*, vol. 3. Frankfurt am Main: Klostermann.
- (1995) *Augustinus und der Neuplatonismus. Frühe Freiburger Vorlesung 1921*. In *Gesamtausgabe*, vol. 60. Frankfurt am Main: Klostermann, 157–299.
- (1997) *Die Grundprobleme der Phänomenologie*. In *Gesamtausgabe*, vol. 24. Frankfurt am Main: Klostermann.

Heine, Heinrich (1959) John Snodgrass, trans. *Religion and Philosophy in Germany*. Boston: Beacon Press.

Heinze, Max (1894) *Vorlesungen Kants über Metaphysik aus drei Semestern*. Leipzig: Hirzel.

Henrich, Dieter (1967) "Kants Denken 1762/3. Über den Unterschied synthetischer und analytischer Urteile." In Heinz Heimsoeth, Dieter Henrich, and Giorgio Tonelli, eds. *Studien zu Kant's philosophischer Entwicklung*. Hildesheim: Olms, 9–38.
- (2012) "Concerning Kant's Earliest Ethics: An Attempt at a Reconstruction." In Susan Shell and Richard Velkley, eds. *Kant's "Observations" and "Remarks": A Critical Guide*. Cambridge: Cambridge Univ. Press, 13–37.

Herder, Johann Gottfried (1846) Emil Gottfried von Herder, ed. *Johann Gottfried von Herder's Lebensbild. Sein chronologisch-geordneter Briefwechsel, verbunden mit den hierhergehörigen Mittheilungen aus seinem ungedruckten Nachlasse, und mit den nöthigen Belegen aus seinen und seiner Zeitgenossen Schriften.* Vol. 1, part 1. Erlangen: Theodor Bläsing.
– (1877–1913) Bernhard Suphan, ed. *Sämtliche Werke*. 33 vols. Berlin: Weidmann.
– (1977–96) Wilhelm Dobbek and Günter Arnold, eds. *Briefe. Gesamtausgabe.* 10 vols. Weimar: Böhlau.
– (1985) Ulrich Gaier, ed. *Frühe Schriften, 1764–1772.* Vol. 1 of *Werke*, 10 vols. Frankfurt am Main: Deutscher Klassiker Verlag.
– (1991) Hans Dietrich Irmscher, ed. *Briefe zu Beförderung der Humanität.* Vol. 7 of *Werke*, 10 vols. Frankfurt am Main: Deutscher Klassiker Verlag.
– (1998) Hans Dietrich Irmscher, ed. *Schriften zu Literatur und Philosophie, 1792–1800.* Vol. 8 of *Werke*, 10 vols. Frankfurt am Main: Deutscher Klassiker Verlag.
Herder, Maria Caroline (1830) "Erinnerungen aus dem Leben Johann Gottfried von Herder." In Georg Müller, ed. *Johann Gottfried von Herders Sämtliche Werke*, vols. 20–22. Stuttgart, Tübingen: J. G. Cotta.
Herman, Barbara (1993) *The Practice of Moral Judgment.* Cambridge, MA: Harvard Univ. Press.
Hinske, Norbert (1970a) *Kants Weg Zur Transzendentalphilosophie.* Stuttgart: Kohlhammer.
– (1970b) "Verschiedenheit und Einheit der transzendentalen Philosophien." *Archiv für Begriffsgeschichte* 14, 41–68.
– (1983) "Wolffs Stellung in der deutschen Aufklärung." In Werner Schneiders, ed. *Christian Wolff 1679–1754.* Studien zum achtzehnten Jahrhundert, vol. 4. Hamburg: Meiner, 306–20.
– ed. (1986a) *Eklektik, Selbstdenken, Mündigkeit.* Hamburg: Meiner.
– (1986b) *Stellenindex und Konkordanz zu G. F. Meiers "Auszug aus der Vernunftlehre."* Stuttgart-Bad Cannstatt: Frommann-Holzboog.
– (1990) "Die tragenden Grundideen der deutschen Aufklärung: Versuch einer Typologie." In Raffaele Ciafardone, ed. *Die Philosophie der deutschen Aufklärung: Texte und Darstellung.* Stuttgart: Reclam, 407–58.
– (1995) *Stellenindex und Konkordanz zur "Logik Pölitz."* Stuttgart-Bad Cannstatt: Frommann-Holzboog.
– (1998) *Zwischen Aufklärung und Vernunftkritik: Studien zum Kantschen Logikcorpus.* Stuttgart-Bad Cannstatt, Frommann-Holzboog.
– (2000) "Die *Jäsche-Logik* und ihr besonderes Schicksal im Rahmen der Akademie-Ausgabe." In Reinhard Brandt and Werner Stark, eds. *Zustand und Zukunft der Akademie-Ausgabe von Immanuel Kants Gesammelten Schriften.* Kant-Studien 91, Sonderheft. Berlin and New York: De Gruyter, 85–93.
Hirsch, Philipp-Alexander (2012) *Kants Einleitung in die Rechtslehre von 1784.* Göttingen: Universitätsverlag Göttingen.
Hißmann, Michael (1778a) *Anleitung zur Kenntnis der auserlesensten Literatur in allen Theilen der Philosophie.* Göttingen: Lemgo.
– (1778b) *Briefe über Gegenstände der Philosophie, an Leserinnen und Leser.* Gotha: Carl Wilhelm Ettinger.
Hohenegger, Hansmichael (2004) *Kant, filosofo dell'architettonica. Saggio sulla* Critica della facoltà di giudizio. Macerata: Quodlibet.
– (2014) "La terminologia della spazialità in Kant." In Delfina Giovannozzi and Marco Veneziani, eds. *Locus-Spatium* 122. Florence: Olschki, 519–80.

Holzhey, Helmut (1977) "Der Philosoph für die Welt – eine Chimäre der deutschen Aufklärung?" In Helmut Holzhey and Walther Ch. Zimmerli, eds. *Esoterik und Exoterik der Philosophie: Beiträge zu Geschichte und Sinn philosophischer Selbstbestimmung*. Basel and Stuttgart: Schwabe, 117–38.

Home, Henry, Lord Kames (2005) *Elements of Criticism*, ed. Peter Jones. Reprint of 6th edn., 1785. Indianapolis: Liberty Fund.

Hotson, Howard (2007) *Commonplace Learning: Ramism and its German Ramifications 1543–1630*. Oxford: Oxford Univ. Press.

Hügelmann, Karl (1879) "Ein Brief über Kant. Mitgeteilt von Karl Hügelmann." *Altpreußische Monatsschrift* 16, 607–12.

Hume, David (1985) "Of National Characters." In Eugene F. Miller, ed. *Essays Moral, Political, and Literary*. Indianapolis: Liberty Fund, 197–215.

— ([1739–40] 2007) *A Treatise of Human Nature*, ed. David Fate Norton and Mary J. Norton. 2 vols. Oxford: Clarendon Press.

Huneman, Philippe, ed. (2007) *Understanding Purpose: Kant and the Philosophy of Biology*. Rochester: Univ. of Rochester Press.

Husserl, Edmund (1985) *Texte zur Phänomenologie des inneren Zeitbewußtseins (1893–1919)*. Hamburg: Meiner.

Hutter, Axel (2003) *Das Interesse der Vernunft. Kants ursprüngliche Einsicht und ihre Entfaltung in den transzendentalphilosophischen Hauptwerken*. Hamburg: Meiner.

Illetterati, Luca (1996) *Figure del limite. Esperienze e forme della finitezza*. Trento: Verifiche.

Ingensiep, Hans Werner (1994) "Die biologischen Analogien und die erkenntnistheoretischen Alternativen in Kants *Kritik der reinen Vernunft* B § 17." *Kant-Studien* 85, 381–93.

Irmscher, Hans Dietrich, ed. (1964) *Immanuel Kant. Aus den Vorlesungen der Jahre 1762 bis 1764. Auf Grund der Nachschriften Johann Gottfried Herders*. Kant-Studien Ergänzungsheft 88. Cologne: Kölner-Universitäts-Verlag.

Ischreyt, Heinz, ed. (1995) *Zentren der Aufklärung II. Königsberg und Riga*. Wolfenbütteler Studien zur Aufklärung, vol. 16. Tübingen: Niemeyer.

Isen, Alice M. and Paula F. Levin (1972) "The Effect of Feeling Good on Helping: Cookies and Kindness." *Journal of Personality and Social Psychology* 21, 384–8.

Jachmann, Reinhold Bernhard (1804) *Immanuel Kant geschildert in Briefen an einen Freund*. Königsberg: Friedrich Nicolovius.

— (1993) "Immanuel Kant geschildert in Briefen an einen Freund." In Felix Gross and Rudolf Malter, eds. *Immanuel Kant*. Darmstadt: Wissenschaftliche Buchgesellschaft, 103–87.

Jacobs, Brian and Patrick Kain, eds. (2003) *Essays on Kant's Anthropology*. Cambridge: Cambridge Univ. Press.

Jäsche, Gottlieb Benjamin, ed. (1800) *Immanuel Kant's Logik*. Königsberg: Nicolovius. [In *Kant's gesammelte Schriften*, vol. 9].

Johnston, James Scott (2013) *Kant's Philosophy: A Study for Educators*. New York: Bloomsbury.

Jorgensen, Larry (2009) "The Principle of Continuity and Leibniz's Theory of Consciousness." *Journal of the History of Philosophy* 47 (2), 223–48.

Jünemann, Franz (1904) "Pädagogische Aussprüche Immanuel Kants. Aus verschiedenen Schriften chronologisch zusammengestellt." *Aus der Schule – für die Schule* 16, 394–403.

Justinian, Caesar Flavius (1913) J. B. Moyle, trans. *The Institutes of Justinian*. 5th edn. Oxford: Clarendon Press.

Kant, Immanuel (1802) Friedrich Theodor Rink, ed. *Physische Geographie*. 2 vols. Königsberg: Goebbels & Unzer.

- (1803) Friedrich Theodor Rink, ed. *Über Pädagogik*. Königsberg: Nicolovius.
- (1804) Friedrich Theodor Rink, ed. *Über die von der königl. Akademie der Wissenschaften zu Berlin für das Jahr 1791 ausgesetzte Preisfrage: Welches sind die wirklichen Fortschritte, die die Metaphysik seit Leibnitz's und Wolff's Zeiten in Deutschland gemacht hat?* Königsberg: Goebbels & Unzer.
- (1817) Karl Heinrich Ludwig Pölitz, ed. *Vorlesungen über die philosophische Religionslehre*. Leipzig: Taubert.
- ([1817] 1830) Karl Heinrich Ludwig Pölitz, ed. *Vorlesungen über die philosophische Religionslehre*. 2nd edn. Leipzig: Taubert
- (1833) Fr. Ch. Starke [Johann Adam Bergk], ed. *Immanuel Kant's Vorzügliche kleine Schriften und Aufsätze. Nebst Betrachtungen über die Erde und den Menschen aus ungedruckten Vorlesungen*. 2 vols. Leipzig: Expedition des europäischen Aufsehers.
- (1838–42) Karl Rosenkranz and Friedrich Wilhelm Schubert, eds. *Immanuel Kant's sämtliche Werke*. 12 vols. Leipzig: Leopold Voss.
- (1900–) *Kant's gesammelte Schriften*, ed. the Royal Prussian, subsequently German, then Berlin-Brandenburg Academy of Sciences. 29 vols. Berlin and New York: Reimer, subsequently De Gruyter.
- (1923) Friedrich Theodor Rink and Paul Natorp, eds. *Über Pädagogik*. [In *Kant's gesammelte Schriften*, vol. 9].
- (1934) Theodore M. Greene and Hoyt H. Hudson, trans. *Religion within the Limits of Reason Alone*. Chicago: Open Court.
- (1950) Lewis White Beck, trans. *Prolegomena to Any Future Metaphysics*. Indianapolis: Bobbs-Merrill.
- (1961) Gerhard Lehmann, ed. *Vorlesungen über Enzyklopädie und Logik*. Vol. 1: *Vorlesungen über Philosophische Enzyklopädie*. Berlin: Akademie Verlag.
- (1963) Hans-Hermann Groothoff and Edgar Reimers, eds. *Ausgewählte Schriften zur Pädagogik und ihrer Begründung*. Paderborn: Schöningh. [2nd edn., 1982].
- (1967) Alexis Philonenko, trans. and ed. *Réflexions sur l'éducation*. Paris: Vrin.
- (1970) James Ellington, trans. *Metaphysical Foundations of Natural Science*. Indianapolis: Bobbs-Merrill.
- (1982) Karl Heinrich Ludwig Pölitz, ed. *Vorlesungen über die philosophische Religionslehre*. Darmstadt: Wissenschaftliche Buchgesellschaft. [Reprint of 2nd edn., 1830].
- (1992) David Walford, trans. and ed., in collaboration with Ralf Meerbote. *Theoretical Philosophy 1755–1770*. Cambridge: Cambridge Univ. Press.
- (1996a) Mary Gregor, trans. and ed. *Practical Philosophy*. Cambridge: Cambridge Univ. Press.
- (1996b) George di Giovanni and Allen Wood, trans. and eds. *Religion and Rational Theology*. Cambridge: Cambridge Univ. Press.
- (1997a) Peter Heath, trans. and ed., and Jerome Schneewind, ed. *Lectures on Ethics*. Cambridge: Cambridge Univ. Press.
- (1997b) Karl Ameriks and Steve Naragon, trans. and eds. *Lectures on Metaphysics*. Cambridge: Cambridge Univ. Press.
- (1997c) Reinhard Brandt and Werner Stark, eds. *Vorlesungen über Anthropologie*. [*Kant's gesammelte Schriften*, vol. 25]. 2 vols. Berlin: De Gruyter.
- (1998a) Paul Guyer and Allen Wood, trans. and eds. *Critique of Pure Reason*. Cambridge: Cambridge Univ. Press.

- (1998b) Allen Wood and George di Giovanni, trans. and eds. *Religion within the Boundaries of Mere Reason*. Cambridge: Cambridge Univ. Press.
- (1998c) Tillmann Pinder, ed. *Logik-Vorlesung: Unveröffentlichte Nachschriften*. Hamburg: Meiner.
- (1999) Arnulf Zweig, ed. and trans. *Correspondence*. Cambridge: Cambridge Univ. Press.
- (2000a) Kowalewski, Sabina Laetitia and Werner Stark, eds. *Königsberger Kantiana*. [Kant, Werke. Volksausgabe, vol. 1, ed. Arnold Kowalewski]. Kant-Forschungen, vol. 12. Hamburg: Meiner.
- (2000b) Paul Guyer, ed. and trans., and Eric Matthews, trans. *Critique of the Power of Judgment*. Cambridge: Cambridge Univ. Press.
- (2001) Karl Ameriks and Steve Naragon, trans. and eds. *Lectures on Metaphysics*, revised edn. Cambridge: Cambridge Univ. Press.
- (2003) Norman Kemp Smith, trans. *Critique of Pure Reason*. Basingstoke: Palgrave Macmillan.
- (2004a) Werner Stark, ed., with preface by Manfred Kuehn. *Vorlesung zur Moralphilosophie*. Berlin: De Gruyter.
- ([1992] 2004b) Michael Young, trans. and ed. *Lectures on Logic*. Cambridge: Cambridge Univ. Press.
- (2004c) Jabik Veenbaas and Willem Visser, trans. and eds. *Kritiek van de zuivere rede*. Amsterdam: Boom.
- (2005) Paul Guyer, ed. and trans., Curtis Bowman and Frederick Rauscher, trans. *Notes and Fragments*. Cambridge: Cambridge Univ. Press.
- (2007) Günter Zöller and Robert B. Louden, eds. *Anthropology, History, and Education*. Cambridge: Cambridge Univ. Press.
- (2009a) Robert B. Louden, trans. *Lectures on Pedagogy*. In Steven M. Cahn, ed. *Philosophy of Education: The Essential Texts*. New York: Routledge, 253–80.
- (2009b) Werner Stark, ed., in collaboration with Reinhard Brandt. *Vorlesungen über Physische Geographie*. [Kant's gesammelte Schriften, vol. 26.1]. Berlin: De Gruyter.
- (2009c) Werner Pluhar, trans., with an Introduction by Stephen Palmquist. *Religion within the Bounds of Bare Reason*. Indianapolis: Hackett.
- (2012a) Robert B. Louden and Allen Wood, eds., Robert R. Clewis, Robert B. Louden, Felicitas Munzel, and Allen Wood, trans. *Lectures on Anthropology*. Cambridge: Cambridge Univ. Press.
- (2012b) Robert B. Louden, trans. *Lectures on Pedagogy*. In Steven M. Cahn, ed. *Classical and Contemporary Readings in the Philosophy of Education*. New York: Oxford Univ. Press, 153–73.
- (2012c) Eric Watkins, ed. *Natural Science*. Cambridge: Cambridge Univ. Press.
- (2013) "Kant's Handwritten Notes to the Metaphysics." In Alexander Gottlieb Baumgarten, *Metaphysics: A Critical Translation with Kant's Elucidations, Selected Notes, and Related Materials*, trans. and ed. Courtney Fugate and John Hymers. London: Bloomsbury, 35–51.
- (2016) Frederick Rauscher, ed., Frederick Rauscher and Kenneth Westphal, trans. *Lectures and Drafts on Political Philosophy*. Cambridge: Cambridge Univ. Press.

Kästner, Abraham Gotthelf (1758) *Anfangsgründe der Arithmetik, Geometrie, ebenen und sphärischen Trigonometrie, und Perspektiv*. Göttingen: Vandenhoek & Ruprecht.

Karsten, Wenceslaus Johann Gustav (1783) *Anleitung zur gemeinnützlichen Kenntniß der Natur, besonders für angehende Aerzte, Cameralisten und Oeconomen*. Halle: Renger. [Reprinted in *Kant's gesammelte Schriften*, vol. 29.1,1].

Kauder, Peter and Wolfgang Fischer (1999) *Immanuel Kant über Pädagogik. 7 Studien.* Hohengehren: Schneider.
Käuser, Andreas (1990) "Anthropologie und Ästhetik im 18. Jahrhundert." *Das achtzehnte Jahrhundert* 14 (2), 196–206.
Kelemen, Deborah (1999) "Why Are Rocks Pointy? Children's Preference for Teleological Explanations of the Natural World." *Developmental Psychology* 35, 1440–53.
Kemp Smith, Norman (1918) *A Commentary to Kant's "Critique of Pure Reason."* New York: Humanities Press.
Kerszberg, Pierre (2001) "Entre science et speculation: Kant et la chimie." In Volker Gerhardt, Rolf-Peter Horstmann, and Ralph Schumacher, eds. *Kant und die Berliner Aufklärung. Akten des IX. Internationalen Kant-Kongresses.* Berlin and New York: De Gruyter, 572–80.
Kleingeld, Pauline (2001) "Nature or Providence? On the Theoretical and Moral Importance of Kant's Philosophy of History." *American Catholic Philosophical Quarterly* 75, 201–19.
– (2007) "Kant's Second Thoughts on Race." *The Philosophical Quarterly* 57, 573–92.
– (2012) *Kant and Cosmopolitanism: The Philosophical Ideal of World Citizenship.* Cambridge: Cambridge Univ. Press.
Klemme, Heiner, ed. (1994) *Die Schule Immanuel Kants. Mit dem Text von Christian Schiffert über das Königsberger Collegium Fridericianum.* Kant-Forschungen, vol. 6. Hamburg: Meiner.
– (1996) *Kants Philosophie des Subjekts.* Hamburg: Meiner.
Kneale, William and Martha Kneale (1962) *The Development of Logic.* Oxford: Oxford Univ. Press.
Knittermeyer, Hinrich (1920) *Der Terminus transzendental in seiner historischen Entwicklung bis zu Kant.* Dissertation. Marburg.
– (1953/54) "Von der klassischen zur kritischen Transzendentalphilosophie." *Kant-Studien* 45, 113–31.
Kopitzsch, Franklin (1983) "Die Aufklärung in Deutschland: Zu ihren Leistungen, Grenzen und Wirkungen." *Archiv für Sozialgeschichte* 23, 1–21.
Kötter, Rudolf (1991) "Kants Schwierigkeiten mit der Physik. Ansätze zu einer problemorientierten Interpretation seiner späten Schriften zur Philosophie der Naturwissenschaft." In Siegfried Blasche, ed. *Übergang: Untersuchungen zum Spätwerk Immanuel Kants.* Frankfurt am Main: Klostermann, 157–84.
Kowalewski, Arnold and Elisabeth-Maria Kowalewski, eds. (1925) *Philosophischer Kalender für 1925. Im Zeichen Immanuel Kants.* Berlin: Reuther & Reichard.
Kreimendahl, Lothar (1990) *Kant – Der Durchbruch von 1769.* Cologne: Dinter.
Kuehn, Manfred (1983) "Dating Kant's 'Vorlesungen über Philosophische Enzyklopädie'." *Kant-Studien* 74, 302–13.
– (1987) *Scottish Common Sense in Germany, 1768–1800.* Kingston: McGill-Queens Univ. Press.
– (1998) "Skepticism: Philosophical Disease or Cure?" In Johan van der Zande and Richard Popkin, eds. *The Skeptical Tradition around 1800: Skepticism in Philosophy, Science and Society.* Dordrecht: Springer, 81–110.
– (2001a) *Kant: A Biography.* Cambridge: Cambridge Univ. Press.
– (2001b) "Kant's Teachers in the Exact Sciences." In Eric Watkins, ed. *Kant and the Sciences.* Oxford: Oxford Univ. Press, 11–30.
– (2012) "Kant on Education, Anthropology, and Ethics." In Klass Roth and Chris W. Surprenant, eds. *Kant and Education.* New York and London: Routledge, 55–68.

- (2015) "Collins: Kant's Proto-critical Position." In Lara Denis and Oliver Sensen, eds. *Kant's Lectures on Ethics: A Critical Guide*. Cambridge: Cambridge Univ. Press, 51–67.
Kühnemann, Eugen (1912) *Herder*. 2nd edn. Munich: C. H. Beck.
La Rocca, Claudio (2007) "L'intelletto oscuro. Inconscio e autocoscienza in Kant." In Claudio La Rocca, ed. *Leggere Kant. Dimensioni della filosofia critica*. Pisa: Edizione ETS, 63–116.
Lærke, Mogens, Justin E. H. Smith, and Eric Schliesser, eds. (2013) *Philosophy and Its History: Aims and Methods in the Study of Early Modern Philosophy*. Oxford: Oxford Univ. Press.
Lakoff, George and Mark Johnson (1980) *Metaphors We Live By*. Chicago: Univ. of Chicago Press.
Landucci, Sergio (1994) *Sull'etica di Kant*. Milan: Guerini e Associati.
Lang, Ossian H. (1891) *Basedow: His educational work and principles*. New York: Kellogg.
Langel, Hans (1909) *Die Entwicklung des Schulwesens in Preussen unter Franz Albrecht Schultz (1733–1763)*. Halle: Karras.
Larrimore, Mark (1999) "Sublime Waste: Kant on the Destiny of the Races." *Canadian Journal of Philosophy* 25, 99–125.
Laywine, Alison (1993) *Kant's Early Metaphysics and the Origins of the Critical Philosophy*. Atascadero, CA: Ridgeview.
- (2001) "Kant in Reply to Lambert on the Ancestry of Metaphysical Concepts." *Kantian Review* 5, 1–48.
Lazzari, Alessandro (2004) *"Das Eine, was der Menschheit Noth ist." Einheit und Freiheit in der Philosophie Karl Leonhard Reinholds (1789–1792)*. Stuttgart-Bad Cannstatt: Frommann-Holzboog.
Lee, Seung-Kee, Riccardo Pozzo, Marco Sgarbi, and Dagmar von Wille, eds. (2012) *Philosophical Academic Programs of the German Enlightenment*. Stuttgart-Bad Cannstatt: Frommann-Holzboog.
Lehmann, Gerhard (1961) "Einleitung zur Enzyklopädievorlesung." In Kant, *Vorlesungen über Enzyklopädische Philosophie*. Berlin: Akademie Verlag, 69–74.
- (1969) *Beiträge zur Geschichte und Interpretation der Philosophie Kants*. Berlin: De Gruyter.
- (1979) "Einleitung." In *Kant's gesammelte Schriften*, vol. 27. Berlin: De Gruyter, 1037–68.
Leibniz, Gottfried (1691) "De legibus naturae et vera aestimatione virium motricium contra Cartesianos." *Acta Eruditorum*, September 1691, 439–47.
- (1875–90) Carl Immanuel Gerhardt, ed. *Die philosophischen Schriften*. Berlin: Weidmann.
- (1962a) Leibniz-Forschungsstelle of the Universität Münster, ed. *Sämtliche Schriften und Briefe*. Series VI: *Philosophische Schriften*. Vol. 6: *Nouveaux Essais*. Berlin: Akademie Verlag.
- (1962b) Carl Immanuel Gerhardt, ed. *Mathematische Schriften*. Vol. 7: *Die mathematischen Abhandlungen*. Hildesheim: Olms.
- (1996) Peter Remnant and Jonathan Bennett, trans and eds. *New Essays on Human Understanding*. Cambridge: Cambridge Univ. Press.
- (1997) R. S. Woolhouse and Richard Francks, eds. and trans. *Leibniz's "New System" and Associated Contemporary Texts*. Oxford: Oxford Univ. Press.
Lessing, Gotthold Ephraim ([1766] 1984) *Laocoön: An Essay on the Limits of Painting and Poetry*, trans. Edward Allen McCormick. Baltimore: The Johns Hopkins Univ. Press.
Lindemann-Stark, Anke (1990). *Kants Vorlesungen zur Anthropologie in Hippels "Lebensläufen."* Magisterarbeit. Marburg.

Livingstone, David N. (1992) *The Geographical Tradition: Episodes in the History of a Contested Enterprise*. Oxford: Blackwell.
Livingstone David N. and R. T. Harrison (1981) "Immanuel Kant, Subjectivism, and Human Geography: A Preliminary Investigation." *Transactions of the Institute of British Geographers* 6, 359–74.
Locke, John (1975) P. H. Nidditch, ed. *Essays Concerning Human Understanding*. Oxford: Oxford Univ. Press.
— (1996a) Ruth W. Grant and Nathan Tarcov, eds. *Some Thoughts Concerning Education; Of the Conduct of the Understanding*. Indianapolis: Hackett.
— (1996b) Terry Boswell, Riccardo Pozzo, and Clemens Schwaiger, eds. *Anleitung des menschlichen Verstandes: Eine Abhandlung von den Wunderwerken*. In der Übersetzung Königsberg 1755 von Georg David Kypke. Stuttgart-Bad Cannstatt: Frommann-Holzboog.
Longuenesse, Béatrice (1998) *Kant and the Capacity to Judge*, trans. Charles T. Wolfe. Princeton: Princeton Univ. Press.
Louden, Robert B. (2000) *Kant's Impure Ethics: From Rational Beings to Human Beings*. New York: Oxford Univ. Press.
— (2007) "Translator's Introduction to *Lectures on Pedagogy*." In Kant, *Anthropology, History, and Education*, ed. Günter Zöller and Robert B. Louden. Cambridge: Cambridge Univ. Press, 434–6.
— (2011a) "'The Play of Nature': Human Beings in Kant's Geography." In Stuart Elden and Eduardo Mendieta, eds. *Reading Kant's Geography*. Albany: SUNY Press, 139–60.
— (2011b) *Kant's Human Being: Essays on His Theory of Human Nature*. New York: Oxford Univ. Press.
— (2012a) "Translator's Introduction to *Menschenkunde*." In Kant, *Lectures on Anthropology*, ed. Robert B. Louden and Allen W. Wood. Cambridge: Cambridge Univ. Press, 283–7.
— (2012b) "'Not a Slow *Reform*, but a Swift *Revolution*': Kant and Basedow on the Need to Transform Education." In Klas Roth and Chris W. Surprenant, eds. *Kant and Education: Interpretations and Commentary*. New York: Routledge, 39–54.
— (2014) "The Last Frontier: Exploring Kant's Geography." *Society and Space* 32 (3), 450–65.
— (2015) "*Vigilantius*: Morality for Humans." In Lara Denis and Oliver Sensen, eds. *Kant's Lectures on Ethics: A Critical Guide*. Cambridge: Cambridge Univ. Press, 84–99.
Loughlin, Martin (2003) *The Idea of Public Law*. Oxford: Oxford Univ. Press.
— (2010) *Foundations of Public Law*. Oxford: Oxford Univ. Press.
Lu-Adler, Huaping (2012) *Kant's Conception of Logical Extension and Its Implications*. Ph.D. Dissertation. Univ. of California-Davis.
— (2013) "The Objects and the Formal Truth of Kantian Analytic Judgments." *History of Philosophy Quarterly* 30, 177–93.
— (2014) "Kant on the Logical Form of Singular Judgements." *Kantian Review* 19 (3), 367–92.
Ludwig, Bernd (1988) Reinhard Brandt and Werner Stark, eds. *Kants Rechtlehre*. Kant-Forschungen, vol. 2. Hamburg: Meiner.
Makkreel, Rudolf (2012) "Relating Aesthetic and Sociable Feelings to Moral and Participatory Feelings: Reassessing Kant on Sympathy and Honor." In Susan Shell and Richard Velkley, eds. *Kant's "Observations" and "Remarks": A Critical Guide*. Cambridge: Cambridge Univ. Press, 101–15.
Maliks, Reidar (2012) "Revolutionary Epigones: Kant and his Radical Followers" *History of Political Thought* 33, 647–71.

Malpas, Jeff and Karsten Thiel (2011) "Kant's Geography of Reason." In Stuart Elden and Eduardo Mendieta, eds. *Reading Kant's Geography*. Albany: SUNY Press, 195–214.
Malter, Rudolf (1987) "Physische Geographie Kaehler." *Kant-Studien* 78, 259.
— ed. (1990) *Immanuel Kant in Rede und Gespräch*. Hamburg: Meiner.
Marcuzzi, Max (2011) "Writing Space: Historical Narrative and Geographical Description in Kant's *Physical Geography*." In Stuart Elden and Eduardo Mendieta, eds. *Reading Kant's Geography*. Albany: SUNY Press, 115–36.
Martin, Geoffrey J. (1989) "*The Nature of Geography* and the Schaefer-Hartshorne Debate." In Nicholas J. Entrikin and Stanley D. Brunn, eds. *Reflections on Richard Hartshorne's The Nature of Geography*. Washington, D. C.: Association of American Geographers, 69–90.
Martin, Gottfried (1936) "Herder als Schüler Kants. Aufsätze und Kolleghefte aus Herders Studienzeit." *Kant-Studien* 41, 294–306.
— (1967) "Die mathematischen Vorlesungen Kants." *Kant-Studien* 58, 58–61.
— (1985) *Arithmetic and Combinatorics. Kant and His Contemporaries*, trans. and ed. Judy Wubnig. Carbondale and Edwardsville: Southern Illinois Univ. Press. [Originally published as *Arithmetik und Kombinatorik bei Kant*. Berlin and New York: De Gruyter, 1972].
Marx, Karl (1971) *Frühschriften*. Stuttgart: Kröner.
Massimi, Michela (2011) "Kant's Dynamical Theory of Matter in 1755, and Its Debt to Speculative Newtonian Experimentalism." *Studies in History and Philosophy of Science* 42, 525–43.
Mauser, Wolfram (1989) "Geselligkeit: Zu Chance und Scheitern einer sozialethischen Utopie um 1750." In Karl Eibl, ed. *Entwicklungsschwellen im 18. Jahrhundert*. Hamburg: Meiner, 5–36.
May, Gerhard (2003) "Augustinus als Prediger, Seelsorger und Bischof." In Gerhard May and Geesche Hönscheid, eds. *Die Mainzer Augustinus-Predigten. Studien zu einem Jahrhundertfund*. Mainz: Philipp von Zabern, 95–105.
May, J. A. (1970) *Kant's Concept of Geography and its Relation to Recent Geographical Thought*. Toronto: Univ. of Toronto Press.
Mayhew, Robert J. (2010) "Geography as the Eye of Enlightenment Historiography." *Modern Intellectual History* 7, 611–27.
McLear, Colin (2011) "Kant on Animal Consciousness." *Philosopher's Imprint* 11 (15), 1–16.
McNulty, Bennett (2014) "Kant on Chemistry and the Application of Mathematics in Natural Science" *Kantian Review* 19 (3), 393–418.
Meer, Frederik van der (1951) *Augustinus der Seelsorger. Leben und Wirken eines Kirchenvaters*. Cologne: Bachem.
Meier, Georg Friedrich (1746) *Gedancken von dem Zustande der Seele nach dem Tode*. Halle: Hemmerde.
— (1752a) *Vernunftlehre*. Halle: Gebauer.
— (1752b) *Auszug aus der Vernunftlehre*. Halle: Gebauer. [In *Kant's gesammelte Schriften*, vol. 16].
Meiners, Christoph (1772) *Revision der Philosophie*. Göttingen and Gotha: Dieterich.
— (1773) *Kurzer Abriß der Psychologie*. Göttingen and Gotha: Dieterich.
— (1787) *Grundriß der Theorie und Geschichte der schönen Wissenschaften*. Lemgo: Meyer.
— (1780) *Historia doctrinae de vero Deo omnium rerum auctore atque rectore*. Lemgo: Meyer.
Meister Eckhart (1993) *Werke*, ed. Niklaus Largier. 2 vols. Frankfurt am Main: Deutscher Klassiker Verlag.
Melton, James Van Horn (1988) *Absolutism and the Eighteenth Century Origins of Compulsory Schooling in Prussia and Austria*. Cambridge: Cambridge Univ. Press.

– (2001) *The Rise of the Public Sphere in Enlightenment Europe*. Cambridge: Cambridge Univ. Press.
Mendelssohn, Moses (1989) *Schriften über Religion und Aufkärung*, ed. Martina Thom. Berlin: Union Verlag.
– (2013) *Phädon oder über die Unsterblichkeit der Seele*, ed. Anne Pollok. Hamburg: Felix Meiner.
Mensch, Jennifer (2013) *Kant's Organicism: Epigenesis and the Development of Critical Philosophy*. Chicago: Univ. of Chicago Press.
Mikkelsen, Jon, ed. and trans. (2013) *Kant and the Concept of Race*. Albany: SUNY Press.
Mittelstraß, Jürgen (1999) *Die Häuser des Wissens: Wissenschaftstheoretische Studien*. Frankfurt am Main: Suhrkamp.
Montucla, Jean Etienne (1758) *Histoire des Mathématiques*. Vol. 1. Paris: Ch. Ant. Jombert.
Moran, Kate A. (2012) *Community and Progress in Kant's Moral Philosophy*. Washington, D. C.: Catholic Univ. of America Press.
Moravia, Sergio (1973) *Beobachtende Vernunft: Philosophie und Anthropologie in der Aufklärung*. Munich: Hanser.
Moretto, Antonio (1986) "'Limite' e 'analogia' in alcuni aspetti della filosofia critica di Kant." *Verifiche* 15 (4), 341–64.
– (1999) *Dottrina delle grandezze e filosofia trascendentale in Kant*. Padua: Il Poligrafo.
– (2004a) "Tempo e memoria nella fondazione kantiana della matematica." In Antonio Moretto, ed. *Scienza e conoscenza secondo Kant*. Padua: Il Poligrafo, 527–51.
– (2004b) "Die Auffassung des Endlichen und des Unendlichen in der Mathematik nach Kant und Hegel." In Francesca Menegoni and Luca Illetterati, eds. *Das Endliche und das Unendliche in Hegels Denken*. Stuttgart: Klett-Cotta, 58–80.
– (2007) "Matematica e psicologia empirica in Wolff." In Ferdinando L. Marcolungo, ed. *Christian Wolff tra psicologia empirica e psicologia razionale*. Vol. 106 of Jean Ecole, Hans Werner Arndt, Robert Theis, Werner Schneiders, and Sonia Carboncini-Gavanelli, eds. Christian Wolff, *Gesammelte Werke. Materialien und Dokumente*. Hildesheim: Olms, 145–65.
– (2008) "Zur Auffassung des Begriffs der mathematischen Relation in Christian Wolffs Ontologia." In Jürgen Stolzenberg and Oliver-Pierre Rudolph, eds. *Christian Wolff und die europäische Aufklärung*. Part 4, Section 8: Mathematik und Naturwissenschaften. Hildesheim: Olms, 25–37.
– (2010) "Matematica." In Stefano Besoli, Claudio La Rocca, and Riccardo Martinelli, eds. *L'universo kantiano. Filosofia, scienze, sapere*. Macerata: Quodlibet, 261–313.
– (2012) "La teoria elementare della misura delle grandezze da un punto di vista filosofico-matematico." In Paola Di Nicola, ed. *La sfida della misurazione nelle scienze sociali*. Milan: Franco Angeli, 17–35.
– (2013) "Con Euclide e contro Euclide: Kant e la geometria." *Studi Kantiani* 26, 71–91.
Morgenstern, Karl (1821) "Litterarische Berichtigungen." *Dörptische Beyträge für Freunde der Philosophie, Litteratur und Kunst* 3 (2), 485.
– (1843) *D. Gottlob Benjamin Jäsche. Kathedervortrag [...] gehalten am 3. September 1842 [...]*. Dorpat: Laakmann.
Mortier, Roland (1974) "Diderot, Ernesti, et la 'Philosophie populaire'." In John Pappas, ed. *Essays on Diderot and the Enlightenment in Honor of Otis Fellows*. Geneva: Droz, 207–30.
Munzel, G. Felicitas (1999) *Kant's Conception of Moral Character: The "Critical" Link of Morality, Anthropology, and Reflective Judgment*. Chicago: Univ. of Chicago Press.

— (2012) *Kant's Conception of Pedagogy: Toward Education for Freedom*. Evanston: Northwestern Univ. Press.
Murphy, Daniel (1995) *Comenius: A Critical Reassessment of His Life and Works*. Dublin: Irish Academic Press.
Muthu, Sankar (2003) *Enlightenment against Empire*. Princeton: Princeton Univ. Press.
Naragon, Steve (2000) "The Metaphysics Lectures in the Academy Edition of Kant's *gesammelte Schriften*." In Reinhard Brandt and Werner Stark, eds. *Zustand und Zukunft der Akademie-Ausgabe von Immanuel Kants Gesammelten Schriften*. Kant-Studien 91, Sonderheft. Berlin and New York: De Gruyter, 190–216.
— (2015a) "Kant in the Classroom." http://www.manchester.edu/kant/Home/index.htm. [For all of the following entries from Naragon's website: accessed 11 May 2015].
— (2015b) "Introduction: Kant's Lectures." http://www.manchester.edu/kant/Lectures/lecturesIntro.htm
— (2015c) "Moral Philosophy Notes." http://www.manchester.edu/kant/Notes/notesMoral.htm
— (2015d) "Kant's Lecture Announcements." https://www.manchester.edu/kant/lectures/lecturesAnnouncements.htm
— (2015e) "Contemporary Accounts of Kant's Lectures and Notes." http://www.manchester.edu/kant/lectures/lecturesListAccounts.htm
— (2015f) "Kant's Textbooks." http://www.manchester.edu/kant/Lectures/lectures-Textbooks.htm
— (2015g) "Production of the Notes." http://www.manchester.edu/kant/notes/notesProduction.htm
— (2015h) "Past Evaluations of the Notes." http://www.manchester.edu/kant/Notes/notesPastUse.htm
— (2015i) "Glossary." http://www.manchester.edu/kant/Helps/Glossary.htm
— (2015j) "Introduction: The Student Notes." http://www.manchester.edu/kant/Notes/notesIntro.htm
— (2015k) "Kant's Lectures by Discipline." http://www.manchester.edu/kant/Lectures/lectureslistdiscipline.htm
— (2015l) "Academic Instruction." http://www.manchester.edu/kant/Professors/profsInstruction.htm
Newton, Isaac ([1729] 2010) *The Principia: Mathematical Principles of Natural Philosophy*, trans. Andrew Motte, based on 3rd Latin edn., 1726. London: Snowball Publishing.
Nietzsche, Friedrich (1888–89) *Der Antichrist. Fluch auf das Christenthum*. In Giorgio Colli and Mazzino Montinari, eds. *Kritische Studienausgabe*, vol. 6. Munich, Berlin and New York: dtv/ De Gruyter, 165–254.
— (1918) H. L. Mencken, trans. *The Antichrist*. New York: Knopf. [Reprinted in Costa Mesa, CA: The Noontide Press, 1998.]
Oberhausen, Michael and Riccardo Pozzo, eds. (1999) *Vorlesungsverzeichnisse der Universität Königsberg: 1720–1804*. Forschungen und Materialien zur Universitätsgeschichte. Division I, Vol. 1. Stuttgart-Bad Cannstatt: Frommann-Holzboog.
Palmquist, Stephen R. (1992a) "Kant's 'Appropriation' of Lampe's God." *Harvard Theological Review* 85 (1), 85–108.
— (1992b) "Does Kant Reduce Religion To Morality?" *Kant-Studien* 83 (2), 129–48.
— (1997) "Kant's Critical Hermeneutic of Prayer." *The Journal of Religion* 77 (4), 584–604.

- (2000) *Kant's Critical Religion: Volume Two of Kant's System of Perspectives*. Aldershot: Ashgate.
- (2008a) "Kant's Moral Panentheism." *Philosophia* 36 (1), 17–28.
- (2008b) "Kant's Quasi-Transcendental Argument for a Necessary and Universal Evil Propensity in Human Nature." *The Southern Journal of Philosophy* 46 (2), 261–97.
- (2010) "Kant's Ethics of Grace: Perspectival Solutions to the Moral Difficulties with Divine Assistance." *The Journal of Religion* 90 (4), 530–53.
- (2013) "Could Kant's Jesus Be God?" *International Philosophical Quarterly* 52 (4), 421–37.
- (2015a) "What is Kantian *Gesinnung*? On the Priority of Volition over Metaphysics and Psychology in Kant's *Religion*." *Kantian Review* 20 (2), 235–64.
- (2015b) *Comprehensive Commentary on Kant's Religion within the Bounds of Bare Reason*. Chichester: Wiley-Blackwell.

Palmquist, Stephen R. and Steven Otterman (2013) "The Implied Standpoint of Kant's *Religion*: An Assessment of Kant's Reply to (and an English Translation of) an Early Book Review of *Religion within the Bounds of Bare Reason*." *Kantian Review* 18 (1), 73–97.

Parsons, Charles (1992a) *Kant's Philosophy of Arithmetic*. In Carl Posy, ed. *Kant's Philosophy of Mathematics. Modern Essays*. Dordrecht: Kluwer, 43–79.
- (1992b) *Arithmetic and the Categories*. In Carl Posy, ed. *Kant's Philosophy of Mathematics. Modern Essays*. Dordrecht: Kluwer, 135–58.

Pasternack, Lawrence (2013) *Routledge Guidebook to Kant on Religion within the Boundaries of Mere Reason*. Abingdon, U.K.: Routledge.

Paulsen, Friedrich ([1899] 1920) *Immanuel Kant. Sein Leben und seine Lehre*. Stuttgart: Fromann.

Petrus, Klaus (1994) "'Beschrieene Dunkelheit' und 'Seichtigkeit,' Historisch-systematische Veraussetzungen der Auseinandersetzung zwischen Kant und Garve im Umfeld der Göttinger Rezension." *Kant-Studien* 85, 280–302.

Pfotenauer, Helmut (1987) *Literarische Anthropologie*. Stuttgart: Metzler.

Piaget, Jean (1929) *The Child's Conception of the World*. New York: Harcourt.

Piché, Claude (2001) "The Precritical Use of the Metaphor of Epigenesis." In Tom Rockmore, ed. *New Essays on the Precritical Kant*. Amherst: Humanity Books, 182–200.

Pinzani, Alessandro (2008) "Representation in Kant's Political Theory." *Jahrbuch für Recht und Ethik* 16, 203–26.

Pisanski, Georg Christoph and Rudolf Philippi, eds. (1886) *Entwurf einer preußischen Literärgeschichte in vier Büchern. Mit einer Notiz über den Autor und sein Buch*. Königsberg. [Reprint in *Sonderschriften des Vereins für Familienforschung in Ost- und Westpreußen e. V.*, No. 80 (1), 1994].

Plaaß, Peter (1965) *Kants Theorie der Naturwissenschaft. Eine Untersuchung zur Vorrede von Kants Metaphysischen Anfangsgründen der Naturwissenschaft*. Göttingen: Vandenhoeck & Rupprecht.

Platon (1972) *Werke*, ed. Günther Engler. 8 vols. Darmstadt: Wissenschaftliche Buchgesellschaft.

Pollok, Konstantin (2008) "'An almost single inference' – Kant's Deduction of the Categories Reconsidered." *Archiv für Geschichte der Philosophie* 90 (3), 323–45.
- (2012) "Wie sind Erfahrungsurteile möglich?" In Holger Lyre and Oliver Schliemann, eds. *Kants Prolegomena. Ein kooperativer Kommentar*. Frankfurt am Main: Klostermann, 103–25.

Pontynen, Arthur (2006) *For the Love of Beauty: Art, History, and the Moral Foundations of Aesthetic Judgment*. New Brunswick: Transaction Publishers.
Pozzo, Riccardo (1986) "Kant sulla questione della chiusura di Cina e Giappone: Discrepanze tra gli scritti a stampa e le *Vorlesungen über die physische Geographie*." *Rivista di storia della filosofia* 41, 725–45.
— (1989) *Kant und das Problem einer Einleitung in die Logik: Ein Beitrag zur Rekonstruktion der historischen Hintergründe von Kants Logik-Kolleg*. Frankfurt am Main: Lang.
— (1991) "Catalogus Praelectionum Academiae Regiomontanae." *Studi Kantiani* 4, 163–87.
— (1998) "Kant within the Tradition of Modern Logic: The Role of the 'Introduction: Idea of a Transcendental Logic'." *The Review of Metaphysics* 52, 295–310.
— (2000) *Georg Friedrich Meiers "Vernunftlehre": Eine historisch-systematische Untersuchung*. Forschungen und Materialien zur deutschen Aufklärung. Division II, Vol. 15. Stuttgart-Bad Cannstatt: Frommann-Holzboog.
— (2001) "Dallo 'intellectus purus' alla 'reine Vernunft': Note sul passaggio dal latino al tedesco prima e dopo Kant." *Giornale critico della filosofia italiana* 82, 231–45.
— (2015) *Kant y el problema de una introducción a la logica*, trans. Jaime Gonsález-Capitel. Madrid: Maia.
Priestley, Joseph (1767) *The History and Present State of Electricity, with Original Experiments*. London: J. Dodsley, J. Johnson, B. Davenport, and T. Cadell [sic].
Rausch, Alfred (1924) *Immanuel Kant als Pädagoge. Zur zweihundertsten Wiederkehr seines Geburtstages*. Annaberg im Erzgebirge: Neupädagogischer Verlag.
Rauscher, Frederick (2012) "Review Essay: A New Resource for Kant's Political Philosophy." *Kantian Review* 17, 357–65.
Redekop, Benjamin W. (2000) *Enlightenment and Community: Lessing, Abbt, Herder, and the Quest for a German Public*. Montreal: McGill-Queens Univ. Press.
Reicke, Rudolf (1881) "Scheffner über Herders Metakritik." *Altpreußische Monatsschrift* 18, 438–45.
Reimarus, Hermann Samuel (1766) *Die vornehmste Wahrheiten der natürlichen Religion*. Hamburg: Johann Carl Bohn.
Reinhardt, Olaf (2011) "Translating Kant's *Physical Geography*: Travails and Insights into Eighteenth Century Science (and Philosophy)." In Stuart Elden and Eduardo Mendieta, eds. *Reading Kant's Geography*. Albany: SUNY Press, 103–14.
Reinhold, Karl Leonhard (1797) "Einige Bemerkungen über die in der Einleitung zu den metaphysischen Anfangsgründen der Rechtslehre von J. Kant aufgestellten Begriffe von der Freyheit des Willens." In K. L. Reinhold, *Auswahl vermischter Schriften*, vol. 2. Jena: Mauke, 364–400.
— (2004) *Beiträge zur Berichtigung bisheriger Mißverständnisse der Philosophen. Zweiter Band, die Fundamente des philosophischen Wissens, der Metaphysik, Moral, moralischen Religion und Geschmackslehre betreffend*, ed. with introduction and notes by Faustino Fabbianelli. Hamburg: Meiner.
— (2008) *Briefe über die Kantische Philosophie. Zweyter Band*. In K. L. Reinhold, *Gesammelte Schriften. Kommentierte Ausgabe*, ed. Martin Bondeli, vol. 2,2. Basel: Schwabe Verlag.
Reisert, Joseph (2012) "Kant and Rousseau on Moral Education." In Klas Roth and Chris Surprenant, eds. *Kant and Education*. New York and London: Routledge, 12–25.
Richards, Paul (1974) "Kant's Geography and Mental Maps." *Transactions of the Institute of British Geographers* 61, 1–16.

Riedel, Wolfgang (1992) "Influxus physicus und Seelestärke." In Jürgen Barkoff and Eda Sagarra, eds. *Anthropologie und Literatur um 1800*. Munich: Iudicium, 24–52.
Rink, Friedrich Theodor, ed. (1800a) *Sammlung einiger bisher unbekannt gebliebener kleiner Schriften von Immanuel Kant*. Königsberg: Friedrich Nicolovius.
— (1800b) *Aphorismen über Volkserziehung und das Landschulwesen insbesondre: mit Hinsicht auf die vorgeschlagenen Verbesserungen des letztern in den Preußischen Staaten*. Königsberg: Goebbels & Unzer.
— ed. (1802) *Immanuel Kant's physische Geographie*. 2 vols. Königsberg: Göbbels & Unzer.
— ed. (1803) *Immanuel Kant über Pädagogik*. Königsberg: Nicolovius.
— (1805) *Ansichten aus Immanuel Kant's Leben*. Königsberg: Göbbels & Unzer.
— (1811a) *Verzeichniß der hinterlassenen Bibliothek des wohlseligen Herrn F. T. Rink, der Philosophie u. Theol. Doktors, des Danziger Gymnasii Rektors, der S. Trinitatis-Kirche Pastors, der Theologie, der griech. u. der morgenländischen Sprachen Professors, welche 1811, den 23. Septbr. durch öffentlichen Ausruf, in der Holzgasse Nro. 26 verkauft wird*. (Danzig, printed with Müllerschen writings) [Copy: UB Tübingen / Ke XXIV 732].
— (1811b) *Memoria viri summe venerabilis atque doctissimi Friderici Theodori Rinkii [...]*. Danzig: Gymnasialprogramm.
Rink, Friedrich Theodor and Gottlob Benjamin Jäsche, eds. (1800) *Mancherley zur Geschichte der metacritischen Invasion von Johann Georg Hamann genannt Magnus in Norden, und einige Aufsätze die kantische Philosophie betreffend. Nebst einem Fragment einer älteren Metakritik*. Königsberg: Nicolovius. [Reprint: Brussels 1968].
Ritter, Christian (1971) *Der Rechtsgedanke Kants nach den frühen Quellen*. Frankfurt am Main: Klostermann.
Robinson, Hoke (2000) "Logik-Vorlesung: Unveröffentlichte Nachschriften" (Review). *Journal of the History of Philosophy* 38, 603–5.
Rosenkranz, Karl and Friedrich Wilhelm Schubert, eds. (1838–42) *Immanuel Kant's sämtliche Werke*. 12 vols. Leipzig: Leopold Voss.
Roth, Klass and Chris W. Suprenant, eds. (2012) *Kant and Education*. New York and London: Routledge.
Rousseau, Jean-Jacques (1973) *The Social Contract and Discourses*, trans. G. D. H. Cole. London: Everyman Library.
— (2010) *Emile: or on Education*, trans. Allan Bloom and Christopher Kelly. In Roger Masters and Christopher Kelly, eds. *The Collected Writings of Rousseau*, vol. 13. Hanover: Dartmouth College Press.
Sala, Giovanni B. (2004) "Das Reich Gottes auf Erden. Kants Lehre von der Kirche als 'ethischem gemeinen Wesen'." In Norbert Fischer, ed. *Kants Metaphysik und Religionsphilosophie*. Hamburg: Meiner, 225–64.
Santos, Robinson dos (2007) *Moralität und Erziehung bei Immanuel Kant*. Kassel: Kassel Univ. Press.
Schaefer, Fred K. (1953) "Exceptionalism in Geography: A Methodological Examination." *Annals of the Association of American Geographers* 43, 226–49.
Scheffner, Johann Georg (1918–38) Arthur Warda and Carl Diesch, eds. *Briefe von und an Johann Georg Scheffner*. 5 Vols. [Vols. 1–4: Munich and Leipzig: Duncker & Humblot 1918–31. Vol. 5: Königsberg: Gräfe & Unzer 1938].
Schiavone, Aldo (2005) *L'invenzione del diritto in Occidente*. Turin: Einaudi.
— (2012) *The Invention of Law in the West*, trans. Jeremy Carden and Antony Shugar. Cambridge: Belknap Press.

Schiffert, Christian (1741) *Nachricht von den jetzigen Anstalten des Collegii Fridericiani.* In *Erleutertes Preußen* 5 [1742]. Königsberg: Hartung, 587–672. [Reprinted in Heiner Klemme, ed. *Die Schule Immanuel Kants.* Kant-Forschungen, vol. 6. Hamburg: Meiner, 1994].
Schings, Hans-Jürgen (1977) "Der philosophische Arzt: Anthropologie, Melancholie und Literatur im achtzehnten Jahrhundert." In *Melancholie und Aufklärung.* Stuttgart: Metzler, 11–40.
— ed. (1994) *Der ganze Mensch: Anthropologie und Literaatur im achtzehnten Jahrhundert* Stuttgart: Metzler.
Schlichtegroll, Friedrich, ed. (1803) *Nekrolog der Teutschen für das neunzehnte Jahrhundert*, vol. 2. Gotha: Perthes.
Schmid, Carl Christian Erhard (1975) *Versuch einer Moralphilosophie* [Jena 1790]. In Rüdiger Bittner and Konrad Cramer, eds. *Materialien zu Kants "Kritik der praktischen Vernunft."* Frankfurt am Main: Suhrkamp, 241–51.
Schmucker, Josef (1961) *Die Ursprünge der Ethik Kants in seinen vorkritischen Schriften und Reflexionen.* Meisenheim: A. Hain.
Schneewind, Jerome (1997) "Introduction." In Kant, *Lectures on Ethics*, ed. Peter Heath and Jerome Schneewind. Cambridge: Cambridge Univ. Press, xiii–xxvii.
Schneider, Ulrich J. (1996) "Intellectual History and the History of Philosophy." *Intellectual News* 1, 28–30.
Schneiders, Werner (1983) "Zwischen Welt und Weisheit: Zur Verweltlichung der Philosophie in der frühe Moderne." *Studia Leibnitiana* 15 (1), 2–18.
Schnepf, Robert (2001) "Metaphysik oder Metaphysikkritik? Das Kausalitätsproblem in Kants Abhandlung *Über die negativen Größen.*" *Archiv für Geschichte der Philosophie* 83, 130–59.
Schönfeld, Martin (2000) *The Philosophy of the Young Kant: The Precritical Project.* Oxford and New York: Oxford Univ. Press.
Schulting, Dennis (2012) *Kant's Deduction and Apperception. Explaining the Categories.* Basingstoke and New York: Palgrave Macmillan.
— (forthcoming a) "'Pure Consciousness Is Found Already in Logic': On Apperception, Spontaneity, and Judgement."
— (forthcoming b) "In Defence of Reinhold's Kantian Representationalism." *Kant Yearbook* 8 [2016].
Schulz, Günter Eberhard (1960) "Christian Garve und Immanuel Kant: Gelehrten-Tugenden im 18. Jahrhundert." *Jahrbuch der Schlesischen Friedrich-Wilhelms-Universität zu Breslau* 5, 123–88.
Schwaiger, Clemens (2000) "Die Vorlesungsnachschriften zu Kants praktischer Philosophie in der Akademie-Ausgabe." In Reinhard Brandt and Werner Stark, eds. *Zustand und Zukunft der Akademie-Ausgabe von Immanuel Kants Gesammelten Schriften.* Kant-Studien 91, Sonderheft. Berlin and New York: De Gruyter, 178–88.
Schwartz, Paul (1910–12) *Die Gelehrtenschulen Preußens unter dem Oberschulkollegium (1787–1806) und das Abiturientenexamen.* 3 vols. Berlin: Weidmann. [Monumenta Germaniae Paedagogica: Nos. 46, 48, 50].
— (1925) *Der erste Kulturkampf in Preußen um Kirche und Schule (1788–1798).* Berlin: Weidmann. [Monumenta Germaniae Paedagogica: No. 58].
— (1931) "Die Schulen der Provinz Ostpreußen unter dem Oberschulkollegium 1787–1806." *Zeitschrift für Geschichte der Erziehung und des Unterrichts* 21, 54–78 and 280–307.

Schwarz, Walter (1915) *Immanuel Kant als Pädagoge.* Langensalza: Beyer. [*Systematische Darstellung der pädagogischen Anschauungen Kants.* Dissertation. Königsberg].
Segner, Johann Andreas von (1747) *Deutliche und vollständige Vorlesungen über die Rechenkunst und Geometrie.* Lemgo: Meyer.
— (1756) *Cursus matematici pars I. Elementa Arithmeticae, Geometriae et Calculi Geometrici.* Halle: Renger.
— ([1764] 1773) *Anfangsgründe der Arithmetik, Geometrie und der Geometrischen Berechnungen.* 2nd edn. Halle: Renger.
Seifert, Arno (1976) *Cognitio historica: Die Geschichte als Namengeberin der frühneuzeitlichen Empirie.* Berlin: Duncker & Humblot.
Sensen, Oliver (2012) "The Role of Feelings in Kant's Moral Philosophy." *Studi Kantiani* 25, 45–58.
— (2013) "Kant's Constructivism." In Carla Bagnoli, ed. *Constructivism in Ethics.* Cambridge: Cambridge Univ. Press, 63–81.
— (2014) "Universalizing as a Moral Demand." *Estudos Kantianos* 2 (1), 169–84.
Sgarbi, Marco (2010) *Logica e metafisica nel Kant precritico: L'ambiente intellettuale di Königsberg e la formazione della filosofia kantiana.* Frankfurt am Main: Lang.
Shabel, Lisa A. (2003) *Mathematics in Kant's Critical Philosophy. Reflections on Mathematical Practice.* New York and London: Routledge.
Shell, Susan Meld (1996) *The Embodiment of Reason: Kant on Spirit, Generation, and Community.* Chicago: Univ. of Chicago Press.
— (2009) *Kant and the Limits of Autonomy.* Cambridge, MA: Harvard Univ. Press.
Shell, Susan and Richard Velkley, eds. (2012) *Kant's "Observations" and "Remarks": A Critical Guide.* Cambridge: Cambridge Univ. Press.
Siegmund-Schultze, Reinhard (2014) *Zur Entwicklung des Begriffs der Angewandten Mathematik von Wolff bis Mises.* In Michael Fothe et al., eds. *Mathematik und Anwendungen.* Bad Berka: Thüringer Institut für Lehrerfortbildung, Lehrplanentwicklung und Medien (Thillm), 21–5.
Sloan, Phillip R. (1973) "The Idea of Racial Degeneracy in Buffon's *Histoire Naturelle.*" *Studies in Eighteenth-Century Culture* 3, 293–321.
— (2002) "Preforming the Categories: Eighteenth-Century Generation Theory and the Biological Roots of Kant's A Priori." *Journal of the History of Philosophy* 40, 229–53.
Solomon, Robert C. and Lori D. Stone (2002) "On 'Positive' and 'Negative' Emotions." *Journal for the Theory of Social Behaviour* 32 (4), 417–35.
Sonderling, Jakob (1903) *Die Beziehungen der Kant-Jäscheschen Logik zu George Friedrich Meiers "Auszug aus der Vernunftlehre."* Berlin: A. Scholem.
Spalding, Johann (1908) *Betrachtung über die Bestimmung des Menschen.* In Horst Stephan, ed. *Spaldings Bestimmung des Menschen (1748) und Wert der Andacht (1755).* Giessen: Töpelmann.
Stark, Werner (1992) "Die Formen von Kants akademischer Lehre." *Deutsche Zeitschrift für Philosophie* 40, 543–62.
— (1993) *Nachforschungen zu Briefen und Handschriften Immanuel Kants.* Berlin: Akademie Verlag.
— (1995) "Kant als akademischer Lehrer." In Heinz Ischreyt, ed. *Königsberg und Riga.* Tübingen: Niemeyer, 51–68.
— (2000) "Vorlesung – Nachlass – Druckschrift? Bemerkungen zu *Kant über Pädagogik.*" In Reinhard Brandt and Werner Stark, eds. *Zustand und Zukunft der Akademie-Ausgabe von*

Immanuel Kants Gesammelten Schriften. Kant-Studien 91, Sonderheft. Berlin and New York: De Gruyter, 94–105.
— (2003) "Krótkie wyjasnienie historyczne odnoscie Fragmentu krakowskiego" [Polish: Brief Historical Clarification of the "Krakauer Fragment"]. In Immanuel Kant, *Spór Fakultetów* [Polish Translation of *Streit der Fakultäten*], ed. and trans. Mirosław Żelazny. Toruń and Lubicz, 169–186. [Original, German edn. at: http://archiv.ub.uni-marburg.de/es/2010/0012/. Accessed 11 February 2015].
— (2004) "Nachwort." In Kant, *Vorlesung zur Moralphilosophie*, ed. Werner Stark. Berlin: De Gruyter, 371–407.
— (2009) "Das Manuskript Dönhoff – eine unverhoffte Quelle zu Kants Vorlesungen über Physische Geographie." *Kant-Studien* 100, 107–9.
— (2011a) "Kant's Lectures on 'Physical Geography'. A Brief Outline of Its Origins, Transmission, and Development: 1754–1805." In Stuart Elden and Eduardo Mendieta, eds. *Reading Kant's Geography*. Albany: SUNY Press, 69–85.
— (2011b) "Historical and Philological References on the Question of a Possible Hierarchy of Human 'Races', 'Peoples', or 'Populations' in Immanuel Kant – A Supplement." In Stuart Elden and Eduardo Mendieta, eds. *Reading Kant's Geography*. Albany: SUNY Press, 87–102.
— (2012) "*Über Pädagogik*: Eine Vorlesung wie jede andere?" *Jahrbuch für historische Bildungsforschung* 18, 147–68.
— (2013) "Dokumentation der Vorlesungen über Physische Geographie." http://kant.bbaw.de/base.htm/. Accessed 17 November 2014.
— (2014a) "Rousseau und Kant." In Christian Ritzi, ed. *Jean-Jacques Rousseaus Émile. Erziehungsroman, philosophische Abhandlung, historische Quelle*. Bad Heilbrunn: Julius Klinkhardt, 169–92.
— (2014b) "Naturforschung in Königsberg – ein kritischer Rückblick aus den Präliminarien einer Untersuchung über die Entstehungsbedingungen von Kant's Vorlesung über Physische Geographie." *Estudos Kantianos* 2 (2), 29–60.
— (2015) "Albertus-Universität Königsberg: Die Philosophische Fakultät im 18. Jahrhundert." http://staff-www.uni-marburg.de/~stark/albert.ine/al_phil.htm. Accessed 23 February 2015.
— (forthcoming) *Erneute Untersuchungen zu Kant's Vorlesungen über Physische Geographie*.
Starke, Fr. Ch. [Johann Adam Bergk], ed. (1833) *Immanuel Kant's vorzügliche kleine Schriften und Aufsätze. Nebst Betrachtungen über die Erde und den Menschen aus ungedruckten Vorlesungen*. 2 vols. Leipzig: Expedition des europäischen Aufsehers.
Stattler, Benedikt (1788) *Anhang zum Anti-Kant in einer Widerlegung der Kantischen Grundlegung zur Metaphysik der Sitten*. Munich: Lentner.
Stavenhagen, Kurt (1949) *Kant und Königsberg*. Göttingen: Deuerlich.
Stratton-Lake, Philip (2001) *Kant, Duty, and Moral Worth*. London: Routledge.
Streidel, Paul (2003) *Naturrecht, Staatswissenschaften und Politisierung bei Gottfried Achenwall (1719–1772)*. Munich: Herbert Utz.
Stroud, Scott R. (2014) *Kant and the Promise of Rhetoric*. University Park, PA: Penn State Press.
Strube, Werner (1990) "Die Geschichte des Begriffs 'schöne Wissenschaften'." *Archiv für Begriffsgeschichte* 33, 136–216.
Stuckenberg, J.H.W. (1882) *The Life of Immanuel Kant*. London: Macmillan & Co.
Sturm, Thomas (2009) *Kant und die Wissenschaften vom Menschen*. Paderborn: Mentis.

Suprenant, Chris (2008) "Kant's Postulate of the Immortality of the Soul." *International Philosophical Quarterly* 48, 85–98.
Sutherland, Daniel (2006) "Kant on Arithmetic, Algebra, and the Theory of Proportions." *Journal of the History of Philosophy* 44 (4), 533–58.
Tacquet, Andrea (1761) *Elementa Geometriae planae ac solidae, quibus accedunt selecta ex Archimede Theoremata*. Superiorum permissu. Patavii.
Tertullian (1961) *Apologeticum*, ed. Carl Becker. Munich: Kösel.
Thiel, Udo (2011) *The Early Modern Subject. Self-Consciousness and Personal Identity from Descartes to Hume*. Oxford: Oxford Univ. Press.
Thiele, Gunnar (1938) *Geschichte der preußischen Lehrerseminare Berlin*. Monumenta Germaniae paedagogica, vol. 62, Part 1. Berlin: Weidmannsche Verlagsbuchhandlung.
Timmermann, Jens (2015) "Mrongovius II: A supplement to the *Groundwork of the Metaphysics of Morals*." In Lara Denis and Oliver Sensen, eds. *Kant's Lectures on Ethics: A Critical Guide*. Cambridge: Cambridge Univ. Press, 68–83.
Tonelli, Giorgio (1955) *Kant dall'estetica metafisica all'estetica psicoempirica: Studi sulla genesi del criticismo (1754–1771) e sulle sue fonti*. Turin: Accademia delle Scienze di Torino.
— (1966) "Die Anfänge von Kants Kritik der Kausalbeziehungen und ihre Voraussetzungen im 18. Jahrhundert." *Kant-Studien* 57, 417–56.
— (1994) *Kant's Critique of Pure Reason within the Tradition of Modern Logic*, ed. D. H. Chandler. Hildesheim: Olms.
Turner, R. Steven (1974) "University Reformers and Professional Scholarship in Germany, 1760–1806." In Lawrence Stone, ed. *The University in Society*. Vol II: *Europe, Scotland, and the United States from the 16th to the 20th Century*. Princeton: Princeton Univ. Press, 495–531.
Ulrich, Johann August Heinrich (1788) *Eleutheriologie, oder über Freiheit und Nothwendigkeit. Zum Gebrauch der Vorlesungen in den Michaelisferien*. Jena: Crökersche Buchhandlung.
Untersteiner, Mario (1980) *Problemi di filologia filosofica*, ed. Livio Sichirollo and Massimo Venturi Ferriolo. Milan: Cisalpino Goliardica.
Vázquez Lobeiras, María J. (1998) *Die Logik und ihr Spiegelbild: Das Verhältnis von formaler und transzendentaler Logik in Kants philosophischer Entwicklung*. Frankfurt am Main: Lang.
— (2001) "Kants Logik zwischen Tradition und Innovation." In Michael Oberhausen et al., eds. *Vernunftkritik und Aufklärung: Studien zur Philosophie Kants und seines Jahrhunderts: Norbert Hinske zum 70. Geburtstag*. Stuttgart-Bad Cannstatt: Frommann-Holzboog, 365–82.
Vogel, Peter (1990) *Kausalität und Freiheit in der Pädagogik. Studien im Anschluß an die Freiheitsantinomie bei Kant*. Frankfurt am Main: Peter Lang.
Vollmer, Johan J. W. (1801–05) *Immanuel Kants physische Geographie*. 7 vols. Hamburg and Mainz: Gottfried Vollmer. [A second, enlarged but still incomplete edition, prepared by Joh. Jak. Wilh. Vollmer and F. Stiller, likewise appeared in Hamburg in 4 vols. (1808–17).]
Vorländer, Karl (1924) *Immanuel Kant. Der Mann und das Werk*. 2 vols. Leipzig: Meiner.
Warda, Arthur (1905) "Aus dem Leben des Pfarrers Christian Friedrich Puttlich." In *Altpreußische Monatsschrift* 42. Königsberg: Rosbach, 253–304.
— (1922) *Immanuel Kants Bücher. Mit einer getreuen Nachbildung des bisher einzigen bekannten Abzuges des Versteigerungskataloges der Bibliothek Kants*. Berlin: Martin Breslauer.

Warren, Daniel (2001) "Kant's Dynamics." In Eric Watkins, ed. *Kant and the Sciences*. Oxford: Oxford Univ. Press, 93–116.
Waschkies, Hans-Joachim (1987) *Physik und Physikotheologie des jungen Kant. Die Vorgeschichte seiner Allgemeinen Naturgeschichte und Theorie des Himmels*. Amsterdam: Gruner.
Waterman, W. B. (1899) "Kant's Lectures on the Philosophical Theory of Religion." *Kant-Studien* 3, 301–10.
Watkins, Eric, ed. (2001) *Kant and the Sciences*. Oxford: Oxford Univ. Press.
— (2005) *Kant and the Metaphysics of Causality*. Cambridge: Cambridge Univ. Press.
— ed. and trans. (2009) *Kant's Critique of Pure Reason. Background Source Materials*. Cambridge: Cambridge Univ. Press.
— (2012) "General Introduction." In Kant, *Natural Science*, ed. Eric Watkins. Cambridge: Cambridge Univ. Press, xiii–xviii.
Watkins, Eric and Olaf Reinhardt (2012) "Introduction to *Physical Geography*." In Kant, *Natural Science*, ed. Eric Watkins. Cambridge: Cambridge Univ. Press, 434–8.
Waxman, Wayne (2006) "Kant's Debt to the British Empiricists." In Graham Bird, ed. *A Companion to Kant*. Malden: Blackwell, 93–107.
Weatherson, Brian and Dan Marshall (2014) "Intrinsic vs. Extrinsic Properties." In Edward N. Zalta, ed. *The Stanford Encyclopedia of Philosophy*. http://plato.stanford.edu/archives/spr2014/entries/intrinsic-extrinsic/Spring 2014 edn.
Weiss, Georg (1913) *Die Anfänge des pädagogischen Universitätsseminars zu Königsberg 1809–1815*. Dissertation. Jena, 1912. In *Deutsche Blätter für erziehenden Unterricht* 40, 3–5, 13–16, 23–6, 33–5.
Weisskopf, Traugott (1970) *Immanuel Kant und die Pädagogik. Beiträge zu einer Monographie*. Zurich: Editio Academica.
Wenzel, Uwe Iustus (1992) *Anthroponomie. Kants Archäologie der Autonomie*. Berlin: Akademie Verlag.
Williams, Bernard (2006). Myles Burnyeat, ed. *The Sense of the Past: Essays in the History of Philosophy*. Princeton: Princeton Univ. Press.
Wilson, Holly L. (2006) *Pragmatic Anthropology: Its Origins, Meaning, and Critical Significance*. Albany: State Univ. of New York Press.
— (2011) "The Pragmatic Use of Kant's *Physical Geography* Lectures." In Stuart Elden and Eduardo Mendieta, eds. *Reading Kant's Geography*. Albany: SUNY Press, 161–73.
Wimmer, Reiner (1990) *Kants kritische Religionsphilosophie*. Berlin and New York: De Gruyter.
Winter, Aloysius (2005) *Kann man Kants Philosophie "christlich" nennen?* In Norbert Fischer, ed. *Kant und der Katholizismus. Stationen einer wechselhaften Geschichte*. Freiburg: Herder, 33–57.
Withers, Charles W. J. (2009) "Place and the 'Spatial Turn' in Geography and History." *Journal of the History of Ideas* 70, 637–58.
— (2011) "Kant's *Geography* in Comparative Perspective." In Stuart Elden and Eduardo Mendieta, eds. *Reading Kant's Geography*. Albany: SUNY Press, 47–68.
Wolff, Christian (1720) *Vernünfftige Gedancken von Gott, der Welt und der Seele des Menschen, auch allen Dingen überhaupt*. Halle: Renger.
— (1730) *Philosophia prima sive ontologia methodo scientifica pertractata qua omnis cognitionis humanae principia continentur*. Frankfurt: Renger.
— (1750a) *Anfangsgründe aller mathematischen Wissenschaften*. Erster Theil. Frankfurt and Leipzig: Renger.

- (1750b) *Anfangsgründe aller mathematischen Wissenschaften*. Dritter Theil. Halle: Renger.
- (1750c) *Anfangsgründe aller mathematischen Wissenschaften*. Letzter Theil. Halle: Renger.
- (1750d) *Kurtzer Unterricht von den vornehmsten mathematischen Schriften*. Frankfurt and Leipzig: Renger. In Christian Wolff, *Anfangsgründe aller mathematischen Wissenschaften*, letzter Theil. Halle: Renger. [Content as *Anhang*, with its own pagination].
- ([1713] 1755) *Auszug aus den Anfangsgründen aller mathematischen Wissenschaften*. Frankfurt and Leipzig: Renger.
- (1757) *Anfangsgründe aller mathematischen Wissenschaften*. Anderer Theil. Halle: Renger.
- (1968a) *Elementa matheseos universae*. Tomus I. Ed. and prepared by J. E. Hofmann. In *Gesammelte Werke*, Division II, vol 29. Reprint of the edn., Halle 1742. Hildesheim: Olms.
- (1968b) *Elementa matheseos universae*. Tomus II. Ed. and prepared by J. E. Hofmann. In *Gesammelte Werke*, Division II, vol. 30. Reprint of the edn., Halle 1733. Hildesheim: Olms.
- (1968c) *Elementa matheseos universae*. Tomus III. Ed. and prepared by J. E. Hofmann. In *Gesammelte Werke*, Division II, vol. 31. Reprint of the edn., Halle 1735. Hildesheim: Olms.
- (1968d) *Elementa matheseos universae*. Tomus IV. Ed. and prepared by J. E. Hofmann. In *Gesammelte Werke*, Division II, vol. 32. Reprint of the edn., Halle 1738. Hildesheim: Olms.
- (1968e) *Elementa matheseos universae*. Tomus V. Ed. and prepared, with an epilogue and index by J. E. Hofmann. In *Gesammelte Werke*, Division II, vol. 33. Reprint of the edn., Halle 1741. Hildesheim: Olms.
- (1968f) *Psychologia empirica*. Ed. and prepared by Jean Ecole. In *Gesammelte Werke*, Division II, vol. 5. Reprint of the edn., Frankfurt and Leipzig 1738. Hildesheim: Olms.
- (1968g) *De praecipuis scriptis mathematicis brevis commentatio*. In Christian Wolff (1968e), 1–164.
- (1972) *Psychologia rationalis*. Reprint of the 2nd ed., Frankfurt am Main 1740. In *Gesammelte Werke*, Division II, vol. 6. Hildesheim: Olms.
- (1977) *Philosophia Prima sive Ontologia*. Ed. and prepared by Jean Ecole. In *Gesammelte Werke*, Division II, vol. 3. Reprint of the edn., Frankfurt and Leipzig 1736. Hildesheim: Olms.
- (1978) *Mathematisches Lexicon*. Ed. and prepared by J. E. Hofmann. Reprint of the edn., Leipzig 1716. Hildesheim: Olms.
- (1983a) *Philosophia rationalis sive logica*. Ed. and prepared by Jean Ecole. In *Gesammelte Werke*, Division II, vols. 1–3. Reprint of the edn., Frankfurt and Leipzig 1740. Hildesheim: Olms.
- (1983b) *Vernünfftige Gedancken von Gott, der Welt und der Seele des Menschen, auch allen Dingen überhaupt*. Ed. Charles A. Corr. Reprint of the edn., Halle 1751. Hildesheim: Olms.
- (2005) *Erste Philosophie oder Ontologie: Lateinisch-Deutsch*. Trans. and ed. Dirk Effertz. Hamburg: Felix Meiner.

Wood, Allen (1984) "Kant's Compatibilism." In Allen Wood, ed. *Self and Nature in Kant's Philosophy*. Ithaca: Cornell Univ. Press, 73–101.
- (1991) "Unsocial Sociability: The Anthropological Basis for Kant's Ethics." *Philosophical Topics* 19, 325–51.
- (1999) *Kant's Ethical Thought*. Cambridge: Cambridge Univ. Press.

Wubnig, Judith (1969) "The Epigenesis of Pure Reason." *Kant-Studien* 60, 147–52.

Wunderlich, Falk (2005) *Kant und die Bewußtseinstheorien des 18. Jahrhunderts*. Berlin and New York: De Gruyter.

Wundt, Max (1924) *Kant als Metaphysiker*. Stuttgart: Enke.

Young, J. Michael (1992) "Translator's Introduction." In J. Michael Young, ed. *Lectures on Logic*, Cambridge: Cambridge Univ. Press, xv–xxxii.
Zabarella, Jacopo (1578) *Opera logica*. Venice: Meietus.
Zammito, John (1992) *The Genesis of Kant's* Critique of Judgment. Chicago: Univ. of Chicago Press.
— (1998) "'Method' vs 'Manner'? – Kant's Critique of Herder's *Ideen* in Light of the Epoch of Science, 1790–1820." *Herder Yearbook*, 1–25.
— (2002) *Kant, Herder, and the Birth of Anthropology*. Chicago: Univ. of Chicago Press.
— (2003) "'This Inscrutable Principle of an Original Organization': Epigenesis and 'Looseness of Fit' in Kant's Philosophy of Science." *Studies in History and Philosophy of Science* 34, 73–109.
— (2006) "Policing Polygeneticism in Germany, 1775: (Kames) Kant and Blumenbach." In Eigen, Sara and Mark Larrimore, eds. *The German Invention of Race*. Albany: SUNY Press, 35–54.
— (2012a) "The Pursuit of Science as Decadence in Kant's *Remarks in 'Observations on the Feeling of the Beautiful and Sublime'*." In Susan Shell and Richard Velkley, eds. *Kant's "Observations" and "Remarks": A Critical Guide*. Cambridge: Cambridge Univ. Press, 234–46.
— (2012b) "The Second Life of the 'Public Sphere': On Charisma and Routinization in the History of a Concept." In Christian Emden and David Midgley, eds. *Changing Perceptions of the Public Sphere*. New York and Oxford: Berghahn Books, 90–119.
Zande, Johan van der (1992) "Popular Philosophy and the History of Mankind." *Storia della Storiografia* 22, 37–56.
— (1998) "The Moderate Skepticism of German Popular Philosophy." In Johan van der Zande and Richard Popkin, eds. *The Skeptical Tradition around 1800: Skepticism in Philosophy, Science and Society*. Dordrecht: Kluwer, 69–80.
Zedler, Johann Heinrich (1732–54) *Grosses vollständiges Universallexicon aller Wissenschaften und Künste*. 64 vols. with 4 supplemental vols. Halle and Leipzig. [Digital Version: http://www.zedler-lexikon.de/index.html. Accessed 14 January 2014].
Zimmerli, Walther (1978) "Arbeitsteilige Philosophie? Gedanken zur Teil-Rehabilitierung der Popularphilosophie." In Hermann Lübbe, ed. *Wozu Philosophie? Stellungnahmen eines Arbeitskreises*. Berlin and New York: De Gruyter, 181–212.
— (1981) "'Schulfuchsische' und 'handgreifliche' Rationalität – oder: Stehen dunkler Tiefsinn und Common sense im Widerspruch?" In Hans Poser, ed. *Wandel des Vernunftbegriffs*. Freiburg and Munich: Albers, 137–76.
— (1983) "'Schwere Rüstung' des Dogmatismus und 'anwendbare Eklektik': J. G. H. Feder und die Göttinger Philosophie im ausgehenden 18. Jahrhundert." *Studia Leibnitiana* 15 (1), 58–71.
Zinkin, Melissa (2006) "Respect for the Law and the Use of Dynamical Terms in Kant's Theory of Moral Motivation." *Archiv für Geschichte der Philosophie* 88, 31–53.
— (2012) "Kant on Negative Magnitudes." *Kant-Studien* 103 (4), 397–414.
Zöller, Günter (1988) "Kant on the Generation of Metaphysical Knowledge." In Hariolf Oberer and Gerhard Seel, eds. *Kant: Analysen – Probleme – Kritik*. Würzburg: Königshausen & Neumann, 71–90.
— (1989) "From Innate to A Priori: Kant's Radical Transformation of a Cartesian-Leibnizian Legacy." *The Monist* 72, 222–35.

- (2007) "Bibliography." In Kant, *Anthropology, History, and Education*, ed. Günter Zöller and Robert B. Louden. Cambridge: Cambridge Univ. Press, 565–83.
- (2010) "Autokratie. Die Psycho-Politik der Selbstherrschaft bei Platon und Kant." In Hubertus Busche and Anton Schmitt, eds. *Kant als Bezugspunkt philosophischen Denkens*. Würzburg: Königshausen & Neumann, 351–77.
- (2015a) *Res publica: Plato's "Republic" in Classical German Philosophy*. Hong Kong: The Chinese Univ. Press.
- (2015b) "'Allgemeine Freiheit.' Kants *Naturrecht Feyerabend* über Freiheit, Recht und Gesetz." In Bernd Dörflinger, Dieter Hüning, and Günter Kruck, eds. *Zum Verhältnis von Recht und Ethik in Kants praktischer Philosophie*, Hildesheim: Olms.

Zopf, Johann H. (1731) *Logica enucleata*. Halle: Hemmerde.

List of Illustrations

Fig. 1. Reproduction of a page from Herder's first day of notes from Kant's metaphysics lectures 32
Fig. 2. Reproduction of page 1 ("Prolegomena") of Kant's copy of A. G. Baumgarten's *Metaphysica*, with Kant's handwritten notes 63
Fig. 3. Reproduction of page 292 ("Psychologia Rationalis") of Kant's copy of A. G. Baumgarten's *Metaphysica*, with Kant's handwritten notes 88
Fig. 4. Reproduction of page 318 ("Status Post Mortem") of Kant's copy of A. G. Baumgarten's *Metaphysica*, with Kant's handwritten notes 114
Fig. 5. Reproduction of page 3 ("Einleitung in die Vernunftlehre") of Kant's copy of G. F. Meier's *Auszug aus der Vernunftlehre*, with Kant's handwritten notes 136
Fig. 6. Reproduction of sheet 101' (verso) inserted between printed pages 100 and 101 of G. F. Meier's *Auszug aus der Vernunftlehre* 159
Fig. 7. Reproduction of page 199 ("Phantasia") of Kant's copy of A. G. Baumgarten's *Metaphysica*, with Kant's handwritten notes 222
Fig. 8. Reproduction of page 179 ("Sectio II. Facultas Cognoscitiva Inferior") of Kant's copy of A. G. Baumgarten's *Metaphysica*, with Kant's handwritten notes 242
Fig. 9. Reproduction of the title page from the handwritten student notes from Kant's course on philosophical encyclopedia 300
Fig. 10. Reproduction of the title page from the manuscript "Naturrecht Feyerabend" 322
Fig. 11. Reproduction of page 35 (sheet 19 recto) from the manuscript "Naturrecht Feyerabend" 323
Fig. 12. Kant's *Religion* as "einem Leitfaden." Photo-reproduction of page xix from the original 1793 publication of Kant's *Die Religion innerhalb der Grenzen der bloßen Vernunft* 364
Fig. 13. Reproduction of page 386 ("Sectio II. Finis Creationis") from Kant's copy of A. G. Baumgarten's *Metaphysica*, with Kant's handwritten notes 391
Fig. 14. Reproduction of page 1 from Herder's notes on mathematics, "Mathematik Herder" 410
Fig. 15. Reproduction of page 7 from Herder's notes on mathematics, "Mathematik Herder" 414
Fig. 16. Reproduction of sheet 14 verso from the "Danziger Physik" manuscript 456
Fig. 17. Reproduction of sheet 15 recto from the "Danziger Physik" manuscript 457
Fig. 18. Reproduction of the title page of a printed copy of Kant's essay "Von den verschiedenen Racen der Menschen" ("Of the Different Races of Human Beings") (1775) 524
Fig. 19. Reproduction of the title page (7 recto) from the "Kaehler" handwritten notes on physical geography 525

Figures 1, 11, 14, 15, 16, and 17 are followed by English translations of the corresponding German text.

Contributors

Henny Blomme is Visiting Professor at the Universidade Federal do Rio Grande do Norte. He was recently Postdoctoral Fellow at the Max Planck Institute for the History of Science (Berlin), Postdoctoral Researcher at the University of Edinburgh, and Visiting Research Fellow at the Centre for Classical German Philosophy (Bochum). His research on Kant includes several articles and chapters as well as two forthcoming books: *Kant et la matière de l'espace* (Olms), and *Kant und das Nichts: Ein Beitrag zur kritischen Ontologie* (Walter de Gruyter). In 2015, he received the quinquennial junior International Kant Prize (Preis Silvestro Marcucci), awarded by the jury of the Kant-Gesellschaft.

Robert R. Clewis is Associate Professor of Philosophy at Gwynedd Mercy University. He is the author of *The Kantian Sublime and the Revelation of Freedom* (Cambridge University Press, 2009). Between 2012 and 2014 he held an Alexander von Humboldt Fellowship for Experienced Researchers as a Visiting Scholar at the University of Munich / Ludwig-Maximilians-Universität München and he is currently a Visiting Scholar at the University of Pennsylvania. He is the translator of the Mrongovius lecture in *Lectures on Anthropology* (Cambridge University Press, 2012) in The Cambridge Edition of the Works of Immanuel Kant.

Alix Cohen joined the University of Edinburgh as a Chancellor's Fellow in 2014. She is the author of *Kant and the Human Sciences: Biology, Anthropology and History* (Palgrave, 2009) and has published papers on Kant as well as Hume and Rousseau. She is editor of *Kant's Lectures on Anthropology: A Critical Guide* (Cambridge University Press, 2014) and *Kant on Emotion and Value* (Palgrave, 2014). She is Associate Editor of the British Journal for the History of Philosophy and the Oxford Bibliography Online (Oxford University Press), and Executive Member of the British Society for the History of Philosophy and the UK Kant Society.

Corey W. Dyck is Associate Professor of Philosophy at the University of Western Ontario. He specializes in the history of German philosophy, with an emphasis on the eighteenth century. His recent research has focused on metaphysics and the philosophy of mind in the period from Wolff to Kant. He is the author of *Kant and Rational Psychology* (Oxford University Press, 2014), has published articles in *Journal of the History of Philosophy*, *Kant-Studien*, *British Journal for the History of Philosophy*, *Philosophy Compass*, *Kantian Review*, and *Kant Yearbook*, and is the co-translator (with Daniel Dahlstrom) of Moses Mendelssohn's *Morning Hours: Lectures on God's Existence* (Springer, 2011).

Faustino Fabbianelli is Associate Professor at the University of Parma. He has also taught at the Università della Calabria, Ludwig-Maximilians-Universität München, and Universität of Freiburg im Breisgau. He was Fellow of the Istituto Italiano per gli Studi Filosofici di Napoli (1997), the Deutscher Akademischer Austauschdienst (1998–99), the Deutsche Forschungsgemeinschaft (2000–02) and the Alexander von Humboldt-Stiftung (2008–10). His areas of specialization are German Idealism, Italian Philosophy, German Phenomenology, and German Enlightenment. Since 2005 he has been a co-editor of Karl Leonhard Reinhold's *Correspondence* (Frommann-Holzboog).

Norbert Fischer's work on Kant includes (with Dieter Hattrup) *Metaphysik aus dem Anspruch des Anderen: Kant und Levinas* (Schöningh, 1999); *Kants Metaphysik und Religionsphilosophie*

(Meiner, 2004); *Kants Grundlegung einer kritischen Metaphysik* (Meiner, 2010); and (as co-editor) *Die Gottesfrage in der Philosophie Immanuel Kants* (Herder, 2010). He studied philosophy, theology, and German philology at the universities of Mainz and Freiburg im Breisgau and earned his Ph.D. and *Habilitation* in philosophy. He was Professor of Philosophy at Mainz (1985–88), Trier (1989–90), Paderborn (1991–95) and Eichstätt (1995–2013). His research interests include Plato, Augustine, Kant, Heidegger, and Levinas; philosophical theology; metaphysics; the foundations of practical philosophy; and philosophy of religion.

Courtney D. Fugate is Assistant Professor at the American University of Beirut and Post-Doctoral Fellow at Emory University. He is co-editor, translator, and author (with John Hymers) of *Baumgarten's Metaphysics: A Critical Translation with Kant's Elucidations, Selected Notes and Related Materials* (Bloomsbury, 2013) and author of *The Teleology of Reason: A Study of the Structure of Kant's Critical Philosophy* (Walter de Gruyter, 2014). He has also published on Kant's moral and religious philosophy in the *European Journal of Philosophy*, *History of Philosophy Quarterly*, and *Skepsis*.

Paul Guyer is the Jonathan Nelson Professor of Humanities and Philosophy at Brown University, and Florence R. C. Murray Professor *emeritus* at the University of Pennsylvania. He is the author of nine books and editor of five anthologies on the philosophy of Kant, general co-editor of The Cambridge Edition of the Works of Immanuel Kant, and an editor and translator of Kant's *Critique of Pure Reason*, *Critique of the Power of Judgment*, and *Notes and Fragments* within that series as well as of Kant's *Observations on the Feeling of the Beautiful and Sublime and Other Writings* in the Cambridge Texts in the History of Philosophy. He is the author of *A History of Modern Aesthetics* in three volumes (Cambridge University Press, 2014). He is a past President of the Eastern Division of the American Philosophical Association and of the American Society for Aesthetics, and a Fellow of the American Academy of Arts and Sciences.

Robert B. Louden is Distinguished Professor of Philosophy at the University of Southern Maine. His publications include *Kant's Impure Ethics* (Oxford University Press, 2000) and *Kant's Human Being* (Oxford University Press, 2011). Louden is also co-editor and translator of *Anthropology, History, and Education* (Cambridge University Press, 2007) and *Lectures on Anthropology* (Cambridge University Press, 2012) in The Cambridge Edition of the Works of Immanuel Kant. He is a former President of the North American Kant Society.

Huaping Lu-Adler is Assistant Professor at Georgetown University. In 2012 she completed her Ph.D. dissertation, "Kant's Conception of Logical Extension and Its Implications" under the supervision of Henry E. Allison. Her recent journal publications and current interests explore various aspects of Kant's philosophy of logic, and she has been especially interested in Kant's relation to Locke, Leibniz, Wolff, and Euler.

Antonio Moretto is Professor of Logic at the Università di Verona. He is the author of numerous articles or essays on the relationship between science and philosophy in Kant, including: "Die Auffassung des Endliches und des Unendliches in der Mathematik nach Kant und Hegel" (2004); "Philosophie transcendantale et géométrie non-euclidienne" (2009); "Kant and the Riemannian geometry" (2010); "L'infini potentiel et actuel dans la philosophie des mathématiques de Kant" (2011); and "Kästner und Kant über die Grundlagen der Geometrie und das Parallelenproblem" (2011).

Steve Naragon is Professor of Philosophy at Manchester University (Indiana, USA), where he has taught since 1991. He received his Ph.D. in philosophy from the University of Notre Dame, working with Karl Ameriks and Neil Delaney. To help us understand the lecture notes from Kant's classroom and to offer insights into their historical and intellectual contexts, he developed and currently maintains the website "Kant in the Classroom." He co-edited and translated (with Karl Ameriks) Kant's *Lectures on Metaphysics* (Cambridge University Press, 1997) and is currently re-transcribing Herder's notes from Kant's metaphysics lectures for the Berlin-Brandenburg Academy of Sciences.

Chris Onof is Honorary Research Fellow in Philosophy at Birkbeck College (University of London), and Reader at the Faculty of Engineering, Imperial College London. He has published on Kant's ethics and metaphysics (in *Kant-Studien, Kant Yearbook, Kantian Review*), on Heidegger and Sartre as well as on the nature of consciousness (in *Philosophy and Phenomenological Research, Journal of Mind & Behavior*). He is co-founder of the journal *Episteme* and serves on the Editorial Board of *Kant Studies Online*.

Stephen R. Palmquist is Professor in the Department of Religion and Philosophy at Hong Kong Baptist University, where he has taught since receiving his doctoral degree from Oxford University in 1987. His works include ten books, among them *Kant's System of Perspectives* (University Press of America, 1993); *Kant's Critical Religion* (Ashgate, 2000); *Kant and the New Philosophy of Religion* (co-edited with Chris L. Firestone, Indiana University Press, 2006); *Cultivating Personhood: Kant and Asian Philosophy* (as editor, Walter de Gruyter, 2010); and *A Comprehensive Commentary on Kant's Religion within the Bounds of Bare Reason* (Wiley-Blackwell, 2015). His 100+ articles have been published in over 60 different journals, such as *Kant-Studien, Dialectica*, and *The Review of Metaphysics*, located in at least 25 countries.

Riccardo Pozzo is Director of the Department of Humanities and Social Sciences, Cultural Heritage of the National Research Council of Italy. He has published monographs on Kant (Maia, 2015; Akal, 1998; Lang, 1989), the Renaissance (Schwabe, 2012), the Enlightenment (Frommann-Holzboog, 2000), and Hegel (La Nuova Italia, 1989). He has edited or co-edited the lecture catalogues of the University of Königsberg (Frommann-Holzboog, 1999) and books on Dilthey and the methodology of the history of ideas (Meiner, 2010; Harrassowitz, 2011; Frommann-Holzboog, 2011), Kant on the Unconscious (Walter de Gruyter, 2012), the philosophical academic programs of the German Enlightenment (Frommann-Holzboog, 2011), and the impact of Aristotelianism on modern philosophy (Catholic University of America Press, 2003). His articles have been published in *Journal of the History of Philosophy, Studi Kantiani, Kant-Studien, Archiv für Begriffsgeschichte, Giornale critico della filosofia italiana, Hegel-Jahrbuch, History of Science, History of Universities, Jahrbuch für Universitätsgeschichte, The Review of Metaphysics, Rivista di storia della filosofia*, and *Topoi*.

Frederick Rauscher is Professor of Philosophy at Michigan State University. He is the author of *Naturalism and Realism in Kant's Ethics* and several articles on Kant's meta-ethics and political philosophy, among other topics. He is editor of *Lectures and Drafts on Political Philosophy* (Cambridge University Press), which includes his translations of Kant's course on natural right and related *Nachlaß* (literary remains), as well as translator of Kant's *Nachlaß* on ethics for *Notes and Fragments*, both in The Cambridge Edition of the Works of Immanuel Kant.

Dennis Schulting is former Assistant Professor of Metaphysics and the History of Philosophy at the University of Amsterdam, the Netherlands, where he taught from 2006 until 2011. He earned his Ph.D. in philosophy from the University of Warwick, England, in 2004. Among many chapter contributions and articles in journals such as *Algemeen Nederlands Tijdschrift voor Wijsbegeerte*, *Kantian Review*, *Kant-Studien*, *Studi kantiani*, *The Philosophical Review*, and *Tijdschrift voor Filosofie*, he is the author of *Kant's Deduction and Apperception: Explaining the Categories* (Palgrave Macmillan, 2012). He also edited the essay collection *Kant's Idealism: New Interpretations of a Controversial Doctrine* (Springer, 2011) as well as *The Bloomsbury Companion to Kant* (1st edn., Continuum, 2012; 2nd edn., Bloomsbury, 2015).

Oliver Sensen is Associate Professor and Director of Graduate Studies at Tulane University. He is the author of *Kant on Human Dignity* (Walter de Gruyter, 2011), editor of *Kant on Moral Autonomy* (Cambridge University Press, 2012), as well as co-editor of *Kant's* Tugendlehre (Walter de Gruyter, 2013), and *Kant's Lectures on Ethics: A Critical Guide* (Cambridge University Press, 2015). He has published articles on key concepts in Kant's ethics such as autonomy, the categorical imperative, conscience, dignity, freedom, friendship, heteronomy, obligation, respect, and value.

Susan Meld Shell is Professor and Chair of the Department of Political Science at Boston College. Her most recent books include *Kant and the Limits of Autonomy* (Harvard University Press, 2009) and (with Richard Velkley), *Kant's* Observations *and* Remarks*: A Critical Guide* (Cambridge University Press, 2012). She has also written on Kant's cosmology, the problem of embodiment, and other topics in eighteenth- and nineteenth-century political and moral philosophy.

Werner Stark is Honorary Professor at the Philipps-Universität Marburg and member of staff at the Berlin-Brandenburg Academy of Sciences. He co-edited (with Reinhard Brandt) the *Akademie-Ausgabe*'s volume on anthropology (vol. 25) and edited (in collaboration with Brandt) the volume on physical geography (vol. 26). He has also prepared and published online digital transcriptions of numerous lecture notes. He edited the student transcriptions from Kant's ethics course, *Vorlesung zur Moralphilosophie* (Walter de Gruyter, 2004) and is author of *Nachforschungen zu Briefen und Handschriften Immanuel Kants* (Akademie Verlag, 1993). He has written and edited numerous articles and books on Kant's published works, letters, notes, and lectures in their philosophical and institutional contexts.

John H. Zammito is a historian of philosophy and science, concentrating on the German eighteenth-century, especially Kant and Herder. He also works on theoretical issues in science studies and in historical theory. Author of *The Genesis of Kant's* Critique of Judgment (University of Chicago Press, 1992) and *Kant, Herder, and the Birth of Anthropology* (University of Chicago Press, 2002), his current research explores the emergence of life sciences in eighteenth-century Germany.

Günter Zöller is Professor of Philosophy at the University of Munich/Ludwig-Maximilians-Universität München. He has recently held visiting appointments at Seoul National University, McGill University, Chinese University of Hong Kong, Huazhong University of Science and Technology, Venice International University, University of Venice, and Fudan University. His recent book publications include *Fichte lesen* (Frommann-Holzboog, 2013) and *Res publica: Plato's "Republic" in Classical German Philosophy* (The Chinese University Press, 2015). He is the author, editor, and coeditor of 35 books and the author of over 300 articles on Kant and German idealism published in sixteen languages worldwide.

Name Index

Abegg, Johann Friedrich 264
Achenwall, Gottfried 4, 326, 328–329, 336, 340, 344–345, 359
Addison, Joseph 314
Adickes, Erich 1, 9, 11, 15–16, 18, 38, 51, 56, 95, 139, 163–164, 265–266, 328–329, 344, 421, 438, 452, 499, 506, 513, 515, 529–530, 532, 535
Aertsen, Jan A. 80
Albrecht, Michael 305, 308, 313
Allison, Henry E. 219, 228–229
Ameriks, Karl 1, 64, 91, 100, 115, 121–125, 128, 214
Anaximenes 486
Aquinas, Thomas 21
Archimedes (Archimède) 433–435, 450
Arendt, Hannah 1, 21
Aristotle 1, 21, 23, 85, 141, 144, 153, 156, 167–168, 310, 347–348, 486
Arnoldt, Emil 1, 8, 40, 122, 129–131, 170–172, 179, 262, 301–302, 307, 345, 418
Augustine 286, 392–394, 396, 398, 401, 403–404, 407
Averroes 21

Baron, Marcia 244
Basedow, Johann Bernhard 4, 267, 278, 280–282, 520
Baum, Manfred 219, 459
Baumgarten, Alexander Gottlieb 2, 4, 13, 17, 21–22, 37–38, 40, 43, 48–56, 59–61, 63–67, 71–75, 87–89, 93, 96, 105, 109, 114, 116–120, 130, 153, 167, 179–181, 207, 222–223, 229, 234–235, 242, 270, 275, 365, 380–381, 391, 401, 526
Becher, Johann Joachim 489
Beck, Lewis White 1, 121, 127, 129, 318
Beiser, Frederick C. 42, 326
Bergk, Johann Adam; *see* Starke, Friedrich Christian
Bernasconi, Robert 506, 522, 529
Bernet, Rudolf 393
Beyer, Kurt 266
Bien, Günther 306

Black, Joseph 487
Blomme, Henny 11, 28–29, 158, 484–485, 501
Bock, Friedrich Samuel 267, 419
Bock, Karl Gottlieb 43
Bödeker, Hans-Georg 304
Bojanowski, Jochen 202, 207
Bolin, Ronald 29, 505
Bondeli, Martin 219
Bonnet, Charles 308, 312
Borowski, Ludwig Ernst 6, 46, 161, 534
Boswell, Terry 138–140, 164
Böttiger, Karl August 27, 45
Bowen, Margarita 519
Boxill, Bernard 529
Boyer, Carl B. 441
Brandt, Reinhard IX, 10, 89, 93, 185, 269, 276, 303, 309, 517, 536
Brentano, Franz 187
Brewer, Daniel 511
Buchner, Edward Franklin 277, 507
Büchner, Ludwig 394
Buck, Friedrich Johann 27, 40, 419, 462
Buffon, Georges-Louis Leclerc 534, 538
Burger, Anton 268
Busch, Werner 326
Butler, Joseph 194
Byrd, Sharon 326, 331, 336

Callanan, John 145
Carrier, Martin 475, 485, 489, 495
Cassirer, Ernst 1
Cavendish, Henry 488
Caygill, Howard 509
Chiereghin, Franco 446
Chignell, Andrew 129
Church, Michael 520, 531
Churton, Annette 507
Cicero, Marcus Tullius 165–166, 346
Clewis, Robert R. 1, 66, 68, 89, 158, 184, 199, 243, 259, 457, 505, 526
Cohen, Alix 2, 5, 24, 243–245, 251, 395
Collins, Georg Ludwig 299
Comenius, Jan 278

Conrad, Elfriede 137–140, 163–164, 174
Cramer, Konrad 308
Crugott, Martin 272, 295
Crusius, Christian August 38, 48–50, 52–55, 58–59, 69, 71–72, 153, 167, 192, 310

D'Alembert, Jean Le Ronde 303, 308
d'Este, Isabelle 355
Dangerfield, Rodney 508
Darwin, Charles 273, 515
de Boer, Karin 526
Delekat, Friedrich 405
Delfosse, Heinrich 322–323, 335, 356, 361
Denis, Lara 2, 5, 255
Descartes, René 49, 54, 167, 404
DiCenso, James 377
Diderot, Denis 303, 308
Dobbek, Wilhelm 40, 44
Dohna-Wundlacken, Heinrich Ludwig Adolph Graf zu 500, 543
Dörflinger, Bernd 2, 398
Dorrien, Gary 367
Du Bois-Reymond, Emil 394
Du Prel, Carl 1
Dussort, Henri 500
Dyck, Corey 22, 100–101, 115, 117, 133

Eberhard, Johann August 365, 380, 401, 526
Eberhard, Johann Peter 462, 487
Eckhart (Meister Eckhart) 401, 406
Eigen, Sara 529
Elden, Stuart 14, 505–506, 508–509, 512, 528
Elisabeth of Bohemia 1
Ellendt, Georg Albrecht 261
Empedocles 486
Erdmann, Benno 1, 139
Erhard, Johann Benjamin 500
Erler, Georg 261
Borowski, Ludwig Ernst 534
Erxleben, Johann Christian Polykarp 4, 28, 462, 487–488
Euclid (Euclides) 421–423, 431, 433, 435–436, 439–440, 444, 447–450, 452
Euler, Werner 275
Eze, Emmanuel Chukwudi 529
Fabbianelli, Faustino IX, 24, 200, 214

Faggiotto, Pietro 446, 449
Falkenstein, Lorne 50
Feder, Johann G. H. 4, 26, 174, 301–304, 307–313, 316–317
Feinberg, Joel 194
Fichte, Johann Gottlieb 19, 21, 394
Firestone, Chris L. 375
Fischer, Norbert IX, 27, 200, 393–396, 398–400, 403–404
Fisher, Mark 527
Fordyce, David 127
Formosa, Paul 292
Forstreuter, Kurt 275
Frederick the Great 169, 279, 281, 283, 287
Frederick William I 279–280
Frederick William II 279, 281, 366
Frederick William III 280
Friedländer, David Joachim 462
Friedman, Michael 443, 466–467, 476, 478, 485, 495, 500
Friedrich, Carl J. 18
Frierson, Patrick 180, 184, 194, 243, 249
Fugate, Courtney 21, 64, 67, 158
Funke, Gerhard 292, 395

Galilei, Galileo 444, 490
Gallie, Walter Bryce 511
Garber, Jörn 280
Garve, Christian 302, 310
Genova, Anthony C. 145
George, Rolf 127
Gerard, Alexander 235
Göbel, Christian X, 392, 394
Goethe, Johann Wolfgang von 280, 398, 407
Gollwitzer, Helmut 407
Goy, Ina 193
Green, Ronald M. 378
Greene, Theodore 374, 378, 384, 386
Gregory, Tullio 160
Grenberg, Jeanine 244
Grimm, Gunter 305–306
Grimm, Jacob and Wilhelm 165
Grotius, Hugo 348
Guyer, Paul IX, 24, 166, 184–185, 223–224, 228–229, 238, 508, 510, 521

Haller, Albrecht von 44, 308

Hamann, Johann Georg 19, 42, 50, 264
Hardtwig, Wolfgang 306
Harrison, R. T. 509, 520
Hartshorne, Richard 508–509, 511–513, 520
Harvey, David 508, 512–513, 519
Hasenkamp, Xaver von 418
Heath, Thomas 436, 440, 444, 447
Hegel, G. W. F. 1, 21, 347, 394
Heidegger, Martin 393, 395, 398–399
Heine, Heinrich 383
Hales, Stephen 487–488
Heinze, Max 1, 73, 108–109, 113, 119–123, 127–130
Henrich, Dieter 50, 66, 199
Heraclitus 486
Herder, Johann Gottfried 12, 14, 17–19, 21–22, 27–28, 32, 37–51, 54–61, 65–71, 73, 75, 79–80, 89–90, 103, 105–106, 125, 179–181, 183–185, 189, 191, 193–195, 199, 245, 309, 316, 410, 414, 418–429, 431, 433–445, 447–453, 461–462, 476, 478–479, 533
Herder, Maria Caroline 44
Herman, Barbara 182
Herz, Marcus 10, 15, 18, 38, 46, 94, 305, 463
Hesse, Georg 530
Hill, Jr., Thomas E. 529
Hinske, Norbert 11, 80, 164–165, 170–171, 173, 265, 305, 314
Hirsch, Philipp-Alexander 326, 356
Hißmann, Michael 311
Hobbes, Thomas 348
Hohenegger, Hansmichael 162
Holstein (Friedrich Karl Ludwig von Holstein-Beck) 10, 29, 274, 507–508, 520–522, 530–536, 541, 546, 549
Holzhey, Helmut 303, 305
Home, Henry (Lord Kames) 14, 19, 43–45, 48, 66, 179, 235, 276, 280, 297
Hotson, Howard 160
Hruschka, Joachim 326, 331, 336
Hudson, Hoyt 374, 378, 384, 386
Hügelmann, Karl 20
Hume, David 17, 49–51, 55, 167, 238, 312–313, 316–318, 510, 522
Huseyinzadegan, Dilek 505
Husserl, Edmund 393

Hutcheson, Francis 21, 188
Hutter, Axel 396

Illetterati, Luca 449
Ingensiep, Hans Werner 145
Irmscher, Hans Dietrich 410, 414, 419–420, 435, 450–452
Isen, Alice M. 195

Jachmann 1, 39, 180
Jacobs, Brian 243, 375
Jäsche, Gottlieb Benjamin 10, 22, 112–113, 137–140, 143, 150–152, 157–158, 164, 264–265, 428, 430, 433, 507
Jaspers, Karl 393
Jesus 34–35, 372, 374, 377, 394, 406
Job 292, 392, 397, 405, 516
Johnson, Mark 509
Johnston, James Scott 507
Jorgensen, Larry 97, 112
Justinian, Caesar Flavius 352–353

Kaehler, Johann Sigismund 535
Kain, Patrick 243
Kames; see Home, Henry (Lord Kames)
Karsten, Wenceslaus Johann Gustav 4, 28, 462, 480, 487–489
Kästner, Abraham Gotthelf 28, 420, 422–424, 426–433, 437, 439, 442–443, 452–453
Kauder, Peter 268
Käuser, Andreas 310
Kelemen, Deborah 550
Kemp Smith, Norman 156, 174
Kepler, Johannes 17, 50, 433, 466
Kerszberg, Pierre 495
Kleingeld, Pauline 14, 254, 522–523, 529
Klemme, Heiner 94, 275
Kneale, William 156
Knittermeyer, Hinrich 80
Knutzen, Martin 167
Kopitzsch, Franklin 304
Kötter, Rudolf 495
Kowalewski, Arnold 6, 13, 162
Kreimendahl, Lothar 50
Krummacher, Friedrich Wilhelm 407

Name Index

Kuehn, Manfred 1, 180–181, 186, 191, 198, 277, 279, 301, 304, 310, 318
Kühnemann, Eugen 40

Lærke, Mogens 3
La Rocca, Claudio 99
Lakoff, George 509
Lambert, Johann Heinrich 153, 469, 473–475, 480
Lampe, Martin 383
Landucci, Sergio 207
Lang, Ossian H. 280
Langel, Hans 170
Langhansen, Christoph 27, 40, 419
Larrimore, Mark 529
Lavater, Johann Caspar 392, 405
Lavoisier, Antoine 488–489, 499–501
Laywine, Alison 41
Lazzari, Alessandro 214
Lee, Seung-Kee 161, 174
Lehmann, Gerhard 9, 46–47, 61, 161, 179–181, 183, 301–303, 335, 418–420, 434, 441, 450–452, 456–457, 461, 487
Leibniz, Gottfried 1, 17, 22, 49–51, 90, 94–98, 103, 112, 153–154, 167, 266, 353, 403, 405, 425, 428, 441–442, 477, 511
Lessing, Gotthold Ephraim 233
Levin, Paula F. 195
Lichtenberg, Georg Christoph 488
Lindemann-Stark, Anke 15
Linnaeus (Carl Linné) 492
Livingstone, David N. 509, 512, 520
Locke, John 23, 49, 96, 153–155, 157, 164, 167–168, 278, 280, 309–311, 313, 511, 519–520
Longuenesse, Béatrice 51
Louden, Robert B. IX, 1–2, 10, 29, 243, 259, 280, 505, 507, 514, 517–518, 520–522, 526, 528, 535
Loughlin, Martin 354
Lu-Adler, Huaping 10, 22–23, 137, 141, 150–151
Ludwig, Bernd 1, 89, 174, 229, 262, 266, 326, 392, 394, 534

Machiavelli, Niccolò 348, 350
Makkreel, Rudolf 251, 255
Malebranche, Nicolas 49, 153

Maliks, Reidar 328
Malpas, Jeff 510
Malter, Rudolf 6, 8, 17–20, 325, 535
Marcuzzi, Max 516
Marshall, Dan 480
Martin, Geoffrey 512
Martin, Gottfried 418, 429
Marx, Karl 394
Massimi, Michela 480, 483
Mauser, Wolfram 304
May, Gerhard 393
May, J. A. 512–513, 516
Mayhew, Robert J. 511, 513
McLear, Colin 106
McNulty, Bennett 495–496
Meer, Frederik van der 393
Meier, Georg Friedrich 4, 17, 22–23, 98, 109, 120, 136–137, 153, 159–160, 163–170, 316, 432, 526
Meiners, Christoph 4, 308, 310–312, 365, 380, 389, 401–402
Melton, James Van Horn 278, 304
Mendelssohn, Moses 64, 115, 127, 463
Mendieta, Eduardo 509
Mensch, Jennifer 145, 526, 534
Merzbach, Uta 441
Mikkelsen, Jon 14, 529, 533, 540, 545
Montesquieu, Charles Louis de Sécondat 348
Montucla, Jean Etienne 434, 441
Moran, Kate 277
Moravia, Sergio 305
Moretto, Antonio 27–28, 418, 423–425, 430–431, 434–435, 440, 443, 446, 449
Morgenstern, Karl 263–265
Mortier, Roland 308
Mrongovius, Krzysztof Celestyn 463
Munzel, G. Felicitas 4, 277, 281
Murphy, Daniel 278
Muthu, Sankar 522

Naragon, Steve IX–X, 1–2, 4, 6–9, 12, 14, 16–18, 20–21, 27, 29, 32, 37, 66, 80, 89, 96, 100, 106, 162, 179, 345, 410, 414, 483, 526
Natorp, Paul 259–260, 395
Newton, Isaac 17, 49–50, 95, 167, 466–467, 469, 476–477, 480
Nicomachus 433, 435–436

Nietzsche, Friedrich 394–395
Oberhausen, Michael 7, 161–163, 170, 174–175, 259–260, 267
Onof, Christian 28, 461
Ortelius, Abraham 513
Otterman, Steven 375

Palmquist, Stephen R. 27, 29, 365–366, 370–372, 375, 383–388
Paracelsus 486
Parsons, Charles 442–443
Pascal, Blaise 392
Pasternack, Lawrence 377
Paulsen, Friedrich 1, 12, 403
Petrus, Klaus 167, 308, 310
Pfotenauer, Helmut 310
Piaget, Jean 550
Piché, Claude 145
Pirrone, Amanda X, 526
Pisanski, Georg Christoph 262
Plaaß, Peter 485
Plato 1, 26, 85, 347, 350, 353, 393–396, 398, 453
Plotinus 21
Pluhar, Werner 365, 374, 378, 384, 386, 388
Pölitz, Karl Heinrich Ludwig 265–266, 392
Pollok, Konstantin 107
Pontynen, Arthur 383
Pope, Alexander 44, 237, 313
Pozzo, Riccardo 6–7, 11, 23, 140, 160–164, 166, 168–171, 173–175, 259–260, 267
Priestley, Joseph 483, 488
Proclus 21
Psellus 434
Pütter, Stephan 336, 359

Rauscher, Frederick 26, 323, 325, 336
Rawls, John 1, 21
Reicke, Rudolf 6, 16, 264
Reimarus, Hermann Samuel 127
Reinhardt, Olaf 506, 508, 518–519
Reinhold, Karl Leonhard 19, 24, 39, 91, 200, 213–219
Reisert, Joseph 281–282, 289, 520
Richards, Paul 518
Ricoeur, Paul 393
Riedel, Wolfgang 310

Rink, Friedrich Theodor 1–2, 10, 25, 29, 259–268, 271, 274, 276–277, 506–508, 513–517, 520–522, 527–528, 532–533, 535–536
Ritter, Christian 326
Robinson, Hoke 143
Rosenkranz, Karl 10–11
Roth, Klass 277, 507
Rousseau, Jean-Jacques 17, 25, 44, 49–50, 167, 247–248, 268–269, 277, 280–284, 286–291, 293–295, 302–303, 313–314, 316, 330, 348–350, 380, 520, 538
Russell, Bertrand 1

Sala, Giovanni B. 400
Santos, Robinson dos 260, 268
Schaefer, Fred K. 512
Scheele, Carl Wilhelm 488
Scheffner, Johann Georg 44, 264
Scheler, Max 393
Schelling, Friedrich W. J. 394
Schiavone, Aldo 352
Schiffert, Christian 261
Schings, Hans-Jürgen 310
Schliesser, Eric 3
Schmid, Carl Christian Erhard 24, 200, 213–216, 219
Schmucker, Josef 184
Schneewind, Jerome 180
Schneider, Ulrich J. 161
Schneiders, Werner 305
Schönfeld, Martin 41
Schubert, Friedrich Wilhelm 10–11
Schulting, Dennis IX, 22, 29, 89, 91, 101, 103, 110, 113, 483, 526
Schulz, Günter Eberhard 263, 308
Schwaiger, Clemens 180–181
Schwartz, Paul 275
Segner, Johann Andreas von 425–426, 438–439, 452
Seifert, Arno 305
Sensen, Oliver 2, 5, 23, 179, 183, 188, 193, 207
Sgarbi, Marco 160–161, 174
Shabel, Lisa 430, 443
Shell, Susan Meld 10, 25, 34, 277, 281, 286, 296, 298, 522, 526
Siegmund-Schultze, Reinhard 427

Simplicius 21
Sloan, Phillip 145, 534
Smith, Justin E. H. 3
Socrates 127, 314, 394
Solomon, Robert C. 244
Sonderling, Jakob 10–11
Spalding, Johann 314
Spinoza, Baruch 1, 383–384, 404
Stahl, Georg Ernst 488–490, 499–501
Stark, Werner IX–X, 1–2, 7–8, 10, 14–15, 25, 44, 57, 179–181, 259–261, 264–265, 269–271, 273–274, 276–277, 306, 505, 507–508, 522, 526, 528, 530–533, 535–536
Starke, Friedrich Christian (Johann Adam Bergk) 1, 11, 274, 507, 530–531, 547
Stattler, Benedikt 200, 212
Stavenhagen, Kurt 7
Stone, Lori D. 244
Stratton-Lake, Philip 196
Stroud, Scott R. 389
Strube, Werner 309
Stuart, Elden 505, 509
Stuckenberg, J. H. W. 5
Sturm, Thomas 243, 316
Sulzer, Johann Georg 50, 368
Suprenant, Chris 121, 277
Sutherland, Daniel 422, 426, 434, 443

Tacquet, Andrea 433, 435, 448
Tertullian 394
Teske, Johann Gottfried 40, 167, 419, 462
Tetens, Johannes Nikolaus 95
Thales 486
Thiel, Udo 95–97, 99, 510
Tieftrunk, Johann Heinrich 276
Timmermann, Jens 180–181
Tonelli, Giorgio 160, 167
Torricelli, Evangelista 490
Trescho, Sebastian Friedrich 534
Turner, R. Steven 305

Ulrich, Johann August Heinrich 24, 200, 212–213, 215–216

Valentin, Weigel 441
Vogel, Peter 268

Vollmer, Johann J. W. 1, 11, 173, 265
Vorländer, Karl 1, 8, 418

Warda, Arthur 52, 96, 261, 263, 487, 500
Warren, Daniel 474–475, 479–480
Waterman, W. B. 401
Watkins, Eric 41, 50–51, 467, 474, 506, 516
Waxman, Wayne 520
Weatherson, Brian 480
Weisskopf, Traugott 25, 260, 266, 268, 274, 281, 507
Wenzel, Uwe Iustus 19, 400
Wilpert, Jakob Friedrich 43–44
Williams, Bernard 20
Wilson, Holly 243, 518–519
Wimmer, Reiner 399
Winter, Aloysius 405
Withers, Charles 505, 511, 516
Wolff, Christian 4, 8, 17, 23, 27–28, 37, 49–52, 54–55, 66, 71, 92, 95–96, 98–101, 116–117, 122, 153–155, 157, 165, 167, 266, 305, 313–314, 418–437, 439–444, 446–449, 452–453, 477
Wöllner, Johann C. 279, 366
Wood, Allen IX, 202, 247, 392, 508, 510, 529
Wubnig, Judith 145
Wunderlich, Falk 96, 103
Wundt, Max 10, 12–13, 395

Xenophon 380
Xylander 434–435

Young, J. Michael 138–139

Zabarella, Jacopo 167–168
Zammito, John 1, 19, 25–26, 145, 243, 301, 304, 309, 314, 316, 536
Zande, Johan van der 303
Zedler, Johann Heinrich 351
Zedlitz, Karl Abraham von 15, 170–172, 260, 279, 306
Zimmerli, Walther 303, 305, 308, 310–311
Zinkin, Melissa 55, 193
Zöller, Günter IX–X, 1, 26, 29, 75, 89, 145, 346–347, 351–352, 357, 507, 526
Zopf, Johann H. 166

Subject Index

a posteriori 73–74, 78–79, 81, 110, 121–122, 125, 312, 464, 466–467, 470, 491, 499
a priori cognition 22, 146, 188, 389
a priori synthesis 100–101
Abschrift (copy of student notes) 15, 171; see also under lectures
accountability 202–203, 206, 215, 219, 285
acoustics 413, 427, 465
Acroasis Logica (Baumgarten) 66, 96
action and reaction 467, 477
action, free 201, 210–211, 360
adaptation (of nature) 540
aesthetic response 225
affection, empirical 29, 485, 495, 497–498, 501
Africa 521, 536
afterlife 115–120, 125, 128–133, 388
agency 29, 243, 256, 527–528, 531, 535, 538
agents, moral 256
aggregate 518, 537
agreeable, the 235, 293
agriculture 163, 521
air 52, 286, 290–291, 427, 460, 465, 468, 480, 486–490, 500, 533–534
Albertina University 2, 6, 25, 169, 207, 259–262, 274, 279, 345, 418, 531
alchemists 486
algebra 153, 411–413, 422, 424–427, 433–434
algorithms 28, 453
alteration 57, 61, 85, 122, 230–231, 329, 385, 459–460, 465, 469, 477, 486
America (continent) 521, 536, 539
Analogies of Experience 469
analytic 38, 51, 58, 85, 101, 110, 174, 204, 217, 224, 227, 238, 432, 440, 444, 496, 498
Analytic of the Beautiful 224, 238
analytic unity 101, 110
animality 128, 285, 287, 297, 383, 386
animals 29, 94, 105–106, 111, 128, 254, 272–273, 292, 369, 526–528, 530–535, 538

animation (*Belebung*) 227, 229–230, 235–236
Anlage (predisposition) 283, 287, 297, 459, 530, 533, 535
"Announcement of the Organization of His Lectures in the Winter Semester 1765/66"; see "Nachricht von der Einrichtung seiner Vorlesungen in dem Winterhalbenjahre von 1765–1766"
"Answer to the Question: What is Enlightenment?" 172, 337, 369
Anthropology from a Pragmatic Point of View 10, 25, 167, 243, 269–270, 521
anthropology lectures 49, 91–92, 94, 229, 231, 521–522
anthropology of morals 256
Anticipations of Perception 494
antinomies 479
apperception 22, 89–93, 95–101, 103–111, 113, 131
apprehension 226
arbitrium divinum 194
archeology 163, 542–543
architectonic 64–65, 140, 493–494
argument 315
Aristotelianism 167
arithmetic 27–28, 58, 173, 412, 420–422, 424–427, 432–436, 439, 441–442, 444–445, 447, 452–453
art
– work of 233, 235, 237
artifice 283
ascription (agency) 200
Asia 521, 536, 546
astronomy 27, 44, 126, 173, 413, 427, 514
atheism 382–383, 394, 396
"Attempt to Introduce the Concept of Negative Magnitudes into Philosophy" 6, 37, 42, 50, 55–58, 60–61, 73, 94, 162, 421, 452–453, 475
Aufklärung 164, 175, 305, 317; see also Enlightenment

autonomy 23, 179, 182, 188, 192, 198–199, 211–212, 214, 283, 350–351, 358, 400–401
axiom 430–432, 436, 440, 494, 511
Axioms of Intuition 494

beautiful sciences 163, 316
beauty
– intellectual interest in 223
– social interest in 24
belief
– in God 394, 402
– in immortality 116, 121, 128–134
beneficence 184, 400–401
Betrachtungen über *die Erde und den Menschen* (ed. Starke) 7, 274, 547–548
Bildung 304–305, 315, 453; *see also* culture, cultivation
bindingness (*Verbindlichkeit*) 26, 346–347, 349, 351–355, 357–361
biology 145, 529
blacks (race theory) 522, 546
bodies (physics)
– characterizations of 479
– metaphysics of material bodies 495
– properties of 464
boundaries
– of knowledge (reason) 82–83, 87, 156, 396, 509–510; *see also* limits

calculating 425, 435, 441, 443
calculus 413, 424–426, 444, 452
caloric 481–482, 500
Canon of Pure Reason 129
capacity of the understanding 106, 144–145, 147, 151
catechism 279, 291
categorical imperative 181, 188, 199, 349, 358, 361; *see also* moral law
categories
– of quality 113, 475, 480–481
– of quantity 424, 429, 481
– origin of 144–145, 151
cause, free 200–201
censorship, religious 366, 369
change
– concept of 498

character
– empirical 202–206, 210, 216–217
– intellectual 204
chemistry
– chemical theories 486
– developments in 28, 500
– history of 486–487
– organic 29, 488, 500
– phlogistic 489, 500
– pneumatic 487–488
– principles of 490, 499
children 517; *see also* education
China 173, 520–521
Christianity 279, 366, 370, 380–381, 394, 399, 404–406
chronology 413, 427, 429
church
– the "true church" 372, 374–375, 377
citizens 169, 248, 276, 294, 329, 331, 334, 340, 348, 350, 355, 517
citizenship 292
civil constitution 253, 287
civil society 276, 290, 352–353
civilization 244, 246, 253–255, 281, 286, 296
clarity and distinctness 98, 118, 137
clean copy (notes) 14; *see also Reinschrift*
climate 20, 514–515, 533–534, 536
coercion 291, 324, 326, 357
cognition
– theoretical 121, 128, 545
color 233–234, 274, 325, 420, 465, 482, 515, 532
combustion 463, 489
common sense 70, 239, 304, 307, 310, 318, 512
common understanding 165
communicability 223, 238, 241
community
– ethical 355, 369
– religious 27, 367, 390
compatibilism 202–203, 206–207
compendia 10, 302–303, 435, 518, 526; *see also* textbooks (compendia)
composite concepts 68
comprehensibility 230–233, 235–236
comprehension 294, 492

Conflict of the Faculties 25, 276, 283–284, 298, 306, 327
conscience 96, 189, 206, 250, 270, 287, 337, 349, 372, 375, 377–379, 389, 402
consciousness
– gradual conception of 22, 90, 112
consequences
– ground and consequence 56–59, 72–74, 81, 142, 490, 492
constraint
– juridical 357, 359–360
continents 536
contingency 120, 395
contract
– contractual relations 352, 354
– original 330–331, 341
contradiction in conception 182–183, 185–186
contradiction in the will 182, 186
correspondence (letters) 6, 15, 264, 303, 346
countries 514, 519–521, 536
course catalog (university) 7, 161, 170, 267, 345
creation
– artistic 236–237
– purpose of 27, 395, 403–405
credit, moral 296
critical
– mysticism 384, 390
Critique of Practical Reason 181, 198, 202–203, 205, 209, 211, 218, 256, 431
Critique of Pure Reason 5, 23, 26, 78–79, 82–85, 87, 89–90, 109, 115–116, 126–128, 137, 160, 164–166, 170, 173–174, 202, 204–206, 211–212, 219, 279, 302, 392, 398, 423, 425, 430–431, 433–434, 437, 440, 442–443, 446, 448–450, 461, 466, 468–470, 479, 488, 493, 496, 505, 528
– as a textbook 174
Critique of the Power of Judgment 24, 166–167, 223–225, 233
– section §9 237
cultivation 66, 87, 284, 286, 293–295, 305, 315, 373, 389–390; *see also* moralization
culture (*Bildung*)
– vices of 244, 247, 285

death
– of the body 115, 117–119, 121–122, 128–133
deduction 23, 90–91, 104, 107, 109, 137, 141, 144, 150–151, 156–157, 227
deed 200–204, 206, 208–209, 211, 213, 216–219, 284, 296, 386
degrees of freedom (agency) 24, 208–211, 236; *see also* freedom
degrees of morality 208
deism 384
delirium (*Schwärmerei*) 376, 384–385; *see also* fanaticism
delusion, religious 375–376, 385, 387
demerit 201, 208
democracy 330–331, 334, 339, 342–343
desert 539; *contrast also* wilderness
design
– apparent design in nature 29, 527–529, 534–535, 548–550
despotism 337, 339
determinate concept 81–82, 224–228, 231, 235, 237–238, 240
determinism 212–217
development 39
dignity 168, 172, 184, 255, 270, 279, 282, 295, 357, 381, 383, 385, 387
dimensions 69, 448
Discipline of Pure Reason 433
diversity (of natural kinds) 491, 511, 514, 546, 548
dividing 476, 478
divine grace 372, 376, 386, 388
Division (of the Academy Edition) 6, 267, 272–273, 356
division, chemical 500
doctrinal belief 22, 129, 132
dogmatic 12–13, 40, 45, 77, 154–156, 158, 164–165, 284, 313, 318, 382–383, 396, 419, 464, 493
Dreams of a Spirit-Seer 42, 58, 124, 303
duties
– ethical 349, 361
– of right 295
– to oneself 270, 295
– to others 270
duty; *see also* moral law; morality
– performance of 249, 256

dynamics 429, 480, 482, 501
earth
- physical features of 307, 413, 513–518, 528, 531–533, 537–539, 542–543, 546–547; see also geography
earthquake (Lisbon) 532
educated, the 27, 393, 405
education
- educational reform 292
- moral 252, 269–270, 283, 286, 288, 292, 294–295, 368, 371, 379–380, 388, 520
- popular 25, 277, 279, 281
- public 292
- religious 278, 283, 287, 369, 371, 375, 377, 381, 388–389
- science 517
electricity 462–463, 482–483; see also subtle material (electricity)
elements
- fifth element (quintessence) 487
- four elements 486, 488
eloquence 18, 45, 166, 229, 236–237; see also rhetoric, oratory
embodiment (human agency) 24, 256
Emile (Rousseau) 17, 25, 50, 277, 280–282, 284, 286, 289, 291, 293, 295, 380
emotion 5, 24, 190, 255–256, 296
empirical apperception 92–93, 109, 111
empirical psychology 46, 49, 109, 121–123, 157–158, 207, 223, 275, 301, 307, 309–310, 315, 426
empiricism 85, 167, 520
end in itself 374, 400
enlightenment (Enlightenment) 167, 303–304, 308–310, 314, 337, 368–370, 374, 377, 511, 516, 519
Enthusiasmus (enthusiasm) 384; *contrast also* fanaticism (*Schwärmerei*)
Entwurf eines Collegii der physischen Geographie 6, 162, 306, 532
epigenesis 141, 144–145
equations 413, 424–425; see also mathematics
Erlangen Gelehrten Zeitung 303
essence 57, 187, 347, 398, 472, 486–487, 493
Estates General 26, 329, 343

eternity 44, 401, 404
ether 463, 481–482, 487
Ethica philosophica (Baumgarten) 180
ethics; see moral philosophy, morality
Eurocentrism 521–522
Europe 352, 441, 521, 535–536
evil
- radical evil 269, 283, 369, 400
evolution (Darwinian) 188, 515, 550
executive power 333, 339
experiments 278, 280, 370, 464, 467, 483, 490, 500
extensive magnitude 499; see also intensive magnitude
extraordinarius (professor) 262

fact of reason 203–204, 209
faculties (mental) 76, 82, 106, 126, 128, 130, 168, 225–229, 236–237, 289, 314, 353
faculty of desire 126, 218
faith
- moral 402
- rational 373, 405
"False Subtlety of the Four Syllogistic Figures" (*Falsche Spitzfindigkeit*) 6–7, 41, 161–162
fanaticism (*Schwärmerei*) 193, 384, 402
feeling
- of pleasure 111, 189, 194, 226–227, 229, 236, 238
finality 126, 156
finitude 74
fire 53, 84, 465, 480, 486, 488–489
"First Introduction" to the third *Critique* 226, 353
force
- attractive 28, 460, 464, 469, 471, 473, 475, 480; *contrast also* repulsive
- magnetic 482
- original 463, 474–475
- repulsive 28, 464, 471–473, 475, 478, 480
Formula of Autonomy 182, 198; see also categorical imperative
Formula of Humanity 183; see also categorical imperative
fractions 161, 420, 438, 443, 452; see also mathematics

free will 201, 211, 360–361
free-acting beings 522
freedom
– causality through 205, 215
– of choice 213–219
– of human action 358
– of the will 214, 217, 219
French Revolution 26, 276, 283, 325–329, 331, 333–335, 337, 339–341, 343–345
friendship 264, 295
fusion (air and phlogiston) 489

gardens 240
Garve-Feder review 302
Gefühl (feeling) 316, 535; *see also* feeling
general will 330, 334, 349
generatio aequivoca 144
Genesis 11, 14, 276, 301, 350, 394, 403, 430, 538
genius 46, 165, 169, 172, 229, 235, 237, 291, 314–316
geography
– as a science 512, 515
– geographical metaphors 509–511
– mathematical 513, 532
– nature and status of 511, 513, 527
– orthodox 512
– regional 520
geometry 27, 95, 173, 396, 413, 421, 426–427, 429, 435–436, 444, 447, 449–453, 478, 493
German Idealism 394
Germanizations (of Latin) 165; *see also* Latin
germs 297, 533–534, 536, 539, 544, 549; *see also* Keime (germs)
germs-and-predispositions theory 533–534; *see also* race theory
globe 519
gnomonics 413, 427, 429
God
– as supreme intelligence designing nature 528
– existence of 86, 382, 387, 402
– God's love 404
– moral argument for God's existence 382–383
– relation to 385, 396

good, the 42, 196, 250, 269, 284–285, 297, 355, 371–372, 386, 388, 406
government 172, 281, 297, 328–330, 332, 337, 339–344, 372, 418, 526
grace 95, 372, 376, 378, 385–388, 404, 407
gravity 465, 469
ground
– and consequence 57, 73, 81
– determining 205, 209, 216–218
– logical 21, 37–38, 50, 52, 56–59
– real 37–38, 49–53, 55–61, 71, 94
Groundwork of the Metaphysics of Morals 26, 199, 211–212, 269, 336, 347, 350, 356–357, 360–361, 406
growth (organic) 548

Halle 49, 276, 305
handwritten notes (Kant's) 63, 88, 114, 136–139, 151, 157, 222–223, 242, 391; *see also Reflexionen* (Kant's notes)
happiness 86, 184–185, 196, 297, 305, 392, 400–401, 403
harmony 49, 51, 53, 117, 185, 226–228, 235–236, 331, 401, 477
harmony of the faculties 228
health 19, 173, 239, 284
heat
– absolute notion of 481
– measurement of the quantity of 481
– sensation of 481
helps and hindrances (moral agency) 256
Herder student notes
– caution about using 46
– courses Kant taught during the Herder years 41
– importance of 21, 37
– mathematics notes 28, 418–427
– metaphysics notes 21, 37, 65, 103, 105–106, 125, 533
– moral philosophy notes 179–180, 184, 191
– physics notes 462
– why they are special 40
hereditary factors 515
heteronomy 211
highest good 198, 254, 366, 394, 400, 402–403, 517
historical knowledge 73, 84, 313, 513

holiness 209, 380, 386–387, 401–402
homogeneity 436
honor 24, 172, 243–255, 392, 404, 406; see also love of honor
hope
- and fear 26, 346, 355
- for a future life 128–129; see also immortality
human beings; see also human species
- as animals 530, 539–540
- as social animals 302
- behavior of 533–534
- human nature 50, 129, 184, 238, 247, 256, 269, 275, 282, 284, 289, 369, 400, 520
- practices of 514
- skin colors of 515
human species 244–246, 251, 253–254, 271–276, 287–288, 290–291, 307, 535
humanities 305, 308; see also liberal arts
humanity 17, 50, 172, 183, 187, 245, 254–255, 270, 275, 285, 287–290, 295, 297, 327, 337, 342, 369, 378, 383, 400, 522, 538
hylozoism 123

"Idea for a Universal History with a Cosmopolitan Aim" 273, 290, 543
idea of humanity 295, 383
ideal
- influence 53
- of beauty 223
- moral ideals 517
image, sensible 28, 438–439, 453
imagination 58, 106, 111, 118, 152, 157, 166, 223–229, 237–238, 240, 246, 295, 372, 431, 517
imitation 197, 314
Immanuel Kant's Logik (Jäsche) 265
Immanuel Kant's physische Geographie (Rink) 265
Immanuel Kants Vorlesungen über die philosophische Religionslehre (Pölitz) 266, 392
immortality 22, 115–125, 127–134, 388, 398, 401
impenetrability 28, 464, 470–474
imputatio
- absolute 202
- *imputatio facti* 201
- *imputatio legis* 201
- relative 206–207, 210
imputation
- absolute model 24, 202, 207, 210, 219
- models of 24, 209
- moral 24, 201, 205–208, 210–211, 214–217, 219
- relative model 24, 210
Inaugural Dissertation (*De mundi sensibilis atque intelligibilis forma et principiis*) 93–94, 188, 191, 231, 318, 368, 448, 479, 536
inclinations 193, 195–197, 243–244, 246, 248–250, 285, 291, 295, 308, 430, 532
indeterminism 212–213, 216–217
indifferentism 318
inertia 123, 463, 467, 472
infinity 97, 476, 479
Initia philosophiae practicae primae (Baumgarten) 180
innatism 145
inner end 529
inner sense 22, 90, 92–94, 97, 105–106, 108–109, 111, 133, 231, 494, 498, 522
"Inquiry concerning the Distinctness of the Principles of Natural Theology and Morality" 42
instruction; see also education
- academic 265, 364, 366
- moral 295, 373
- religious 278, 295
integers 422
intellect 67, 101, 118
intelligible 85, 202–207, 212–215, 218–219, 254, 469, 472, 479; contrast also sensible
intelligible character 202–206, 213
intensive magnitude 99, 104, 112, 425; see also extensive magnitude
intentionality, artistic 236–237
intermixing (of subspecies) 538, 547
intersubjectivity 26, 361
intrasubjectivity 26
intuition
- empirical 495
intuitive understanding 383

Inuit 539–540, 547

Japan 173
Jena 262, 441
judging 29, 94, 106, 110, 137, 141, 144, 149, 157, 200, 238, 247, 282, 340, 529
judgments
- categorical 150
- fundamental 68–69
- of beauty 5
- of taste 24, 223–225, 227, 229, 238–239, 241; *see also* beauty
- primitive 72
- reflecting 225, 529
- teleological 29, 529
justice 120, 183, 185, 189, 205, 279, 286, 326, 337, 347, 349, 385, 388–389

K2 (metaphysics lecture) 108–109, 113, 119–123, 127–130
K3 (metaphysics lecture) 122
Kant
- academic teaching 2, 4
- contemporary accounts of Kant as professor 17
- announcements of lectures (program writings) 6–7, 29, 161, 259, 420, 452, 531
- as a lecturer (*Privatdozent*) 1, 3, 5, 17, 21, 42–43, 89, 345
- courses taught (discipline and frequency) 8
- daily teaching schedule (1760s) 41
- intellectual activity 3, 14
- intellectual development 3, 13, 39, 65, 528
- lecturing activity 89, 345, 531
- letters 3, 6, 9, 12, 17, 46, 50, 214, 425, 534
- mature philosophy 421
- pedagogical practice 531
- why Kant abandoned Philosophical Encyclopedia 316–319
Kant's copy of Achenwall's text 326, 328–329, 336, 344–345, 359
Keime (germs) 459, 533; *see also* germs
kinematics 463
kingdoms (animal, plant, mineral) 273, 519, 528, 541

knowledge of the world 18, 256, 306–307, 516–518; *see also* Weltkenntnis
Königsberg 2, 7, 9, 19, 37–38, 40–43, 48, 50, 161–162, 165, 170, 174–175, 207, 229, 260–264, 266, 268, 273–275, 279, 306, 418–419, 428, 462–463, 520, 531, 534, 538; *see also* Albertina University
Königsbergsche Gelehrte und Politische Zeitungen 42

L1 (metaphysics lecture) 46, 73–78, 80–85, 93, 100, 102, 105–106, 108, 119–124, 130–133, 146
L2 (metaphysics lecture) 102, 106, 108, 121–122, 124, 126–127
Latin
- in class 23, 160–161, 163, 165, 167, 169, 171, 173, 175
- use of 23
law; *see also* moral law
- contract 352
- empirical 202, 355
- juridical 348–349, 357
- of nature 17, 44, 57, 202–203, 205, 210, 212, 217, 357
- Roman 26, 346–347, 352
lawfulness 90, 155, 227, 358, 360–361, 371, 494
lecture announcements 29, 161, 259
lectures
- debate about value of lecture notes 10–13
- explanation of terms for notes 14–15
- issues posed by the notes 9
- manuscripts available 16
- scholarly interest in 1
- using the student lecture notes 21, 37–39
legal theory 340, 352
legality 182, 193, 349, 356, 359
legislative authority (power) 325, 327–328, 330–335, 337–344
legitimate state 330
Lehmann, editing by 46
Leibnizian-Wolffian background 22, 89, 93; *see also* Wolffian philosophy
liberal arts 173, 305; *see also* humanities
limiting, the 448–449

limits
- Grenzen 448–449; see also boundaries
- of knowledge 168, 540
literary genre 23, 160–162
logic
- formal 498
- general 142, 146, 151, 157, 227
- Kant's corpus 22, 137, 139–141, 143, 145, 147, 149, 151, 153, 155, 157–158, 164
- rules 137, 139, 141, 143, 145–147, 149–153, 155–157; see also rules
- modern 140, 142, 151–153, 157–158, 167
- philological problems with Kant's corpus 138–139, 151, 164
Logik Blomberg (lecture) 98, 102
Logik Busolt (lecture) 171
Logik Dohna-Wundlacken (lecture) 22, 102, 173
Logik Philippi (lecture) 171
Logik Wiener (lecture); see Wiener Logik
Louis XVI (King of France) 329–330, 332–333, 335
love of honor
- degenerate forms of 247
- feeling of 243–255
- moral role of 24, 255
lying 23, 40, 57, 183, 185–187, 190–192, 203, 247, 276, 293, 376

mania 247, 255, 384
manifold, temporal 231
marginal notes (Kant's, student's) 6, 10, 15, 38, 100, 171, 532; see also Reflexionen (Kant's notes)
materialism 394
mathematical sciences 418, 420–421, 427, 429
mathematicians 420, 435, 468, 474, 480, 511
mathematics
- application of 484, 499
- applied 28, 428–429, 453
- mathematical laws 425
- pure 419, 424, 429, 466
- special 413, 429
mathesis applicata 28, 421, 426, 447, 453; see also mathematics

mathesis universalis 28, 412, 421, 424–425, 453; see also mathematics
matriculation age (university) 271
matter
- concept of 469–470, 473, 479, 485, 496–497
- divisibility of 28, 463, 470–471, 476, 478–479
- empirical nature of 496
- gas 427, 481, 488, 500
- liquid 465, 468, 481, 486
- solid 413, 427–429, 448–449, 459, 468, 481, 486
maturity, sexual 271, 289, 295
maxims
- in ethics 186, 218, 269–270, 292, 294, 358, 361, 371
- of reason 528
measurement 412, 421–425, 427, 434, 437, 447, 450, 465, 481
mechanics 8, 413, 418, 421, 427–429, 460, 474–475
mechanism 26, 144, 196, 245, 247–248, 275, 488, 533
Menschenkunde (anthropology lecture) 49, 267, 269–270, 273
merit 120, 201, 208, 210, 215, 217, 219, 247, 252, 292
meta-cognitive approach (beauty) 228
metaphysical deduction 23, 137, 141, 150–151, 156–157
Metaphysical Foundations of Natural Science 5, 28, 425–426, 429, 461, 466–469, 473–474, 476, 479, 484, 490, 492, 494
metaphysics
- dogmatic 493
- knowledge in 67, 71, 74, 76–78, 87
- scientific 67, 155
- special 83, 485, 494
- the tradition of 64, 474
Metaphysik Dohna (lecture) 101, 109
Metaphysik Mrongovius (lecture) 46, 106
Metaphysik Volckmann (lecture) 101, 106, 396

method
- mathematical 165, 421, 429–430, 466; see also mathematics
- philosophical 154, 165
migration (human) 533–534
mineralogy 8, 418, 487
Mitschrift (original class notes) 14, 171; see also under lectures
modality 149, 354, 359, 429, 481, 495
monad 96, 472, 477–479
monarchy 26, 279, 281, 327, 329, 338–339
moral cultivation 284, 295, 373; see also cultivation
moral feeling 184, 189–191, 193–194, 196–197, 385; see also respect
moral law
- content of 23, 179, 181–187
moral panentheism 383–384; see also panentheism
moral philosophy
- Collins (lecture) 180, 186–187, 190–192, 195–198, 201, 208, 217, 245, 252, 398–399
- development of 180–181
- Herder's lecture notes 179–181, 183–185, 189, 193–195
- Mrongovius I (lecture) 180, 335
- Mrongovius II (lecture) 23, 180–181
morality; see also supreme principle of morality
- aid to 24, 243–245, 247, 249, 251–253, 255; see also helps and hindrances (moral agency)
- content of 23, 184, 186
- law of 184, 205, 208, 217, 377
moralization 244, 253–255, 281, 348–349
motion
- predicable of 498–499
- speed and direction of 499; see also movement
motivation, moral
- early view of 193
- mature view of 192–193
movement 126, 205, 463–465, 472, 474, 477, 485, 490; see also motion
multiplication 417, 437–439, 441–442, 444; see also mathematics

Nachlass (Kant's literary remains) 95, 108
"Nachricht von der Einrichtung seiner Vorlesungen in dem Winterhalbenjahre von 1765–1766" 7, 161, 164–165, 174, 307, 535
Nachschrift 14–15, 25, 171, 265, 438, 440–441, 452, 533
national character 521
natural drive 208, 243–245, 247
natural history 278, 491, 514–516, 536, 538; see also under nature
natural teleology 526–527, 529, 531, 533, 535, 537
nature
- agency of 29, 527–528, 531
- causality of 202–203, 210, 215–216
- corporeal 485, 494
- counter-purposive tendency of 288
- description of 464, 466–467, 491, 512, 514–515, 519; contrast also history of nature
- doctrine of 28, 142, 426, 464, 467, 484–485, 490–494
- ends of 246, 529, 538
- history of 464, 487, 491, 512, 514, 516; see also natural history
- purposiveness of 126, 129, 528
Naturrecht Feyerabend 17, 26, 322–323, 326–327, 335–344, 346–347, 349, 351, 353, 355–361
New Elucidation (*Principiorum primorum cognitionis metaphysicae nova dilucidatio*) 37, 47, 49, 54, 61
normativity 358, 361
noumenon 202, 216, 330, 446, 509
novelty 232, 316; contrast also beauty
numbers; see also mathematics
- science of 424–425
- theory of 435

obedience 278, 285, 291–294, 328, 337, 401, 430
objective validity 152, 494, 498
objectivity 91, 107
obligatio 26, 323–324, 347, 351–354, 360; see also obligation

obligation
- moral 179, 192, 355
"Observations on the Feeling of the Beautiful and Sublime" 42, 183–185, 189, 193, 247, 251, 521–522, 535, 546; see also Remarks (Bemerkungen) in the "Observations"
obstacles
- moral 209–210, 219
- natural 152, 208, 219
- physical 208, 211
ontological argument 381
ontology 43, 46, 49, 51, 55, 64, 83, 317, 427
optics 413, 427, 465
optimism 275, 403, 419, 421, 532
Opus Postumum 481, 501
oratory 166; see also rhetoric
organism 29, 526–530, 532, 535
organization (purposive) 134, 460, 529–530
organized being 144, 528–529
oxidation 489

paleontology 542; see also archeology
panentheism 383–384; see also moral panentheism
pantheism 383
paralogisms 102–103, 105, 115–117, 119, 121, 123, 125, 127, 129–133
passion 61, 243, 249, 295, 315
pastoral care 390, 392–393, 402
pedagogy
- moral-religious 27, 365, 367, 377, 380, 387, 389–390
- religious 27, 367–368, 370, 373, 377, 379
- seminar in Königsberg 275
peoples 521, 534–535, 546, 548
perception 22, 90, 96–99, 107–108, 110, 118–119, 225, 235, 464, 481, 494, 496–497
perfection
- of humanity (human beings) 194, 230, 274, 297, 383, 401, 405, 522; see also virtue
- of world 117, 245, 403
perfectionism 234
personality 94, 118–119, 130–133, 280, 285, 383, 386, 400

Pflicht (duty) 354, 359, 430; see also duty
phenomenology (*Metaphysical Foundations of Natural Science*) 429
phenomenon 18, 71, 95, 106, 200, 205–206, 218, 330, 353, 384, 425, 432–433, 463–465, 468, 474, 476, 478, 480–483, 509, 513, 519; contrast also thing in itself
Philosophical Encyclopedia 4–5, 8, 14, 16, 25, 162, 299–300, 304, 307, 312, 316–318
philosophical knowledge 306, 309, 313
philosophy
- academic (German school) 20, 302
- ancient 160
- for the world 25, 29, 303–304, 314; see also knowledge of the world; *Weltkenntnis*
- for the schools 25, 304–305, 308, 314; see also scholastic knowledge
- history of 3, 20, 160, 303, 307, 311, 526
- of biology 529
- of religion 27, 366–367, 395, 397, 399, 509
- transcendental 29, 82, 90, 167, 315, 317, 437, 479, 494–495
phlogiston 488–489
phoronomy 413, 426–429, 463, 498, 501
phylum (*Stamm*) 530, 536
physical geography lectures
- far less studied 509, 527
- Manuscript Dohna 530–531
- Manuscript Dönhoff 530–531
- Manuscript Holstein 530–536
- Manuscript Kaehler 267, 530–531, 533, 535–538
- Rink's poor editing of 506–507, 527
- seen as irrelevant 508
physical influx 50, 477
physico-theology 534
physics
- experimental 479, 483
- mathematical 462, 466–467, 477–479, 490–491, 496
- theoretical 461
physiological approach 154–155, 308, 310
Pietism 261, 278, 373–374

play
- free 24, 223–225, 228, 235–238, 240–241
- harmonious 228, 234–237
pleasure 24, 111, 189, 193–194, 196, 198, 225–227, 229, 231–232, 235–236, 238–241, 388–389, 518–519
plurality 28, 361, 412, 423
poetry 229, 233, 235–237
politics 26, 84, 287, 347–348, 350, 427
Popular philosophy 25, 304–305, 308–309, 314, 318–319
postulate 123, 204, 326, 366, 401, 430–432, 435, 476, 481
power of choice 124, 214–218, 284, 386
powers, cognitive 24, 126, 152, 223–225, 227–229, 231–232, 241
practical philosophy 26–27, 201, 213, 217, 350–351, 354–356, 397, 401
practical reason
- pure 204, 211, 224, 401
Prädisposition 533; *see also Anlage* (predisposition)
pre-established harmony 49, 51, 53
predicable 485, 497–499
preformationism 144–145
priestery 374, 377
principii cognoscendi 76
principium diiducationis 198
principle
- of contradiction 60, 71, 74, 440
- of identity 56–57
- of right 288, 324, 326, 336
principles
- a priori 81, 142–143, 158, 382, 431, 464, 466–467, 469, 491–492, 496
- ethical 26
- formal 69–70
- material 69–71
- teleological 29, 515, 527–528
probability 413, 428
Programmschriften 161–162; *see also* lecture announcements
Prolegomena to Any Future Metaphysics 64, 103, 107, 174, 302, 304, 308, 423, 438, 446, 448, 466–467, 481

proofs
- of immortality 115–117, 119–121, 123, 125, 127, 129, 131, 133
properties, chemical 488
proportions 443–447, 452; *see also* mathematics
propriety 248–251, 253, 282–283
Providence 251, 254, 398, 527–528, 535, 538
prudence 18, 270, 288, 297, 358, 402
Prussia 25, 169, 275, 277, 279, 337, 418; *see also* Königsberg
pseudoservice (of God) 373, 375–376, 387
psychometry 425
psychopannychia 118
public right 336, 340
public sphere 304
pure concepts 74–76, 78, 82, 84–86, 107–108, 144, 146, 405, 495
purpose of creation 27, 392, 395, 403–405
purposiveness 126–127, 129, 226, 528, 537
Pythagorean theorem 450–451

quid iuris 85

race theory
- climatological (vs. germs-and-predispositions) 533
- Hume's notorious remark 522, 546
- race essays 515
- races 515–516, 522, 524, 536
- racial difference 533–534, 536
racism 522
ratio (reason) 37, 52, 204, 209, 420, 444–445, 447; *see also* ground
rational creatures 403, 537
rational psychology 22, 46, 49, 64, 76, 78, 115–116, 124, 127, 130–131, 133, 315, 494
rationalism 49
rationality 24, 256, 305
reactions, chemical 487, 499
real opposition 56, 59–60
reality
- objective 104, 130, 396, 430, 495
- of freedom (morality) 192, 203–205, 379
realm of ends 361
reason
- fact of 203–204, 209

- faculty of 83, 86, 154, 225
- idea of pure 78–79
- idea of 380, 388, 493
- pure practical 204, 211, 224, 401
- speculative 86
- theoretical 389
- use of pure 85

rebellion 325, 328, 337
receptivity 109, 385, 464
Recht, difficulty of translating 26, 326
Reflexionen (Kant's notes) 3, 6, 9, 12, 18, 50, 106, 108, 137, 163–164, 166–167, 316–317, 326, 432, 444, 452, 499, 510
reform 25, 275, 279–281, 292
refutation of idealism 132
regeneration (organic) 529, 548
region (geographical) 520, 532–533, 537–539
Reinschrift 14; *see also under* lectures
religion, rational 365, 373, 375–376
Religion within the Boundaries of Mere Reason 25, 216, 267, 283–284, 286, 295–296, 397, 400, 404–405, 509
Remarks (*Bemerkungen*) in the "Observations" 185, 193, 282, 290
repetitoria (practicals) 6–7, 15, 23, 160, 169–171
representation
- obscure 22, 89, 93, 101–105, 111–113, 232
- of the people 329–330, 332, 334–335, 338, 341

reproduction (organic) 285, 515, 543, 547–548; *see also* sexual maturity
republic 293, 327, 329–331, 337, 394, 396
republican spirit 282, 287, 291
resistance 285, 292, 325, 328, 474
respect
- feeling of 193
- giving Kant's geography 508–509
- Rodney Dangerfield not getting any 508

responsibility, personal 394
revolution (political) 26, 276, 283, 325–329, 331, 333–335, 337, 339–341, 343–345; *see also* French Revolution
rhetoric 164, 166–167, 173, 236; *see also* oratory
right of nations 336
rights 187, 282, 292, 326, 328–329, 344, 353–354
rigor 26, 169, 307, 311, 314, 436
Rink's life events 263
rituals 354, 365, 373, 376, 378, 388
rules
- demonstration of logical rules 137, 139, 141, 143, 145, 147, 149, 151–153, 155–157; *see also* logic

Russians 8, 50, 418–419, 428–429, 521

satisfaction (*Wohlgefallen*) 214, 388
schema 285, 311, 437, 439
scholastic knowledge 17, 531, 541
schönen Wissenschaften 309, 312
schooling 278–279
science
- empirical 29, 74, 315, 518, 526
- natural 28, 95, 396, 461–462, 464, 466–470, 476, 485, 491–493, 511, 527, 531–532, 544–545, 549, 552
- proper 28–29, 142–143, 151–153, 156–157, 484–486, 488–493, 495, 499–501
- rational 74–76, 79, 84, 86, 142–143, 490, 492
- spatial 514, 518

scientists 488
Scottish Enlightenment 309–310
scripture 366, 370, 379
sculpture 231, 233
self-consciousness 90, 92–93, 99–101, 105, 108, 111, 132–133
self-determination 214, 217, 219
self-legislation, ethical 350
self-love 247, 251–252, 386
self-mastery 248–250, 351
selfhood 393–394
sensation 92, 97, 103–104, 106, 109, 112, 131–132, 181, 190, 227, 233–237, 250, 368, 464, 481–482, 497
sensibility 92, 101, 106, 111, 155, 196–197, 206, 212–213, 219, 228, 230, 256, 315, 317, 383, 385
sensus communis 251
silent decade (Kant's) 461, 536
skepticism 72, 152, 308, 512
sleep 92, 103, 118, 130, 377

sociability 239, 247–248, 250, 270, 285, 291, 295, 304, 543
social intercourse 249–250, 351
soul
– immortality of the 115–117, 119–120, 122, 129, 133, 401
– perdurance of the 115
sovereignty 26, 327, 330, 332–342
space
– and time 19, 108, 162, 230, 469, 472, 477–478, 497
– cosmic 481
– geography as a science of 512
species (animal) 491–492, 529, 547–548; see also animals
spirit 34–36, 44, 87, 111, 131, 235, 281, 286–287, 291, 315, 348, 532
spirituality 118, 130–131, 133
spontaneity 109, 123–125, 144–145, 148, 188, 216, 350
stone 489, 519, 534, 541
student notes; see lectures
Sturm und Drang 316
style 179, 313, 316
subjects (areas of study) 38, 169, 278, 467
sublime, the 184, 223, 225, 318
subspecies 538; see also races
substance
– category of 469
– relations among substances 478
– simple 476, 478
subsumption 227
"subtle material" (electricity) 482
subtraction 416, 437–438, 442
suicide 187
superstition 314, 376, 519
supreme principle of morality
– development of 23
– source of the 187–190, 192
symbol 223, 365, 376, 379, 437
sympathy 125, 166, 189, 243–244, 302
synthesis 100–101, 107, 316, 430–431
synthetic
– a priori 82, 431, 437, 494, 496
– unity 101, 108, 110, 146
system
– of duties 256

– nature as a 538
– systematic art (chemistry) 28, 484, 490, 492, 499
– systematic whole 81
systematicity 305, 492–493; see also system

taste 24, 44, 223–225, 227, 229–230, 235, 237–241, 309, 314, 316, 519
teleological proof of immortality 116, 125, 127–129, 131, 133; see also soul
teleology
– natural 526–527, 529, 531, 533, 535, 537
temperament (natural) 204, 207–208, 217, 251, 256, 270, 295, 533–534
temperature 481, 486
temporality 385, 512–513
textbooks (compendia)
– authors of textbooks Kant used 4, 336, 526
– manuals 158, 346
"The Only Possible Argument in Support of a Demonstration of the Existence of God" 37, 42, 50, 56
theism 382–383, 396–397
theology
– Christian 397, 404; see also Christianity
– moral 380, 382–383, 402
– natural 4, 8, 16, 42, 46, 49, 55, 58, 64, 73, 76, 78, 264–265, 363, 365, 380–381, 389, 425, 472, 527, 534
– philosophical 19, 365–369, 371, 373, 375, 377–383, 385, 387, 389–391
– rational 381, 392
theorem 416, 431–432, 440, 442, 447, 450–451, 511
thing in itself 91, 93, 202, 205, 213, 472, 479; contrast also phenomenon
thinking
– formal conditions of 22
Third Antinomy 202–203, 212, 215–216
time; see under space and time
totality 334, 423–424, 494, 511
Toward Perpetual Peace 173, 328
transcendental
– apperception 22, 89–93, 95, 97–99, 101, 103, 105–107, 109–111, 113
– deduction 90, 109, 144

- freedom 213; see also freedom
- ground 125; see also ground
- idealism 202, 205, 207
- logic 90, 142, 146, 152, 174, 227; see also logic
- theology 78, 80, 381–382; see also theology

Transcendental Aesthetic 470–471
Transcendental Analytic 85, 217
Transcendental Dialectic 85, 168, 204
transcriptions; see lectures
trigonometry 27, 413, 421, 426–427, 429, 451; see also mathematics
truth
- aesthetic play and 235–236
- criterion of 310, 317
- revealed 376, 381
- telling the 185, 187

truthfulness 185, 270

"Über den Gebrauch teleologischer Principien in der Philosophie" 529, 529, 544
unconditioned, the 82, 205, 254, 287
understanding
- pure 64, 75–77, 80, 83–85, 110, 147, 168, 188, 191, 466, 510

uniformity 9, 38, 232, 271
united people 329–335, 340, 343–344
united will of the people 330–332, 335, 340; see also united people
unity
- of apperception 101, 110
- of consciousness 92, 100–101, 107, 109–111, 150

universal validity 188, 223–224, 229, 238, 240–241, 355
university; see also Albertina University
- teaching 1, 5, 7, 20, 29, 301; see also under Kant

unsocial sociability 247, 291; see also sociability
utility
- and beauty 229–230, 240
- and mathematics 442, 447

variation (race theory) 533
velocity 474
"Versuch, den Begriff der negativen Größen in die Weltweisheit einzuführen"; see "Attempt to Introduce the Concept of Negative Magnitudes into Philosophy"
vices of brutishness 285–286; contrast also virtue
virtue
- and vice 368
- doctrine of 158, 355, 377

vocation of humanity 314, 318
volume
- in physics 471, 474
- measurement of 447

"Von den Verschiedenen Racen der Menschen" 7, 524, 529, 533, 536

war 16, 170, 172, 189, 278, 332, 336, 400, 407, 418
water 34–35, 468, 486, 488–490, 500, 519, 538
way of thinking (Denkungsart) 166, 205, 251, 281, 294, 371, 389, 397
weight 412, 465, 488, 490
Weltkenntnis 306, 517–518, 522
"What Real Progress has Metaphysics Made in Germany Since the Time of Leibniz and Wolff?" 266
whites (race theory) 536
Wiener Logik (lecture) 22, 112, 153, 550
wilderness 239
wisdom 18, 119–120, 129, 254, 304, 314, 358, 387, 400, 402, 407
Wolffian philosophy 165, 167, 305; see also Leibnizian-Wolffian background
world
- at large 517; see also knowledge of the world; Weltkenntnis
- intelligible 472, 479
- sensible 209, 401, 472

worthiness, moral 244, 248–250, 253

Zweck (end) 528, 532